THE CAMBRIDGE COMPANION TO

SPINOZA

The Cambridge Companion to
SPINOZA

Edited by Don Garrett
University of Utah

CAMBRIDGE
UNIVERSITY PRESS

Published by the Press Syndicate of the University of Cambridge
The Pitt Building, Trumpington Street, Cambridge CB2 1RP
40 West 20th Street, New York, NY 10011-4211, USA
10 Stamford Road, Oakleigh, Melbourne 3166, Australia

© Cambridge University Press 1996

First published 1996

Printed in the United States of America

Library of Congress Cataloging-in-Publication Data

The Cambridge companion to Spinoza / edited by Don Garrett.
   p. cm.
  Includes bibliographical references.
  ISBN 0-521-39235-7 (hc). – ISBN 0-521-39865-7 (pb)
  1. Spinoza, Benedictus de, 1632–1677. I. Garrett, Don.
B3998.B32 1995
199'.492 – dc20   95-11445
                                         CIP

A catalog record for this book is available from the British Library.

ISBN 0-521-39235-7 hardback
ISBN 0-521-39865-7 paperback

This volume is dedicated to the memory of Alan Donagan, our friend and colleague.

CONTENTS

viii   Contents

CONTRIBUTORS

JONATHAN BENNETT is Professor of Philosophy at Syracuse University. He is the author of, among other works, two books on Kant, one on the British empiricists, and more recently *A Study of Spinoza's Ethics* (1984). He has also, with Peter Remnant, edited and translated Leibniz's *New Essays on Human Understanding* (1981). His most recent book is *The Act Itself.*

EDWIN CURLEY is Professor of Philosophy at the University of Michigan, the editor and translator of *The Collected Works of Spinoza* (Vol. I, 1985; Vol. II, forthcoming) and *A Spinoza Reader* (1994), the editor of Hobbes's *Leviathan* (1994), and the author of *Spinoza's Metaphysics* (1969), *Descartes Against the Skeptics* (1978), and *Behind the Geometrical Method* (1988).

MICHAEL DELLA ROCCA is Assistant Professor of Philosophy at Yale University. He is the author of *Representation and the Mind–Body Problem in Spinoza* (forthcoming from Oxford University Press) and of articles on Spinoza and on metaphysics.

The late ALAN DONAGAN was Doris and Henry Dreyfuss Professor of Philosophy at the California Institute of Technology; he was the author of *The Later Philosophy of R. G. Collingwood* (1962), *The Theory of Morality* (1977), *Human Ends and Human Actions: An Exploration in St. Thomas's Treatment* (1985), *Choices: The Essential Element in Human Action* (1986), *Spinoza* (1988), and *Philosophical Papers of Alan Donagan* (two vols., 1994).

ALAN GABBEY is Professor of Philosophy and Chair of the Philosophy Department at Barnard College, Columbia University, and is a *Membre effectiv* of the Académie Internationale d'Histoire des Sci-

ix

ences. Among his publications are "Force and Inertia in the Seventeenth Century: Descartes and Newton," in S. Gaukroger, ed., *Descartes: Philosophy, Physics, Mathematics* (1980), and "Philosophiae cartesiana triumphata: Henry More 1646–1671," in T. Lennon et al., eds., *Problems of Cartesianism* (1982). He is a member of the editorial boards of the *Journal of the History of Philosophy* and the monograph series *International Archives of the History of Ideas*.

DON GARRETT is Professor of Philosophy at the University of Utah. He is the author of numerous articles on Spinoza and early modern philosophy. He is also the author of *Cognition and Commitment in Hume's Philosophy* (1996) and coeditor of the journal *Hume Studies*.

W. N. A. KLEVER is Professor of Philosophy at the Erasmus University of Rotterdam (Netherlands) and cofounder and chief editor of *Studia Spinozana*. He published the recently discovered *Vrye Politijke Stellingen* of Spinoza's master Franciscus van den Enden (1992) and is the author of *Verba et sententiae Spinozae according to Lambertus van Velthuysen* (1990), *Zuivere economische wetenschap; een ontwerp on basis van Spinozistische beginselen* (1991), and *Zicht op Spinoza* (1994).

PIERRE-FRANÇOIS MOREAU is Professor of Philosophy at the Ecole Normale Supérieure of Fontenay/Saint-Cloud and Chairman of the Groupe de Recherches Spinoziste (CNRS). He is the author of *Le Récit utopique. Droit naturel et roman de l'Etat* (1982), *Hobbes. Science, philosophie, religion* (1989), and *Spinoza. L'Expérience et l'Eternitié* (1994). He is the translator of Spinoza's *Tractatus politicus* (1979) and (in collaboration with J. Lagrée) L. Meyer's *Philosophia S. Scripturae Interpres* (1988).

RICHARD H. POPKIN is Professor Emeritus, Washington University, St. Louis, and Adjunct Professor at the University of California, Los Angeles. He is the author of the *History of Scepticism from Erasmus to Spinoza* and many articles on Jewish and Christian intellectual history in the seventeenth and eighteenth centuries.

MARGARET DAULER WILSON is Professor of Philosophy at Princeton University, where she has taught since 1970. She has published a book, *Descartes*, as well as many papers on early modern philosophy. Among her previous publications are a number of essays concerned with Spinoza's *Ethics*.

ACKNOWLEDGMENTS

I wish to thank Kelly Sorensen for assistance with preparation of the manuscript, including assistance with the bibliography; and my wife Frances for her invaluable support during the preparation of this volume.

METHOD OF CITATION

Where references are by author and year of publication, full reference information may be found in the Bibliography.

The following common abbreviations have been used in referring to Spinoza's writings:

CGLH   *Compendium of Hebrew Grammar (Compendium Grammatices Linguae Hebraeae)*

DPP   *Descartes's "Principles of Philosophy" (Renati Des Cartes Principiorum Philosophiae, Pars I et II, More Geometrico demonstratae)*

E   *Ethics (Ethica Ordine Geometrico demonstrata)*

Ep   *Correspondence (Epistulae)*

ST   *Short Treatise on God, Man, and His Well-Being (Korte Verhandeling van God, de Mensch en des zelfs Welstand)*

TdIE   *Treatise on the Emendation of the Intellect (Tractatus de Intellectus Emendatione)*

TP   *Political Treatise (Tractatus Politicus)*

TTP   *Theological-Political Treatise (Tractatus Theologico-Politicus)*

References to the *Short Treatise on God, Man, and His Well-Being,* the *Treatise on the Emendation of the Intellect,* the *Political Treatise,* and the *Theological-Political Treatise* are by chapter and, within chapters, by the section numbers introduced in the Bruder edition of Spinoza's works and reproduced in many subsequent editions.

References to the *Correspondence* are by letter number.

References to *Descartes's "Principles of Philosophy"* and the *Ethics* begin with an arabic number denoting the Part, and use the following common abbreviations:

xii

a   Axiom
ap Appendix
c   Corollary
d   Definition (when not following a Proposition number)
d   Demonstration (when following a Proposition number)
da Definition of the Affects (located at the end of *Ethics* Part 3)
ex Explanation
le Lemma (located after *Ethics* 2p13)
p   Proposition
po Postulate
pr Preface
s   Scholium (Note)

For example, "E 1p14d,c1" refers to *Ethics* Part 1, Proposition 14, Demonstration and Corollary 1.

Introduction

In many ways, Benedict (Baruch) de Spinoza appears to be a contradictory figure in the history of philosophy. From the beginning, he has been notorious as an "atheist" who seeks to substitute Nature for a personal deity; yet he was also, in Novalis's famous description of him, "the God-intoxicated man." He was an uncompromising necessitarian and causal determinist, whose ethical ideal was to become a "free man." He maintained that the human mind and the human body are identical; yet he also insisted that the human mind can achieve a kind of eternality that transcends the death of the body. He has been adopted by Marxists as a precursor of historical materialism, and by Hegelians as a precursor of absolute idealism. He was a psychological egoist, proclaiming that all individuals necessarily seek their own advantage above all else and implying that other individuals were of value to himself only insofar as they were useful to him; yet his writings aimed to promote human community based on love and friendship, he had many devoted friends, and even his critics were obliged to acknowledge that his personal conduct was above reproach. He held that the state has the right to do whatever it has the power to do, while at the same time he defended democracy and freedom of speech. He denied supernatural revelation, and criticized popular religion as a grave danger to the peace and stability of the state; yet he devoted himself to the careful interpretation of scripture, and argued for complete toleration and freedom of religion. Rarely employing figures of speech or rhetorical flourishes of any kind, his works are nevertheless among the most magisterial and uplifting of all philosophical writings, and have inspired more poets and novelists than those of any other philosopher. Providing explicit definitions of his terms and formal demonstra-

I

tions of his doctrines, he sought to clarify his meaning and reasons more diligently than has perhaps any other philosopher; yet few philosophers have proven more difficult to interpret.

To understand how all of these things can be true of one man and his philosophy is to do more than merely to resolve some fascinating interpretive puzzles. It is more, even, than to gain insight into the seventeenth-century intellectual world that produced him and the subsequent eras that have tried to understand him. It is both of those things, of course; but it is also to see into one of the deepest philosophical minds of the modern or any other era, and thereby to see deeply into philosophy itself.

The seventeenth century was a period of scientific, intellectual, political, and religious turmoil that gave birth to many philosophical "systems." Of these, it is Spinoza's monistic and naturalistic system, so initially forbidding in language and presentation, that ultimately speaks most cogently and persuasively to the twentieth century. As Alan Donagan has written:

Most philosophies, whatever their superficial attractions, are incoherent, and so impossible. Others, while not impossible, either gratuitously assume what there is no reason to believe, or deny what there is good to believe. . . . [T]he number of possibly true philosophies there is some reason to believe is very small indeed, and the philosophical interest of every one of them is correspondingly great. Spinoza's is of that number. (Donagan 1988: xiv)

Born and educated in the Jewish community of Amsterdam, and strongly influenced by his study of Descartes, Spinoza was excommunicated in his early twenties, changed his name from "Baruch" ("blessed") to its Latin equivalent "Benedict," and lived out the remaining two decades of his life quietly as a tutor and lens-grinder in and near Leiden and the Hague. His personal insignia bore the motto "*Caute*" ("caution"), and he was indeed a cautious intellectual revolutionary, expressing new and even radical doctrines in traditional terminology and formulae. Always careful about sharing his views with others, he published his *Theological-Political Treatise* (which examines the relation between religion and political theory through interpretation of the scriptures and the history of the Hebrew nation) anonymously under a false imprint; and he declined to publish his masterwork, the *Ethics*, during his own lifetime. He was not, however, a solitary individual working in a personal or intellectual vacuum, as many have supposed. On the contrary, he influenced and was influenced by many of his contemporaries, and was part of a lively Dutch intellectual community. In Chapter 1, W. N. A. Klever relies on recent historical discoveries – many of them his own – to retell the story of Spinoza's life and works in their seventeenth-century Dutch context. In the process, he provides new perspectives on Spinoza's aims and motivations, devoting particular attention to Spinoza's early secularization, his commitment to "science" in a broad sense, and his concern to address, from the standpoint of his own philosophical conception of God, the practical political problems posed by the nature of popular religion.

The bold and striking full title of Spinoza's mature presentation of his philosophical system is *Ethics, Demonstrated in Geometrical Order*. This "geometrical order," modeled on Euclid's *Elements*, corresponds to what Descartes had called the "synthetic" method of demonstration:

As for the method of demonstration, this divides into two varieties: the first proceeds by analysis and the second by synthesis. Analysis shows the true way by means of which the thing in question was discovered methodically. . . .

Synthesis, by contrast, employs a directly opposite method. . . . It demonstrates the conclusion clearly and employs a long series of definitions, postulates, axioms, theorems, and problems, so that if anyone denies one of the conclusions it can be shown at once that it is contained in what has gone before, and hence the reader, however argumentative or stubborn he may be, is compelled to give his assent. (Descartes 1985: II,110–11)[1]

Spinoza had already used this synthetic method, or geometrical order, as an expositor of Descartes in the only work that Spinoza published under his own name during his lifetime, *Descartes's "Principles of Philosophy."*

In the *Ethics*, Spinoza sought to demonstrate his ethical doctrines in proper order from the metaphysical principles on which, he believed, they depend and through which they must be understood. His metaphysical ontology, like Descartes's, consists of substance, attributes (what Descartes called "principal attributes"), and modes. According to Spinoza, a substance is that which is "in itself and conceived through itself"; an attribute is that which "the intellect perceives of a substance, as constituting its essence"; and modes are "the affections of substance, or that which is in another through which also it is conceived."

Because he maintained that all other things are causally dependent on God for their creation and conservation, Descartes had recognized a strict sense of the term "substance" in which God is the only substance. In a looser and more everyday sense of the term, however, he recognized two kinds of created substance, each with its own principal attribute: extended substances, whose principal attribute is extension (i.e., spatial dimensionality); and minds, whose principal attribute is thought. From Cartesian-seeming definitions and axioms – which, however, embody a strong requirement that everything be intelligible through a sufficient cause or reason – Spinoza in his *Ethics* deduced a strict substantial monism, according to which God is the only substance. Spinoza's God is a self-caused substance of "infinite" attributes, including both extension and thought, from whose nature everything possible necessarily flows. It follows that individual things, such as human beings, can only be *modes* of this one substance – which Spinoza sometimes called "God or Nature" (*"Deus, sive Nature"*). In Spinoza's view, *every* mode of extension is identical with a corresponding mode of thought, so that everything is thinking, as well as extended. One application of this doctrine is that the human body is identical with the human mind. Nevertheless, because extension and thought are each independent and self-contained attributes of God or Nature, there can be no causal interaction or explanatory relation between them. In Chapter 2, Jonathan Bennett traces the roots of Spinoza's metaphysics to four underlying assumptions – "explanatory rationalism" (i.e., the principle that everything must have a sufficient reason), "concept dualism," "impact mechanics," and "size neutrality" – and to Spinoza's attempt to solve two fundamental metaphysical problems: (i) What material substances are there? and (ii) What underlies the systematic correlation between mental states and physical states? In the course of doing so, he further develops the distinctive interpretation of the relations among Spinozistic substance, attributes, and modes that he first set out in his *Study of the Ethics of Spinoza* (Bennett 1984).

Spinoza appropriated Descartes's distinction between two human representational faculties, the intellect and the imagination. He regarded the former as nonimagistic and the source of adequate ideas, the latter as imagistic and the source of inadequate ideas. As the title of his early and unfinished *Treatise on the Emendation of the Intellect* suggests, part of Spinoza's philosophical project was to improve and strengthen the intellect. In Part 2 of the *Ethics*, he proposed to demonstrate – as consequences of his metaphysics – the character of the human mind as the "idea" of the human body, the nature of sense perception, the relation between true and false ideas, and the way in which all ideas (including human minds) are contained in the infinite intellect of God. He also distinguished three kinds of knowledge, or cognition *(cognitio)*: the first kind, *opinion* or *imagination*, includes random or indeterminate experience, and hearsay or knowledge from mere signs; the second kind, *reason*, depends on "common notions" (features of things that are equally in the part and in the whole) and on adequate knowledge of "properties" (rather than essences) of things; the third kind, *intuitive knowledge*, "proceeds from an adequate knowledge of the essence or attributes of God to knowledge of the essence of things," in proper order, from causes to effects. Both the second and the third kinds of cognition are true and adequate, but the third kind provides the greater understanding and insight into the essences of things. In Chapter 3, Margaret D. Wilson comprehensively explains the many interrelated aspects of Spinoza's theory of knowledge, showing what is distinctive or idiosyncratic about it, and emphasizing the ethical character and purposes of Spinoza's epistemological doctrines.

The theory of knowledge, on the one hand, and natural science, on the other, were closely related for Spinoza. In his view, the former serves as the basis from which the methods of natural science, like those of any inquiry, must be derived and through which they must be understood. In addition, however, it follows from the parallelism of the two attributes of thought and extension and the identity of their corresponding modes, that the power of logical entailment itself – by which adequate ideas produce or give rise to other adequate ideas under the attribute of thought – is literally *identical* with the causal power by which modes of extension produce or give rise to other modes of extension. That is, logical power and physical power are the very same power, considered in two different ways, under two different attributes. The *Ethics* itself devotes somewhat less discussion to the sciences of extended bodies, or what we would now call natural science, than it does to the sciences of thinking things, or what we would call psychology. Nevertheless, Spinoza's concern with both the methods and the content of natural science is evident throughout his writings, from his *Treatise on the Emendation of the Intellect* to his geometrical presentation of Cartesian physics in *Descartes's "Principles of Philosophy,"* and from his so-called physical excursus following *Ethics* 2p13 to his sometimes-detailed correspondence with Henry Oldenburg (first Secretary of the British Royal Society, and friend of Robert Boyle). In Chapter 4, Alan Gabbey locates Spinoza's scientific interests in the context of the disciplinary categories of the seventeenth century, investigates the authorship of two small treatises (on the rainbow, and on the calculation of chances) often attributed to him, describes his scientific correspondence, evaluates his strengths and weaknesses as an expositor of Cartesian physics, assesses the role of Cartesian physics in his own philosophy, and explores his conception of methodology in the natural sciences.

Spinoza's doctrine that there is only one substance raises the question of how individual things can be distinguished from one another. Because different individuals are not different substances, they must be distinguished, within the one substance, in some other way. Within the attribute of extension, individual things are constituted by "fixed proportions of motion and rest" – that is, persisting patterns in the distribution of fundamental physical forces. Within the attribute of thought, individuals are constituted by the ideas of such actually persisting patterns. Individuals each have a definite nature or essence, and are, to that extent, finite approximations to substances. Part 3 of the *Ethics* argues that a thing's essence or nature must seek to exclude from itself what is incompatible with its own persistence, so that a thing can be understood as *active* – that is, as the adequate cause of effects – only to the extent that it endeavors, through its own nature, to persist. This striving or endeavor (*conatus*) to persevere in its own being is thus a consequence of the conditions for being an individual at all, and constitutes each individual's own power.

In this way, Spinoza's solution to the problem of individuation involves a doctrine of necessary individual psychological egoism that applies throughout all of nature. He sought to derive the nature of human psychology by adding to this general doctrine two further postulates about human beings in particular: (i) that they are affected in many ways that can increase or decrease their power of *acting* (in the sense of being an "adequate cause"); and (ii) that they are sufficiently complex to form and retain sensory images or traces of other things. On this basis, Spinoza defined three primary emotions or "affects": (i) desire (*cupiditas*), which is "appetite [i.e., the endeavor for self-preservation] together with consciousness of the appetite"; joy (*laetitia*), which is an affect "by which the Mind passes to a greater perfection" or capacity for action; and sadness (*tristitia*), which is an affect "by which the Mind passes to a lesser perfection" or capacity for action. When an affect is produced by external causes, rather than through the agent's own power, the affect is a *passion*. Part 3 of the *Ethics* goes on to analyze and define a large number of additional affects in terms of these three – by varying their combinations, their causes, and their objects – and deduces from these definitions a number of consequences for emotional and motivational phenomena. In Chapter 5, Michael Della Rocca analyzes and evaluates in detail Spinoza's argument for the metaphysical conclusion that "each thing, insofar as it can by its own power, strives to persevere in its being"; he describes and assesses Spinoza's attempt to apply this metaphysical doctrine to human psychology; and he critically examines Spinoza's account of the particular laws governing human psychology. In doing so, he emphasizes the naturalistic character of Spinoza's project, which requires Spinoza to regard human psychological states as subject to laws that are instances or applications of more general laws operative throughout nature.

Spinoza's analysis of the emotions, or "affects," and his doctrine that each person necessarily endeavors to persevere in being, provide, together with his metaphysics and his theory of knowledge, the basis for the ethical theory that he developed in Parts 4 and 5 of the *Ethics*. There he sought to explain human susceptibility to passions (i.e., affects of which the individual is not the adequate cause), the ways in which the understanding provides power to control those passions, and the elements of "the right way of living." The "good," as Spinoza defined it, is whatever we know to be useful for preserving our being. Since all human beings do necessarily endeavor to persevere in their being, all human beings will be motivated, at least to some extent, so far as their own power permits, to pursue the good as they understand it. Ethics, as knowledge of the "right way of living," is for Spinoza a kind of knowledge of nature that is at the same time knowledge that is necessarily motivating (to some extent) for human beings. He argues that the highest human good lies in adequate knowledge, which is itself eternal and thereby allows a part of the human mind to be eternal. Those who are most able to pursue their own advantage through adequate knowledge are "free men," who are "guided by reason" and possess virtue. The existence of human freedom is compatible with necessitarianism because freedom involves, not chance or indeterminism, but rather action from the necessity of one's own self-preservatory nature, in contrast to necessitation by external causes. Accordingly, only those who are guided by reason, rather than passion, are truly free. Part 4 of the *Ethics* evaluates a variety of affects and behaviors from an ethical perspective, praising friendship and nobility (because nothing is more advantageous to a human being than other human beings who are guided by reason), but condemning such Christian virtues as humility, repentance, and pity (because they are kinds of sadness). In Chapter 6, I outline Spinoza's ethical theory and related doctrines and examine several crucial but often neglected or misunderstood aspects of that theory: (i) the meaning of ethical language, (ii) the nature of the good, (iii) the practicality of reason, (iv) the role of virtue, (v) the requirements for moral freedom and moral responsibility, and (vi) the possibility and moral significance of altruism.

Spinoza's psychological egoism also provides the basis for his political theory. Like his ethical theory, his political theory is a branch of the study of nature; but whereas his ethical theory primarily concerns the power and advantage of human individuals, his political theory, as detailed in his *Theological-Political Treatise* and his later unfinished *Political Treatise*, primarily concerns the power and advantage of the political collectives that human individuals compose. Fundamental to his political theory is his doctrine that "right" and "power" are coextensive. Like Machiavelli, he sought to understand relations of political power practically, scientifically, and dispassionately. Like Hobbes, he held that citizens are well-advised to give up their right and power to the state in return for the protection that it can provide to them in their pursuit of self-preservation. Unlike Hobbes, however, Spinoza emphasized the breadth of the practical limitations on the individual's concession of power to the state; and also unlike Hobbes, he located a human being's highest advantage not in mere continued life and the pursuit of pleasure, but in the achievement of adequate knowledge and its resulting peace of mind.

For Spinoza, the state is itself an "individual," with its own endeavor for self-preservation. However, it is usually in greater danger from its own citizens than it is from external enemies, and in order to preserve itself, it must take care how it seeks to exercise its power over them. The wisest and most stable state, he maintained, is a limited constitutional democracy that allows freedom of expression and religious toleration. A free state is thus "free" in three different but related senses, for Spinoza: It places no restrictions on speech or religion; it is conducive to the development of "free men," in the sense of Spinoza's ethical ideal; and it is *itself* a free individual, because it acts through its own nature to achieve its own self-preservation. In Chapter 7, Edwin Curley explains Spinoza's relation to Machiavelli, to Hobbes, and to the concept of a social contract, and he critically assesses Spinoza's subordination of the concept of political right to that of political power.

Although he was a naturalist – in the sense of holding that nothing exists outside of or beyond Nature – Spinoza was no simple atheist hiding impiety in conciliatory or ironic theistic terminology. Rather, by reconceiving Nature as active and self-causing, and at the same time reconceiving God as nonpurposive and extended, he was able to conceive of God as identical with, rather than as the transcendent creator of, Nature. His God, like the God of the theologians, is perfect and infinite, is the self-caused cause of all, has an essence identical with his existence, and is (through the "third kind" of knowledge) the object of an eternal religious contemplative love and blessedness. Unlike the God of the theologians, however, Spinoza's God is directly intelligible to the intellect, through the divine attributes of thought and extension. Indeed, since Spinoza's God is the only substance, in which everything is and through which everything must be conceived, *all* knowledge is knowledge of God, for Spinoza, just as all effects are effects of God's power. Spinoza's natural, intellectualistic theology, concerned with knowledge of God as the absolutely infinite substance, is largely coextensive with his metaphysics, presented in Part 1 of the *Ethics*. However, Spinoza sought not only to provide a philosophical understanding of theology, but also to describe the kind of imaginative theology – that is, theology as grasped by the faculty of imagination – that could serve as the basis of a universal popular religion. Although he does not take divine revelation supernaturally, he does, in the *Theological-Political Treatise*, take it seriously. In Chapter 8, Alan Donagan interprets Spinoza's natural theology, as embodied in Parts 1 and 2 of the *Ethics*; Spinoza's account of revelation and revealed theology, as embodied in the *Theological-Political Treatise*; and also Spinoza's account of practical theology, or human action in relation to God.

Spinoza saw the Bible as a work of great importance, capable of exacerbating social conflict and motivating persecution, but also capable of exercising a beneficial influence on the unphilosophical masses, depending on the manner in which it was interpreted. In consequence, he himself sought to interpret it with great care, as a historical product of nature, on the basis of careful attention to the meaning of its authors, philological understanding of its language, and historical knowledge of its composition and transmission. In addition to writing a *Compendium of Hebrew Grammar*, he devoted considerable attention to the interpretation of scripture in the *Theological-Political Treatise*. He concluded, from the content of scripture itself, that prophets are distinguished not by the strength of their intellects but by the vividness of their imaginations; that revelations were accommodated to the minds of the prophets who received them; and that Scripture itself teaches nothing as essential to salvation except justice (i.e., obedience to the laws of the state) and charity toward one's neighbor. In Chapter 9, Richard H. Popkin locates some of the antecedents and influences of Spinoza's interpretive approach to the Bible in the work of Aben Ezra, Isaac La Peyrère, the Quaker Samuel Fisher, and the Socinians; he explains Spinoza's own principles for the interpretation of Scripture; he examines Spinoza's treatment of the status of Jesus; and he concludes that the originality of Spinoza's interpretation of Scripture lies less in the details of the interpretive theses he proposed than in the radically secularizing spirit that his naturalism made possible.

Spinoza and his philosophy have meant many things to many people. His own contemporaries generally regarded his philosophy as a thinly disguised form of atheism, while Bayle's *Dictionnaire historique et critique* (1697) served to reinforce the image of an absurd and heretical metaphysician who nonetheless lived an exemplary life. First German, and then English, Romanticism found Spinoza's pantheism in keeping with the striving and unorthodox spirit of their age. Absolute idealists of the nineteenth century saw his monism and his conception of the infinite attribute of thought as anticipations of Hegel, while Marxists saw in his necessitarianism and his power-based scientific political theorizing a foreshadowing of Marx. Later philosophers have classified Spinoza, alongside Descartes and Leibniz, as one of the three most important figures of "Continental Rationalism." Succeeding generations of natural scientists and psychologists, novelists and poets have found in his writings a continuing source of inspiration. In Chapter 10, Pierre-François Moreau (with translation by Roger Ariew) chronicles the varied history of Spinoza's reception and influence from the seventeenth century to the present.

Spinoza regarded all knowledge – like its objects – as closely interrelated. In addition, as Gabbey emphasizes, his conception of disciplinary boundaries differed considerably from our own. It is inevitable then that some topics are addressed, from different angles, in more than one chapter of this volume. For example, Chapters 5 and 6 both take up the rationality of action and the weakness of will; Chapters 8 and 9 both take up Christology; and Chapters 3, 6, and 9 each touch in some way on the eternality of the mind. It is my hope that readers will find these multiple perspectives on some of the doctrines that lie at the intersections of Spinoza's many interests to be helpful. In no case, I think, is there mere repetition.

In spite of – and sometimes because of – his use of "geometrical order," Spinoza is among the most difficult philosophers to interpret; and as Moreau makes clear, he has been the subject of many divergent interpretations up to and including the present. Even such a fundamental matter as the question of what Spinoza meant by saying that modes are "in" substance is a topic of ongoing debate, as Bennett explains in Chapter 1. Thus, it is not surprising that some differences of interpretation and of interpretive emphasis are manifested in this volume. (For one example, see the different treatments of dishonesty in Chapters 6 and 8.) What is surprising, under the circumstances, is not how many but how few such disagreements there are. Our understanding of what Spinoza meant to convey to his readers is not complete; it is, however, considerably greater than it has been at any time in the past. Taken as a whole, the essays in this volume present a detailed, coherent, and – I believe – accurate portrait of one of the most original and fruitful thinkers that humankind has yet produced.

NOTES

1 Descartes also used the term "geometrical order," but he did so in a broader sense than did Spinoza. For Descartes, geometrical order required only that "the items which are put forward first must be known entirely without the aid of what comes later; and the remaining items must be arranged in such a way that their demonstration depends solely on what has gone before" (Descartes 1985: II,110). For Descartes, both the analytic and the synthetic methods of demonstration are examples of geometrical order.

1   Spinoza's life and works

Benedict (Baruch) Spinoza's life is usually summarized in a few lines, as follows. He was born in 1632 in Amsterdam as a son of Jewish Marrano immigrants from Portugal. After having been educated as a Jew, he was excommunicated in 1656. While earning his livelihood, first by commerce and later by grinding lenses, he learned Latin in the school of Franciscus van den Enden and conversed with a circle of Amsterdam Collegiants, who were dedicated to Cartesianism. He lived in Rijnsburg near Leiden (1660–3), in Voorburg near The Hague (1663–70), and in The Hague (1670 onward). He published in 1663 under his own name Descartes's "Principles of Philosophy" (Renati Des Cartes Principiorum Philosophiae, Pars I et II, More Geometrico demonstratae), and anonymously in 1670 the Theological-Political Treatise (Tractatus Theologico-Politicus). After his death (February 21, 1677) his Opera Posthuma – containing in Latin his main work the Ethics, Demonstrated in Geometrical Order (Ethica, Ordine Geometrico demonstrata), the Correspondence (Epistulae), the unfinished Political Treatise (Tractatus Politicus), the unfinished Treatise on the Emendation of the Intellect (Tractatus de Intellectus Emendatione), and a Compendium of Hebrew Grammar (Compendium Grammatices Linguae Hebraeae) – was published by his friends. They also produced a Dutch translation of the Opera Posthuma (without the Hebrew Grammar), called De Nagelate Schriften, in the same year. An early forerunner of the Ethics, in Dutch and entitled Short Treatise on God, Man, and His Well-Being (Korte Verhandeling van God, de Mensch en des zelfs Welstand), was discovered and published in the nineteenth century. Spinoza was a seventeenth-century rationalist philosopher much decried on account of his atheism.

Even in this rough survey some features are false, inaccurate, or slightly misleading. For the purpose of a reliable biography, a critical discussion of the available biographical documents is unavoidable. This is the more necessary because the old biographies sometimes show considerable differences in their presentation. I warn the reader that this chapter is a reconstruction of Spinoza's life story on the basis of a new interpretation of the sources and the presentation of some new sources. I will, however, offer the basic material so that the reader may judge whether I am right or not.

Baruch's father, Michael Spinoza, born in 1587 in Vidiger (Portugal), was a respected and influential member of the Jewish community in Amsterdam. He was regularly elected a member of the *Parnassim* (*Senhores Quinze*), a board which discussed common affairs. He earned his living as a merchant; he must have traded in dried citrus fruit. Business was successful in the period before 1652; his bank balances were high. He lived in the Amsterdam Jewish quarter Vlooienburg, the place where today the Music House and Townhall are erected.[1] Michael married three times within his own family: first to Rachel de Spinoza, who died in 1627; then to Hanna Debora Despinosa, who died in 1638; and finally to Ester d'Espinosa, who died in 1653. Two children, Isaac and Rebecca, were born to Michael and Rachel; Baruch, Mirjam, and Gabriel were born to Michael and Debora.

Spinoza was born on November 24, 1632 and given the Jewish name "Baruch," although his family called him "Bento." "Baruch," "Bento," and the later latinization "Benedict" or "Benedictus" have the same meaning, namely "blessed person." His mother tongue was Portuguese, but as a young child Bento would very quickly have picked up some Dutch words when playing on the street with Dutch children. Spanish was the cultural language among the Sephardim Marranos, whose forefathers had been expelled from Spain to Portugal. But the education, of course, was primarily an introduction to Hebrew, the language of the Holy Scripture, and the study of the Law and the Talmud. His parents sent him to the excellent Talmud Torah school, which was famous because of its well-planned educational system. A certain rabbi Sabattai Scheftel Hurwitz, who visited Amsterdam in 1649, wrote: "I also came in their school, which was lodged in a large building. I saw that the small children learned the Pentateuch from the first to the last words, after this the other twenty-four Books of the Bible and then the whole Mischna." Among Spinoza's schoolmasters were the famous Saul Levi Morteira[2] and Menasseh ben Israel.[3] He must have attended the school until he was a young man of about fourteen years old.[4]

Historians suggest today that he did not finish the higher education which prepares for the rabbinate, but that he became involved in commercial activities, first together with his father and then, from 1654 onward, when his father had died, together with his brother Gabriel in the firm of "Bento y Gabriel Despinoza." In April and May 1655 the young merchant had a bitter experience with a debtor named Anthonij Alveres who failed to repay a large amount of money. Alveres even assaulted him, as is attested in an official document:

Today, the 7th of May, 1655, appeared before me, Adriaen Lock, notary &c. in the presence of the witnesses mentioned hereafter, Hendrick Fransen, about 35 years old and Jan Lodwijcxsen, about 32 years old, both in the service of the honourable Cornelis de Vlamingh from Outshooren, chief-sheriff of this city, and in true words and offering to take the oath, they solemnly testified, declared and attested at the request of Bento Dispinose, *merchant here*, that it is true that about a week and a half ago, without remembering the exact day, they arrested *at the request of the requisitionist*, the person of Anthonij Alveres for debt and that they took him to the inn De Vier Hollanders in the Nes here, to obtain payment of a certain bill of exchange of five hundred guilders that the requisitionist owned, chargeable to him and that said Anthonij Alveres then asked the requisitionist to come to the inn to reach an agreement with him; that when the requisitionist arrived there, the said Anthonij Alveres hit the requisitionist on the head with his fist without there having been spoken a word in return and without the requisitionist doing anything. (Vaz Diaz and Van der Tak 1982: 160; emphasis added)

In March 1656 we see Spinoza – through the mediation of the Orphan-master Lous Crayer – abstain from all claims on his father's inheritance "since he is afraid that after the strictest application of the law the judicial allocation of the claim could be an encumbrance to him, which might be used against him by the creditors." Also in 1656 Spinoza stopped paying his *finta* and his *imposta*, the usual contribution and tax for the benefit of the community that were calculated according to the wealth and the sum of the merchandise that had been traded. We do not know whether the reason was that business had declined or that he had already drifted away from the orthodox Jewish way of life and Jewish customs. The latter interpretation seems the most probable, because a few months later (July 27, 1656) he was formally excommunicated on account of his heresies and behavior. The text of the act of excommunication is preserved, and reads in translation:

The Senhores of the Mahamad make it known that they have *long* since been cognizant of the *wrong opinions and behavior of Baruch d'Espinoza,* and tried various means and promises to dissuade him from his evil ways. But as they effected no improvement, obtaining on the contrary more information every day of the *horrible heresies* which he *practiced and taught,* and of the *monstrous actions* which he performed, and as they had many trustworthy witnesses who in the presence of the same Espinoza reported and testified against him and convicted him; and after all this had been investigated in the presence of the rabbis, they decided with the consent of these that the same Espinoza should be excommunicated and separated from the people of Israel, as they now excommunicate him with the following ban. . . . We order that nobody should communicate with him orally or in writing, or show him any favor, or stay with him under the same roof, or come within four ells of him, or read anything composed or written by him. (emphasis added)[5]

The document makes a clear distinction between Spinoza's deviant behavior and his unorthodox opinions. It also supposes, however, that they had already been practiced and taught during a long period. Endeavors on the part of Jewish authorities to bring him back to the right path had remained without any result. One must realize, moreover, that the act of excommunication, as quoted above, speaks about Spinoza in the third person. Spinoza himself was already gone beforehand[6] and was already "converted" to another worldview and another lifestyle.

After experience had taught me that all the things which regularly occur in ordinary life are empty and futile, and I saw that all the things which were the cause or object of my fear had nothing of good or bad in themselves, except insofar as my mind was moved by them, I resolved at last to try to find out whether there was anything which would be the true good.[7]

I surmise that Spinoza's conversion took place at least half a year before he was excommunicated. The excommunication was not at all a tragic experience in his life. Other things were more so, including the violence of human emotional reactions and the life-threatening danger of human greed, ambition, and bigotry.

Spinoza's intellectual power, which emerged shortly after 1656 in his *Treatise on the Emendation of the Intellect*, must have had a long incubation. A philosophical genius cannot come from nowhere; ideas have their causes, like other things, and need time for their development. It is dangerous to propose a history of Spinoza's mental evolution. But one may at least speculate. In 1648 Spinoza was a young man of sixteen. He had refused to continue his studies in the higher courses in Jewish theology given by his masters, although his father, a faithful and perhaps also conservative member of the community, recommended them forcefully. He read the Jewish theological authors, first of all Maimonides, but they could not satisfy his inquisitive mind. His critique of the Jewish system, the many prescriptions and their vindication, deepened. He could only free himself from their pressure by a commercial participation in public life in his father's business; this seemed to him a promising way out. Along this line he came into contact with other merchants, many of them of Mennonite origin, who had free minds and were much interested in the new philosophy of Descartes. Pieter Balling[8] and Jarig Jelles,[9] both of them merchants and later friends, as we know from the correspondence, were among them; he could have met them on the Bourse. Descartes was praised for his new physics and geometry. Although he left Holland for Sweden in 1649, where he died a year later, Descartes's writings were published in Holland and raised much discussion. The religious freethinkers held special meetings – "colleges" – in which everyone was welcome. Perhaps Spinoza joined these *Collegianten*. He soon realized that he could not avoid learning Latin. There was a marvelous opportunity to become acquainted with the language of the sciences and with the new science itself in the newly (since 1652) established Latin school of the medical doctor Franciscus van den Enden. This Van den Enden participated in scientific disputations, attended the meetings of the *Collegianten*, and instructed the youth of the well-to-do citizens, who did not want to send their sons and daughters to the official, but reformed, Latin school of the town. Many biographical documents confirm that Spinoza learned Latin and atheism from Van den Enden, without saying whether this was before or after the excommunication.[10]

In my view, we cannot doubt that Spinoza's process of secularization must have started four or five years before 1656. The reformed theologian Salomon van Til, professor in Leiden, writes in 1694 about Spinoza's development and his *"Apologia"*:

A great instrument for the dispersion of the evil owned the Prince of Darkness some years ago in an Amsterdam schoolmaster [Van den Enden], who in this turbulent town tried to spread on all occasions his sentiment, that *nature had to be considered the only God.* . . . Who tried to build further on those fundaments and to give a nice glimmer to this sentiment, was Benedictus de Spinoza, a deserted Jew, who in the beginning played the admirer and expositor of the Cartesian Philosophy, attracted pupils for instruction under that pretension, but started to contradict some of Descartes' fundaments inconspicuously. His familiarity with mathematics and experience in grinding lenses opened the door for him, to have access to many great men. *Afterwards* manifesting himself a bit clearer, this assaulter of religious doctrine first endeavored to overthrow the authority of the books of the Old and New Testament. And he tried to show the world, how these writings of human industry were transformed and recast various times. And how it could happen that they were lifted up to the esteem of divinity. Such objections were extensively collected by him in a Spanish treatise under the name of *A Justification of his Departure from Judaism.* But holding back this writing on the advice of friends, he dared to introduce these things more skillfully and more economically in another work, published by him under the name of *Tractatus theologico-politicus* in the year 1670. (Van Til 1694: 5; emphasis added)[11]

I stressed the word "afterwards" (*"Daarna"*). According to Van Til, Spinoza became interested in science and became familiar with mathematics and optics before the break with Jewish tradition.

A confirmation of this new chronology of his life may be found in the biography of Jean Maximilien Lucas, who had been, as he states himself, Spinoza's friend. His *La vie et l'esprit de Mr. Benoit de Spinoza* (which appears in Freudenthal 1899) was published rather late, in 1719, but certainly written not longer than a year after Spinoza's death. In it one finds a fairly reliable report of Spinoza's life, which in my opinion is much underestimated by scholars because they do not like the tone of admiration, even adoration, which runs through the pages. I think that Lucas, though not always precise in his details, is very close to Spinoza's intellectual level. This French immigrant to the Low Countries, who had conversed with Spinoza and may have asked him questions about his youth, twice explicitly gives an early date to Spinoza's critical attitude concerning the Jewish articles of belief:

His father . . . decided to let him learn the Hebrew Literature. This kind of study, which constitutes the whole science of the Jews, could not satisfy his brilliant mind. He had not yet fifteen years, when he proposed objections, which could not be solved by the most learned among the Jews. . . . He concluded that he henceforward could better consult himself and had to take all pains to discover the truth himself. One needs a great mind and an extraordinary power to conceive *under the age of twenty (au-dessous de vingt ans)* such an important plan. (emphasis added)

Lucas continues that Spinoza went on to analyze for himself the biblical texts and Jewish theological authors and that, as an autodidact, he came to his heretical conclusions, for which the rabbis, especially Morteira, would sentence him. He has the rabbis declare

that they had heard him scoff the Jews because they were superstitious people, born and educated in ignorance, who do not know what God is and nevertheless are so audacious as to consider themselves as his people, despising thereby other peoples. And the Law would have been instituted by a man who was much more adroit than they concerning the truth in political matters but who was not at all so much enlightened in physics neither in theology; and that if one had only an ounce of common sense, one could easily unveil the imposture; one had to be equally stupid as the Hebrews in the time of Moses, in order to keep oneself to the orders of this man.

Spinoza's departure (*sortie*) from the Jewish community as well as his entry into Van den Enden's school and his being lodged in the latter's private house are both dated by Lucas *before* his solemn condemnation (the *herem*) in the Synagogue. The study of the sciences and their language (Latin) kept Spinoza already busy for quite a time before the *Parnassim* thought it necessary to drive out his shadow. "Spinoza, who had found an asylum, only thought of making progress in the human Sciences" (Freudenthal 1899: 10).

It should not be supposed that the "human Sciences" (*"Sciences humaines"*) referred to in this text are identical with today's "soft" sciences of man. There was only one science in the days of Galileo, Descartes, Huygens, and Newton, the science of nature, alternatively called *"philosophia"* or *"mathematica"*; and this was the science to which Spinoza henceforth was dedicated. One may read this also in the other biographies available. Colerus, a Lutheran minister, who came to The Hague some years after Spinoza's death, lived in a house where Spinoza had dwelled, did some research on his famous forerunner, and then wrote the *Korte, dog waaragtige Levens-Beschrijving van Benedictus de Spinosa, uit Autentique Stukken en mondeling getuigenis van nog levende Personen, opgestelt* (*Short but true Biography of Benedictus de Spinosa, drawn up from authentic pieces and oral testimonies of still living people*), is also very clear about this point:

Spinoza now understanding the Latin Language . . . and finding himself more capable for research into physical things (*natuurkundige zaaken*), dropped theology and dedicated himself totally to philosophy (*wysgeerte*). For some time he looked for a good Master and for writings which served his intentions, until he finally hit upon Renatus Descartes. He often pretended to have received the greatest light in his natural science (*in zijn natuurkunde*) from Descartes, and that he had learned through him, to accept nothing that could not be proved with sound and clear reasons. . . . As a consequence (*Dienvolgens*) he started to avoid more and more the intercourse with his Jewish Masters and to appear only seldom in the Synagogue, whereupon they started to hate him. (Colerus 1705: 6)

There is no misunderstanding possible concerning the reference of "*sciences humaines*" or "*natuurkunde.*" The testimony of a third biographer, the critical Pierre Bayle in his influential article, "Spinoza," in *Dictionnaire historique et critique,* must be interpreted in the same vein:

He studied Latin language under a medical doctor, who taught in Amsterdam, and he applied himself very early to the study of theology to which he spent several years; after this he dedicated himself totally to the study of philosophy. Since he had the attitude of a geometrician (*l'esprit géomètre*) and he wanted to be paid with reasons for all things, he soon understood that the doctrine of the rabbis did not fit his taste. . . . He withdrew little by little from the Synagogue. (Bayle 1697)

According to the evidence of these documents, the departure from the Synagogue was more the end point of an introduction into natural science than its starting point, as is usually supposed. The new physics of Descartes must have played an important role in Spinoza's process of enlightenment. This is confirmed by Lucas.[12] I will come back to this influence in a moment.

The period 1656–61 is rather invisible for the eyes of the Spinoza historian. We may suppose that Spinoza was for one or two years still in the Latin school of Van den Enden; independent evidence for this hypothesis is the fact that Spinoza's latinity shows much familiarity with the Latin of Terence. We know from other sources that this Latin comedy writer had an important place in Van den Enden's educational method. Under his leadership, the pupils played the *Andria* and the *Eunuchus* in the Town Theater of Amsterdam several times during the first months of 1657 and 1658. Many of Spinoza's crypto-citations of Terence may be traced back to certain roles of the comedies which, therefore, could have been played by Spinoza himself, one of the older pupils.[13] A curious thing is that quotations from Terence seem to be completely absent from the *Treatise on the Emendation of the Intellect*; this absence could be interpreted as an indication for a very early date of this text, namely before Spinoza's participation on the stage.[14] The content and Latin of this work are much nearer to the tragedies and letters of Seneca and the *Metamorphoses* of Ovid.[15] An early origin of the *Treatise on the Emendation of the Intellect* not only fits Mignini's theory about a later origin of the *Short Treatise* (to be discussed later), but is also confirmed by Jarig Jelles in his *Voorreeden* (Preface) to the *Nagelate Schriften*, in which he provides us with a very reliable survey of Spinoza's life, works, and philosophy. He writes, "The *Treatise on the Emendation of the Intellect* was one of the first works of the Author as is testified by its style and concepts themselves."[16] Jelles must have known about Spinoza's "*Apologia.*" It is tempting to substantiate his plural, "one of the author's first works," by connecting the esoteric *Treatise on the Emendation of the Intellect* with the time of the exoteric "*Apologia*" as an unfinished endeavor to render an account of his conversion to philosophy. The first pages of the *Treatise on the Emendation of the Intellect* can only be explained as being very close to Spinoza's personal experiences and the beginning of his new "institution," his new point of view: the unity of the mind with the whole of nature. They are, as it were, notations drawn from his private journal, from the time of his transition to a new "system."[17]

Apart from the orthodox majority there were also Jewish freethinkers in the Amsterdam Jewish community. The tragedy of Uriel da Costa, who, after a life of humiliation, defamation and repeated excommunication, finally committed suicide, must have made a deep impression in the family of Spinoza. Bento was eight years old when the news came that Uriel da Costa had shot himself. His rejection of the Law of Moses had brought him into deep misery and drawn upon him the hatred of the rabbis.[18] Another radical type in "Freetown" ("*Vrijstad*"), as Amsterdam was called in underground literature, was a certain Juan de Prado, a Spanish medical doctor, born in 1610 in Alcalà in Spain, who had settled in Amsterdam in 1641. His works show that he was a naturalist who identified God with nature and rejected superstitious dogmatic doctrines. C. Gebhardt was the first to point to a possible relationship between Spinoza and De Prado at the end of the 1650s (Gebhardt 1923), but it is the merit of the historian I. Révah to have discovered interesting documents in the archive of the Inquisition in Madrid, which demonstrate that Spinoza and De Prado were in contact with each other (Révah 1959, 1964). The monk Solano y Robles answers to the questions of the Inquisitors on 8 August 1659, referring to his stay in Amsterdam the year before, that:

He also got acquaintance with Dr. Juan de Prado, physician, who called himself Juan – he did not know his Jewish name – who had studied in Alcalà and a fellow named De Espinosa, who he thought was a native from one of the Dutch towns, because he had studied in Leiden and was a good philosopher. Those two persons had confessed the Law of Moses, and the Synagoge had expelled and excommunicated them since they had turned atheists. And they themselves had said to the witness, that they had been circumcised and had observed the Law of the Jews, but that they had changed their opinion, because it seemed to them that the Law mentioned was not true and that the souls died with the bodies and that there is no God other than philosophically (*ni havia Dios sino filosofalmente*).

In this hearing, Spinoza was described as "a small man, with a beautiful face, a clear tint, black hair, black eyes. He is twenty-four years old [sic]. He had no job and was Jewish from birth." The next day (August 9, 1659) the captain Miguel Perez de Maltranilla was heard, who confessed that he had often (*muchas veces*) spoken with Dr. Prado and Spinoza in the house of a chevalier of the Canaries. He painted Spinoza's appearance thus: "a young man with a well-formed body, slight, long black hair, a small moustache of the same color, a beautiful face; his age is thirty-three years." Moreover, Spinoza told him that he never had seen Spain but that he wished to see this country.

It is important to find the two heterodox Jews, who had suffered the same fate of excommunication in 1656–7, together in the years 1658–9. The *"Dios de la naturaleza"* was their common ground, the foundation of their enlightenment. It is not impossible that Spinoza and De Prado arrived, with each other's help, at the distinction between the several kinds of knowledge, explicitly presented in the *Treatise on the Emendation of the Intellect* 19–29. There is a letter from De Prado to the *Parnassim* of the Talmud Torah, written in 1658, in which one discovers the distinction:

When I taught him [i.e. the spy sent by the rabbis] about the norms of certainty, asserting that we know some things by natural light, other things from a syllogistic order, other things from experience, other things finally from belief, I gave him at last this example: "I don't believe from experience that there exists a reward and punishment neither do I, forced by reason, assent to the immortality of the soul" (Albiac 1987: 509)

The documents from the Inquisition Archive show that there were contacts between Spinoza and De Prado in the years 1658–9. I cannot, however, follow Révah's overestimation of De Prado's influence, which brings him to the conclusion "that the historians of Spinoza have exaggerated the precocity of the philosophical development of the young Baruch" (Révah 1959: 37). One may imagine that Spinoza opposed De Prado's rejection of the immortality of the soul on account of his early insight into the mind's eternity, as already expressed in the *Treatise on the Emendation of the Intellect.*

A third testimony about the "dark period" in Spinoza's life is contained in the journal of a Danish traveler in the Low Countries, Olaus Borch (Klever 1989b). The notations in the diary of this learned anatomist bring us to the threshold of the slightly better known period of Spinoza's life from which we have at least some letters and other writings. They also show that Spinoza in his Amsterdam period belonged to a group of radical Cartesians. As I noted earlier, the works of Descartes were much discussed in intellectual circles and in the universities.[19] On May 17, 1661, Borch was told, "that there were certain atheists in Amsterdam, most of them Cartesians, among which an impudent atheist Jew." Some months later, on the 10th of September of the same year, when he was traveling in the neighborhood of Leiden, Borch again had something to report about this Jew: People said, that here in the village Rijnsburg lived somebody who had become a Christian from a Jew and now was nearly an atheist. He does not care about (non curat) the Old Testament. The New Testament, the Koran and the fables of Aesop would have the same weight according to him. But for the rest this man behaves quite sincerely and lives without doing harm to other people; and he occupies himself with the construction of telescopes and microscopes.

In 1661 Spinoza was already well-known for his atheism and the fabrication of optical instruments. This text, only recently discovered, is historically the earliest attestation of Spinoza's work in optics, the scientific technology in which he later cooperated with Huygens and the mathematician Hudde. One should not underestimate the value of Borch's testimony. Borch had no special interest in this field and was more fascinated by anatomical lessons than optical theories or theological disputes. What he writes in his diary are the things he casually picks up in his many contacts with other scientists and with professors of the Leiden University. He is, as it were, the echo of the renown that Spinoza already enjoyed in that period. In the same month he once more writes about Spinoza, saying this time "that he *excelled in the Cartesian philosophy*, what is more that he *superseded Descartes*, namely with his distinct and probable ideas; that all those [Cartesian] ideas were far converted by the Amsterdammer Hudde, who added his 'de forkeren' to the recent edition of Descartes' geometrical works" (emphasis added).

It is not quite clear what he means with his reference to Hudde's activity, but it is nonetheless very intriguing to find the famous Hudde[20] already as a neo-Cartesian in Spinoza's companionship and those two among the radical Cartesians of the early 1660s. A third man in this stream of Cartesianizing philosophers was Franciscus van den Enden, probably the mastermind of the circle. He is the first named participant on another day (April 3, 1662), on which Borch, being in Amsterdam, writes in his journal, that:

there are here atheists and they are principally Cartesianists, like Van den Enden, Glasemaker etc.; and they also teach other people. They don't preach openly atheism, because they often speak about God, but by God they do understand nothing else than this whole universe, as appears more clearly from a *certain Dutch writing*, which was recently artificially written while the name of the Author was suppressed.[21] (emphasis added)

It is tantalizing to suppose that this mention of a "certain Dutch writing" is a reference to Spinoza's *Short Treatise* and thereby also a confirmation of its then fairly recent composition. In the same month (April 1662) Spinoza writes to Oldenburg:

As for your question how things have begun to be, and by what connection they depend on the first cause, I have composed a whole *short* work devoted to this matter. I am engaged in transcribing and emending it, but sometimes I put it to one side because I do not yet have any definite plan regarding its publication. I fear, of course, that the theologians of our time may be offended and with their usual hatred attack me, who absolutely dread quarrels. . . . I regard as creatures many attributes which they – and everyone, so far as I know – attribute to God. Conversely, other things, which they, because of their prejudices, regard as creatures, I contend are attributes of God, which they have misunderstood. Also, I do not separate God from nature, as everyone known to me has done. (Ep 6; emphasis added)

It was F. Mignini who first proposed on internal evidence the theory that the *Short Treatise* was written after the *Treatise on the Emendation of the Intellect*, probably in the years 1661–2.[22] The *Short Treatise* is clearly an esoteric work, destined for private use in the circle of friends, as is stated explicitly at its conclusion:

To bring all this to an end, it remains only for me to say to *the friends to whom I write this*: do not be surprised at these novelties. . . . And as you are also aware of the age in which we live, I would ask you urgently to be very careful about communicating these things to others. I do not mean that you should keep them altogether to yourselves, but only that if you ever begin to communicate them to someone, you should have no other aim or motive than the salvation of your fellow man, and make as sure as possible that you will not work in vain. (KV II.26.10; emphasis added)

As far as I can see, all evidence converges on the hypothesis that the treatise referred to in Borch's journal must be Spinoza's *Short Treatise*. This work is, though not yet in geometrical form, a systematically (and in that sense also artificially) composed treatise, a provisional presentation of the material that later would be geometrically deduced in the *Ethics*.

As Borch states elsewhere in his journal, Van den Enden had also written some works and handed over to certain friends "*quaedam philosophiae suae arcaniora . . . manuscripta*," ("certain more secret things of his philosophy . . . in manuscript"). We do not actually have manuscripts of Van den Enden from this period; but we do have a printed pamphlet written by him in 1661 and 1662 with the title *Kort Verhael van Nieuw-Nederlants* . . . (1662) and another one, published in 1665 under the title *Vrije Politijcke Stellingen*, but written in 1663. These pamphlets were recently unearthed by this author[23] and were also discovered nineteen years earlier, but not published, by M. Bedjai, as I came to hear some weeks later. On the basis of the mentioned works I came to the conclusion that Van den Enden must be considered a proto-Spinoza, the genius behind Spinoza; Bedjai defends in his thesis the same idea, by claiming that the so-called Amsterdam Spinoza circle could better be named "Van den Enden and his circle" (Bedjai 1990). The works of Van den Enden contain a political theory which is in fact the same as the one worked out by Spinoza in his *Theological-Political Treatise* and *Political Treatise*. One finds moreover between the lines all the items which would later be proven deductively by Spinoza in his *Ethics*: full-fledged determinism, the distinction between three kinds of knowledge (and other epistemological claims), human passivity, the *conatus* theory, the intellectual love of God, and so on. Much research has still to be done, but one may already conclude that the group of Amsterdam friends, to which Meyer and Bouwmeester also belonged, had a common philosophy, to which they were inspired by the Latin schoolmaster, the radical Cartesian and medical doctor Franciscus van den Enden. This man is very much praised by contemporary poets on account of his extraordinary capacities in science and letters, in education and politics.[24] He appears to have been strongly occupied with political theory and practice. Spinoza's intention to contribute as much as possible to the formation of society, about which he spoke on the third page of his earliest writing, may be interpreted as an echo of Van den Enden's main interest.[25]

Spinoza's preoccupation with Descartes can also be demonstrated from other sources. In the early 1660s (1660–3), he had many contacts with the Danish anatomist Niels Stensen (Steno), who was at the time a medical student in Leiden. In the letter which Steno addressed to him in 1671, not quite four years after his conversion to Roman Catholicism in 1667,[26] he described Spinoza as "a man who once was very familiar with me." He explicitly acknowledges in this letter, that Spinoza was very much at home in the Cartesian philosophy, which is "very diligently elaborated and *reformed by you*" (emphasis added). In the same year, 1671, Steno wrote to the famous Malpighi: "I have certain friends in Holland who are altogether lost to (*dati tutti alla*) Cartesian philosophy, in such a way that they make philosophy the judge about all knowledge of grace" (Stenonis 1952: 248).

It cannot be doubted that Spinoza had chosen the career of a scientist, that is, the "investigation of nature" in all its aspects. For some years he had concentrated on the laws of human nature, the results of which were laid down in his *Short Treatise on God, Man, and His Well-Being*. Nature was a continuum for him, of which all things were simply modes or modifications. Man is such a mode of the one, divine, infinite nature, determined by other modes in a never-ending series, but always according to the eternal laws, partly known to us in the so-called common notions. For a scientist, everything is caused by something else in the same attribute. This principle is also valid for human behavior, that is, for the motions of human bodies, which must be considered as effects of other motions, inside or (mainly) outside those bodies. This was the point on which he criticized his master in physics, Descartes, as he said in his first letter (September 1661) to the Secretary of the English Royal Society, Henry Oldenburg: "particular volitions cannot be called free (because they require a cause in order to exist), but must be as their causes have determined them to be" (Ep 2).

The English scientists, foremost Robert Boyle, and Spinoza, with other Dutchmen like Huygens and Hudde, had a common field of interest and research, and entertained considerable communication with each other. Oldenburg had told Spinoza about Boyle's physiological essays and his experiments about the elasticity of air, about fluidity and fixity of matter (Ep 1), and he wrote:

In our Philosophical College we devote ourselves as energetically as we can to making experiments and observations, and are much occupied with putting together a History of Mechanical Arts. For we regard it as settled that the forms and qualities of things can best be explained on mechanical Principles, that all nature's effects are produced by motion, shape and texture, and their various combinations, and that there is no need for us to seek a refuge for our ignorance in inexplicable forms and occult qualities. (Ep 3)

Spinoza must have been fascinated by this news because he fully subscribed to this research program himself. In his Letter 6 he commented as an expert on the results of Boyle's experiments concerning the constitution of saltpeter (niter), using for his criticism the upshot of the three experiments he had done himself. This proves that he must have been introduced to this type of work in an earlier period. In fact, we know that Van den Enden also, together with a certain Johan Glauber,[27] was devoted to chemical analysis. It is likely that Spinoza also had participated in this work when he was still living in Amsterdam. His critique of Boyle's book was that Boyle was not consistent enough in his endeavor to give only mechanical explanations of natural phenomena:

In paragraph 25 the Distinguished Gentleman seems to wish to demonstrate that the alkaline parts are carried here and there by the impulse of the saline particles, but that the saline particles *raise themselves into the air by their own impulse.*

In explaining this Phenomenon I have said that the particles of Spirit of Niter acquire a more violent motion because, when they enter wider passages, they must necessarily be surrounded by a very fine matter and *driven upwards* by it, as particles of wood are by fire, but that the alkaline particles receive their motion from the impulse of particles of Spirit of Niter penetrating through the narrower passages. (Ep 6; emphasis added)

Another remark, on a passage in which Boyle supposes that nature has designed birds and fishes for flying and for swimming, could not be shorter and sharper: "He seeks the cause in the purpose." A natural scientist is not allowed to explain by final causes.

The reader should consult Letters 6 and 13 in order to discover how much Spinoza was involved in empirical science – without, however, neglecting the principles of mathematical method.[28] We should realize that this was the type of work to which he was mostly dedicated as a "philosopher." His philosophy was not a kind of "armchair philosophy," far away from the center of natural science. On the contrary, he conceived and practiced a type of philosophy which was continuous with what we call today "natural science." This claim can also be proved in another way.

The Amsterdam friends, who in early 1663 already possessed some of Spinoza's writings and discussed them in their circle,[29] suddenly discovered that Spinoza, as a professional tutor, had explained Cartesian philosophy to a Leiden University student named Casearius. This made them jealous. "Fortunate, indeed, most fortunate is your companion, Casearius, who lives under the same roof with you, and can talk to you about the most important matters at breakfast, at dinner, and on your walks" (De Vries, in Ep 8). In fact, Casearius received from Spinoza a very professional introduction in Cartesian physics; in their contact hours they concentrated on the second and following books of Descartes's *Principles of Philosophy*.

Here is how Lodewijk Meyer, a learned friend and himself a *doctor medicinae* from Leiden University, introduces the 1663 edition of Spinoza's *Descartes's "Principles of Philosophy."* After having declared "that the best and surest method of seeking and teaching the truth in the sciences is that of the mathematicians, who demonstrate their conclusions from definitions, postulates, and axioms, since a certain and firm knowledge of anything unknown can only be derived from things known certainly beforehand," he says that his time is privileged because it is enlightened by the "brightest star" of the age, René Descartes, whose writings contain a mathematical method, though not yet fully formalized. Because unskilled readers need some help with their study of Descartes's work, Meyer had often wished that someone who possessed "a thorough knowledge of Descartes's writings and philosophy" would be able to bring these people some assistance by rendering in the synthetic order what Descartes had written in the analytic order, thereby demonstrating everything in the manner familiar to the geometricians. He felt himself unequal to so great a task and was, moreover, occupied by other things:

Therefore I was very pleased to learn from our Author that he had dictated, to a certain pupil of his, whom he was teaching the Cartesian Philosophy, the whole Second Part of the *Principles*, and part of the Third, demonstrated in that geometric manner, along with some of the principal and more difficult questions, which are disputed in Metaphysics and had not yet been resolved by Descartes, and that in response to the entreaties and demands of his friends, he had agreed that, once he corrected and added to them, these writings might be published. So I too commended this project to him, and at the same time gladly offered my help in publishing, if he should require it. Moreover, I advised him – indeed entreated him – to render also the first part of the *Principles* in a like order, and set it before what he had already written, so that by having been arranged in this manner from the beginning, the matter could be better understood and more pleasing. When he saw the soundness of this argument, he did not wish to deny both the requests of a friend and the utility of the reader. And he entrusted to my care the whole business of printing and publishing, since he lives in the country, far from the city, and so could not be present. (DPP Preface)

Having summarized, then, the contents of the work, Meyer continues by asserting that Spinoza not only often deviates from Descartes
in the arrangement and explanation of the axioms, demonstrations,
and conclusions, but also that Spinoza himself in many cases does
not agree with Descartes's propositions, which are faithfully presented by him. "So let no one think that he is teaching here either
his own opinions, or only those which he approves of." Spinoza, for
example, does not think that the will is distinct from the intellect,
much less that it is endowed with freedom. According to him, Descartes is only assuming and does not prove that the human mind is a
substance thinking absolutely. Another important point of disagreement between Descartes and his expositor is that Descartes is too
quick in stating that this or that surpasses the human understanding
concerning things which in the opinion of Spinoza are entirely clear
and can be explained satisfactorily. The foundations of Descartes's
science, says Meyer, are not the same as those of Spinoza's. Meyer's
introduction to *Descartes's "Principles of Philosophy"* is extremely
valuable as an authentic document about an early period in Spinoza's career, containing a clear statement of Spinoza's position on
Cartesian science.

Meyer was an important scientist and author in his own right. He
held Spinoza in high respect, but the converse is also true, as may be
concluded from Spinoza's letters to him (Ep 12, 12A, 15). It is not
impossible that it was he who pushed Spinoza towards the geo-
metrization of his philosophy. After having written his medical and
physical doctoral dissertations in 1662 at Leiden University, he returned to Amsterdam as a *"liberalium artium magister"* and dedicated his powers first to the question of the interpretation of the
Scripture, which was an important topic in the theological disputes of
those years. The results of this research program were published in
his *Philosophias s. scripturae interpres* (Meyer 1666).[30] The text of
this work, however, was written a few years before (in 1663–4) as
Meyer remarks in his postscript.[31] I will attend to this work in order
to clarify the meaning of the word "philosophy" in that period and,
also, to use the work as a source which not only refers to Spinoza's
early influence but likewise to its effects on Spinoza. Secondary literature constructs an opposition between Meyer and Spinoza,[32] in my
opinion without any foundation. Both Spinoza and Meyer maintain
that the true sense (*sensus verus*) of scriptural phrases, paragraphs,

sections, or works can only be discovered in a rational, that is, scientific, way. They both reject the idea that the meaning of words and sentences would depend on or should have to be accommodated to a certain philosophical system or to other prejudices of readers and interpreters. When they call "philosophy" or "the understanding" the judge of revelation, they do not intend anything other than scientific treatment, professional reading with the help of philology, history, and so on. One should, as a real expert, show and prove by means of linguistic principles, grammar and lexicography, and practical methods like comparison of words and metaphors, that a certain sense is indeed the meaning of the author, even when it is not at all understandable why he wants to say it. "Philosophy" is equivalent to "knowledge of the liberal arts and sciences" (Meyer 1666: 53), "especially grammar, rhetoric, dialectics, and physics" (Meyer 1666: 122), and knowledge of particular languages – in the case of the Scripture, the oriental languages. On the last page of his work Meyer alludes to people (plural) who, following in Descartes's footsteps, "will bring to light such things of God, the rational soul, and human highest happiness and similar things, belonging to the acquisition of eternal life." The sequence of words in this sentence is, for the insiders, a salute to the title of Spinoza's *Short Treatise on God, Man, and His Well-Being.* Some pages earlier, however, Meyer had referred to an anonymous singular: "the most illustrious and experienced man in those things" (i.e. philology), or to "this same man, by far the most exercised in all sort of similar knowledge and learning, who does not hesitate to declare in clear words that *when somebody would compare all the written books of the New Testament with each other, he would find as many differences in them as words*" (Meyer 1666: 131).[33] Elsewhere, this man is called the "eminent philosopher of our age" (Meyer 1666: 134). Meyer, who must have been very close to Spinoza and was fully trusted by him, pays great honor to his scientific companion with these words. His own scientific career was filled with philological, grammatical, and poetical studies. He composed a famous Dutch dictionary, *Woordenschat,* which ran into various editions; an Italian grammar; a Latin vocabulary; and many plays for the theater. He also cooperated with another friend of Spinoza, Johannes Bouwmeester, in the art academy *"Nil Volentibus Arduum"* (NVA), which was the collective author of *Onderwijs in de tooneelpoëzy* (*Science of theater poetry*).[34]

Spinoza continued his work in the science of letters with his *Theological-Political Treatise* (to which I will refer later) and with his *Compendium of Hebrew Grammar* – an unfinished but still quite voluminous work – published in the *Opera Posthuma*, which he must have started in the same years in which NVA flourished (1669–71).[35] The editors of the *Opera Posthuma*, which included the same linguists Meyer and Bouwmeester, declared in their "admonition to the reader" that Spinoza had written this grammar "at the request of some of his friends (*rogatu amicorum quorundam suorum*) who very much studied the holy language," by which words they probably indicated themselves. It is very likely that this work was meant as a contribution from Spinoza to the linguistic research program of the academy NVA of his friends. They further said in their foreword that they knew that he was "imbibed with this language from his early youth, that he had studied it during many years with great effort and understood its 'genius' very well, and that he was an excellent expert in it." In Spinoza's (and Meyer's) view the scientific analysis of the Hebrew language was very important for the interpretation of the Scripture. Spinoza would demonstrate this in the seventh chapter of the *Theological-Political Treatise*, but said it also in his satirical remark in the *Compendium of Hebrew Grammar* that "there have been many people who wrote a grammar [explication] of the Scripture but none who wrote one of the Hebrew language" (CGLH vii.2). It is very misleading, to say the least, that historiographers of philosophy do not even mention that this "philosopher," Spinoza, spent a considerable amount of his valuable time in the analysis and description of the linguistic structures of Hebrew, and composed a grammar of it which manifested a very personal style.[36]

Jelles testifies in retrospect about Spinoza in his biographical Preface to the *Nagelate Schriften*, that:

He has exercised himself in linguistics and literature (*Letteren*) from childhood on.... He has, apart from his usual occupation in the sciences (*wetenschappen*) taken his special exercise in the optics (*Gezichtkunde*), and in the grinding of magnifying glasses and telescopes.... He spent most of his time in the *research of the nature of things* and in ordering the things he had found in order to communicate them to other people. (Akkerman 1980: 216; emphasis added)

Spinoza was – I cannot repeat it enough – a man of science rather than a twentieth-century kind of philosopher. Optics had his special interest. I must now say a few words more about this topic, because historians tend to neglect also this aspect of his work, in the opinion that it was only marginal. All biographical sources, however, stress that Spinoza was very much occupied with and interested in this field of research, on a theoretical level but also practically. When Leibniz called him an *"insignis opticus"* (Freudenthal 1899: 193), this was not a rhetorical trick in order to avoid the title (and praise) of the philosopher, but a telling assessment.

I have already said that Spinoza's work was more than handicraft, and may be compared with optical industry, which implied optical theory. The German travelers Stolle and Hallmann (Freudenthal 1899: 225), Pierre Bayle (Bayle 1697: 346), Colerus, Jelles, Lucas, Christiaan Huygens, Theodor Kerckringh, and many others relate that Spinoza personally constructed microscopes and telescopes which were highly praised by the scientists of his day. Leibniz praised him as the maker of famous peeptubes and confessed in his letter to him (October 5, 1671) that "he would not easily find somebody who in this field of studies could judge better." In his *Observationes anatomicae*, Kerckringh, a comrade of Spinoza's in Van den Enden's Latin school who had become a famous anatomist, wrote: "I own a first class microscope (*microscopium praestantissimum*) made by that Benedictus Spinoza, that noble mathematician and philosopher, which enables me to see the lymphatic vascular bundles. . . . Well, this that I have clearly discovered by means of my marvelous instrument, is itself still more marvelous" (Kerckringh 1670: 177).

The famous astronomer and mathematician Christiaan Huygens spoke about the excellent instruments fabricated by "that Israelite" (a somewhat deprecative expression) living nearby in Voorburg. Being in Paris, he frequently requested his brother to give him all possible information about the theoretical and technical progress Spinoza made in this field. After some disagreement, he had in the end to confess that Spinoza was right: "It is true that experience confirms what is said by Spinoza, namely that the small objectives in the microscope represent the objects much finer than the large ones" (Huygens 1888–1950: IV,140; letter of May 11, 1668). A trace of the scientific discussions between Huygens and Spinoza can also be found in Spinoza's letter of May 1665 to Oldenburg:

Mr. Huygens also has the book on microscopic observations, but unless I am mistaken, it is in English. He has told me wonderful things about these microscopes and also about certain Telescopes, made in Italy, with which they could observe eclipses of Jupiter caused by the interposition of its satellites, and also a certain shadow on Saturn, which looked as if it were caused by a ring. These things make me astonished at Descartes's haste. He says that the reason why the Planets next to Saturn – for he thought its projections were Planets, perhaps because he never observed them touching Saturn – do not move may be that Saturn does not rotate around its own axis. But this does not agree very well with his principles. (Ep 26)

Spinoza certainly joined Huygens during one of his nightly observations of Jupiter by means of his thirty-foot telescope. Spinoza was quite sure of his own position in optics and was not afraid to criticize Huygens. After having summarized in Letter 30 some points of Huygens's *Dioptrics* for Oldenburg in London, he adds to it the remark: "Until now this seems to me fully impossible." Of another mathematician, the later Amsterdam Burgomaster Johannes Hudde, Spinoza asked advice. Letter 36 from June 1666 shows that Spinoza in one and the same letter explained to him the properties of the infinite divine nature and proposed to him an optical formula which would enable him to construct the best new dishes for grinding lenses. Optical questions were also the subject of some correspondence with Jarig Jelles (Ep 39).[37]

Spinoza not only specialized in optical theory and technology but also tried to make observations himself as well as possible, where it was appropriate by means of instruments. To Ostens he wrote that "the nicest hand looks terrible when seen through a microscope" (Ep 54). And the famous Letter 32, in which the harmony in the infinite world is illustrated by the example of a worm living in the blood and pushing against other particles and viruses, clearly suggests that Spinoza practiced the study of the blood by means of his microscope. In Colerus's biography we find a trace of this pleasure in microscopic observation, where he relates about Spinoza:

He also often took his magnifying glass, observing through this the smallest mosquitoes and flies, at the same time reasoning about them.
He knew, however, that things cannot be seen as they are in themselves.

The eternal properties and laws of things and processes can only be discovered by deduction from common notions and evident axioms. "The eyes of the mind, by which it sees and observes the things, are the demonstrations."[38]

The practice of science to which Spinoza was fully dedicated[39] raised much criticism against his person on the side of the ministers of the Reformed Church, who, having discovered that he identified God with nature in unpublished manuscripts, and being afraid of his growing influence, accused him of atheism and tried to warn their flocks against his "pernicious" doctrines. In a local dispute in Voorburg concerning the appointment of a new minister – in which Spinoza's landlord Daniel Tydeman was also involved – the pious people of the church council spread the following report:

That the aforesaid Daniel Tydeman has rented an apartment to an A . . . Spinosa, born from Jewish parents, who is now (as it is said) an atheist or someone who scoffs at all religions and therefore is a harmful instrument in this republic, as so many learned men and preachers, among which Rev. Lantman and who know him, may testify, who has written the request presented to the Burgomasters. (Freudenthal 1899: 117-19)

The preachers did not shrink from instigating theological hatred and so, with an appeal to divine revelation, calling a halt to the threatening natural science. From the pulpit and with many polemical pamphlets, the political authorities were accused of negligence in the campaign against this evil. The pressure of the Orangistic party directed by them drove the liberal states-party, the party of the so-called *regenten* (i.e., the political governors), more and more into the corner. The tensions between the Reformed Church and the government resulted in a grim relationship.

Spinoza was not the only one to experience the negative consequences of a life of reason devoted to the causal explanation of things. His friend Lodewijk Meyer wrote in 1665 in the Postscript of his *Interpres*, "The discomfort and harm, which hang above my head, is the hatred of the theologians, who will despise and reject my sentiments. . . . They usually elevate themselves above all scientists, imagining that the divine enunciations are only confided to them." His prediction was accurate. Six undignified refutations followed immediately upon the publication of his scientific treatment of the Scriptures, in which he had done nothing more than to try to discover the "true sense" (*verus sensus*) of the prophecies with linguistic proofs. The first words written in *Onderwijs* by another friend, Johannes Bouwmeester, read: "Everywhere and in all times are the Arts and Sciences most hated by the ignorant," and he stated that especially the ministers of all religious sects tried to darken the truth for their audience in favor of their own profit.

It seemed to Spinoza that it would become impossible for him to remain in security and at the same time explain to his fellow citizens the principles of nature and their application to human behavior, as he had done according to the method of the geometricians in the first drafts of his *Ethics*, already sent to his friends in Amsterdam. Hence, he decided to interrupt this work, which would likely end in disaster, in order first to pave the way for a truly free communication of thoughts. And had it not always been his intention to do his utmost for the well-being of the state in order to derive for himself the maximum of happiness and safety from it? Personal safety depends on the stability of the state. But a sound state is impossible where freedom of thought, speech, and publication is excluded or restricted by the narrow-mindedness of the bigots. In October 1665 he informed Oldenburg about his new activity:

I have now started writing a treatise with my insights concerning the Scripture. I am motivated to do so by:

1. The prejudices of the theologians, because I realize that they are the main obstacles which restrain people from the dedication to science.[40] Therefore I exert myself to reveal them and to ban them from the mind of the more prudent people.

2. The opinion that the common people cherish concerning me: it does not stop to accuse me of atheism. I feel myself compelled to avert as far as possible also this evil.

3. The freedom to practice science and to express our thoughts. I wish to defend with all means this freedom, which is suppressed here by the too great authority and brutality of the preachers.

The first objective, the unmasking and dismantling of the prejudices of the theologians, consisting in false interpretations and a political misuse of the Scripture, was fulfilled in the first part of the *Theological-Political Treatise* (i.e., Chapters i–xv). An elucidation of this target is also given in the Preface. Having stated that those who call themselves Christians only see mysterious and incredible things in the Scripture, Spinoza continued:

When I revolved this in my mind, namely that the natural light was not only despised but that it was also damned by many as the source of impiety, that human fictions were considered as divine doctrines and credulity was estimated as belief, that in church and court the highest emotions were stirred by philosophical controversies and as a consequence the most cruel hatred and discord originated by which people easily came to rebellion . . . I made the serious decision, to study the Scriptures again, to examine them with a free mind, to neither affirm nor admit anything as its doctrine, that could not be most clearly demonstrated to be so.

The method to fulfill this project is the same as that indicated and practiced by Meyer. Spinoza explained his principles for the scientific understanding and explanation of a text such as the Scriptures in Chapter vii. They consist mainly in the knowledge of the Hebrew language, in a historical approach to the separate books, in a comparison of various parts of a book, and so on. The method of explaining texts does not differ from the method of explaining natural phenomena: In both cases the phenomena are deduced from general principles.

Spinoza's second purpose, namely his defense of himself, as a scientist, against the charge of atheism, is fulfilled in Chapter vi, where he rejects the possibility of miracles and claims that we have a better knowledge of God in the degree we have more knowledge of nature. "If there would happen something in nature, which would not follow from its laws . . . , that would be against nature and its laws and consequently the belief in it would make us doubt everything and lead us to atheism" (TTP vi.28).

Spinoza realizes the third objective, the defense of the freedom of science, of publication of scientific results, and of discussion on all kinds of topics, in the five last chapters. According to the theory of the state developed in Chapters xvi–xx, the "libertas philosophandi" constitutes the very essence of a political society, as is likewise indicated in the formulation of the subtitle, "that this freedom can only be taken away (tolli) together with the peace and piety of the republic." Doctrinal prescriptions can only cause dissension, sectarianism, and schisms among the people, by which the freedom of the state (not to mention the possibility of sciences and arts) is necessarily undermined. A government which mixes itself in questions of theology will stimulate the fury of parties and change piety into rage. Dutch history had provided a tragic example of such a rage, which should

serve as a warning for all times that laws about religion are pernicious. This example was the battle between the Remonstrants and
the Contra-Remonstrants, mentioned by Spinoza on the penultimate
page of the *Theological-Political Treatise* (TTP xx.41). The puritani-
cal Calvinists, together with Prince Maurice, had succeeded in bringing the state of Holland to the edge of the abyss. The great statesman
of the time, the pensionary Oldenbarnevelt, a Remonstrant with liberal ideas, had to pay with his life (in 1619). It is to him that Spinoza
cynically alludes in *Theological-Political Treatise* xx.35:

What, I say, can be more hurtful than that men who have committed no
crime or wickedness should because they are enlightened, be treated as
enemies and put to death and that the scaffold, the terror of the delinquents,
should become the finest theatre to show the highest example of tolerance
and virtue to the sharp disgrace of the majesty?

Amsterdam, in contrast, was a positive example in the eyes of Spinoza. "In this most flourishing republic and excellent town people of
all nations and sects live together with highest unanimity" (TTP
xx.40). As a member of a community of political refugees, the minority of Portuguese Jews, Spinoza had had no notably bad experiences
with the state authorities and their justice. But was Amsterdam still
so tolerant in the late 1660s?

As Spinoza was writing his treatise, the situation worsened because of a serious economic malaise and the political isolation of the
Dutch Republic. Intolerance was aggravated also, and came very
close to Spinoza himself. To the circle of his friends and followers
belonged a certain Adriaan Koerbagh, who had studied medicine and
law in Utrecht and Leiden. He had (with his brother Johan) become
persuaded by Spinoza's naturalism, and was also acquainted with
Franciscus van den Enden. This man, only two years younger than
Spinoza, started to spread all the essentials of the Spinozistic theory
from 1665 onward, and published them in 1668, in plain Dutch.[41]
His main work, *Een ligt*, was on many pages more open about Spinoza's esoteric doctrine than the *Theological-Political Treatise*. God
is defined as "the essence of all modes of existence, consisting of
infinite attributes, of which each one is infinite in its kind." The
work as a whole may be considered as a parallel to the *Theological-
Political Treatise*, with chapters on Essence (God is consequently
called "*Wesen*"!), the Savior (Jesus), the Holy Spirit (reason), good

and evil, religion, the Bible, heretics, heaven, miracles, and so on.[42] Nowhere in the book is Spinoza's name mentioned, but his doctrine is elaborated on many pages. The author was, however, much less prudent than Spinoza himself, and launched strong attacks on the preachers and theologians. When he was arrested, he confessed at his trial to his relations with Spinoza and Van den Enden. He was sentenced, in the free town of Amsterdam, to ten years in the house of correction (*tuchthuis*), ten years exile afterward, and a fine of 6,000 guilders. He was thrown into the *Rasphuis*, a prison with very bad circumstances, in which he died a year later (in 1669).

This case of theological fury resulting in political repercussions – to which his friend and pupil Adriaan Koerbagh fell a victim, in a town which according to his own memory was so tolerant to every kind of religion – must have made a deep impression on Spinoza, occupied with the later chapters of the *Theological-Political Treatise*. The authorities had sentenced Koerbagh under the pressure of the ministers of the Reformed Church, who had decried Koerbagh as a very great danger to public life. Having explained how the Pharisees had accused the Sadducees of impiety, Spinoza continued in *Theological-Political Treatise* xviii.24, probably thinking of the unhappy fate of his friend: "Following this example of the Pharisees the vilest hypocrites, agitated by the same frenzy (*rabie agitati*) which they call zeal by divine right, have always persecuted men distinguished by their honesty and their virtue and therefore envied by the mob; they do this by publicly despising their opinions and inflaming the anger of the furious multitude against them."

The *Theological-Political Treatise* was published in 1670, anonymously and under a false impress.[43] The work soon proved to be counterproductive. It neither helped to reduce the influence of theological prejudices among philosophically-minded readers nor furthered the freedom required for the enlightened citizen. In fact, the *Theological-Political Treatise* did not at all prepare the way for the publication and reception of Spinoza's overall philosophy. Its publication, on the contrary, aggravated the situation by unchaining a series of devastating refutations and defamations.[44] A good example of a negative reaction in a person who was considered a liberal philosopher, and therefore especially addressed by Spinoza in his preface as a "philosophical reader," was Lambert van Velthuysen, a member of the Utrecht "*College der sçavanten,*" who attacked the *Theological-*

Political Treatise as an atheistic writing in a letter to Ostens. Spinoza was disappointed and even indignant about this "sinister" interpretation, as he called it in his Letter 43 to Jacob Ostens. Van Velthuysen had consciously misrepresented the claims and objectives of the treatise in his summary, the "*libellum*" that he had sent to their common friend. How could he call him an atheist? "Atheists are used to strive immoderately to honors and riches, which I always have despised, as all know who are acquainted with me. . . . In this way was Descartes formerly denounced by Voetius, and so the best people are everywhere betrayed!"[45]

The Councils and Synods of the Reformed Church showed a high degree of vigilance. They immediately condemned the *Theological-Political Treatise* as "a harmful book" (Amsterdam), a "treatise of idolatry and superstition" (The Hague, July 1670), as "the vilest and most sacrilegious book the world has ever seen" (Schiedam, July 1670). The theologian J. Melchior published in the same year a refutation in which Spinoza's name was spoiled to "Xinospa" and he was characterized as a freak (*monstrum*). A professor in Utrecht, a certain J. G. Graevius, wrote in a letter to Leibniz about the "*liber pestilentissimus*," full of "monstrous opinions." The effect of the book, in which Spinoza "talked as a scientist about the Scripture" was nothing less than "a torrent of persecutors."[46]

The upheaval, though, was soon overshadowed by a political revolution of far-reaching consequences. The regime of the liberal grand-pensionary Jan de Witt, who had been in power uninterruptedly since 1654, came to a bloody end with the invasion of the French and German armies in the so-called disaster year (*rampjaar*) of Dutch history (1672). The whole country was "*radeloos, redeloos en reddeloos*," that is, desperate, irrational, and past recovery. Jan de Witt, together with his brother, was abducted by the mob and cruelly murdered. The dynasty of the Orange lieutenants (*Stadhouders*) returned in the person of the young prince William III (later king of England). It was said by Leibniz, who visited Spinoza in 1676, that Spinoza, who must have conversed with Jan de Witt,[47] was in great distress[48] at this rebellion and at the death of his political friend and protector, and therefore wanted to protest against it by means of a placard on which he had written "*Ultimi Barbarorum*." But the landlord restrained him from such a dangerous demonstration.[49]

Notwithstanding the grim rejection of the *Theological-Political*

Treatise by the ministers of the Reformed Church, the work became a commercial success for the publisher, Spinoza's friend Jan Rieuwertsz. The gales of indignation could not withhold the presses from printing new editions. After five quarto editions in 1670, a series of octavo editions with misleading title pages was laid up. In 1673 the *Theological-Political Treatise* appeared as *Francisci Henriquez de Villacorta, doctoris medici Opera Chirurgica omnia* (Amstelodami: apud Jacobum Paulli). Another edition from the same year was baptized *Danielis Heinsii Operum Historicorum collectio prima. Editio secunda, priori editione multo emendatior & auctior. Accedunt quaedam hactenus inedita* (Lugd. Batav: Apud Isaacum Herculis). A third edition in octavo was named *Totius Medicinae idea nova, seu Francisci de le Boe Sylvii, medici inter Batavos celeberrimi Opera Omnia novas potissimum super morborum causis, symptomatis & curandi ratione meditationes & disputationes continentia* (Amstelodami: apud Carolum Gratiani).[50] Rieuwertsz was a courageous entrepreneur, not deprived of some humor. His shop, called *"In het Martelaersboeck"* (*In the Book of the Martyrs*), was a center of freethinkers' discussions in which news was exchanged between radical Cartesians and Spinozists.

Spinoza knew, however, that he had to be careful and that his life could be in danger when the common people were stirred against him. He had not forgotten the case of Adriaan Koerbagh, who had published his ideas in plain Dutch. Therefore, he tried with all available means to forestall the publication of the Dutch translation of his *Theological-Political Treatise*. On February 17, 1671, when he still enjoyed the protection of Jan de Witt, he wrote to his Amsterdam friend Jarig Jelles:

When recently the professor . . . paid a visit to me, he told me among other things that he had heard that my *Tractatus theologico-politicus* was translated into Dutch and that somebody – he did not know who – intends to give it in print. Therefore I beseech you urgently to do your best to get information and, if possible, to prevent the printing. This is not only my request but also that of many of my friends and acquaintances, who would not like to see that the book would be forbidden, as will undoubtedly happen when it will be published in Dutch. (Ep 44)

Spinoza's fame, which had already begun to spread by 1665[51] now reached a higher pitch. His ideas reached through the whole of Europe: London, Paris, Florence, Rome, Stockholm, and other cities. The court of Heidelberg invited him for a professorship in the newly founded academy of the illustrious monarch Karl Ludwig of the Palts. But Spinoza did not hesitate to decline this offer. In his letter of invitation, the councillor Fabricius (who was himself against the invitation) had mentioned a condition that was impossible for Spinoza to fulfill because it did not depend on himself. He was to receive the amplest freedom of philosophizing ("*philosophandi libertatem*"), but it was expected that he would not "misuse it in order to disturb the publicly established religion" (Ep 47; February 16, 1673). Spinoza's answer was to the point: "I think that I do not know in what boundaries that freedom of philosophizing should be included in order not to make the impression that I have the intention to perturb the publicly-instituted religion." Spinoza did not want to take the risk. He had already experienced how easily he could be misunderstood and misinterpreted, even when he aimed for a very clear presentation of his thoughts. "And since I have already experienced this while leading a private and solitary life, how much more have I to fear this in case I will ascend towards such a degree of dignity" (Ep 48; March 30, 1673). Another reason Spinoza offered for not accepting the invitation was that it never had been his wish to be a professor with public teaching responsibility. The instruction of the youth would hinder him from being free for the promotion of science. The background of this argument must be the same as the other motive just mentioned: A man who is employed by certain authorities and paid for his academic work is in fact a subordinate, who has to keep himself to certain prescriptions and expectations, and has no full freedom of speech. As Spinoza wrote: "Academies that are founded at the public expense are instituted not so much to cultivate men's natural abilities as to restrain them. But in a free commonwealth, arts and sciences (*scientiae et artes*) will be best cultivated to the full if everyone that asks leave is allowed to teach publicly, and that at his own cost and risk" (TTP viii.49). A scientist must be completely independent. One's freedom is unavoidably restrained when one allows oneself to be paid for one's work.

It is not impossible that a third reason played a role in Spinoza's declining the invitation of Karl Ludwig, who was known to be a monarch with a free mind. Fabricius himself was an orthodox theologian who had studied reformed theology in Utrecht under Voetius and had many relations with Dutch Contra-Remonstrant theologians such as Frederik Spanheim. A certain J. H. Heidegger later said in his obituary of this Fabricius that Fabricius, after having read the "horrible book" (the *Theological-Political Treatise*), had told him that he hoped that this blasphemous material would never be allowed to enter and be promulgated inside the German borders. He further had remarked that he much preferred that similar pernicious opinions be suppressed rather than refuted.[52] In a small world with only a few networks of relationships this attitude of the Dutch Fabricius may have been known to Spinoza.

Another invitation, however, was not refused: Spinoza was asked by the general, the Prince De Condé, to come to the headquarters of the French Army in Utrecht. The sources (Bayle, Colerus) do not reveal the reason why he was invited. The prince was an "*esprit fort*" or libertarian, who could have wished to meet the famous Dutch thinker who had already entertained contacts with many other French libertarians. Spinoza, on the other hand, may have thought that he might profit from the opportunity to meet the French authorities, in order to do something in favor of his country, which was still in great distress because of the war with the French invaders. This latter seems probable, inasmuch as it was a principle of Spinoza's behavior to contribute as much as possible to the well-being of the state, wherever he could. "I am a sincere republican," he said (Colerus 1705: 38).[53] In any case, he made use of the passport presented to him and went to Utrecht in July of 1673. When he arrived there, the Prince de Condé was gone, having been called back by his superior, King Louis XIV. Colerus says that Spinoza conversed with Lieutenant Stouppe instead of with Condé. Our information remains too scarce to say anything definite on this curious visit of Spinoza to Utrecht. Did he have a permit or even a mandate from the States of Holland, or from the Stadhouder prince William III? One cannot imagine that Spinoza went without any political charge – perhaps the preparation of negotiations – to the camp of the enemy.

Stouppe, who had been a Protestant minister before he began his military career, published in the same year a small book on *La religion des Hollandais* in which he paid much attention to the influence of Spinoza's views on religion. Although he of course did not acknowledge it, he had first-hand information:

I don't believe I have spoken enough about the religions of this country, if I have not said a word about an illustrious and learned man, who, as I have been assured, has a great number of followers (Sectateurs) who are wholly attached to his sentiments. It is a man born as a Jew, who is called Spinosa, who has not abjured the religion of the Jews neither embraced the Christian religion; he is therefore a very bad Jew nor a better Christian. Before some years he has written a book in Latin, of which the title is Tractatus Theologico-Politicus, in which his main objective is the destruction of all religions, particularly the Jewish and Christian religion, and to introduce atheism, libertarianism (le Libertinage) and freedom in all religions. He maintains that they are altogether invented for public utility, with the purpose that the citizens live honestly and obey their magistrates, that they keep themselves virtuous, not in the hope of a compensation after death, but simply for the excellency of virtue itself and for the advantages for virtuous people in this life. (Freudenthal 1899: 195)

Spinoza must have been disappointed by the many refutations of the *Theological-Political Treatise* he saw appearing in the book-markets. Whoever had some influence in public life or in the academies seemed to turn himself against Spinoza, if only to protect himself against suspicion. But he could also be ironic about what he found. Concerning the refutation of a Reinier van Mansvelt, a professor in Utrecht, whose book he had seen in the window of a bookseller, he wrote to his friend Jelles: "And laughing to myself, I pondered how precisely the ignorant are the first with their pen and most audacious in their writing" (Ep 50).

Spinoza was not a pessimistic type nor an ascetic, and had a positive attitude towards anything that could contribute to his well-being. He enjoyed the good things of life, including a glass of wine and a pipe of tobacco, and wrote in a letter that "I seek to pass my life not in sorrow and sighing, but in peace, joy and cheerfulness."[54] It was not his custom, however, to laugh publicly at other people or to despise them. He wrote that it was his principle "to try, not to laugh at human actions neither to mourn about them or to detest them, but to understand them" (TP i.4).[55] Spinoza does not say that he always succeeded, but only that he earnestly tried to follow this maxim. It is well known that he sometimes failed and confessed as much, saying (with Terence): "Nothing human is alien to me."[56] It is not my intention to make a saint of Spinoza, who himself was deeply convinced of everyone's weakness, including his own. His way of life, however, was sober and honest. He did not seek after superfluous goods.[57] This conduct constituted a problem for many people: How could an atheist behave so virtuously? That was also the problem of one of his later biographers, Pierre Bayle, after he had to characterize him as *"un homme d'un bon commerce, affable, honnête, officieux et fort règlé dans ses moeurs"* (Bayle 1697: 347).

During the life and government of Jan de Witt, the supreme court of Holland had already tried to prohibit officially the printing and spreading of the *Theological-Political Treatise*, but the Grand Pensionary had succeeded in preventing this prohibition. After the political change, the situation was quite different in this respect. In July of 1674, the Court of Holland published a *"placcaet"* against some harmful books, among which was the *Theological-Political Treatise*. Spinoza must have felt this as a bitter disappointment. In the text of the announcement, his book was declared one of the "sacrilegious and soul-destructive books, full of unfounded and dangerous propositions and horrors, to the disadvantage of the true religion and church service." Severe punishments were put on the printing, promulgating, or selling of those books.

By this act of the judicial – that is, political – authorities he, who so loved his country and its much-praised freedom, had become infamous, a subject for further defamations. Many famous scientists from all over Europe had paid visits to him and discussed the progress of arts and sciences. Now it became more and more quiet in his apartment. One of his best friends and followers, the young Baron von Tschirnhaus, who was at the time in Paris, asked him whether he could pass manuscripts of parts of his *Ethics* to a certain Gottfried Leibniz, who had consulted Spinoza some years earlier about questions of optics. Spinoza refused to give him the permission: "I don't think it advisable to entrust my writings so quickly to him. I first would like to know what he is doing in Paris" (Ep 72). What was the reason? No doubt he was not convinced of the sincerity of Leibniz, of his endeavor to strive only after truth. But we may guess also that another thing made Spinoza fear bad consequences. It was not unlikely that the spreading of his *Ethics* would have had repercussions for his life. His master Van den Enden, who had lived in Paris since 1670, had been arrested and sentenced to death, for his political activities but probably also for other reasons. He was hanged on December 6, 1674; his writings were burned a day later. Dutch newspapers such as *De Amsterdamsche Courant* reported the trial and the execution in all its details.

In spite of Spinoza's warning that Tschirnhaus should be reluctant in communicating what he had received for private use, we know that Tschirnhaus nonetheless revealed many secrets to the inquisitive Leibniz. This appears from a note written by Leibniz, which he must have made shortly after a meeting. I think it worthwhile to quote this note here in full because it enables us to see how Spinoza's doctrine was perceived, understood, and explained by his friends and followers in or around 1675. A second reason is that this note, which is not known by many scholars and is not yet available otherwise in English, contains several interesting points which cannot be found elsewhere, and is also for that reason relevant.

Sir Tschirnhaus told me many things about the handwritten book of Spinoza. There is a merchant in Amsterdam, called Gerrit Gilles [Jarig Jelles] I think, who supports Spinoza. Spinoza's book will be about God, mind, happiness or the idea of the perfect man, the recovery of the mind and the recovery of the body. He asserts the demonstration of a number of things about God. That he alone is free. He supposes that freedom exists, when the action or determination originates not from an external impact, but only from the nature of the actor. In this sense he justly ascribes freedom to God alone.

According to him the mind itself is in a certain sense a part of God. He thinks that there is sense in all things to the degrees of their existence. God is defined by him as an absolutely infinite Being, which contains all perfections, i.e. affirmations or realities or what may be conceived. Likewise only God would be substance or a Being which exists in itself or which can be understood by itself; all creatures are nothing else than modes. Man is free in so far as he is not determined by any external things. But because this is never the case, man is not free at all, although he participates more in freedom than the bodies.

The mind would be nothing but the idea of the body. He thinks that the unity of the bodies is caused by a sort of pressure. Most people's philosophy starts with the creatures, Des Cartes started with the mind, he [Spinoza] starts from God. Extension does not imply divisibility as was unduly supposed by Descartes; although he supposed to see this also clearly, he fell into the error that the mind acts on the body or is acted upon by the body.

He thinks that we will forget most things when we die and retain only those things that we know with the kind of knowledge he calls intuitive, of which only a few are conscious. Because knowledge is either sensual or imaginative or intuitive. He believes a sort of Pythagorical transmigration, namely that minds go from body to body. He says that Christ is the very best philosopher. He thinks that apart from thought and extension there are an infinity of other positive attributes, but that in all of them there is thought like here in extension. How they are constituted cannot be conceived by us but every one is infinite like space here. (Leibniz 1980)

We may conclude from this substantial document that the young Tschirnhaus, who had been in contact with Spinoza when he was a student in Leiden in the early 1670s,[58] was well initiated into the essentials of the *Ethics*. It is very striking how sharply he distinguishes between Spinoza's and Descartes's methods, saying that the latter starts from the soul whereas Spinoza develops his philosophy from the idea of God. The kernel in this Spinozistic physics is determinism, which includes that *"oriri unionem corporum a pressione quada"* – things are constituted as individuals by the pressure of the surrounding particles.[59] Descartes's dualism and anthropological interactionism are superseded in Spinoza's theory of the attributes of the one substance, of which individual things are the modes. Moreover, Tschirnhaus credits Spinoza – and this is completely new in comparison with other sources – with a kind of Pythagoreanism, implying that souls in a certain sense transmigrate from one form of matter to another. This idea is not entirely alien to the theory of the mind's eternity, based on the adequate ideas of the "fixed and eternal things" of extension. It is likely that the comparison with Pythagoras's transmigration theory originates from Spinoza himself, who probably had recognized the similarity in his reading of Ovid's *Metamorphoses* (Book XV), one of his classical sources.

When Spinoza had finished the five parts of his *Ethics* a year before, he had gone to his Amsterdam friend Jan Rieuwertsz in order to present to him the text for publication. Good friends warned him, however, not to do so, because the situation was too dangerous. Spinoza relates the story to Oldenburg (in September or October 1675):

Just when I received your letter from 22 July, I departed for Amsterdam with the intention to trust the book, about which I had written to you, to the press. When I was busy with this, the rumor spread that a certain book of mine about God was on the press and that I tried to demonstrate in it, that there is no God. This rumor was believed by many. Certain theologians, (probably themselves the authors of this rumor) were occasioned by it to complain about me to the Prince and the magistrates. Further stupid Cartesians – probably in order to clear themselves from the suspicion that they sympathized with me – did not stop to express their abhorrence over my opinions and writings; and they still continue doing so. When I had heard this from certain credible men, who likewise warned me that the theologians set everywhere traps for me, I decided to postpone the publication which I was preparing and to wait first how things would develop; and I planned to tell you later what I was going to do. *But it seems that the situation is becoming worse from day to day; and I don't really know what I have to do.* (Ep 68; emphasis added)

Ultimately, Spinoza was anxious and felt himself insecure, perhaps also alone. He had no contacts with relatives. Many good friends, like Simon Joosten de Vries and Pieter Balling, had died; others had been persecuted until death, like Koerbagh, Jan de Witt, and Franciscus van den Enden. Two of his former comrades (Niels Stensen and Albert Burgh) had converted to Roman Catholicism and now tried to draw him towards orthodoxy.[60] Oldenburg, his first correspondent, could not follow his radical determinism and secularism; he beseeched him, in effect, to change his mind. What would happen to him? "*Sub specie aeternitatis,*" death was not noxious. In the last part of the now finished *Ethics* he had written "that death is less harmful to us, the greater the Mind's clear and distinct knowledge, and hence, the more the Mind loves God" (E 5p38s). But he remained a human being, like everyone else, with fears and hopes, liable to passions, caught by imaginations of all kinds. Clear insights into the eternal laws of nature and reasoning could not dispel from his mind the "first" (lowest, imaginative) kind of knowledge, although they helped him to acquiesce in the unavoidable processes and defeats of human life.

His health left much to be desired. In his correspondence, Spinoza now and then intimated to his friends that not everything was well with him and that he sometimes had to excuse himself on account of not being able to work. Lucas says that he died in midlife, "after having suffered during the last years of his life." According to Jelles it was the "*tering*" (phthisis, or consumption) which caused him many troubles. But the situation was not always so bad that he could not work. His interest in the well-being of the state was so deeply rooted in his mind that he could not refrain from a new endeavor to contribute to it. After hiding in his desk the text of the *Ethics*, brought home from the fruitless trip to Amsterdam, he laid new blank paper on it. Spinoza now began to present a political architecture in a treatise, the *Political Treatise*, in which he demonstrated how different types of political societies (monarchies, aristocracies, democracies) should be organized in order to make them stable and secure for their citizens. He had gathered considerable material for his proposals from his reading of the books of the brothers De la Court; the works of his master Franciscus van den Enden, including his lecture on Machiavelli; and the Roman historians such as Livius, Tacitus, Curtius, and Flavius Josephus. What is more, he now could also use the laws of human behavior, formulated and deduced in Parts 3 and 4 of the *Ethics*, for his new enterprise.

Jarig Jelles wrote in his Preface to the *Nagelate Schriften:*

Our writer has made the Treatise about Politics not long before his death, which also prevented that it could be finished. His thoughts in this treatise are very accurate and his style is clear. Without discussing the opinions of many political writers, he proposes in this work his conception very solidly and draws everywhere conclusions from his premises. (Freudenthal 1899: 248)

Jelles reported that a work about "the nature of motion and in what way the differences in matter could be deduced a priori" was also on his program, had life given him the opportunity. We also read about this intention in the correspondence with Tschirnhaus. In Letter 59, Tschirnhaus asked about Spinoza's *Generalia in physicis* and when he could expect the publication of this work. Spinoza answered in Letter 60 (January 1675) that "he had not yet orderly composed" this material and that Tschirnhaus, therefore, would have to wait until another occasion. A short *Algebra* was likewise still on the list of works to be written according to Jelles.

Spinoza had not enough time to accomplish all the things he wished.[61] Many of his works remained unfinished – the *Treatise on the Emendation of the Intellect*, Descartes's *"Principles of Philosophy (Part III)"*, the *Political Treatise*, the *Compendium of Hebrew Grammar* – while others were not more than planned. Only the *Theological-Political Treatise* and the *Ethics* lay before us in perfect completeness. Yet we need not be discontent about the fruits of his life. I fully agree with the fine words of his friend J. M. Lucas: "*Ses jours ont été courts; mais on peut dire néanmoins qu'il a beaucoup vécu*" (Freudenthal 1899: 23). His life lasted not more than forty-four years, but its significance can hardly be equaled by other lives. He "lived much," though not long.

Death arrived on the 23rd of February in 1677. Colerus carefully inquired into the circumstances of it by checking the original documents. He says (three times) that the Amsterdam "*medicus* L. M." (Lodewijk Meyer) was with Spinoza in his last days and was also present at his deathbed. He assures us that Spinoza did not take opium in order to die insensible of pain. He only took the bouillon, which the wife of the landlord Van der Spyk had cooked from a chicken on the request of Lodewijk Meyer. Being very thin from the disease he had had for many years, he must have expired quietly, from lack of power. His manuscripts were immediately sent to Amsterdam:

The still-living landlord of Spinoza, Mr. Hendrik van der Spyk tells me, that Spinoza had ordered that after his death his desk with the writings and letters lying in it would be sent without any delay to Jan Rieuwertzen, cityprinter in Amsterdam, as he also has executed. And Jan Rieuwertzen, in his answer to the aforementioned Mr. van der Spyk, dated Amsterdam the 25th March 1677 confesses to have received such desk. The last words of this letter were: "The friends of Spinoza wanted to know, to whom the desk was sent, since they judged that it contained much money and they intended to call in upon the skippers to whom it was delivered. Because in The Hague the packets delivered on the towboat are not registered, I don't see how they could get it to know. It is best that they don't know it." (Colerus 1705: 51)

In an earlier letter dated March 6, Jan Rieuwertsz had written to Van der Spyk that he stood surety for all costs of the burial and that the friend of Schiedam (a brother of Simon Joosten de Vries) had paid to him the rent which Spinoza owed for the apartment (Colerus 1705: 78). Van der Spyk had to dispose of the body. Colerus continues with his report: "On the 25th February the corpse was buried in the New Church on the Spuy with 6 state-carriages (*karossen*) and shown out by many persons of high rank (*aanzienlijke luiden*). . . . Coming from the burial the friends drank, according to civil custom, a glass of wine."

Six coaches drawn by horses on a cold or misty day with prominent and distinguished people followed the corpse! No, Spinoza had not been entirely alone in his last years. The bigots had attacked him increasingly,[62] but among intelligent people, and evidently many highly placed persons, he had become a much respected man. The "*grand nombre de sectateurs*," about which the French colonel Stouppe had spoken, was as it were visualized in the spectacular funeral of the humble philosopher. Bayle testified that "*les esprits forts accouraient àlui de toutes parts*" (i.e., that the libertarians came to him from all sides). One may suppose that many of those political persons and *esprits forts* paid him the last honor.

Before they were sold, the books of Spinoza's library were put on a short title catalog which has come down to us.[63] It is worthwhile to examine this list, since it may convince one about Spinoza's fields of interest and the sources he used.[64] The collection is one of a scientist who wanted to keep abreast of developments in various fields of research. Most books are about mathematics, mechanics, astronomy, anatomy, chemistry, grammar, biblical hermeneutics, classical literature,[65] political history and theory, or Spanish literature. There are only very few items which would fit in philosophical libraries of today. Aristotle is present in a Latin edition, but Plato is absent. The works of Descartes, in contrast, are represented with many editions, including a Dutch translation.

J. M. Lucas concluded his obituary with the words "*Baruch de Spinosa vivra dans le souvenir des vrais Sçavants*": Spinoza will survive in the memory and the practice of the true scientists (Freudenthal 1899: 24). This may be verified by looking to the work of his friends after his death. Tschirnhaus, for example, a friend who was very concerned about the precise meaning of Spinoza's propositions, as is manifest in the correspondence, dedicated his life to mathematics and medicine. His Spinozistic naturalism is elaborated in his *Medicina mentis sive Artis inveniendi praecepta generalia* (Tschirnhaus 1686).[66] On many pages he insinuates his adherence to Spinoza's principles and propositions. The human mind is only cured from its errors by the "science of nature."

I know that many will disagree with me when they read this. The reason of this is not unknown to me. Until now they did not form yet a correct idea of the physics about which I speak neither did they recognize or taste in effect its fruits. By physics I understand nothing else than the science of the universe demonstrated a priori by the rigorous method of the mathematicians and confirmed a posteriori by the most evident experiences which even convince the imagination. . . . This science is truly divine. One here exposes the laws . . . according to which everything produces invariably its effects. The knowledge of this sciences liberates us also of innumerable prejudices. . . . In this way, through the mediation of the true physics, one becomes so to say a completely new man and one is regenerated philosophically. . . . One learns here to see the things from a higher point of view and to consider that nothing is more evident for the understanding than our continuous dependence on God alone, which is such that we cannot even raise our hand or produce a thought and, in a word, that never, neither in our mind nor in our body, can we absolutely do anything without the actual concurrence of God. . . . Ultimately *thanks to physics* we are prepared for still more important knowledge.[67] Since when we bring the study of all the general items of this science to a good end, then not only the knowledge of our mind and its eternity, but also of God himself, of his real and necessary existence and his infinitely perfect attributes . . . becomes clear and evident for us. (Tschirnhaus 1686: 245–7; emphasis added)

Thus was Spinoza's legacy interpreted and practiced by one of his most intelligent correspondents: Human salvation and happiness are the products of human understanding of the laws of nature, a kind of science which is the privilege of everyone but may be professionally improved in physics. It can be shown from various documents[68] that Spinoza's Amsterdam friends continued his work as linguists and mathematicians. This was the way Spinoza's reception was in fact realized: not by philosophizing about the end of life and proper morals, but by doing science as Spinoza himself had always done. An interesting example of this naturalistic Spinozism is Burchard de Volder, who once had been in contact with Spinoza in Amsterdam. He was appointed a professor in (traditional) philosophy in the Leiden University, but soon afterwards asked permission from the Curators to lecture on physics and mathematics.[69] He began a tradition of natural science which became famous with the name of Boerhaave.[70]

The *Opera Posthuma* were published in the year of Spinoza's death, 1677. The title page showed the initials "B. d. S." but not the name of the author or of the publisher, Rieuwertsz.[71] Apart from the *Ethics*, the *Correspondence* and the *Political Treatise*, the work also contained the unfinished *Treatise on the Emendation of the Intellect*, which the editors indicated was one of Spinoza's earliest works. In this work Spinoza had already delineated, after having enumerated and explained the four kinds of perceiving, the program of his *Ethics*. He wrote:

To choose the best mode of perceiving from these, we are required to enumerate briefly the means necessary to attain *our end*:

    1. To know exactly our nature, which we desire to perfect, and at the same time,

    2. [To know] as much of the nature of things as is necessary,

    (a) to infer rightly from it the differences, agreements and oppositions of things,

    (b) to conceive rightly what they can undergo and what they cannot,

    (c) to compare [the nature of things] with the nature and power of man.

This done, the highest perfection man can reach will easily manifest itself. (TdIE 25)

The *Ethics* appears to be the fulfillment of this research program. On the basis of general laws of nature (Part 1) it presents an analysis of the properties of human nature, of its power and its weakness in confrontation with other things, its passions and servitude, but also its (relative) freedom, perfection, and happiness.

On the 25th of June 1678 the States of Holland and West-Friesland officially proclaimed in a *Placcaet* their interdiction of the "trading, selling, printing, and translating" of Spinoza's *Opera Posthuma* because they considered it to be a "profane, atheistic, and blasphemous book." The prohibition is no longer valid, but that does not mean that the text has finally become the intellectual possession of our enlightened times. There is still enormous work to do before we fully understand Spinoza's life and works.

NOTES

1 See Vaz Diaz and Van der Tak 1982.
2 See Salomon 1988.
3 See Méchoulan and Nahon 1979.
4 Nearly all possible details about Spinoza's early youth and education may be found in *Spinoza. Troisième centenaire de la mort du philosophie* (catalog), Paris: Institut Néerlandais, 1977.

5 The original Portuguese text is kept in the *Livro dos Acordos* of the Jewish-Portuguese community.

6 Pierre Bayle says that Spinoza wrote *"un Apologie de sa sortie de la Synagoge."* The title of this work, written in Spanish, would have been (according to C. G. von Murr): *"Apologia para justificarse de su abdicacion de la synagga."*

7 These are the first lines of the oldest text we possess from Spinoza's pen, the *Treatise on the Emendation of the Intellect* (in Edwin Curley's translation, Spinoza 1985a).

8 See Klever 1988b. With his small work, *Het licht op den kandelaar* (a small pamphlet, printed "for the author"), Balling was the first to publish some of Spinoza's ideas on language, knowledge, determinism, and the passions.

9 See Akkerman and Hubbeling 1979.

10 Apart from new findings to be mentioned later on, see Meinsma 1896. This fundamental work is also translated in French and extended with many valuable notes as Meinsma 1983. See also Meininger and van Suchtelen 1980.

11 For an analysis of this passage see Gebhardt 1987: 224–8.

12 *"Ses amis, dont la plupart étoient Cartésiens . . ."* (Freudenthal 1899: 12).

13 The first to have demonstrated this point was the Dutch classical philologist and poet, J. H. Leopold, in Leopold 1902. See also Akkerman 1980 and especially Proietti 1985. Proietti gives an extended list of crypto-quotations in Spinoza from the different works of Terence and suggests that Spinoza had the parts of Simo and Parmeno.

14 As is remarked by O. Proietti in Proietti 1989a. After stressing the fact that we find many utilizations of Terence in Spinoza's works, he writes: *"Leggere il TIE [Tractatus de Intellectus Emendatione] è invece constatare l'enigmatica assenza di Eunucus e Andria: enigmatica se collochiamo l'opera nel 1662–63, ancor più enigmatica se la collochiamo negli anni 1957–59. Si dovranno porre perciò, con molta prudenza, una domanda e un problema: non è possibile che Spinoza utilizzi, in quell'opera, blocchi di* materiale accumulati negli anni 1655–1657? *La discussione critica di Seneca, Epist. 57, 7–9 in TIE, p. 28, 20–26 mostra ad esempio la presenza di una tematica 'urielique,' in dubbiamente lontana dalla* KV [Korte Verhandeling] *e dall'E"* (page 255; emphasis added).

15 See Proietti 1989b.

16 The text of the *Voorreeden* of the *Nagelate Schriften* and of the *Praefatio* of the *Opera posthuma* (i.e., Meyer's translation of Jelles's Dutch preface) has been recently republished in Akkerman 1980. The quotation is on page 250.

17 For a fine analysis of the introductory section of the *Treatise on the Emendation of the Intellect*, see Zweerman 1983.

18 The works of Da Costa are collected and annotated in Osier 1983. For a survey of the problems in the Amsterdam community, see Albiac 1987 and Fuks-Mansfeld 1989.

19 See Thijssen-Schoute 1989 and Verbeek 1988.

20 Hudde, at the time already known as a young mathematical genius, would very soon become one of the most influential politicians of Amsterdam, in which town he acted as a burgomaster for more than twenty-five years. For a short biography and bibliography, see Klever 1989a.

21 See further my publication of these documents in Klever 1989b.

22 See now his *opus magnum*, Mignini 1986a.

23 See my publication of the findings in *NRC Handelsblad* (May 8, 1990).

24 See Van Suchtelen 1987. It may be demonstrated that Van den Enden's interest in politics dates at least from 1648, when he played a role in the Peace of Münster, and 1650, when he republished a Dutch political pamphlet, in which the sovereignty of the States of Holland and West-Friesland was defended against the claims of the king of Spain.

25 See *Treatise on the Emendation of the Intellect* 13–14:

> This, then is the end I aim at: to acquire such a nature, and to strive that many acquire it with me. That is, it is part of my happiness to take pains that many others may understand as I understand, so that their intellect and desire agree entirely with my intellect and desire. To do this it is necessary . . . to form a society of the kind that is desirable, so that as many as possible may attain it as easily and surely as possible.

26 This letter (Letter 67A, dated 1675 in Spinoza 1928) was published, not written, in 1675.

27 Glauber's *Miraculum mundi* (1660) was in fact an essay on saltpeter.

28 See Klever 1988d.

29 Letter 8, written by Simon Joosten de Vries on 24 February 1663, says: "Next, I thank you very much for *your writings*, which were imparted to me by P. Balling and which have given me great joy, particularly the remark to proposition 19" (emphasis added), from which we may conclude that a first part of the later *Ethics* belonged to the writings sent. Spinoza reacted in Letter 9 to the "questions proposed in your circle." It is important to take notice of the fact that Spinoza had urged his friends to imbibe the whole of natural science. This is presupposed in De Vries's closing remark: "I have entered an anatomy course (*collegium anatomiae*), and am about half through. When it is finished, I shall begin chemistry, and *following your advice* (*suasore te*), go through the whole Medical Course" (emphasis added).

30 The full title is: *Philosophia s. scripturae interpres; Exercitatio Para-doxa, in qua, veram Philosophiam infallibilem S. Literas interpretandi Normam esse, apodictice demonstratur, & discrepantes ab hac Senten-tiae expenduntur, ac refelluntur.* A Dutch translation by the author himself appeared in 1667. There is also a recent French translation, Meyer 1988.

31 He writes that "I have kept this treatise already some years from the press."

32 See Zac 1965; Matheron 1969; Meyer 1988. See Klever 1990c.

33 The italicization is in the text of Meyer and must be read as a literal quotation from what Spinoza said.

34 This text, written in the years 1669–71 and recently edited by A. J. E. Harmsen (*Nil Volentibus Arduum* 1989) contains many essays from the pen of Bouwmeester and Meyer, in which one may easily recognize the influence of their conversations with Spinoza and Van den Enden. Meyer wrote, to give only one striking example, in the first chapter:

> Everybody is bound by nature to seek his own well-being; and the more capacities my fellow-man have to further my well-being and the more I have to expect from him, the more also am I bound to seek his well-being in which the aforesaid capacities are contained. This is the ground, on which stand all teachings and instructions and whatever one would be able to do for his fellow-man. And nobody directing his behavior to the right reason will toil and moil with work for another, without the expectations that some fruit from this labor will return to him. (*Nil Volentibus Arduum* 1989: 31)

> Compare this passage with the already quoted *Treatise on the Emenda-tion of the Intellect* 13–14. For more information about *NVA* see Van Suchtelen 1987.

35 See Proietti 1989c.

36 Relevant literature includes: Spinoza 1968; Klijnsmit 1986; Levi 1987; and Porges 1924–6.

37 For a more elaborate discussion of all aspects of Spinoza's optics, see Klever and van Zuylen 1990.

38 The quotation is from E 5p23s.

39 He also did experiments in hydrostatics (Letter 41) and metallurgy. See Klever 1987.

40 As noted earlier, the meaning of the seventeenth century word *"philosophia"* is not the same as the meaning of our twentieth-century "philosophy" but is indeed closer to that of our "science."

41 First in *Een Bloemhof van allerley lieflijkheyd sonder verdriet door Vreederijk Waarmond / ondersoeker der waarheyd / tot nut en dienst*

van al die geen die der nut en dienst uyt trekken wil. Of een vertaaling en uytlegging van al de Hebreusche / Grieksche / Latijnse / Franse / en andere vreemde bastartwoorden en wijsen van spreeken . . . , a dictionary in which foreign words from theology, medicine and law were explained. Then also a systematical work: *Een ligt schijnende in duystere plaatsen / om te verligten de voornaamste saaken der Godsgeleertheyd en Gods-dienst / ontsteeken door Vreederijk Waarmond / ondersoeker der Waarheyd. Anders Adr. Koerbagh.* The text of *Een Ligt* is republished in a critical edition by H. Vandenbossche, Koerbagh 1974. Also see: Vandenbossche 1978; and Evenhuis 1971: IV,351–61. At his trial, Koerbagh explicitly confessed, "that he was in contact with Spinoza and had visited him sometimes."

42 The work is masterfully written, testifies to the strong ability of the author in linguistics and natural science, and is a first class antitheological treatise which deserves to be taken into consideration by Spinoza scholars. One must conclude that the *Theological-Political Treatise* is only one of many similar writings from members of the Amsterdam circle, which all defend the same ideas. I have already mentioned Balling's *Licht op den kandelaar* (1662) and Meyer's *Interpres* (1666), but one must also mention Jelles's *Belijdenisse des algemeenen en christelijken geloofs* (1673).

43 "Hamburgi, apud Henricum Künraht" instead of "Amsterdam, Jan Rieuwertsz." Spinoza later (around 1675) made many annotations, some of which were quite long, to the text of the *Theological-Political Treatise*, which were first published in the original Latin by Chr. Th. de Murr in de Murr 1802. They were earlier published in French as *Remarques curieuses et nécessaires pour l'intelligence de ce livre*, added to the French translation of the *Theological-Political Treatise* by Saint-Glen, which first appeared under the title: *La clef du Sanctuaire* ([Spinoza] 1678). For an erudite discussion of the problems around these annotations and their variants, see Totaro 1989.

44 See Van Bunge 1989.

45 For the later relations between Spinoza and Van Velthuysen see my monograph, Klever 1990d.

46 The last two quoted phrases are from J. M. Lucas, in Freudenthal 1899.

47 J. M. Lucas (Freudenthal 1899: 15) writes: "He had the advantage to be known by the sir pensionary De Witt, who wished to learn from him mathematics and who gave him often the honor to consult him on important matters." The relationship between Spinoza and De Witt is confirmed by Sebastian Kortholt in the preface to Kortholt 1700, where it is said that Spinoza would have preferred to be torn to pieces "with the De Witts, his friends" than to look after vain glory.

48 Lucas confirms this writing, "that he shed many tears when he saw how his fellow citizens lacerated their common father" (Freudenthal 1899: 19).

49 The story seems to be truthful, since there is no reason why Leibniz would have fabricated it. We know moreover, that Spinoza was well read in Suetonius, in whose *The twelve Caesars* one finds an expression which is very close to *"ultimi barbarorum,"* namely *"ultimi Romanorum."* This expression could have inspired Spinoza to his crypto-citation.

50 For full and precise bibliographical information see Kingma and Offenberg 1977.

51 Spinoza's name *"coepit inclarescere."* See Klever 1989c.

52 See John Henrico Heidegger, *Joh. Ludovici Fabricii Theologi Archipalatini Celeberrimi Opera Omnia quibus praemittitur Historia Vitae et Obitus ejusdem* (Tiguri: Gessner, 1698).

53 Cf. Sebastian Kortholt's remark in Kortholt 1700: 27, *"Politici enim nomen affectabat"* – he wanted the name of a politician, i.e., a good citizen.

54 The passage appears in Letter 21, to Blijenbergh. A persuasive presentation of this attitude also occurs in *Ethics* 4p45s2:

> My account of the matter, the view I have arrived at, is this: no deity, nor anyone else, unless he is envious, takes pleasure in my lack of power and my misfortune; nor does he ascribe to virtue our tears, sighs, fear, and other things of that kind, which are signs of a weak mind. . . . To use things, therefore, and take pleasure in them as far as possible – not, of course to the point where we are disgusted with them, for there is no pleasure in that – this is the part of a wise man. It is the part of a wise man, I say, to refresh and restore himself in moderation with pleasant food and drink, with scents, with the beauty of green plants, with decoration, music, sports, the theater, and other things of this kind, which anyone can use without injury to another. For the human Body is composed of a great many parts of different natures, which constantly require new and varied nourishment, so that the whole Body may be equally capable of all the things which can follow from its nature, and hence, so that the Mind also may be equally capable of understanding many things.

55 See also Letter 30, *Ethics* 2p49s, and the Preface to *Ethics* Part 3.

56 One example is his anger consequent on the murder of the brothers De Witt. Another example is indicated in a letter of Philippus van Limborch to Jean Le Clerc (January 23, 1682) in the University Library of Amsterdam (printed as appendix 10 in Meinsma 1896): "I remember that I was six years ago invited to a dinner, to which beyond my expectation also

this author was present. During the prayer he showed signs of an irreligious soul by means of gesticulations by which he seemingly tried to demonstrate our stupidity in praying to God."

57 *"Les richesses ne le tentoient pas."* He tried to be economically self-supporting by means of grinding and selling lenses. S. J. de Vries wanted to grant him 2,000 guilders but Spinoza refused to accept the gift. A yearly pension of 500 guilders, offered to him by the brother of that friend (the De Vries from Schiedam) was, at his request, reduced to 300 guilders (Freudenthal 1899: 17–18).

58 See Vermij 1988.

59 Compare Spinoza's definition of *"individuum"* in the physical excursus following *Ethics* 2p13.

60 See the interesting remark of Proietti 1989c: 266: *"Il 1675 rappresenta un punto di crisi e di svolta per il cammino intellettuale di Spinoza."* The year 1675 represents a turning point in Spinoza's life. He now puts everything aside (see Letter 84) for the transition from the theological-political to the political order. Spinoza prepares for a decisive battle: *"un intervento politico di natura teorica." "C'è battaglia aperta, nuova, decisiva e ultima"* (Proietti 1989c: 269).

61 Jelles sees Spinoza's "untimely" death as a confirmation of a general rule: "But the death has demonstrated that human intentions are seldom executed" (Akkerman 1980: 254).

62 To mention a few of them: Van Blijenbergh 1674; Mansvelt 1674; Cuper 1676; Melchior 1671; Batalier 1674; Musaeus 1674; Spizelius 1675. Spizelius calls Spinoza a "most irreligious author." Mansfelt says that the *Theological-Political Treatise* should be condemned forever. Similar remarks are made by the other authors.

63 The list may be found in *Catalogus van de bibliotheek der Vereniging 'Het Spinozahuis' te Rijnsburg*, Leiden: Brill, 1965. A more extended description appears in the *Catalogus van de boekery der Vereniging Het Spinozahuis* (n.d.). The list is also printed in Préposiet, J. *Bibliographie spinoziste*, Besançon: Centre de Documentation (n.d.).

64 See Vulliaud 1934.

65 The authors here are: Tacitus, Livius, Virgilius, Arrianos, Petronius, Lucianus, Julius Caesar, Seneca, Sallustius, Martialis, Plinius, Ovidius, Plautus, Cicero, Curtius, and Justinianus.

66 There is also a French translation, with introduction and notes: Tschirnhaus 1980.

67 *"Grâce à la physique nous sommes préparés à des connaissances beaucoup plus importantes encore."*

68 See Klever 1991a.

69 See Klever 1988a.

70 Other examples of Spinoza's friends who became scientists are: Dr. P. van Balen, author of *De verbetering der gedachten* (1684 and 1691) (edited by M. J. van Hoven in van Balen 1988); Dr. P. van Gent (see Klever 1991a); and Dr. A. Cuffeler, author of *Artis ratiocinandi naturalis et artificialis ad pantosophiae principia manuducens*, 1684.

71 Concerning Rieuwertsz, the Dutch bishop Neercassel wrote in 1677 to the Roman Catholic cardinal Barberini: "This bookseller usually publishes whatever exotic and impious is thought out here by impudent and conceited minds," alluding to the *Opera posthuma* and its author. See Klever 1988c.

2   Spinoza's metaphysics

In this chapter I shall present two problems which dominate Spinoza's metaphysics (sections 1–2), and then present his solution of one of them through his doctrine that there is only extended substance (sections 3–6). After a brief interlude looking at his views about necessity and time (sections 7–8), I then turn to Spinoza's treatment of the second problem, in his theory about how mentality fits into the universe (sections 9–14). Most of the references are to the *Ethics* Part 1 and the first few propositions of Part 2.

I.   SOME UNDERLYING ASSUMPTIONS

The main outlines of Spinoza's metaphysical system are his response to two problems inherited from Descartes's philosophy. They existed as problems for him because of certain assumptions that he made at too deep a level for him to recognize them as items of doctrine. I shall pick out four of these.

(1) Explanatory rationalism. There is a satisfying answer to every "Why?" question. (Leibniz was also a rationalist in this sense; Descartes was not.) Associated with this is a view about, or attitude toward, causation. Spinoza did not distinguish what is absolutely or logically necessary from what is merely causally necessary. In his way of thinking, there is a single relation of necessary connection, which links causes with effects in real causal chains and premises with conclusions in valid arguments. Those of us who do distinguish these will want to know *how* Spinoza collapses them into one. Does he regard absolute necessity as weaker than it really is, or does he regard causal necessity as stronger than it really is? There may be no clear-cut answer to this, but the latter is closer to the truth than the former.

(2) *Concept dualism.* The concepts pertaining to the material aspects of things have no overlap with the concepts pertaining to thought. No fact about the realm of thought has any logical relations with any fact about the realm of matter. This intensely Cartesian assumption of Spinoza's is expressed by him in the statement that mentality and materiality (or, as he said, thought and extension) are "attributes," that is, fundamental and mutually nonoverlapping ways that things can be.

(3) *Impact mechanics.* Bodies affect one another only through impact – there are pushes but no pulls, repulsive forces but no attractive ones. Spinoza shared this assumption with Descartes; it was also accepted by Locke and Leibniz; the former recanted in face of the evident success of Newton's *Principia*, but Leibniz held firm even then. The price to be paid for denying "traction" was high: It included a complete inability to explain "cohesion," that is, the fact that some portions of matter clump together to form separate things. But there was a reason for it, namely that traction cannot be explained by the basic nature of matter, whereas repulsion can. From the supposedly necessary truth that bodies are mutually impenetrable it follows that if body A moves into a region which contains body B, the latter must move away. That does not yield any particular laws, but it does yield – as absolutely necessary – the result that there is such a causal phenomenon as impulse, this being required by the essence of body as such; whereas there is no comparable reason why there must be traction. As Leibniz said, if there is traction it is "miraculous." In his mind as presumably in Spinoza's, explanatory rationalism is at work in this area.

(4) *Size neutrality.* There is nothing special about being small. It was common ground in the seventeenth and eighteenth centuries that small things differ from large ones only in size. C. D. Broad called this a blank check that philosophers wrote on Nature's bank and that did not visibly bounce until late in the nineteenth century.

2. TWO PROBLEMS

The two biggest problems that Spinoza's metaphysic was meant to solve are these:

(i) What material substances are there? That modest question poses a problem for anyone who believes, as did many seventeenth-century philosophers and physicists, (a) that whatever is material is spatially extended, (b) that any extended thing, however small, is splittable into parts which can go their separate ways, and (c) that if something is splittable it is not a substance but, at best, an aggregate of substances. It seems to follow that there are no material substances, which is to say that if the world is made up of basic things they are not bits of matter. Since it looks as though the world is made up of bits of matter, this is a problem. Premise (a) comes from the assumption of size neutrality, which stopped philosophers from thinking of the possibility – which did occur to Kant – that extended things might be made up of physical points, and that the extension of familiar matter results from each point's exerting force throughout a region. Premise (b) is true if impact mechanics is the whole of physics, but otherwise might be false. Premise (c) does not need much explaining; but observe that it overlooks the possibility that there are no substances (basic things) although there is substance (basic stuff). I shall begin expounding Spinoza's solution to this problem in section 3.

(ii) The facts about the world in its mental aspects clearly have something to do with the facts about it under its material aspects: It is not a coincidence that a person's sensory states correlate somewhat with how things are in his material environment, or that physical damage is associated with pain, or that wanting something is more likely to be associated with getting closer to it than moving away from it. Something systematic is going on here; what is it? The obvious answer is that it is causal interaction: Sensory states are caused by the environment, pain is caused by damage, bodily movements are caused by desires. That answer, however, is forbidden to Spinoza. His strong understanding of causal connection implies that there are causal links only where there are what we would call conceptual connections: Minds do not act upon bodies or vice versa unless there are suitable conceptual overlaps between the two realms. Concept dualism is precisely the denial that there are such overlaps. Spinoza boldly concluded that the mental and material realms are causally fenced off from one another, but he needed to explain the appearance of interaction as something other than an absurd, brute-fact series of coincidences. He had, therefore, a problem: There is a systematic relation, and it is not causal; so what is it? I shall start on this topic in section 10.

3. SUBSTANCE MONISM

According to Spinoza there is only one substance, namely the whole world, which he usually calls "Nature" or "God." His official argument for this substance monism (E 1p14d) has satisfied nobody. It goes like this:

(a) There is a substance that has every attribute.
(b) There cannot be two substances that have an attribute in common.
(c) There cannot be a substance that has no attributes.

Therefore:

(d) There cannot be two substances.

The argument is valid, and premise (c) seems to be true. But (a) depends on a special version of the "ontological argument" for the existence of God (E 1p11d), which is no sounder than any of the other versions of that notorious paralogism. It infers God's existence from God's being by definition a substance. Spinoza accepted the then standard view that no substance can depend on anything else for its existence; so any substance must depend on itself for its existence. This sounds like self-causation, which is not clearly meaningful, but Spinoza found a way of interpreting it that, he thought, enabled it to make sense. He takes the self-dependence of a substance in a logical rather than a causal way, saying that the existence of any substance is explained by the substance's nature, by which he means that the substance has a nature which absolutely must be instantiated. (In Spinoza's terminology, the essence of a substance involves existence.) So God, or a substance which . . . etc., necessarily exists.

As for the argument for (b): Even Spinoza scholars for whom charity comes first agree that this argument (E 1p5d) seems to be confined to substances that have only one attribute each. Two such substances that shared an attribute would (trivially) share every attribute, but that does not yield the substance monism that Spinoza wants. There could be hundreds of substances, each with a different selection of attributes and only one having all the attributes.

However, there is a much better route than *Ethics* 1p14d to the conclusion that there is only one substance – an argument that goes by respectable moves from premises for which Spinoza had reasons. One premise in this unofficial argument says that there is only one *extended* substance. The second premise says that any thinking that gets done must be done by extended substances. Those two premises entail that the world of thought and extension consists of only one substance, which both thinks and is extended. I believe that this route to his substance monism was at work in Spinoza's mind; otherwise it is a sheer coincidence that a solid Spinozistic case can be made for a doctrine for which Spinoza offered such a rickety official argument. In this respect as in some others, I submit, his official apparatus of "demonstrations" is not a good guide to his actual reasons for his metaphysical doctrines.

The better argument, which I shall start on in section 4, involves two of the world's "attributes," namely extension and thought. However, Spinoza seems to imply that there are others – he says indeed that God or Nature has "infinite attributes." Surprising as it may seem, there are reasons to think that by this Spinoza did not mean anything entailing that there are more than two attributes. (i) Thought and extension are the only two attributes that play any active role in the *Ethics*. (ii) The role of infinity in *Ethics* 1p14d shows that Spinoza takes "God has infinite attributes" to entail that God has all the attributes. This entailment does not hold when "infinite" is used in our way; so Spinoza's meaning for the term differs from ours, and the question is, "How?" One possible answer is that he used "infinite attributes" to mean "all (possible) attributes," so that Nature's having infinite attributes is consistent with its having only two. (iii) Spinoza has a solid, intelligible reason for saying that Nature has all attributes: If there were an attribute – a basic way of being – that was not instantiated, nothing could explain this fact, and that conflicts with explanatory rationalism. There is on the other hand no respectable reason for Spinoza to say that Nature has (in our sense) infinitely many attributes. (iv) He gets "infinite attributes" into the story through his statement that God has infinite attributes, and we should ask why. Spinoza's use of the term "God" as one name for the natural world is evidently based on his believing that descriptions of God in the Judeo-Christian tradition come closer to fitting the natural world than to fitting anything else: infinite, not acted on from the outside, not criticizable by any valid standard, omniscient (in the sense of containing all the knowl-

edge there could possibly be), omnipotent (in the sense of being able
to do anything that it is possible for anything to do). If in that spirit
the attribution to God of "infinite attributes" is to be justified, it
must be through the tradition that God is the *ens realissimum*, the
most real being, the being that exists in every basic way in which it
is possible to exist. That leads us to God's having all (possible)
attributes, and does not entail anything about how many of them
there are.

On the other hand, it was a little perverse of Spinoza to say "infinite" if he only meant "all." And in his last two letters he addresses
the question of how it is that we do not know anything about any
attributes except thought and extension. The mere fact that he faces
the question does not show that he was convinced that there are
more than two attributes. He certainly did not rule out there being
more than two, so that he needed to explain how it *could* happen
that there are attributes with which we are not acquainted. (His
explanation of this is bad.) Still, if he really thought that there *might*
be only two, and did not mean to have implied otherwise, it is
strange that he does not say so in these letters.

4. MONISM ABOUT EXTENDED SUBSTANCE

Spinoza believed, and had good reason for believing, that there is just
one extended substance, namely the entire extended world – not the
totality of all matter, but the totality of everything that is extended.
If space extends beyond the edges of the *material* world, then all that
extra space is also part of the extended substance (and in that case
the difference between matter and space does not show up at the
level of basic metaphysics). This candidate for the role of "an extended substance" is unique in not being splittable: It cannot be
split from side to side, because it is infinite in all directions and has
no sides, and it cannot have pieces taken away from it because there
is nowhere for them to go. We can make divisions within it, but not
of it.

This puts it in strong contrast with any lesser, finite portion of the
material world. Every such portion is divisible, Spinoza thinks;
there are no atoms. So every such portion is an aggregate (and thus
not a single substance), and can be destroyed by dissipation (and is
thus not substantial); and can be acted upon from the outside (which

Spinoza also seems to think disqualifies it as a substance). Whatever other reasons he may have had, the sheer divisibility of all matter put him under pressure to say that the whole world is the only extended substance.

If the extended world is the one extended substance, what is the status of ordinary finite bodies such as pebbles? One possible answer is that they are parts of the one substance, this being tolerable because in this one unique case a thing could have parts without being in any danger of being taken apart and thus without prejudice to its status as a substance, a basic thing, an item whose existence is not at the mercy of the existence of other items. The reasons Spinoza could have had for not handling finite bodies in that way are rather complex, and I am not sure that he ever actually considered this possibility. Anyway, I shall pass it by.

Spinoza's actual answer to the question, "What is the metaphysical status of a pebble?" is that a pebble is a "mode" of the one substance. For Spinoza as for his contemporaries, a "mode" of a thing is a property or quality of it. Descartes, for example, says that he uses "mode" to mean "exactly the same as what is elsewhere meant by *attribute* or *quality*," though he goes on to recommend reserving "mode" for those aspects of a substance that it may gain and lose, retaining "attribute" for such properties of it as it must have at all times when it exists at all (Descartes 1985: I,56). This use of "mode" to stand for what is predicable of a substance or possessed by or instantiated by a substance was standard in philosophical writing in the sixteenth and seventeenth centuries. Spinoza says nothing to suggest that he is using the term in any other way, and his definition – "By *mode* I understand the affections of a substance, or that which is in another through which it is also conceived" – strongly points to his using "mode" in its normal meaning.

A mode was often thought of not as a universal property, but rather as a particular property instance. A blush is a mode: For a face to have a blush on it is just for the face to be red in a certain way; we do not have two things, a face and a blush, standing in a certain relation; rather, we have a single thing, a face, and it is blushing; but there is such an item as *the blush*, it is this *instance of blushingness*. So even if you and I are blushing in exactly the same way, your blush is one item and mine is another: They are qualitylike items, except that they are particular rather than universal. According to various theorists from Locke and Leibniz through to Jaegwon Kim and myself, modes or property-instances also figure as events: The fall of a sparrow is one particular instance of fallingness. I do not use "instance of property P" to refer to the thing that instantiates P. If I did, I would be identifying the blush with the face, and the fall with the sparrow. The instances I am talking about are *abstract particulars*. Spinoza's view, then, is that a pebble relates to the entire extended world as a blush does to a face or a fall to a sparrow.

How can this be? We grasp the grammar of the sentence, and we know what each of its words means, but that does not tell us what Spinoza is getting at, that is, how it could possibly be true that a pebble is a mode. Commentators on Spinoza have usually repeated his statement and superficially explained its meaning (as I have done) without seriously addressing the problem of what he can be getting at. It was left to Edwin Curley to challenge this procedure, saying that we should not understand Spinoza to have meant such a thing if we cannot tell a reasonable story about how it might be true. It may be false, but it must at least be intelligible and *prima facie* defensible.

Finding no way of presenting the doctrine in that light, Curley concluded that it has been a mistake to attribute to Spinoza the view that a pebble relates to the extended world as a blush does to a face (Curley 1969: 36–43). The term "mode," Curley noted, was used in the seventeenth century to do two things at once: to call something a mode was *both* to classify it as an instance of a quality *and* to say that it is a dependent entity, something that depends for its existence on another thing. (We have already seen this at work twice: in the self-dependence element in Spinoza's ontological argument for God's existence, and in the view that finite portions of matter are destructible and therefore not substantial.) In the absence of any coherent account of what it could really mean, in detail, to say that pebbles are "modes" when that word is given its full meaning, Curley conjectured that Spinoza meant it to have only the second part of its meaning, namely that of "dependent item." That implies that Spinoza is using "substance" to mean "independent item," so that his substance monism, as applied to extension, becomes merely the thesis that the entire extended world is the only extended item that could not be destroyed from without.

That metaphysical position is almost certainly true, and I am sure that Spinoza held it. What is at issue is whether that was *all* he meant when he said that the whole world is the only extended substance and that finite bodies are modes of it. To say that it was is to credit him with good sense but not with boldness or originality, yet the latter virtues are commonly thought to be more typical of him. Curley's reading of substance monism has another count against it too: Nothing in Spinoza's uses of "substance" and "mode" prepare us for these terms' being stripped of what had hitherto always been the more central and important part of their meaning. The main thing in Curley's favor was the lack of any story about how bodies could conceivably relate to the extended world as blushes do to faces.

That lack has been made good. Curley is on record as agreeing that in my *Study of Spinoza's Ethics* (Bennett 1984) I have presented a basically coherent metaphysical story according to which finite bodies do indeed relate to the extended world as blushes do to faces or as falls do to sparrows. Although he agrees that his challenge has been met, Curley is not convinced that Spinoza really did mean to advance the metaphysic which I have attributed to him, and he stands by his theory that Spinoza thinned out the meanings of "substance" and "mode." Our interchange on the issue occurs elsewhere, and will not be repeated here. (See Curley 1991b, and Bennett 1991.) In this chapter I stand by the interpretation of Spinoza presented in my book, the outlines of which I shall now present.

5. FINITE BODIES AS MODES

Start by thinking of the one extended substance as *Space*, which can be arbitrarily divided into regions shaped however you like and any size you like. (These regions do not compete with Space for the title of substance or most basic kind of thing because no region is privileged: There are no constraints on how finely or coarsely Space can be "divided" into regions.) Now, consider a pebble P which exactly fills a certain region R. We think that R existed before P moved into it, and will exist when P moves on, but right now P and R exactly coincide. That makes it sound as though P and R are two extended items that have exactly the same coordinates, items of kinds that enable them to be precisely co-located, which we assume two material things could not be. If we do not like that account of the situation (and nobody does), it seems that we must give primacy to either P or R: Either there is a pebble here, and the so-called region is to be explained away, or there is a region, and the so-called pebble is to be explained away. Leibniz took the former option, Descartes and Spinoza the latter.

If primacy is given to the pebble (not necessarily saying that it is fundamentally real, but giving it more reality than the region), what is to be said about the region? Descartes anticipated one answer to this, namely that the region is *nothing* (Descartes 1985: II,18). He attacked this through an argument that is approvingly echoed by Spinoza: If the region is nothing, then if the pebble is annihilated there will be nothing between the pebbles that now touch its opposite edges; if there will be nothing between them then they will be in contact; since they are not now in contact, that means that they will have moved; so we get the result that the annihilation of one thing will absolutely necessitate the movement of something else; this is intolerable, so the premise is wrong, and the region is not nothing. This argument, which is sometimes derided, seems to me sound, deep, and important. I have fleshed out its details a little, but the core of it is in Descartes and in Spinoza (for references to the latter, see section 6).

Leibniz had a different device for explaining away the region. He contended that every so-called region, and indeed Space as a whole, is an ideal entity – a logical construct out of relations between bodies. This account of space implies, for example, that the crucial fact about the two pebbles on opposite sides of P is not that *there is something between them* but rather that *they are apart from one another*; so we have the language of relations between bodies and (regions of) space, but it is to be understood as a way of expressing facts about relations among bodies. It is not easy to carry through in detail this relational view of space, and it has had a better press than any specific version of it has earned (Earman 1989, Chapter 1). Still, it is a possibility, and it seems not to have occurred to either Descartes or Spinoza.

They, and especially Spinoza, went the other way: We should start with the region, and explain away the statement that there is a pebble in it. If there is (as we should ordinarily say) a pebble in region R, what makes this true is the fact that R is *pebbly*, where "pebbly" stands for a certain monadic property that a spatial region can have. If the pebble moves (as we should ordinarily say), what makes this true is the fact that there is a continuous change in which regions are pebbly: The so-called movement of a pebble through space is like the so-called movement of a panic through a crowd. Nothing literally moves, but there is a change in which people are calm and which are agitated. And if the pebble were to be annihilated, what would really be happening is that a region ceased being pebbly and no adjoining region became pebbly; the going out of existence of a pebble is like the going out of existence of a blush or a panic or a freeze – nothing goes out of existence, but something alters.

6. SOME TEXTUAL EVIDENCE

That is my interpretation of Spinoza's doctrine that there is only one extended substance, and that finite bodies are modes of it. It gives the doctrine a chance of being true, and uses the technical terms "substance" and "mode" in their entire normal meanings. Furthermore, it makes sense as nothing else does of the principal passage in the *Ethics* where this matter is actually discussed – as distinct from the apparatus of official "demonstrations." I refer to the wonderful *Ethics* 1p15s, which includes this:

Matter is everywhere the same, and parts are distinguished in it only insofar as we conceive matter to be qualitatively various, so that its parts are distinguished only modally, but not really. Water is divided and its parts separated from one another – *qua* water, but not *qua* corporeal substance. For *qua* substance it is neither separated nor divided. Again, water *qua* water comes into and goes out of existence, but *qua* substance it does neither.

The parts of matter are not separated really (that is, "thingwise," from the Latin *"res,"* meaning "thing") but they are separated modally (that is, qualitywise). And the last sentence says that when water is annihilated no thing goes out of existence, but a region of the one substance becomes unwatery. This is all just what Spinoza should say if he has the metaphysic that I have attributed to him; I can find no other basis for it.

Spinoza connects this with Descartes through his reference in *Ethics* 1p15s to an earlier treatment that he has accorded to "vacuum." The treatment is in his *Descartes's "Principles of Philoso-*

phy" 2p2,3, where Descartes's argument that space cannot be *nothing* is explicitly invoked.

One dramatic bit of evidence that this really is Spinoza's position can be found in Letter 4. The passage consists of two sentences, of which the first is this: "Men are not created, only generated, and their bodies existed before, although formed differently." This sounds like a claim about the permanence of particles of matter: My body "existed before" in the sense that its constituent atoms existed in 1929 although they did not then make up a human body; and that could be said by someone who did not accept the metaphysic I have been expounding. But I think that Spinoza did mean to be stating that metaphysic, implying that Space is basic and my body is not: My body "existed before" in the sense that my body at this moment is a certain Bennettish region of space, and that region existed in 1929 although it was not then Bennettish. (It was not Bennettish three minutes ago, either. I have [to speak idiomatically] moved to this position two minutes ago, which is true because [to speak with metaphysical strictness] this region became Bennettish at that time.) That must be what Spinoza was getting at; otherwise, his next sentence is lunatic. He has just said that your beginning was not a true origination, and has implied that your ending will not be a true annihilation either. What, for him, would count as a true annihilation of an extended item? It would have to be the *annihilation of a region*. But if there is just one Euclidean space, that would have to involve *the annihilation of Space*: It does not make sense to suppose that a region might go out of existence leaving the rest of Space intact. Now look at the two sentences together: "Men are not created, only generated, and their bodies existed before, although formed differently. From this it follows, as I freely acknowledge, that if one part of matter were annihilated, the whole of extension would also vanish at the same time." On my interpretation of Spinoza, that second sentence is just right. I know of no other basis on which it makes any sense at all.

This metaphysical view, that the "occupants" of Space are really modes of Space which is the one extended substance, has been sympathetically entertained by Plato, Descartes, Newton, Locke, Quine, and others. In attributing it to Spinoza, I am putting him in worthy company.

A couple of "matters arising" should be dealt with here, before we move to other topics.

(i) In the apparatus of lemmas etcetera that Spinoza inserts between *Ethics* 2p13 and 2p14, he presents an abstract physics, based on the view that the material world is made up of "simplest bodies." Many questions arise about these – questions that are not answered by Spinoza's characterization of them as items "that are distinguished from one another only by motion and rest, speed and slowness" (E 2p13a2"). For present purposes, however, what mainly matters is that none of the material presented between 2p13 and 2p14 belongs at the most basic level of Spinoza's metaphysic. That basic level leaves open the possibility that the qualitative variations that are found in Space, the one substance, might be such as not to support a physics of material particles at all; it might, for example, modally differentiate regions from one another in wavelike rather than thinglike patterns. Spinoza as a child of his times accepted the "corpuscularian hypothesis," and he had no good reason not to do so. I am a little sorry, though, that he was not inspired by his own metaphysic to see the possibility that the world at its next-to-basic level might have been unimaginably different from the world we think we have. The main point, however, is that the physics of simplest bodies does not compete with the substance monism; it belongs at a different, shallower level.

(ii) In addition to finite modes, says Spinoza, there are infinite modes. If modes are features or qualities of a substance, then the infinite modes of extension – described as Spinoza describes them – must be features of the extended world that it instantiates everywhere and always, features that it will continue to have no matter what alterations it undergoes. What could such features be? The only convincing answer to this that I know of is Curley's. He says that infinite modes are causal features of the world, and a statement attributing such a mode to the world would be a basic causal law (Curley 1969: 55–74).

That seems pretty clearly to be right, and Curley turns it to good effect in explaining 1p28,d. He interprets this passage as saying that each finite mode (thing or event) is caused by a previous finite mode, which means that the causal chain leading up to any particular thing that happens runs back to infinity; and each succession of one finite mode by another takes place by virtue of an infinite mode, that is, a causal law. Thus, as Curley felicitously puts it: "The previously existing singular facts give us the infinite series of finite causes. The general facts [causal laws] give us the finite series of infinite causes, terminating in God" (Curley 1969: 66). Note, incidentally, that Curley must say that infinite modes depend on the one substance because they are laws about it, while finite ones depend on it because they are causally at its mercy. On my more traditional account of "mode" and "substance," the notion of modal dependence is more unitary as well as being less central.

8. NECESSITY AND CONTINGENCY

Spinoza's account of the causation of particular events, namely through an infinite chain of earlier events linked through infinite and eternal causal laws, brings us to the question of his views about necessity and contingency. He certainly holds that causal laws are absolutely necessary: It is necessary, as strongly as you like, that if a world is extended then it conforms to such and such physical laws. From that, together with Spinoza's view – based on his peculiar onto-logical argument – that there absolutely must be an extended world, it follows that the laws of physics are themselves absolutely neces-sary. That satisfies the demands of explanatory rationalism so far as physical laws are concerned. If P is a causal law, then the answer to "Why is it the case that P?" is that it could not possibly not be the case that P. Causal laws involve no element of brute fact.

What about particular matters of fact, such as the fact that a slate just fell from my roof? Well, it was caused to fall by a puff of wind, which was caused by some other movement of the air, which was caused by . . . , and so on backwards; strict determinism reigns, and the causal chain must run back forever. Furthermore, each link in it is supported by a causal law, which means that the link is absolutely necessary. Given that a gust like that occurred in precisely those circumstances, it was absolutely impossible for the slate not to fall.

So the fall of the slate, like every other matter of particular fact, was *inevitable* in the sense that: Given the previous history of the world, it could not possibly have not happened exactly as it did happen. That, however, is not to say that such facts are *necessary*. The proposition about the slate might be inevitable yet contingent, which is just to say that the world might have had a different previous history, in which case the slate would not have fallen.

When Spinoza writes, "Things could not have been produced by God in any other way or in any other order than they have been produced" (E 1p33), one can reasonably take him to mean that the world could not have had a different history, which is to say that each matter of fact is absolutely necessary, or that this is the only possible world. But such a reading is not forced upon us, I think. Taken in context, *Ethics* 1p33 might express only the thesis that each particular matter of fact is (not necessary, but) inevitable, that is, necessitated by the previous history of the world.

Spinoza also writes: "In nature there is nothing contingent" (E 1p29). That might seem definitively to imply that this is the only possible world, but it does not because Spinoza does not mean by "contingent" what we do. For him a contingent truth is one that is not necessary or even inevitable. His determinism implies that nothing is "contingent" in that sense, because it implies that every particular matter of fact is inevitable. The question whether all such truths are judged by Spinoza to be in themselves necessary remains open.

I am not sure what his considered opinion was on this issue, this being a subject of disagreement among his interpreters. Some hold that he consistently maintained that all truths are absolutely necessary, some that he consistently denied this, and some that he inconsistently asserted and denied it. I have been inclined to belong to the third camp, though I am swayed by the defense of the first position – that Spinoza was a consistent necessitarian – in Garrett 1991.

The view that this is the only possible world seems on the face of it to be tremendously implausible – even more so than the view that each matter of particular fact is inevitable. Still, Spinoza is under pressure to adopt the necessitarian position, the pressure coming from his explanatory rationalism. The slate's fall was the latest event in an infinite causal chain – one that had no beginning, each item in it being caused by an earlier one. Any question of the form "Why did E_i occur?", where E_i is a member of that chain, can be answered by adducing some previous event and the laws of nature. But now consider the question "Why did that whole causal chain occur?" There seems to be no way of answering this that will satisfy the demands of explanatory rationalism unless it can be said that the entire chain is absolutely necessary.

It would therefore not be surprising if it eventually turned out that Spinoza was an outright necessitarian, though I do not think it has yet been conclusively shown that he was. In addition to Garrett 1991, it might be worthwhile to read Bennett 1984, Chapter 5.

9. TIME

The concept of absolute necessity is involved in Spinoza's use of the term "eternal," and I make that my excuse for bringing in at this point the question of what Spinoza's view was about time. There has been disagreement and controversy about this too, but I contend that the situation is straightforward, untangled, and unambiguous.

(i) By "eternal" Spinoza means "absolutely necessary" (E 1d8), and when he uses that word to express this concept it is because he is thinking of the fact that whatever is necessarily true is always true. (ii) By "duration" Spinoza means the passage of time. (iii) By the Latin word "*tempus*" (usually translated as 'time') he means time thought of as cut or divided in some way: The concept of *tempus* is at work in any proposition that distinguishes some part of time from some other. Thus, it is used in all statements about measured periods of time, all uses of tenses, and all statements about what happened before or after what else. The phrase "an hour" involves *tempus* because it refers to a slice of time, a small amount of time cut out from the whole time-line; the phrase "what color the sky *was*" involves *tempus* because it distinguishes one time as past from another that is present; and "The rain ended before the snow began" involves *tempus*, quite apart from its past tense, because it distinguishes the time of the rain's ending from that of the snow's starting.

Spinoza says that duration "can be made definite by *tempus*" (E 5p23d), meaning that a statement involving the former concept can be made more specific by a use of the latter. For example, we can go from "The Milky Way lasts [tenseless] through time" to the more specific "The Milky Way lasts [tenseless] through at least a billion years." In short, to attribute duration to an item is just to say that it lasts through time, saying nothing about how long its time of existence is, whether past or future, or how related to other times; any such further details involves *tempus*.

Eternity, as I have implied, involves sempiternity; that is, it involves something's being the case at all times. Spinoza says of the existence of an eternal thing that "it cannot be limited by *tempus* or explained through duration" (E 5p23s). That it cannot be limited by *tempus* is something it shares with merely sempiternal things (if there are any), that is, things that exist at all times though not necessarily. In talking about the time of existence of a sempiternal thing, we do not need tenses, clocks, calendars, or relatings of times to other times. But sempiternity could be "explained through duration," for it is just unlimited duration, or duration through all times. Eternity cannot be so explained, as it involves not only sempiternity but also the additional concept of absolute necessity.

Some commentators have made heavy weather of all this. It is in fact simple and straightforward. The only tricky question has to do with which of these temporal concepts Spinoza is willing to apply to God or Nature. In his early *Metaphysical Thoughts* (published as an Appendix to *Descartes's "Principles of Philosophy"*), he said that God has no duration, which amounts to saying that no temporal concepts are applicable to the universe. His reasons for this were bad, and he seems to have changed his mind in the *Ethics*. He is of course committed to attributing duration to God given that he attributes eternity to God, because eternity is necessary sempiternity, which is a special case of duration.

What about *tempus*? In Letter 12 Spinoza speaks of it as "nothing but a mode of the imagination," which ought to mean that in a true fundamental account of the whole of reality the concept of *tempus* would not be used. In the *Ethics*, however, it is not clear that Spinoza meant to go so far. When he speaks of *tempus* he usually has in mind the measurement of time, and he did think that all our measures – of time and space and of things spatial and temporal – are superficial and "imaginative" and not part of the basic, objective story (see 1p15s). I do not think that he seriously meant to declare that none of the other uses of the concept of *tempus* would come into a fundamental description of the world.

If he did, then he must have held that the universe does not alter, and that apparent change is unreal. Some things he says could be taken in that way, especially "God, or all of God's attributes, are immutable" (E 1p20c2), but such remarks do not force us to conclude that Spinoza thought change to be unreal, and I am reluctant to attribute to him anything so manifestly false.

10. THREE THESES, ESPECIALLY PARALLELISM

What happens to my body is systematically tied to states of my mind. This has to be explained, and Spinoza will not explain it causally. His explanation relies on a doctrine I shall call *parallelism*: "Mental items can be mapped onto bodily items in a way that preserves causal connectedness. That is, if M1 causes M2, and B1 corresponds to M1 and B2 to M2 under the mapping, then B1 causes B2. And conversely." As Spinoza says: "The order and connexion of ideas is the same as the order and connexion of things" (E 2p7). The mental correlate of any material item x is called "the idea of x." The most striking instance of this is that the mind of any human being is the "idea of" his or her body.

This thesis of mind–body parallelism is supposed to explain why minds seem to interact with bodies. It seems to us that a stab causes a pain which causes a cry; but really the stab causes the bodily counterpart of the pain, which causes the cry; and the "idea of" the stab causes the pain which causes the "idea of" the cry. There are two parallel causal chains; we are aware of bits of each, and we mentally assemble these into a single spurious chain – one that moves, impossibly, from extension to thought and back again.

It is wholly in character that Spinoza should see the correlations as complete rather than partial: There could not be a reason why some material items should have mental counterparts while others did not, and what cannot have a reason cannot be the case. Faced with the apparent fact that the mental world is partly harnessed to the world of matter, Spinoza is saying "It's not a harnessing and it's not partial."

As it stands, this is not much of an explanation of the facts as we find them! We know *what induces Spinoza to believe it*, but it will not explain the facts unless he also says *what makes it true*. He says that parallelism follows from *Ethics* 1a4, "The knowledge of an effect depends on, and involves, the knowledge of its cause," though I think help is also supposed to come from 2p3, "In God there is necessarily an idea both of his essence and of everything that necessarily follows from his essence," together with *substance monism*, which says that there is only one substance, so that whatever it is that is extended is also whatever it is that thinks. This is discouraging. For one thing, the official argument for substance monism is weak (see section 3 above), and even with substance monism on board one cannot get, or even seem to get, parallelism out of *Ethics* 1a4 and 2p3. If one thinks that Spinoza was a genius, or even that he was a solidly competent philosopher, one must think that he could do better for parallelism than that. If he cannot, I give up: What remains is mere history, with not enough followable content to engage our philosophical interests. What is at stake here is the question of whether parallelism is sober metaphysics or a mere shot in the dark.

The clue to that is *mode identity*, that is, the thesis that if M is correlated with B under the parallelism, then M is B. This startling statement is first made in 2p7s, and we cannot get any further without finding out what Spinoza means by it.

II. THE MODE IDENTITY THESIS

To understand Spinoza's doctrine that a mode of extension and the idea of it "are one and the same thing," that is, that my body and my mind are one and the same thing, we have to take the term "mode" seriously. According to Spinoza my body is a mode – that is, an "affection" or state or quality – of the extended substance. This entails that the fact that

There is a body which is . . . ,

with the blank filled by a complete account of the physical nature and history of my body, is really the fact that

Space is F

for some complex value of F. The same applies *mutatis mutandis* for my mind: It is a mode of the thinking substance, the item that is to thought what Space is to extension, so that the fact that

There is a mind which is . . . ,

with the blank filled by a complete account of the nature and history of my mind, is really the fact that

> The thinking substance is G

for some complex value of G. Those must be Spinoza's views if he seriously and literally holds that finite particular things are modes.

Now, when Spinoza says that my body is my mind, or that a circle and the idea of it are one and the same thing, he ought to mean *that F is G*. That is, what it takes for there to be a physical object such as my body is for there to be an extended substance that is F, and what it takes for there to be a mind such as mine is for there to be a thinking substance that is F – for the very same value of F. My mind is a mode, my body is a mode, and my mind is my body; so the mode that is my mind is the mode that is my body; and so the "affection" or quality or state which, added to extension, yields the whole nature of my body is the very one which, added to thought, yields the whole nature of my mind. What Spinoza means by the mode identity thesis, therefore, is precisely what his words imply when understood in their complete standard meanings.

The doctrine is that each mode is a mode under all of the attributes; we should think of the mode that constitutes my body not as a complex quality that *includes* extendedness but rather as a complex quality that *can be combined with* extendedness and also with thinkingness. The modes are transattribute, logically speaking; that is, each is combinable with thought and with extension, and with any other attributes there may be.

Spinoza usually uses the term "mode" differently from this, taking a mode to be a complex property that includes an attribute: "The modes of each attribute involve the concept of their attribute," he says (E 2p6d). But in 2p7s he has changed his tune and now uses "mode" to stand for what would remain if the attribute were removed. My interpretation of the mode-identity thesis brings this fact into the spotlight, but even if my interpretation is wrong the fact is undeniably there. Put together these: (a) concept dualism, (b) the thesis that modes of extension involve extension and modes of thought involve thought, and (c) our present thesis that a mode of extension is a mode of thought. If (c) is maintained, one of the others must be dropped or qualified. It cannot be (a) concept dualism, because that is a load-bearing part of the structure of the *Ethics*. So we must suppose that (b) is intermittent because Spinoza moves in 2p7s to using "mode" in a special sense in which it refers not to attribute-involving modes but rather to modes from which the attribute has been deleted, the result being something which, he now says, could be combined with any attribute.

12. EXPLAINING PARALLELISM

Not only are these modes transattribute in the sense that each is *combinable* with any attribute; furthermore each mode actually is *combined* both with thought and extension. That is guaranteed by the substance monism doctrine, which says that there is just one substance that instantiates both the attributes. If there were two substances, one extended and one thinking, it would not follow from the fact that something is extended and F that anything is thinking and F. The potentially transattribute mode that combines with extension to yield my body might not be possessed by the thinking substance, in which case my mind would not exist.

That is the key to explaining why parallelism is true. The doctrine of mode identity says that corresponding to any extended mode (F-and-extension) there *could be* a corresponding thinking mode (F-and-thought); the doctrine of substance monism says that any mode that is instantiated in combination with extension is also instantiated in combination with thought; put the two together and you get the thesis that corresponding to any actual mode involving one attribute there is a mode involving the other. Thus, from substance monism and mode-identity we get parallelism.

That pattern of argument exactly fits the details of 2p7s. In that scholium, Spinoza does the following things in the following order. (1) He reminds us that there is only one substance, so that the thinking substance and the extended substance are one and the same. (2) He goes straight on to say that any mode of extension is identical with the idea of it, that is, with the corresponding mode of thought. For example, a circle and an actual idea of the circle are "one and the same thing which is explained through different attributes." He does not infer (2) from (1), but merely says they are similar, as indeed they are. *Just as* there is only one substance that is comprehended under this or that attribute, *so also* any thought–extension complex is only one mode, which can be explained through this or that attribute. (3) Having asserted (1) and (2), Spinoza says that "that is why" (*ideò*) we shall find one and the same order and connection of causes, no matter which attribute we investigate Nature under. That is, he offers substance monism and mode-identity as *explaining* the parallelism that he has asserted in 2p7.

What comes after that in the scholium (its penultimate paragraph in Curley's layout) is puzzling if one pauses to look at it carefully. I shall explain the puzzle and the solution in section 14, but first I must devote a part to the most formidable objection to the line of thought with which I have been crediting Spinoza.

13. A CONJECTURE ABOUT TRANSATTRIBUTE MODES

My interpretation of the three doctrines seems to conflict with Spinoza's thesis that there is no causal flow across any boundary between attributes. This is vital to many of his lines of thought, that is, his view that to explain human physical behavior we should resort not to psychology but to biology. The threatened conflict, however, does not result from anything controversial that I have said, but is plainly there on any unstupid reading of Spinoza's text. On the one hand: "The modes of each attribute have God for their cause only insofar as he is considered under the attribute of which they are modes, and not insofar as he is considered under any other attribute" (E 2p6). This clearly entails that what happens in my mind does not cause what happens in my body, and vice versa. On the other hand: "A mode of extension and the idea of that mode are one and the same thing, but expressed in two ways (E 2p7s). The object of the idea constituting a human mind is a human body" (E 2p13). These two entail that my mind is my body. How can my mind be my body, and yet not be causally relevant to my body? The threat of absurdity comes straight out of Spinoza, with no exegetical help from me. *Something* must be done to render all this consistent.

The only remedy I can find requires me to accept a certain hypothesis about Spinoza's thought – a risky hypothesis, attributing to him a philosophical doctrine that he does not state explicitly. Still, I think the attribution is right: As well as removing the threatened inconsistency, it solves some textual and philosophical problems for which no other solutions have been offered, one being the problem of what Spinoza is getting at in the strange later part of 2p7s.

Spinoza held, I conjecture, that the transattribute modes are not accessible to intellect in isolation, and can be thought only in combination with some attribute. One can think that the one substance is *extended and F*, thereby thinking the whole truth about my body; and one can think that the one substance is *thinking and F*, that being the whole truth about my mind. But no intellect – not even an unlimited or "infinite" one – can dismantle either of those thoughts into its attribute component and its F component, conceptually isolating the transattribute mode.

That would give Spinoza a reason for saying that no explanation can run from one attribute through to another. To explain something across a boundary between attributes would be to go from the premises

> The one substance is extended and F, and
> The one substance is thinking,

to the conclusion

> The one substance is thinking and F.

That would get a conclusion about my mind from a premise about my body in conjunction with the thin premise that the universe has a mental aspect. But to conduct such a prediction or explanation, one must detach F from extension and bring it across into combination with thought. I conjecture that Spinoza believed that we cannot do that, which is why he said that no legitimate intellectual operation runs from premises under one attribute to a conclusion under another, and why this is consistent with the thesis that a single mode appears under both attributes. Tracking such a mode through would involve thinking certain concepts in abstraction from any attribute, and (according to my hypothesis) Spinoza holds that to be impossible.

14. EXPLANATION AND CAUSATION

That would explain how Spinoza, consistently with his doctrine of the identity of modes across the different attributes, can deny that there are *followable explanations* running from one attribute to another, but not how he can deny that there are *entailments* or *causal chains* running from one attribute to another. Indeed, he seems to be

committed to there being entailments across attribute boundaries:
The transattribute modes create a system of logical relationships
between the attributes, whether or not anyone can think them in
abstraction. Or so one might think.

This looks like trouble for my interpretation, and for any other
that takes him to be using "mode" with its full normal meaning. In
showing how the trouble can be dealt with, I shall not discuss the
logical and causal possibilities separately, because Spinoza does not
distinguish them. So the difficulty is this: My hypothesis reconciles
mode identity with the denial that there are *followable explanations* that go across boundaries between attributes, but not, apparently, with the denial that there are *causal chains* that go across
boundaries between attributes.

This difficulty, however, rests on a distinction which Spinoza rejects. When he says there are no causal chains which . . . , etc., he
means only that there are no followable explanations which . . . ,
etc. He says as much, just where he needs to, namely at the point
where an alert reader would start to suspect that the doctrine is
inconsistent. This is the strange nearly final episode in *Ethics* 2p7s,
to which I have referred (the emphases are mine):

> When I said that God is the *cause* of the idea . . . of a circle only insofar as he
> is a thinking thing, and the *cause* of the circle only insofar as he is an
> extended thing, this was only because the intrinsic being of the idea of the
> circle can be *perceived* only through another mode of thinking as its proxi-
> mate cause, and . . . so on to infinity. Hence, so long as things are *considered*
> as modes of thinking, we have to *explain* the order of the whole of nature, or
> the connection of causes, through the attribute of Thought alone. And inso-
> far as they are *considered* as modes of Extension, the order of the whole of
> nature has to be *explained* through the attribute of Extension alone.

This passage picks up the doctrine about the causal insulation
between the attributes and psychologizes it, explains it as meaning
something about how things must be explained, perceived, considered. This is the place to do it. Spinoza has just finished explaining
why the parallelism obtains; the explanation asserts the identity of
modes across the attribute boundaries, which seems to offer a basis
on which there could be a logico-causal flow across those boundaries; and Spinoza needs to explain why it does not. He does this by
psychologizing the notion of causal flow.

This is the only place in the *Ethics* where Spinoza does such a thing, presumably because this is the only place where he needs to. It is just here, and nowhere else, that he explains the metaphysical underlay of the 2p7 parallelism; that explanation involves mode identity of a kind that *prima facie* threatens the causal separateness of the attributes; and Spinoza has to remove the threat. Notice that psychologizing causation removes the threat only with help from the premise that the transattribute modes cannot be thought in abstraction from any attribute. My hypothesis that Spinoza accepted that premise thus gets some confirmation from the penultimate paragraph of 2p7s. If the hypothesis is wrong, then so is my account of what the paragraph is there for. But then what other account can be given?

15. WHAT IS AN ATTRIBUTE?

My hypothesis also lets me explain something that has plagued Spinoza scholars for centuries, namely his strange definition of the term "attribute." The general outline of how things go in the *Ethics* seems to indicate that the items that are predicable of the one substance divide into the *attributes*, which are the basic ones, and the *modes*, which are all the rest. For example, to call something "square" is to say that it is extended and . . . ; to call something "afraid" is to say that it is thinking and . . . But to call something "extended" or "thinking" is not to assign it to some species of a still broader genus; there are no broader genera. That, I repeat, seems to be how Spinoza distinguishes attributes from modes.

But the official definition of "attribute" says, strangely, that an attribute is "that which intellect perceives of substance as its essence" (E 1d4). The term "intellect" brings in just one of the attributes, namely *thought*. What special privilege does thought have that entitles it to help define "attribute" generally? More urgent and more specific is the question:

- If Spinoza does not think that attributes are essences, what does he think about them, and why does he explain the term "attribute" in terms of something that is not true of attributes though it is perceived as being true of them? If on the other hand Spinoza holds that an attribute is an essence of any substance that has it, why does not he say so outright, instead of saying only that it is "perceived as" an essence?

Or perceived *as if* it were an essence – the much debated difference between "as" and "as if" is of no importance. Either way, by bringing in what "intellect perceives" Spinoza powerfully suggests that attributes are not really essences, and one wants to know why. An answer to this question falls out from the interpretation I have been offering for mode-identity and more generally for 2p7s.

Why does the *definiens* say that an attribute is "perceived as," rather than that it *is*, an essence of the substance that has it? Because according to Spinoza it *is not* an essence of the substance that has it. The relevant sense of "essence" is the one given by Descartes:

Each substance has one principal property which constitutes its nature and essence, and to which all its other properties are referred. Thus extension in length, breadth and depth constitutes the nature of corporeal substance, and thought constitutes the nature of thinking substance. Everything else which can be attributed to body presupposes extension, and is merely a mode of an extended thing; and similarly, whatever we find in the mind is simply one of the various modes of thinking. (Descartes 1985: I,53)

According to my hypothesis, Spinoza's attitude to this could be expressed as follows:

- Setting aside the bit about "*one* principal property," which is just a mistake, the rest of this account of the "nature and essence" of a substance reports accurately on how the situation must be perceived by any intellect. If you start with the various specific features of an extended thing, and ask what they all have in common – what they are all specifications of – the answer will inevitably be *extension*. In fact, each feature consists of something of the form "F and extended," where F could be combined also with other attributes; but that fact is not accessible to any intellect, and so extension will be *perceived by any intellect as* a Cartesian essence of the substance that has it. It is not really a Cartesian essence, however; it is not the most basic thing that is predicable of the substance. On the contrary, the transattribute modes are in a clear sense more basic, in that they can spread across all the attributes.

So what the definition of "attribute" does is to permit us to treat the attributes as basic in the way that Cartesian "essences or natures" are said to be, while including a hint ("what intellect perceives . . .") that what makes this a safe procedure is a limitation on what intellect can do rather than a fact about how things stand in the rest of reality. Spinoza explains "attribute" in this way because he has no other way of explaining it. That explains why Spinoza proceeds as he does in 1d4, and this explanation enables 1d4 to count as textual support for my hypothesis.

This account also explains why one attribute (thought) should be implicitly mentioned in a definition of "attribute" in general. The definition gives a privileged status to one attribute because it has such a status in Spinoza's whole metaphysical structure: His account of attributes in general involves the concept of causation, which he ultimately cashes out in terms of thought, as he explains at the end of 2p7s.

When Spinoza puts "what intellect perceives" into the definition of "attribute," he distinguishes appearance from reality. That is what Wolfson said too, and refuting him has become a standard exercise for Spinoza scholars (Wolfson 1934: I,151ff). But he took Spinoza to hold that the attributes are not really distinct from one another though they are perceived by intellect as being so. That is altogether indefensible: It ignores the wording of the definition of "attribute," which says nothing about distinctness. I interpret Spinoza as holding that the attributes are real, and really distinct, but that they are not really basic, are not really "essences" in Descartes's sense. That fits the wording of the definition ("perceives as . . . its essence"), and harmonizes with my treatment of 2p7s.

If Spinoza really held that an attribute *is* an essence of the substance that has it, there is not only the puzzle about "perceives as" in *Ethics* 1d4, but also the question of why he repeatedly says that each attribute *expresses* the (or an) essence of God. (See, for example, E 1d6, 1p16d, and 1p19d.) I explain it as follows: The nearest Spinoza will come to using the concept of essence in a metaphysically serious way involves him in saying that the system of trans-attribute modes is the essence of God. We can get at this only in its combination with some attribute or other. So the role of the attributes is to combine with the transattribute modes to get the latter into a form in which we can think them. The attributes let the modes come through. It is as though the modes were words written in a script to which intellect is blind, and the attributes make the message of the modes accessible to intellect by reading them aloud, *expressing* them.

There is another striking bit of evidence that this is right. At the start of 2p7s Spinoza reminds us of substance monism by saying that all the attributes belong to one substance. But instead of writing that every attribute pertains to one substance only, he writes, "Whatever can be perceived by an infinite intellect as constituting an essence of substance pertains to one substance only." In this one place, and nowhere else in the *Ethics*, Spinoza replaces the word "attribute" by its 1d4 definiens. Why do it at all? Why do it just here? I answer that this scholium is the only place in the work where the full force of 1d4 is relevant to what is going on. Throughout the rest of the work, we can proceed as though the attributes were basic, that is, were Cartesian "essences"; it is safe for us to do this, and indeed we have no alternative because our intellects are bound to perceive them as basic. Only here, where transattribute modes have to be introduced in Spinoza's explanation of parallelism, does Spinoza need to admit that as a matter of sheer metaphysics the attributes are not really basic after all.

Another benefit of this line of interpretation is that it answers the old question as to what content there is to Spinoza's substance monism. The statement that thought and extension are attributes of a single substance does not imply that they interact causally, Spinoza tells us, so what difference *does* it make whether they are possessed by one substance or two? I answer that there is a lot of content to the thesis: The unity of the one substance – its being one rather than two or more – is secured by the fact that the entire modal story about the whole of reality reappears under each of the attributes. The single "order and connection of things" and "order and connection of causes" – that is, the entire network of transattribute modes – runs across, through, under all the attributes, giving the one substance its integrity, its unity, its wholeness. There is not the slightest threat that Nature, just because its attributes are so disconnected from one another, will conceptually fall apart.

3   Spinoza's theory of knowledge

The human mind is part of the infinite intellect of God."
(E 2p11c)

I. INTRODUCTION

Spinoza's theory of knowledge is a strange and hybrid creature. An organic, inseparable part of his total philosophical system, it blends highly distinctive, original (even bizarre) formulations with both "modern" – especially Cartesian – influences, and ideas and aspirations rooted in much older thought.

Many recent commentators on Spinoza's epistemology have particularly stressed the Cartesian background of Spinoza's position, presenting him as evolving his own views in response to what he perceived as deficiencies in Descartes's.[1] Up to a point this approach is a sensible one. Fundamental features of Spinoza's framework and terminology do clearly derive from the Cartesian philosophy; and much that Spinoza says about such topics as skepticism, certainty, judgment, and "ideas" is unquestionably directed against Descartes. Further, focusing on those features of Spinoza's epistemology that can plausibly be represented as deliberate alternatives to well-known tenets of the *Meditations* (and related works of Descartes's) helps domesticate the epistemological elements of the *Ethics*, releasing them from their exotic theological/moral/eschatological context, and qualifying Spinoza as a comprehensible disputant in recognizably modern debates about knowledge.

Still, I believe that efforts to subordinate Spinoza's treatment of epistemological topics to the Cartesian tradition can all too easily

89

distract us from coming to terms with the basic thrust of his system, and the role of knowledge in it. For better or worse, Spinoza simply is *not* a "modern" ("post-Cartesian") thinker, if this designation implies accepting a merely extrinsic or instrumental relation between the pursuit of human knowledge and the achievement of personal happiness, both in ordinary life and in relation to the prospect of eternity. "The endeavor to understand," he writes, "is the first and only foundation of virtue, and it is not for some further purpose that we endeavor to understand things" (E 4p26). For Descartes, knowledge even of *God* plays a primarily instrumental role, isolating from any threat of doubt the clear and distinct perceptions on which he seeks to found a "firm and permanent" science of nature. Spinoza, on the contrary, denies that we legitimately seek to know God for the sake of something ulterior: "The mind's highest good is the knowledge of God, and the mind's highest virtue is to know God" (*"Summum Mentis bonum est Dei cognitio, et summma Mentis virtus Deum cognoscere")* (E 4p28).[2]

Of course for Spinoza, knowledge of God is knowledge of the one substance, "God or Nature," whose essence is equally and alternatively expressed by the infinite attributes of Thought and Extension. As we will see, however, the "highest kind of knowledge" is not bare knowledge of God's absolute or infinite essence through these attributes; rather it involves an intuitive grasp of how the essences of dependent things (or "modes") necessarily follow from the divine nature. Thus Spinoza's theory of knowledge, directed as it is towards "the mind's highest good," is at the same time firmly anchored in his monistic and necessitarian metaphysical position.

The brief comment which introduces the central exposition of Spinoza's epistemology, Part 2 of the *Ethics* ("Of the Nature and Origin of the Mind"), both refers back to the necessitarian position of Part 1 – specifically the central 1p16 – and points ahead to the conception of human freedom and salvation to be expounded later in the work:

I now pass to the explication of those things that must necessarily have followed from the essence of God, the eternal and infinite Being; not indeed all of them – for we proved in Proposition 16 of Part 1 that from his essence there must follow infinite things in infinite ways – but only those things that can lead us as it were by the hand to the knowledge of the human mind and its utmost blessedness.

The primary concern of the present chapter will be to explain as clearly as possible Spinoza's claims about knowledge and related topics in this Part of the *Ethics*, without losing sight of the metaphysical/theological commitments that underlie them, or of the ultimate goal of salvation or "blessedness" systematically expounded in Part 5. (A major phase in the search for salvation through knowledge is the "remedy for the passions" that distinct understanding provides [Parts 4 and 5]. I will not attempt to address this topic in detail, however, since it is dealt with at length in Chapter 6.)

The other major epistemological text in Spinoza's *corpus* is an earlier, unfinished essay, the *Treatise on the Emendation of the Intellect (Tractatus de Intellectus Emendatione*, abbreviated as "TdIE"). This work supplements the *Ethics* position in certain ways: for instance, through its explicit discussion of issues of "method" – an important seventeenth-century philosophical topic which does not directly figure in the *Ethics*. A thorough discussion of Spinoza's views about knowledge would have to include close critical examination of the *Treatise on the Intellect* as well as of Part 2 of the *Ethics* (and other relevant portions).³ Unfortunately, the *Treatise on the Intellect* poses formidable interpretive challenges of its own, and appears to diverge from the later, definitive doctrine of the *Ethics* in certain important respects. (Further, it lacks much of the detailed metaphysical framework within which that doctrine is developed.)⁴ It seems to me best, therefore, to deal with the *Treatise on the Intellect* for the most part only incidentally in this chapter; that is, I will turn to it only when Spinoza's statements there seem genuinely helpful in interpreting his later claims. My main intention, again, is to provide a reading of his epistemological doctrine in the *Ethics* that will be as clear, correct, and intelligible as possible.

But in order to underscore the main theme of this introduction – the intimate interconnections between Spinoza's position on knowledge and his conceptions of God, the dependent world, and the human search for salvation – I will conclude the section with a brief summary of the famous opening passage of the *Treatise on the Intellect*. The *Treatise* begins with an autobiographical sketch of Spinoza's conversion from pursuit of such ordinary objects of desire as fame, wealth, and sensual pleasure to seeking the "true good" – "something which once discovered and acquired would afford me a continuous and supreme joy to all eternity" (TdIE 1). Spinoza conveys the urgency of his new quest in powerful phrases reminiscent of Pascal and other mainstream religious thinkers:

I saw that I was in the greatest danger, and that I was forced to seek a remedy with all my strength, however uncertain it might be, like a sick man suffering from a fatal disease who, foreseeing certain death unless a remedy is forthcoming, is forced to seek it, however uncertain it might be, with all his strength, for in that lies all his hope. (TdIE 7)

[L]ove towards an eternal and infinite thing feeds the mind with joy alone, unmixed with any sadness. This is greatly to be desired, and sought with all our strength. (TdIE 10)

Up to this point Spinoza has spoken of the true good as an object to be sought and "loved"; but soon he begins to stress that his quest (which he hopes to share with others as well) has, at the least, a strong epistemological dimension. The supreme good, he says, is enjoyment of a perfected human nature: "What that nature is we shall show in its proper place: namely, the knowledge of the union which the mind has with the whole of nature" (TdIE 13). He goes on to observe that various "sciences" are indispensable to this endeavor, listing Moral Philosophy, Theory of Education, Medicine, and Mechanics. "But," he continues,

before anything else we must work out a method of emending the intellect and of purifying it, as far as is feasible at the outset, so that it may succeed in understanding things without error and as well as possible. So now it will be evident that my purpose is to direct all the sciences to one end and goal, that is (as we have said) the achievement of the highest human perfection. Thus everything in the sciences which does nothing to advance us towards our goal must be rejected as useless. (TdIE 16)

It seems then, that the intellect is to be emended and purified in order to suit it for progress in (only) those sciences that conduce to the supreme good for man: itself a form of "knowledge."

2. *ETHICS* 2: BACKGROUND ASSUMPTIONS AND TERMINOLOGY FROM PART I

Much of the metaphysical doctrine expounded in Part 1, concerning substance, attributes, modes, and causality, is directly or indirectly implicated in the theory of mind and knowledge to which Spinoza turns in Part 2. While a reasonable general grasp of Part 1's basic claims must largely be taken for granted in the present chapter, there are a few points that are worth calling to attention before we proceed.

As already mentioned, Spinoza himself recalls a particular central proposition of Part 1 at the very beginning of Part 2; namely, 1p16: "From the necessity of the divine nature infinite things in infinite ways (that is all that can fall under infinite intellect) must follow." The primary intention behind this proposition – as its demonstration and subsequent elaboration in Part 1 make clear – is to establish that all dependent beings follow from God's essence necessarily and ineluctably. As he elaborates in the scholium to *Ethics* 1p17: . . . "I think I have shown quite clearly (p16) that from God's supreme power or infinite nature an infinity of things in infinite ways – that is, everything – have necessarily flowed or are always following from that same necessity, just as from the nature of a triangle it follows from eternity to eternity that its three angles are equal to two right angles." An important feature of this doctrine is the denial – against Descartes in particular – that God brings about the world, including both laws of matter and principles of human reason, through an act of creation that is radically arbitrary. Like Descartes, Spinoza holds that creation from God is wholly free or "unconstrained"; for Spinoza, however, this conception implies only that "God acts solely from the laws of his own nature": It implies, that is, no arbitrariness or contingency.

Another important feature of 1p16 is the explicit introduction (for the first time in the *Ethics*) of the concept of "infinite intellect." This reference to infinite intellect signals the fundamental *intelligibility* of the generation of modes from the nature of substance – as does, in a more homely way, the geometrical analogy that Spinoza goes on to provide. The concept – often expressed by the apparently equivalent term "idea of God" (*idea Dei*) – will play an absolutely fundamental role when Spinoza comes to articulate his theory of human knowledge in Part 2.[5]

Also especially important to the development of Part 2 are the claims from Part 1 that (a) attributes, though expressing the essence of the one sole substance, are conceived independently of each other (E 1p10); (b) modes can "only be in the divine nature and be conceived through the divine nature" (E 1p15); and (c) (a consequence of (b)) "God is the *immanent* . . . cause of all things" (E 1p18; emphasis added). Further, (d) any finite thing "which has a determinate existence" requires another *finite* cause, which itself "has determinate existence," in order to exist or act (E 1p28).

Finally, we should take note of two axioms from Part 1 which play especially salient roles in Part 2. According to 1a4, "Knowledge of an effect depends on knowledge of the cause, and involves it." In several propositions of Part 1 Spinoza interprets this axiom as implying that an effect must be *conceived through* its cause, and therefore must *have something in common* with its cause (E 1p3, 1p6, 1p25; cf. 1a5). We will find that this axiom is very important to certain aspects of the epistemological position Spinoza develops in Part 2, particularly with respect to the relation between the causal order of material nature and knowledge of material things.[6]

According to 2a6, "A true idea must agree with its ideatum [i.e., its object]." This seemingly bland axiom figures in Part 1 only rather marginally and unobtrusively (cf. E 1p5 and 1p30). It begins to take on more importance, however, when Spinoza comes to expound his views about truth in Part 2. The axiom indeed is implicated in certain apparent conflicts in his statements which present some difficult interpretive challenges.

3. *ETHICS* 2: INITIAL ORIENTATION

Among the several definitions at the beginning of Part 2, there are two so centrally important for all that follows that they ought to be quoted in full. *Ethics* 2d3 expresses Spinoza's own understanding of the Cartesian term "idea": "By idea I understand a conception of the Mind which the Mind forms because it is a thinking thing." This definition is meant to have an important implication. As Spinoza goes on to explain: "I say 'conception' rather than 'perception' because the term perception seems to indicate that the Mind is passive to its object, whereas conception seems to express an activity of the Mind." In fact, Spinoza seems to use several terms as equivalent to "idea" throughout Part 2 – including "perception."[7] But the notion that having ideas involves some sort of mental activity is never lost sight of. (Its significance is only made clear at the very end of Part 2, however.)

Descartes contrasted his "clear and distinct" ideas (primarily belonging to intellect or reason) with those that were "obscure and confused" (associated primarily with imagination and sense). Spinoza follows Descartes in this terminology to some extent, but he tends to favor a different terminology to mark the distinction between favored and disfavored "ideas": Ideas are either *adequate* or *inadequate*. As he explains in 2d4: "By an adequate idea I mean an idea which, in so far as it is considered in itself without relation to its object, has all the properties – that is, intrinsic denominations (*denominationes*) – of a true idea." He adds (with implicit reference back to 1a6):[8] "I say 'intrinsic' so as to exclude what is extrinsic – that is, the agreement of the idea with its ideatum [i.e., its object]." But what *are* these "intrinsic denominations"? And how do they relate to the extrinsic "agreement" required by 1a6? Unfortunately Spinoza never addresses these important questions very concretely, and the remarks he does make (later in Part 2) tend to produce more confusion than they remove. The unfolding of his general position on ideas and knowledge in the earlier phases of Part 2 does suggest (as we shall see) that an appropriate rational *ordering* of ideas is central to his conception of "adequacy."

One other definition should be noted here, because it explains a term of art that we will find to be prevalent throughout Part 2, namely "singular things": "By singular things I mean things that are finite and have a determinate existence" (E 2d7).

The other four definitions and the five axioms of Part 2 do not need to be examined separately at this stage (though I will touch on one or two of them later). In fact, it is rather notable that *no* definition or axiom from Part 2 figures (explicitly, anyway) in *any* reasoning that Spinoza puts forward up to 2p10! In other words, the first nine propositions of Part 2, with their various corollaries and scholia, ostensibly follow without supplemental premises from the principles and theorems of Part 1. (These early propositions are still focused on God, not on human knowledge.) They do, however, involve a new departure: specific focus on mind and body. (Part 1 dealt with substance, attribute and mode more abstractly.) They also provide the essential framework for virtually everything else that Spinoza tries to establish in Part 2. They are, to be sure, in many ways obscure and strange – at least from the points of view of both ordinary discourse and the relatively accessible Cartesian philosophical system. I will now sketch my understanding of the gist of these early theorems, without particularly trying to show how they fit with what "we" (or Descartes) "would say."

4. THE IDEA OF GOD AND THE ORDER OF THINGS (E 2pp19)

In 2p1 and 2p2 Spinoza argues that Thought and Extension are "infinite attributes of God, [each] expressing God's infinite and eternal essence" (E 2p1; cf. E 2p2). According to 2p3, "In God there is necessarily the idea both of his essence and of everything that necessarily follows from his essence." The demonstration of this proposition relies partly on 1p16, where, as we have seen, Spinoza introduced the concept of the "infinite intellect": All that "can fall under infinite intellect" was said to follow necessarily from God's essence. The point of 2p3 is that God not only "can" but *does* "form the idea of his own essence and of everything that necessarily follows from it." *Ethics* 2p4 explicitly connects the expression "infinite intellect" with "the idea of God," and argues that the idea of God "is one only" (on the grounds that God is one). The issue of the relation between God's infinite intellect or "idea" and the human mind will turn out to be the fundamental concern of Part 2 (and, derivatively, of Part 5 as well). Any legitimate account of Spinoza's theory of knowledge must take full account of the role of "*idea Dei.*"

The next several propositions concern the equally important, and closely related, issue of causal order. According to 2p5, ideas considered in their "formal being" – that is, as modes of thought, without relation to their objective contents – have their full causality ("have God for their cause") under the attribute of Thought, rather than depending causally on their objects. *Ethics* 2p6 generalizes this point: "The modes of any attribute have God for their cause only in so far as he is considered under that attribute, and not in so far as he is considered under any other attribute." The whole demonstration of this proposition, and one of the two demonstrations offered for the preceding one, rests on the claims from Part 1 that any two attributes are conceived independently of each other (E 1p10), and that an effect must be known (or conceived) through its cause (E 1a4).

But although the causes of a mode must be found exclusively under its own attribute, there is an extremely intimate relation between the "order" of causes, and hence the order of knowledge, under the different attributes, specifically Thought and Extension: "The order and connection of ideas is the same as the order and connection of things" (E 2p7). This proposition, one of the most important in the *Ethics*, has one of the shortest demonstrations: "This is evident from 1a4; for the idea of what is caused depends on the knowledge of the cause of which it is the effect." While this "demonstration" has been dismissed as both incomplete and (even when supplemented) unsuccessful,[9] at a certain level of intelligibility Spinoza's point seems fairly straightforward. To have the idea of an effect is to "know" the effect; but knowledge of the effect (by 1a4) depends on knowledge of the cause. In other words, *just as* an effect depends on its cause, *so* the knowledge or idea of that effect depends on the knowledge or the idea of its cause. In still other words, Spinoza is holding that "the order" of understanding is the same as "the order" of being.

Spinoza makes virtually the same point in yet another way in 2p7c: "Hence it follows that God's power of thinking is on a par with his power of acting. That is, whatever follows formally from the infinite nature of God, all this follows from the idea of God in the same order and the same connection in God objectively." Here he simply expresses in Cartesianese the notion that in whatever order things follow from God's nature, in that same order God thinks, knows, or (so to speak) ideates them: Their order considered as caused things ("formal" order) is the same as their order considered as objects of understanding ("objective" order). In the famous scholium to 2p7, he further underpins the identification of the formal *order* of modes (of Extension, specifically) with the order of their ideas, by observing that it follows from the oneness of God or Substance (conceived under the different attributes) that the *modes* of Extension and their ideas in the attribute of Thought are "one and the same thing, conceived in two ways."

Ethics 2p8, with its corollary and scholium, concerns "the ideas of non-existing singular things." Implicit in this proposition is a distinction – important throughout the *Ethics*, but often overlooked – between existence purely as essence ("existence in the attributes of God"), and existence in time and place, or "duration." The distinction is particularly important to Spinoza's account of the several "kinds" of knowledge, and his theory of eternity of mind; we will come back to it later, in connection with these topics. For now, it is sufficient to note that Spinoza takes 2p7 to imply that the ideas of nonexisting things have the same status in the idea of God that the nonexisting things have in God's attributes: Both equally have a sort of essential reality, but lack determinate existence. (Thus, by 2d7, quoted above, they do not qualify for the designation "singular things.")

Ethics 2p10, drawing on 1p28, argues that the idea of a singular thing must be caused by the idea of some other singular thing; or, in Spinoza's words, it must "have God for its cause in so far as he is considered as affected by another definite mode of thinking" (and the chain of such causes goes on to infinity). In the corollary to this proposition Spinoza maintains that God has knowledge of "what happens in" a singular thing that is the object of an idea, only insofar as he has the idea of that object. The demonstration (which I find rather obscure) seems to rely on the implicit assumption that a thing is the *cause* of "what happens in it" (so an idea of a thing, by 2p7, is the cause of the idea or knowledge of what happens in the thing).

At this point (beginning with 2p10) Spinoza finally turns to the human mind (and its body). Some of the material he develops from 2p10 through the end of Part 2 – some of what he says about the "essence of man," and the mind–body relation, for instance – is more appropriately considered in another chapter. At the same time, much of this material – more, I think, than commonly recognized – is really quite important for approaching an understanding of Spinoza's basic doctrines about knowledge.

5. THE HUMAN MIND

Spinoza first explains at some length (in 2p10, its scholia and corollary) that the essence of man does not have the status of substance, but is rather "constituted by definite modifications of the attributes of God." He goes on to argue (E 2p11) that an actually existing human mind is necessarily the "idea of" an actually existing "singular thing" (soon to be identified with the human body (E 2p13)). In the important corollary of 2p11 he asserts:

Hence it follows that the human mind is part of the infinite intellect of God; and therefore when we say that the human mind perceives this or that, we are saying nothing else but this: that God – not in so far as he is infinite but in so far as he is explicated through the nature of the human mind, that is, in so far as he constitutes the essence of the human mind – has this or that idea.

The corollary continues (and concludes):

And when we say that God has this or that idea not only in so far as he constitutes the essence of the human mind but also in so far as he has the idea of another thing simultaneously with the human mind, then we are saying that the human mind perceives a thing partially or inadequately.

The reader who responds with bewilderment to these resonant pronouncements will find that his or her reaction has been anticipated by the author: "At this point our readers will no doubt find themselves in some difficulty and will think of many things that will give them pause" (E 2p11s). Spinoza asks that we follow his argument to the end before passing judgment.

While this seems basically a reasonable request, it may still be helpful at this point to restate briefly some features of the remarkable position that is beginning to take shape.

First, Spinoza maintains that there is an infinite system of actual thought, constituting knowledge of everything that exists, as necessarily produced from the essence of God or nature: He calls this system infinite intellect, or the idea of God.

Second, the order and connection of the determinate ideas that fall within infinite intellect are the same as the causal order obtaining among the determinate things (bodies) that are the objects of these ideas. (In fact, an idea and its bodily object are the same thing, conceived in two ways.)

Third, human minds are themselves "ideas," and as such have their place in the infinite system that is the idea of God: They are "parts" of this system. (Actually, as becomes clear as Spinoza goes along, human minds, like the idea of God itself, are constituted of a plurality of subsidiary ideas. See especially 2p15.)

Fourth, the "object" of a human mind – the corresponding mode under the attribute of Extension – is that human being's body. The human mind is dependent for its "determinate existence" on the determinate existence of its body.

Finally, fifth, an idea in the human mind may be incomplete ("partial or inadequate"), in the sense that it is dependent (in the infinite system of thought or knowledge) on other ideas which that human mind does not include.

6. SENSE AND IMAGINATION (E 2pp10–18)

Spinoza's reference to inadequate perception at the end of 2p11c heralds the beginning of his account of sense perception (which Spinoza, like Descartes before him, primarily associates with confused or inadequate ideas). *Ethics* 2p12 provides the starting point for this account by enunciating a very strange claim that proves to be one of its fundamental premises:

Whatever happens in the object of the idea constituting the human mind is bound to be perceived by the human mind; i.e. the idea of that thing will necessarily be in the human mind. That is to say, if the object of the idea constituting the human mind is a body, nothing can happen in that body without being perceived by the mind.

The demonstration of this startling claim appeals to 2p9c, "Whatsoever happens in the singular object of any idea, knowledge of it is in God only in so far as he has the idea of that object." I have already suggested that the demonstration of this corollary is obscure; and I do not think tracing the antecedents of the demonstration of 2p12 helps very much in telling us what to make of the proposition. One point that seems to be overwhelmingly forced upon us by common sense is that Spinoza *must* be dissociating the notion of the human mind's *perceiving* some thing (or occurrence) from that of its being *consciously aware* of that thing (or occurrence).[10] This point is reinforced by what he goes on to say about minds in general in 2p13.

As already mentioned, Spinoza proclaims in 2p13 that the human body is the object of the human mind. This proposition is based on an axiom to the effect that "we feel a certain body to be affected in many ways" (E 2a4). Thus, he says, "it follows that man consists of mind and body, and the human body exists according as we sense it" (E 2p13c). Further, "From the above we understand not only that the human Mind is united to the Body but also what is to be understood by the union of Mind and Body" (E 2p13s). Clearly, Spinoza is trying to replace the Cartesian account of mind–body union based on causal interaction (which his system deliberately rules out) with an account based on the proposition that the mind is "the idea of" the body (or the body "the object of" the mind). This does not seem the right context in which to evaluate this particular anti-Cartesian move.[11] But it is important to take note of two points that Spinoza immediately goes on to make. First, just as the idea of God includes the idea of the human body (i.e., the human mind), so also it includes ideas of every body whatsoever: Thus *all* individual things are animate, "although in different degrees." Second, the minds of different individuals vary in excellence according to the perfection of their bodies: The human mind, Spinoza implies, excels all others, because of certain perfections of its bodily "object":

... in proportion as a body is more apt than other bodies to act or be acted upon simultaneously in many ways, so is its mind more apt than other minds to perceive many things simultaneously; and in proportion as the actions of one body depend on itself alone and the less that other bodies concur with it in its actions, the more apt is its mind to understand distinctly. (E 2p13s)

Here is a further indication that distinct perception is going to be tied to internal determination: (relatively) self-caused bodily behavior is the flip side (in the attribute of Extension) of ideas that are adequate *within* the human mind. But the passage also encourages the speculation that the ideas or minds of relatively imperfect and non-autonomous bodies (such as pebbles) might be something like those ideas of relatively simple and nonautonomous components of the human body which (by E 2p12) necessarily occur within the human mind.[12] Perhaps in general these low-level ideas are quite remote from articulate conscious awareness, or even ordinary sensation.

The similarity of nature of all bodies is stressed in a series of "lemmata" and (new) axioms that follow *Ethics* 2p13. This sustained passage also provides some account of the general principles governing bodily motion, and of the dynamic constitution of complex bodies (including their continuing existence despite replacement of their component bodies).[13] Here, however, we need only quote part of one of the axioms – which turns out to be quite important to Spinoza's account of sense experience: "All the ways in which a body is affected by another body follow from the nature of the affected body together with the nature of the body affecting it" (E 2p13a1"). After the lemmata Spinoza lays down a set of "postulates" concerning the composition and efficacy of the human body, and its dependence on external things. He then goes on, in 2p14–16, to offer an account of sense perception which avoids the Cartesian assumption that changes brought about in our bodies and brains by the impingement of external things ultimately cause the production of ideas of sense in our minds. According to Spinoza's clever noninteractionist position, our minds, by virtue of "perceiving everything that happens in our bodies," "perceive" changes brought about in our bodies by the external bodies that interact with it. By 2p13a1" (just quoted) these changes "follow from the nature of the body affected together with the nature of the affecting body"; that is, both "natures" are causally relevant. Hence, on the assumption that "knowledge of an effect depends on knowledge of the cause, and involves it" (E 1a4), knowledge or perception of these changes involves "the nature of both bodies" (2p16); that is, we (as minds) perceive external bodies, but only derivatively, through our "perception" of our own bodies. In fact, Spinoza concludes, "the ideas that we have of external bodies indicate the constitution of our own body more than the nature of external bodies" (E 2p16c2). This seems to be his own way of expressing the characteristic seventeenth-century view that sense perception fails to reveal bodies to us as they really are – particularly so far as the so-called secondary qualities, such as color, taste, and sound, are concerned.[14] (But Spinoza has another, more systematic basis, for construing sense perception as "inadequate knowledge," as we shall shortly see.)

This account of sense experience provides the basis for Spinoza's account of imagination and memory as well. In imagination the mind regards an external body as present, as a result of its *earlier* effects on the human body (E 2p17).[15] Further, if two or more bodies have ever affected a human body at the same time, the mind's subsequent imagination of one of them will bring the other to mind as well (E 2p18).[16] Memory, then, "is just a linking of ideas involving the nature of things outside the human body, a linking which occurs in the mind according to the order and linking of affections of the human body" (E 2p18s). In this same scholium Spinoza makes two very important points about his account of imagination and memory. First, he calls attention to an easily overlooked distinction between "involving the nature of" and "explicating the nature of":

I say, firstly, that [memory] is only the linking of those ideas that involve the nature of things outside the human body, not of those ideas that explicate the nature of the said things. For they are in fact (2p16) ideas of the affections of the human body which involve the nature both of the human body and of external bodies.

Second, he begins to place emphasis on a distinction between two sorts of "order" or "linking" (*concatenatio*) among ideas that will prove to be perhaps the single most fundamental element in his general theory of knowledge:

I say, secondly, that this linking is according to the order and linking of the affections of the human body, so as to distinguish it from the linking of ideas which is according to the order of the intellect, by which the mind perceives things through their first causes, and which is the same in all men. (E 2p18s)

The notion of an idea "explicating the nature" of a thing also figures in Spinoza's explanation of the distinction between the "idea of" a given individual which is that individual's mind, and the idea of the individual in *another* mind. Thus, the idea of Peter that "constitutes the essence of Peter's mind . . . directly explicates the essence of Peter's body, and does not involve existence, except as long as Peter exists" (E 2p17s). On the other hand, the idea of Peter which is in another man – say, Paul – "indicates the constitution of Paul's body rather than the nature of Peter; and so, while that constitution of Paul's body continues to be, Paul's mind will regard Peter as present to him although Peter may not be in existence."

Thus ideas that are in my mind – while presumably always in one sense "of" my body – can also be (derivatively, so to speak) "of" other, external bodies as well. (Spinoza goes on to state that he will use the term "images of things" to designate "those affections of the human Body *the ideas of which* present external Bodies as present to us.")[17] What should be further noticed, however, is that he is here also distinguishing among the two readings of "idea of" in terms of issues of essence and existence. The essence of Peter's mind "directly explicates the essence" of Peter's body: Spinoza ties this characterization to the claim that the idea of Peter that constitutes the essence of Peter's mind can only exist as long as "its" (i.e., Peter's) body exists. *Paul's* idea of Peter, on the other hand, only indicates the effect that Peter has had on the "constitution" of Paul's body. These effects can linger as affections of Paul after Peter has ceased to be (as long as *Paul* continues to exist). The result of the latter circumstance, Spinoza goes on to say, is that Paul may *erroneously* believe that Peter continues to exist. (He adds that the error in this case is not inherent in the image itself of the external thing – which, we may say, as far as it goes is a veridical "perception" of a state of Paul's body, resulting from his past encounters with Peter. Rather, it arises from the fact that Paul's mind lacks the *further* piece of knowledge that Peter has meanwhile ceased to be. But it is not yet time to consider in detail Spinoza's theory of error.)

7. THE HUMAN MIND'S INADEQUATE KNOWLEDGE OF ITSELF, ITS BODY, AND EXTERNAL BODIES (E 2pp19–31)

In *Ethics* 2p19 Spinoza maintains that the human mind "has no knowledge of" its body, nor of its body's existence, except insofar as its body is affected by external things. The basic drift of his argument in behalf of this claim is that (by one of the earlier-stated Postulates) the human body is causally dependent for its existence on many external bodies. Thus (by E 2p7) God "knows" the human body only insofar as he has the ideas of these external bodies, "not in so far as he constitutes the nature of the human mind." But the human mind does perceive the affections of its body (E 2p12), thereby perceiving its body as actually existing.

This at first seems a rather perplexing development. Granted that the body is the "object of" the mind, how can Spinoza categorically deny that God knows the human body "in so far as he constitutes the nature of the human mind?" But reconsideration of some of the earlier reasoning of Part 2 – especially the demonstration of 2p13, "The object of the idea constituting the human mind is the body – i.e., a definite mode of extension actually existing" – reveals that this aspect of his position is *based on* the claim that we have ideas of the affections of our body. (See also 2a4: "We feel a certain body to be affected in many ways.")[18] So, it seems, up until now claims about our knowledge of our body have been predicated on our knowledge (or "perception") of the effects produced in our body by external things.

In the following three propositions (E 2pp20–22) Spinoza argues for the view that "there is in God" the idea or knowledge *of the human mind*, which relates to the mind in the same way that the mind is related to the body. This "idea of an idea" includes as subparts the ideas of the mind's "perceptions" of the affections of its body. There are a number of much-discussed problems that arise in connection with Spinoza's theory of "ideas of ideas": for example, the question of how the relationship between two items *within* an attribute can legitimately be assimilated to a relationship between modes of *different* attributes. Fortunately, these need not delay us here. What is worth noting, though, is that Spinoza, drawing in part on 2p19, maintains that the human mind knows *itself* only insofar as it "perceives ideas of affections of the body" (E 2p23). This claim is important, because it will lead to a conclusion about the *inadequacy* of the mind's knowledge of itself – a conclusion that parallels one that Spinoza is also about to draw concerning the inadequacy of the mind's knowledge of its body and of external bodies. For Spinoza the mind's perceptions take place within a causal context just as the body's affections depend on external causality. The mind no more has an immediate and direct knowledge of itself, independent of these external causes, than it has a direct knowledge of its body independent of external factors sustaining the body's existence.

In the next several propositions Spinoza defends several claims concerning the "inadequacy" of much of human knowledge. The human mind has no adequate knowledge of the component parts of its body (E 2p24). Its ideas of its body's affections do not involve adequate knowledge of an external body (E 2p25). Insofar as it imagines external bodies it lacks adequate knowledge of them (E 2p26c). Its ideas of its body's affections do not involve adequate knowledge of its body (E 2p27); they "are not clear and distinct, but confused" (E 2p28). Similarly, "the idea that constitutes the nature of the human mind," the idea of that idea, and "the ideas of the ideas of the body's affections" are seen not to be clear and distinct (E 2p28s). Further, "the idea of the idea of any affection of the human body does not involve adequate knowledge of the human mind" (E 2p29).

In general, the arguments for these claims turn on a distinction between what is available to the human mind, with regard to the various objects of knowledge in question (and hence to God "in so far as he constitutes the nature of the human mind"); and the system of ideas in infinite intellect that constitutes knowledge of those objects according to the order of their causes. For instance, the component parts of a given human body are not essentially tied to that body, but can also exist alone, or as constituents of other bodies: "Therefore (2p3) the idea or knowledge of any component part will be in God, and will be so (2p9) in so far as he is considered as affected by another idea of a singular thing, a singular thing which is prior in Nature's order to the part itself (2p7)" (E 2p24). It is notable that Spinoza omits to cite his earlier definition of "adequate idea" in these propositions concerned with the *in*adequacy of ideas in the human mind. (He will soon turn to direct discussion of truth, adequacy, and error, however.) Nevertheless, it is quite clear what is supposed to be amiss with the human ideas in question. They cannot really be *understood* by the human mind because their causes – the ideas of the causes of their objects – fall outside of the human mind. From the point of view of the human mind they occur only fortuitously: "after the common order of nature," as Spinoza puts it (cf. E 2p29c). In this way their status in the human mind contrasts with their status in the divine mind, where they *are* understood in relation to their full causal history, and according to "Nature's order." Within the human mind they are – to cite one of Spinoza's famous phrases – "like conclusions without premises" (E 2p28s).[19] Or, as he also says, in summary of *Ethics* 2pp24–29, "whenever the human mind perceives things after the common order of nature, it does not have an adequate knowledge of itself, nor of its body, nor of external bodies, but only a confused and fragmentary knowledge" (E 2p29s).

Of course, it is not Spinoza's intention to imply that *all* ideas in the human mind are inadequate. Soon enough he will be discussing in detail its capacity to share with the divine mind ideas that are adequate. This point is foreshadowed in the scholium to 2p29, which also formulates nicely the contrast between the two sorts of "order" of ideas which has figured in the previous discussion:

I say expressly that the Mind does not have an adequate knowledge, but only a confused and mutilated knowledge, of itself, its own Body, and external bodies so long as it perceives things from the common order of nature, that is, so long as it is determined externally – namely, from fortuitous encounters with things (*ex rerum nempe fortuito occursu*)[20] – to consider this or that; and not so long as it is determined internally, from the fact that it considers a number of things at once, to understand their agreements, differences, and oppositions. For so often as it is disposed internally, in this or another way, then it regards things clearly and distinctly, as I shall show below.

The principal contrast in this passage is between the mind's having within itself sufficient knowledge to provide a genuine understanding of something that it contemplates, and its merely "encountering" a certain thing through the thing's external impingement on its body. Normally, I assume, understanding requires a grasp of the causal determinates of the thing in question.[21]

Spinoza's exotic terminology – and, indeed, the far from commonsensical assumptions that underlie his whole discussion – need not blind us to the essential elegance and simplicity of his position as so far sketched. If one is willing to grant him (at least for the sake of discussion) his conception of infinite intellect, his conception of the human mind as the "idea of" the human body, his various assumptions about causality, and his commitment to the identity of "the" order of knowing (in infinite intellect) and the causal order of being, much of what he has just been saying makes perfectly good sense (or so it seems to me). Not that I wish to deny that all this "granting" adds up to a pretty tall order. But, as I mentioned at the outset, I am not concerned here to make Spinoza's epistemological position seem intuitively attractive and "common sensical" from the late twentieth century point of view – an objective I would regard as fundamentally misguided.[22]

In the next two propositions (E 2pp30–31) Spinoza concludes his exposition of what is known only inadequately by arguing that the human mind has only inadequate knowledge of the duration of its own body and of external bodies. The basic line of thought is closely tied in with what has just preceded (though Spinoza places special emphasis on 1p28). The duration of all bodies depends on a whole array of external causes – indeed, an infinite series – i.e., "on the common order of nature and the structure of the universe." But God, of course, does not have an adequate idea of this structure only insofar as he "constitutes the nature of the human mind."

8. TRUTH, ADEQUACY, AND FALSITY (E 2pp32–36)

Although I think it is in general much easier to understand Spinoza if one resists making him out to be a different, more commonsensical and/or Cartesian, type of philosopher than he ever meant to be, there is no denying that certain notoriously difficult sections of the *Ethics* remain perplexing, even from the approach I prefer. A case in point is presented by the propositions now to be considered: statements which constitute the core of what Spinoza has to say directly concerning the nature of truth and falsity.

According to 2p32, "All ideas in so far as they are related to God are true." The demonstration runs as follows: "All ideas, which are in God, agree completely with the objects of which they are ideas (2p7c), and so they are all true (1a6)." One anomaly presented by this short demonstration is the use of 1a6, "A true idea must agree with its ideatum." As originally stated, the axiom appears to present only a *necessary* condition of truth; yet in this demonstration he cites the axiom as permitting an inference from ("complete") agreement to truth, as if it expressed a *sufficient* condition. But if we turn back to 2d4 – the definition of "adequate idea" – we see that Spinoza there already characterized "agreement with its object" as the "extrinsic denomination" of a true idea. So probably the most sensible interpretive move at this point is simply to suppose that 1a6 was misleadingly formulated: that Spinoza really intends "agreement with the object" to provide both necessary and sufficient conditions for the truth of ideas.[23]

But the other part of the demonstration of 2p32 presents a problem, too. Spinoza says that all ideas *which are in God* agree completely with the objects of which they are ideas, citing 2p7c. Now, the scholium that immediately follows that corollary tells us that any idea and its object are "one and the same thing, expressed in two ways." This might well seem to suggest that every idea *without qualification* must agree with its object, and hence that the phrase "which are in God" should be dropped. But certainly this restriction is crucial to Spinoza's purposes. (He is about to go on to provide a theory of false ideas.)

What I think we need to notice, however, is that the scholium to 2p7, like 2p7 itself, is fundamentally concerned with the "order and connection" of ideas and things. And this is certainly the focus of the corollary to 2p7 cited in the demonstration of 2p32: "[w]hatever follows formally from the infinite nature of God, all this follows from the idea of God in the same order and the same connection in God objectively." Thus, I suggest, we ought to infer that when Spinoza speaks of "complete agreement" between ideas and objects in 2p32 he is including in the concept of "agreement" (never directly explained) the notion of identity with regard to "Nature's order."[24]

This suggestion leads to another one, concerning Spinoza's conception of the relation between truth and adequacy, or between "extrinsic" and "intrinsic" denominations of truth. According to the commitments of his system, especially the thesis that the order and connection of ideas is the same as the order and connection of things, these characterizations turn out to be effectively equivalent. "Intrinsic denominations" of truth have to do with the order intrinsic to the divine intellect; "extrinsic" ones with correspondence of intellectual order to the order of things in extension; but these orders are the same.[25]

Ethics 2p32 plays an important role in the deployment of Spinoza's position on falsity. Ideas cannot be false by virtue of some positive feature, since that feature would (like everything else) have to be "in God"; but all ideas considered in relation to God are true (E 2p33). The only alternative, Spinoza holds, is that falsity consists in a *privation*. Not just in a lack, however (for error with regard to something is different from mere ignorance): rather, "[F]alsity consists in the privation of knowledge which inadequate ideas, that is, mutilated and confused ideas, involve" (E 2p35). What Spinoza seems to mean is that ideas give rise to falsity when they occur in finite minds in separation from the full causal order in which they stand in the divine mind. Take, for example, a person who has a visual idea of the sun, but no knowledge of the causal determinates of her idea; that is, no knowledge of optics, astronomy, etc. That person may be expected to take her idea at, so to speak, face value: Her judgments about the sun's size and distance will reflect only the contents of the sensory idea (cf. E 2p35s). Now her idea of the sun will also be in God, for it is in itself a "positive" thing – and (as we have noted above) not *inherently* erroneous. But God will understand the way the sun appears to the person on Earth as the inevitable result of a body of such-and-such a size, at such-and-such a distance, transmitting light in such-and-such a way to such-and-such an eye and nervous system. (We must remember, of course, that the physical chain does not "cause" the idea; the latter is a result of a chain of *ideas* coinciding with the physical causal order.)[26]

This is another one of Spinoza's clever systematic solutions, which fits in well with a lot of what he has said.[27] It does seem to be glaringly open to at least one serious objection, however. It might be all right to hold that the *reason or explanation for* my having a false idea about, say, the distance of the sun is to be found in my lack of other relevant ideas needed to "place" the sensory idea in an intellectually adequate causal system. It further seems reasonable to hold that *in a sense* my "idea of the sun as being at such-and-such a distance" can be "in God," without it following that God has false ideas. For, as we have seen, "ideas of" external objects in a given finite mind are (in the first instance, so to speak) ideas of the affections of that mind's body; and *that* the body is affected in a certain such way is *true*.[28] Finally, there seems no reason to deny that (on another epistemic level) there could be in God the reflexive idea *that I have* an erroneous idea of the distance of the sun from me. So, from several points of view one may be able to preserve Spinoza's reconciliation of human error with the dictum that all ideas, insofar as they are related to God, are true. All that said, one problem seems to remain: a problem that is not, I think, very easy to get around. The uninstructed person *does have the idea that*, say, *the sun is 200 feet away*. But, one is tempted to insist, *this* idea is false, period. But it *is* an idea; and thus presumably it has to be conceived as a mode of God. It would seem to follow that ideas which are false are among God's modes: That is (to put the matter colloquially), Spinoza's God *must* after all have false ideas.[29]

In any case (returning to Spinoza's own exposition), we should take note of one final point he makes in connection with his theory of inadequate ideas. He goes on to observe that inasmuch as "there are no inadequate or confused ideas except in so far as they are related to the particular mind of someone," "inadequate and confused ideas follow by the same necessity as adequate, or clear and distinct ideas" (E 2p36). That is (as should probably be obvious by now), all ideas without exception have their place in the infinite ideational order constituting God's true and adequate knowledge. An idea is only inadequate, or cut off from this intellectual order, insofar as it is "considered in relation to" a finite mind which possesses the idea as a "conclusion without premises." That, at least, is what Spinoza wishes to hold.

9. IDEAS WHICH ARE ADEQUATE IN US
(E 2pp 34,37–40)

At the heading of this chapter I quoted a remark from *Ethics* 2p11c: "The human mind is part of the infinite intellect of God." It is time to point out that this dictum is in an important respect ambiguous. On the one hand, it might be taken to cover the aspect of Spinoza's position we have just been considering, according to which even inadequate ideas in the human mind also belong to the divine mind (in relation to which they are not, however, supposed to be inadequate). Alternatively, it can be interpreted more narrowly, as covering just those cases in which God has an idea "in so far as he is explicated through the nature of the human mind, that is in so far as he constitutes the essence of the human mind" (E 2p11c): in other words, just insofar as the human mind perceives things adequately. Spinoza makes clear in 2p35 that he intends the latter reading.[30] According to that proposition, "Every idea which in us is absolute, that is, adequate and perfect, is true." And the demonstration relies on 2p11c: "When we say that there is in us an adequate and perfect idea, we are saying only this (2p11c), that there is an adequate and perfect idea in God in so far as he constitutes the essence of our mind. Consequently we are saying only this, that such an idea is true (2p32)."

In 2pp37–39 Spinoza specifies a circumstance under which our ideas and God's come to the same thing. "Those things that are common to all things and are equally in the part as in the whole, can only adequately be conceived" (E 2p38). Because such things will be equally in the human body, the affections of the human body, and external things that affect the human body, the ideas of them "will necessarily be in God both in so far as he has the ideas of affections of the human body and external bodies"; and thus "will necessarily be adequate in God in so far as he constitutes the human mind; that is, in so far as he has the ideas which are in the human mind" (E 2p38). The basic thrust of this argument, as I understand it, is that the divine or perfect ideas of "properties" common to the human body and other bodies contrast with ideas of sense and imagination in *not* requiring knowledge of those things that the human mind apprehends only confusedly, in virtue of their *effects* on its body.

The logic of this reasoning seems clear enough, but the interpretation of its content is certainly elusive. Let us follow Spinoza's thought for a few more steps, then see what light can be shed on the notion of "what is common to all things."

In the corollary to 2p38 Spinoza draws on one of his earlier lemmata (E 2p13le2) to conclude that "there are certain ideas or notions common to all men." According to this lemma, "All bodies agree in certain respects"; for they all involve the conception of the attribute of extension; and also they all "may move at varying speeds, and may be absolutely in motion or absolutely at rest."

In 2p39 and its corollary Spinoza uses similar reasoning to establish that the more that a body has in common with the things that customarily affect it, the more its mind is capable of perceiving more things adequately. The point again is that the idea of any such property will be "adequate in God" *simply* insofar as he has the idea of the human body; that is, insofar as he "constitutes the nature of the human mind." Hence, Spinoza concludes, "the mind is more capable of perceiving more things adequately in proportion as its body has more things in common with other bodies" (E 2p39c). Again, in 2p40 he maintains that it is "evident" that "whatever ideas follow in the mind from ideas that are adequate in it are also adequate." For, once again, the inherent limitations of sense and imagination are irrelevant in these cases: The human mind has knowledge of what follows from ideas that are adequate in it even though it is not infinite, and even though it has only confused knowledge of the causes of its affections insofar as their properties are not wholly contained in its own body.

The theory of human adequate ideas that Spinoza is working on here has, I think, three fundamental components. First, because the mind is just the "idea of" the body, whatever is *wholly* contained in the body will be directly and wholly ("adequately") apprehended by the mind. Second, there are basic features of material nature that are in fact wholly present in any body (or "affection" of body) whatsoever. Third, from the ideas of these features follow the ideas of *other* things, of which the human mind is therefore also capable of achieving adequate knowledge. These ideas of other things, it is going to turn out – and this is the most important result for Spinoza – are ideas of the essences of singular things *in general*, not only of the essence of the body of which the particular human mind is the "idea." That is, amazingly, the human mind is able to achieve a God's-eye understanding of the essences of singular things, as they follow from the essence of God, thereby replicating the insight into the divine creative power expressed in 1p16 in terms of "infinite intellect": "From the necessity of the divine nature infinite things in infinite ways, that is all that can fall under infinite intellect, must follow."

The latter point is touched on in 2p40s2 where Spinoza distinguishes the "kinds of knowledge" (and it will be at the center of his account of the "eternity" of mind in Part 5). But before taking up his remarks in that scholium, let us see what more can be said in clarification of his conception of what is "common to all things" – or, as he writes in the *first* scholium to 2p40, "those notions that are called 'common,' and which are the basis of our reasoning processes." This is one point on which his treatment in the *Treatise on the Intellect* both seems reasonably consonant with what he says in the *Ethics*, and provides somewhat more explicit detail.

The first thing to notice is that Spinoza contrasts his conception of what is common to all things with mere "abstractions" or "universals." In the *Ethics* this contrast is largely implicit. In 2p40s1 he maintains that both traditional "transcendental" terms, such as "being," "thing," and "something," and ordinary universal terms, such as "man," "horse," and "dog," signify mere confused ideas of imagination. (Terms of the former type are said to be "confused in the highest degree.") That is, they signify confused ideas which result from the body's lacking the capacity to retain separate images of all the individuals that affect it. For instance, someone who has seen hundreds of horses is unable to retain in imagination all the "unimportant differences" among them, but "imagines distinctly only their common characteristic in so far as the body is affected by them." A term like "being" is even more loosely tied to particular experiences: It results from the mind imagining confusedly *all the bodies* by which its body has been affected. (Unfortunately, Spinoza does not bother to defend this account against either obvious objections, or traditional rival theories of universals; and I will pass over the many problems here.) The clear implication is that when he writes about "what is common to all things" as the basis of reasoning, he has in mind something quite different from these confused ideas of imagination.[31]

But what? This is a point on which the *Treatise on the Intellect* perhaps offers a little help. If we turn to the *Treatise*, we find Spinoza maintaining that the aim of his method is "to have clear and distinct ideas, i.e. such as have been made from the pure mind, and not from the fortuitous motions of the body." He stresses that the mind, in achieving such ideas, reproduces the order of nature: "And then, so that all ideas may be led back to one, we shall strive to link (*concatenare*) and order them so that our mind, as far as possible, reproduces objectively (*refereat objective*) the formal character of nature, both as to the whole and as to the parts" (TdIE 91). He goes on to assert quite definitely that in order to have clear and distinct ideas, in contrast to ideas deriving from fortuitous effects of external things on our body, we must avoid abstractions, and base our thought on particulars. "[W]e must never infer anything from abstractions" (TdIE 93); rather, "the best conclusion will have to be drawn from a particular affirmative essence" (TdIE 98). "For," he continues, "the more specific (*specialior*) an idea is, the more distinct. . . . So we ought to seek knowledge of particulars as much as possible" (TdIE 98). Thus we ought to proceed from "one real being to another real being, in such a way that we do not pass over to abstractions and universals" (TdIE 99) in pursuit of our epistemological goal – which is simply to understand "the inmost essence of things."

Spinoza goes on to explain that there is no question of human beings understanding the infinite series of "singular, changeable things," which would involve intellectual grasp of the infinite circumstances that determine their existence or nonexistence (TdIE 100). Our aim is, rather, knowledge of the *essences* of things, and,

> The essences of singular, changeable things are not to be drawn from their series, *or* order of existing, since it offers us nothing but extrinsic denominations, relations, or at most, circumstances, all of which are far from the inmost essence of things. That essence is to be sought only from the fixed and eternal things, and at the same time from the laws inscribed in these things, as in their true codes [*tanquam in suis veris codicibus*: "codes" in the sense of written systems or compendia of laws], according to which all singular things come to be, and are ordered. (TdIE 101)

He goes on to state that singular, changeable things depend essentially on the fixed and eternal things; they can "neither be nor be conceived without them."[32] "So," he concludes, "although these fixed and eternal things are singular, nevertheless, because of their presence everywhere, and most extensive power, they will be to us like universals, or genera of the definitions of singular, changeable things, and the proximate causes of all things" (TdIE 101).

I assume we can identify the powerful, ubiquitous but singular "fixed and eternal things" of the *Treatise on the Intellect* with the "things common to all things" that figure in Part 2 of the *Ethics*. In the *Ethics*, as we have seen, the "common things" are said to include (via Lemma 2 after E 2p13) the attribute of extension, and principles of motion and rest. In the *Treatise on the Intellect* they are described as the source of the essences of singular things, and as registers of "laws." Spinoza seems to have in mind the productive power of material nature, as it operates according to eternal, necessary "laws" of motion and rest.[33] (Since thought is coextensive with materiality according to Spinoza, and governed by the same causal order, though really distinct in conception, the conclusion seems inescapable that principles of mentality should be included among the common natures as well, though Spinoza does not explicitly say so in either work.)[34]

Certain features of Spinoza's conception of "what is common to all things" are fairly easy to understand, at least as long as one stays within the terms of his system. Obviously, he wants to contrast the shaky, superficial, and shifting inferences and abstractions that we make imaginatively as a result of our random encounters with various bodies, with direct intellectual insight into the fundamental principles that cause things to be what they (essentially) are. Because these causes are implicit in the essence of the human body, which the human mind "explicates," they are directly accessible to the human mind – and in fact "can only adequately be conceived" by it.

Another way to approach Spinoza's position on common notions is to compare it with Descartes's conception of rational knowledge of nature. Descartes seems to hold that the basic explanatory principles of material nature are innate in the mind.[35] In Descartes's writings this conception is involved with that of the mind as a mental substance, which God endows with certain ideas, independent of any embodiment. Spinoza seems to be holding that the mind, by virtue of being "the idea of the body," automatically has access to such principles (conceived by him as "particular").[36]

Descartes's and Spinoza's positions, while different in their ontological and theological commitments, run into the same major difficulty, from the point of view of twentieth century understanding of
scientific knowledge. What both philosophers say is true seems to be
totally unbelievable; namely, that every human being enjoys a direct (if implicit) insight into the nature and fundamental laws of
material things.[37] Consideration of the clumsy and antiquated laws
of interaction of bodies that Spinoza deploys in the lemmata following 2p13 only tends to reinforce this negative judgment. Perhaps the
simplicity of mechanistic principles of the Cartesian era fostered the
illusion that the basic principles of material nature are directly accessible to all human beings – much as simple arithmetical and geometrical principles are often held to be.

10. THE KINDS OF KNOWLEDGE (E 2p40S2–2p42)

In *Ethics* 2p40s2 Spinoza distinguishes, on the basis of what he has
already said, four ways in which "we perceive many things and form
universal notions." The first two he calls (together) "knowledge of
the first kind," "opinion," or "imagination."[38] They include, first,
"knowledge from fortuitous experience" (*"experientia vaga"*)[39], or
"from individual objects presented to us through the senses in a
mutilated and confused manner without any intellectual order." (Spinoza here refers us to the corollary to 2p29, concerning "knowledge
after the common order of nature.") The second type of "knowledge
of the first kind" (not previously discussed at any length), is knowledge from symbols (*ex signis*): "For example [he illustrates], from
having heard or read certain words we call things to mind and we
form certain ideas of them similar to those through which we imagine the things." (Here he refers us to the scholium to 2p18, concerning habitual association, in which one of the examples was a Roman
coming to connect the spoken word *"pomum"* [apple] with the visual perception of a certain fruit.) Thus it seems that both types of
knowledge of the first kind involve associations resulting from fortuitous encounters with sensible individual things and sensible signs.
With this type of knowledge Spinoza goes on to contrast what he
calls "reason," or "knowledge of the second kind." This "second
kind of knowledge" arises "from the fact that we have common
notions and adequate ideas of the properties of things." In support of

his description of this "type of knowledge" Spinoza cites the corollary to 2p38, 2p39 "with its corollary," and 2p40. From these citations we can infer that perception of many things and forming of universal notions through "reason" is meant to encompass all of the following: things that are common to all bodies; things that are common to the human body and the things that customarily affect it; and (E 2p40) things that follow from the common things.

The point that Spinoza is really leading up to, however, is that even the second kind of knowledge ("reason") is deficient from the perspective of achieving human perfection: "Apart from these two kinds of knowledge there is, as I shall later show, a third kind of knowledge, which I shall refer to as "intuitive science" (*scientia intuitiva*). This kind of knowledge proceeds from an adequate idea of the formal essence of certain attributes of God to an adequate knowledge of the essence of things." This characterization fits well with Spinoza's stress on knowledge of particular essences in the *Treatise on the Intellect* (as well as with the recurrent stress in that work on our mind's coming to reproduce the order of nature – in other words, to correspond with infinite intellect). However, the distinction between the second and third kind of knowledge is in several ways perplexing.

For one thing, knowledge of the second kind ("reason") is ranked as a way of forming "universal notions": yet it is based on the common notions, which I have suggested (drawing on the *Treatise on the Intellect*), are contrasted with ordinary universals. Perhaps this catch can be brushed aside, when we remind ourselves that Spinoza does say of the "fixed and eternal things" that they are *to us* as universals.[40] Further, as I will show shortly, Spinoza goes on to subsume knowledge of God's essence under the common notions so far discussed. What then is the difference between knowledge of the third kind, and that part of knowledge of the second kind which does involve inference? Is it that the former proceeds to knowledge of the essences of singular things, whereas the latter infers only to other "common things"? Spinoza's mention of "the properties of things" in his explanation of reason can be construed as supporting this suggestion. For it seems to be his view that the most fundamental knowledge of singular things is of their "inmost essence," from which their properties flow (see, for instance, TdIE 95).[41]

The example Spinoza goes on to give to illustrate the distinctions among kinds of knowledge presents a problem for this otherwise attractive reading. For the example suggests that all three kinds can have the same type of conclusion:

> I shall illustrate all these kinds of knowledge by a single example. Three numbers are given; it is required to find a fourth which is related to the third as the second to the first. Tradesmen have no hesitation in multiplying the second by the third and dividing the product by the first, either because they have not yet forgotten the rule they learned without proof from their teachers, or because they have in fact found this correct in the case of very simple numbers, or else from the force of the proof of Proposition 19 of the Seventh Book of Euclid, to wit, the common property of proportionals. But in the case of very simple numbers, none of this is necessary. For example, in the case of the given numbers 1, 2, 3, everybody can see that the fourth proportional is 6, and all the more clearly because we infer in one single intuition the fourth number from the ratio we see the first number bears to the second. (E 2p40s2)

In each case, it seems, one comes to "know" *that a certain number is the solution to a certain problem*: the difference lies in whether one arrives at a number by rules derived from fortuitous external inculcation, or by applying a rigorous proof, or by direct intuition.

Despite the *apparently* contrary implications of the example, however, it seems to me most likely that Spinoza does intend the contrast between knowledge of properties, and knowledge of essences, suggested by his way of describing reason and intuitive science respectively. The appropriateness of the mathematical example, I suggest, lies not in the fact that all the procedures result in the same type of conclusion, but rather just in the differences among the procedures. On this interpretation, the second kind of knowledge differs from the third both in requiring steps of reasoning, as distinct from direct mental vision, and in failing to arrive at the inmost essences of things.

I believe that this reading receives some slight additional support from the discussion of the kinds of knowledge in the *Treatise on the Intellect*, where Spinoza gives the same example. He there concludes that geometers solving a proportionality problem by Euclid's proof "do not see the adequate proportionality of the given numbers; and if they do, they see it not by means of that Proposition, but intuitively, without performing any operation" (TdIE 24).[42]

None of this, of course, throws any significant light on Spinoza's conception of intuitive knowledge of the essences of things. The definition of "essence" that he has offered at the beginning of Part 2 is too abstract to be much help with understanding this conception.[43] A couple of relevant points will come to light as we complete our discussion of Part 2, and take up the role of the third kind of knowledge in Part 5. But I cannot, regrettably, promise any dramatic elucidation of this important notion.[44]

According to 2p41: "Knowledge of the first kind is the only cause of falsity; knowledge of the second and third kind is necessarily true." The demonstration is uninteresting, indicating only that inadequate and confused ideas have, by the preceding scholium, been consigned to the first kind of knowledge, whereas adequate ideas have been "asserted" to belong to the second and third kinds. But, by 2p34, adequate ideas are all true. (While any connection between "knowledge" and "falsity" might strike the English-language reader as solecistic, we must remember that the term translated "knowledge" is *cognitio* – not, for instance, *"scientia."*)[45]

According to 2p42, knowledge of the second and third kinds alone "teaches us to distinguish true from false"; for only they can provide adequate ideas, including the adequate idea of the difference between the true and the false. *Ethics* 2p43, however, asserts a more interesting claim.

II. TRUTH AND CERTAINTY (E 2p43; *TdIE*)

Most of what Spinoza has to say in the *Ethics* about doubt and certainty is contained in 2p43, together with its demonstration and scholium. According to the proposition: "He who has a true idea knows at the same time that he has a true idea, and cannot doubt its truth." The demonstration depends on the theory of ideas of ideas, together with the corollary to 2p11, which has so often figured in this chapter. The gist of the argument is as follows: An idea that is true in us is adequate in God "in so far as he is explicated by the nature of the human mind"; the (adequate) idea of that idea will be in God in the same way, and thus will itself be included in the human mind. "So," Spinoza concludes, he who has an adequate idea, that is, "he who knows a thing truly (2p34) must at the same time have an adequate idea, that is, a true knowledge of his knowledge; that is, (as is self-evident) he is bound at the same time to be certain." This line of reasoning depends on the tight connection between adequacy, or "intrinsic denominations," and the "external denominations" of agreement with the objects that Spinoza has tried to establish in 2pp32–34. (In fact he claims at the end of the scholium to 2p43 to have explained how one can know that he has an idea that agrees with its object; that is, by virtue of having an adequate idea, and therefore necessarily knowing, by 2p44, that such an idea is true.) But whereas in 2p34 he seemed to be presenting adequacy as a *sufficient* condition of truth, he now seems to be *restricting* "true ideas" to those that are adequate. In fact he goes farther. As he elaborates in the scholium to 2p43, "To have a true idea means only to know a thing perfectly, that is, to the utmost degree." Thus, "nobody who has a true idea is unaware that a true idea involves absolute certainty." He makes similar claims in the *Treatise on the Intellect*, where he insists, for instance, that "for the certainty of the truth, no other sign is needed than having a true idea" (TdIE 35). And he there holds that everyone does have, natively, a true idea (TdIE 39).[46]

Part of Spinoza's position on this issue is the view that Cartesian "hyperbolic doubt" is misguided. An idea is true in us just in case we fully understand the subject of the idea – and we cannot possibly err in our apprehension that we do understand the thing perfectly. Thus, no external guarantee, such as Descartes sought to provide in his "proof" of God's nondeceiving nature, is required. Indeed, no *general standard* is required: for (Spinoza asks rhetorically), "what standard of truth can there be that is clearer and more certain than a true idea?" (E 2p43s).[47] Further, and unsurprisingly, Spinoza again invokes the corollary to 2p11: "[T]he human mind, in so far as it perceives things truly, is part of the infinite intellect of God (2p11c), and thus it is as inevitable that the clear and distinct ideas of the mind are true as that God's ideas are true" (E 2p43s).

Descartes's attempt to "guarantee" his clear and distinct ideas in the face of "hyperbolic doubt" is notoriously subject to the objection of "circular reasoning" (among others). Spinoza's bold insistence that "truth is its own standard" does have the merit of avoiding that morass. Further, as the reference to 2p11c suggests, Spinoza's rejection of hyperbolic doubt is not a mere *ad hoc* epistemological convenience, but has roots deep in his general anti-Cartesian metaphysics. Descartes's strategy for calling into question even those things he perceives as most evident enlists explicitly the notion of "a God who can do anything, by whom I have been created such as I am," for whom it would be "easy" to cause me to be mistaken even in the clear and distinct deliverances of my reason (Meditation III). Implicitly it seems to rest on a conception of the human mind as a creature separate from God, and on Descartes's commitment to the view that all truth depends on God's unconstrained will, so that even things that seem incomprehensible and contradictory to us are not beyond the divine power to bring about. On Spinoza's contrary position, all things follow from the necessity of the divine nature, according to its "laws." And the human mind, through its insight into that nature (soon to be affirmed directly), shares in infinite intellect's understanding of the necessary sequence; indeed, is "part" of God's mind.

But of course Spinoza's position presents problems of its own. His insistence that true ideas, by their very nature, involve "absolute certainty" and "understanding a thing perfectly" results in an extremely restrictive conception of what is to count as a "true idea" – one that has little connection with either ordinary discourse or much traditional philosophizing about the concept of truth.[48] (It seems that *only* what is absolutely certain can be true in his system.)[49] Further, it is by no means easy to get a comfortable handle on this notion of self-revealing truth, bound up as it is with Spinoza's less than detailed accounts of "adequate ideas," "agreement with the object," and the second and third "kinds of knowledge."[50]

12. KNOWLEDGE UNDER THE ASPECT OF ETERNITY (E 2pp44–47)

In the following proposition (E 2p44), Spinoza points out that "it is in the nature of reason" to regard things as necessary, not as contingent. This result follows rather trivially from the position defended throughout Part 1, that there is no contingency in nature (and reason must regard things as they are, or truly). In a long scholium to 2p44 he explains that when we conceive of things as contingent, we do so only because inconstant sensory associations result in a "wavering of imagination" involving uncertain expectation. The following corollary (E 2p44c2) then introduces one of the most famous phrases in the *Ethics*: "It is in the nature of reason to perceive things under a certain aspect of eternity (*sub quadam specie aeternitatis*)." In perceiving things as necessary, reason perceives them in relation to "the very necessity of God's eternal nature" (by E 1p16). Further, the "basic principles of reason," being (as we have seen) "common to all things," must be conceived "without any relation to time, but under the aspect of eternity."[51] The following three propositions build up to the claim (E 2p47) that "the human mind has an adequate knowledge of the eternal and infinite essence of God." Most of the argument through this passage seems at first unremarkable, given what has gone before. Things "existing in actuality" must be conceived in God; and they "have God for their cause" insofar as he is conceived under the attribute of which they are modes; that is (by the definition of "attribute" [E 1d6]), through the eternal and infinite essence of God (E 2p45). But this essence is common to all things, and therefore (by E 2p38) will be known adequately in every idea. The human mind will then know it adequately, since, as previously stated, it has ideas of itself, its body, and external bodies.

There are, however, two related remarks in these three propositions that deserve special comment. In the scholium to 2p45 Spinoza stresses that he is not here concerned with durational existence, which requires determination under the series of finite causes. Rather, he is speaking "of the very nature of existence, which is attributed to singular things because from the necessity of God's nature infinite things follow in infinite ways (see 1p16)." The final sentences of this scholium give some further clue to what he means by "the very nature of existence": "I am speaking . . . of the very existence of singular things in so far as they are in God. For although each singular thing is determined by another singular thing to exist in a certain way, the force by which each perseveres in existing follows from the eternal necessity of God's nature." At the end of this statement Spinoza provides a reference to an exceptionally difficult passage from Part 1, 1p24c, which involves a distinction between coming into existence and continuing to exist, and includes some quite murky remarks on existence and essence. There simply is not space in the present context to try to sort out all the distinctions he may have in mind. What needs to be noticed, mainly, is that Spinoza (here in 2p45s) appears to be focusing on a special sort of relation that singular things have to God. Apart from their determination by other finite things, each has a force of persevering in existence, *which follows from the eternal necessity of God's nature.*

In an early proposition of Part 3 he affirms that "Each thing, in so far as it is in itself, endeavors to persist in its own being" (E 3p6). In the demonstration he ties this claim to the conception of singular things as "modes which express in a definite and determinate way the power of God whereby he is and acts." And in the following proposition he identifies "the *conatus* with which each thing endeavors to persist in its own being" with "the actual essence of the thing itself" (E 3p7).

The relevance of all this to Spinoza's theory of knowledge is indicated in 2p46s:

Hence we see that God's infinite essence and his eternity are known to all. Now since all things are in God and are conceived through God, it follows that from this knowledge we can deduce a great many things so as to know them adequately and thus to form that third kind of knowledge I mentioned in 2p40s2, of the superiority and usefulness of which we shall have occasion to speak in Part 5.

I take these passages to suggest that the third kind of knowledge involves an intuitive grasp of the relation of things' essential, individual force of persistence to God's power. Of course this suggestion does not get us *very* far in understanding just what Spinoza has in mind. But given the limited amount that he tells us about *scientia intuitiva*, and the central importance of this notion in the final Part of the *Ethics*, it seems that even vaguish clues ought to be noted explicitly.

13. WILL, IDEAS, AND JUDGMENT (E 2pp48–49)

The remaining few pages of Part 2 are largely devoted to the energetic exposition of a position on the nature of ideas and judgment which Spinoza contrasts with that of (apparently numerous) unnamed opponents. This is one of the most accessible, and most discussed, passages in Part 2. I will accordingly keep my account brief.

Many aspects of Spinoza's treatment seem particularly directed against Descartes. Descartes's account of judgment was developed in the service of the need to reconcile human error with the goodness of God (on which his attempt to establish a guarantee of clear and distinct perceptions relies). Descartes maintains a distinction between the faculties of will and intellect in man. The will he takes to be free – not determined by external causes. It is essentially involved in judgment, affirming or denying ideas presented to it in the mind. Intellect is limited (there are many things we do not perceive distinctly); but the will is unlimited; that is, capable of affirming or denying any idea at all that may be presented to it. Error arises when we use our wills wrongly, affirming or denying things that we do not distinctly perceive (instead of simply suspending judgment). Spinoza has little patience with any aspect of this account.

First, by the necessitarian argument of Part 1, there is no "free" volition: The mind "must be determined to will this or that . . . by a cause, which likewise is determined by another cause, . . . etc." (E 2p48). Further, there are no "faculties" of will or intellect, only individual acts of mind (E 2p48s). In fact "volitions" (conceived as acts of affirmation – not, as Spinoza notes, desires) are nothing distinct from ideas: Ideas as such necessarily involve affirmation or negation. For example, we can neither affirm that the three angles of a triangle are equal to two right angles without having the idea of a triangle, *nor can we separate this idea of a triangle from the affirmation* (E 2p49; cf. E 2p48s).

In these two propositions (especially the long scholium to 2p49) Spinoza stresses that the mistaken tendency to think of judgment as involving arbitrary acts of will directed at inert ideas, and conversely, to overlook the essentially judgmental nature of ideas, is bound up with a failure to distinguish correctly the nature of thought from that of extended things, both images and words. An idea is "a conception of the mind" – a mental act – not to be confused with "a dumb picture on a tablet," nor with merely verbal affirmation. Some of what Spinoza says in this connection seems to me confusing, especially if one supposes that his *main* target is the Cartesian position. For instance, he attributes to certain opponents the view that "ideas consist in images formed in us from the contact of external bodies," so that "those ideas whereof we can form no like image are not ideas, but mere fictions fashioned arbitrarily at will" (E 2p49s). Now certainly the identification of mental ideas and physical images is no part of Descartes's position; and the Cartesian voluntarist theory of judgment has nothing to do with "fashioning fictions." (Spinoza's contrast between ideational and verbal "affirmation" raises other questions, but I will pass over them here.)

Still, Spinoza's basic position is clear and interesting enough to deserve the attention it has often received. Judgment is not something *added* to distinct mental entities; rather, thought, or the mental, is inherently and essentially judgmental (and in this regard "the nature of thought . . . is quite removed from the concept of extension").[52] Inadequate ideas of sense or imagination cannot be separated from affirmation or negation any more than can ideas of reason. There is, Spinoza allows, such a thing as suspension of judgment, but this must not be thought of as resulting from free control of the will. Rather, suspension of judgment is itself really a perception: "For when we say that someone suspends judgment, we are saying only that he sees that he is not adequately perceiving the thing" (E 2p49s). This position doubtless does have advantages over Descartes's. (In my view almost any theory would.)[53] What "seeing that one is not adequately perceiving" consists in is not entirely clear, however. (Seeing that one's evidence is not conclusive? Experiencing "wavering imagination" resulting from inconstant relations among perceived objects?) But there is no space to pursue the details of this issue here. Similarly, I have to forego consideration of the other issues Spinoza takes up in defense of his conception of ideas in 2p49s. I will conclude this section with one brief (but two-sided) observation on Spinoza's conception of mental modes as inherently judgmental ("involving affirmation or negation").

On the one hand, the interest of Spinoza's position goes well beyond its role in undercutting an inherently implausible earlier theory of judgment. Through post-Kantian eyes, it is not hard to see him as anticipating such seminal propositions as "It is necessary for the 'I think' to accompany all my representations," and "Intuitions without concepts are blind." People who wonder how a philosopher such as Berkeley could get from the exiguous sensory atoms that he takes to be the mind's primary contents to any coherent epistemology may feel that Spinoza was well ahead of major philosophers who wrote after him. (And not only with regard to rejecting the "dumb," atomistic, receptive view of perception: Spinoza's conception of *the mind* as, so to speak, a very big meta-judgment shows one way of avoiding conceiving of it as a mysterious sort of nonphysical container.) But, on the other hand, it needs to be noted that Spinoza's position about the nature of ideas is, on the whole, announced rather than argued. His texts generally fail to offer the evocative, concrete observations and precise, innovative distinctions that could solidify claims to major advances in the philosophy of knowledge and mind. Further, interpretation of his philosophy cannot (in my opinion) legitimately detach even those views that seem like nice alternatives to others we think we understand from systematic constraints which, while endlessly intriguing, are not infrequently arcane.

14. *SCIENTIA INTUITIVA*, INTELLECTUAL LOVE OF GOD, AND ETERNITY OF MIND

The last three Parts of the *Ethics* are concerned to depict "the nature and strength of the emotions, and the power of the mind in controlling them" (E 3pr). A major aim of Spinoza's argument is to show us how to pass from a state of unfreedom or "bondage" – domination by the "passive affects" – to the kind of freedom we are capable of achieving. The distinction between adequate and inadequate ideas looms large throughout this discussion: The passions, according to Spinoza, "depend solely on inadequate ideas" (E 3p3). Thus his treatment of this issue does tie in closely with topics we have been considering in this chapter. It can reasonably be said, however, that most of the material directly bearing on the passions and the mind's power over them belongs more properly to the area of moral psychology than to epistemology. But Spinoza's conception of the general goal of knowledge, in relation to human nature and human happiness, is also developed in certain portions of these parts of the *Ethics*, culminating in the last half of Part 5. In accordance with my own view of how Spinoza should be read, this phase of his argument is of essential importance to any serious exposition of his theory of knowledge. I will summarize (without detailed scrutiny) the most important claims of Parts 3 and 4 that contribute to this theme, then proceed to a more detailed and critical examination of Part 5, particularly 5pp21–40.

At the beginning of Part 3 Spinoza introduces the point that we are *active* insofar as the cause of something is wholly within our own nature: "I say that we are active when something takes place, in us or externally to us, of which we are the adequate cause; that is . . . when from our nature there follows in us or externally to us something which can be clearly and distinctly understood through our nature alone" (E 3d2). In other words (by the ubiquitous 2p11c) our minds are active insofar as our ideas are adequate in God insofar as he constitutes the essence of our mind; that is, insofar as we have adequate ideas (E 3p1; cf. E 3p3). Conversely, our minds are passive insofar as our ideas are inadequate or caused from without: hence, ultimately, Spinoza's assimilation of passive affects to inadequate ideas, touched on above. Our minds can pass to a greater or lesser state of activity or perfection. (Such transitions are always correlated, of course, with an increase or decrease of the *body's* power of activity: In 3p2 Spinoza explicitly draws out the implication of 2p6 and 2p7s that mind and body do not interact, while also affirming in the long scholium that the conditions of the two vary correlatively.) Transitions to greater activity Spinoza identifies with pleasure; transitions in the other direction with pain (E 3p11). The third basic emotion, desire, is identified with the *conatus* to persevere in being (insofar as we are conscious of it) (E 3p9). When the mind regards its own power of activity it thereby passes to a greater state of activity, and therefore feels pleasure (E 3p53). Most important for present purposes is the subordinate point that the mind experiences pleasure – and desire, too – insofar as it conceives adequate ideas (E 3p58).[54] Spinoza has a wonderful term for the "pleasure arising from the fact that man contemplates himself and his power of activity": *acquiescentia in se ipso* (E 3da25). ("Self-contentment" is a correct, but somehow inadequate, English rendering.)

In certain passages of Part 4 Spinoza takes the first steps toward identifying this activity and the accompanying pleasure with the mind's highest good, and connecting it with both eternity of mind, and the love of God. First, at the end of the preface to Part 4 he gives an explicit explanation of the meaning of "perfection," which stresses the relation between essence and perfection, and the distinction between both of these concepts and (mere) duration:

[B]y perfection in general I shall understand reality . . . ; that is, the essence of any thing in as far as it exists and acts in a certain way, having no regard to its duration. For no singular thing can be said to be more perfect on the grounds that it has persevered in existence a longer time. Indeed, the duration of things cannot be determined from their essence, since the essence of things involves no certain and determinate time of existence.

Also important is 4d8, which links virtue, essence, and power: "By *virtue* and *power* I understand the same thing; that is . . . virtue, in so far as it is related to man, is man's very essence, or nature, in so far as he has power to bring about something that can be understood solely through the laws of his own nature." This definition (skipping over some further details of argument) yields the claims that "The *conatus* to preserve oneself is the primary and sole basis of virtue" (E 4p22c); and that a man can be said to be acting from virtue only insofar as he is determined to some action from the fact that he understands (E 4p23). Further, the *conatus* of the mind to preserve its own being is "only the endeavor to understand," and so the endeavor to understand is "the primary and only basis of virtue, and it is not for some further purpose that we endeavor to understand things" (E 4p26). But since the "highest object we can understand" is God, "The mind's highest good is knowledge of God, and the mind's highest virtue is to love God" (E 4p28). In 4p52 Spinoza also says that self-contentment is the highest good we can hope for. Thus, it seems, self-contentment, as previously explained, and knowledge of God, are one and the same. These themes are rounded out at the end of Part 4, where Spinoza concludes: "Therefore it is of the first importance in life to perfect the intellect, or reason, as far as we can, and the highest happiness or blessedness of mankind consists in this alone. For blessedness is nothing other than the self-contentment that arises from the intuitive knowledge *(cognitio)* of God" (E 4ap4). This remark prefigures the more developed argument of Part 5, to which I now turn.

At the end of the scholium to 5p20, Spinoza summarizes some of the claims he thinks he has already established concerning the value of reason, or clear and distinct knowledge. It (and especially "the third kind of knowledge, whose basis is the knowledge of God") can relate the passive emotions to God, thereby understanding them adequately (E 5pp3–4), and experiencing pleasure (E 3p53). Since God is perceived as the cause of this pleasure, it carries with it love of God (for we love what we conceive to be the external cause of our pleasure) (E 3da6).[55] Picking up phrasing from the *Treatise on the Intellect* that I quoted in section 1, he adds that such clear and distinct knowledge "begets love towards something immutable and eternal . . . which cannot be defiled by any of the faults that are to be found in the common sort of love, but can continue to grow more and more . . . and engage the greatest part of the mind . . . and pervade it" (E 5p20s).

At this point Spinoza makes a remark that many have found a baffling fundamental departure from all that has gone before in the *Ethics*, even amounting to direct contradiction of previously stated doctrines:

> And now I have completed all that concerns this present life; for as I said at the beginning of this scholium, in this brief account I have covered all the remedies against the emotions. . . . So it is now time to pass on to those matters that concern the duration of the mind without respect to the body. (*Tempus igitur jam est, ut ad illa transeam, quae ad Mentis durationem sine relatione ad Corpus pertinent.*)

Surely up until now Spinoza has consistently maintained the complete inseparability of mind from body: They are, after all, said to be "one and the same thing" (E 2p7s). In 2p8 (concerning "the ideas of non-existing modes") Spinoza even appears specifically to tie the duration of the mind to the duration of the body: "[W]hen singular things are said to exist not only in so far as they are comprehended in the attributes of God but also in so far as they are said to have duration, their ideas also will involve the existence through which they are said to have duration." Although I am generally reluctant to "solve" interpretive problems by simply throwing out texts, the transition to 5p21 seems to me to present a nearly unquestionable example of a case where such a move is warranted. Spinoza, I claim, has simply "misspoken"; what he meant to say was this:

> Now it is time to pass on to those matters that concern the reality of the mind without respect to the duration of the body.[56]

Nearly *everything* Spinoza goes on to say in the next few propositions supports this suggestion about what he has in mind. Before looking at some of the details of the position he develops, let me cite one sentence (from the demonstration of 5p23) that seems to me in itself virtually conclusive evidence: "[W]e assign to the human mind the kind of duration that can be defined by time only in so far as the mind expresses the actual existence of the body, an existence that is explicated through duration and can be defined by time. That is, we do not assign duration to the mind except while the body endures" (2p8c).[57]

The doctrine of "eternity of mind" that Spinoza deploys after 5p20 can be summarized fairly briefly, since the basic elements have been well prepared for. First, the inadequate knowledge of external bodies found in imagination, sense, and memory (and also implicated in the passive emotions) ceases when the human body ceases to endure (E 5p21,34). Yet, the *essence* of the human body is in God (without regard to duration) and is conceived through God "by a certain eternal necessity"; thus: "[T]here is necessarily in God an idea which expresses the essence of this or that human body under the aspect of eternity" (E 5p22). That is, the human mind, insofar as it expresses the essence of the human body – and so is "part of the infinite intellect of God" – is itself eternal; or, as Spinoza somewhat misleadingly expresses the point (E 5p23): "The human mind cannot be absolutely destroyed along with the body, but something of it remains, which is eternal." Here again we find Spinoza succumbing to a temptation to exalt mind over body, with regard to some kind of permanence; yet correctly (in accordance with his own carefully developed principles) he could and should be holding simply this: that the human mind has a noneternal part that perishes when the body ceases to endure; but also an eternal part, to be understood as knowledge of the essence of the body from the point of view of eternity: "[W]e nevertheless sense that our mind, in so far as it involves the essence of the body under the aspect of eternity, is eternal, and that this existence of it cannot be defined by time, nor explained through duration" (E 5p23s; cf. E 5p29).[58]

As I have already mentioned, one of Spinoza's central views, with regard to knowledge and the achievement of human perfection, is that our mind's ability to understand the essence of various things under the aspect of eternity is a function of its ability to understand or know or conceive the essence of its own body under the aspect of eternity. Because such knowledge, like all knowledge, involves understanding its object in relation to its cause – God – this knowledge that the mind has in relation to its body and external bodies satisfies the definition of "the third kind of knowledge."

The mind conceives nothing under the aspect of eternity except in so far as it conceives the essence of its body under the aspect of eternity (5p29), that is (5p21,23), except in so far as the mind is eternal. Therefore . . . in so far as it is eternal, it has knowledge of God, knowledge which is necessarily adequate. . . . Therefore the mind, in so far as it is eternal, is capable of knowing all the things that can follow from this given knowledge of God . . . : that is, of knowing things by the third kind of knowledge. . . . of which the mind is therefore . . . the adequate or formal cause in so far as it is eternal. (E 5p31)[59]

The third kind of knowledge, Spinoza goes on to argue, brings pleasure "accompanied by the idea of God as its cause," and hence (partly by some previous remarks about the nature of love) love of God, conceived as eternal (E 5p32). Thus it is tied not only to self-contentment, but also to what Spinoza calls "intellectual love of God" (amor intellectualis Dei), which is itself "eternal" (E 5p32c and 5p33). This condition Spinoza identifies, in succeeding propositions, with perfection of mind, and blessedness or salvation or freedom (E 5p33s and 5p36s). He explicitly holds that the third kind of knowledge – or "intuitive knowledge of singular things" is "superior" to the second, "abstract" kind of knowledge (E 5p36s). However, the second kind, too, consists of adequate ideas, and thus (it seems) contributes to enlarging the part of the mind that enjoys eternity (E 5p38).[60] Still,

from the third kind of knowledge there arises the highest possible content-ment, hence it follows that the human mind can be of such a nature that that part of it that we have shown to perish with the body [i.e. that part consisting of inadequate ideas] (5p21) is of no account compared with that part of it that remains. (E 5p38s)

The more things a given human mind understands adequately, the larger portion of it belongs to the infinite intellect of God, and so is eternal; and the less reason is there to fear death (E 5pp38–40). The passionate concern expressed at the beginning of the Treatise on the Intellect, to find the key to experiencing "a continuous and supreme joy to all eternity," has now been met.

15. CONCLUSION

Unlike some other commentators, I do not find that Part 5 of the Ethics (particularly the propositions following 5p20) is discon-tinuous or at variance with previously announced doctrine. On the contrary, it seems to me that virtually everything in Part 5 is care-fully prefigured in earlier material (some of it often neglected, such as the distinction between senses of "existence" in 2p45s, picked up in 5p29s). It is true that I have had to acknowledge one anomaly in Part 5, in contrast to earlier parts: In deploying his doctrine of eternity of mind Spinoza perversely tends to imply that the mind achieves existence *separate* from the body (and even speaks of its achieving "*duration* without relation to the body"). To this extent Spinoza's language doubtless evokes a less esoteric conception of the "eternity of mind" than his principles permit. But this lapse does not seem inherently unmanageable: Texts of Part 5 itself show that his earlier conception of the mind–body relation, as asserted in Part 2 especially, persists under the inconsistent language (which can accordingly largely be disregarded). The more serious problem, I believe, is quite a different one: namely, explaining how Spinoza really understands the "third kind of knowledge" – or, for that matter, the second.[61]

The third kind of knowledge, as we have seen, involves grasping the "inmost essence" of singular things in relation to the essence of God. I pointed out that Spinoza gives us some reason to suppose that what he has in mind is (at least in part) our coming to grasp intuitively the "force to persevere in existence" that defines the essence of singular things as a manifestation and consequence of God's power. Unfortunately – and exasperatingly – he says little else to elucidate this fundamental notion. (I have suggested that the mathematical example he provides in both the *Ethics* and the *Treatise on the Intellect* may actually be misleading in certain respects.) We are told, of course, that the third kind of knowledge (and to a lesser extent the second), in virtue of presenting things "under the aspect of eternity," renders the mind itself (or a "part" of it) "eternal." Such understanding carries with it the "intellectual love of God," and feeds the mind with unmixed joy. Much of this language suggests a transformation of the mind in relation to God that might be construed as "mystical." At the same time, the theory of "what is common to all," or the "fixed and eternal things," especially as developed in the *Treatise on the Intellect*, seems to suggest some kind of intellection in terms of causal laws, closer to what we now think of as "scientific" understanding. But, it seems to me, this is about as far as the texts take us. So in the end we are left with a riddle: What is it, exactly, to come to perceive the "inmost essences" of singular things as they follow from the necessity of the divine nature? A good solution to this riddle would be, I think, a more fundamental contribution to understanding

Spinoza's position on knowledge than even the best commentaries on his response to Cartesian hyperbolic doubt, or Descartes's theory of judgment. But, unfortunately, I know of none.[62]

NOTES

1 See, for instance, Curley 1988; Donagan 1988; and Walker 1989, Chapter 3.

2 Spinoza, as we shall see, also denies the *need* for an external "guarantee" of our distinct perceptions; but this aspect of his position itself is bound up with un-Cartesian views about the relation of our minds to God's intellect.

Note that the term *'cognitio'*, here (as elsewhere in the *Ethics*) most naturally translated 'knowledge', does not have quite the same connotations as the English term: In this particular passage, for instance, its sense seems closest to our "apprehend." The translations in this chapter often follow those of Edwin Curley, especially in citations of the *Treatise on the Improvement of the Understanding*, and Samuel Shirley in some citations from the *Ethics*. But I have made changes in both Curley's and Shirley's versions.

3 Other works of Spinoza, including the *Short Treatise on God, Man, and His Well-Being* and the *Theological-Political Treatise*, also contain material that bears on his views about knowledge.

4 For an interesting discussion of the relation between the accounts of knowledge in the *Treatise on the Intellect* and the *Ethics* see Carr 1978. Carr argues that the discussions in the two works are not as hard to reconcile as some earlier interpreters have held.

5 In Spinoza's system the infinite intellect is conceived as an infinite mode of the attribute of Thought. See 1p31 and (for a discussion of infinite modes, though one that focuses on the modes of Extension) Donagan 1988: 102ff.

6 The axiom is the linchpin of Spinoza's denial of mind–body interaction, which, while not formally asserted until 3p2, underlies several of the central doctrines of Part 2, including his noninteractionist account of sense perception.

7 I discuss this point, as well as others relevant to the current discussion, in Wilson 1991.

8 Although, it seems, with a new twist on the reading of 1a6: see below.

9 See Bennett 1984: 127ff. Bennett takes a particularly negative view of the use of 1a4, which, he says, Spinoza gives us "no reason" for accepting (131). I criticize Bennett's treatment of the axiom in detail in Wilson 1991.

10 For a critical discussion of this issue see Wilson 1980; and for a detailed, ingenious apologetic approach, Robinson 1991.

11 It is worth noting though, in the context of a discussion of epistemological cal issues, that part of Spinoza's aim is to undercut Descartes's treatment of the existence of body as problematic: See 2p17s (end of the first paragraph).

12 Note that the lemmata of Part 2 (following E 2p13) suggest a naively mechanistic conception of the component parts of the human body, far from the complex informational conception we are familiar with today.

13 In this passage Spinoza distinguishes the "simplest bodies" from the "composite bodies" that are made up of them. The "form" of the latter consists in the "union" of simplest bodies which make it up; and the union is explained in terms of "unvarying relation of movement [or motion-and-rest] among themselves." The relation – and hence the individuality of the composite body – can be retained even if some of the simplest bodies are replaced by others.

14 Spinoza touches on this issue somewhat more explicitly towards the end of the appendix to Part 1.

15 In the demonstration of 2p17 Spinoza provides a quaint mechanistic account of how imagination works on the physical level, based on the "postulates" he has set forth earlier (between E 2p13 and E 2p14).

16 In the proposition and its demonstration Spinoza seems to indicate that one case of simultaneous exposure is sufficient to set up imaginative association. In the scholium, however, he places emphasis on frequent experienced conjunction, and habitual connection: "[E]very person will pass on from thinking of one thing to thinking of another according as he is in the habit of joining together and linking the images of things in various ways." The key point in any case is that imagination is *subjective*, in the sense that it depends on vagaries of experience that will vary from person to person.

17 Emphasis has been added. (Spinoza continues: "And when the mind regards bodies in this way, we shall say that it 'imagines' [*imaginari*].") The Latin verb translated as "present" is "*repraesentant*."

18 According to 2p13c, "[M]an consists of mind and body, and the human body exists as we are aware of it (*prout ipsum sentimus*)." (The translation of the latter phrase is somewhat controversial: see Curley's note to this passage in Spinoza 1985a for some discussion.)

19 "Therefore these ideas of affections [of the human body], insofar as they are related only to the human mind, are like conclusions without premises; that is, as is self-evident, confused ideas."

20 Here I follow Curley's reading, which seems to me both exact and inspired.

21 The reference in this passage to understanding the "agreements, differences, and oppositions" among things does seem to depart from the issue of causal determination that Spinoza usually stresses, and brings to mind (for a specialist in modern philosophy, anyway) Hume's account of "comparison of ideas" (cf. *A Treatise of Human Nature*, Book I, part I, section 5). Spinoza uses a very similar phrasing in the *Treatise on the Intellect* (TdIE 25).

22 It strikes me that the interpretation of early modern philosophy has generally suffered (if that is the right word) much more from a felt need to bring its subjects into line with outlooks and assumptions prevalent today than has the interpretation of ancient and medieval philosophy.

23 In Part 1 the axiom is used just twice; and both times only as providing a necessary condition. Possibly Spinoza just failed to look ahead to his needs in Part 2 in formulating the axiom.

24 I don't mean to deny that the stress in 2p7s on the general proposition that ideas are the same as their objects in extension still stands in some tension with the assumption that some ideas are false, once "agreement with the object" is interpreted as a sufficient condition of truth. I am only suggesting that Spinoza thought of "agreement with the object" as incorporating the identity of *order* stressed in 2p7; or at least that the texts hang together better if we assume that he did.

25 Confusingly, in 2p36 Spinoza cites 2p7c as establishing the *adequacy* of ideas in relation to God – apparently in distinction from their truth, as established in 2p32! "All ideas are in God (1p15), and in so far as they are related to God, they are true (2p32) and adequate (2p7c)." There has been considerable discussion of whether Spinoza's theory of truth should be construed as a "correspondence" or as a "coherence" theory. Since Spinoza's position on truth is incomprehensible apart from his metaphysical assumptions, and since these are (to say the least) unusual, I am inclined to think it is unproductive to try to type his views in relation to this rather anachronistic contrast.

26 There are some tantalizing parallels between Spinoza's notion of infinite intellect and Bernard Williams's exposition of an inclusive "absolute conception of reality." (See Williams 1978: 64–8, among other passages.)

27 It is interesting to note that error (or false judgment) presents difficulties for both Descartes and Spinoza in relation to their conceptions of God, and that both adopt traditional responses to the problem of evil in addressing the problem of error. Unlike Spinoza, Descartes is not satisfied with the explanation that error is "nothing positive" (though he does seem to endorse the claim, at the beginning of Meditation IV). Rather, he goes on to exploit the notion that error arises from human beings' misuse of their free wills (in affirming or denying what they do not suffi-

ciently clearly "perceive"). Spinoza's attack on the latter view is discussed below.

28 Though known "adequately" only, again, when understood in relation to
the full system of causes.

29 In the demonstration of 2p30 Spinoza does speak of ideas being "inadequate in God" – but "insofar only as he is considered to constitute the
nature of the human mind." Is it possible that he means to hold, at the
same time, that a false idea is to be considered a *mode* of God, "insofar
only as he is considered to constitute the nature of the human mind"?
This does not seem an acceptable solution: An idea is said to be a mode
because it is conceived through, and dependent on, an infinite attribute.

I do not mean to imply that there clearly is *no* satisfactory way of
resolving the seeming conflict among Spinoza's commitments: i.e., to
the status of all ideas as modes of God (and therefore "in God"); to
falsity in human ideas; and to the denial of falsity in God (except "insofar as he constitutes" finite minds). In fact a quite remarkable variety of
resourceful responses have been proposed to me, on Spinoza's behalf, by
a number of people (especially participants in a joint Amherst College/
University of Massachusetts [Amherst] colloquium [December, 1992];
and Jonathan Vogel [in correspondence]). However, no approach that I
know of is sufficiently straightforward to be appropriately entered into
here.

For a closely similar objection to Spinoza's position on falsity (in
relation to God) see Barker 1972 (especially page 118). (This essay was
originally published in 1938.) In Radner 1971, Daisie Radner offers a
reply to Barker (see especially page 349); but it seems to me that her
reply fails to address the crucial issue (as restated here).

30 Actually, a careful reading of 2p11c itself yields the same interpretation.
(Or so it seems to me. For a different view, see Barker 1972: 163–4.)

31 At the end of 2p40s1 Spinoza stresses that subjective factors, such as
whether one is impressed by height in humans, will influence how
one forms universals. He concludes: "Therefore it is not surprising
that so many controversies have arisen among philosophers who have
sought to explain natural phenomena through merely the images of
these phenomena."

32 See *Ethics* 2d2, on his understanding of "essence."

33 For a particularly detailed development of a view of the attributes and
infinite modes as lawlike entities, see Curley 1969.

34 In the *Treatise on the Intellect* Spinoza does write that what he has
claimed (concerning *"scientia"*) is "the same as what the ancients said,
i.e., that true science proceeds from cause to effect – except that so far
as I know they never conceived the soul (as we do here) as acting accord-

ing to certain laws, like a spiritual automaton (*quasi aliquod automa spirituale*) (TdIE 85).

35 See the beginning of Meditation V. For a more recent defense of the "rationalistic" point of view – one which has interesting affinities with Spinoza's position as well as with Descartes's – see Thomas Nagel's section on "Rationalism" in Nagel 1986: 82–9.

36 The question of whether a philosopher accepts or denies the existence of "innate ideas" has sometimes been considered important to whether or not he is appropriately labeled a "rationalist." Spinoza's position on this issue is a little hard to categorize, partly because he does not think of the mind as a substance in which ideas might be imprinted, independently of its connection with the body. But on the whole it seems to me that he is best thought of as aligned with the innatist camp. That is, he holds that the mind, by virtue of being what it is (the "idea of the body") has certain ideas, independently of particular, fortuitous learning experiences (namely, the ideas of "what is common to all"). Additionally, he repeatedly indicates in the *Treatise on the Intellect* that the mind possesses certain true ideas as "inborn tools," or "arising from the very power of the mind." (See, for example, TdIE 39, 86.)

37 Spinoza says virtually nothing about the "accessing" of the common notions by a given mind – I mean having these notions in conscious or explicit awareness. Descartes says a good deal about transforming innate ideas from potential to actual knowledge, but some have felt that his position is not fully clear or consistent across various texts. One thing to note is that Spinoza implies that the most fundamental notions are truly common among men, and not even subject to obscuring by "prejudice" (as Descartes seems to have allowed). See Spinoza's remarks at the beginning of 2p40s1.

38 Spinoza's categorization of the several kinds of knowledge has certain clear affinities with Plato's famous "divided line" categorization in *The Republic*. This is one of many respects in which Spinoza's position seems more readily compared with ancient Greek philosophical notions than with Descartes's views.

39 "*Experientia vaga*" is a rather odd phrase, for which a variety of translations have been proposed: "vagrant experience", "random experience," and "casual experience" are all legitimate suggestions (though "vague experience" is not). I believe that the most important connotation of the phrase is "what things and conjunctions of things one *happens to encounter in one's own individual course of life*" (as opposed to what others may encounter in theirs). There is, of course, no suggestion that the oddities of an individual's experience are strictly contingent: only that under the necessitarian laws of nature, different people with differ-

ent careers through the world inevitably develop different "imaginative" associations. "Fortuitous experience" seems to me to capture this connotation better than the alternatives.

40 In the *Treatise on the Intellect* Spinoza interprets knowledge from "universal axioms" as a form of knowledge from experiential induction, in contrast with rational demonstration (TdIE 23). Incidentally, the *Treatise on the Intellect* seems to me to suggest that even the highest kind of knowledge, which grasps things' inmost essences, may well rely in part on experiments (see TdIE 102).

41 Cf. *Treatise on the Intellect* 93: "from universal axioms alone the mind cannot descend to particulars."

42 It should be mentioned that there are some notable differences between the accounts of the kinds of knowledge in the *Treatise on the Emendation of the Intellect* and in the *Ethics*, and scholars disagree on their significance. Perhaps most important is the fact that in the *Treatise on the Intellect* the middle type of knowledge is identified as "the Perception that we have when the essence of a thing is inferred from another thing, but not adequately" (TdIE 19). "This happens," Spinoza continues, "either when we infer the cause from some effect, or when something is inferred from some universal, which some property always accompanies." In a footnote to this passage Spinoza registers (among other comments) a distinction between knowing *propria* and knowing the essence of particular things – a distinction which seems to fit with what I have proposed with regard to the *Ethics* discussion. But it seems unlikely that consideration of the obscure and apparently somewhat divergent *Treatise on the Intellect* account would help to *clarify* Spinoza's later position, so I largely pass over it here. (As we shall soon see, in the *Ethics* Spinoza takes pains to portray knowledge of the second kind, too, as *adequate.*)

43 "I say that there pertains to the essence of a thing that which, when granted, the thing is necessarily posited, and by the annulling of which the thing is necessarily annulled; or that without which the thing can neither be nor be conceived, and, vice versa, that which cannot be or be conceived without the thing" (E 2d2).

44 In the *Treatise on the Intellect* Spinoza admits that the things he has so far "been able to know by this kind of knowledge are very few" (TdIE 22).

45 See note 2.

46 In the *Treatise on the Intellect* 34–9 Spinoza seems concerned to head off the possibility of infinite regress by denying that it is necessary, in order to know, that one knows that one knows. There seems to be a shift on this issue in the *Ethics*, where the doctrine of ideas of ideas assures

knowledge of one's knowledge through what Spinoza appears there to consider a nonvicious regress.

47 Is this position compatible with Spinoza's notion that there are "intrinsic denominations" of a true idea? Perhaps so, if this notion can be understood in terms of an individual idea presenting itself as true (as opposed to being identified as true by comparison with some general standard).

48 Oddly, Spinoza also claims in the scholium to 2p43 that to doubt the proposition that "to have a true idea means only to know a thing perfectly," one must mistakenly think of an idea as "a dumb thing like a picture on a tablet," as opposed to an act of understanding. (Recall that Spinoza explained at the beginning of Part 2 that ideas involve mental acts; he will soon explain this point in greater detail. But even if one agrees that to have a true idea involves some act of understanding, it does not clearly follow that it requires self-conscious awareness that one "knows a thing perfectly.")

49 At the beginning of the scholium to 2p49 Spinoza distinguishes the mere absence of doubt that may attend someone's false ideas (which results from the mere happenstance that he has not encountered anything to "cause his imagination to waver") from certainty (which is "something positive," not "privation of doubt"). "But" he adds, "by privation of certainty we mean falsity."

50 Spinoza also claims that the true is related to the false as being to nonbeing (E 2p35, E2p43s) and that it "is the standard both of itself and falsity," "just as light makes manifest both itself and darkness" (E 2p43s). (For another instance of the former comparison, apparently drawn from the neo-Platonic tradition, see also Descartes, *Discourse on the Method*, Part V, toward the end.) These comparisons, however venerable, seem more hopeful than helpful with regard to clarifying the essential issues of why we are so often *wrong*, and how we are supposed, after all, to be able in principle to distinguish false beliefs or assertions from true ones. Note, further, that Spinoza's improbable hard line on truth and certainty apparently extends to endorsing the view that reasoning is strictly impervious to error: cf. *Ethics* 2p47s.

51 In 2p44s Spinoza ties time to the imagination, saying it arises from our perceptions of varying movements of different bodies.

52 One sometimes reads that Spinoza regards ideas as "propositional," but this seems a very misleading characterization (unless one somehow identifies propositions with individual mental acts). On this point see also Mark 1978: 13ff. (Mark in fact argues that we should reject not only the characterization of Spinozistic ideas as propositional, but also the identification of them as judgments, in favor of thinking of them as "acts of

perception or apprehension." I have doubts about his argument for the latter point – especially with regard to false ideas – but I will not here pursue the semantic issue to this degree of detail.)

53 See Wilson 1978, Chapter 4.

54 Spinoza holds that "Desire is the very essence of man in so far as his essence is conceived as determined to any action from any given affection of itself" (E 3da1).

55 It is admittedly odd that Spinoza's logic here requires thinking of God – our "immanent" cause – as "external." The real point, I think, is that God, the cause of our pleasure, is understood to be greater than we are, and hence not *identical* to us.

56 Not *quite* unquestionable, however, because there is an alternative interpretive move that would allow us to retain Spinoza's words as written: namely, that of assuming he is using "duration" in a different sense in the troublesome sentence than elsewhere in the *Ethics*. This possibility – suggested to me by James Ross on the basis of varying traditional understandings of "duration" – receives a bit of support from the curious wording (quoted below in my text) from 5p23: "But we assign to the human mind *the kind of duration that can be defined by time*." I by no means consider it beyond Spinoza to use "duration" suddenly and without warning in a different sense than the one that he has been insisting on for many pages. The point in any case is that there is little or no real ambiguity about the sense of Spinoza's discussion of eternity of mind in 5pp21–40; and (in my opinion) little or no basis to believe that he here "sells out" earlier phases of his position on the status of mind. Perhaps some interpreters have been inclined to make this allegation partly because they would like to be able to present Spinoza as a "tough-minded" type of philosopher, with (perhaps) materialist leanings. (Unpublished writing by Shawn Travis has made me newly aware of a number of complex issues connected with Spinoza's treatment of eternity, particularly with regard to the "eternity" of modes, in relation to the "eternity" of substance. Regrettably, time constraints have prevented my reconsidering what I say here in the light of these issues – which, in any case, are too complex to be addressed in detail in the present context.)

57 See also 5p23s, toward the end.

58 See also the scholium to 5p29, where Spinoza restates the distinction between two senses of "actuality" or "existence" (i.e., with regard to essence and eternity, and with regard to duration) that we have previously touched on.

59 Further, Spinoza indicates (E 5p30) the mind can know itself, too, in relation to God's essence, and therefore under the aspect of eternity. In

5p36s he puts special emphasis on this knowledge as a component of human blessedness:

"[S]ince the essence of our mind consists solely in knowledge, whose principle and basis is God (1p15 and 2p17s), it follows that we see quite clearly how and in what way our mind, in respect of essence and existence, follows from the divine nature and is continuously dependent on God."

60 The word Spinoza uses here is, again, "remains" (remanet). Perhaps one can mitigate the temporal connotations of this term by thinking of arithmetical "remainders."

61 Underlying the difficulties in interpreting Spinoza's position on eternity of mind in Part 5 of the Ethics are difficulties connected with what he says about "nonexistent modes" in 2p8 – on which a good deal of his position in the last Part of the work relies. Alan Donagan addresses this problem resourcefully and insightfully in Donagan 1973b. But his reading is in some ways unsatisfying. Diane Steinberg has plausibly criticized details of Donagan's paper in Steinberg 1981.

62 I am grateful to Roger Woolhouse for pointing out a problem in an earlier draft, with regard to my treatment of 2p17s. (I have made changes in response to his criticism; but may well not have fully accommodated it.) My comments on Spinoza's theory of error were to some degree influenced by remarks of members of a Spinoza seminar I taught at Princeton in the fall of 1992 (especially, perhaps, Ben Friedman).

4 Spinoza's natural science and methodology*

I. INTRODUCTION

The question of Spinoza's involvement with science depends initially on the kinds of scientific pursuit in which he is thought to have been involved. To judge by the prestigious *Dictionary of Scientific Biography*, Spinoza was not importantly involved in any kind of science, since he does not merit an entry in its ostensibly comprehensive sixteen volumes (Gillispie 1970–80). This judgment is shared by the authors of most histories of science that cover the seventeenth century, where Spinoza's name appears, if at all, only in passing as part of the historical furnishing. A minority of historians of science takes a more constructive view. In Wolf's *History of Science, Technology, and Philosophy in the 16th and 17th Centuries*, where one enjoys the wider vision of an older historiography of science, Spinoza joins Hobbes, Descartes, Locke, and Leibniz in the chapter on psychology, and he is accorded a chapter or section in most histories of psychology, including collections of source material. Furthermore, many articles and book-length studies deal in one way or another with Spinoza's psychology (however understood); biology, medicine and psychoanalysis also figure topically in Spinoza bibliographies.[1] Again, there is an entry on Spinoza in a recent one-volume encyclopedia of political science and in each of the two main (English-language) encyclopedias of the social sciences.[2] And prominent among those who recognize Spinoza's role in the emer-

*In addition to sharing in the memorial tribute of this volume as a whole to Alan Donagan, I should like this essay to stand also as a personal tribute to Marjorie Grene.

gence of scientific hermeneutics are Savan, Curley, and Popkin, though they disagree about its nature and importance.[3]

As for Spinoza's engagements with optics, the science of motion, physics in general, and scientific methodology, they have received a mixed treatment in monographic studies. The authors of some standard accounts say next to nothing about these aspects of his intellectual life, writing about Spinoza the way some do about Descartes, that is, as a philosopher-colleague of the twentieth century unburdened by the antique science of the seventeenth. In some Spinoza studies, the scientific themes appear only as nudging undercurrents to the "philosophical" thought. Even Wolfson is disappointingly remiss in saying little about the scientific dimensions of Spinoza's thought, sidelining (for example) the account of Descartes's *Principles of Philosophy* as at best "only introductory" to a reading of the *Ethics*. Among those who recognize the scientific dimension of Spinoza's thought, though dealing with it in varying degrees of detail, are Pollock, Curley, Parkinson (especially useful on Spinoza's methodology), Delahunty, and McKeon, who provides a useful survey of the scientific episodes in Spinoza's life and letters. There are several valuable articles on Spinoza and the physical sciences, especially those by Lachterman and Savan. Complementing Biasutti's monograph on Spinoza's "doctrine of science" broadly understood, there is now a volume of collected papers devoted centrally to Spinoza and particular sciences.[4]

2. THE DISCIPLINARY BACKGROUND

Spinoza's absence in the *Dictionary of Scientific Biography* and other history of science texts broadcasts two messages: (1) that he made no positive contribution to the natural or mathematical sciences, and (2) that his positive achievements do not merit the label "science," or at least not "proper" science. The first of these messages is unexceptionable, but whether the second is valid depends on the disciplinary classifications tacitly and more often unthinkingly assumed by today's scientists, historians, and compilers of biographical dictionaries.[5] For example, for those who think that Political "Science" is a bogus classification, the usurper of a respectable name, the *Political Treatise* and *Theological-Political Treatise* will not even qualify as science. In this essay, however, I am not concerned with the otiose question of whether or how much of what Spinoza did was "science" by whatever twentieth-century criteria.[6] The intellectual traditions and relations between disciplines that Spinoza and his contemporaries knew are the proper contexts within which his thought can be understood, and a competent assessment of his originality and subsequent influence be grounded.

To see something of the disciplinary categories that were generally recognized in Spinoza's day, we might look at the philosophical and logical manuals with which he was familiar during his formative years. (Precisely because these categories were common coin – *praecognita philosophica* – it is only in didactic or propaedeutic texts that one can expect to find fully informative accounts of them.) Among the works Spinoza knew were the textbooks of neoscholastics such as Burgersdijk and his disciple Adriaan Heereboord, and of others such as Bartholomew Keckermann,[7] which Spinoza began to study in Franciscus van den Enden's Latin school after his expulsion from the Amsterdam Synagogue in 1656. Keckermann's *Systema logica* was in Spinoza's library, its influence is discernible in the *Short Treatise*, and the same holds for Burgersdijk's *Institutiones logicae* and Heereboord's *Meletemata philosophica*. Spinoza was sympathetic to Heereboord's way of philosophizing, and he quotes directly from the *Meletemata* in the *Metaphysical Thoughts* (appended to *Descartes's "Principles of Philosophy"*), during the writing of which he also seems to have had at his elbow Burgersdijk's *Institutiones metaphysicae*.[8] These treatises do not exhaust the sum of Spinoza's instruction in the major philosophical tradition of his day, nor should it be assumed that they concur on all issues, but as far as the taxonomy of disciplines is concerned, they represent enough of a broad consensus to improve our understanding of Spinoza's achievements.

In the wide sense employed "by teachers and professors of philosophy today," as Keckermann puts it, and as distinct from theology, jurisprudence, and medicine (the three higher *facultates*),[9] *philosophia* comprises all the liberal disciplines: grammar, rhetoric, logic, physics, mathematics, metaphysics, ethics, economics,[10] and politics. But in the strict sense, though not properly speaking, *philosophia* means theoretical or contemplative philosophy, that is, the three *scientiae* (metaphysics, physics or natural philosophy, and mathematics) or even metaphysics alone. Properly speaking, however, *philosophia* comprises just six disciplines: the three *scientiae* and the three *prudentiae* (branches of practical philosophy), which are ethics, home economy, and politics. There is a corresponding division within philosophy according to nature and purpose. The purpose of the *scientiae* is contemplation, *theoria*, knowledge for its own sake; the purpose of the *prudentiae* is *praxis*, practical knowledge with a view to human action.[11] As for logic, it is not part of philosophy. Like grammar and rhetoric, it is an "instrumental art" *(ars instrumentaria)*, one of whose *instrumenta* is method, which teaches how best to find truth through the illative process, and how best to retain in the memory the knowledge thus acquired.[12]

While warning that philosophy cannot be perfectly defined (in the sense of stating its essence), Heereboord offers the conventional "knowledge *(cognitio)* of divine and human things inferred from principles known per se through the natural light of the intellect" (Heereboord 1659: *Collegium logicum*, p. 1, Theses 1–3,5). *Scientia*, properly speaking, arises from demonstration with respect to "the why", and is knowledge *(cognitio)* of necessary things through their proximate causes. Loosely speaking, however, *scientia* can be said to be knowledge, in some accepted sense, of virtually anything (Heereboord 1659: *Collegium Physicum*, p. 1, Thesis 1). In his philosophical dictionary, the most comprehensive of the early seventeenth century, Goclenius notes that *scientia*, when used in the proper sense, is *scientia* absolutely speaking; when used loosely, it becomes adjectival or the science *of* something (political science, the science of medicine, etc.).[13]

Spinoza's writings reflect both senses of *"scientia."* To judge by the opening chapter of the *Theological-Political Treatise*, *scientia* properly speaking – *vera scientia* – is knowledge acquired through causal explanation. The third kind of knowledge in the *Ethics* is *scientia intuitiva* because it involves proceeding "from an adequate idea of the formal essence of certain attributes of God to the adequate knowledge of the essence of things" (E 2p40s2).[14] It is a nice question whether this process *("procedit ab . . . ad")* is to be interpreted as causal or illative, but at least it reflects the causal dependence on God of the essence of particular things, and allows for whatever purely demonstrative bridge Spinoza thought was possible between the infinite attributes and finite modes. In one respect the *Treatise on the Emendation of the Intellect* (henceforth, *Trea-*

tise on the Intellect) is more explicit than the *Ethics*: the fourth mode of perception (*perceptio* – i.e., the "third kind of knowledge" of the later *Ethics*) obtains when "a thing is perceived through its essence alone, or through knowledge (*cognitio*) of its proximate cause" (TdIE 19).

On the other hand, Spinoza often uses the umbrella phrase *"artes et scientiae"* ("arts and sciences") notably to argue that freedom is an absolute prerequisite for their advancement or that they in turn are prerequisites for human perfection. Such instances indicate that he would not reject *"scientia"* (in the loose sense) as a suitable label for all six divisions of philosophy.[15] More telling is the passage in the *Treatise on the Intellect* where Spinoza lists the disciplines required to reach the human perfection that consists in the union of mind and Nature: moral philosophy, educational doctrine, the whole of medicine, mechanics (as an *ars*!), and the subject of the *Treatise on the Intellect*, "corrective method" (*modus medendi intellectûs*). This is a very heterogeneous group, yet Spinoza reveals their common identity in the footnote referring to the passage: "I take the trouble only to enumerate the sciences (*scientia*) necessary for our purpose, without attending to their order (*series*)" (TdIE 16n).

In seventeenth-century terms, therefore, Spinoza was a major contributor to two branches of practical philosophy (*prudentia*), to one *scientia* and part of another (psychology and the science of animate bodies were then subdivisions of *physica specialis*), to an *instrumentum* of logic, and to the special disciplinary medley labeled by Alsted as *critica theologica*.[16] As for his daily bread, Spinoza *mechanicus* earned it by practicing the art of lens-grinding. He was not a significant figure in mathematics, nor in any of the *scientiae mediae* such as optics.[17] Nor was he a significant natural philosopher, except qua expositor of Descartes, or to the extent that physics underpins his psychology and ethical[18] and political philosophy. The aim of the natural philosopher was to explain the physical world: Spinoza's central purpose was to know how human beings do and should behave as individuals and as social creatures. As Brunschvicg puts it: "*Spinoza s'est consacré à la philosophie parce qu'il s'est demandé comment il devait vivre. Les hommes ont des genres de vie différents, chacun doit choisir le sien; il s'agit de faire le choix le meilleur, et c'est là le problème que Spinoza s'est proposé de résoudre*" (Brunschvicg 1951: 1; see also Roth 1929: 43). Nancy

Maull, on the other hand, "cannot conscript [Spinoza] into the ranks of Descartes and Boyle, Leibniz and Newton," nor, "alas," can she press-gang him into "the lineup of scientific 'greats' either theoretically or by virtue of some concrete scientific achievement" (Maull 1986: 3). But why expect Spinoza to be something other than he was? To ask why Spinoza did no serious mathematics or natural philosophy, implying almost a dereliction of duty on his part, or regret on the part of the inquirer, is like asking why Wagner wrote no piano concertos. Or why Descartes, Boyle, or Newton wrote no political philosophy. . . .

The disciplinary taxonomies I have outlined illuminate some of the grounds of Spinoza's originality. The very title of the *Ethica ordine geometrico demonstrata* signaled a disciplinary incongruity for the more traditional of Spinoza's contemporaries, a feature of the work of which he was fully aware:

[T]hose who prefer to abuse or deride the emotions and actions of men rather than to understand them . . . will doubtless find it surprising that I should attempt to treat of the faults and follies of mankind in the geometric manner, and that I should wish to demonstrate through secure reasoning what they cry out is repugnant to reason, and is vain, absurd and horrifying. (E 3pr)

In accordance with Peripatetic tradition, Burgersdijk (for example) distinguished between "natural" method, which observes and preserves both the order of nature and the order of our distinct cognitions of things in the order of nature, and "arbitrary" method, which ignores the natural order to deal in confused cognitions for the purposes of persuasion or entertainment. All parts of natural method must be homogeneous, a rule that decrees "not only that the disciplines not mix, and that ethical matters be not committed to mathematical matters, nor mathematical matters to ethical matters; but also that every single thing be committed in its place . . ." (Burgersdijk 1651: *Institutiones logicae*, pp. 275–6,280). Yet the commingling of ethical content and goals with a species of mathematical form of presentation was precisely what Spinoza attempted in the *Ethics*. The *Ethics* was a hybrid disciplinary foursome consisting of one *prudentia* (ethics), two *scientiae* (metaphysics and parts of natural philosophy), and a measure of *methodus* (*modo geometrico*). In this respect the *Ethics* was more radical than (say) Newton's *Philosophiae naturalis prin-*

cipia mathematica (1687), where at least the *mathematica* and the *philosophia naturalis* were both parts of *philosophia speculativa*.[19] When one of Spinoza's critics, Noël Aubert de Versé, sardonically labeled him *"ce géomètre"* (Versé 1684: 29), he was not targeting some imagined prowess in geometry, but the supposed apodictic respectability conferred on the dangerous doctrines in the Euclideanly veneered *Ethics*, and, by implication, the impious absurdity of trying to geometrize the moral life. Again, according to the Peripatetic tradition the subject of each *prudentia* is contingent things (in the absolute sense) dependent on human will and action, and the subject of each *scientia* (in the strict sense) is necessary things produced by divine or natural cause. Spinoza's strict necessitarianism abolished that distinction (E 1p29),[20] making the principal subjects of the *Ethics* and the two political *Treatises* formal impossibilities within a Peripatetic perspective.

3. NATURAL AND EXPERIMENTAL PHILOSOPHY IN THE CORRESPONDENCE

Spinoza's contributions to two domains of *philosophia practica*, to *critica theologica*, to two *scientiae* (metaphysics and psychology), and to a subdomain of logic (epistemology),[21] are examined elsewhere in this volume. That leaves for this chapter the mathematical sciences, aspects of Spinoza's method, and natural philosophy minus the psychology and (unfortunately through lack of space) minus Spinoza's teachings on animate bodies.[22] Although Spinoza made no important contribution to the natural or mathematical sciences, he took a serious interest in the latest advances, and knew or corresponded with leading mathematicians and natural philosophers.[23] Here I think it sensible not to exaggerate Spinoza's participation in the natural philosophy of his day. In this role he joined the ranks of the many *"esprits curieux"* of the age, not the select band of innovators that conventional historiography associates with "The Scientific Revolution." In addition to the caveats advanced in the previous section, and not forgetting the question of innate ability, it was also simply a matter of personal interest and commitment. A significant measure of Spinoza's engagement with the topics of this chapter is the proportion of relevant titles that made up his library, which at his death numbered about one hundred and sixty volumes. This was the residue of what had probably still been a very modest collection, taking cognizance of the fact that some valuable items were sold off before the inventory was prepared. Yet the titles that relate to the concerns of this chapter make up only about thirty percent of the total (Van Rooijen 1888: 110–220).[24] The size of a private library is in no way a measure of its owner's intellectual capacities, but the *proportionate* holding in a given domain is normally an index of the owner's interest in that domain. Certainly, the inventory of Spinoza's library does not support Klever's claim that he "devoured all [the] literature of the new physical science" (Klever 1990a: 126).

For the purposes of this chapter, a reading of Spinoza's correspondence is disproportionately rewarding in comparison with the meager expectations that a perusal of his library holdings might raise. Twenty-eight letters make up the exchanges between Spinoza and the first Secretary of the Royal Society, Henry Oldenburg,[25] and accentuating their importance is the fact that five of them (Ep 6,7,11,13,16) are effectively letters to and from Robert Boyle, with Oldenburg as intermediary. Stretching over the period 1661–76, with a ten-year break from 1665 to 1675, the Spinoza–Oldenburg letters throw light on many aspects of Spinoza's reactions to the natural and experimental philosophy of his day. In the initial exchanges they discussed God, the mind–body union, Thought and Extension, and the philosophical infirmities of Descartes and Bacon: their imperfect knowledge "of the first cause and origin of all things," their ignorance of the "true nature of the human mind," and their failure to grasp "the true cause of error." Oldenburg sent Spinoza a copy of Boyle's *Certain physiological essays* on its publication in 1661,[26] an important gesture that was instrumental in eliciting from Spinoza his critique of Boyle's interpretation of his experiments on fluidity and firmness, and on nitre (see Section 6 below). In 1663 Oldenburg sent a copy of Boyle's reply to Francis Linus's attack on "the spring of the air" championed by Boyle in his *New experiments physico-mechanicall* (1660).[27]

Elsewhere the Spinoza–Oldenburg letters are rather more run-of-the-mill, though they are still informative. Oldenburg sends Spinoza news of experimental researches in the Royal Society and at Oxford, of Boyle's treatise on colors, and of the publications of Kircher and Hevelius. Hevelius has told Oldenburg (1665) that his *Cometographia* is in press (it did not appear until 1668), and that he has sent

Oldenburg his *Prodromus cometicus* (1665), containing descriptions of two recent comets whose explanation is a matter of controversy among astronomers. Spinoza has "not yet heard that any Cartesian explains the phenomena of the recent comets on Descartes's [vortex] hypothesis," and doubts "whether they can rightly be thus explained." Oldenburg too remarks that no one yet has tried to explain them using the Cartesian hypothesis (Ep 30, Spinoza to Oldenburg, September or October 1665; Ep 31, Oldenburg to Spinoza, October 12 [O.S.] 1665; Oldenburg 1965–86: II,540–2,565,568). In return for the news from England, he asks Spinoza about theoretical and experimental advances in Holland, notably Huygens's work on the pendulum clock, on collision theory, on dioptrics, and in astronomy. Spinoza writes to Oldenburg that Huygens has been telling him about Boyle and his treatise on colors, about "the book on the observations with the Microscope" that Oldenburg had already mentioned (Robert Hooke's *Micrographia*, 1665), and about new telescopes from Italy that had been used to observe the rings of Saturn and the shadows cast on Jupiter by its satellites.

As one would expect, dioptrical matters figure prominently in Spinoza's correspondence. Spinoza asks Johan Hudde if he does not agree, on the basis of calculations derived from Hudde's own *Dioptrics* (now lost), that plano-convex lenses are better for telescopes than concavo-convex lenses. Jarig Jelles consults Spinoza on a difficulty in Descartes's *Dioptrics* (see Section 4). Leibniz sends Spinoza his *Notitia opticae promotae* (1671), mentions the dioptrical work of Francisco Lana and Johannes Oltius and his own *Hypothesis physica nova* (1671), and proposes a way of eliminating spherical aberration. Spinoza replies that he has not yet seen the latter three works and, confessing that he does not quite follow Leibniz's argument in the *Notitia*, asks for further clarification and offers an idea of his own that he had already used in his reply to Jelles's difficulty over Descartes. There are no further extant letters between Leibniz and Spinoza. In the last of the nine letters of the 1670s between Spinoza and Tschirnhaus, the penultimate extant letter in Spinoza's whole correspondence, Spinoza asks him if he can find out about recent dioptrical discoveries in Paris.

Viewing these "dioptrical letters" as a whole, there is little doubt about Spinoza's enthusiasm for the subject and its well-being, yet the overall impression is of only a moderate theoretical competence.

Lucas might claim that Spinoza so excelled in his lens-making that "if death had not prevented it, he would have discovered the most beautiful secrets of Optics" ([Lucas] 1927: 60), but the evidence suggests that after 1666 his contemporaries, at least in Holland, quickly became aware of his limited talents as an optical theorist.[28]

In a letter now lost, and in conversation, Jarig Jelles apparently asked Spinoza if he thought that the pressure and speed of water flowing through a horizontal tube under gravitational pressure from a raised tank varies along the length of the tube. To answer the question Spinoza built appropriate apparatus and conducted a series of careful experiments, with two assistants to help him. He found that for still water the pressure remained constant along the tube, and that for flowing water the speed remained constant independent of the length of the horizontal tube. The experiments seem to have been well thought out, and the results are empirically sound, but Spinoza's theoretical explanations are shaky, especially his application of Galileo's law of fall, which he misunderstood. There is no sign in the letter (Ep 41, Spinoza to Jarig Jelles, September 5, 1669) that Spinoza (or Jelles) was aware of the seminal researches in the same field that Pascal had published in Paris six years earlier.[29]

Two letters indicate something of Spinoza's attitude to alchemy. In March 1667 Jarig Jelles had asked him about a reported successful transmutation carried out by J. F. Helvetius, physician to the Prince of Orange. Spinoza replied that he had mentioned it to Vossius, who ridiculed the whole idea. "Taking no notice" of Vossius's views, Spinoza visited the silversmith who had tested the gold, to learn that the transmutation had taken place and that the silversmith thought the gold used to initiate the process "contained something uncommon," a view shared by others who were present.[30] Finally Spinoza visited Helvetius himself, who explained what had happened and showed Spinoza the apparatus, adding that he planned to publish an account of the transmutation (Ep 40, Spinoza to Jelles, March 25, 1667). Eight years later, writing to the Hague physician G. H. Schuller, Spinoza said he had not yet tested the claims of an anonymous (alchemical) *Processus* Schuller had sent him, nor did he think he would be able to apply his mind to the task at a later date. He doubted, on technical grounds, Schuller's claim that he himself had made gold (Ep 70, G. H. Schuller to Spinoza, November 14, 1675; Ep 72, Spinoza to Schuller, November 18, 1675). These two letters suggest that Spinoza's views on transmutation were not unusual for the time. Like many of his contemporaries, he had an open mind on the subject, tinged probably with a tincture of skepticism. Ignoring Vossius's contemptuous dismissal of Helvetius's claims, he set out to check the story himself, and seems to have been satisfied with Helvetius's own account of events. As for his doubts about Schuller's claims, they were evidently not on the grounds that transmutation is absurd in principle. Nor could transmutation have been absurd in principle for Spinoza, given his Cartesian view of matter and the teaching in Descartes's "Principles of Philosophy" Part 3 that "matter, with the aid of these Laws [of Nature], successively takes on all the forms of which it is capable" (Spinoza 1985a: 296). Spinoza was evidently interested in alchemy, but probably not inordinately so: there was only one alchemical book in his library, Theodore Kerckring's Commentarius in Currum Triumphalem Antimonii Basilii Valentini (Amsterdam, 1671).

Spinoza's most extended essays in natural philosophy were Descartes's "Principles of Philosophy" (as commentator) and parts of the Ethics. But before examining them I must address an undecided issue in Spinoza scholarship.

4. SPINOZA THE AUTHOR OF THE TWO
REECKENING?

Two mathematical texts have conspired to complicate the life of Spinoza scholars since the mid-nineteenth century: the Stelkonstige Reeckening van den Regenboog (Algebraic Calculation of the Rainbow) and the Reeckening van Kanssen (Calculation of Chances), first published anonymously in The Hague in 1687 by Levyn van Dyck. Despite the expository and editorial labors of McKeon, Dutka, Moreau, and Petry, all of whom take Spinoza to be the author of both treatises, it is not universally agreed that he wrote either of them. Klever and De Vet reject Spinoza as their author, and Freudenthal doubted that he wrote the Reeckening van Kanssen. In particular, De Vet's critique (De Vet 1986) of the assumptions informing Petry's edition introduces a range of historical, archival, and linguistic considerations that suggest the wisdom of assuming that Spinoza was not the author of these mathematical exercises, rather than nourishing the hopeful assumption (as I suspect) that he, one of the great

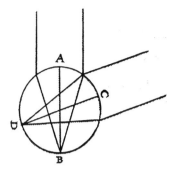

Figure 1

minds of the seventeenth century and a practical optician, must have published *something* on mathematical science.[31]

In addition to the historical work of Klever and De Vet, I might add two pieces of internal textual evidence that seem to count against the supposition of Spinoza as the author of either *Reeckening*. Whatever the value of *Regenboog* as an original contribution to optics, its author had a measure of competence in the mathematical management of Cartesian dioptrical principles. Yet Spinoza's letter to Jarig Jelles of March 3, 1667 contains an unaccountable blunder (as I see it) that would scarcely have been made by the author of *Regenboog*. Replying to a question Jelles had raised (in a letter now lost) about Descartes's account in *La Dioptrique* of image size on the retina, Spinoza writes that the account is faulty because Descartes "does not consider the size of the angle which these rays make when they cross each other at the surface of the eye." This is something Descartes ignored, because he "knew of no means of gathering the rays coming in parallel lines, from different points, in as many other points." Perhaps, Spinoza suspects, Descartes "was silent about it in order not to put the circle in any way above the [other] figures which he had introduced." Then Spinoza explains:

For it is certain that in this matter the circle surpasses all other figures which can be discovered. For the circle being everywhere the same, has everywhere the same property. For instance, the circle ABCD [Fig. 1] has this property, that all rays parallel to the axis AB or coming from the direction A, are refracted at its surface in such a way that they afterward all come together at the point B. Similarly, all rays parallel to the axis CD, and coming from the direction C, will be refracted at the surface in such a way that they will all come together at the point D. This can be said of no other figure, although Hyperbolas and Ellipses also have infinite diameters. (Ep 39)[32]

One's immediate suspicion of error and confusion is readily confirmed by a straightforward application of Descartes's law of refraction. For the circle to have the dioptrical property Spinoza claims, the refractive index of the glass would have to be a function of the angle of incidence,[33] a condition of which there is not the slightest hint in the letter. In his next letter (March 25, 1667) to Jelles, who had asked for clarification, Spinoza explained that light rays from a relatively distant object are in fact only approximately parallel, since they arrive as "cones of rays" from different points on the object. Yet he maintained the same property of the circle in the case of ray cones, apparently unaware of the importance of the "[other] figures" (the famous "Ovals of Descartes") that Descartes had constructed in Book 2 of *La Géométrie* to provide a general solution to the problem of spherical aberration (Ep 40). I suggest therefore on these grounds alone that though Spinoza may well have written a treatise on the rainbow (which he allegedly burned shortly before his death; Spinoza 1985b: 8), it is very unlikely that he wrote *Stelkonstige Reeckening van den Regenboog*.

As for the five questions of the *Reeckening van Kanssen*, they are taken verbatim from Huygens's pioneering treatise on games of chance (Van Schooten 1657),[34] and only the First Question receives a solution (First and Second Propositions). To tackle the First Question, the author applies the second rule of what he mystifyingly calls "de Denckonst van de Heer Descartes," which Petry italicizes as "Descartes' *Art of Thinking*" and identifies without comment as the *Discours de la méthode* (Spinoza 1985b: 80–1). But since it is indeed the second rule of the *Discours* that is in question, one wonders if it is at all likely that Spinoza would have thought *"Denckonst"* a suitable translation for any part of the full title of Descartes's *Discours*, or (another even more unlikely possibility) that he (of all people) would have confused the titles of the *Discours* and the Port-Royal Logic.[35] And is it likely that he would have referred to "Heer" Descartes? Only once in his works and letters did Spinoza refer to Descartes in that way – in the *Short Treatise*, where the conventionally respectful "D[ominus]. des Cartes" of the Dutch text is presumably an untranslated import from the lost Latin original. Spinoza worked on the doctrine of chances, as we know from his clear solution to a problem posed by Van der Meer (Ep 38, Spinoza to John van der Meer, October 1, 1666), but while that is not incompatible with the supposition that he wrote the *Reeckening van Kanssen*, it seems to me not to strengthen it.

5. SPINOZAN PHYSICS AND CARTESIAN PHYSICS

Spinoza's propaedeutic reworking of Descartes's *Principles of Philosophy* (1644) is selective, frustratingly incomplete, and its "geometric" presentation does not reflect the format of the original, whose purpose was to replace the Peripatetic *summae philosophiae* in Europe's colleges and universities. Nor is it unspotted by misunderstandings of Descartes's text. Yet in many instances Spinoza's *Descartes's "Principles of Philosophy"* is a faithful résumé of Descartes's intentions, it clarifies important points that were unexplained in the original, and resolves difficulties that Descartes left hanging. Its Euclidean *mos demonstrandi* reflects the epistemological security that characterized the principles of Descartes's natural philosophy (if not its explanatory hypotheses), and it is a harbinger of the *ordo geometricus* whose apotheosis in the domain of practical philosophy was to be the *Ethics*.[36] It is also the harbinger of the natural philosophy in which the *Ethics* is grounded. Johannes Casearius, the nineteen-year-old student for whom Spinoza wrote the text, was fortunate to have as his tutor such a perceptive reader of the *Principles of Philosophy*, though whether he appreciated his teacher's didactic method is another matter.[37]

I can deal with only a few examples to illustrate notable features of Spinoza's exposition of Part 2 of Descartes's *Principles of Philosophy*. I take my cue from his instructions to Lodewijk Meyer, who saw the text through the press, to explain to readers in the preface that "I [Spinoza] demonstrate many things in a way different from the way Descartes demonstrated them, not to correct Descartes, but to retain my own order better and not increase the number of axioms so much, and that for the same reason I demonstrate many things Descartes asserts without any demonstration, and have had to add others that he omitted" (Ep 15, Spinoza to L. Meyer, August 3, 1663).[38]

My first example is not so much a difference in demonstration as a difference in nomenclature signaling a deeper difference relating to demonstration. Articles 37–8, 39, and 40–2 of the original Part 2 present the three foundational "laws of nature" of Cartesian physics, "*leges naturae,*" as Descartes terms them. However, the term "*lex (leges) naturae*" does not reappear in Spinoza's text, and the three laws are redrafted as demonstrated propositions (DPP 2p14–18,20, with their corollaries and scholia). Though unspecified necessary *leges Naturae* (*sive Dei Spinozani*) will become the ground of all change and action in Spinoza's mature conception of Nature, it is not clear from *Descartes's "Principles of Philosophy"* that in 1663 he wholly appreciated the function or status of the "laws of nature" that appear in Descartes's *summa* of natural philosophy. Descartes certainly derives his laws of nature from the attributes and actions of (Descartes's) God, which in turn he derives from the irreducible primacy of the *cogito*, but once that ontological authentication is achieved, the laws of nature constitute the single nomological starting point of Descartes's program of natural philosophy. Descartes's arguments in support of his laws of nature may reappear (*grosso modo*) as Spinozan demonstrations, but there is a great difference between conceiving and calling something a "Law of Nature," and labeling it "Proposition XIV." The appellation "law of nature" identifies not a proposition to be demonstrated, but a principle of explanation, with or without a demonstration or justification. The propositions in Spinoza's version of Part 2 derive from nine definitions and twenty-one "axioms," and most of the latter could change places (*mutatis mutandis*) with some of the "propositions" that follow them. Indeed, just before the demonstrations of each of 2p14 (part of Descartes's First Law) and 2p15 (part of Descartes's Second Law), Spinoza notes that though these propositions can be viewed as axioms, nonetheless he will demonstrate them.[39] Here, as in the *Ethics,* Spinoza's "axioms" are not intuitively evident and incontrovertible Euclidean premises from which all else flows "unidirectionally" so to speak, but a set of starting points selected in preference to other sets (i.e., the propositions), some of which could also have served as axioms. But that does not mean that 2p14 and 2p15, renamed as "axioms," would retain the nomological primacy Descartes intended for them.

In other respects, however, this aspect of Spinoza's earliest publication is instructive in that it announces, in its own way, his ideal of a unified body of interrelated demonstrative truths *de Natura sive*

Deo. Spinoza's real *terminus a quo* is the Whole, rather than any of its constituent parts. Grene's characterization of Spinoza's philosophy effectively makes the point:

As atomism, the effort to explain the whole of reality through its least parts, recurs from time to time as a style of metaphysical thinking, so, if more rarely, does Spinozism, the effort to understand the parts of reality in terms of the ultimate nature of the whole. Thus the *Ethics* represents, as few texts do, a permanent possibility of human vision, one of the possible ultimates of philosophical reflection. (Grene 1973: xvi)[40]

Within that perspective the categorization of truths as axioms or propositions becomes almost a matter of choice. There is no Spinozan equivalent of the Cartesian *cogito*.

Another instance of Spinoza's demonstrations differing from Descartes's in a significant way is the trio of propositions 2p15,16,17, corresponding to Descartes's presentation of his Second Law of Nature:

that every motion is from its own nature rectilinear, and so bodies moving in a circle always tend to recede from the center of the circle they describe. [Commentary:] The next law of nature is that each single particle of matter, considered individually, never tends to continue moving along any deviating lines, but only along straight lines – although many particles are often compelled to deviate, because of collisions with others. (*Principles of Philosophy* 2.39)

Descartes's justification of the law per se is only fairly clear and is insufficiently distinct. He grounds the law in the immutability and simplicity of the conserving activity of God, who conserves motion

precisely as it is only at the very moment of time at which he is conserving it, it being of no relevance how it might have been a short time previously. And although no motion takes place in an instant, it is still evident that in each single instant which can be designated during the motion of anything that moves, it is determined (*determinatum*) to continue its motion in some direction along a straight line, never along any curved line.

Spinoza does better than that (DPP 2p15), though he is still at one remove from clarity and distinctness. Because God creates motion at each instant, Spinoza argues, we cannot attribute to motion, as pertaining to its nature, a duration that can be conceived to be longer than another. In other words (mine, not Spinoza's), there is no nonzero shortest duration of continuously re-created Cartesian motion (irrespective of speed) that belongs to its nature. But if someone claims that it pertains to the nature of motion that a moving body naturally describes a curved line, this motion would by its nature be of longer duration than if it moved in a straight line, which (by DPP 2a17) is the shortest distance between two points. Hence the proposition follows.

In the scholium to the proposition, Spinoza raises and rejects an objection based on the fact that for any given line (whether curved or straight) there is always another one (whether curved or straight) that is shorter. His demonstration has to do solely with the "universal essence or essential difference" of the lines, not with their quantities or accidental differences. To avoid obscuring what is already clear, Spinoza refers the reader to the definition of motion (Descartes's Article 25, Spinoza's 2d8) as the *translatio* of one part of matter from the vicinity of immediately contiguous bodies taken to be at rest to the vicinity of other similarly disposed bodies, and signs off with the claim that if we conceive the simplest *translatio* to be other than rectilinear, we attribute to the motion something foreign to its nature. Evidently, the scholium does little to clear up the difficulties in the demonstration. It is not clear what Spinoza takes the "universal essence" of the straight and of the curved to be, nor why 2d8 is relevant, and he could have avoided the scholium altogether had he simply compared rectilinear and curved motion between the same arbitrary points A and B. Given 2a17, any curve AB is necessarily longer than the straight line AB, and so for a given body moving with a given speed, its motion along curve AB is necessarily of longer duration than motion along the straight line AB. The corollary states that curvilinear motion results from an external cause continually making the body deviate from its natural rectilinear motion.

Descartes illustrates the Second Law with the example of a stone whirled in a sling. At any point in its circular motion the stone tends or "tries" to move along the tangent to the circle at that point, and in that sense away from the center of the circle, but is prevented from doing so by the sling. The stone *per se* is not determined to move along the circle, because curvilinearity is not naturally "in" its motion, although it is continually being *forced* to move in a circle, as is shown by the tension in the sling.[41] Rather than repeat

Descartes's analysis, Spinoza offers two ingenious alternative demonstrations which owe nothing to Descartes.

Descartes's "Principles of Philosophy" 2p16 states that "every body moving in a circle, for example a stone in a sling, is continuously determined to continue moving along the tangent." There is a textual difficulty at the beginning of the first of the two demonstrations. The first sentence (Latin text; two sentences in Curley's translation) is a straightforward application of 2p15 and its corollary to circular motion. But Curley's third sentence (translating the second Latin sentence) reads: "I say, moreover, that a body moving in a circle is determined by an external cause to continue to move along a tangent." This sentence leads Curley to note: "It is not clear that Spinoza's exposition is even consistent with Descartes's, since Spinoza treats the sling as a cause of the stone's tendency to continue along a line tangential to the circle in which it is moving . . . whereas Descartes treats the sling as an impediment to a tendency to rectilinear motion" (Spinoza 1985a: 278–9n42). The situation is worse than that, however, since Spinoza's original second sentence flatly contradicts his own opening sentence! Yet Curley's translation is an accurate rendering of the original Latin: *"Dico praeterea corpus, quod circulariter movetur, à causâ externâ determinari, ut secundùm tangentem pergat moveri."*[42] I cannot believe that Spinoza would perpetrate a formal contradiction in two successive sentences, so I conclude that the original Latin text is defective. Happily it can be restored quite simply by transposing a single comma: from after *"movetur"* to after *"externâ,"* and possibly deleting the comma after *"determinari."* The sentence would then read (modifying Curley): "I say, moreover, that a body moving in a circle by an external cause is determined to continue to move along a tangent."

To come to the first demonstration itself, it depends on 2a18: "If A is moved from C towards B [along the straight line CB], and is forced back by a contrary impulse, it will move towards C along the same line."[43] Spinoza proceeds by *reductio ad absurdum*. Suppose that a stone, moving from L to B, is not determined to move along the tangent BD when it arrives at B, but along some other line BF (Fig. 2). Now suppose that the same stone arrives from the other direction along CB, and suppose similarly that it is determined to move not along the tangent BA but along BG, with angle GBH equal to angle HBF, because of the symmetry about B. The motion along CB can be

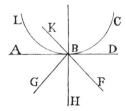

Figure 2

seen as arising from an impulse that is contrary to the impulse that brought the stone from L to B (Spinoza does not spell this out, but that is what he means). So it follows from 2a18 that when the stone arrives at B from C, its determination should be in the direction BK, that is, in the direction opposite to the supposed direction in which the stone is determined to move when it arrives at B from L. But that is contrary to the hypothesis of a determination in the direction BG for the stone arriving from C. The only directions of determination that do not lead to absurdity are BD and BA, that is, the two segments of DBA, the tangent at B. *Q.E.D.*

The second demonstration (*"Aliter"*) begins not with a circle but with a hexagon ABH inscribed in the circle radius DB (Fig. 3). A body is at rest at the midpoint C of the side AB of the hexagon, and the ruler DBE swings counterclockwise round the fixed center D. When the ruler strikes the body at C the ruler will be perpendicular to AB, and so will determine the body to move along the straight line FBAG toward G. (This step in the argument assumes what has to be proved, but let it pass. . . .) Now the same will hold for any figure inscribed in the same circle radius DB, so go to the limit and replace the hexagon with a figure with an infinite number of straight sides (*"hoc est, circulum ex def. Archimedis,"* Spinoza explains). When the ruler DBE strikes the body sitting at the midpoint C of a side of this Archimedean circle, it will determine the body to move along the tangent to the circle at C. Replace the ruler with a sling, and the proposition follows. Note that the second demonstration is Archimedean in inspiration, a feature that it shares with the mathematical work (both pure and mixed) of Spinoza's friend Christiaan Huygens.[44]

Spinoza notes at the end of the second demonstration that both demonstrations "can be accommodated to any curvilinear figure

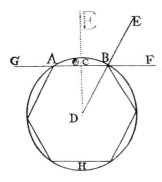

Figure 3

whatever." This is a fine insight, in that a body moving along any curve does continually tend to move along the tangent. But one wonders how much accommodation Spinoza thought the two demonstrations would require. Curves in general are not symmetrical on either side of a point lying on them, as required in the first demonstration; and a radius vector does not in general cut chords at right angles within the curve, as DBE does AB at C in the second demonstration. Spinoza rounds off his account of the Second Law with 2p17, that "every body moving in a circle endeavors (*conatur*) to recede from the center of the circle it describes."

An excellent example of the "many things that Descartes merely proposed without any demonstration," or in this case without explanation, is his concept of "determination" (*determinatio*), which we have just seen Spinoza using in his version of the Second Law, and of which of course he made important use in his own mature philosophy. In classical Greek and Latin, "determination" denoted a specification of some kind, or a bounding of something within limits or *termini*. In the medieval and early modern periods *"determinatio"* and its cognates were frequent currency in philosophical texts, one relevant sense of *"determinatio"* being a specific, particular actualization of a general power or cause. Descartes picked up the concept and shaped it for his own purposes in *Le Monde, La Dioptrique,* and the *Principles of Philosophy.* It is one of the more slippery notions in Descartes's thought, a condition not improved by the absence in his writings of a precise explanation of what he meant by it. In a lengthy attempt elsewhere to pin down its Cartesian sense, and taking account of the attempts of others to do likewise, the best I have come up with is that Descartes's *determinatio* is *not* the direction of a body's motion (as some still think), but is its "directional mode of motive force."[45]

Spinoza saw that the concept would create difficulties, especially for students like Casearius, and he would have learned from Descartes's published correspondence the misunderstanding it had created in disputes with Fermat, Roberval, and Hobbes. At the same time, he appreciated, as few have then or since, the crucial role that *determinatio* plays in Descartes's collision theory and in his physics as a whole. Accordingly, to remove confusion in the minds of his readers, Spinoza follows the corollary to 2p27 (Descartes's Third Rule of collision, 2.48) with a scholium in which he sets out clearly his understanding of the distinction between the "force of determination" (*vis determinationis*) and "the force of motion" (*vis motûs*). The corollary says in effect that the determination a body has to move along a (straight) line is proportional to its speed. But the same is true of a body's force of motion, so in the scholium (modeled on the arguments in *La Dioptrique, Discours Second*) Spinoza shows that additionally force of determination, unlike force of motion, is inseparably associated with a given direction, and can be resolved and compounded directionally according to the parallelogram rule. He then goes further than Descartes by using *vis determinationis* to try to solve the illustrative example of two bodies in oblique collision. His solution is incorrect and confused, but the fault is not Spinoza's qua commentator. Descartes's law of conservation (*Principles of Philosophy* 2.36) applies only to motion, not to determination, the parallelogram rule applies only to determinations, not to motions, and his rules of collision apply only to collisions along the same straight line – all of which makes it formally impossible to analyze oblique collisions in Cartesian terms.[46] Spinoza can scarcely be expected to have made the necessary emendations to Descartes's theories of motion and of collision that were to be the combined revolutionary contributions of Huygens, Leibniz, and Newton.

A major element in Descartes's collision theory that is missing from the original *Principles of Philosophy*, but which Spinoza accurately supplies, is what I describe elsewhere as "The Principle of Least Modal Mutation" (PLMM), Descartes's version of the principle of economy. Presumably because of its teleological nature, Descartes excluded the principle from the major public presentation of his natural philosophy, though his rules of collision are unintelligible without it, as is clear from his letter to Claude Clerselier of February 17, 1645: "they [the rules of collision] depend on only a single [!] principle, which is that when two bodies collide and have in them incompatible modes, there must undoubtedly occur some mutation of these modes to make them compatible, but this mutation is always the least possible" (Descartes 1964–74: V,185).[47] Spinoza's version is 2p23: "When the modes of any body are forced to undergo a variation, the variation will always be the least possible."[48] However, the one-sentence demonstration comes as a surprise: "This proposition follows clearly enough from Proposition 14." Now 2p14 is Spinoza's rewording of Descartes's First Law of Nature, and reads: "Each thing, in so far as it is simple and undivided, and is considered in itself alone, perseveres, as far as possible, always in the same state." Why does 2p23 follow from 2p14? Spinoza never tells us, either in *Descartes's "Principles of Philosophy"* or elsewhere.[49] (Neither does Descartes explain why *his* PLMM is true, though we can guess it is because God's simplicity of action permits nothing superfluous in corporeal interactions.)

Perhaps the simple and undivided things of 2p14 change their modes as little as possible so as to remain as close as possible to the state they happen to be in at any given instant. If that is the right answer, it has interesting implications. *Ethics* 3p6 says essentially the same thing as Spinoza's Cartesian 2p14. So if *Descartes's "Principles of Philosophy"* 2p23 follows as clearly from the earlier 2p14 as Spinoza claims, why does *Ethics* 3p6 not *imply* with equal clarity a Spinozan equivalent of Descartes's PLMM? There is no hint of a minimal principle in the *Ethics*, and the closest Spinoza comes anywhere near to one is *Ethics* 5a1: "If two contrary actions are set up in the same subject, a change *(mutatio)* must necessarily occur in both, or in one alone, until they cease to be contrary."[50] The terminology and associated concepts have changed from Cartesian (incompatible modes of interacting bodies) to Spinozan (incompatible actions in the same finite modes), but the echo of Descartes's PLMM in *Ethics* 5a1 raises a suspicion that lurking in Spinoza's ostensible text is the supplementary axiom that the required *mutatio* must be the least possible. The suspicion is strengthened by the beginning of Spinoza's explanation of the harmonious interconnections of the parts of Nature in the letter to Oldenburg of November 20, 1665: "So by the coherence of parts, all I mean is that the laws, or if you like the nature, of one part so accommodate themselves to the laws or nature of another part, that there is the least possible amount of contrariety between them (*ut quàm minimè sibi contrarientur*)" (Ep 32; Oldenburg 1965–86: II,597,600). This is not quite the equivalent of Descartes's PLMM, but it is very close. At least, it is plainly teleological. *Ethics* 3p6, *Ethics* 5a1 and its echo of Descartes's PLMM, and of course Spinozan *conatus*, all conspire to cast the gravest doubts on the conventional view that Spinoza's mature philosophy is wholly free of finalism.[51] This is not the place to explore the matter further, except to suggest that the problem of teleology in Spinoza (and in Descartes) is best approached by recognizing at the outset the distinction that generally holds (in the real world, that is) between the actual content of an original philosophical system and the accompanying philosophical propaganda that aims to ensure its acceptance and influence.

Spinoza's care with Descartes's *determinatio* and the PLMM prepares one to be not at all surprised to discover that he does something about the collision Rule that Descartes unaccountably omitted. Descartes's Rule 1 (*Principles of Philosophy* 2.46) states that two equal (hard) bodies colliding with equal speeds rebound with speeds unchanged. Rule 2 (*Principles of Philosophy* 2.47) adds that if the bodies are unequal in size, only the smaller one rebounds, and as before the speeds remain unchanged. If the bodies are equal but one is faster than the other, Rule 3 (*Principles of Philosophy* 2.48) specifies that only the slower body rebounds, receiving motion from the faster body so that both bodies move together with the mean speed.[52] However, Descartes offers no Rule that specifies what happens when the sizes and (nonzero) speeds are *both* unequal. Spinoza sees the *lacuna*, and between Rules 2 and 3 (between Rules 3 and 4 would have been a better spot) places 2p26: "If the bodies are unequal in bulk (*molis*) and speed, with B twice as big as A but A's motion twice as fast as B's, with everything else as before, then both bodies will be reflected in the opposite direction with each retaining the speed it had."[53]

This is not the general case that one would have liked Spinoza to tackle, but at least it is a numerical example of the important special case where the ratio between the bodies' sizes is the inverse of the ratio between their speeds. In the demonstration, Spinoza notes that the bodies have the same quantity of motion, so there is no contrariety between their motions, and their forces of motion are equal. The outcome is therefore the same as in Rule 1, where the equal determinations are in opposition, but not the motions. Here Spinoza has modified Descartes's theory. In *Principles of Philosophy* 2.44 Descartes had argued that there is no contrariety between motions of equal speed, but only between motion and rest or between speed and slowness ("in so far as it participates in the nature of rest"), and between determinations in opposite directions. To solve the new Rule, Spinoza sees the convenience (perhaps the necessity) of extending the denial of contrariety to equal *quantities* of motion, as he had already done in the corollary to 2p19. Finally, in the corollary to 2p26, Spinoza takes the opportunity to highlight two important points about *determinatio* that follow from 2pp24–26, and which he would have found Descartes explaining to Clerselier in the letter of February 17, 1645. To change the determination of one body requires as much force as it does to change its motion, so a body that loses more than half of its determination and more than half of its motion, suffers a greater mutation than one that loses the whole of its determination.

It is unfortunate that we do not know in detail what prompted Oldenburg to write to Spinoza in 1665: "In talking about Huygens's *Tractatus de motu*, you intimate that Descartes's Rules of motion are nearly all false" (Ep 31, Oldenburg to Spinoza, October 12 (O.S.), 1665; Oldenburg 1965–86: II,565).[54] There are no extant letters in which Spinoza talks about these matters. Oldenburg goes on to ask Spinoza to explain what is wrong with Descartes's rules, and mentions *Descartes's "Principles of Philosophy."* Spinoza replies that it was Huygens who found fault with Descartes's collision rules, that he (Spinoza) objected only to Rule 6, and that there he found Huygens at fault as much as Descartes (Ep 32, Spinoza to Oldenburg, November 20, 1665; Oldenburg 1965–86: II,598,601). Oldenburg asked once more that Spinoza explain to him where Descartes and Huygens had gone astray in their collision theory (Ep 33, Oldenburg to Spinoza, December 8 (O.S.), 1665; Oldenburg 1965–86: II,634,636), but at that point in their correspondence began a ten-year break, and there is no (extant) answer to Oldenburg's request.

I cannot guess what might have been Spinoza's reasons for simultaneously (*a*) accepting six of Descartes's Rules, (*b*) rejecting Rule 6, (*c*) rejecting Huygens's solution to the same problem, *and* possibly by implication (*d*) accepting the rest of Huygens's collision theory. Descartes's Rule 6 (*Principles of Philosophy* 2.50) states that if the two bodies B and C are equal and C is at rest, then C will be set in motion by B, and B will be reflected by C, each with a different quantity of motion. Huygens's (correct) solution is that B comes to rest, and C moves off with B's initial speed (Huygens 1888–1950: XVI, 33–9). If both solutions are in error, did Spinoza have one of his own? Probably not.[55] Rivaud has suggested that Spinoza rejected Rule 6 because the bodies' change of speed implies "changing their nature and losing their essence," which is characterized in each of them by a fixed speed (Rivaud 1924–26: 31). But the final speeds in Rule 6 are as fixed and calculable as those in the other Rules, and as Gueroult points out (Gueroult 1968–74: II,552), Spinoza accepts the other Rules, in three of which (Rules 3, 5, and 7) the bodies also change their speed on collision.

In any event, is Rivaud not mistaken in supposing that for Spinoza bodies change their nature or essence when they change their speeds? If the colliding bodies are taken to be the *corpora simplicissima* of *Ethics* Part 2, then motion, rest, speed, and slowness are their sole distinguishing characteristics, according to *Ethics* 2p13l1 and the paragraph at the end of *Ethics* 2p13a2″. But neither of these kinematic characteristics constitutes the essence of a *corpus simplicissimum*, to judge by *Ethics* 2d2, since a simple body can exist and be conceived (per *Ethics* 2p13,a1″,a2′,a2″) whether it is in motion or not, and whatever its speed if in motion.[56] The problem then arises (not for the first time) of unravelling what exactly Spinoza means in *Ethics* 2d1 (body as "a mode which expresses in a certain and determinate way the essence of God in so far as he is considered as an extended thing"). If the "certain and determinate way" excludes (or does not necessarily include) the kinematic characteristics that distinguish a simple body (presumably empirically), what does it necessarily include, in addition to extension? Clearly the body's own essence, which by *Ethics* 3p6–7, is simply the *conatus* or endeavor "by which it endeavors [sic] to persevere in its own being." But then, persevering in its own being necessarily involves the body persevering in its present rest, or in its present motion with this or that speed. Perhaps Rivaud is not mistaken after all.

On the other hand, if a body in collision is taken to be a *corpus compositum*, or "individual" in Spinoza's sense, its nature depends on the preservation of the same proportionate internal exchanges of motion between the simple bodies out of which it is composed (definition following *Ethics* 2p13). Provided those proportionate internal relations of motions (and rest) remain the same, the nature or essence of the composite body certainly does not change or perish if it changes speed when moving as a whole or qua individual. That much is clear from *Ethics* 2p13le6–7,s.

Despite his many insights into and elucidations of Descartes's natural philosophy, Spinoza's concept of the individual is striking evidence of an apparent disinclination or inability to disentangle and clarify a fundamental difficulty in Descartes's doctrine of motion. The difficulty arises from the couple "motion and rest." In *Principles of Philosophy* 2.36, Descartes introduces the familiar thesis that God is the universal and primary cause of motion, and describes his creative and conservative power in the following terms:

[T]he general cause of all motion in the world . . . is none other than God himself, who in the beginning created matter together with motion and rest, and who through his ordinary concourse alone now conserves in all of matter as much motion and rest as he put in it then. For although this motion in moved matter is nothing other than its mode, it has nonetheless a certain and determined quantity, which we can easily understand is always the same in the whole totality of things, although it might change in its individual parts.

The creation and conservation of a quantity of motion seem unproblematic (assuming in the first place we can accept Descartes's concept of motion), as does the creation of bodies at rest. But does rest have "a certain and determined quantity," and if so how can it be quantified and conserved on all fours with motion? In the special context of Descartes's collision theory, rest is quantifiable and functions as a quantity in the explication and operation of the Rules,[57] but it is unclear what Descartes means by the quantitative conservation of "motion *and rest*" in the universe as a whole. God conserves all things with the same power, but the translation of that power into quantifiable rest remains obscure. Descartes does not explain himself here or elsewhere, and Spinoza's *Descartes's "Principles of Philosophy"* is no help either (2p11,s,12,13).

Whether Spinoza saw the difficulties or not, "rest and motion" became a leitmotiv in his own philosophy (as in many Spinoza commentaries), and in particular it is the central notion in his concept of the individual, defined in *Ethics* 2p13:

> When a number of bodies of the same or different magnitude are constrained by other bodies to press on each other, or if they are moved with the same or diverse grades of speed so that they communicate (*communico*) among themselves their motions in a certain fixed proportion (*certâ quâdam ratione*), we may say that those bodies are united among themselves, and that all together they compose one body, or Individual, which is distinguished from other bodies through this union of bodies.[58]

There is no mention of *rest* here, almost certainly because Spinoza was unhappy with the idea of bodies "communicating rest" among themselves,[59] but it is implicitly and ineluctably present, not only because of *Ethics* 2p13a1' and 2p13le1, but more unambiguously because of (for example) 2p13le5,s, and *Ethics* 4p39. *Ethics* 2p13le5 reads: "If the parts composing an Individual become greater or smaller, yet do so in a proportion (*eâ . . . proportione*) so that they all maintain among themselves the same proportion of motion and rest (*motûs, & quietis ratio*) as before, the Individual will likewise retain its nature as before, without any mutation of form."[60]

We can appreciate what Spinoza is trying to do in these texts, since it is exceptionally difficult to say what constitutes the unity-in-diversity characteristic of organic and inorganic individuals. We admire his intuition into what much later will become known as homeostasis – and personally I admire what to me is possibly an ingenious neo-Cartesian reformulation of the traditional Galenic medical doctrine of humoral balance (good health) and imbalance (illness). Yet that intuition is vitiated by the "motion and rest" riddle inherited from Descartes's natural philosophy. To talk of bodies maintaining among themselves "the same proportion of motion and rest," or communicating motion to each other "in a certain fixed proportion," is to say nothing effective, unless a mathematical account is provided of those proportions and of the measures of motion and rest from which they are formed, and unless there is some account of the laws that ensure the claimed invariance in proportionalities. Spinoza provides no such laws, nor does he say how the proportions are to be mathematically expressed. In the worm-in-the-blood illustration of the harmonious interrelation of all parts of Nature, the formula *"motûs, & quietis ratio"* encouragingly becomes *"ratio motûs ad quietem."* Spinoza writes to Oldenburg that all bodies:

are surrounded by others, and are determined to exist and to act, each by the other, in a fixed and determined way (*ratio*), the same proportion of motion to rest (*eâdem ratione motûs ad quietem*) always being preserved in all things as a whole, that is, in the whole universe. (Ep 32, Spinoza to Oldenburg, November 20, 1665; Oldenburg 1965–86: II, 598)

But this still lacks quantitative anchoring, and is therefore much too vague to allow an assessment of what exactly is being claimed.

Matheron courageously attempts to make sense out of this aspect of the Spinozan individual, but fails, largely because of an unintelligible mathematical reconstruction of Spinoza's presumed intentions (Matheron 1969: 37–41).[61] The mathematical irretrievability of Spinoza's doctrine of the individual has not dissuaded Gueroult from an excursion into the theory of rigid bodies in an attempt to restore to the doctrine mathematical intelligibility. In an Appendix devoted entirely to the matter, he goes to great lengths to establish the eccentric claim that Spinoza's definition of the individual (*certa quadam ratio*) can be found in the relationship between speed and distance in the investigations on center of oscillation carried out by Descartes, Roberval, and above all Huygens. According to Gueroult, Spinoza could have taken the idea of his distinction between *corpora simplicissima* and *composita* from Huygens's distinction between simple and compound pendulums, and the arguments in the famous letter to Oldenburg of November 20, 1665 show the "probable influence" on Spinoza of the researches on pendulums of Roberval and Huygens, notably *"le principe de la conservation du mouvement du centre de gravité."* Gueroult admits that

On doit préciser que si l'hypothèse d'une influence de la théorie pendulaire de Huygens sur la théorie spinoziste des corps n'est pas historiquement prouvée par des documents, des allusions précises ou des textes formels, mais ne s'impose que de par leur convergence indéniable, en revanche, les circonstances historiques, à tout le moins, l'autorisent. . . . (Gueroult 1968–74: II,557)

Unfortunately, the historical circumstances (e.g., Spinoza's friendship with Huygens) authorize nothing of the sort. There is no evidence, either in Spinoza's historical circumstances or in his writings or letters, that he had any grasp of the mathematical intricacies of

Huygens's investigations into the theory of rigid-body motion, or that there is any link between these investigations and Spinoza's concept of the individual. It is painful to say so, but Gueroult's Appendix 5 is an unaccountable aberration in an otherwise distinguished Spinoza commentary.[62]

6. SCIENTIFIC METHOD

The criticisms of Bacon in Spinoza's first letter to Oldenburg do not imply that he repudiated the whole of Bacon's philosophy, any more than the criticisms of Descartes in the same letter imply that Spinoza's philosophy is free of Cartesian ideas. Indeed the first-order fact-gathering business of natural philosophy was viewed by Spinoza in a Baconian way. In Chapter vii of the *Theological-Political Treatise* he bracketed the methods of scriptural exegesis and natural philosophy in the following terms:

I say that the method of interpreting Scripture is scarcely different from the method of interpreting nature, but accords with it closely. For just as the method of interpreting nature consists above all in compiling a natural history from which, as from established facts, we infer definitions of natural things; so also to interpret Scripture we must prepare a sound Scriptural history, and from that, as from established facts and principles, to reach legitimate conclusions about the intentions of the authors of Scripture.... Scripture very often deals with matters that cannot be deduced from principles known to the natural light, for it comprises for the most part historical accounts and revelations ... therefore the knowledge (*cognitio*) of ... nearly everything contained in Scripture, must be sought only from Scripture itself, just as the knowledge of nature is sought from nature itself. (TTP vii.6–9; Spinoza 1925: III,98)

The compilation of "natural and experimental histories" was the first step in Bacon's method, and Spinoza's inference of definitions (i.e., of essences or natures) parallels Bacon's inductive extraction of forms and natures. In the *Treatise on the Intellect* Spinoza lists four steps assisting the selection of the best among the four *modi percipiendi*. The first two of these read: "I. That we know exactly our nature, which we desire to perfect, and at the same time know as much of the nature of things as is necessary. II. That we collect therefore the differences, agreements, and oppositions of things" (TdIE 25). I think Savan is right to see in the second of these the influence of Bacon's inductive tables of "Degrees or Comparison," "Presence and Essence," and "Deviation or Absence in Proximity" (Savan 1986: 122n8).

The same Baconian spirit leads Spinoza to advise Oldenburg, during his discussion of Boyle's "The History of Fluidity and Firmness," that

... for an understanding of the nature of fluids in general, it suffices to know that we can move our hand in a fluid in all directions with a motion proportionate to it (*motu fluido proportionato*) and without any resistance [?]. This is clear enough to those who pay sufficient attention to those notions (*notio*) that explain Nature as it is in itself, not as it is related to human sense. I do not therefore despise this history as useless. On the contrary, if [a history] of each liquid could be compiled as accurately as possible and that was of the utmost reliability, I should judge it to be most useful for understanding their individual differences, which being highly necessary is something to be greatly desired by all philosophers. (Ep 6, Spinoza to Oldenburg, [April 1662]; Oldenburg 1965–86: I,456 [text of autograph in the Royal Society]).[63]

Indeed in the same letter he goes beyond Baconian natural history to cite Bacon as having "more than adequately demonstrated" before Descartes that tangible qualities depend only on motion, shape, and other mechanical affections – though I suspect Spinoza is using Bacon here to scold Boyle for making too much of an experimental meal out of something that his illustrious compatriot had already cleared up years before.

More decisive perhaps is the letter to Bouwmeester in which Spinoza argues that our clear and distinct perceptions are not caused by anything outside ourselves, but only by *other* clear and distinct perceptions. This means that our clear and distinct perceptions arise only from

the certain and fixed laws of our nature alone, that is, from our absolute power (*potentia*), not from chance (*fortuna*), that is, from causes, though also certain and acting through fixed laws, that are unknown to us and alien to our nature and power. As for other [kinds of] perceptions, I acknowledge that they depend wholly and utterly on chance.

Accordingly, the true Method consists in

the knowledge alone of the pure understanding, of its nature and of its laws. To acquire this method, you must first of all distinguish between intellect and imagination, or between true ideas and the others, that is fictitious, false, and doubtful ideas, and, absolutely speaking, all those that depend on memory alone. To understand this, at least as far as the Method requires, there is no need to know the nature of the mind through its first cause; it is sufficient to compile a short history (*historiola*), in the way taught by Verulamius [Bacon], of the mind or of its perceptions. (Ep37, Spinoza to Jan Bouwmeester, June 10, 1666)

The "true method" envisioned by Spinoza is scarcely Baconian, insofar as it charts the generation of clear and distinct perceptions from each other, but the materials on which it is supposed to work are to be collected in a Baconian manner. Without those empirical materials, we cannot ascend to a knowledge of the nature of things. Or rather, following the account of the fourth kind of *perceptio* in the *Treatise on the Intellect*, we cannot acquire a knowledge through their proximate causes of the essences or definitions of finite modes (TdIE 19).[64]

If there is such a Baconian influence in Spinoza's methodology, there reemerges the question of his presence in the Spinozan taxonomy of knowing. I refer to Spinoza's notion of *experientia vaga*, which has traditionally been taken to be a straightforward allusion to or borrowing from Aphorism 100 of *Novum Organum*, Book I:

But not only is a greater abundance of experiments (*experimentum*) to be sought for and procured, and that too of a different kind from what has been done hitherto; but an entirely different method, order, and process for continuing and advancing experience (*experientia*) must also be introduced. For random experience (*experientia vaga*), when it just follows its own nose, is, as was said above, mere groping in the dark, and confounds men rather than instructs them. But when Experience proceeds by fixed law, without interruption and in regular order, then we may hope for something better of the sciences. (Bacon 1857–74: I,203; IV,95, translation modified)[65]

Certainly there is a parallel between the *experientia vaga* of the two philosophers; and Spinoza, who had closely studied *Novum Organum* by September 1661, can scarcely have been unaware of Bacon's use of the expression. Yet the link with Bacon seems to have been assumed by default, rather than inferred after an examination of other sources of *prima facie* relevance. Spinoza and Bacon may well have been the only philosophers to couple "*experientia*" and "*vaga*" to make a philosophical point, but they were not the first to use the latter term for that purpose. Since the thirteenth century (at the latest)[66] "*vagus*" had functioned in logical treatises in ways that invite us to reconsider Spinoza's use of the term.

To take once again the manuals that Spinoza knew, Burgersdijk, in his *Institutiones logicae* (1626), introduces "*vagus*" in his discussion of universals, singulars, and individuals. The singular is that which is predicated of one thing through its own nature (Theorem VII), and singulars are "atoms," or individuals, in the sense that they cannot be subdivided into entities that retain the same name and nature (Theorem VIII). Furthermore (Theorem IX), each individual is either determined (*determinatum*), or undesignated (*vagum*). An individual is determined in four ways (Theorem X): through a proper name ("Alexander," "Bucephalus"), through a common name ("The Philosopher," meaning Aristotle), through a demonstrative pronoun ("this person"), and periphrastically ("The Apostle to the Gentiles," meaning St Paul). An individual is *vagum* in one way (Theorem XI): through an indefinite pronoun ("someone," "some person"). As Heereboord puts it in his *explicatio* of Theorem IX, "Individuals are said to be determined, when they are delimited to a certain place and time. They are undesignated, when the contrary obtains."[67]

A useful source from earlier in the century is the article on "*confusa*" in Goclenius's *Lexicon philosophicum* (1613). After "*confusa*" as "*indistincta*," and Aristotle's and Zabarella's "*confusum*" as a "Whole comprising a multitude of parts," Goclenius goes on to note:

> *Confusum* is also taken by some Scholastics to be *Vagum*, & in Fonseca's teaching *De suppositionibus* it is the opposite of "specified" *(signatum)* and "determined" *(determinatum)*. Children first know confused particulars as *particularia vaga*, later they know *particularia signata*. First they know father or mother only as another person who is no different from other people but who resembles them. Later, however, they know him or her as this specified person *(ut hunc signatum)*, that is, they distinguish father and mother from other persons. John the Grammarian also took it *[confusum]* in this sense in [his commentary on Aristotle's] *Physics* I. (Goclenius 1613: 439)

Given this traditional technical sense of "*vagus*," as expressed in Burgersdijk, Heereboord, and Goclenius, Spinoza seems to be using the term in the same way, as a description of the logical status of the individuals on which *experientia vaga* is based. First, the opposition between *vaga* and *determinata* is explicitly mentioned in the *Trea-*

tise on the Intellect, and the way Spinoza presents it implies that some of what he is saying will be familiar to his readers:

II. There is the perception we have from *experientia vaga,* that is, from experience that is not determined (*determinatur*) by the intellect, but is spoken of in just this way because it happens by chance (*casu*) and we have to hand no other counter-instance (*nullum aliud habemus experimentum, quod hoc oppugnat*), and so to us it remains an unshaken perception. (TdIE 19)

Second, Spinoza illustrates *experientia vaga* by noting that

through *experientia vaga* I know that I shall die, for I affirm this because I have seen that others like myself have died, though they did not all live through the same interval of time, or die from the same disease. Again, I know also from *experientia vaga* that oil is suited to feeding fire, but that water is suited to extinguishing it; I know also that the dog is a barking animal, and that man is a rational animal, etc. (TdIE 20)

Now each of these items of knowledge, and the knowledge the non-mathematician has of simple arithmetical algorithms (including the Rule of Three, the illustration that appears in the *Treatise on the Intellect,* the *Short Treatise,* and the *Ethics*), is inferred from or grounded on individual experiences that merit the epithet *"vaga"* because they are not "determined by the intellect" in one or other of the four ways listed by Burgersdijk. When we say that "man is rational," we do not mean only that Alexander or The Apostle to the Gentiles is rational, but that any human is rational. When we say that "oil feeds fire," we do not mean just *this* or *that* measure of oil, but simply "oil," that is, any and every measure of oil. We are reminded of William of Sherwood's third mode of simple supposition, whose own example was: "Pepper is sold here and in Rome" (see note 66). Spinoza says – significantly for my argument – that those he has seen die did not live the same life-spans or die from the same causes, meaning that the death of anyone at all, and of no one in particular, has played its part in leading him to infer that he too will die. He does not know this merely through having seen the lifeless body of his father on a certain day in March 1654, of Simon de Vries on a certain date in 1667, of Adriaan Koerbagh on a certain date in 1669, or the bodies of the murdered Jan and Cornelis de Witt on or after August 20, 1672.[68] Had Spinoza inferred his own mortality from these deaths alone, the knowledge acquired would have been from *experientia determinata,* but because of its narrower observational base, it would have been less assured (in this instance) than the knowledge acquired from *experientia vaga*.

Similar considerations hold for *Ethics* 2p40s1,2. In *Ethics* 2p40s1 the discussion is partly of universals (as was Burgersdijk's above), which we form in varying ways according to the dispositions of our individual bodies. Accordingly, Spinoza claims in *Ethics* 2p40s2, "we perceive many things and form universal notions: I. from singular things which have been represented to us through the senses in a way that is mutilated, confused, and without order for the intellect (see p29c); for that reason I have been accustomed (*consuevi*) to call such perceptions knowledge from random experience (*experientia vaga*).[69] Note how "*consuevi*" significantly alters the sense of the last phrase: Shirley omits it, leaving only "and therefore I call such perceptions . . ." (Spinoza 1982: 90), which breaks the direct link – implied in the Latin text – with the *Treatise on the Intellect*, and possibly the indirect link with the Peripatetic logical tradition.

We must not overlook the fact that in the *Treatise on the Intellect* Spinoza describes knowledge from *experientia vaga* as "unshaken," provided there are no counter-instances, and as constituting nearly all the practical knowledge we need in life. Each of the items of knowledge with which Spinoza illustrates *experientia vaga* is in itself anything but "vague" or "undetermined." Each item is clear, unambiguous, and, like death (yes, the ideal example) and taxes, is one of the certainties of this life. Each product of *experientia vaga* is either an empirical generalization, a scientific law, or a mathematical truth. But because there *might* be counter-instances, at least in principle (even human mortality is open to experiential disconfirmation, it seems), knowledge from *experientia vaga* is not absolutely certain. Those who believe, on the basis of their own random experience, that all sheep have short tails, are surprised to discover that Moroccan sheep have long tails (ST II,3). And although Spinoza is unclear on the question, I assume that even the Rule of Three is open to correction in the sense that a mathematician might show that there are exceptions to the algorithm assumed without benefit of Euclid through extrapolation from a simple case, though no one is likely to come across them in ordinary circumstances. To convert these items of knowledge from *experientia vaga* into absolute certainty requires knowing the essence of dogs, oil, water, humans, and the Euclidean theory of proportions, from which the respective accidents could be deduced.

It cannot be assumed, therefore, that Bacon is the direct source for Spinoza's *experientia vaga*. It is more likely that the Peripatetic logical tradition is the source for *both* Bacon and Spinoza, each of them using *vagus* in his own way and for his own quite different purposes. Bacon's purpose in the aphorisms on either side of Aphorism 100 (*Novum Organum*, Book I) is to assess methods that others have chosen to attain truth in the sciences. Some have resorted to authority, some to logic, and some to simple experience (*experientia mera*), "which if it [just] occurs, is called chance (*casus*), and if sought for, is called experiment." Simple experience therefore includes *experientia vaga*, which Bacon brackets with chance experience earlier in the same aphorism (Aphorism 82, Bacon 1857–74: I,189–90). But all these methods are useless as means of discovering causes, in contrast to the proper method, which proceeds "by fixed law, without interruption and in regular order" (*experientia determinata*). Spinoza's purpose in the contexts where "*experientia vaga*" appears, on the other hand, is not to emulate Bacon with a critique of methodologies or with proposals for a new method, but to set out three or four kinds of perception or knowledge. And although Spinoza's *experientia vaga* does not uncover causes or essences, at least it yields empirical generalizations (and mathematical algorithms) that form a useful part of one's general knowledge of things. The difference here between Bacon and Spinoza is that for Bacon *experientia vaga* is an ineffectual *method* of finding the causes of things: for Spinoza it is an *empirical base of a specific logical kind* from which are inferred general propositions which are useful in life, but which do not reveal the essences or causes of things.

So what is Spinoza's method for revealing the essences of things? How does one obtain "adequate ideas of the properties of things," or the *scientia intuitiva* that consists in the move from "an adequate idea of the formal essence of certain attributes of God to the adequate knowledge of the essence of things" (E 2p40s2)? It is difficult to shape an answer, since it is not clear how precisely Spinoza's method is supposed to yield an understanding of causes or essences. Where he counsels Baconian recipes, as in the letter to Bouwmeester or in the letter to Oldenburg advocating a history of liquids (both quoted above), that preliminary part of the method is straightforward, but as a means of unveiling essences and proximate causes it would have been as powerless as Bacon's own method proved to be.

Where Spinoza adumbrates his own method, the matter is much less straightforward. The optimistic Bouwmeester had asked Spinoza if there exists a method by means of which "we can proceed safely and without weariness [!] in the consideration of the most exalted subjects." Spinoza replied that there is such a method, "by which we can direct and concatenate our clear and distinct conceptions," which however "can only arise from other clear and distinct conceptions which are in us; they acknowledge no other cause outside us." So as we saw above, the true method consists "in the knowledge alone of the pure understanding, of its nature and of its laws" (Ep 37). It is impossible to envisage such a method "rightly controlling the Reason in acquiring knowledge of unknown truths," as Tschirnhaus characterized the method he vainly sought from Spinoza in 1675 (Ep 59, E. W. von Tschirnhaus to Spinoza, 5 January 1675). In the *Treatise on the Intellect*, Spinoza's only extended essay in methodology, though admittedly an unfinished draft, he explains that

Method is not the reasoning itself by which we understand the causes of things, much less the understanding of the causes of things; it is understanding what a true idea is by distinguishing it from the rest of the perceptions. . . . From this it may be inferred that Method is nothing but a reflexive knowledge (*cognitio reflexiva*), or an idea of an idea. (TdIE 37–8)

As Parkinson puts it, Spinoza's method "consists in thinking about what is known, rather than in trying to prove that a given proposition is known." It is difficult to disagree with his verdict that the rules in *Treatise on the Intellect* "are of little value for the discovery of new truths" (Parkinson 1954: 11,21).[70]

As for experimentation, Spinoza valued it, as we saw earlier, because it reveals new things and their qualities, and new phenomena. But it cannot uncover the nature of things: sensory knowledge belongs to the imagination, the knowledge of essences and causes to the intellect alone.[71] In the controversy with Boyle (cf. Section 3), there is no suggestion that Boyle's experiments might have helped, however minimally, to improve Spinoza's knowledge of the nature of nitre or of fluidity and solidity. Spinoza's response to Boyle's *Essays* was essentially an examination of Boyle from a Spinozistic Cartesian standpoint. The natural contrast was with Descartes, who Spinoza imagined had uncovered the real natures of all these things through rational demonstrations, and whose explanations of these natures had not been amplified or improved on by Boyle's experimental investigations. I will pass over Spinoza's (idiosyncratically Cartesian) comments on the essays on fluidity and solidity, and look briefly at some of his critique of the experiment of which "On Nitre" was the published account in Boyle's *Essays*.

Boyle had dropped a piece of glowing coal onto nitre (saltpetre, potassium nitrate), thereby decomposing it into a fixed part (fixed nitre, potash, potassium carbonate[72]), and a volatile part (spirit of nitre, nitric acid) which he distilled. On recombining the two parts he retrieved the "redintegrated" nitre, and a rough quantitative check showed that almost as much nitre was recovered as had been "divided" initially. Boyle concluded that nitre is a chemical compound (as opposed to a mechanical mixture of different substances), the constituent parts being substances of different specific chemical and physical natures, the spirit of nitre showing acidic properties, the fixed nitre showing "an Alkalizate nature," each of them being of a different nature from the nitre itself, which exhibited other properties. Boyle inferred that the corpuscles of the constituent parts persist unchanged throughout the reactions, and that the reactions were explicable on the basis of his corpuscular chemistry, but not by the doctrine of substantial forms, according to which the form of nitre is destroyed in the substantial change brought about in the experiments.[73]

Spinoza objected that Boyle would need an additional experiment to show that the nitre and the spirit of nitre are in fact different substances and that the spirit of nitre cannot be crystallized without the fixed nitre, which Spinoza took to be only an impurity both in the original nitre and in the spirit of nitre. Furthermore, Boyle's quantitative check did not support his case. He should at least have investigated further to see if a given quantity of nitre always produces the same quantity of fixed nitre and if the fixed nitre is always proportional to the amount of nitre required to produce it. Whether or not this intriguing quantitative critique of Boyle's methodology (which elicited no response from Boyle) is cognate with Spinoza's doctrine of the individual (see section 5), as it probably is, it is unclear why Spinoza thought this additional experiment might have tested just Boyle's interpretation of his results, any more than it might have tested his own. A priori, one would expect the proportionate relationship to apply equally to the fixed nitre interpreted as a mere impurity.

According to Spinoza's Cartesian explanation of Boyle's results, the two products of the experiment were nothing more than the observed effects of different mechanical states of the same fundamental particles. Nitre and the spirit of nitre consist of rigid, carrot-shaped particles.[74] The particles of nitre are at rest, those of spirit of nitre are in rapid motion; the fixed nitre slows the faster particles of the spirit of nitre to produce nitre, and it has pores whose sizes change and whose walls become brittle when the nitre is forced out by the fire. As for the difference in taste that Boyle noted between the fixed nitre (alkaline) and spirit of nitre (acidic), their particles lie lengthways on the tongue when slow, and prick it when they move fast. The inflammability of nitre and non-inflammability of spirit of nitre, also noted by Boyle, arise from the inability of fire to carry the motionless particles of nitre upwards as quickly as it does the already quickly moving particles of spirit of nitre, which thereby extinguishes the fire rather than feeding it. To support his interpretation of Boyle's experimental results, Spinoza describes three experiments he performed to show that spirit of nitre is really volatile nitre. Though the experiments are of interest in themselves, they neither confirm nor deny their Cartesian theoretical parentage. Boyle had little difficulty in accounting for them without having to revise his own position.[75]

To prove Boyle's claimed specific differences between the substances would have meant actually showing that their particles have different geometrical forms. However, Boyle was content to show their different chemical properties, without explaining precisely how they derive from the presumed corresponding corpuscular states, though he had no doubt that that was their origin. His principal purpose in the experiment, according to his spokesman Oldenburg, was not to present "a really perfect and philosophical analysis of niter," but to show the weakness of the doctrine of substantial forms and qualities (which Spinoza thought could be taken as read), to show that forms and qualities can themselves be explained in mechanical terms (Ep 11, Oldenburg to Spinoza, April 3, 1663; Oldenburg 1965–86: II,37, 40).[76] Yet in the essay itself Boyle claimed that his experiment proved the reducibility of sensible qualities to the "primary and mechanical affections" of bodies. Since Boyle censured Spinoza for making gratuitous (Cartesian) assumptions about the nature of nitre and the associated substances, the dispute as a whole, including the arguments over fluidity and solidity, comes across as a case of the pot calling the kettle black. As Meinel has effectively shown (at least for the earlier seventeenth century), alleged experimental confirmations of mechanical hypotheses were far from being as conclusive as the theoreticians and experimentalists of the mechanical philosophy pretended (Meinel 1988). We ought to look afresh at Spinoza's insistence on the epistemological insufficiencies of the experimental way.

7. NATURA VEXATA (SIVE DEUS VEXATUS)?

Bacon's familiar distinction between *natura libera* and *natura vexata* is among the earliest of a number of related distinctions that categorize modern notions of Nature and of the Natural Sciences. We have assumed, often uncritically, the distinction between observation and experiment, between the observational and the experimental sciences, between Natural History and Experimental History, between Nature left free for human inspection and Nature subjected to human inquisition, between listening passively to what Nature tells us and "torturing" Nature to tell us more, between Nature and Art. In all philosophical and cultural traditions, the mechanical or manual arts, for example, have consisted in the construction and operation of machines and devices whose purpose has been to benefit human society by moving things *contra naturam*. The Peripatetics distinguished between *secundum naturam* (according to nature), *contra naturam* (against nature), *praeter naturam* (beyond though not strictly contrary to the natural, e.g., being born with six fingers), and *supra naturam* (the supernatural, e.g., miracles). Presiding over and lending intelligibility to these distinctions is the belief that the human species and Nature are distinct and (for some) separable entities, and that we can thereby exercise our will to *intervene* in the "natural" world, to *disturb* the "natural" run of things, to have dominion over the creatures, to make ourselves masters and possessors of Nature.

Philosophically speaking, Spinoza cannot admit any of these distinctions, except only as *entia rationis*. They are not demarcations within the real, because human beings, as modes of infinite sub-

stance, are integral parts of Nature and not distinct from it as technological or experimental agents intervening in Nature in a Baconian
way. Everything that happens is *secundum Naturam* (*sive Deum*),
that is, strictly according to the Laws of Nature (or God). Nothing
can conceivably act *contra naturam*, as Spinoza emphatically proclaims in Chapter vi ("On miracles") of the *Theological-Political
Treatise*, so there cannot be a distinction *in re* between Art and
Nature. Substance cannot *intervene* in its own operations to change
them in accordance with some presumed non-nomological act of
will; here the notion of "intervening" makes no sense. As an ordinary citizen using ordinary language, Spinoza at his lathe grinding
lenses would describe the activity as *ars mechanica*, but according
to his philosophical doctrines he cannot say that he is *intervening* in
Nature through an act of will to produce lenses *contra naturam*. The
will, being an *ens rationis*, cannot cause volitions, whose real causes
lie hidden elsewhere (Ep 2, Spinoza to Oldenburg, September 1661;
Oldenburg 1965–86: I,425,427). Spinoza, his lathe, and the manufac-
tured lenses behave strictly and solely according to the Laws of
Nature expressed through his and their own essence.

In the Preface to *Ethics* Part 3 Spinoza censures those who, writing
about the passions and human conduct,

seem to treat, not of natural things, which follow the common laws of
nature, but of things that are outside nature (*extra naturam*). Indeed they
seem to conceive man in nature as a dominion within a dominion (*imperium in imperio*). For they believe that man disturbs, rather than follows, the
order of nature, that he has absolute power over his actions, and that he is
determined only by himself. (Spinoza 1985a: 491)

This idea, one of Spinoza's most powerful, reappears in the *Political
Treatise*. There is no difference between desires engendered within
us through reason, and desires arising from external causes, because
both are the products of the laws of nature:

Whether wise or ignorant, a human being is part of nature, and every single
thing by which each individual person is determined to act must be attributed to the power of nature, that is, in so far as that thing can be defined by
reference to the nature of this or that person. Whether led by reason or by
desire alone, no human being does anything except in accordance with the
laws and rules of nature.

Nevertheless,

most people believe that the ignorant perturb the order of nature rather than follow it, and conceive of men in nature as a kingdom within a kingdom (*imperium in imperio*). They decree that the human mind is produced not by any natural causes, but is created immediately by God, and is so independent of other things that it has absolute power (*potestas*) to determine itself and to use reason correctly. (TP ii)[77]

Reflecting on the Second Anglo–Dutch War (1665–67), Spinoza wrote to Oldenburg:

these disorders . . . do not move me to laughter nor even to tears, but rather to philosophizing, and to the better observation of human nature. I do not think it right for me to laugh at nature, much less to weep over it, when I consider than men, like the rest, are only a part of nature, and that I do not know how each part of nature is connected with the whole of it, and how with the other parts. (Ep 30, Spinoza to Oldenburg, September or October 1665; Oldenburg 1965–86: II,541)[78]

Perhaps that is the noblest lesson Spinoza took from his own philosophical vision of Man and Nature. Among the many lessons we today might draw from the same rich source, the most disturbing, yet the most exciting, must be that "Modern Technological Man" and "Man in the State of Nature" are one and the same thing. It is a lesson whose implications we show no sign of beginning to comprehend.[79]

NOTES

1 See Wolf 1935: 564–81 especially at pp. 571–75. Spinoza re-appears of course in the chapter on philosophy, pp. 650–6. It is worth recalling that the author of this serviceable history of early modern science is the eminent Spinoza scholar. See also Brett 1965: 394–406; Sahakian 1970: 34–8; and Klein 1970: 402–49 ("Spinoza's Hormic Psychology"). Oddly, Spinoza makes no appearance in Herrnstein and Boring 1965. For a list of other relevant studies see Nails 1986, to which may be added Neu 1977.

2 See Seligman and Johnson 1930–5: XIV,299–301 (by Benjamin Ginzburg); Sills 1968–79: XV,135–7 (by Rosalie L. Colie); and Miller 1987: 502–3 (by Robert J. McShea).

3 See Savan 1986: 97–9; Popkin 1986 and his chapter in this volume; and Curley 1995.

4 See Wolfson 1934: I,32; Pollock 1912; Parkinson 1954; Biasutti 1979;

Curley 1973a; Delahunty 1985; Lachterman 1978; McKeon 1928; Savan 1986; and Grene and Nails 1986.

5 Not forgetting bibliographers: see the thoughtful introduction (p. 305) to Nails 1986.

6 Nor can I examine Spinoza's presence in post–seventeenth-century scientific contexts, which would be a possibly more difficult assignment. At all events, I intend to stay at a safe distance from that special corner of Spinoza studies where one finds congregating, like wasps round a jamjar, authors of bizarre meditations on "Spinoza and" this or that twentieth-century scientist or scientific notion. Predictably, Einstein, Freud, Field Theories, and the Space–Time Continuum are the usual victims of these surreal diachronic assignations. For some examples the reader is invited to peruse Nails 1986, Bennett 1984: 91 et seq., and Hessing 1977. As a corrective to Bennett in this context, see Ariew 1987: 652–3.

7 On scholasticism and neoscholasticism in Dutch universities during the first half of the seventeenth century, especially the influential works of Burgersdijk, Heereboord, and Keckermann, see Dibon 1954. On Burgersdijk's thought, historical context, and influence see Bos and Krop 1993.

8 See Van Rooijen 1888: 180; Siebrand 1986: 65–66; Wolf's commentaries in Spinoza 1910: xxxi,190–2,194,198; and Wolfson 1934: I,64n2,81n1.

9 Plus ça change. . . . Theology, Law, and Medicine (add Dentistry) have succeeded to this day in fooling citizens and governments into believing that they are "higher" occupations, as is confirmed by the salary scales of all but the first profession.

10 In this period "economics" ("oeconomica") meant what we would today call "home management," "home economics," or "domestic economy."

11 See Keckermann 1614, "Praecognitorum philosophicorum liber primus, qui est de philosophiae natura"; Cap. I, "De nomine et definitione philosophiae," col. 7; Cap. II, "De philosophiae partitione," cols. 11–18. In Cap. II, Keckermann gives a long commentary on some of the drawbacks of partitioning philosophy into theoretical and active. See also Heereboord 1659: "Collegium logicum," "Positionum logicarum disputatio prima, de philosophiae et logicae natura," Theses 8–14, p. 1,. See also Burgersdijk 1651: "EPMHNEIA Logica: sive Synopseos logicae Burgersdicianae Explicatio," p. 277. Except where otherwise stated or indicated, all translations are my own.

12 Heereboord 1659: Collegium logicum, Positionum logicarum disputatio prima, de philosophiae et logicae natura, Theses 15–18, p. 1. Burgersdijk 1651: Lib. II, Cap. I (De definitione in genere, déque definitione nominali), Theorema II; p. 143, Lib. II, Cap. XXVIII (de methodo), and

Heereboord's *explicatio* in *"EPMHNEIA Logica: sive Synopseos logicae Burgersdicianae Explicatio,"* p. 127.

13 Goclenius 1613: 1010. Though it is probably not irrelevant in this context, I leave aside the other sense of *"scientia"* as *habitus*, that is, as an intellectual state attained, or quality or disposition possessed, by the "scientist." See Goclenius 1613: 623–5,1012; Heereboord 1659: *Collegium logicum, Positionum logicarum disputatio quarta, de Qualitate*, p. 6; Keckermann 1614: cols. 871–5, Lib. I, Cap. VI *(De explicatione qualitatum)*, *Exemplum primae speciei qualitatis nempe* Habitus.

14 In his otherwise valuable analysis of *scientia intuitiva*, Mignini fails to ask what Spinoza might have understood by *scientia* (Mignini 1990).

15 *Tractatus de Intellectus Emendatione*: Spinoza 1925: II, p. 6. C.I: 8, note a. *Tractatus Theologico-Politicus*, cap. V, XV, XX; *Tractatus Politicus*, cap. VIII. Spinoza 1925: III, pp. 73, 187, 243, 346.

16 Alsted 1649: Tom. IV *(Praecipuae Farragines disciplinarum)*, Lib. 35 *(Apodemica, Critica)*. Spinoza's *Theological-Political Treatise* might be described in Alstedian terms as a *farrago* of *politica, historia*, and, as Alsted's Tabula XXXVIII (Tom. I) puts it, *critica specialis theologica de libris Scripturae Sanctae*.

17 The *scientiae mediae* (middle sciences), a sub-division within speculative philosophy, operated "midway" between mathematics and physics, treating physical and empirically accessible objects in a mathematical way. The principal *scientiae mediae*, or "mixed mathematics," as they became known in seventeenth-century England, were optics, music, astronomy, and mechanics. See for example Keckermann 1614, *Generalis introductio in praecognita philosophica*, Cap. II *(De Philosophiae Partitione)*, col. 17. See also Gabbey 1992: 308–12.

18 ". . . Ethics, which, as everyone knows, must be founded on metaphysics and physics" (Ep 27, Spinoza to Willem van Blijenbergh, June 3, 1665).

19 See Gabbey 1992.

20 The contingent things defined in *Ethics* 4d3 are contingent only *for us*, who, attending only to their essence, find nothing that necessarily posits or excludes their existence. On Spinoza's necessitarianism see Garrett 1991; 1990c: 32–7.

21 "Epistemology" belongs to logic *de re* though not by name. I do not know when the term *epistemologia* first appeared, if it ever did, other than in modern neoscholastic manuals. The English term dates from as recently as 1856 (O.E.D.).

22 However, on Spinoza's model of organic structure, see the excellent studies Jonas 1973 and Duchesneau 1974, and on the possible influence on Spinoza's general physical thought of Lambert van Velthuysen's biological and medical writings, see Dunin-Borkowski 1933.

23 For valuable surveys of the scientific side to Spinoza's intellectual life, see McKeon 1928: 130–57; Siebrand 1986; Savan 1986; also the Introduction to Spinoza 1928, especially pages 39–43. For a defense of the unusual view that "his philosophy was strikingly disconnected from the sifting and interrogating science that went on around him," see Maull 1986.

24 Parkinson sees more significance in the number of Spinoza's "scientific" books than I do (Parkinson 1954: 2–3).

25 Originally there were more, since the internal evidence of the correspondence is that (at least) five letters are lost.

26 Since Spinoza did not read English, Oldenburg would have sent in fact the Latin translation that appeared in London in 1661: see Spinoza 1985a: 173n14. See also Letter 25, Oldenburg to Spinoza, April 28 (O.S.), 1665, where he tells Spinoza that the *Essays* has already appeared in Latin in England, and asks him therefore to try to prevent it being printed in Holland (Oldenburg 1965–86: II,381–2 [see also note 2]).

27 The reply was included in the second edition of *New experiments physico-mechanicall* (Oxford, 1662), and the Latin version (presumably sent to Spinoza) was published in 1663, though there is no extant evidence that Spinoza responded to Oldenburg's invitation to send him his comments on it.

28 See Petry's remarks in Spinoza 1985b: 96–7.

29 See Pascal 1663, also Spinoza 1985a: 187n51.

30 Klever misreads Spinoza's account of the transmutation, taking it to mean that Spinoza himself did the experiment, and moreover that its purpose was "to find out the structure of gold" (Klever 1990a: 124). The purpose of the operation was not to discover the *structure* of gold, but to find a way of *making* it from (in this instance) silver.

31 See McKeon 1965; Dutka 1953; Spinoza 1984–5; Freudenthal 1904: 298; Klever 1983; De Vet 1983, 1986; and Petry in Spinoza 1985b. De Vet 1986 produces an alternative author for the *Reeckening van den Regenboog*: Salomon Dierquens, a magistrate in The Hague. Petry 1994 rejects this hypothesis in the context of a more comprehensive critique of De Vet's position on the subject.

32 By "circle" (*"circulus"*) Spinoza presumably means a circular disc of glass.

33 If i is the angle of incidence between the ray and the radius of the globe or circular disc, with r the radius and μ the refractive index of the glass, then the distance from A to the intersection X of refracted ray and diameter AB is given by:

$$AX = \frac{r}{\sqrt{(\mu^2 - \sin^2 i)} - \cos i} + r$$

If X were always to coincide with B, that is, if AX = $2r$ for all values of i, then μ would have to depend on i, with $\mu^2 = 2 + 2 \cos i$. Equivalently, the angle of refraction would have to be always half the angle of incidence, as Wolf points out in his annotation to Letter 39 (Spinoza 1928: 434). An analysis of this sort would have been within the competence of the author of *Reeckening van den Regenboog*.

34 Huygens's *Tractatus de ratiociniis in aleae ludo*, originally written in Dutch, first appeared in Van Schooten's (unsatisfactory) Latin translation in the latter's *Exercitationes mathematicae*, a copy of which was in Spinoza's library (Van Rooijen 1888, no. 27, p. 154). See further Huygens 1888–1950: XIV,3–6;29–31n7, where the editors give the first French translation of the two propositions provided in answer to the first question in the *Reeckening van Kanssen* (attributed to Spinoza).

35 Antoine Arnauld and Pierre Nicole, *La logique, ou l'art de penser* (Paris, 1662). Cf. De Vet 1986: 297. Though it proves nothing either way, it is worth noting that Spinoza had in his library both *L'Art de penser* and the 1659 edition of J. H. Glazemaker's Dutch translation of the *Discours*. See Van Rooijen 1888: 141–2,187–8.

36 In the *Praefatio* Meyer writes confusingly that he often wished that someone well versed in analysis and synthesis, and in Descartes's writings and philosophy, would "render in the Synthetic order what Descartes wrote in the Analytic, and to demonstrate it in the manner familiar to the geometricians" (Spinoza 1985a: 227). But Descartes's *Principles of Philosophy* is not written in analytic form (nor is the *Meditations*, properly speaking: Garber 1992: 47–8), which leads Curley to infer from the *Praefatio* that Spinoza was unclear about Descartes's distinction between analysis and synthesis: Curley 1977, also Spinoza 1985a: 224n3. Siebrand disagrees, suggesting that the confusion is Meyer's alone, not Spinoza's: Siebrand 1986: 69. See also Garber and Cohen 1982: 141–7. On Spinoza's *Descartes's "Principles of Philosophy"* and his reception of Cartesian physics, see Dunin-Borkowski 1933–6: III,95–146; Siebrand 1986: 65–73; and Van der Hoeven 1973a, 1973b. To economize on notes in this section, I use only in-text references to the articles of Descartes's *Principles of Philosophy*, which can easily be located in Descartes 1964–74: VIII (1). I should make it clear that the text of the *Principles of Philosophy* that Spinoza used was the original Latin edition of 1644, not Picot's French translation of 1647.

37 Spinoza disliked Casearius, whom he found disagreeable and "more anxious for novelty than for truth." See Letter 9, Spinoza to Simon de Vries, March 1663.

38 Spinoza's instructions are duly reflected in Meyer's Preface. Readers are warned that Halbert Hains Britan's translation of Spinoza's text (Spinoza 1974) is thoroughly unreliable, and in places is quite appalling.

39 Proposition 14: "Each thing, in so far as it is simple and undivided, and is considered in itself alone, perseveres, as far as possible (*quantum in se est*), always in the same state." Proposition 15: "Every moved body tends, of itself, to continue to move along a straight line, not along a curved line."

40 See also the equally insightful McKeon 1928: 155–6.

41 Later, in *Principles of Philosophy* 3.57–9, Descartes examines circular motion in greater detail. See Gabbey 1980: 290–7 and Garber 1992: 218–23,285–8.

42 Gebhardt's reading of the sentence (Spinoza 1925: I,204, lines 6–10) is identical to that of the first edition, and the Dutch translation of 1664 conveys accurately the sense of the Latin text (Spinoza 1663: 64; 1664: 74).

43 It is clear from the simple diagram, which I omit, that CB is assumed to be a straight line.

44 Huygens was an Archimedean through and through. See the relevant articles in Bos 1980.

45 See Gabbey 1980: 248–60, and also Garber 1992: 188–93. For a survey of Scholastic senses of "*determinatio*" and cognates, see Goclenius 1613: 523–5.

46 See Gabbey 1980: 256–7. Note that although in *La Dioptrique, Discours Second*, the collisions are oblique, one of the bodies (earth, water, etc.) is assumed to be immovable, and the changes in speed of the ball are arbitrary. These devices are legitimate in the context of a demonstration of the law of optical refraction, but in the general case of oblique collision, both bodies are in motion, and the changes in speed (and direction) are precisely what one is trying to find.

47 It is modes in the Cartesian sense that are at issue here, not the modes of the mature Spinoza. I have translated Descartes's "*changement*" as "mutation," which is inelegant but technically precise. He is thinking of *mutatio* in the Peripatetic sense that includes instantaneous change, which is the case during hard-body collision, as in the Rules in the *Principles of Philosophy*. See further Gabbey 1980: 306–307n77,313n147. On the tangled relations between the PLMM and Descartes's collision Rules, see Gabbey 1980: 263–5.

48 Spinoza places 2p23 immediately before his account of Descartes's Rules of collision, and uses it to demonstrate them.

49 Lecrivain claims, without explanation, that in Descartes's "*Principles of Philosophy*" Descartes's minimal principle is "an application of the law of inertia," and states, without any justification, that in Spinoza's hands the principle "can perhaps be understood as the beginning of a principle of internal regulation – of an almost statistical nature – which will make possible a dynamic definition of individuality, notably in the *Ethics*" (Lecrivain 1986: 50).

50 Note Spinoza's use of *"mutatio"*; see note 47.

51 In their objection-and-reply on teleology in Spinoza, neither Curley nor Bennett mentions the appearance of Descartes's PLMM in *Descartes's "Principles of Philosophy,"* nor *à fortiori* does either of them examine its relevance to the issue in hand (Bennett 1990b; Curley 1990).

52 For a useful synopsis of Descartes's Seven Rules, together with translations of the Latin and French texts (1644, 1647) and of the important letter to Clerselier of February 17, 1645, see Garber 1992: 255–62.

53 I put "bulk" for *"molis"* rather than the equivalent "mass," which has a misleading Newtonian connotation.

54 Wolf mistakenly translates *"Cartesii Regulas motûs"* as "Descartes's Laws of Motion" (Spinoza 1928: 207). The treatise of Huygens that Spinoza had told Oldenburg about was the *De motu corporum ex percussione*, written about 1656 but not published until 1703, in which Huygens set out the first successful general theory of (perfectly elastic) collision.

55 It is possible that Spinoza simply could not reconcile Huygens's empirically respectable collision theory with Descartes's, which he seems to have accepted (apart from Rule 6) to the end of his life. After meeting him in 1676, Leibniz wrote: "*Spinoza ne voyait pas bien les défauts des règles du mouvement de M. Descartes; il fut surpris quand je commençai à lui montrer qu'elles violaient l'égalité de la cause et de l'effet*" (quoted from Gueroult 1968–74: II,552). Spinoza told Tschirnhaus that it is absolutely impossible to demonstrate the existence of bodies from Descartes's conception of extension, for matter at rest will stay at rest unless moved by a stronger external cause. "For that reason," concluded Spinoza, "I did not hesitate at one time to affirm that the Cartesian principles of natural things are useless, not to say absurd" (Ep 81, May 5, 1676). Whether this implies that the impact Rules too are useless *en bloc* is a moot point. The evidence of the *Ethics* is that for Spinoza many Cartesian principles of natural things were anything but useless.

56 On the difficulties attending Spinoza's simple and composite bodies in the context of his physics, and indeed on his physics as a whole, see Lachterman 1978.

57 See for example Gabbey 1980: 265–72.

58 Shirley ignores Spinoza's crucial use of *"communico"* (*"ut motûs suos invicem . . . communicent"*), thereby weakening his translation of the definition: "so as to preserve an unvarying relation of movement among themselves" (Spinoza 1982: 74).

59 I think it significant that in none of Descartes's impact Rules is any body *brought to rest* by the collision. That could be accidental (in the sense of being nothing more than a side effect of Descartes's faulty Rules), but I think it more likely that Descartes believed that bodies

coming to rest in his theory of collision might threaten his conservation law. I suspect that Spinoza felt the same in the case of his own system, though neither of them of course could deny that rest must have always existed. To pursue this story would take us too far afield, but see Gabbey 1973.

60 Like some Spinoza scholars, Shirley uses the hyphenated formula "motion-and-rest" for Spinoza's "*motus & quies*" (Spinoza 1982: 75). I think this is a mistake. The hyphens imply inseparability (like "Amos-'n-Andy" or "Punch-and-Judy"), but all Spinoza intends by "*motus & quies*" is that at any given time some bodies are in motion, some are at rest, without either state entailing the other. Yet one cannot be absolutely sure, since Spinoza never defines motion or rest. Tschirnhaus asked Spinoza for "the true definition of motion" in January 1675 (Ep 59). Spinoza replied that he had not yet formalized his ideas on the subject, but was reserving that for another time (Ep 60). The time seems not ever to have arrived, since we hear nothing further from Spinoza on the nature of motion and rest (other than their being infinite modes).

61 Matheron expresses Spinoza's "motion and rest" invariance as a meaningless (and dimensionally incorrect) formula in which the quantity of rest is measured by and indeed made equal to the mass, while the quantity of motion is measured by the more conventional "mass × speed." I have not incorporated into my own analysis the precise "1/3" given as an example of the "motion and rest" ratio in the *Short Treatise* II Preface Section 12, 14 (Spinoza 1985a: 96), because the passage in question is an addition possibly not by Spinoza. Anyway, the ratio 1/3 to express the motion/rest relation in the human individual means nothing in the absence of quantitative measures of both modes.

62 "*Appendice Nº 5. Disques tournants, pendules composés, corps composés, corps vivants.*" (Gueroult 1968–74: II,555–58). The problems of center of oscillation and (equivalently) center of percussion arise from properties of a rigid body (of any shape) rotating about an axis through the body. If the body is oscillating under gravity, find the length of the simple "string-and-bob" pendulum that oscillates with the same frequency (the center of oscillation problem). If it is swinging under any force, like a baseball or cricket bat, find the point on the body where the maximum force can be felt (the center of percussion problem). These problems, which were among the most difficult of mid–seventeenth-century mechanics, were solved partially by Descartes, Roberval, and others, and more comprehensively by Huygens.

63 See Savan 1986: 113.

64 On the whole question of experience in Spinoza's epistemology, see Curley 1973a; Parkinson 1954 passim; also Klever 1990a. On Spinoza

the empiricist and on seventeenth-century usages of and distinctions between "reason" and "experience" see Francks 1985, especially p. 180, and (on Spinoza and Bacon) pp. 187–91.

65 See Joachim 1901: 164; 1940: 25–26n2; and Curley 1973a: 35. The original Latin of the penultimate sentence of Aphorism 100 reads: "*Vaga enim Experientia et se tantum sequens (ut superius dictum est) mera palpatio est, et homines potius stupefacit quam informat*" (Bacon 1857–74: I,203). The precision of "*vaga experientia*" vanishes in the Ellis-Spedding-Heath translation: "For experience, when it wanders in its own track, is, as I have already remarked, mere groping in the dark, and confounds men rather than instructs them" (Bacon 1857–74: IV,95).

66 In Chapter 5 ("Properties of Terms") of his *Introductiones in logicam*, William of Sherwood (thirteenth century) distinguishes three modes of simple supposition, the third of which he explains in the following way:

The third mode occurs as follows: "pepper is sold here and in Rome." This supposition is unlike the first, since the species itself is not sold, and unlike the second, since "pepper" is not used here [for everything belonging to the species] insofar as it is pepper. Instead, "pepper" here supposits for its significatum [as] related in a general, unfixed way to the things belonging to it. Thus it is often said that this is unfixed (*vaga*) supposition. [A term having this third mode of simple supposition] supposits for a species insofar as [it does so] through individuals belonging to the species, but undesignated (*non signata*). It is as if someone asked "what animal is useful for plowing?" and one answered "the ox"; in answering one does not intend to speak of a particular ox, but simply *ox*. Likewise, whoever says "pepper is sold here and in Rome" does not intend to speak of some pepper in particular, but simply of *pepper.*" (Sherwood 1966: 112; brackets as in printed text)

Note Kretzmann's translation of "*vaga*" as "unfixed." Although in William's text "unfixed" could be replaced without loss by "undetermined," "unfixed experience," as a possibility for Spinoza's "*experientia vaga*," would sound silly. A better alternative for "undetermined" is given in the next sentence: "undesignated" ("*non signata*"). Note also that the use of "*vaga*" in this way pre-dates William's treatise ("thus it is often said"): cf. the quotation from Goclenius's *Lexicon philosophicum* below in text.

67 See Burgersdijk 1651: lib. I, cap. II (*De themate simplici & complexo, universali & singulari*) p. 9; and *EPMHNEIA Logica: sive Synopseos logicae Burgersdicianae Explicatio*, p. 5.

68 For the sake of illustration, I assume that Spinoza did not just hear about the deaths of the last four, but saw the bodies as well. Merely

hearing about the deaths, without seeing the bodies, would be *perceptio ex auditu.*

69 The terms *"mutilatè"* and *"confusè"* used here and elsewhere by Spinoza also function in technical senses in Peripatetic texts, but to explore the question would take us too far afield. However, as an *entrée* to this unexplored aspect of Spinoza's thought, see Goclenius's article on *"confusum,"* partly quoted above.

70 See further McKeon 1928: 133–7; Joachim 1940: 102–11; Curley 1973a; and Savan 1986: 110.

71 See the important analysis in McKeon 1928: 152–3, also pages 133–5 and 144–5.

72 Boyle was not aware that the coal contributed to the formation of the fixed nitre.

73 For further details on the Boyle–Spinoza dispute see McKeon 1928: 137–57; Daudin 1948; Hall and Hall 1964; Oldenburg 1965–86: I,466–70 (editors' notes on Spinoza to Oldenburg, April 1662); Yakira 1988; and particularly Clericuzio 1990: 573–9.

74 See Descartes, *Principles of Philosophy* 4.110, and Plate XXI, Figure iii.

75 See Letter 6, Spinoza to Oldenburg, [April 1662]; Letter 11, Oldenburg to Spinoza, April 3 (O.S.), 1663; Oldenburg 1965–86: I,448–54 (autograph in the Royal Society), 458–63 (translation); II,38 (Latin), 41 (translation).

76 The same point is reiterated in Letter 16, Oldenburg to Spinoza, 4 August 1663 (O.S.) (Oldenburg 1965–86: II,101–3). See Clericuzio 1990: 574–5.

77 Commenting on this passage in some notes he wrote on Spinoza's philosophy around 1707, Leibniz countered with his view that "every substance whatsoever is a kingdom within a kingdom, but one in precise harmony with everything else" (Leibniz 1989: 280). For Leibniz, too, humans are therefore part of Nature, though not of course in a Spinozistic sense. Leibniz's notes on Spinoza appear in a longer discussion on Johann Georg Wachter's *Elucidarius Cabalisticus* (Rome, 1706), one chapter of which is "On the agreement between the Cabala and Spinoza." See Leibniz 1989: 272–3.

78 Oldenburg included this part of Spinoza's letter in his letter to Boyle of October 10 (O.S.), 1665 (Oldenburg 1965–86: II,557–8).

79 I am grateful to Marjorie Grene, Michael Petry, and Samuel Shirley for helpful comments and suggestions arising out of their reading of an earlier draft of this chapter.

5 Spinoza's metaphysical psychology

Spinoza is a metaphysician. I emphasize this fact here (and in my title) because one can discover what is most exciting and important about Spinoza's psychology only by seeing it as emerging from his metaphysics. Spinoza is a systematic philosopher and nowhere is his system more ambitious and under more strain than in his attempt to derive an account of human motivation, affects, and other mental states from his general metaphysics.

This project of deriving psychology from metaphysics stems from Spinoza's guiding belief in naturalism about human beings – a belief he famously expresses as the view that man in nature is not a kingdom within a kingdom (E 3pr). For Spinoza, the principles at work throughout nature in general also govern human psychology. The clearest statement of his view occurs in the Preface to Part 3 of the *Ethics*:

[N]ature is always the same, and its virtue and power of acting are everywhere the same, i.e., the laws and rules of nature, according to which all things happen, and change from one form to another, are always and everywhere the same. So the way of understanding the nature of anything, of whatever kind, must also be the same, viz. through the universal laws and rules of nature. The affects, therefore, of hate, anger, envy, etc., considered in themselves, follow from the same necessity and force of nature as the other singular things.[1]

As this passage indicates, in order to establish his naturalism, Spinoza would need to show that the following two claims are true:

    (1) There are laws or rules governing the psychological states of human beings.[2]

192

(2) These laws or rules are instances of more general laws or rules operative throughout nature.

The main task of this chapter is to analyze and evaluate Spinoza's way of carrying out this naturalistic program in psychology. In light of (1) and (2), I will divide this task into three parts. First, I will investigate those general metaphysical principles which are central to Spinoza's psychology, but without, at this stage, delineating their purported psychological ramifications. I will then determine the way in which Spinoza applies these metaphysical principles to human beings and their psychology. It will become clear that despite his naturalistic pronouncements, Spinoza sometimes veers from a strict naturalistic path. In the third section of the chapter, I will focus on (1)'s claim that laws govern psychological phenomena. As we will see, in many instances, one can usefully explain these principles on their own terms, without paying specific attention to the way in which Spinoza attempts to derive these principles from more general metaphysical views.

One should be aware at the outset that Spinoza does not successfully carry out his project for psychology. The general metaphysics, the application of this to psychology, and the psychology taken on its own all fall prey to grave gaps and incoherencies. The reasons for this will become apparent soon enough. But this failure should not obscure the fact that Spinoza's general program of naturalizing psychology is a valuable and appealing one and that Spinoza's execution of it, even where unsuccessful, is a rich source of philosophical insight.[3]

I. THE METAPHYSICAL ACCOUNT: STRIVING, SELF-PRESERVATION, AND POWER OF ACTING

Let us begin with the metaphysical claims that will be relevant to psychology. The most important of these is: "Each thing, insofar as it is in itself, strives to persevere in its being" (E 3p6).[4] In this section, I will show what this claim means, why it is false, and why Spinoza might have been led to make it. I will also chart and explain some of the general metaphysical implications Spinoza takes *Ethics* 3p6 to have. A particular theme of this section is that the metaphysical claims central to Spinoza's psychology are often subject to conflicting interpretations. This suggests that, in this area, Spinoza may be guilty of conflating importantly different theses.

The meaning of 3p6

The first thing to note about 3p6 is that for Spinoza the striving of a thing to persevere in its being is equivalent to its striving to persevere in existence or its striving to preserve itself (for example, E 4p22). A more difficult issue in interpreting 3p6 concerns the meanings of the key terms "strives" ("*conatur*") and "insofar as it is in itself" ("*quantum in se est*"). Although commentators have often investigated the meanings of these terms, they have not, I believe, recognized the potential significance of Spinoza's inclusion of *both* terms in a *single* proposition. For that reason, after examining the meaning of each of these terms separately, I will investigate the import that they have together.

Unfortunately, 3p6 and the immediate context do not provide enough information for us to be able to separate out the different contributions these two locutions make to the meaning of the proposition as a whole. For that reason, when unpacking these locutions, I will often turn to other, related texts in which they occur. A comparison with Descartes's use of these terms will also prove quite illuminating.

I will focus on the meaning of "strives" first. It is important to realize at the outset that this term by itself does not carry any genuinely psychological implications. The point in 3p6 is supposed to apply to things in general: rocks and tables can be said to strive as well as dogs and human beings. Spinoza is, of course, a panpsychist – for him each thing is animate to some degree (E 2p13s). Thus a striving table is an animate thing that strives. But the fact that a table strives does not, for Spinoza, presuppose that it has mentality. Spinoza's attribution of striving to all things is made independently of the considerations that lead to his panpsychism.[5]

Striving is, then, for Spinoza a nonpsychological notion. This accords with Descartes's use of the term. But this is not the only point of agreement here and, for this reason, examining Descartes's positive characterization of striving will shed much light on Spinoza's own account. Descartes offers his definition of striving in terms of the striving of a certain kind of physical object:

When I say that the globules of the second element strive (*conari*) to move away from the centres around which they revolve, it should not be thought that I am implying that they have some thought from which this striving (*conatus*) proceeds. I mean merely that they are positioned and pushed into motion in such a way that they will in fact travel in that direction, unless they are prevented (*impediantur*) by some other cause. (*Principles of Philosophy* 3.56; Descartes 1985: I,259)

This passage suggests the following Cartesian definition of striving in general:

> x strives to do F (e.g., move in a certain direction) iff x's state is such that it will do F unless prevented by external causes.

It is clear from this definition and from the above quote that what x strives to do is, in part, a function of what its state is at a given moment. The globules, for example, strive to move in a certain direction only because of their current position and motion. This shows that a given object can strive for different things at different times, depending on its state at those different moments.

A related passage is *Principles of Philosophy* 2.39 (Descartes 1985: I,241–2) where Descartes says that a moving body will continue moving in a rectilinear fashion, unless it is deflected by other bodies: "All motion is in itself rectilinear; and hence any body moving in a circle always *tends* (*tendere*) to move away from the centre of the circle which it describes" (emphasis added). Descartes elaborates this as follows: "[E]very piece of matter, considered in itself (*seorsim spectatam*), always tends to continue moving, not in any oblique path but only in a straight line. This is true despite the fact that many particles are often forcibly deflected by the impact of other bodies." Descartes's point here concerns tending and not, apparently, striving. However, by eliciting the general account of tending implicit in this passage, we can see that the notions of striving and tending are equivalent for Descartes. Notice that whether or not a body tends to move in a straight line depends in part on its state, on whether or not it is already moving at a given moment. So tending, like striving, is a function of one's state. The above passage also makes clear another similarity between tending and striving: Both concern what a given object will do unless prevented by external causes. Thus the general account of tending at work here seems to be:

x tends to do F iff x's state is such that it will do F unless prevented by external causes.

Since "tending" is defined in the same way as "striving," these terms are synonymous for Descartes.[6]

I think that Spinoza (at least most of the time) uses "strives" in the way that Descartes uses this term and the term "tends." Important evidence for this claim comes from the fact that Spinoza is, of course, thoroughly familiar with the Cartesian usage and represents it accurately in *Descartes's "Principles of Philosophy." Descartes's "Principles of Philosophy"* 3d3 is Spinoza's version of the definition of "striving" contained in *Principles of Philosophy* 3.56: "By striving for motion (*conatum ad motum*) we do not understand any thought, but only that a part of matter is so placed and stirred to motion, that it really would go somewhere if it were not prevented by (*impediretur*) any cause." The counterpart of *Principles of Philosophy* 2.39 is *Descartes's "Principles of Philosophy"* 2p17.[7]

Further evidence for Spinoza's understanding of the term "strives" comes from the appendix to *Descartes's "Principles of Philosophy," Metaphysical Thoughts* I.6. There Spinoza speaks of a body A that strives to persevere in its state of motion. He says that in such a case A cannot be "losing, of itself, its force of moving." That is, its loss of motion can only be explained by things external to A. Spinoza's point, then, is that for A to strive to continue moving is for it to be such that external causes are required for it to be the case that it does not continue moving. This seems to fit perfectly with the Cartesian account of striving.

Let us turn to the phrase "it is in itself." This also is a Cartesian term with which Spinoza is familiar. The phrase famously occurs in *Principles of Philosophy* 2.37: "[E]ach thing, insofar as it is in itself (*quantum in se est*), always continues in the same state; and thus what is once in motion always continues to move" (Descartes 1985: I,240–1).[8] What is it for a thing, insofar as it is in itself, to do something, to continue moving? The subsequent passage provides an answer:

[E]ach thing, insofar as it is simple and undivided, always remains in the same state, insofar as it is in itself (*quantum in se est*), and never changes except as a result of external causes. Thus, if a particular piece of matter is square, we can be sure without more ado that it will remain square for ever, unless something coming from outside changes its shape. If it is at rest, we hold that it will never begin to move unless it is pushed into motion by some cause. And if it moves, there is equally no reason for thinking it will ever lose this motion of its own accord (*sua sponte*) and without being checked by (*impeditam*) something else. Hence we must conclude that what is in motion always, insofar as it is in itself (*quantum in se est*) continues to move. (*Principles of Philosophy* 2.37)

Descartes's point here seems to be that when simple and undivided things change their state, this change must be a result of factors external to the thing. The qualifier "insofar as it is in itself" in the initial statement of the law of motion thus seems to mark the fact that a simple and undivided thing that is moving will continue to do so unless prevented by external causes.[9]

On the basis of this example we can arrive at a general definition of what it is for a thing, insofar as it is in itself, to do F:

> x, insofar as it is in itself, does F iff x's state is such that it will do F unless prevented by external causes.

Here we can see that for Descartes, what it is for x, insofar as it is in itself, to do F is the same as what it is for x to strive to do F.[10]

The same equivalence seems to hold for Spinoza. In *Descartes's "Principles of Philosophy"* 2p14 and its demonstration, he accurately captures the Cartesian meaning of the qualifier "insofar as it is in itself." Further, this reading of the locution fits nicely with Spinoza's technical use of the term "in itself" ("*in se*"). For Spinoza, as Curley and others have pointed out, to say that something is in itself is to say that it is independent of external causes.[11] Things can, of course, be more or less subject to outside influences and that is why it makes sense to speak of the extent to which something is in itself. This suggests that, for Spinoza, to say that x, insofar as it is in itself, does F is equivalent to saying that x, insofar as it is independent of outside causes or insofar as it is left to itself, does F. This is completely in line with the Cartesian sense of the sentence "x, insofar as it is in itself, does F." Because, for Descartes, this sentence is equivalent to the sentence "x strives to do F" and because, as we have seen, Spinoza also accepts the Cartesian reading of this latter sentence, it follows that Spinoza, like Descartes, treats the two sentences as equivalent.

With this understanding of the terms "insofar as it is in itself" and "strives," we can offer an interpretation of *Ethics* 3p6. All we need to do is substitute the appropriate defining phrases for the key terms in the proposition:

> Each thing, insofar as it is in itself, strives to persevere in its being.

First let us substitute for the phrase "insofar as it is in itself." The result is:

> (a) For each thing x, x's state is such that, unless prevented by external causes, it will strive to persevere in its being.

Now let us substitute for the term "strives" as it appears in (a):

> (b) For each thing x, x's state is such that, unless prevented by external causes, x's state will be such that, unless prevented by external causes, x will persevere in its being.

It is not immediately clear that (b) makes sense at all. There is an air of redundancy or even incoherence about it. The problem arises from the fact that Spinoza uses both crucial terms ("insofar as it is in itself" and "strives") in a single proposition.[12] This difficulty does not arise in Descartes, who is careful (as far as I can tell) to separate occurrences of the two terms.[13]

Nevertheless, there is an interesting way of making sense of (b). And, although I will ultimately conclude that this is not the way Spinoza primarily intends 3p6, this reading is important to consider because it will provide a clue to claims Spinoza makes elsewhere in the *Ethics*. To see how to make sense of (b), let us return for the moment to (a):

> (a) For each thing x, x's state is such that, unless prevented by external causes, it will strive to persevere in its being.

This can be read as saying that each thing is such that it will strive to persevere in its being unless external causes prevent it from so striving. (a) is opening up the possibility that external causes can act on x in such a way that x no longer strives to persevere in its being. Now to say that x strives to persevere in its being is to say that external causes are required in order for it to be the case that x ceases to exist or does not persevere in its being. Thus (a) is opening up the possibility that external causes can act on x in such a way that external causes are no longer required to bring about x's nonexistence. The external causes will have brought it about that x's state is sufficient, without any further input from outside, for the nonexistence of x. The point behind (a), and thus (b), is that x will be such that external causes are no longer required for its nonexistence only if external causes have caused x to be in a state in which external causes are no longer required for x's nonexistence. This reading does, I believe, show (a) and (b) to be coherent.

Nevertheless, I do not think that (a) and (b), so understood, capture Spinoza's meaning in 3p6. The main problem is that, as I have pointed out, on this reading Spinoza is leaving open the possibility that some things do not strive to persevere in their being. And, however plausible such a claim might be, it conflicts with a thesis at the heart of Spinoza's ethics. In 3p7, Spinoza claims: "The striving by which each thing strives to persevere in its being is nothing but the actual essence of the thing." This proposition grounds Spinoza's egoistic ethical standpoint as expressed in the view that "the striving to preserve oneself is the first and only foundation of virtue" (E 4p22c). Since Spinoza's ethical egoism is absolutely crucial to his system, 3p7 must be seen as of paramount importance. From the fact that, according to 3p7, the striving to persevere in its being is the essence of a thing, it follows that a thing cannot exist without such striving.[14] However, if we interpret 3p6 along the lines of (b), we must regard it as saying that a thing can exist without such striving. Thus (b) is incompatible with 3p7. Given the significance of 3p7, I think we should avoid any interpretation of 3p6 which renders it incompatible with 3p7. A related reason for avoiding such an interpretation would be that the claims that it must see as incompatible are juxtaposed in the text. It is not very likely that Spinoza would have in mind a certain understanding of 3p6 and then immediately make an incompatible claim in 3p7.

How then should we interpret 3p6? I think the best course is to read it as if Spinoza had used only one of the pair of terms "insofar as it is in itself" and "strives." There is support for such a move in the fact that Spinoza often uses "strives" without "insofar as it is in itself" when he makes claims derived from 3p6 (see, e.g., 3p28 and 3p29). *Ethics* 3p6 would then be interpreted as:

(c) For each thing x, x's state is such that, unless prevented by external causes, x will persevere in its being.

Although (c) does not do as good a job as (b) does of accounting for the presence of both "insofar as it is in itself" and "strives" in 3p6, it does convey the import which each term taken individually would have. Further, (c) does not entail that a thing could exist without striving to persevere in its being and thus, unlike (b), (c) is compatible with the important 3p7. This is not to say that there is no support for reading 3p6 along the lines of (b). In the next subsection, I will present evidence for the view that Spinoza, in a certain application of 3p6, inclines towards a reading like (b).[15] Nevertheless, I think that (c), instead of (b), expresses Spinoza's primary understanding of 3p6.

Is 3p6 true?

The evidence that Spinoza has some tendency to understand 3p6 in terms of (b) emerges by considering counterexamples to 3p6 construed as:

(c) For each thing x, x's state is such that, unless prevented by external causes, x will persevere in its being.

As many have noted, there seem to be many counterexamples to this view. Consider an example from Wallace Matson: "The sun will perish, and it is possible, indeed highly probable that it will perish by burning itself out, by depleting its nuclear and then its gravitational energy" (Matson 1977a: 407). The sun seems to be such that it will go out of existence, even if external causes do not prevent the sun from existing – say by being struck by a bigger star. Matson discusses a similar example which Curley describes as follows: "Imagine a candle, burning on Spinoza's table. . . . Will it not, if left to itself, burn itself out, and thereby destroy itself?"[16] Even if external causes, such as an exploding bomb, do not prevent the candle from existing, the candle will still go out of existence. Also relevant here is the case of a person who commits suicide. A person in a suicidal frame of mind seems to be such that even if external causes, such as a murderer, do not prevent this person from existing, he will still cease to exist. All of these cases seem to be counterexamples to 3p6. Now I do not think we can get Spinoza completely out of difficulty here. While some potential counterexamples may be able to be explained away, it does seem quite plausible that at least some things can destroy themselves and thus can be such that they are able to cease to exist, even if external causes do not prevent them from existing. This would undermine 3p6 – or at least 3p6 interpreted as (c). Although, for the reasons given earlier, I do think (c) expresses Spinoza's primary understanding 3p6, there is, as I said, evidence that Spinoza sometimes understands 3p6 in terms of:

(b) For each thing x, x's state is such that, unless prevented by external causes, x's state will be such that, unless prevented by external causes, x will persevere in its being.

To the extent that Spinoza understands 3p6 in this way, he may be able to avoid at least some of the above counterexamples.

To see why this is so, recall that, construed as (b), 3p6 does not assert or imply that each thing always strives to persevere in its being. Spinoza would, on this interpretation, be allowing that external causes might act on a thing in such a way that it no longer strives for persistence or, equivalently, external causes might act on a thing in such a way that it can cease to exist even if not prevented from existing by external causes.

This reading would help with the potential counterexamples to 3p6 in the following way. Consider a person who commits suicide – a person who, it is natural to say, does not strive to persist. 3p6, read as (b), can allow this as long as the person's failure to strive for persistence is a result of external causes. This is indeed how Spinoza accounts for suicidal persons in 4p20s: "No one . . . unless he is defeated by causes external, and contrary, to his nature, neglects to seek (*appetere*) his own advantage, or to preserve his being." Since Spinoza uses the verb "*appetere*" here and since appetite (*appetitus*) is, for Spinoza as we will see, the striving of a human being, Spinoza seems to be saying that a suicidal person fails to strive to preserve his own being. But, Spinoza emphasizes, this can be the case only if external factors have caused this person no longer to strive for his own persistence.[17]

Similarly, one might grant that a burning candle is such that external causes are no longer required to bring about its nonexistence, and thus that the candle does not strive for persistence. One might reconcile this claim with 3p6, interpreted as (b), by pointing out that the candle is in such a state because of external factors. The external thing that lit the candle caused it to be the case that the candle does not strive for persistence.[18]

Thus reading 3p6 along the lines of (b) would enable us to avoid at least some of the counterexamples to that proposition and, significantly, 4p20s indicates that Spinoza himself would handle the counterexamples in this way. Nevertheless, I still do not think that we can see (b) as expressing Spinoza's primary understanding of 3p6. Despite the fact that interpreting 3p6 as (c) leaves it open to counterexamples, such an interpretation, as I have explained, accords best with Spinoza's overall ethical position.[19] Spinoza's apparent leaning toward (b) in 4p20s together with his apparent espousal of (c) does reveal, however, that there are conflicting and perhaps conflated strands in Spinoza's thought on the striving for self-preservation.

The argument for 3p6

Yet another conflation in Spinoza's thought on these matters emerges from an examination of the way Spinoza argues for 3p6. This argument is based on 3p4: "No thing can be destroyed except through an external cause."[20]

Since x would be destroyed, but not through external causes, iff x's state at a given moment sufficed for its destruction, I take 3p4 to amount to the claim: "(d) For each thing x, it cannot be the case that x's state suffices for its destruction." *Ethics* 3p6 follows directly from 3p4 understood in this way. On this reading, 3p4 is saying that factors beyond x's state must be responsible for x's destruction. Thus, in the absence of such responsible factors, x is not destroyed and thus x persists in existence. This is just the claim of 3p6, interpreted as (c).

Ethics 3p4, interpreted as (d), is subject to the kinds of counterexamples that seemed to undermine 3p6. The state of the burning candle does, for example, seem to suffice for its destruction. Thus 3p4, interpreted in this way, seems to be false. However, as with 3p6, there is evidence that Spinoza accepts a different reading of 3p4, a reading that is not subject to the familiar counterexamples. After introducing this other reading of 3p4, I will present evidence that Spinoza may understand 3p4 in this way.

To set up the discussion of this other reading, I need to say a little about the distinction between x's state and x's essence or nature and also about Spinoza's views on nonessential properties. x's essence, of course, would only include x's essential features. x's state at a given moment would include all of its properties at that moment. Because x's essence remains the same no matter what state it is in, it follows that x's state at any given moment includes all of its essential features. Thus, if Spinoza allows that x has nonessential features, then he would hold that x's state is broader than x's essence.

Spinoza does explicitly allow that things have nonessential properties. Consider, 3p8: "The striving by which each thing strives to persevere in its being involves no finite time, but an indefinite time." As we have seen, Spinoza identifies this striving with the thing's actual essence (E 3p7). Thus, it seems that, from x's essence alone it cannot be determined how long x will exist. So, if x does have the property of being, say, ten years old, it does not have this property by virtue of its essence alone. This shows that this property is not essential to x.[21] Spinoza would, I believe, also hold that very many other properties of a thing are nonessential. Thus, for him, x's state is broader than x's essence.

Let us turn now to an alternative reading of 3p4. As I will explain shortly, at one point in the demonstration of 3p4, Spinoza does not seem primarily concerned with cases in which x's state at a given moment suffices for x's destruction; rather Spinoza's focus in 3p4d seems to be on cases in which x's *essence* suffices for x's destruction. On such a reading, 3p4 is equivalent not to

(d) For each thing x, it cannot be the case that x's state suffices for its destruction,

but rather to

(e) For each thing x, it cannot be the case that x's essence suffices for x's destruction.

Because, as we have just seen, Spinoza holds that a thing's essence is narrower than its state at a given moment, it is clear that for him (e) is a weaker claim than (d); (e) is implied by, but does not imply, (d). It follows that if Spinoza is merely saying in 3p4 that x's essence is not sufficient for x's destruction, he may not be intending to rule out all cases in which x's state suffices for x's destruction. That is, he could allow that x's state suffices for x's destruction, as long as the set of x's features that do suffice for its destruction contains some nonessential features.

This opens up a way of handling potential counterexamples to 3p4. Although the candle's destruction follows from its state, that destruction seems to depend on nonessential features of the candle. The destruction of the candle seems to follow from the fact that it has been lit and, arguably, the property of having been lit is not essential to the candle. Since the destruction of the candle depends on a nonessential feature, such a case would not violate 3p4 understood in the above way. Other potential counterexamples to 3p4 could, perhaps, be dealt with in a similar manner.

As I mentioned, there is evidence in 3p4d that Spinoza understands 3p4 in this way.[22] Here is 3p4d: "[T]he definition of any thing affirms, and does not deny, the thing's essence, or it posits the thing's essence, and does not take it away. So while we attend only to the thing itself, and not to external causes, we shall not be able to find anything in it which can destroy it." The first sentence suggests that Spinoza is claiming that, by focusing on x's essence, we cannot find anything that would account for its destruction. This emphasis on the thing's essence suggests that when, in the second sentence, Spinoza says that by attending to the thing itself (*rem ipsam*) we cannot find anything which would destroy it, the phrase "the thing itself" is meant to refer to x's essence in particular (and not, e.g., to x's state at a given moment). This suggests, in turn, that 3p4 itself should be read simply as ruling out the destruction of a thing by virtue of its essence alone. Thus there is some indication that Spinoza understands 3p4 along the lines of (e).

If such an interpretation of 3p4 allows it to avoid counterexamples and seems to be suggested by Spinoza's own 3p4d, then perhaps we should read 3p4 as (e) rather than as (d). The problem is, however, that Spinoza sees 3p4 as entailing 3p6; and while (d), as we have seen, does entail 3p6 interpreted as (c), (e) does not. 3p6 interpreted as (c) requires that x's state not suffice for its destruction. However, 3p4 interpreted as (e) does not rule this out – it merely excludes the possibility that x's essence suffices for its destruction.[23]

Because

(i) (as we have seen) there is good reason to construe 3p6 as (c),

(ii) 3p4 interpreted as (e) does not entail 3p6 interpreted as (c), and

(iii) Spinoza clearly sees 3p4 as entailing 3p6,

there is some reason against interpreting 3p4 as (e). Reading 3p4 as (d), by contrast, enables us to preserve the validity of the inference to 3p6 interpreted as (c). But despite this relative advantage of (d), there is some evidence (in 3p4d) that Spinoza does understand 3p4 as (e). And (d), while providing a natural understanding of the terms in which Spinoza expresses 3p4, has the liability of being subject to some obvious counterexamples to which (e) is not subject. There is, then, no one reading of 3p4 that is both free from obvious counterexamples and such as to entail 3p6 interpreted as (c). In light of all this, I think we must view Spinoza as conflating the two different readings of 3p4. (d) seems to be at work in the derivation of 3p6 from 3p4, but (e) seems to be at work in 3p4d itself.[24]

In order to keep track of the various conflations and conflicts in 3p4 and 3p6, the following summary may be helpful. One potential reading of 3p6 is as

(b) For each thing x, x's state is such that, unless prevented by external causes, x's state will be such that, unless prevented by external causes, x will persevere in its being.

(b) faithfully accounts for the presence of both "strives" and "insofar as it is in itself" in 3p6. (b) also enables 3p6 to avoid certain counterexamples by a strategy apparently employed by Spinoza himself in 4p20s. However, (b) conflicts with the all-important claim in 3p7 that the striving for persistence is the essence of a thing. This fact indicates that what Spinoza generally has in mind by 3p6 is not (b), but rather the closely related

(c) For each thing x, x's state is such that, unless prevented by external causes, x will persevere in its being.

(c) is subject to the counterexamples that (b) avoids, but perhaps Spinoza fails to see this because he conflates (c) with (b). Thus it must be admitted that Spinoza does not properly distinguish (b) from (c).

Spinoza regards 3p4 as entailing 3p6 and this immediately suggests that 3p4 is to be read as

(d) For each thing x, it cannot be the case that x's state suffices for its destruction.

However, (d) is subject to counterexamples. Moreover, there is evidence in 3p4d that Spinoza understands 3p4 as

(e) For each thing x, it cannot be the case that x's essence suffices for x's destruction.

(e) is not subject to these counterexamples, but, unfortunately (e) does not entail 3p6 interpreted as (c); though, I believe, it entails 3p6 interpreted as (b). Since there are reasons for and against interpreting 3p4 as (d) and interpreting it as (e), we must conclude that in his understanding of 3p4 Spinoza does not properly distinguish (d) from (e).

I think that the above account goes a long way toward explaining what Spinoza means by 3p4 and 3p6 and why he accepts them despite their apparent falsity. I have not, however, attempted to deal with all the interpretive difficulties arising from what can now be seen as the rather rich text in and around 3p6. In particular, I have not explored 3p5's role in demonstrating 3p6. I have treated 3p4 (on some reading) as more or less directly entailing 3p6 and Spinoza, in effect, treats 3p4 in this way too. For, although he cites 3p5 in his proof of 3p6, 3p5 is proved with the help only of 3p4. Thus, formally speaking, 3p5 is a superfluous middle man here. Exactly why Spinoza includes 3p5 is an intriguing matter, but I do not have space to take this up here.[25]

The truth in 3p6

I have been very critical of Spinoza's conclusion in 3p6 and of his way of reaching it, but now I want to sketch briefly why I think that Spinoza was onto an important truth here, even if he ultimately mischaracterizes it.

Ethics 3p6 says that all things strive to preserve themselves. While this may be false as it stands, I think Spinoza is right to this extent: The striving for self-preservation is *in some way* built into the notion of at least some things – viz. complex individuals.[26] I will show how this is so by outlining a largely Spinozistic account of complex individuality. Then I will consider how much of this account Spinoza actually accepts.

What makes a certain collection of physical objects itself a complex individual? Consider, for example, my dining room chair which is made up of several different pieces of wood, nails, etc. Or consider my telephone which is made up of a receiver, buttons, etc. In each case, the members of a certain collection of physical objects unite to form another, unified physical individual.

But other collections of physical objects do not achieve such unity – e.g., consider the collection made up of my chair and telephone. This is not in any intuitive sense a single physical individual, but rather a nonunified, mere collection. Why does the collection of the parts of the chair constitute a single individual, while the chair–telephone collection does not?

A plausible answer is as follows.[27] The members of the chair–telephone collection are not responsive to changes in one another in any systematic way. If I move the chair from my dining room to my office or if I start cutting up the chair, nothing happens to the telephone. Similarly, changes in the telephone leave the chair unscathed. By contrast, the pieces of wood, etc. that make up the chair itself are responsive to one another. If I move the back of the chair then, typically, the rest of the parts follow. The parts of the chair have a tendency to stay in a certain overall relation. I can, of course, disrupt the relation these parts bear to one another. I can, as I said, cut up the chair. But, in very many cases at least, the members of the collection that is the chair respond to changes in one another in a way that enables them to maintain the same overall relation to one another. The parts do, in other words, quite often keep the shape of a chair. By contrast, there is little or no tendency for the members of the chair–telephone collection to maintain a certain overall relation. The changes in the telephone do not typically cause changes in the chair that enable the chair and the telephone to remain in the same overall relation.

Thus a complex individual, qua complex individual, has constituents that are, quite often at least, sensitive to one another in such a way that they preserve a certain overall relation among themselves.[28]

Out of this account of what constitutes complex individuality, we can construct an account of what constitutes the persistence of such an individual over time. The members of the collection of bodies constituting an individual do not, of course, always succeed in preserving a certain overall relation among themselves. Outside forces and perhaps internal forces can overwhelm the individual. But, when the members of the collection do succeed in preserving this overall relation among one another, it is plausible to say that the complex individual persists. Thus the preservation of the relation among the parts is sufficient for the preservation of the chair. It also seems to be necessary. The chair persists only if this relation is maintained. If the relation is not maintained (as when, for example, a bomb explodes near the chair), the chair ceases to exist. Given this necessary and sufficient condition, it seems that the preservation of a complex individual over time consists of its constituents' maintaining a certain relation among themselves.[29]

Thus, given that each individual is necessarily such that, in very many situations, its constituents preserve a certain relation among one another, and given that such preservation is tantamount to the preservation of the individual itself, it follows that an individual is necessarily such that, in very many situations, it succeeds in preserving itself. The point is that we could not make sense of something as being a complex individual if it did not have parts which, in a large number of circumstances, were sensitive to one another in such a way as to preserve the individual itself.

The fact that, in very many circumstances, the parts of an individual are sensitive in this way to one another indicates that, in those circumstances, the individual *strives* (in Spinoza's sense) to preserve itself. Because of the responsiveness of the parts to one another, the individual is, in the relevant circumstances, such that it will preserve itself, unless prevented by external causes. Thus an individual is necessarily such that, in general, it strives to preserve itself.

The fact that the striving for self-preservation is built into the concept of an individual in the above way is compatible with the claim that, in certain circumstances, an individual may fail to strive for self-preservation and, in fact, strive for self-destruction. The striving for self-destruction may, of course, be successful and so it is possible for an individual to destroy itself. We can make sense of such cases of self-destruction and failing to strive for self-preservation just in case, in keeping with the concept of a complex individual as I have outlined it, we see the individual as striving to preserve itself in very many other circumstances. The failure to strive for self-preservation, we might say, can be understood, but only against a general background of cases in which the individual strives to preserve itself.

The way the striving for self-preservation figures into the concept of a complex individual is much like the way in which, in Donald Davidson's view, rationality figures into the concept of a person. For Davidson, the attribution of mental states to a person is constrained by the following principle: A person's mental states and actions cannot be, in general, irrational. The more the pattern of mental states we attribute to an agent exhibits irrationality, the more evidence we have that such an attribution is incorrect. Agents, as such, have mental states that are by and large rational. We can, of course, make sense of irrationality in others, but only against a prevailing background of rationality.[30] The concept of a complex individual is subject to a similar constraint. Individuals, as such, strive to preserve themselves in very many circumstances. We can, of course, make sense of an individual's self-destruction and of its failure to strive for self-preservation, but only against a broad background of cases in which that individual strives to preserve itself.

Now how much of the above account is Spinoza's? He does define complex individuality in terms of the ability of the members of a collection of objects to preserve a certain relation among themselves.[31] Spinoza also holds that the preservation of this relation is constitutive of the preservation of the complex individual.[32] So Spinoza is committed to the view that complex individuals, as such, have the ability to preserve themselves. This is in keeping with the foregoing account of individuality and it is, I believe, an important insight of Spinoza's. To the extent that 3p6 – Spinoza's claim that each thing strives to persist – reflects this insight into the general self-preserving nature of individuals, it is importantly correct. But this is not a complete endorsement of 3p6. For, as we have seen, there is some evidence that Spinoza takes this claim as involving a denial of the possibility of self-destruction. To the extent that Spinoza holds this view, he goes against the conception of individuality just outlined. This conception – quite plausibly – accepts the possibility of self-destruction.

Although Spinoza captures the insight that the concept of the striving for self-preservation is connected with the concept of a complex individual, his characterization of this connection is too rigid. He fails to see the Davidsonian escape clause that allows us to make sense of self-destruction and of failing to strive for self-preservation. Spinoza's apparent mistake of ruling out self-destruction is analogous to the mistake of holding that, because rationality is somehow connected with the concept of a person, persons can never be irrational.[33]

3p6 and power of acting

Before we leave Spinoza's metaphysics in general and turn to his psychology in particular, we must examine an important conclusion that he draws from 3p6. Spinoza actually couches this claim in psychological terms (in 3p12 and 3p13), but it is clear that he sees a general metaphysical thesis at work here.[34] It is this general thesis that I want to explore in this subsection before turning to its psychological version in the next section. The general claim is that each thing not only strives to persist in existence, but also strives to prevent any decrease in what Spinoza calls power of acting (*agendi potentia*) and indeed strives to do whatever will increase its power of acting.

In order to see what these further claims mean and how they are connected with 3p6, we must, for reasons that will soon become apparent, turn to Spinoza's notion of an adequate cause: "I call that cause adequate whose effect can be clearly and distinctly perceived through it. But I call it partial or inadequate if its effect cannot be understood through it alone" (E 3d1). Because, for Spinoza, to perceive an effect through a cause is to explain it,[35] we can say that for Spinoza an adequate cause is a complete or sufficient explanation of it.

The notion of adequate causation is crucial to Spinoza's notion of activity:

I say that we act when something happens, in us or outside us, of which we are the adequate cause, i.e. (by 3d1), when something in us or outside us follows from our nature, which can be clearly and distinctly understood through it alone. On the other hand, I say that we are acted on when something happens in us, or something follows from our nature, of which we are only a partial cause (E 3d2).[36]

This definition indicates that something is active to the extent to which it is an adequate cause of some effect. Correspondingly, something is passive to the extent to which it is only a partial cause of some effect.[37]

Activity and passivity, so defined, are clearly matters of degree. Consider, e.g., a stone A that, at t_1, is held in a moving sling. The stone's motion at t_2 is a function of its motion at t_1 together with the motion of the sling at t_1. Let us say that at t_2 the sling drops away and so it no longer plays a role in determining the stone's motion. The motion of the stone at t_3 will then solely be a function of the stone's motion at t_2 (on the assumption that at t_2 no other object interferes with the stone's motion). In this case, we can say that initially (at t_1) the stone's motion is determined to a large extent by something apart from the stone (viz. the sling). However, since at t_2 the sling is no longer determining the stone's motion, the stone itself becomes more nearly the complete cause or explanation of the stone's motion. To this extent, the stone is more active at t_2 than at t_1.

Of course, there is a sense in which the stone at t_2 is not completely active. Although the stone's state at t_2 may suffice for its being in another state of motion at t_3, that state at t_2 is due in part to external causes that were operative before t_2. Thus the explanation of the stone's motion at t_3 will, at some stage, have to appeal to outside causes. However, this undeniable passivity in the stone does not alter the fact that at t_2 the stone is less subject to outside forces and relatively more independent than it was previously.

Given this account of degrees of activity, we can define an increase in *power* of acting in the following way: "An object comes to have a greater power of acting to the extent to which it comes to be able to be active to a greater degree with regard to a certain effect." In other words, something's power of acting increases to the extent to which it becomes less dependent on external things in the production of some effect. A decrease in power of acting can be defined in a corresponding fashion.[38]

A different example will help to clarify this point. Let us say that prior to my breakfast of Wheaties I am able to move my refrigerator only with the help of someone else. However, after my Wheaties, I have the ability to move the refrigerator without assistance from another person. Such a case is one in which my power of acting increases. After the Wheaties, I have a greater ability than I had previously to approximate being the complete cause of the refrigerator's moving.

A decrease in power of acting can be illustrated in a similar way. If, after my Wheaties, I inadvertently take a mild poison, I may cease to be able to move the refrigerator by myself. I then have less ability to approximate being the complete cause here and so my power of acting has decreased.

Before turning to Spinoza's claim that each thing strives to increase its power of acting, there are three important points to notice about the general notions of increase and decrease in power of acting. (1) Something's power of acting can simultaneously increase in certain respects and decrease in others. This is because power of acting is defined in terms of one's ability to bring about (on one's own) a certain kind of effect. Since a certain change can make one more adept at bringing about one kind of effect, but less adept at bringing about another, it can happen that one's power of acting increases in one respect, but decreases in another. (Consider, for example, a drug that increases my ability to lift heavy weights, but decreases my ability to perform delicate movements with my fingers, leaving me unable to play a musical instrument.) These simultaneous transitions in opposite directions form the basis of Spinoza's account of psychological vacillation (see 3p17s).

(2) The above account enables us to represent dying or being destroyed as involving a decrease in one's power of acting to nothing, a complete elimination of one's power of acting. This is because when an object is destroyed, it no longer has any power to be even the partial cause of anything and so it no longer has any degree of activity.[39]

(3) Finally, it is clear that an increase or decrease in one's power of acting can be due to external objects. That is, external objects can make one more or less dependent on external objects in the production of certain effects. For example, the poison or the Wheaties – themselves external objects (at least initially) – make me more or less dependent on external objects when it comes to producing the effect of moving the refrigerator.

This third point is simply a more general version of an implication of the reading of 3p6 as (b). On that reading (toward which Spinoza is inclined to some extent) Spinoza is implying that external causes can make an object more or less dependent on external causes when it comes to bringing about that thing's destruction. (b) concerns the specific effect of destruction, while the claim elicited in the previous paragraph from Spinoza's notion of power of acting simply makes the same point for effects in general.

Let us turn to the claims about striving with which I began this section. Consider first the claim that each thing strives to do whatever will increase its power of acting. In particular, if doing F would increase x's power of acting, then x strives to do F. The point of such a claim is that an object will not, on its own, fail to increase its power of acting. If doing F would increase x's power of acting, then external causes are required for x to fail to do F.

Such a claim is evident in 3p12d. There Spinoza says that if the mind imagines certain things, then its power of acting is increased.[40] Spinoza concludes from this that the mind strives to think of those things.[41] Although the point here concerns the mind in particular, the form of the inference would seem to be quite general. Thus we can conclude that for Spinoza each thing strives to increase its power of acting and to do those things that will increase this power.[42] Spinoza expresses this general point in the *Short Treatise*: "each thing in itself has a striving to preserve itself in its state, and *bring itself to a better one*" (KV I.5; emphasis added).

Since each thing strives in this way, it follows directly that it also strives to prevent any decrease in its power of acting. Again, this simply means that if left to itself, a thing will not undergo any decrease in its power of acting. Spinoza seems to be making this kind of claim for the mind in 3p13d.

Spinoza bases these claims on 3p6, but, like 3p6, they seem to be false. Since, as we have seen, we can make sense of a thing striving to destroy itself or to eliminate completely its power of acting, there seems to be no reason why we cannot also make sense of its failing to strive to prevent a partial decrease in its power of acting or of its merely failing to strive to increase its power of acting. So, Spinoza's additional claims about striving seem to be false.

Moreover, not only do 3p6 and these further claims seem to be false, the further claims do not, contrary to what Spinoza seems to hold, follow from 3p6. A thing can persevere in its being – that is, continue to exist – even if its power of acting does not increase and even if its power of acting decreases (as long as that decrease is not to zero). Since persistence is compatible with a lack of increase in, and also with a decrease in, one's power of acting, it seems that striving to persist is also compatible with failing to strive to increase one's power of acting and also with failing to strive to prevent a decrease in one's power of acting. The only restriction stemming from 3p6 is that one cannot strive to eliminate completely one's power of acting. So, even if each thing must strive to persist, it does not follow that each thing must strive to prevent a decrease in its power of acting and indeed to increase its power of acting. Not only, then, are Spinoza's additional claims about striving false, they do not seem to follow from the (false) basis on which he makes them.43

What led Spinoza to make these further claims? Perhaps here, as in the earlier passages, a conflation between things and their essences is at work.44 It may well be true that a thing's *essence* cannot by itself suffice for a thing's failure to increase its power of acting. Perhaps, in any explanation of a thing's failure to increase its power of acting, factors apart from the thing's essence must play at least some role. Spinoza may be conflating this somewhat plausible claim with the clearly false claim that a thing's state at a given moment cannot suffice for its failure to increase its power of acting. Because the latter claim is false, there is a meaningful sense in which things can indeed fail to strive to increase their power of acting. Spinoza may fail to recognize this sense since he may be conflating the causal powers of the essences of things with the, perhaps broader, causal powers of the things themselves.

It is important to note that a weaker, Davidsonian version of these further claims does not seem to be true. Earlier, we saw that although it is not true that each thing *always* strives to preserve itself, it may well be true that each thing (or at least each complex individual) is such that there are *many circumstances* in which it strives to preserve itself. Can we say something similar for the striving to increase one's power of acting and the striving to prevent a decrease in one's power? I do not think so. We can, I think, make sense of an individual that in most circumstances fails to strive to increase its power of acting and indeed fails to strive to prevent a decrease in its power of acting. As long as an individual is such that, in general, it strives to preserve itself, that is, strives to prevent a *complete elimination* of its power of acting, we can coherently say that it, in general, fails to strive to increase its power of acting and even, in general, fails to strive to prevent a decrease in its power of acting. Significantly, however, as we will see in the next section, psychological analogues of the Davidsonian claims concerning power of acting may well be true.

2. THE APPLICATION OF METAPHYSICS TO PSYCHOLOGY

We are now ready to turn to Spinoza's naturalistic derivation of psychology proper from the general account of the metaphysics of striving and power of acting. For such a derivation to be successful, Spinoza must show that the principles at work in human psychology are instances of principles at work throughout nature. The aspect of our psychology that Spinoza is most concerned to derive in this way consists of what he calls affects.[45] There are, for Spinoza, three basic affects: desire, joy, and sadness. In this part, I will first examine the way in which Spinoza presents his naturalistic account of these affects. For each of the three, I will ask: What is Spinoza's account of this affect and does this account draw only on elements already found in the general metaphysical story we have outlined? We will see that Spinoza's lack of a naturalistic account of belief generates a gap in his naturalistic derivation of each of the basic affects. After examining these derivations, I will consider the threat that apparent cases of prudence and altruism pose for Spinoza's naturalism. Spinoza neutralizes these threats by means of interesting strategies that contain much that is correct. But, particularly in the case of his handling of apparent cases of altruism, we will see that what is right in Spinoza's naturalistic account only serves to raise grave challenges to the success of that account as a whole.

Desire

To elicit Spinoza's account of desire, I need to introduce his notion of appetite. For Spinoza, as we have seen, everything strives to do certain things. The striving of a human mind in particular Spinoza calls *will*. Given Spinoza's parallelism,[46] whenever the mind strives, the body must be striving as well. In fact, Spinoza would also hold that the striving of the mind is one and the same thing as the striving of the body.[47] This allows Spinoza to consider a single striving as "related" to mind and body together. When Spinoza considers this striving as simultaneously a striving of the mind and the body, he calls it *appetite* (E 3p9s). Following Descartes, Spinoza uses the term "man" (*"homo"*) for the union of mind and body (E 2p13c). I will use this term or the term "human being" to refer to this entity. Thus, an appetite can be seen as the striving of a man or human being.

Initially, it appears that Spinoza considers a desire to be a certain kind of appetite – an appetite accompanied by consciousness (E 3p9s). But in 3da1, we find Spinoza downplaying this distinction: "I really recognize no difference between human appetite and desire. For whether a man is conscious of his appetite or not, the appetite still remains one and the same." Thus he defines desire so as to "comprehend together all the strivings of human nature that we signify by the name of appetite, will, desire, or impulse." And so: "By the word 'desire' I understand any of a man's strivings, impulses, appetites, and volitions."

So for Spinoza, while there is a distinction to be drawn between those appetites or human strivings of which one is conscious and those of which one is not, Spinoza's account of desire does not have to be seen as turning on this distinction.[48] Thus I think it is best to view a desire as simply an appetite, that is, as the striving of a human being.

To begin to evaluate Spinoza's naturalistic account of desire, we must spell out what, on his view, are the objects of desire. As we have seen, for Spinoza, things in general strive to preserve themselves and to increase their power of acting. Spinoza's naturalism dictates that the same is true of human beings and, since the strivings of human beings are their desires, it follows that, for Spinoza, all human beings desire to preserve themselves and to increase their power of acting.[49]

We have already seen that the general metaphysical claims involved here are false and there is no reason to think that the specific versions of these claims concerning human beings are any more satisfactory. (For example, as I mentioned, the cases in which human beings commit suicide clearly seem to falsify the claim that all human beings strive to preserve themselves. Similar counterexamples could be devised concerning human beings who do not strive to increase their power of acting.) I am not, however, primarily concerned at this stage with the falsity of the general metaphysical claims or of the corresponding psychological ones involving desire. I want to focus on the independent issue of whether the latter claims are appropriately derived from the former ones.

That there is indeed a problem with Spinoza's derivation here emerges when we consider an immediate and natural objection to his claim that each human being desires to increase his power of acting. We saw earlier that the general claim that each thing strives to increase its power of acting entails that if doing F would increase x's power of acting, then x strives to do F. External causes would have to prevent x from doing F. Applied to desires, the point is that if doing F would increase human being x's power of acting, then x desires to do F. However, this seems false: There are many things that would increase my power of acting that I have no desire to do simply because I am unaware that they will increase my power of acting. For example, assume that taking a certain drug will cure me of an illness and thus increase my power of acting. On the above account of desire, according to which I desire to do whatever will increase my power of acting, it follows that in this case I desire to take the drug. However, this would surely fail to be the case if I do not happen to know of the curative powers of the drug. It seems that in such a case I do not desire to take the drug, even though taking the drug will increase my power of acting.

A defender of Spinoza's definition of desire might deny this conclusion by invoking a notion of *de re* Spinozistic desire. According to such a concept, it might be said that I desire whatever will *in fact* increase my power of acting: If doing F will increase my power of acting, then even if I am not aware of this fact, I desire to do F. Thus, in the drug case, I would, after all, desire to take the drug.

The notion of desire operative here is found in this familiar kind of example: Joe knows that I dislike loud music and he observes that I am about to go into a room where, unbeknownst to me, loud music is playing. Looking out for my interests, Joe says to me quite appropriately: "You don't want to go in there. You want to stay out here." In the same way that one might say that I want to stay outside, despite my lack of knowledge of the benefits of doing so, it might also be said that I want to take the drug, despite my ignorance of its curative powers.[50]

Spinoza himself clearly sees the difficulty cases like that of the unknown drug pose for his view that each human being desires to increase his or her power of acting. However, he does not attempt to get around this problem by invoking a *de re* sense of desire in the way just described. Rather, Spinoza sometimes qualifies his account of desire in a certain way. Instead of saying, as he does in 3p12, that if doing F will increase human being x's power of acting, x desires to do F, he sometimes more cautiously says that if x *believes or imagines or judges* that doing F will increase x's power of acting, then x desires to do F.[51] Such a qualification handles the drug case nicely. Although I do not desire to take the drug prior to learning that this drug will indeed cure me, it does seem plausible to say that if I do come to learn this, I will desire to take the drug.

So, introducing the qualification concerning one's beliefs is a welcome change, as far as the plausibility of Spinoza's account of desire is concerned. But it may not be a welcome change from the point of view of Spinoza's naturalism. The problem arises in the following way. Spinoza defines desire as the striving of a human being. If the account of desire is to be truly naturalistic, then the principles governing desire or human striving must be the same as the principles governing the striving of things in general. As we have seen, a general principle of striving, according to Spinoza, is:

(1) If doing F will increase x's power of acting, then x strives to do F.

However, Spinoza at least sometimes holds that human beings are not governed by this principle, but by a closely related one:

(2) If human being x believes that doing F will increase x's power of acting, then x strives to do F.

If human striving plays by different rules from the rules that apply to nonhuman striving, then human beings constitute a special case – "a kingdom within a kingdom" – and thus naturalism would be violated.

Perhaps, however, these difficulties do not show that Spinoza violates his naturalism, but rather show that his considered opinion would be that, at the general metaphysical level, something like (2) is true instead of (1). Of course, (2) could not, as it stands, be a general metaphysical claim. This is, in part, because it involves the psychological concept of belief and general metaphysical principles must be neutral when it comes to psychological matters. So, if one is to defend Spinoza along these lines, one must say that Spinoza would hold that a neutral version of (2) is the principle governing striving in general. On this view, desire or human striving would not, after all, be an exception to the laws governing striving in general.

This is, I think, the line Spinoza would have to take to defend his naturalism. But, for such a line to succeed, Spinoza would need to specify a general metaphysical concept of which belief would be the psychological version. The relation between this general concept and the concept of belief would be much the same as the relation that Spinoza claims holds between the general metaphysical concept of striving and the psychological concept of desire. Unfortunately, Spinoza does not, in fact, specify such a concept. Nor is it at all clear what concept of this sort he might accept. Still, I have not shown that his account of desire is doomed to fail as a naturalistic account. It merely has an important gap: a gap that would be filled by a naturalistic account of belief.

Joy and sadness

A similar threat to Spinoza's naturalism arises from a discrepancy between the account of the affects of joy and sadness that seems to be at work in his system and his official definitions of those affects.

In 3p11s, Spinoza defines joy as "that passion by which the mind (*mens*) passes to a greater perfection." Sadness, correspondingly, is there defined as "that passion by which it [the mind] passes to a lesser perfection."[52] This definition seems to make joy and sadness wholly mental states or episodes. But, in his definitions of joy and sadness at the end of Part 3, Spinoza does not restrict these affects to the mental realm: "Joy is a man's passage from a lesser to a greater perfection. Sadness is a man's passage from a greater to a lesser perfection" (E 3da2–3). Notice that here Spinoza defines joy and sadness in terms of a *man's* (*hominis*) transition to a different degree of perfection, not (as in 3p11s) in terms of a *mind's* transition. Now, as I pointed out earlier, a man, for Spinoza, consists of a mind and a body (E 2p13c). This indicates that in the definitions at the end of Part 3, Spinoza regards joy and sadness as related to both mind and body, and not to the mind alone.[53]

In speaking of joy or sadness as related to both mind and body, Spinoza intends the following. Whenever the body increases or decreases in power of acting, the mind changes correspondingly (E 3p11). This follows from Spinoza's parallelism which also entails that whenever the mind increases or decreases in power of acting, the body undergoes a corresponding change. The transitions of the mind and the simultaneous transitions of the body are actually, for Spinoza, one and the same thing (E 3p2s). So we can speak of the transitions involving joy and sadness as transitions equally of the mind and of the body. In this sense of the terms "joy" and "sadness," these affects straddle the attributes in much the same way that appetite and desire do. These latter affects were defined as the striving of a man, a striving that is related to both mind and body (E 3p9s, 3da1).

In what follows, the difference between the 3p11s definitions of joy and sadness and the later definitions of these affects will not be relevant. Since throughout Part 3, desire is defined in terms of a man's striving, I will, for the sake of a more unified overall presentation of Spinoza's views, focus on the account of joy and sadness in terms of a *man's* transition, rather than in terms of a mind's transition.

The first and most important thing to note about these definitions is that they offer a fully naturalistic account of these affects. The notion of a transition to a greater or lesser degree of perfection is a notion that, on Spinoza's view, is applicable not just to human beings, but to all objects in nature. For Spinoza, things in general undergo transitions from one degree of perfection or power of acting to another. Things in general can become more or less dependent on external causes in the production of certain kinds of effect. (Recall the example of the stone which at first is and then is not restrained by a sling.) Spinoza's definitions of joy and sadness suggest that what is going on when human beings experience these affects is not fundamentally different from certain kinds of changes that occur throughout nature.

There is an immediate and obvious objection to this account of joy and sadness – an objection to which Spinoza himself appears to be sensitive. Spinoza may be right that the notions of joy and sadness have something to do with the notion of perfection or power of acting. However, the connection surely cannot be the one asserted in Spinoza's definitions of these affects. This is because whether I feel joy or sadness seems to concern not so much whether there is an actual increase or decrease in my power of acting, but rather whether I *believe* that there is an increase or decrease.

For example, consider Bill, a prisoner in chains. If the chains are removed, Bill's power of acting will increase: He will then be able to move from place to place more quickly and without outside assistance. But, intuitively, this increase in power will be joy or be accompanied by joy only if Bill is aware that the chains have been removed and is aware of the increase in his power. If Bill mistakenly believes that he remains in chains, then he will remain sad or at least will not experience joy. Similarly, if Bill remains in chains, but he mistakenly believes that the chains have been removed, he will, it seems, feel joy even though there has been no increase in his power of acting. He merely *thinks* there has been an increase.

These examples indicate that one should not see joy and sadness as simply an increase or decrease in one's power of acting. Rather, if one is going to explain joy and sadness in terms of power of acting at all, one should see these affects as a function of one's beliefs concerning increase or decrease in power. These reflections suggest that the following accounts of joy and sadness are to be preferred to Spinoza's official definitions:

(1) x feels sadness iff x *believes* that his power of acting is decreasing.

(2) x feels joy iff x *believes* that his power of acting is increasing.

The important point for our purposes is not that these objections can be raised against Spinoza's official account of joy and sadness, but that, as in the case of a similar objection to his official account of desire, Spinoza appears to be sensitive to the challenge to his views. This is significant because, in attempting to deal with this kind of difficulty, Spinoza modifies his account of joy and sadness in a way that threatens to undermine its naturalistic status.

Spinoza's attempt to deal with the problem in his account of joy and sadness emerges most clearly not in his discussion of joy and sadness in general, but rather in his discussion of love and hate which are special kinds of joy and sadness. In what follows, I will focus on love, but parallel points apply to hate.

Spinoza defines love as "joy with the accompanying idea of an external cause" (E 3p13s). Since love involves joy, it involves an increase in one's power of acting. Let us say that x increases my power of acting and that I am aware of this fact. It follows that I love x. If x is destroyed, my power of acting might well decrease. For example, suppose that my car enables me to travel home more quickly than I could prior to owning a car. The car thus increases my power of acting and so I experience joy. If I am aware of this increase as due to the car, I come to love the car. Suppose further that the car is now destroyed. I thus no longer have the power to get home quickly. My power of acting decreases upon the destruction of the car and thus I feel sadness. This would be a case in which the destruction of a loved one would, on Spinoza's official account of love and associated affects, involve sadness.[54]

However, when Spinoza spells out some of the features of love, it is clear that he deviates from this official account and approaches the alternative accounts of joy and sadness elicited above. Consider, for example, 3p19: "He who imagines that what he loves is destroyed will be saddened; but he who imagines it to be preserved, will rejoice."[55] Here Spinoza says that it is a sufficient condition for one's sadness in such a case that one imagine that the loved one is destroyed. Similarly, it is a sufficient condition for joy that one imagine that the loved one is preserved. This is in keeping with the alternative definitions (1) and (2).

Those definitions also entail that imagining the destruction or preservation of a loved one is a necessary condition for joy or sadness in this case. Spinoza, however, does not explicitly make this claim in 3p19. That proposition leaves open the possibility that in some cases in which I neither imagine that the loved one is destroyed nor imagine that it is preserved, I feel joy or sadness (depending on whether or not the loved one is actually preserved). Such a view, however, is very implausible and, given Spinoza's obvious willingness in 3p19 and related passages to tie joy and sadness to one's beliefs, it seems reasonable to think that he would reject such a view. If so, then we can see that in Spinoza's discussion of love, he departs from his official definitions of joy and sadness and inclines toward the more plausible (1) and (2).

However, despite their relative plausibility, these accounts may have an important drawback from a Spinozistic point of view. Unlike the explicit definitions of joy and sadness, the unofficial accounts that I have just described are not clearly naturalistic. This stems from the fact that the unofficial accounts include the notion of belief, while the official ones include only the clearly naturalistic notions of increase or decrease in power of acting. As we saw in connection with Spinoza's account of desire, he does not provide, and does not clearly have the resources to provide, a naturalistic account of belief. Thus to the extent that Spinoza wants to account for joy and sadness in terms of belief he threatens to veer from what had promised to be an austerely naturalistic account of joy and sadness.

Prudence and the primacy of the immediate

A different potential threat to Spinoza's naturalistic psychology emerges when we consider not joy and sadness *per se*, but rather their relation to desire. Consider some commonplace claims about the kinds of desires that human beings have. We often desire to perform immediately (say at t_1) a certain action which leads to (and perhaps which we believe leads to) our joy at a later time t_2.[56] Similarly, we often desire to perform an action immediately which (we believe) has the result that our state at t_2 is less sad than it would otherwise have been.

What is more controversial than such claims is the matter of what kind of explanatory relation (if any) holds between the state at t_2 (or the belief about one's state at t_2) and one's desire to do F at t_1. One natural, but nonetheless contested, claim is that the belief about our state at t_2 does indeed explain why we want to do F at t_1. If there is such an explanation of our desiring to do F and, consequently, of our doing F as a result of that desire, then our action can be explained in a teleological fashion. Bennett has argued that, for Spinoza, there are in some sense no legitimate teleological explanations. I will turn to this interpretation at the end of this chapter.

In this subsection, however, I want to focus on a less general, but still controversial point. Let us grant that my belief about t_2 explains my desire to do F immediately. There can be disagreement as to how this belief explains the desire. It is quite natural to say that in many cases my belief concerning my state at t_2 provides a prudential explanation of my desire to do F immediately. An example will make clear what I mean by a prudential explanation. Suppose that I need to take a certain medication immediately (at t_1) in order to avert great sadness or pain at t_2.[57] I am not in pain now, nor will I be in pain at t_1, the immediately following moment. Rather, there is the threat of pain at t_2 and such pain can be avoided only by taking the medication at t_1. Further, let us assume, for the sake of simplicity, that there are no pleasurable or painful side effects of the medication, either at t_1 or afterwards. If I know all these facts about the medication, I might well desire to take the medication at t_1. It seems that in such a case I desire to take the medication only because it will have the good effect of my not being in pain at t_2. No good effect that obtains earlier seems to be relevant to my desiring to take the medication. It is not, it seems, because I believe that some pain at t_1 will be averted or because I believe that some pleasure at t_1 will be generated that I desire to take the medication. Rather, I take the medication only because I believe that a state of nonpain will, as a result, obtain in the nonimmediate future (at t_2). Since the only benefit that seems to be relevant to my desiring to take the medication at t_1 is a benefit that obtains only after t_1, we can say that my desire here is prudential. In this light also, we can say that my belief concerning the good effect at t_2 provides a prudential explanation of my desire to take the medication at t_1. In general, a prudential desire to do F at t_1 (immediately) is a desire that one has not because of any anticipated benefit *at* t_1 of doing F at t_1, but only because of some anticipated *later* beneficial effect of doing F at t_1.

As I indicated, it seems quite plausible to hold that human beings (and indeed planning creatures in general) have prudential desires. However, as I will now explain, Spinoza's naturalism puts pressure on him to deny that there are any genuinely prudential desires. Thus, from a naturalistic perspective, the familiar claim that there are prudential desires can be seen as controversial after all.

To see why, consider a case of prudential striving in which I believe that doing F at t_1 will avert pain at t_2 because it is in fact true that such an action will avert pain. (This need not be true of all cases of prudential striving – e.g., in some cases the relevant belief may be false.) If this belief in turn explains why I desire to do F at t_1, then it can be said that the fact that doing F at t_1 will avert pain at t_2 explains why I desire to do F at t_1. Further it might well be the case that in addition to desiring to do F at t_1 because of the future benefits of so doing, I do not desire to do F at t_1 because of any benefits at t_1 of so doing. (This would, it seems, be true of the medication case.) In general, then, the possibility of prudential desiring would open up the possibility of desiring to perform an action immediately not because such an action would increase one's pleasure at t_1 or offset pain at t_1, but rather because such an action will increase one's pleasure or offset pain at t_2. It is this latter possibility that generates a threat to naturalism.

Given Spinoza's general metaphysical analogues of desire, joy, and sadness, the naturalistic version of this claim would involve what might be called future-directed striving:

> (FDS) It is possible for an object x to strive to do G immediately (at t_1), not because doing G would increase x's power of acting at t_1 or offset a decrease in that power at t_1, but because such an action would increase x's power of acting *at t_2* or offset a decrease in that power *at t_2*.

Prudential desiring would be a species of future-directed striving.

While it may seem that a psychological analogue of (FDS) holds in the case of human beings (and other planning creatures) who are thus capable of future-directed striving, it does not seem that things in general are capable of such striving. For example, consider the familiar stone whose motion is affected by a sling. Such a stone, as we have seen, strives to preserve its proportion of motion and rest at t_1 and perhaps can be said to strive to be free of the sling at t_1. The objects of these strivings would be of immediate benefit to the stone. Maintaining its proportion of motion and rest at t_1 is, as we saw, necessary for preventing the destruction of the stone itself at t_1, that is, for preventing the stone's power of acting from being reduced to zero. Similarly, becoming free of the sling at t_1 would immediately increase the stone's power of acting. These immediate payoffs seem to explain fully why the stone strives in these ways. There is no basis for saying that the stone strives to do these things at t_1 because of some later benefit that will accrue to the stone. Further, it is hard to see how any of the things the stone strives to do at t_1 (immediately) could fail to be of this character. That is, everything the stone strives to do at t_1 it strives to do only because of the immediate benefit of doing such a thing and not because of any benefit further off in the future. The stone thus does not seem capable of future-directed striving nor do most or all of the objects in the world that are not normally regarded as planning creatures.

Thus there seems to be an important difference between human beings (and other planning creatures) and objects such as the stone. This apparent difference, if accepted by Spinoza, might seem to threaten his naturalism: for if Spinoza holds that human beings are capable of a fundamentally different kind of striving (viz. future-directed striving) from the kind of striving of which most other objects are capable, then would he not be treating human beings as a special case, as a kingdom within a kingdom after all? In the face of such a difference between human beings and others, Spinoza could avoid this conclusion only if he could explain how human beings come to have the special capacity of future-directed striving and explain this by relying exclusively on terms taken from his account of the striving and behavior of objects (including the stone) in general.

To illustrate this last point, consider the fact that sugar melts in water and gold does not. This basic difference between sugar and gold does not mean that we have a violation of naturalism here. This is because we can appeal to other differences between sugar and gold, differences concerning molecular structure, and so forth, which, in conjunction with certain generally applicable laws of nature, serve to explain why sugar dissolves, but gold does not. Similarly, perhaps there is some further difference between human beings and objects such as the stone which, in conjunction with certain principles operative throughout nature, would explain why human beings are capable of future-directed striving, but stones are not. This would be a naturalistic explanation of the important difference concerning striving.

Thus we can see that if Spinoza accepts that human beings, but not stones, are capable of future-directed striving, then, in order to safeguard his naturalism, he must offer such an explanation. A natural way to attempt to carry out such an explanation would be to say that stones have no beliefs about the future, but we do. Perhaps this doxastic difference would begin to explain why we differ from stones in terms of future-directed striving.[58]

However, this is not, I believe, the way that Spinoza would get out of the difficulty here. This is because I do not think that Spinoza accepts the claim that human beings and objects such as the stone differ with regard to future-directed striving. Although he would hold, for the reasons given above, that stones do not engage in future-directed striving, he would deny the plausible claim that human beings are capable of such striving. Given such a denial, there would be no discrepancy between human beings and stones and thus there would be no need for the kind of naturalistic explanation of such a discrepancy that I just described. Spinoza would thus be able to maintain his naturalism by denying the relevant difference in this case. As we have seen, however, there are very many cases in which it is quite plausible to say that human beings do engage in future-directed striving. Thus if Spinoza is to deny that there is such striving, he must offer an alternative account of what is going on in the apparent cases of future-directed striving. My aim for most of the rest of this subsection is twofold: to show how Spinoza would explain away apparent cases of such striving and, concurrently, to explain why Spinoza thinks that human beings (in addition to stones) are not capable of such striving.

The first thing to notice is that apparent cases of future-directed striving in humans involve the anticipation of pleasure or pain. In the medication example, I anticipate being in pain at t_2 and, for this reason, I take the medication immediately (at t_1). Similar cases of future-directed striving involve the anticipation of pleasure. I will, for the sake of simplicity, continue to focus on the anticipation of pain, but corresponding points apply to the anticipation of pleasure.

The reason why Spinoza would deny that there are any genuine cases of future-directed striving in humans turns on his account of anticipation. The basic point here is that, for Spinoza, the anticipation of pain is itself painful. This is evident from 3p18: "Man is affected with the same affect of joy or sadness from the image of a past or future thing as from the image of a present thing."[59] I will briefly discuss the argument for this claim in section 3 of this chapter. For now, however, it will suffice to note that there is something obviously right about Spinoza's position here: The anticipation of a painful experience is itself a painful experience. The pain of anticipation may not be as intense or of the same type as the anticipated pain, but it is pain nonetheless. This point will enable Spinoza to explain away the apparent cases of future-directed striving.

Another point that is crucial in this explanation is the fact that, for Spinoza, whenever we are in pain, we strive to remove that pain. This is because pain is a decrease in power of acting and Spinoza holds, as we have seen, that each thing strives to prevent any decrease (including any further decrease) in its power of acting. Since the anticipation of future pain is itself painful, it follows that in such a case we strive to remove this pain of anticipation; that is, we strive to stop anticipating the future pain. This is indicated by 3p13d where Spinoza says, in effect, that when the mind believes that something painful exists or will exist, it strives to remove that belief.[60]

How does one stop anticipating the future pain (and thus remove the pain of anticipation)? Typically – important exceptions will be discussed a bit later – one stops anticipating the future pain by doing something that, one believes, will avert the pain. This is clearly what happens in the medication case. Taking the medication at t_1 would have, I believe, the result that I am not in pain at t_2. Given this belief, if I take the medication at t_1 and am aware of so doing, I will no longer anticipate pain at t_2 and so no longer feel the pain of anticipation. Thus, in this and other apparent cases of future-directed striving, there is an immediate benefit to doing F at t_1.

But this does not yet show that there is after all no future-directed striving in such cases. This is because, for all I have said so far, it may well be the case that although doing F at t_1 has an immediate payoff (in addition to the long-term payoff of not being in pain at t_2) I desire to do F *only* because of the long-term payoff and not because of the immediate benefit. If this were so, then we would still have a genuine case of future-directed striving.

Spinoza would, however, reject such a situation. For Spinoza, the immediate benefit of doing F at t_1 does explain why I desire to do F. In fact, for Spinoza, I desire to do F *only* because of the immediate benefit. This is evident from 3p37d where Spinoza says: "[A]ll a man affected by sadness strives for is to remove sadness."[61] In the case at hand, since I now anticipate being in pain at t_2, I now experience the pain of anticipation. Further, let us assume that I am not experiencing any other pain now. Thus, for Spinoza, my *conatus* or striving would be wholly directed to removing the pain of anticipation. Since in this case I do strive to do F at t_1, this striving must be solely a function of striving to avoid having any further pain of anticipation. That is, striving to take the medication is a striving I have only because such striving will remove the pain of anticipating pain at t_2. Since, in this apparent case of future-directed striving, my striving to do F at t_1 is not a striving I have because of the future benefit of doing F, the apparent case of future-directed striving is, after all, not a case of future-directed striving. The same conclusion would apply to other apparent cases. Thus we can see that (i) Spinoza's view that our striving is wholly directed to the removal of current pain (if we are in pain)[62] and (ii) his account of anticipation both lead to the conclusion that there are no genuine cases of future-directed striving. At least in respect of such striving, there is, for Spinoza, no fundamental difference between human beings and objects such as the stone in the sling.

In denying that we are capable of future-directed striving, Spinoza is not denying that one can desire to do F at t_1 because so doing will avert pain at t_2. Spinoza is simply offering a particular and controversial account of how it comes to be that one desires to do F at t_1 because of the longer term effects of that action. He makes the explanatory chain explicit in this way: The fact that doing F at t_1 will avert pain at t_2 explains why doing F at t_1 will (if I have the appropriate beliefs) relieve the pain of anticipation that I am experiencing. Since, for Spinoza, if one is in pain one's desire is geared toward the relief of that pain, Spinoza would hold that in this case I desire to do F at t_1. So the fact that doing F will have good long term effects does explain why I desire to do F, but only by way of a desire for an immediate relief from pain (the pain of anticipation).

For Spinoza, outcomes that are relatively distant in the future can lead us to have certain desires only because of their connection (via anticipation) with immediate outcomes. The more distant outcomes cannot by themselves impinge on our desires. Such a view reflects what might be called the primacy of the immediate in Spinoza. This primacy of the immediate is complemented by the primacy of the self in matters of desire as we will see in the next subsection.

As I mentioned earlier, there are cases in which one does not relieve the pain of anticipation by doing something that one believes will avert the anticipated pain at t_2. Some of the most important cases of this kind are ones in which I do not do F (which I believe would avert the anticipated pain) but I believe that I am doing or have done F. Since the anticipation of pain at t_2 involves a belief that the pain will occur, believing that one has done something which will avert that pain serves to undermine the former belief and thus serves to eliminate the anticipation and its attendant pain.

This fact yields an interesting result. Spinoza insists, as we have seen, that we desire the removal of any pain we are currently experiencing. Since a belief that one has performed a certain action (regardless of whether or not one has actually done so) would serve to eliminate that pain, we can see that Spinoza holds that there is some motivation to have the belief that I have done this action, even if I have not actually done so. Our dominant desire to avert pain can, in other words, generate cases of motivated false belief.

Spinoza recognizes the phenomenon of motivated false belief and discusses it in kinds of cases other than the above one concerning anticipation. For example, Spinoza offers reasons for thinking that if I believe that I have made others feel pleasure, then I myself will feel pleasure.[63] Since such a belief would thus involve pleasure, Spinoza says that I desire to have it. However, this desire may outrun the facts and thus, Spinoza says, "it can easily happen that one who exults at being esteemed is proud and imagines himself to be pleasing to all, when he is burdensome to all" (E 3p30s).[64] In general, Spinoza quite rightly allows for the possibility that our desires can blind us to the truth and lead us to espouse falsehood.[65]

The main thrust of this section has been that Spinoza's account of anticipation enables him to avert a threat to his naturalistic psychology posed by apparent cases of future-directed striving. Crucial to this account of anticipation is the plausible point that the anticipation of pain is itself somehow painful (and that the anticipation of pleasure is itself pleasurable). However, despite this intuitive element, many difficulties attend Spinoza's account of anticipation. I will mention some of these later when I explore Spinoza's account of irrationality. I would like to close this subsection, however, not with a criticism of Spinoza's account of anticipation *per se*, but rather with a problem that this account raises for Spinoza's naturalism.

This problem is the now-familiar one involving belief. Spinoza would account for and explain away apparent cases of future-directed striving by invoking his notion of anticipation. If the Spinozistic account of the apparent cases of future-directed striving is to be genuinely naturalistic, Spinoza must, therefore, provide a naturalistic account of anticipation. However, it is not clear whether Spinoza could do so. This is because anticipation involves, of course, a form of belief (about the future) and, as we have seen, Spinoza may not be able to provide a naturalistic account of belief.

Altruism and the primacy of the self

As was the case with the apparent instances of prudential desire, apparent instances of altruistic desire pose a prima facie threat to Spinoza's naturalism. In this subsection, I want to show why this is so and also how Spinoza's way of dealing with apparent altruism mirrors his way of handling apparent prudence.

A case of altruistic desire would be one in which I desire to do F (e.g., assist a stranger in need), not because doing so will give me pleasure or avert some pain that I would have had, but simply because doing so will benefit some other individual. A desire to do F can be altruistic even if doing F is beneficial to me. Altruism simply requires that I do not desire to do F *because* of the benefit to me of such an action.

The possibility of such a desire would threaten Spinoza's naturalism. To see why this is so, consider the general metaphysical analogue of the claim that altruistic desires are possible. Here I use the metaphysical notions that correspond, in Spinoza's system, to desire, joy, and sadness in order to generate a description of what might be called other-directed striving:

> (ODS) It is possible for an object x to strive to do F, not because such an action would increase x's power of acting or offset a decrease in x's power of acting, but because such an action would increase another individual's (y's) power of acting or offset a decrease in y's power of acting.

Altruistic desires would be a species of other-directed striving.

The threat to naturalism emerges from the fact that while human beings (and perhaps certain other creatures) seem to be capable of other-directed striving, objects in general seem not to be. Return for a moment to the example of the stone whose motion is restrained by a sling. Let us embellish the example by saying that the motion of the sling itself is restrained by a person holding it. Now, as we have seen, the stone strives to continue moving and perhaps strives to be free of the sling. Such strivings are directed at states that will maintain or enhance the stone's power of acting. However, there seems to be no plausible way to attribute to the stone a striving for the sling's well-being. For example, the stone does not strive that the sling be free of the person holding it (or if the stone can be said to strive in this way, that is only because such freedom for the sling would generate freedom for the stone). Nor can the stone plausibly be said to strive for the preservation or increase in power of acting of any other object apart from the sling. In general, stones and most other objects do not seem capable of other-directed striving.

If human beings were capable of such striving, while most other objects were not, we would be faced with a potential violation of naturalism. In their capacity for other-directed striving, human beings would seem to depart from the rest of nature. Of course, as we saw in the case of future-directed striving, if this difference between human beings and others were itself explicable naturalistically, then naturalism could be retained. However, as in the previous case, Spinoza does not neutralize the threat in this way, but rather by denying that there is any such difference between human beings and other objects. Spinoza does this by denying that we are capable of altruistic desire. This point is explicit in the way Spinoza applies his *conatus* doctrine to human beings.

For Spinoza, human beings, like any other thing, strive exclusively to preserve themselves and to maintain or enhance their well-being. See, for example, 3p28: "We strive to further the occurrence of whatever we imagine will lead to joy, and to avert or destroy what we imagine is contrary to it, or will lead to sadness." As Spinoza makes clear, the joy or sadness in question here is one's own joy or sadness. This claim indicates that our actions are focused on our own well-being. A denial of a particular kind of altruistic desire occurs in 4p25: "No one strives to preserve his being for the sake of anything else."[66] *Ethics* 3p28 and 4p25 concern human beings in particular, but they are clearly intended to be psychological versions of metaphysical claims that hold generally. Thus we can see that Spinoza would reject other-directed striving in general.

Spinoza is, of course, aware that there are apparent cases of other-directed striving and it is clear how he would explain these away. I will give two examples of this kind of explanation. In many of the cases in which I may be motivated to assist another individual, I am motivated to do so out of pity. Such a motivation cannot be altruistic for Spinoza. This is because, for Spinoza, pity is a form of sadness (E 3p22s).[67] As we have seen, for Spinoza the striving of one experiencing sadness is entirely directed to the removal of that sadness. Thus for Spinoza when I act out of pity, I am striving to ease my own suffering which is involved in that very feeling of pity (E 3p27c3d). In this way, Spinoza would characterize an apparent case of altruism as one that does not involve altruism at all.

Consider another case: A person might desire to instill in others a love of reason and a desire to live one's life according to the dictates of reason (see E 4p37). This noble desire might seem to be a manifestation of an altruistic concern for the quality of life other people can have. But Spinoza could explain such a desire without invoking altruism. Spinoza would likely see such a desire as prompted by the fact, as he sees it, that to the extent that people live according to the guidance of reason, they are more beneficial to one another.[68] For this reason, a given individual might desire to instill in others a desire to live according to the dictates of reason because such a desire in others would ultimately be beneficial to that individual. Again, Spinoza has the resources to explain away an apparent case of altruism. In similar ways, he would, I believe, reconstrue all other cases of altruistic desires and thus preserve his general view that there is no other-directed striving.

Earlier we saw that in the matter of desire, Spinoza espouses what might be called the primacy of the immediate. For Spinoza, the immediate outcomes of an action play a more direct role in the explanation of a desire to perform that action than do the action's nonimmediate outcomes. I can desire to do F immediately because such an action will lead to a good result in the long run, only if and only because that action has an immediate payoff.

In a similar way, we can see that there is also for Spinoza what might be called the primacy of the self. Spinoza holds that the benefits to oneself of a certain action play a more direct role in the explanation of one's desire to perform that action than do the benefits of that action to another individual. I can desire to do F because such an action will help another individual y, only if and only because that action benefits me.[69]

It is interesting to note that there is no logical connection between the primacy of the immediate and the primacy of the self. One might hold that desires are always directed at immediate benefits, but also hold that these immediate benefits need not always be benefits to oneself. Similarly, one might hold that desires are always directed at one's own benefits, without holding that the benefits are always at bottom immediate benefits. Thus Spinoza's primacy of the immediate does not lead to his primacy of the self and his primacy of the self does not lead to his primacy of the immediate. Rather, both positions are generated at least in part by Spinoza's naturalism.

Spinoza's view that the self and its interests are the fundamental objects of all desiring is simply the application to the human case of his general view that each thing strives to preserve itself and increase its power of acting. Earlier we saw a number of problems with this general view and one would expect that the same problems recur in connection with the specific view concerning human desires. Yet a surprise lurks here.

I want to focus on problems concerning the claim that each thing strives to increase its power of acting. Given Spinoza's account of desire and joy, the psychological version of that claim would be the claim that each person desires to experience joy. Both the general claim and its psychological version fell prey to counterexamples involving self-destruction: Some of the examples that we considered earlier were psychological ones (e.g., cases of suicide) and some were not (e.g., the candle case). Thus Spinoza's claim that all things, including human beings, strive to increase their power of acting cannot be correct.

We also saw that a weaker, Davidsonian version of the general claim here fails. The weaker claim would be a claim to the effect that although something may on certain occasions fail to strive to increase its power of acting, that thing must *in general* be such that it strives to increase its power of acting. The failure of a thing to strive to increase its power could be understood, on this view, but only against a broad background of cases in which the thing does strive to increase its power. Such a view, however, does not seem to be correct. We can, I claimed, make sense of a thing that rarely, if ever strives to increase its power of acting (though, perhaps, we must see it as often striving to stay in existence).

Does a weaker version of the relevant psychological claim also fail? That is, is it or is it not the case that although a given person may fail to desire to experience joy or pleasure on certain occasions, that person must be such that *in general* he or she desires to experience joy? On this view, a failure to pursue one's own joy could be understood, but only against a broad background of other cases in which one does pursue one's joy. Unlike the weak version of the general claim, this weak version of the psychological claim does have a great deal of plausibility. To the extent that we see a person as continually and pervasively failing to desire his or her own joy – both in big things and in small – then to that extent we should question whether our interpretation of that person's psychological state is correct.

The general point here derives from Davidson's understanding of the principle of charity. Our attribution of mental states to that agent must always proceed under the constraint that we not attribute a wildly irrational or incoherent system of mental states to an agent. On this view of mentality, each mental state is, by nature, part of a system of mental states that is in general coherent and rational. Davidson expresses the point in this way: "To the extent that we fail to discover a coherent and plausible pattern in the attitudes and actions of others we simply forego the chance of treating them as persons" (Davidson 1980: 221–2). I believe that the claim that an agent fails, in most or all cases, to seek its own joy or pleasure would go against the general coherence of the mental realm as spelled out in Davidson's application of the principle of charity.

Thus a flexible, Davidsonian version of the claim that persons desire their own joy may well be true, even though the rigid, exceptionless version is false, and even though the corresponding general metaphysical claim (both in its rigid and flexible versions) also seems to be false. The fact that some version of the psychological claim seems to be true shows that Spinoza's account of human desire captures an important feature of human desire – viz. its crucial connection to an agent's well-being. Nevertheless, a problem with Spinoza's position here (as well as elsewhere) is that he holds that the connection between two phenomena (such as desire and joy) is much more strict than it actually is. Such a misstep is perhaps to be expected from a philosopher who emphasizes naturalism and laws as much as Spinoza does.

The foregoing reflections, however, raise an even deeper problem for Spinoza and his naturalism. We have seen that the weakened, Davidsonian version of the psychological claim that each person desires his or her own joy is plausible, while the weakened version of the corresponding general metaphysical claim is not plausible. This discrepancy between corresponding psychological and general metaphysical claims indicates that we are, contra Spinoza, willing to treat the psychological as a special case, as somehow obeying principles different from those at work in the rest of nature. Davidson himself makes this point in describing what is, in effect, his anti-naturalistic characterization of the mental:

Any effort at increasing the accuracy and power of a theory of behaviour forces us to bring more and more of the whole system of the agent's beliefs and motives directly into account. But in inferring this system from the evidence, we necessarily impose conditions of coherence, rationality, and consistency. *These considerations have no echo in physical theory.* (Davidson 1980: 231; emphasis added)

So to the extent that we accept what I take to be the plausible Davidsonian account of the nature of the mental realm, we seem to be led to an antinaturalistic, anti-Spinozistic position. A Davidsonian account may help us to see that there is something right about Spinoza's account of desire and joy (viz. the fact that, on Spinoza's view, there is an important connection between these states) but a Davidsonian account also suggests that, in addition, there is something more importantly wrong in Spinoza's account of these matters. The comparisons with Davidson at various points in this chapter show in a new and, I believe, illuminating way exactly why, despite genuine and important insights, Spinoza's thoroughgoing naturalism about psychology is, in the end, difficult to maintain.[70]

3. THE LAW-GOVERNEDNESS OF THE MENTAL REALM

At the outset I represented Spinoza's naturalism about human beings as involving two claims:

(1) There are laws or rules governing the psychological states of human beings.

(2) These laws or rules are instances of more general laws or rules operative throughout nature.

As I explained, these two claims generate two different strategies for analyzing and evaluating Spinoza's naturalistic psychology. The first strategy is to investigate the way in which Spinoza applies to human beings and their psychology metaphysical principles at work throughout the rest of nature. This is what I have done in Section 2 of this chapter. The second strategy is to investigate the nature of the principles that govern psychology, according to Spinoza, without concerning oneself with the extent to which these principles are instances of more general principles. I want to go some distance toward carrying out such an inquiry in this part of the chapter. Of course, we have already explored some of the principles governing psychology by explaining the way in which Spinozistic psychology grows out of Spinozistic metaphysics. But there are many aspects of the law-governedness of psychology that we can profitably examine without direct attention to the extent to which psychological laws and rules are derived from more general metaphysical laws and rules. In this light, I want to explore three central issues in this final section: (i) Spinoza's account of irrational action, (ii) his account of the principles controlling the relations between different affects, and (iii) the extent to which Spinoza allows teleological explanations in psychology. Here, as in the earlier sections of the chapter, Spinoza's views will emerge as interesting and exciting, though not without important flaws.

Irrational action

Irrational action occurs in certain cases in which I have conflicting desires: I desire to do F and I also desire to do G, which is incompatible with F.[71] For example, I might desire to have some spicy food and also desire not to have spicy food because I believe that such food will ultimately cause indigestion. Such a conflict of desires is only a necessary condition of irrational action. It is not sufficient. Irrational action occurs only when, in the face of such a conflict, I intentionally perform one of the actions even though I believe that my interests would in the long run be better served by taking the other course of action. Spinoza seems to accept that there is irrational action in this sense. Quoting Ovid in 4p17s, Spinoza appears to assert that there are cases in which "I see the better and I approve, but I follow the worse."[72]

The phenomenon of irrational action might seem to threaten the law-governedness of psychology in the following way. Even if we do sometimes act irrationally, it is clear that we do not always, or perhaps even often, do so. Thus a naturalist who, like Spinoza, accepts that we can act irrationally faces the challenge of articulating the principles that specify the circumstances under which irrational action occurs and those under which it does not. To explain why irrational action occurs in a given case, it would not be sufficient for a naturalist simply to say that irrationality does sometimes occur, without going on to spell out what it is about this case that accounts for the appearance of irrationality. To deny that any such detailed explanation is forthcoming would be to deny the law-governedness of psychology and thus would be to deny naturalism.

Since Spinoza accepts that there is irrational action, he must offer an account of the principles that govern this phenomenon. Spinoza is sensitive to this requirement and the account he goes on to offer is interesting and coherent with the rest of his system, though, as we will see, it is incomplete in at least one crucial respect.[73]

Spinoza's account of irrationality turns on his account of anticipation. Recall that for Spinoza the anticipation of pain is itself painful.[74] As given in 3p18d, Spinoza's reason for this claim is that when the mind anticipates a given state of affairs, the body is in the same state as it would be if that state of affairs were to obtain. Spinoza assumes that if at two different times the body is in the same state, then at those different times the mind must be in the same state.[75] Given this assumption, it follows that when the mind anticipates a given state of affairs, it is in the same psychological state as it would be if that state of affairs were to obtain. Thus if the anticipation is of a state of affairs that would involve pain, the state of anticipation itself will involve pain. In other words, for Spinoza the anticipation of pain is itself painful.

This argument raises a number of questions, and I will address some of them when I discuss Spinoza's views on memory in the next subsection. What I want to note here is an important way in which Spinoza qualifies his view that in anticipating pain, the mind is in the same state as it would be if this painful state actually obtained. As Spinoza claims in 4p9 and elsewhere, the states are not *exactly* the same. Rather the pain of anticipation is *weaker than* the anticipated pain. The point is that the anticipated pain is stronger when it occurs than the pain of anticipation was at the earlier moment when it occurred. Spinoza does not make completely clear what the weakness or strength of an affect is,[76] but one thing that is clear is that weaker affects are, for Spinoza, less capable of producing action than stronger ones. For example, a weaker pain is less able than a stronger one to prompt action intended to alleviate that pain. This is evident from the very beginning of Part 4 where, while discussing irrational action, Spinoza describes the strength of an affect in terms of its ability to force a certain course of action. See also 4p17s where

Spinoza concludes that there is irrational action after an account of the relative strengths and weaknesses of certain affects. So the upshot of 4p9's claim that the pain of anticipation is weaker than the anticipated pain is that the ability of the pain of anticipation to prompt action directed at its removal is less than the ability of the anticipated pain itself to prompt action directed at *its* removal.

With the help of 4p9, Spinoza demonstrates a further claim that plays a crucial role in his account of irrationality: "We are affected more intensely (*intensius*) toward a future thing which we imagine will quickly be present, than if we imagined the time when it will exist to be further from the present" (E 4p10). Spinoza's point here can be illustrated in this way. Consider two different anticipations that an agent might have at a given time t_1. Anticipation A is the anticipation of having a certain degree of pain at later time t_2. Anticipation B is the anticipation of having that same degree of pain at t_3, a time even further off in the future. In each case, for Spinoza, the pain of anticipation will be weaker than the anticipated pain. However, Spinoza thinks that we can also compare with one another the strength of the pain of anticipation A and the strength of the pain of anticipation B. As 4p10 makes clear, for Spinoza, the pain of anticipation A is stronger than the pain of anticipation B. Spinoza is making the plausible claim that the strength of the pain of anticipation is, in part, a function of the temporal distance from the present of the anticipated pain.[77]

However, for Spinoza, the strength of the pain of anticipation is also a function of something besides the temporal distance of the anticipated pain. Spinoza would also hold that the pain of anticipation is a function of the size of the anticipated pain. This will become apparent by considering two anticipations directed at future pains which are of different degrees, but which are at the same temporal distance from the present. For example, at t_1 an agent might anticipate a very severe pain (the pain of torture) at t_2. That agent might also or instead anticipate at t_1 a very minor pain (the pain of a minor scratch) at t_2. Call the first anticipation, "anticipation C," and the second, "anticipation D."

Intuitively, it would seem that the pain of anticipation C is stronger than the pain of anticipation D. Spinoza's system can deliver this plausible result. For Spinoza, the greater a pain is, the stronger it is, that is, the more capable it is of prompting appropriate action. This is evident in 3p37d where Spinoza says, "the greater the sadness, the greater the power of acting with which the man will strive to remove the sadness."[78] Now the pain of torture is clearly greater than the pain of a minor scratch, so the former pain is stronger than the latter.

How do the *anticipations* of these two pains compare in strength? First of all, recall that for Spinoza the pain of the anticipation of the torture is weaker than the pain of the torture itself and the pain of the anticipation of the scratch is weaker than the pain of the scratch itself. As we saw, the weakness of the pain of anticipation relative to the anticipated pain is a function of the temporal distance between the two. As I have stipulated, in this case, the distance between anticipation C and the torture is the same as the distance between anticipation D and the scratch. This makes it plausible to conclude that the degree to which the pain of anticipation C is weaker than the pain of the torture is the same as the degree to which the pain of anticipation D is weaker than the pain of the scratch.[79]

If this is correct, then since the pain of the torture is stronger than the pain of the scratch, it follows that the pain of anticipation C is stronger than the pain of anticipation D. Here we can see how Spinoza might arrive at the claim that the pain of a certain anticipation is a function not only of the temporal distance from the present of the anticipated pain, but also of the size of the anticipated pain.

All the elements needed for Spinoza's account of irrational action are now in place. We have considered a case (that of anticipations A and B) in which the size of one anticipated affect is the same as another, but the temporal distance of those anticipated affects differ. We have also considered a case (that of anticipations C and D) in which the temporal distance of one anticipated affect is the same as that of another, but the sizes of these affects differ. To see how irrational action arises, according to Spinoza, we need to consider a certain kind of case in which two anticipated affects differ with regard to both size and temporal distance.

Thus return to the spicy food case. I anticipate immediate pleasure, if I eat the spicy food, but I also anticipate the pain of indigestion later on. Let us assume that the pain of indigestion is greater than (and hence stronger than) the immediate pleasure of eating the food. Let us also assume that I am aware of this fact. Now, as we have seen, the strength of the anticipation of a certain affect is, in part, a function of the size of the anticipated affect. Since the pain of indigestion is greater than the immediate pleasure of consuming the food, we can say that, as far as the size of the anticipated affect is concerned, the pain of the anticipation of pain would be stronger than the pleasure of the anticipation of the pleasure. In other words, if the anticipated pleasure and the anticipated pain were at the same temporal distance from the present, then the anticipation of the pain would be stronger than the anticipation of the pleasure.

But the anticipated pain and the anticipated pleasure are not at the same temporal distance. This opens the door to irrational action. Because there is a temporal disparity here, the degree to which the pain of anticipating the pain of indigestion is weaker than the pain of indigestion itself is greater than the degree to which the pleasure of the anticipation of the pleasure of consuming the food is weaker than that pleasure. In such a case, it can happen that the temporal proximity of the anticipated pleasure compensates, or indeed over-compensates, for its relative smallness.

Another way to see this is as follows: Because the pain of indigestion is greater than the pleasure of consuming the food, the pain of the anticipation of the indigestion has an advantage in terms of strength over the pleasure of the anticipation of the pleasure of consuming the food. However, this advantage of the pain of anticipation can be dissipated if the anticipated pain is sufficiently far off in the future and the anticipated pleasure is sufficiently close to the present. The result would be that the pleasure of anticipating the immediate pleasure is stronger than the pain of anticipating the far-off pain, despite the fact that the far-off pain is greater than the immediate pleasure and despite the fact that I am aware of their relative sizes. In such a case, I would be acting irrationally.[80]

In his account of irrational action, Spinoza appeals to temporal disparities of the kind I have just been discussing (see, for example, 4p60s and 4ap30). Further, his claim that there can be irrational action is made in 4p17s immediately after he elaborates his view that an anticipated affect is stronger than the affect of anticipation. These two facts indicate that the above explanation of irrational action is the one Spinoza has in mind. He thus has a way to meet the challenge to his naturalism that irrational action poses. He is able to specify with some precision exactly the kinds of circumstances under which irrational action arises.

Such an account has, I believe, much to recommend it. However, one of its important defects should be noted. This explanation relies heavily on Spinoza's claim in 4p9 that the pain of the anticipation of a certain pain is less strong than that pain itself. As I have said already, such a claim seems plausible. However, Spinoza does not properly argue for it. He makes this claim in 4p9d: "[A]n imagination . . . is more intense (*intensior*) so long as we imagine nothing that excludes the present existence of the external thing."[81] To support this point, Spinoza appeals to 2p17, but as Bennett rightly notes, "2p17 does not contain the concept of intensity or anything like it" (Bennett 1984: 284). That proposition simply concerns the circumstances under which imagining something amounts to regarding it as actually existing. *Ethics* 2p17 does not provide the materials for making a connection between the fact that a given imagining amounts to regarding a thing as actually existing and the fact that that imagining is more intense or stronger than an imagining of that thing as far off in the future. Thus a key element of Spinoza's account of irrational action is without adequate grounding in his system.

Principles of affect constitution and transition

The previous subsection focused on the principles governing the relation between affects and actions. Spinoza's naturalism dictates that there are also principles covering the relations among affects themselves. Because such principles play a number of important roles in the ethical parts of the *Ethics*, I will briefly explain and analyze some of them here. I should note, however, that I will not draw out in any detail the ethical implications of these principles.

One can see Spinoza as employing two basic types of principles concerning the relation among affects. The first type consists of what I call principles of affect *constitution*. The second type consists of principles of affect *transition*. I will discuss these in turn.

To explain the nature of principles of affect constitution, I need to say a little about Spinoza's program for the classification of affects. As we have seen, Spinoza recognizes three basic affects: desire, joy, and sadness. They are basic not in the sense that they are indefinable (as in Hume), but in the sense that each other affect is simply a specific version of either desire, joy, or sadness.[82] Thus, for example, as we have seen, love is a specific kind of joy: It is joy accompanied by the idea of an external cause. Similarly hate is a specific kind of sadness: It is sadness accompanied by the idea of an external cause (E 3p13s, 3da6,7). Since, for Spinoza, joy is partially constitutive of love and sadness is partially constitutive of hate, we might say that Spinoza's definitions here express principles of affect constitution.

Throughout Part 3 of the *Ethics*, Spinoza offers descriptions of many other, often more complex affects that are varieties of the three basic ones. These descriptions are subtle and frequently quite insightful. Nevertheless, in the interests of space and since Spinoza's taxonomy of affects has been well-discussed elsewhere, I will not linger over the details here.[83]

I do, however, want to mention a very important general feature of this taxonomy. For Spinoza, affects are individuated by their cognitive content. This is evident in the cases of love and hate which are defined in terms of the kinds of beliefs or thoughts they contain. In general, for Spinoza, affects are intentional mental states. They are not contentless sensations (as they are in Hume), but rather cognitive states directed at a particular object or state of affairs. Spinoza makes this general claim in 2a3: "There are no modes of thinking, such as love, desire, or whatever is designated by the word affects of the mind, unless there is in the same individual the idea of the thing loved, desired, etc. But there can be an idea, even though there is no other mode of thinking." The cognitive nature of affects plays a central role in Spinoza's account of the means by which we may destroy harmful affects or at least lessen their deleterious effects. Since a harmful affect – like any other – essentially involves beliefs, thoughts, and so forth, if we are able to alter the relevant cognitive state, we will thereby alter or even destroy the harmful affect. In this way, we can see how principles of affect constitution carry important practical and ethical implications for Spinoza.[84]

The other type of principle governing the relations among Spinozistic affects consists of principles of affect transition. Affect transition occurs when one affect A gives rise to affect B, but neither affect constitutes the other. That is, neither affect contains the other in the way that my love of x contains a feeling of joy. An example will make this clear. Let us say that I have an affect of sadness. As we have seen, for Spinoza such an affect gives rise to another affect: the desire to remove the sadness (E 3p37). The desire is not constituted by the sadness. My desire is not my sadness qualified in some way.

Similarly, my sadness is not constituted by my desire. Rather, my desire is a wholly separate affect caused by the affect of sadness. Thus this would not be a case of affect constitution, but instead a case of what I call affect transition.

I want to examine some of the principles governing affect transition. The principle behind the above transition from sadness to desire is one we have already investigated. Such a transition flows simply from the tendency of each thing to preserve itself and enhance its power of acting. However, other cases of affect transition involve different principles.

To see these different principles, I need to explain Spinoza's general doctrine of the association of mental states. This in turn requires focusing for a moment on Spinoza's account of memory. For Spinoza the recollection of an earlier event or object that one experienced requires that one's body be in the same state as it was when it originally experienced that event or object (see E 2p17cd). In this respect, the account of memory parallels Spinoza's account of anticipation. As we saw, for an individual to anticipate a given event requires that the individual's body be in the state that it would be in if the event were actually occurring.

Bracketing the many questions that might arise in connection with this account of memory, I simply want to point out the way in which this account can be seen as stemming from a general doctrine of the association of mental states. In 2p18, Spinoza makes the important claim: "If the human body has once been affected by two or more bodies at the same time, then when the mind subsequently imagines one of them, it will immediately recollect the others also." Spinoza is saying here that if at a certain moment I perceive X and Y and if at a later time I recall X, then at that later time I will also recall Y. His argument is as follows: If I recall X then, by the above account of memory, it must be the case that my body is in the same state as it was when I originally perceived X. Now, as we saw earlier in connection with 3p18d, Spinoza assumes that if at two different times the body is in the same state, then at those different times the mind is in the same state. My bodily state when I originally perceived X was present with certain mental states. These mental states included not only an idea of X, but also an idea of Y. Thus, given Spinoza's assumption, it must be the case that if my body is again in that state, my mind must again have an idea not only of X, but also of Y. This is why, for Spinoza, if I recall X I will recall Y as well (E 2p18d).

At work here is the following claim about the association of ideas of particular objects:

> If at t_1 I have an idea of X and an idea of Y, and if at later time t_2 I again have an idea of X, then at t_2 I again have an idea of Y.

This is a principle concerning the association of ideas of particular objects. But the considerations at work here suggest a claim about the association of mental states in general:

> If at t_1, I am in mental state A and mental state B and if at t_2 I am again in mental state A, then at t_2 I am again in mental state B.

This would be a general doctrine of the association of mental states. Spinoza does not explicitly formulate this general doctrine. However, given 2p18's explicit claim concerning the association of ideas of particular objects and given 2a3's claim that there is an ideational component in mental states in general, it would be quite implausible to reject the general associationist doctrine. In fact, the following Spinozistic line of argument, modeled on 2p18d, indicates that Spinoza is committed to the general view. Let us say that at t_1 I have mental states A and B and that at t_2 I again have mental state A. This can only be the case if my body is in the same state at t_2 as it was at t_1. (Here I am invoking a general version of a claim at work in Spinoza's accounts of memory and anticipation.) At t_1 my body was in a state that was present with certain mental states – in particular mental states A and B. Given Spinoza's superveniencelike assumption that if someone is in the same bodily state at two different times, then he is in the same mental state at those times, it follows that mental states A and B must both be present at t_2. We can see, therefore, that Spinoza is committed to the conclusion that because of the earlier association of mental states A and B, it must be the case that if I subsequently am in mental state A, I will also be in mental state B.[85]

The above Spinozistic arguments for associationist claims do not work. The general problem is this: Spinoza seems to say that the recurrence of a mental state requires the recurrence of the entire physical state of the individual at the time of the original occurrence of the mental state. Surely this is not true. In the case of the recurrence of a mental state, the earlier physical state and the later one must, perhaps, have something in common. However, there is no reason to think that there must be a thoroughgoing similarity that would, by virtue of some kind of supervenience claim, drag along *all* of the mental states originally associated with the one that recurs. Further, there seems to be no reason why the similarity should drag along *any* of the associated mental states. So, Spinoza's reasoning in support of a claim of association seems flawed.

Nevertheless, some version of an associationist doctrine does seem to be true[86] and it is this plausibility that confers plausibility on certain principles of affect transition that depend on the associationist doctrine. Let us begin with a simple case of affect transition. At t_1 I experienced two affects: enjoyment of ice cream and sadness at the loss of a game by my favorite team. Later, when I enjoy ice cream, I experience a revival of the earlier sadness. Since the enjoyment at t_2 gives rise to the sadness at t_2 and since neither the sadness at t_2 nor the enjoyment at t_2 constitutes the other, this is a case of affect transition. Affect transition is also involved in the relation between the earlier affects and the later ones. The later ones are caused, in part, by the earlier ones, but they are not constituted by the earlier ones.

The general doctrine of the association of mental states also makes possible certain more complicated cases of affect transition. For example, at a moment of great sadness for x, another individual, y, happened to be present and x was aware of this presence. y, however, was not at all the cause of x's sadness and did not contribute to it in any way. In this case, an association is established between the affect of sadness and a perception of y. By the general doctrine of the association of mental states, later perceptions of y will give rise to a similar feeling of sadness. y is, therefore, a partial cause of this subsequent sadness and x may well regard y as such a cause. Seeing y as the cause of this sadness, x will come to hate y (E 3p13s). In this case, again, we have affect transition. The original sadness is a partial cause of x's later sadness and hatred of y. Spinoza recognizes this kind of case and offers his account of it in 3p15 and 3p15c. In the terminology of that account, Spinoza would say that y is the "accidental cause" of x's later pain and that that is why x comes to hate y.[87]

Similarity between individuals provides a particularly interesting kind of affect transition that arises out of the general phenomenon of the association of mental states. Spinoza calls attention to this kind of case in 3p16: "From the mere fact that we imagine a thing to have some likeness to an object that usually affects the mind with joy or sadness, we love it or hate it even though that in which the thing is like the object is not the efficient cause of these affects." His demonstration proceeds along the following lines. Assume that y causes x to feel sad and that x is aware of this fact. At the time at which y harms x, x is aware that y has feature F, although this feature is not relevant to the harm y caused x. At a later time, x perceives z, an individual different from y. Despite their distinctness, z, like y, has feature F and x is aware that z has F. Due to x's past acquaintance with y, an association has been established in x's mind between the perception of feature F and sadness. Thus when in encountering z, x perceives F again, x will, by virtue of this association, feel sad. z is the "accidental cause" of this second episode of sadness and if x realizes this, then x will, as a result, come to hate z. Because of the similarity between y and z and because of the phenomenon of the association of mental states, the original sadness caused by y gives rise to further sadness and also hatred of z. This would be another case of affect transition.[88]

Two further facts about this case should be mentioned.[89] (1) The transition of affects as a result of similarity will not occur unless x regards z as F. The transition turns upon an association between a perception of F and a feeling of sadness. Thus without a perception of z as F, no feeling of sadness is due to z and thus no hatred of z can be generated in this case. This is so even if z is in fact F (and x simply does not realize this fact). (2) Further, the transition would occur even if x's belief that z is F is false. The transition turns on the features x regards z (and y) as having, not on what features they actually have. So even if x wrongly thinks that z is F, x will come to hate z.[90]

A different kind of affect transition seems not to operate on a principle of the association of mental states within a given individual. Such transition occurs when an affect in one individual gives rise to a similar affect in another individual. Spinoza calls this the imitation of affects[91] and he introduces it in 3p27: "If we imagine a thing like us, toward which we have had no affect, to be affected with some affect, we are thereby affected with a like affect." Such imitation can arise with any affect. For example, the sadness of another can elicit a corresponding feeling of sadness in me. Spinoza calls this "pity" (E 3p22s, E 3p27s). Another's desire for a certain thing can generate in me a desire for the same thing. Spinoza calls this "emulation" (E 3p27s, E 3da33). Similar points hold for the other affects. It is difficult to deny that Spinoza captures an actual phenomenon here, though, as we will see, his argument for the view that such imitation occurs has serious flaws.

In order to determine the circumstances under which, according to Spinoza, x imitates y's affects, three features of Spinoza's doctrine of imitation must be considered. (1) Spinoza specifies in 3p27 that for x to imitate y's affects, y and x must be similar.[92] This is a plausible point. I am much less likely to be moved by the struggles of a spider than by those of a fellow human being. Spinoza does not spell out the degree of similarity required before imitation takes effect. However, as Curley points out,

[I]t would be expecting too much of him to do that. It seems clear that this is a matter where individual differences are tremendous. Some will feel compassion on the basis of very little similarity, others will be able to identify only with a very limited circle of people like themselves, and most will feel varying degrees of compassion depending on the degree of similarity. (Curley 1988: 118–19)[93]

(2) The phrase "toward which we have had no affect" in 3p27 might seem to suggest that x imitates y's affects only when x has had no previous affect directed toward y. From this phrase, Spinoza might appear to be thinking along the following lines: Normally, if x and y are similar, y's affect of joy will generate a similar affect in x. However, if x hates y, then y's joy will sadden x (E 3p23). Thus, x will not imitate y's joy.

However, it would be wrong to conclude from 3p27 that for Spinoza when x antecedently hates y, affect imitation does not occur. In 3p27d, Spinoza merely says that *to the extent that (eatenus)* x hates y, x is affected by an affect contrary to y's, not by a like affect. This is compatible with affect imitation because it is compatible with saying that *to the extent that* x is like y, x is affected by an affect similar to y's, not by a contrary affect. If this latter claim is correct it follows that if x is like y *and* x hates y, then x experiences conflicting affects.

Spinoza makes precisely this claim in 3p47: "The joy which arises from our imagining that a thing we hate is destroyed, or affected with some other evil, does not occur without some sadness of mind" (see also 3p23s).

(3) x's imitation of affect A in y occurs only if x regards y as having that affect. Further, even if x falsely regards y as having a certain affect, then x will come to have an affect of that type.[94] These claims are implicit in Spinoza's specification that affect imitation involves x's *imagining* y to have a certain affect.

The above three points suggest the following general account of affect imitation:

> x imitates y with respect to affect A iff y is similar to x and x regards y as having affect A.[95]

However, because of the possibility of x's becoming sad on the basis of a false belief that y is sad, such an account must be modified slightly. As stated above, the account implies that in such a case x is imitating y with respect to sadness. But how can x be said to imitate y in this way if y is not actually sad? *Imitation* of affects seems to require an actual matching of affects in two individuals. Spinoza does not deal with this kind of problem facing the above account of imitation. To get out of the difficulty, however, we simply need to coin some new terms. I will say that in the case in which x's belief concerning y is false, there is nonveridical imitation. If x's belief is true, there is veridical imitation. I will use the term "q-imitation" to cover cases of veridical imitation and also cases of nonveridical imitation.[96] Thus to say that x q-imitates y with respect to affect A carries no implication as to whether or not y actually has affect A. The claim simply implies that x believes that y has affect A. With the notion of q-imitation in hand, we can modify the above account of imitation in the following way:

> x q-imitates y with respect to affect A iff y is similar to x and x regards y as having affect A.

This account of q-imitation sets forth a principle governing the generation of affects. However, one should note that not all cases of the q-imitation of affects are cases of the transition of affects from one individual to another. Such transpersonal affect transition occurs only when an affect in one individual gives rise to an affect in another individual. In very many cases of the q-imitation of affects, y's having affect A leads x to believe that y has affect A. This belief in turn leads x to have affect A. This would be a genuine transition from one instance of affect A (in y) to another instance of affect A (in x). But in other cases of q-imitation, there is no genuine transition of affects from y to x. For example, in a case of nonveridical imitation, there need not be any affect in y that is responsible for the affect generated in x.[97]

The notion of imitation throws new light on Spinoza's views on anticipation. Recall that for Spinoza the anticipation of pain is itself painful.[98] In such a case if I believe at t_1 that I will experience sadness at t_2, then I experience sadness at t_1. Although Spinoza does not describe the case in these terms, it might be seen as involving one's present self imitating the affects of one's future self. Let us say that x is my current self and y is my future self. x and y might well satisfy the conditions for affect imitation. y is, it seems, similar to x. Further, if I anticipate being sad at t_2, then we can say that x (my present self) believes that y (my future self) will be sad at that time. Thus, x satisfies the two conditions for imitating y. In anticipating sadness, my present self is imitating my future self with respect to the affect of sadness.[99]

Not only does the account of imitation shed light on Spinoza's views on anticipation, there is also illumination in the reverse direction. As we have seen, for Spinoza, the pain of anticipation is weaker than the anticipated pain (E 4p9). This would be a case in which what might be called the imitating affect is weaker than the imitated affect. This fact suggests the plausible and more general view that when one individual imitates the affects of another, the imitating affect is weaker than the imitated affect. For example, the sadness I feel at watching your suffering may be great, but it is probably not as great as the sadness you yourself are experiencing (or, perhaps, not as great as the sadness I regard you as experiencing). Spinoza does not explicitly make the point that imitating affects are weaker than their imitated counterparts, but such a point does clearly follow from his system.

Spinoza's doctrine of imitation plays very many other key roles in his system. Perhaps most important is the way in which he employs the doctrine to show how a concern for the interests of others emerges from his thoroughgoing egoism (E 4p37d2).[100] The importance of the doctrine only heightens the importance of providing a cogent argument for it. Unfortunately, Spinoza's argument is not cogent. The main problem with 3p27d is that it rests on a general claim to the effect that if x perceives y to be F (for any feature F), then x thereby becomes more like y in respect of F.[101] This is clearly false: For example, if I perceive that Bob is seven feet tall, I do not thereby become a bit taller. Thus 3p27d cannot work.[102]

But all is not lost. Spinoza's own doctrine of the association of mental states can, I believe, go some distance toward providing the kind of argumentative support that the doctrine of imitation needs. It is important to note that this is not a trivial claim: It is *not* the case that the imitation of affects is, by definition, a kind of association of mental states. Association, as I have defined it, is a particular relation between mental states of a given individual, whereas the imitation of affects concerns (purported) cases relating affects in different individuals.[103] Nevertheless, imitation may be regarded as involving association in a subtle way.

Recall that in order for me to imitate y's sadness, I must believe that y is sad. Typically, I become aware of sadness in y by observing y's behavior. In the past, when I was sad I may have behaved similarly and I may have been aware of such behavior on my part. Thus my own experience has established an association between an idea of a certain kind of behavior and a feeling of sadness. When I perceive such behavior in y, the general principle of the association of mental states determines that I will also experience sadness. In this way, I come to imitate y's affect of sadness. We could, in a similar fashion, explain any of the other cases of affect imitation that Spinoza's account is meant to cover.[104]

This line of thought provides genuinely Spinozistic support for his doctrine of imitation. The argument, however, relies on the doctrine of association and, as we have seen, Spinoza does not provide adequate support for this doctrine. This is why I said above only that the doctrine of association goes *some* distance toward providing the requisite support for the doctrine of imitation. Nevertheless, the argument for the imitation doctrine that I have outlined is, I think, an improvement over Spinoza's official argument in 3p27d. Progress often consists in showing how two difficulties stand or fall together and my alternative proof at least accomplishes this.

Human teleology

The aim of the third section of this chapter is to investigate some of the principles governing the relations among psychological states in human beings. In this subsection I will explore the extent to which Spinoza allows teleological explanations in his psychological system.

Human psychology seems to admit of teleological explanations, that is, explanations which view actions as performed for the sake of an end. An example (from Bennett 1984: 216) would be: I raise my hand so as to deflect the stone. Here we are explaining an action in terms of its purpose and it is natural to unpack this explanation in the following way: I desire to deflect the stone and this desire (together with, perhaps, a belief that by raising my hand I will deflect the stone) explains my action. (There is no reason, I believe, not to see the explanation at work here as a causal explanation. The relevant mental states cause my actions.)[105] Such an explanation of an action which proceeds in terms of one's desires or goals and beliefs about the future is a teleological explanation within psychology.[106] That such explanations are possible seems to be a basic fact about psychology.

Yet Spinoza might be regarded as denying this fact. In the appendix to Part 1 of the *Ethics*, he does say that "all final causes are nothing but human fictions." Since final causes are purposes with which things act, this claim might seem to deny the legitimacy of any teleological explanation. However, as Curley carefully explains, the context makes clear that Spinoza is not here rejecting teleological explanation in general, but rather what might be called divine teleology in particular. This is the view that "God himself directs all things to some certain end" and, in particular, "that God has made all things for man, and man that he might worship God" (E 1ap). Spinoza's rejection of such a view does not imply that he would reject teleological explanation in the case of human beings. Indeed, as Curley also notes, Spinoza in the preface to Part 4 juxtaposes a denial of divine teleology with an endorsement of human teleology:

As [God or Nature] exists for the sake of no end, he also acts for the sake of no end. Rather, as he has no principle or end of existing, so he also has none of acting. What is called a final cause is nothing but a human appetite insofar as it is considered as a principle, or primary cause, of some thing. For example, when we say that habitation was the final cause of this or that house, surely we understand nothing but that a man, because he imagined the conveniences of domestic life, had an appetite to build a house. So habitation, insofar as it is considered as a final cause, is nothing more than this singular appetite. It is really an efficient cause, which is considered as a first cause, because men are commonly ignorant of the causes of their appetites.

Thus Spinoza seems to have no difficulty in allowing human teleology into his system.

Bennett, however, demurs. He has recently acknowledged that Spinoza does allow that desires and other psychological states cause or explain human actions (Bennett 1990). This is something of a concession since, in Bennett 1984, Bennett had attributed to Spinoza a more thoroughgoing rejection of teleology.[107] In response to criticism by Curley, Bennett backs off from this extreme position. Nevertheless, while conceding that Spinoza accepts teleology in the above sense, Bennett still wants to maintain that Spinoza rejects a crucial component of teleology. Spinoza's teleology is thus, for Bennett, "a notably half-hearted affair" (Bennett 1990: 53). In the remainder of this section, after describing what Bennett sees as a component of teleology, I will argue that Bennett does not show that Spinoza actually rejects this aspect of teleology.

To explain this aspect, I need to say a bit about the distinction between causally relevant and causally irrelevant features of events or states. Assume that Bill kills Fred by shooting him with a gun.[108] Let us call the firing of the gun "A" and Fred's death "B." A causes B. A has, of course, the property of being a gun-firing. Further, suppose that A also has the property of being loud. These two properties of the same event seem to play different roles in the causation of B. Consider these claims:

(1) It is because A was loud that A caused B.
(2) It is because A was a gun-firing that A caused B.

Intuitively (1) seems false and (2) true. The loudness of A seems to have nothing to do with its causing B, but A's being the firing of a gun does seem to have quite a lot to do with A's causing B. We can mark this difference between the two properties by saying that the loudness is a causally irrelevant feature while being a gun-firing is causally relevant.

Let us return now to teleological explanations, according to which, for example, my raising my hand is caused by a desire to deflect the stone together with my belief that raising my hand will deflect the stone. The claim that there are such causal relations is, however, only a part of a full-blown acceptance of teleology. The further claim that is crucial here is the claim that the representative features of desires and beliefs are relevant to the causation of our actions. A representative feature is, for example, the belief's feature of having a certain content or the desire's feature of being a desire to deflect the stone.[109] It is clear that we do think of representative features as causally relevant to action. Let us call the desire in this case "C" and my action "D." Now consider:

> (3) It is because C is a desire to deflect the stone that C caused D.

(3) seems to be true. This reflects our conviction that representative features of mental states can be relevant to the causation of action.

Accepting such a claim can be seen as a commitment to a further respect in which teleology reigns in the explanation of human action. We can distinguish two components of a full-blown acceptance of teleology. The first component is:

> (4) Desires for certain outcomes and beliefs about how to attain them cause our actions.

As we have already seen, Spinoza accepts such a claim and Bennett acknowledges that Spinoza does so. The second component presupposes (4) but is not entailed by it:

> (5) The representative features of such desires and beliefs are relevant to the causation of our actions.

Since (4) does not entail (5), one can consistently accept (4) but reject (5). But to reject (5) would be to go against much of our thinking about teleological explanations of action. It would, in effect, be to deny that claims like

> (3) It is because C is a desire to deflect the stone that C caused D.

are ever true. Thus a view that accepts (4) but rejects (5) would indeed be a half-hearted espousal of teleology.

This is the position Bennett attributes to Spinoza. He says that despite Spinoza's acceptance of (4), Spinoza holds that the representative nature of a mental state "is irrelevant to its causal powers"

(Bennett 1990: 55). Bennett's reason for this attribution turns on two points: the fact that Bennett insists on a very strong requirement for a feature to be causally relevant and the fact that he thinks that, for Spinoza, representative features do not meet this requirement.

Bennett's strict requirement for causal relevance is this: A feature is relevant to a causal relation only if that feature would be cited in a strict, scientific law covering that causal relation. This requirement is evident in his endorsement of the following claim: "[T]he representative features of mental states, though they figure in rough-and-ready laymen's explanations of behavior, have no place in any disciplined, scientific account of how the mind does its work" (Bennett 1990: 56). Bennett goes on from this to conclude that representative features are causally irrelevant.

According to Bennett, Spinoza holds that representative features do not figure in any disciplined, scientific account of the mind's powers. For the moment, I will forego questioning Bennett's claim here. Instead I want to show that even if this claim is right, it is not at all clear that this would mean, as Bennett claims, that Spinoza is committed to a denial of the causal relevance of representative features. In other words, I want to challenge Bennett's requirement on the causal relevance of properties.

It is far from clear that in order to be able to say that a property is causally relevant, we must be able to say that it would figure in "a disciplined, scientific account." Return to the example of the shooting. The fact that an event is a gun-firing can, it seems, tell us only in "a rough-and-ready laymen's way" what will follow from such an event. Thus it seems rather unlikely that this property will show up in a disciplined, scientific account of the causal relation between A and B. Nonetheless, there is a strong sense in which being a gun-firing is a causally relevant feature of A. This is manifested by the fact that

(2) It is because A was a gun-firing that A caused B.

seems to be true. Thus it is not clear that Bennett's requirement for the causal relevance of a feature is correct.[110]

For this reason it is also not clear that if Spinoza were to hold that representative features do not appear in strict scientific laws, then he would be committed to the causal irrelevance of such features. Before Bennett can make good his claim that Spinoza accepts or would accept such irrelevance, he needs to offer more support than he in fact provides for his strong requirement on causal relevance. Since the claim that Spinoza would accept the causal irrelevance of representative features is essential to Bennett's view that Spinoza is only a half-hearted teleologist, the charge of half-heartedness is also in need of further support.

But the troubles for Bennett's interpretation are not over. As we saw, Bennett's view that Spinoza regards representative features as causally irrelevant is based, in part, on the further claim that for Spinoza representative features would not figure in a scientific account of how the mind works. This latter claim, however, is by no means certain. Bennett's reason for this claim turns on his interpretation of 2p16 and its corollaries as implying that the representative features of a mental state are a function of its causal history.[111] He sees this point, in turn, as entailing that two states could be intrinsically alike, but differ representatively because they have different causal histories. On the assumption (which Bennett makes and also attributes to Spinoza) that only intrinsic features play a role in a scientific account of causal relations of a mental state, it would follow that the representative features of a mental state do not play a role in a scientific account of how the mind works (Bennett 1990: 55).

These are interesting and important implications to draw from Spinoza's views in 2p16 and its corollaries. However, there is no sign that Spinoza appreciates the point that two states could be alike intrinsically, but unalike representationally, and there is certainly no sign that Spinoza recognizes that such a point would have a bearing on the ability of representative features to figure in strict, scientific accounts of the causal powers of the mind. So I do not think that Bennett has made his case for the view that Spinoza reaches such a conclusion. Spinoza may be committed to this conclusion, but it is a commitment he certainly never recognizes. Because the claim that for Spinoza representative features play no role in scientific theorizing about the causal powers of the mind is crucial to Bennett's view that Spinoza rejects a full-blown teleology, we have yet another reason to doubt this view.

Should we then conclude that Spinoza is a full-blown teleologist? To do so, we would need to be convinced that Spinoza is clear about the distinction between a teleology which accepts only

(4) Desires for certain outcomes and beliefs about how to attain them cause our actions,

and one which accepts (4) as well as

(5) The representative features of such desires and beliefs are relevant to the causation of our actions.

This is an important psychological and, indeed, metaphysical distinction; unfortunately, despite the fact that Spinoza is a psychologist and a metaphysician, there is no strong evidence that he recognizes such a distinction.[112]

NOTES

1 Unless otherwise noted, I employ Curley's translations of Spinoza (Spinoza 1985a). See also *Ethics* 4p57s. Bennett captures Spinoza's view well: "[T]he whole truth about human beings can be told in terms which are needed anyway to describe the rest of the universe, and . . . men differ only in degree and not in kind from all other parts of reality" (Bennett 1984: 36).

2 In *Treatise on the Emendation of the Intellect* 85, Spinoza says that he conceives the soul "as acting according to certain laws, like a spiritual automaton."

3 My general assessment here is similar to Bennett's (Bennett 1984: 38). However, as will become apparent, Bennett and I differ on many substantive points of interpretation.

4 "*Unaquaeque res, quantum in se est, in suo esse perseverare.*" Cf. here *Theological-Political Treatise* xvi.2: "It is a supreme law of nature that each thing, insofar as it is in itself, strives to persevere in its state" ("*lex summa naturae est, ut unaquaeque res in suo statu, quantum in se est, conetur perseverare*"). I use the literal translation "insofar as it is in itself" of the phrase "*quantum in se est*" because it highlights the important connection, which I will draw later, between *Ethics* 3p6 and Spinoza's definition of substance as that which is in itself. Curley ("as far as it can by its own power") and Caillois ("*selon sa puissance d'être*") prefer less literal translations. For discussion, see Spinoza 1985a: 498n15 and Spinoza 1954: 1427–8.

5 See Curley 1988: 107–8.

6 See *Principles of Philosophy* 3.57 (Descartes 1985: I,259–60) and Garber 1992: 354n10,355n29.

7 Here Spinoza speaks of the striving to move in a certain way, rather than tending to do so. However, this discrepancy is not significant since, as

we have just seen, these terms seem to be synonymous in Descartes. See Curley's note on this passage in Spinoza 1985a: 280n43.

8 And even more famously in Newton's definition of inertial force as "the power of resisting by which each body, insofar as it is in itself (*quantum in se est*), perseveres in its state of rest or of moving uniformly in a straight line." See Cohen 1964.

9 For the significance of Descartes's restriction to simple and undivided things, see Garber 1992: 212–13. Spinoza's principle concerning the preservation of motion and rest is restricted to what he calls simplest bodies (*corpora simplicissima*). See 2p13le3c and 2p13a2″, after that corollary.

10 And this, in turn, is the same as what it is for x to tend to do F.

11 See Curley 1969 Chapter 1 and Curley 1973b: 367–8. The most important occurrence of the term "*in se*" is, of course, in the definition of "substance" as that which is in itself and is conceived through itself (E 1d3). Interestingly, in Letter 32 Spinoza equates regarding something as independent of external causes with regarding something as a whole. It seems, then, that for Spinoza x is in itself iff x is independent of external causes iff x is a whole.

12 See also the passage from the *Theological-Political Treatise* xvi.2, quoted in note 4.

13 For example, in *Principles of Philosophy* 3.55 Descartes does use both terms, but they occur in different sentences. *Principles of Philosophy* 2.37, though, is something of an exception. There Descartes says that "every piece of matter, *considered in itself*, always tends to continue moving" (my emphasis). The phrase "considered in itself" is not, however, a translation of "*quantum in se est*," but rather of "*seorsim spectatam*." In his definition of inertial force where Newton uses the term "*quantum in se est*," he also does not use terms such as "strives."

14 See 2d2 which says, in part, that a thing cannot be without that which pertains to its essence.

15 See also note 23.

16 Curley 1988: 110. See Matson 1977: 407–8. The example derives from *Treatise on the Emendation of the Intellect* 57.

17 See Bennett 1984: 238.

18 Curley (in Curley 1988: 110) favors something like this diagnosis, though he does not mention any construal of 3p6 along the lines of (b). It is hard to know how to deal with the sun counterexample in the above way because it is not clear what external causes caused the sun not to be such that it will continue to exist unless prevented by external causes.

19 And thus, from now on, in speaking of 3p6, I mean to refer to (c), unless I indicate otherwise.

20 "*Nulla res, nisi a causa externa, potest destrui.*"

21 For further evidence that Spinoza accepts nonessential properties and for an explanation of how this acceptance is compatible with Spinoza's necessitarianism, see Garrett 1991.

22 I am indebted here to Bennett's discussion of 3p4d (Bennett 1984: 236–7).

23 *Ethics* 3p4 interpreted as (e) may, however, entail 3p6 *interpreted as (b)*. If this is so, then there is even further evidence that Spinoza may be inclined toward reading 3p6 as (b) instead of as (c). Here is why I think that (e) entails (b): Consider under what circumstances (b) would be false and also consider whether in these circumstances (e) could be true. (b) would be false only if a thing could be in a state S_1 that sufficed for its destruction, but did not come to be in S_1 as a result of external causes. If the thing did not come to be in S_1 as a result of external causes, then, I believe, the fact that it is in that state must have followed solely from the thing's *essence*. It will not help to say that the thing is in S_1 solely because of some earlier state S_2 of that thing, for then we could inquire as to how the thing came to be in S_2 and a regress would threaten. (It will also not help to say that the thing is in S_1 for no reason at all. Spinoza would clearly disallow any such brute fact.) The only way to account for the thing's being in S_1, short of appealing to external causes, would be to appeal to the thing's essence. The only case in which (b) is false would thus be a case in which the thing's essence accounted for its being in S_1. But notice that this is also a case in which (e) is false: Here the thing's essence can be said to suffice for its destruction because it suffices for its being in S_1 which in turn suffices for its destruction. Since there is no possible situation in which (e) is true and (b) is false, (e) entails (b).

24 Spinoza's conflation of (d) and (e) is not surprising since it is a way of failing to distinguish properly between what a thing is responsible for and what its essence is responsible for. Such a conflation of things with their essences is pervasive in Spinoza. See, e.g., Spinoza's shift from talking about perceiving the nature of bodies in 2p16c1 to talking about perceiving the bodies themselves in 2p16c2. This type of conflation may also be at work in Spinoza's tendency to identify a substance with its attributes, i.e., with that which the intellect perceives as constituting the substance's essence (E 1d4).

25 For some discussion, see Bennett 1984: 240–3. Curley 1988: 109 also holds that 3p5 can be seen as relatively idle.

26 My examples will concern complex physical individuals, but most of what I say would, I think, apply to complex mental individuals as well. Spinoza would certainly regard mental individuals and physical individuals as on a par here.

27 I have been helped here by Hampshire 1951: 76–81 and Bennett 1984: 246–51.

28 This claim needs to be qualified somewhat. There need not be many *actual* occasions on which the constituents of a given complex individual succeed in maintaining a certain overall relation. The chair, e.g., might be blown up immediately after it is created and thus its constituents might have little opportunity to preserve their overall relation. Nevertheless, the chair counts as an individual during the brief moment of its existence because, while there are few actual occasions on which its constituents preserve a certain overall relation, there are many counterfactual cases in which the chair would maintain this overall relation among its parts. The exploded chair was just, in effect, a particularly unlucky chair. That chair *would*, in very many circumstances, maintain the overall relation among its parts, even though it actually did not do so for more than a second. This indicates that the general account of complex individuality should require only very many actual *or counterfactual* cases in which the constituents of the complex object maintain a certain overall relation. I will not, though, make this qualification in the text.

29 I am, of course, omitting to discuss a vast array of problems that would need to be addressed in a fuller account of identity over time. One such problem concerns the ability of objects to gain and lose parts while maintaining their identity over time. Relatedly, various problems of branching also crop up here. Nevertheless, something like the general claim in the text seems to be right.

30 For helpful statements of this view see Davidson, Davidson 1982: 302–3; Davidson 1985: 351–4; and Rovane forthcoming.

31 See the definition after 2p13le3. In the case of physical individuals, Spinoza calls this relation among the parts their "proportion of motion and rest" (e.g., in 2p13le5).

32 See 2p13le4–7, 4p39, *Short Treatise* II Preface.

33 We will see later that Spinoza does not himself make this analogous mistake concerning irrationality.

34 See for example *Short Treatise* I.5, to which I will turn briefly later.

35 See 2p7s and Della Rocca 1993: 209.

36 Spinoza's definition is, strictly, only a definition of activity *in us* (presumably in human beings). But there is clearly no obstacle in formulating a notion of activity for things in general along similar lines.

37 It appears from this definition that changes of which one is not even a partial cause are ones with regard to which one is neither active nor passive.

38 For Spinoza, the notions of increase and decrease in power of acting are equivalent to the notions of increase and decrease in perfection. See 3da3ex and 4pr.

39 Of course, effects brought about by the object prior to its destruction can

go on to produce further effects, after that thing's destruction. We might then say that the object is producing effects even after its destruction. But, in a clear enough sense, the object is no longer *directly* producing any effects and in this sense it is no longer active at all.

40 Spinoza actually speaks of the mind's power of thinking here (not power of acting). But it is clear that the mind's power of thinking is its power of acting. In 3p11s Spinoza describes an increase in the mind's power of thinking as its passage to a state of greater perfection. As I mentioned in note 38, Spinoza equates a thing's passage to a state of greater perfection with an increase in that thing's power of acting. Thus, for Spinoza, an increase in the mind's power of thinking is an increase in its power of acting.

41 Actually, he concludes that the mind strives, *insofar as far as it can* (*quantum potest*), to imagine those things. The qualifying phrase "insofar as far as it can" generates the same interpretive difficulties and options as did "insofar as it is in itself" in connection with 3p6.

42 For example, since being free of the sling would increase the stone's power of acting, it can be said to strive to be free of the sling.

43 While I do attribute a mistaken inference here to Spinoza, I do not agree with Bennett that in these passages Spinoza is guilty of a conflation of a conditional and its converse. Bennett holds – and I agree – that in 3p12 and related passages Spinoza is asserting something like "(1) If it helps him, he does it." Bennett also holds that Spinoza illegitimately makes these claims on the basis of "(2) If he does it, it helps him," which, according to Bennett, is at work in earlier passages such as 3p7 and 3p9. An inference from (2) to (1) would certainly be illegitimate, but I do not think that Spinoza makes such an inference. This is because Spinoza is not asserting (2) in these earlier passages. This point should be clear from my account of Spinoza's notion of striving – a notion at work in 3p7 and 3p9. Bennett's reason for attributing (2) to Spinoza in these earlier passages turns, in large part, on his reading of a sentence from 3p9s as involving (2), and not (1). (See Bennett 1984: 222.) The sentence in question is: "from [man's] nature there necessarily follow those things that promote his preservation." However, this claim is more naturally read along the lines of (1) rather than (2). Oddly enough, Bennett later makes this point himself (Bennett 1984: 245).

44 See note 24.

45 Spinoza's term *"affectus"* is often translated "emotion," but Curley presents good reasons for preferring the translation "affect." See Spinoza 1985a: 625.

46 As expressed in 2p7: "The order and connection of ideas is the same as the order and connection of things."

47 See 2p7s and 3p2s where Spinoza affirms an identity of mental things
    and physical things. I discuss this identity claim in Della Rocca 1993;
    Della Rocca forthcoming, 1996.

48 See Bennett 1984: 259.

49 For the former kind of desire, see 4p20d; for the latter kind, see 3p12d
    (which we discussed earlier).

50 For more on the notion of *de re* desire, see W. V. O. Quine, "Quantifiers
    and Propositional Attitudes," *The Journal of Philosophy*, 53 (1956):
    177–86.

51 See especially 3p28 and 4p19 (which is derived from 3p28). Bennett
    1984: 294–5 discusses the more cautious view.

52 Recall that by "perfection," Spinoza means "power of acting." See note
    38. Spinoza's terms for these affects are *"laetitia"* and *"tristitia."*
    Some have translated these not as "joy" and "sadness," but as "plea-
    sure" and "pain" (e.g., Elwes and Shirley.) I endorse Curley's reasons
    for preferring "joy" and "sadness." See Spinoza 1985: 642,654. How-
    ever, since some of my examples (especially in the next subsection) of
    laetitia and *tristitia* are more naturally construed as examples of plea-
    sure and pain, I will sometimes use these terms instead of, or in addi-
    tion to, "joy" and "sadness." Further, since certain Spinozistic theses
    are somewhat less cumbersomely phrased in the pleasure/pain vocabu-
    lary than in the joy/sadness vocabulary, I will use the former vocabu-
    lary in such cases.

53 Bidney 1940: 75, comments on this difference between 3p11s and the
    later definitions.

54 I am not saying, though, that Spinoza's official account necessarily com-
    mits him to the view that in each case the destruction of a loved one
    involves decrease of power and thus involves sadness. The destruction of
    a loved one merely entails that a source of increase in power has been
    removed. This removal does not necessarily involve a decrease in power
    of acting and thus does not necessarily involve sadness. My point here,
    however, simply relies on the weaker claim that the destruction of a
    loved one can involve decrease of power.

55 For related passages, see 3pp20–24.

56 Here and in what follows, when I speak of desiring or striving to do F at
    t_1, I intend the phrase "at t_1" to apply to the doing and not to the desiring
    or striving. Thus desiring to do F at t_1 is to be contrasted with desiring at
    t_1 to do F.

57 On the terms "sadness" and "pain," see note 52.

58 For such an explanation to be genuinely naturalistic, it would, of course,
    have to be conjoined with a naturalistic account of belief.

59 See also Spinoza's definitions of fear and despair, 3p18s2 and 3da13,15.

60 *Ethics* 3p13d does not explicitly concern anticipation, but it does speak of imaginative states in general and, as Spinoza does claim (E 2p44s), anticipatory beliefs fall under this category.

61 Spinoza makes a parallel claim concerning the preservation of joy in 3p37d. He seems to regard both claims as following directly from his view that each thing strives for self-preservation; it is not clear, however, why this should follow.

62 Our striving is also directed to the preservation of current pleasure (if we are experiencing pleasure).

63 Spinoza's reasons here turn on his doctrine of the imitation of affects which I will discuss in section 3.

64 For related passages, see 3p26s, 3da21,22,28,29.

65 Such motivated false belief need not involve self-deception. Self-deception requires that one's belief in p be part of what generates or sustains one's belief in not-p. The delusion involved in motivated false belief is not necessarily generated or sustained by a contradictory belief.

66 Garrett sums up Spinoza's position in this way: "[For Spinoza] the interests of other individuals enter into one's own considerations only through their usefulness *to oneself*" (Garrett 1990a: 225).

67 The reason why we might feel sadness at the suffering of others stems from Spinoza's doctrine of the imitation of affects.

68 For different and not equally successful reasons for the claim that rational people are beneficial to others, see the two demonstrations of 4p37. See also Della Rocca, forthcoming, 1996.

69 This claim is, of course, subject to qualifications concerning what one believes will help oneself. Similar qualifications apply to the claims in the previous paragraph concerning the primacy of the immediate.

70 Despite these important differences, there are many important similarities between Davidson and Spinoza in the philosophy of mind. In particular, they are both holists about the mental and they both accept some form of a nonreductive identity theory of mental and physical events. See Della Rocca forthcoming, 1996, Chapters 4 and 8.

71 For Spinoza's account of conflicts of desires, see 3p17s.

72 See also 3p2s and 4pr (beginning), as well as Curley's note on 4p17s in Spinoza 1985a: 554n11.

73 In giving Spinoza's account of the circumstances under which one knowingly acts against one's own long-term interests, I am not addressing the separate question of why we *should not* act in this way and thus why such action merits the label "*irrational.*" Since this separate question concerns Spinoza's ethical views more than his purely psychological views, I do not take it up in this chapter. Bennett briefly considers this question (Bennett 1984: 319–20).

74 As before, all the points I will make about the anticipation of pain have corresponding versions concerning the anticipation of pleasure.

75 Spinoza does not justify this assumption, but perhaps it is meant to follow from his thesis of parallelism (E 2p7). Spinoza's assumption here can be seen as a version of a thesis of supervenience: no mental difference without a physical difference.

76 For a helpful grappling with this issue, see Bennett 1984: 282–4.

77 Despite the plausibility of this point, I do not find the demonstration of it in 4p10d completely clear. Spinoza's proof turns on the notion of degrees of imagining something that excludes the present existence of a certain thing, but it is not obvious what such degrees might amount to.

78 Here Spinoza accepts the conditional: "If pain x is greater than pain y, then pain x is stronger than pain y." I am inclined to think that Spinoza would also accept the converse. See, e.g., 5p8 and 5p8d, where Spinoza seems to regard "greater" and "stronger" as equivalent terms.

79 This is only a reasonable conclusion to draw. It is not required. There may well be kinds of pain which are such that the pain of anticipating them is less sensitive to temporal distance than the pain of anticipating other kinds of pain. Still, I think that something like the above conclusion is right and, more importantly for our purposes, I cannot see how to make sense of Spinoza's account of irrational action without attributing this conclusion to him.

80 Notice that, on this account, an apparent case of prudence would be one in which the greater size of one anticipated affect is not overcompensated for in the above way by the relative proximity of another affect.

81 Spinoza uses "more intense" as equivalent to "stronger" ("fortior"). See the last sentence of 4p9d.

82 See Neu 1977: 76–7; and Wolfson 1934: II,208. Spinoza puts the point by saying that all other affects "arise (oriri) from these three" (E 3p11s) and by saying that all other affects are either "compounded" (componitur) or "derived" (derivatur) from desire, joy, or sadness (E 3p56). In recognizing only three basic affects, Spinoza differs from Descartes, who recognized six: wonder, love, hatred, desire, joy, and sadness (Passions of the Soul 2.69, in Descartes 1985: I,353).

83 See Bennett 1984: 262–7. Wolfson 1934: II,209–10 and Voss 1981 each delineate the similarities and differences between Spinoza's list of affects and Descartes's.

84 Spinoza discusses several techniques for overcoming harmful affects in the first half of Part 5 of the Ethics. See especially 5p20s. Neu 1977 emphasizes the cognitive nature of Spinozistic affects and the importance of this feature in psychotherapy.

85 Bennett 1984: 279 also holds that Spinoza is committed to some such general claim.

86 Bennett 1984: 278: "[S]omething like 2p18 is apparently true."

87 For related passages, see 3p36 and 3p36c where Spinoza describes cases in which an object or person is the accidental cause of an affect of joy. See also 3p50's account of accidental causes of hope and fear.

88 A related case is hatred of an entire class or nation. Spinoza sees such hatred as the result of a transition from an affect of sadness caused by one person to an affect of hate directed at all those like that person (E 3p46).

89 As we will see, parallel points apply to the imitation of affects.

90 This point is implicit in Spinoza's phrase in 3p16: "we *imagine* a thing to have some likeness. . . ." (emphasis added). Spinoza allows imaginative ideas to be false (see 2p35 and the definition of imagination in 2p40s2).

91 As I will explain, however, not everything that Spinoza calls affect imitation actually involves affect transition.

92 Actually, 3p27 can be read as requiring not actual similarity, but *perceived* similarity. x must regard y as similar to x in order for imitation to occur, but x and y need not actually be similar. I give my reasons for this reading in Della Rocca forthcoming.

93 See also Bennett 1984: 281, and Matheron 1969: 155.

94 See the parallel claims in the discussion of 3p16 earlier in this subsection.

95 Instead of "y is similar to x," it might be better to say "x perceives y to be similar to x." See note 92. Notice that I have omitted any qualification concerning x's antecedent affects toward y. As we have seen, for Spinoza, such a history of affects does not preclude imitation.

96 "Q-imitation" is short for "quasi-imitation." Compare the notion of quasi-memory found in recent discussions of personal identity. See, e.g., Derek Parfit, *Reasons and Persons* (Oxford: Clarendon Press, 1984): 220.

97 Since in the rest of this section, the difference between veridical and nonveridical imitation will not be at work, I will, for the sake of simplicity, speak of imitation instead of q-imitation from now on.

98 The points I go on to make also apply to the anticipation of pleasurable affects.

99 Similar points apply in the case of certain memories. Spinoza holds that the recollection of pain is itself painful (E 3p18). In such a case, my present self can be said to be imitating my past self with respect to a certain affect.

100 See Della Rocca forthcoming. Other important uses of the imitation doctrine appear in Spinoza's view that hatred breeds further hatred, but can be checked by love (E 3p43, E 4p46) and in his accounts of ambition (E 3p29s), shame, love of esteem (E 3p30s), and envy (E 3p32s).

101 This is, I believe, what the following claim from 3p27d amounts to: "[I]f the nature of the external body is like the nature of our body, then the idea of the external body will involve an affection of our body like the affection of the external body."

102 For a similar criticism, see Bennett 1984: 281 and Broad 1930: 37–8. For a more favorable account of the demonstration, see Matheron 1969: 154–5.

103 Perhaps, however, the imitation of past or future selves by one's present self (in memory and anticipation) can be seen as a case of association.

104 In this paragraph, I am following an argument given in Della Rocca forthcoming.

105 See "Actions, Reason, and Causes," in Davidson 1980.

106 See Curley 1990b: 45.

107 And, for this reason, Bennett found the passage quoted above from 4pr something of an embarrassment for his interpretation. See Bennett 1984: 224.

108 The example here derives from Sosa 1984. See Bennett's example of the fall of a vase (Bennett 1984: 218). I am indebted here to Isaac Wheeler.

109 A nonrepresentative feature would be, e.g., the property of occurring on a Tuesday, or of being a mental state of a baseball fan.

110 For similar doubts about such a requirement, see LePore and Loewer 1987.

111 I think Bennett is right to see these passages as having this implication. The relevant passages are:

2p16: The idea of any mode in which the human body is affected by external bodies must involve the nature of the human body and at the same time the nature of the external bodies.

2p16c1: From this it follows, first, that the human mind perceives the nature of a great many bodies together with the nature of its own body.

2p16c2: It follows, second, that the ideas which we have of external bodies indicate the condition of our body more than the nature of the external bodies.

112 I am grateful to Christine Hayes and Carol Rovane for many valuable comments.

6   Spinoza's ethical theory

So the Philosophers . . . follow virtue not as a law, but from love,
because it is the best thing. (Ep 19)

Spinoza is in many ways – and as many have observed – a philosopher in the Cartesian tradition. His first published work was an
elucidation of Descartes's *Principles of Philosophy*, and Descartes is
the only philosopher named and discussed in the *Ethics*. Some of his
most fundamental metaphysical and epistemological doctrines are
Cartesian, while many others appear to result from reflection on
various difficulties in Descartes's position. His physics, too, is
largely Cartesian.[1] Despite this unmistakable influence, however,
Spinoza's guiding intellectual purpose was quite different from Descartes's. Descartes sought primarily to improve the sciences – for
himself and for others – by providing a better foundation for them.
He justified this endeavor ultimately on the grounds that it would
bring human beings greater mastery over nature. Spinoza, in contrast, sought primarily to improve the character of human beings –
both himself and others – by improving their self-understanding. He
justified this endeavor ultimately on the grounds that it would bring
human beings peace of mind as integral aspects of nature.

While Spinoza's metaphysics, epistemology, and physics are in
many ways Cartesian, his ethical purposes are in many ways
Hobbesian. Like Hobbes, he conceives of human beings as mecha-
nisms in nature that are motivated by self-preservation and individual advantage, and who, by the mutual employment of reason, can
improve their way of life. Hobbes's aim, however, is to show human
beings how best to satisfy their desires by instituting mutually use-

ful political and social constraints on their passions, and so to maximize their chances for a relatively long and pleasant life. Spinoza's aim, while encompassing Hobbes's, is much more ambitious: It is to show human beings how to achieve a mode of life that largely transcends merely transitory desires and which has as its natural consequences autonomous control over the passions and participation in an eternal blessedness.[2]

Ethics, for Spinoza, is knowledge of "the right way of living."[3] The centrality of ethics to his philosophical project is unmistakable in the title of his most systematic presentation of his philosophy: *Ethics Demonstrated in Geometrical Order (Ethica Ordine Geometrico Demonstrata)*. The *Ethics* seeks to demonstrate a broad range of metaphysical, theological, epistemological, and psychological doctrines. Most of these doctrines, however, either constitute, support, or elucidate the premises for his ethical conclusions. Moreover, Spinoza's choices concerning which metaphysical, theological, epistemological, and psychological doctrines to emphasize and develop are largely determined by their usefulness in supporting his ethical conclusions.

Because Spinoza wrote the *Ethics* in what he called "geometrical order" – which Descartes called the "synthetic" method of demonstration[4] – the work itself contains relatively little explicit discussion of his purpose in writing. However, the opening lines of his earlier (and unfinished) *Treatise on the Emendation of the Intellect* – written in what Descartes called the "analytic" method of demonstration[5] – emphasize the personal and ethical character of his philosophical project:

After experience had taught me that all the things which regularly occur in ordinary life are empty and futile, and I saw that all the things which were the cause or object of my fear had nothing of good or bad in themselves, except insofar as my mind was moved by them, I resolved at last to try to find out whether there was anything which would be the true good, capable of communicating itself, and which alone would affect the mind, all others being rejected – whether there was something which, once found and acquired, would continuously give me the greatest joy, to eternity. (TdIE 1)[6]

As its title implies, this early work seeks to develop a method for improving the intellect. That method involves finding remedies against three epistemological hindrances – fiction, falsity, and doubt – which the intellect must learn to distinguish from true ideas. As the initial paragraphs of the work make clear, however, Spinoza seeks improvement of the intellect (and, specifically, his own intellect) not merely as a theoretical exercise, but chiefly as a remedy against three *ethical* hindrances – the overvaluings of wealth, fame, and sensual pleasure – and as an instrument for distinguishing, appreciating, and achieving the one true and eternal practical good.

On the whole, twentieth-century interest in Spinoza's writings has focused – in contrast with Spinoza's own priorities – more on his metaphysics and epistemology (especially in the English-speaking world) and on his social and political theory (especially on the European continent) than it has on his ethical theory proper.[7] It is not, of course, uncommon for a later generation of readers to neglect an aspect of a philosopher's work that the philosopher valued most highly. Nevertheless, Spinoza's ethical theory is innovative, systematic, and important. It is, in fact, despite the brevity of its presentation, one of the most important ethical theories of the modern era.

I will begin by providing an outline of Spinoza's ethical theory as he himself presents it in the *Ethics*. I will then draw on this outline to explore in somewhat greater detail his contributions to a half-dozen central topics of ethics on which his views are often neglected and easily misunderstood. These topics are: (i) the meaning of ethical language; (ii) the nature of the good; (iii) the practicality of reason; (iv) the role of virtue; (v) the requirements for freedom and moral responsibility; and (vi) the possibility and moral significance of altruism. I will conclude by briefly characterizing his ethical theory within the history of ethical theory generally, and assessing its significance.

I. AN OUTLINE OF SPINOZA'S ETHICAL THEORY

Spinoza touches on ethical topics in several of his works, as well as in his correspondence. Part 2 of the early *Short Treatise on God, Man, and His Well-Being* takes up the topics of good and evil, blessedness, and freedom, as well as discussing various affects. The *Theological-Political Treatise* naturally bears on matters of ethics in the political context. By far Spinoza's fullest, most systematic, and most mature discussion of ethical theory, however, is contained in

Part 4 ("Of Human Bondage") and Part 5 ("Of the Power of the Intellect") of his *Ethics*, which I therefore follow.

The natural foundations of ethical theory

In Parts 4 and 5 of the *Ethics*, Spinoza seeks to derive his ethical theory from an understanding of Nature in general, and of human psychological nature in particular, that he has already developed in Parts 1–3. One measure of this dependence is the fact that, although Part 4 begins with eight new definitions, it adds only a single new axiom – an axiom, moreover, that is not distinctively ethical. (The axiom states: "There is no singular thing in nature than which there is not another more powerful and stronger.") Part 5 introduces two additional axioms; but again neither is distinctively ethical, and indeed Spinoza describes the second (despite its official status as an underived axiom) as "evident from" *Ethics* 3p7.[8]

One central feature of nature, for the purposes of Spinoza's ethical theory, is of course the substance/mode relationship between God and individual things that is implied by the monism of 1p15: "Whatever is, is in God, and nothing can be or be conceived without God." Human beings stand, for Spinoza, in an intimate relationship both to God-or-Nature *(Deus sive Natura)* and to other things within Nature, from which they are not "really distinct" in the Cartesian sense.[9] This implies, on the one hand, that human beings cannot act independently of, or separately from, God's own activity, and that every human action must be conceived as a manifestation of nature; but it also implies, on the other hand, that there is a prospect for a kind of direct participation in the divine (see E 4p45c2s).

Equally important is his necessitarianism, expressed in 1p29 ("In nature there is nothing contingent, but all things have been determined from the necessity of the divine nature to exist and produce an effect in a certain way"; see also 1p16 and 1p33,d).[10] This doctrine rules out the possibility of what Spinoza calls "free will" (i.e., freedom understood as the absence of causal determination of the will), helps to determine the character and structure of knowledge (in which 3pp26–28 locate our true good),[11] and provides prospects for consolation in misfortune (E 4ap32; cf. also E 5p6).

Spinoza's doctrine of the identity between modes of extension and their corresponding modes of thought (E 2p7s) entails the identity of the human mind with the human body, and the identity of both cognitions and "affects" (i.e., emotions) with bodily modifications or occurrences. It thereby extends the scope of ethics, as a doctrine about the right way of living, to both the mental and the physical, and proscribes any construal of ethics as involving fundamental conflict between the mind and the body. The distinction between intellect and imagination, and the doctrine of the three kinds of knowledge (*experientia vaga, ratio,* and *scientia intuitiva;* E 2p40s), define more specifically the cognitive categories on which his ethical theory rests and in terms of which it is formulated.

The single most essential underpinning of Spinoza's ethics, however, is clearly the *conatus* doctrine of 3p6, the doctrine that "Each thing, as far as it can by its own power, strives to persevere in its existence,"[12] from which he derives the closely related 3p7: "The striving *(conatus)* by which each thing strives to persevere in its being is nothing but the actual essence of the thing." These propositions constitute (among other things) an innovative solution to a problem that his substance monism raises concerning metaphysical individuation. For Spinoza, individual things in nature cannot be individuated from one another by a difference of substance, because there is only one substance. Individuals emerge instead only as finite approximations to substance: specifically, as finite natures that, within the attribute of extension, are distinguished from one another by the tendency of their essential "fixed proportions of motion and rest" to persist (and, within the attribute of thought, by the tendency of ideas of such extended individuals to persist). The tendency towards self-preservation (perseverance in being) thus becomes, a priori, an essential and defining feature of the natures of all individual things, including all human beings.[13]

Because a thing is truly *active* only to the extent that it is an adequate cause through its own nature (E 3d1) and *passive* to the extent that it is only an inadequate cause through its own nature, and because each individual thing's nature is simply to endeavor to preserve itself as a persistent pattern, it follows that a thing's activity, however much or little it may have, always involves an effort at its own self-preservation. *Desire (cupiditas)* is this striving or *conatus*, as it involves both mind and body, together with consciousness of it (E 3p9s), especially as it is directed toward particular objects. *Joy (laetitia)* and *sadness (tristitia)* are defined as the increase and decrease, respectively, in perfection, or capacity for being *active* (E 3p11s). Hence, desire, joy, and sadness – together with the affects defined in terms of them – play central roles in Spinozistic ethics. It is, in fact, largely the human capacity for so many varieties of desire, joy, and sadness (described throughout *Ethics* Part 3) that makes human ethics, for Spinoza, such a potentially rich and complex domain. Much of his ethics consists in his assessment, from an ethical perspective, of the various human psychological phenomena whose nature and causes he has already deduced, in Part 3, from this metaphysical basis.[14] He concludes Part 3, and signals the transition to a discussion of ethics proper, by designating the source of genuine human activity (as distinguished from passion-driven behavior) as *strength of character (fortitudo)*. He then distinguishes two aspects of strength of character: *tenacity (animositas)*, which is "the desire by which each one strives, solely from the dictate of reason, to preserve his being"; and *nobility (generositas)*, which is "the desire by which each one strives, solely from the dictate of reason, to aid other men and join them to him in friendship" (E 3p59s).

Definitions of ethical terms

Spinoza begins the preface to *Ethics* Part 4 by defining the term "bondage" as "man's lack of power to moderate and restrain the affects." He then sets out two aims for Part 4 itself: first, to demonstrate the causes of bondage; and second, to demonstrate "what there is of good and evil in the affects." The first aim corresponds to *Ethics* 4pp1–18. The second corresponds to *Ethics* 4pp19–73, plus the appendix to Part 4.

Before pursuing these aims, however, Spinoza devotes the remainder of the preface to an account of two pairs of evaluative terms: "perfect" and "imperfect," "good" and "evil." The Latin meanings of "perfect" *("perfectus")* include "accomplished" or "finished." Thus, he explains, something was said, in common usage, to be perfect when the speaker believed that the thing had been completed in accordance with the purpose of its creator. But human beings mistakenly suppose that Nature seeks to produce natural things in accordance with archetypes or forms corresponding to the ideas of imagination that human beings form as models or "universals" (see E 2p40s1). They have therefore accustomed themselves to apply the terms "perfect" and "imperfect" to natural things as well, depending on whether the things in question did or did not conform to their own imaginative models. In addition, because many have supposed that there is a highest genus or universal, that of "being" in general, the term "perfect" has also come to be used as a technical philosophical term for describing a thing's degree of reality (as, indeed, Spinoza himself has already done in 2d6).

Spinoza has already asserted that "good" and "evil" are applied to things in accordance with whether the things happen to affect us with desire or aversion, respectively. We do not desire things *because* they are "good," or avoid them *because* they are "evil," as those terms are generally used; rather, we call things "good" simply because we desire them, and "evil" because we are averse to them (E 3p9s). Here he adds that, at least in common usage, the same thing can be "good" for one individual, "evil" for a second, and indifferent for a third. Thus, these four terms in their common usage "indicate nothing positive in things, considered in themselves"; they "arise because we compare things to one another," and they indicate rather our own personal and idiosyncratic modes of thinking (vague imaginative universal models, and personal desires and aversions, respectively).

Instead of rejecting these terms outright, however, Spinoza retains them and refines their usage. He does so because he holds that it is advantageous to have a particular "model of human nature we set before ourselves." Hence, he proposes definitions of "perfect" and "imperfect," "good" and "evil," in terms of relations to that model. The "good," according to these definitions, is "what we know is certainly a means by which we may approach nearer and nearer to the model," and "evil" the opposite; while "men are more perfect or imperfect, insofar as they approach more or less near to this model" (E 4pr).

In the formal definitions at the beginning of Part 4 proper, Spinoza reaffirms these definitions of "good" and "evil"; however he does so without explicit reference to the "model of human nature we set before ourselves," referring instead simply to what is useful to us:

D1: By good I shall understand what we certainly know to be useful to us.

D2: By evil, however, I shall understand what we certainly know prevents us from being masters of some good.[15]

These reformulations thus embody the assumption that what makes something useful "to us" is its capacity to enable us to approximate the model of human nature that Spinoza sets before us, and vice versa.

Of the remaining six formal definitions of Part 4, only one employs ethical language.[16] This is 4d8, in which Spinoza sets out his definition of "virtue":

> D8: By virtue and power I understand the same thing, i.e., (by 3p7), virtue, insofar as it is related to man, is the very essence, *or* nature, of man, insofar as he has the power of bringing about certain things, which can be understood through the laws of his nature alone.

Bondage and its causes

In explaining "the causes of man's lack of power and inconstancy, and why men do not observe the precepts of reason" (E 4p18s), Spinoza emphasizes that human beings, as finite parts of nature, have a limited amount of power and are always subject to external forces, which may be more powerful than their own natures. These forces may prevent human beings from achieving or acquiring what is most advantageous to them. In particular, these forces can induce *passions* – that is, affects of which the individual alone is not the adequate cause and which, therefore, may or may not be conducive to the individual's well-being. Among the harmful affects, some are affects of sadness, which decrease the individual's capacity for action; some are affects of joy that increase the individual's capacity for action in one respect but only at the expense of rendering the individual less fit for other kinds of actions (e.g., by increasing the power of one part of the body at the expense of others, or by rendering the individual incapable of perceiving or thinking of other things); and some are desires which misdirect the individual's endeavor for self-preservation onto the pursuit of objects that are not truly or entirely advantageous.

Because they arise from external causes, passions may prevent human beings from appreciating where their own true good or advantage lies. However, passions can also prevent human beings from pursuing their advantage even when they do understand it; as

Spinoza remarks (quoting Ovid), we sometimes "see and approve the better, but follow the worse" (E 4p17s). He must therefore explain how this phenomenon can be reconciled with his doctrine that human beings necessarily seek their own advantage as far as they can.

He does so by citing features of affects that contribute to their motivational strength or weakness. Every affect is also at the same time an *idea* (i.e., a representation) of a state of the individual's body, and (indirectly) of external bodies that have contributed to producing that state. However, the motivational *force* of an affect is not directly a function of its truth or falsity as an idea, but rather of its strength as an affect. The constraint or removal of affects – including harmful ones – therefore depends on the occurrence of opposite and stronger affects (E 4p7). An affect is more powerful if we imagine its cause to be present rather than past or future (E 4p9); more powerful if we imagine its object as being in the near, rather than the distant, future or past (E 4p10); more powerful if we imagine its object as free rather than necessary (E 3p49d); more powerful if we imagine its cause as necessary rather than possible (E 3p11); and more powerful if we imagine its object as possible rather than merely contingent (E 4p12; for the distinction between the contingent and the possible, see note 16). But "knowledge of good and evil" is simply the cognition that something affects us with joy or sadness, respectively (E 4p8). Therefore, an affect which is a passion (a desire, for example) can, in virtue of the ways in which it represents its object in the imagination, be stronger than another affect that constitutes knowledge of good or evil. Hence, the affect can overwhelm us into taking an acknowledged lesser good over an acknowledged, but less motivationally effective, greater good. In doing so, we find ourselves driven by passions to "act" (or better, to *behave*, because "passion" and "action" are opposites) against our own acknowledged best interests, interests that we thereby lack sufficient power of action to pursue.

The prescriptions of reason

The remainder of Part 4 (E 4p18–73 and E 4ap) is devoted to the second aim Spinoza sets out in the Preface – specifically, to show "what reason prescribes to us, which affects agree with the rules of human reason, and which, on the other hand, are contrary to those rules" (E 4p18s). He indicates in advance the general character of reason's prescription:

Since reason demands nothing contrary to nature, it demands that everyone love himself, seek his own advantage, what is really useful to him, want what will really lead man to a greater perfection, and absolutely, that everyone should strive to preserve his own being as far as he can. This, indeed, is as necessarily true as that the whole is greater than its part. (E 4p18s)

Spinoza proceeds in several distinct stages. The seven propositions of 4pp19–25 concern the relation between virtue (as already defined at 4d8) and *conatus* – that is, the endeavor at self-preservation that he has attributed, at 3p7, to all individuals as the very essence of their individual existence. Because *conatus* constitutes the actual essence of each individual, it defines the power and activity of the thing's own nature. It follows for Spinoza that a human being's power, and hence virtue, is simply the capacity to strive for and achieve one's own advantage, conceived as self-preservation: "The more each one strives, and is able, to seek his own advantage, i.e., to preserve his being, the more he is endowed with virtue; conversely, insofar as each one neglects his own advantage, i.e., neglects to preserve his being, he lacks power" (E 4p20). Comparison of this account of virtue with 4p18s shows that "acting from virtue" and "acting under the guidance of reason" are equivalent, as Spinoza himself notes at 4p24.

The three propositions of 4pp26–28 concern the intimate relationship between virtue and understanding, and lead to the conclusion that "knowledge of God is the Mind's greatest good; its greatest virtue is to know God" (E 4p28). The mind's highest good is knowledge, according to Spinoza, because the mind's own good must be understood as that which it actively strives for through its own nature – that is, what it tends to produce or acquire insofar as it is genuinely active. But it is genuinely active only insofar as it is an adequate cause of its thoughts, and it is the adequate cause of its thoughts only when it is deriving adequate knowledge from other adequate knowledge through its own rational power. Since the highest object of knowledge is the absolutely infinite being, God, through which everything else must be understood (E 1p15), it follows that knowledge of God is the mind's highest good and that to know God is its highest virtue.

Ethics 4pp29–36 concern relations among human beings and the preconditions for sustained, mutually beneficial cooperation. Spinoza holds, as a general metaphysical thesis, that whenever two things "agree in nature" they will, to that extent, be mutually beneficial, since the nature that each strives to benefit is the same (E 4p31). Human beings necessarily "agree in nature" to the extent that they are guided by reason (E 4p35). For human reason, as reason, is the same in all, and aims at the same thing – namely, knowledge or understanding. Understanding, moreover, is a good that can be shared by all without diminishing anyone's enjoyment of it (E 4p36). In fact, Spinoza holds, nothing is more useful to a human being than another human being who is guided by reason (E 4p35c1). Hence, individuals who are virtuous, or guided by reason, will all seek, from their own self-interest, the same goods for others that they seek for themselves (E 4p37). Indeed to the extent that a community of human beings is guided by reason, its members can "compose, as it were, one Mind and one Body" (E 4p18s) – that is, a complex individual, composed of like-minded human beings, that has its own endeavor for self-preservation.

In contrast, to the extent that human beings are not guided by reason, but are instead subject to passions, they are contrary in nature, and liable to come into conflict with one another (E 4p32). This is so even when the passions themselves seem similar (i.e., passionate love for the same person, prize, or reputation), since being subject to passions is a negation of power, rather than a positive source of agreement in nature (E 4p32). Moreover, individuals subject to such passions come into conflict not through their similarity, but through their difference. For example, they will not passionately desire the same apparent goods for others that they desire for themselves; rather, they will differ in each desiring a different disposition of those "goods" (namely, to themselves exclusively; see 4p33s for a slightly different example).[17]

Ethics 4pp38–66 move from the general to the specific, indicating which things, affects, and behaviors are truly good, virtuous, or in accordance with reason, and which are not. Among things, the good include those that are conducive to preserving the proportion of motion and rest that constitutes the nature of the human body, and thereby serve to keep it alive (E 4p39); those that so dispose the human body that it can either be affected by many things (so that its mind can perceive many things), or affect many other things (E

4p38); and those that enable human beings to live harmoniously together (E 4p40).

Among the affects, cheerfulness – which is the kind of joy in which all parts of the body are equally affected – is always good (E 4p42). More generally, all joy, as such, is good, and all sadness evil (E 4p41). However, pleasure (in contrast to cheerfulness) is joy in which one or several parts of the body are affected more than others; hence, it can be excessive when it prevents us from being affected in other advantageous ways (E 4p43), as also can desire and love (E 4p44). Pain, though directly evil, can be indirectly good when it restrains excessive pleasure (E 4p41). Favor (i.e., love toward one who has benefited another [E 4p51]), self-esteem (E 4p52), and love of esteem (E 4p58) can, when based on adequate ideas, be in accordance with reason. Hate can never be good (E 4p45), however, and the envy, mockery, disdain, anger, and vengeance that result from hate are all evil (E 4p45c1), as are overestimation and scorn (E 4p48). Indignation, pity, humility, and repentance – sometimes regarded as virtues, but all species of sadness – cannot arise from reason, and are not genuine virtues (E 4pp50,51,53,54).

Among behaviors, seeking to repay hate, anger, or disdain with love and nobility is in accordance with reason (E 4p46), as is the policy of "following the greater of two goods or the lesser of two evils" (E 4p65), even when the greater good or lesser evil is in the more distant future. More generally, any behavior leading to harmless pleasure is good:

Nothing forbids our pleasure except a savage and sad superstition. . . . To use things, therefore, and take pleasure in them as far as possible – not, of course, to the point where we are disgusted with them, for there is no pleasure in that – this is the part of a wise man.

It is the part of a wise man, I say, to refresh and restore himself in moderation with pleasant food and drink, with scents, with the beauty of green plants, with decoration, music, sports, the theater, and other things of this kind, which anyone can use without injury to another. (E 4p45c2s).

Ethics 4pp67–73 conclude the main body of Part 4 by providing a description of the ideal "free man," who, it is clear, constitutes Spinoza's promised "model of human nature we set before ourselves." "Free" has already been defined, at 1d7, as follows: "That thing is called free which exists from the necessity of its nature alone." Although only God is completely free in this sense, human beings can have degrees of freedom, corresponding to the degrees to which they are the adequate causes of their own actions. The free man directly pursues the good more than he seeks to avoid evil, so he "thinks of nothing less than of death, and his wisdom is a meditation on life, not on death" (E 4p67). The free man, if born free "would form no concept of good and evil" so long as he remained free (E4p68). The free man exhibits freedom by avoiding dangers as well as by overcoming them (E 4p69); seeks to avoid the favors of the ignorant (E 4p70); is most thankful to other free men (E 4p71); always acts honestly, not deceptively (E 4p72; but see Section 2 below); and is more free in a political state, where he can live in community with others in accordance with a common law, than in a condition of solitude (E 4p73).

In the thirty-two articles of the appendix to Part 4 Spinoza summarizes his ethical doctrines, discusses additional affects, and takes the opportunity to add a number of practical maxims concerning money, marriage, and other matters.

The way to freedom

If human beings are often in bondage to their passions, still they sometimes achieve a degree of freedom over them. Whereas the initial propositions of Part 4 set out the causes of human weakness, the initial propositions of Part 5 (E 5pp1–20) set out "the means, or way, leading to freedom." However, unlike Descartes – who sought to describe the mind's ability to restructure the nature of its command over the body through the interaction of mind and body at the pineal gland – Spinoza seeks to describe the various respects in which the human mind's own cognitive capacity to achieve adequate knowledge naturally gives it a certain degree of power over its own affects. Spinoza summarizes these means in 5p20s.

The first means to freedom lies "in the knowledge itself of the affects." To the extent that we understand a passion (which, as a passion, is a confused idea of a state of the body), our perception of it becomes adequate, and so we are no longer passive, but active; hence, the continuing affect ceases, to that extent, to be a passion (E 5p3). Furthermore, since all states of the body involve some common or pervasive features of extension that are equally in the part and in the whole (E 2p40s2), reason can form at least *some* adequate ideas of any state of the body, including any affect (E 5p4). In understanding the passions *as* bodily states of particular kinds, we gain some ability to control them and moderate them through knowledge of their nature.

The second means lies "in the fact that it [the mind] separates the affects from the thought of an external cause, which we imagine confusedly." Love and hate are forms of joy and sadness, respectively, that are combined with the idea of an external cause as their objects. When we undergo passionate love or hate, the intensity of the passion felt toward the object of the love or hate is decreased when we understand how limited the active causal agency of that object is (E 5p3). If, for example, we understand that a destructive love for a particular individual depends largely on accidental psychological associations, or that a person who has harmed us did so only because of his or her own passions and lack of power, our own passionate love or passionate hate will be diminished.[18] Furthermore, to the extent that we understand the cause's effect on us as a necessary activity of God, we will rejoice in our new understanding – which, like all understanding, increases our power of thinking (E 4p15).

The third means lies "in the time by which the affections related to things we understand surpass those related to things we conceive confusedly, *or* in a mutilated way." Affects which arise from reason (and hence are not themselves passions) are derived from an adequate understanding of the "common properties" of things (E 2p40s2). Because these properties are equally in the part and in the whole of everything, nothing we imagine can exclude the existence of these properties, and hence the affects which arise from an understanding of them are, in the long run, more persistent and permanent. Ultimately, therefore, any affects that are contrary to them will tend either to be destroyed or to become accommodated to them (E 5p7).

The fourth means lies "in the multiplicity of causes by which affections related to common properties or to God are encouraged." Because affects resulting from reason are related to the common properties of all things, they are produced by a greater number of things; but an affect is stronger, Spinoza holds, when more things cause it (E 5p9). Furthermore, the more things cause it, the more frequently it will be produced (E 5p11).

The fifth means lies "in the order by which the Mind can order its affects and connect them to one another." When the mind is not being buffeted by contrary affects, it can understand its own psychology, and from this understanding it can form maxims concerning the best way of living. It can associate these maxims in the imagination with the common circumstances of life to which they are applicable, so that the maxims, and the ethical understanding and active desires that they represent, will come to mind when they are most needed. Although Descartes describes a similar remedy in his *Passions of the Soul* I.50 (Descartes 1985: I,348), Spinoza's version of this method separates it from both the mind–body dualism and the theory of free will with which Descartes connects it.

A sixth respect in which Spinoza holds that reason has power over the affects is inexplicably omitted from his summary at 5p20s.[19] This is the power the mind acquires over the affects when it understands all things – and especially singular things – as necessary. For according to Spinoza, affects are greatest towards a thing that we imagine as free by imagining it "while we are ignorant of the causes by which it has been determined to act" (5p5, derived from 3p49). Understanding a thing – and, in particular, an evil or disappointing thing – as necessitated and inevitable, decreases the power of the affects associated with it. This is a point for which, he thinks, "experience itself also testifies." Thus, necessitarianism is not only true; it has positive psychological value as well.

Not all of the "means" that Spinoza lists at 5p20s are therapeutic techniques that one could consciously adopt in order to increase one's freedom and power over the passions – nor are they intended to be.[20] Indeed, it is arguable that only the fifth directly describes anything like a *technique*. The first and second (like the unlisted sixth remedy) do perhaps suggest the value of regularly undertaking specific lines of thought about affects, but it is hard to see the third and fourth as doing even this. Spinoza's goal in the first half of Part 5, however, is not primarily to describe techniques that could be consciously undertaken as exercises, but rather to list the most important respects in which having adequate knowledge tends to produce a lessened susceptibility to passions over the long run. He believes he has already shown, in Part 4, the value of such a lessened susceptibility to the passions. His authorial purpose in 5pp1–20 is to strengthen the desire of his readers – a desire that is of course already present with some degree of strength in all human beings – to

achieve more adequate understanding. He seeks to achieve this authorial purpose by showing that adequate knowledge has the power
to produce, over time, the very lessening of susceptibility to passion
that he has already shown to be desirable.[21]

Intellectual love of God and blessedness

Spinoza strikingly concludes 5p20s: "With this I have completed
everything which concerns this present life. . . . So it is time now to
pass to those things which pertain to the mind's duration without
relation to the body."[22] The remainder of Part 5 of the *Ethics* accordingly deals with the eternal part of the mind, and with the intellectual love of God and blessedness in which the mind can participate.

The eternality of the mind in Spinoza is a topic that defies easy
categorization. It is at once metaphysical (because concerned with
the relations between existence and essence, duration and the eternal), epistemological (because concerned with the character of the
second and, especially, the third kind of knowledge), theological
(because concerned with the relation between God and human beings), and ethical (because concerned with blessedness, as well as
with the proper attitude toward life and death).[23]

Briefly, Spinoza holds that there is in God an idea which "expresses" the essence (as contrasted with the actual existence) of the
human body. This idea, because it expresses the essence of the human
body, pertains to the essence (as opposed to the actual durational
existence) of the human mind.[24] It consists entirely of adequate
knowledge which, as adequate knowledge, is eternal in God; and in
acquiring adequate knowledge a human being is always acquiring
knowledge that expresses the essence of the human body in just this
way. Thus, as one gains a larger share of adequate knowledge, one's
mind becomes something "whose greatest part is eternal" (E 5p39). It
is not that one achieves continued personal existence after one's biological death. There can be no personal or individual persistence, for
that involves imagination (including sensory awareness) or memory
(E 5p21). Instead, one brings within the scope of one's own mind
adequate knowledge which has always been and always will be eternal in God, and one thus achieves for oneself the *perspective* of the
eternal while one is alive. In consequence, a greater part of one's mind
is composed of ideas that are impervious both to harmful affects –

including fear – and to death itself (E 5p38). That is, the mind is less affected by fear in general, and hence by fear of death in particular; and, at the same time, death becomes less harmful and so less *to* be feared, because the greatest and most important part of the mind will survive (although not, of course, *as* the idea of the actually existing body, since that body will have perished).

But this is not all. In Spinoza's view, human minds, considered as complex ideas or representations, are parts of the "infinite intellect of God" (2p11c), which is God's own thought insofar as it involves or is composed of ideas or representations. However, human thought has not only a representational but also an affective aspect; and this is possible only if God's thought itself – of which human thought is of course a mode – *also* has an affective aspect. Indeed, the existence of this affective aspect is one reason why the infinite intellect of God is *only* an infinite mode of God, and is not the entire attribute of thought itself. To the extent that one achieves knowledge of the third (and highest) kind – which involves understanding the essences of singular things through the attributes of God, effects through their causes (E 2p40s2) – one possesses knowledge in something like the way that God himself does. That is, one's knowledge is in one's own mind in the same way that that knowledge is in God, and so one participates more completely or adequately in the infinite intellect of God. In a similar way, knowledge of the third kind involves having affects in something like the way that those affects are in God, and so enables one to participate more completely in what might be called the affective life of God.

Spinoza's God, although an infinite thinking thing, is not a person. God's eternally supreme perfection is incompatible with desire or purpose (both of which imply some lack), with joy (which requires a transition *from* a lesser perfection or capacity for action), and with sadness (which requires transition *to* a lesser perfection or capacity for action). It follows, of course, that God does not literally love anything, since love is a kind of joy (E 2p13s), implying an increase in something that God already possesses to the maximal degree. Moreover, love is joy accompanied by the idea of an external cause, whereas nothing is or can be external to God.

Nevertheless, because God eternally has the greatest perfection and capacity for action, he has a kind of eternal analogue of joy, an eternal "rejoicing" that we experience as joy whenever we increase our participation in it. Moreover, because God is self-caused, God's eternal rejoicing has God himself as its true object, and so God also has an eternal – and internal – analogue of "love." As we come to participate in the third kind of knowledge, we come to participate in this eternal analogue of love, which Spinoza calls "the intellectual love of God." Insofar as we are still durational existing beings in the process of coming to acquire this affect, we will experience it as actual love. But this affect pertains to that part of our mind that is eternal; and to the extent that we are enabled to take on the eternal viewpoint that is characteristic of adequate knowledge, we can recognize this affect as itself something eternal – not merely a transition to greater perfection, but perfection itself (E 5p33s). This affect of perfection itself – as opposed to the transition toward it – is what Spinoza calls "blessedness" (E 5p33s).

Blessedness, when considered as having an object, is the same thing as the intellectual love of God (E 5p36s). It is, in fact, an intellectual love that is "of" God in two different senses: It has God as its loved *object*, but it is also God's *own* love of himself, and a love in which we, through the third kind of knowledge, can participate. Furthermore, we recognize that, because we are modes of God, the object of this love includes *ourselves* as well. Accordingly, Spinoza says that knowledge of the third kind allows us to love God with the very same love with which God "loves" himself, and the same love with which God "loves" us (E 5pp35–36,36c).

We must, therefore, distinguish two senses of the term "affect." In the narrower sense, Spinoza's God has no affects, because an eternal being cannot have desire, joy, or sadness. In this sense, God does not love us, nor can we can strive that God should love us (E 5p17c,19). Yet in a broader sense, Spinoza's God has the highest kind of affect: not literal joy, but the eternal blessedness of which joy is only a temporal participation.[25] Similarly, while his ideal human being in one sense *acquires* temporal joy, considered as a transition to greater perfection, in another sense he or she takes on a perspective in which all affects are subsumed by participation in God's eternal blessedness, which Spinoza also calls "peace of mind."[26]

Spinoza emphasizes that knowledge of the doctrine of the eternality of the mind is not required for the motivational efficacy of ethics (E 5p41), because the advantageousness of tenacity and nobility were already fully demonstrated in Part 4, independently of this doctrine. Virtue is desirable for whatever duration one has it; to insist that it has no value unless it brings immortality would be "no less absurd . . . than if someone, because he does not believe he can nourish his body with good food to eternity, should prefer to fill himself with poisons and other deadly things" (E 5p41s).

2. SIX CENTRAL TOPICS IN ETHICAL THEORY

The foregoing outline raises a number of important questions concerning Spinoza's position on some of the most central topics in ethical theory. In what follows, I will try to provide answers to some of these questions.

The meaning of ethical language

Spinoza claims to demonstrate ethics in geometrical order. This requires that the ethical propositions of Parts 4 and 5 be deduced, ultimately, from the axioms and definitions of his system. Yet none of his axioms, even those of Parts 4 and 5, are ethical in character. Ethics is a prescriptive discipline; yet Spinoza claims to demonstrate ethical propositions entirely from the descriptive premises provided by his axioms plus a set of mere definitions (including just three definitions of ethical terms, at 4pp1–2,8). How can he suppose this to be possible?

The answer to this question lies in his conception of the meaning of ethical terms. One of the most striking features of Spinoza's ethical writings is his distinctive ethical vocabulary, notable for what it omits as well as for what it contains. For example, despite his reference at 4p18s to "what reason prescribes to us," there is an almost complete absence from his writings of such terms of obligation and duty as "ought," "must," "should," and "may." The concept of permission he introduces only to indicate how much is permissible – namely, whatever seems to be to one's own advantage – without indicating that anything is impermissible:

It is permissible for us to avert, in the way which seems safest, whatever there is in Nature which we judge to be evil, or able to prevent us from being able to exist and enjoy a rational life. On the other hand, we may take for our own use, and use in any way, whatever there is which we judge to be good, *or* useful for preserving our being and enjoying a rational life. And absolutely, it is permissible for everyone to do, by the highest right of Nature, what he judges will contribute to his advantage. (E 4ap8)

Similarly, his uses of the term "right" do not mention anything that is *not* done by right:

Everyone exists by the highest right of Nature, and consequently everyone, by the highest right of Nature, does those things which follow from the necessity of his own nature. So everyone, by the highest right of Nature, judges what is good and what is evil, considers his own advantage according to his own temperament, avenges himself, and strives to preserve what he loves and destroy what he hates. (E 4p37s2; see also TTP xvi.4)[27]

He defines the terms "sin" and "merit," "just" and "unjust," only in political or legal, not ethical, senses: Sin is disobedience to the State, and merit is obedience to it; justice is rendering to each what is judged to be his by the decision of the State, and injustice the opposite (E 4p37s2). These terms receive no ethical use in the *Ethics*, and they are applied to ethical questions in his other writings only in connection with the imaginative idea that God is himself a law-giver.

The ethical propositions of the *Ethics* themselves do not command, exhort, or entreat the reader. Rather, they evaluate, using four primary terms of positive ethical evaluation: "good," "virtue," "guided by reason," and "free man." As Spinoza uses these terms, each is, or can be, defined naturalistically – that is, in natural, descriptive, nonethical terms. He defines "good," as we have seen, as whatever is useful or advantageous (E 4d1), which in turn he defines as that which is conducive to self-preservation (E 4p8d). "Virtue" he defines as (a human being's) power (E 4d8). "The guidance of reason" is definable as the motivational force of the mind's inferential faculty. "Free" is defined as being the adequate (i.e., complete) cause of one's behavior, through one's own nature (E 1d8). Accordingly, ethical propositions can report straightforward natural truths, and the subject matter of ethical propositions is not radically distinct from the study of nature. Rather, ethics is simply that particularly useful branch of the study of nature which compares ways of living in respect of goodness, virtue, reason, and freedom. Its usefulness as a branch of study consists in its ability to aid human beings in pursuing a way of life that will truly suit their purposes.

From the attention that they receive in the preface to Part 4, one might have expected Spinoza's primary terms of ethical evaluation to be "good," and "evil," "perfect," and "imperfect." "Good" and "evil" are, of course, frequently recurring terms in Parts 4 and 5 of the *Ethics*; but "perfect" and "imperfect" are not.[28] Why not? One possible reason for this neglect of the latter pair is that he has already defined "perfection" nonethically, at 2d6, as a synonym for "reality," and used it in that sense throughout the earlier parts of the *Ethics*. Another likely reason, however, is that ethical perfection, as defined in the preface to Part 4, is merely formal: Although it is defined in terms of approximation to a model of human nature that we are to set before ourselves, the definition itself does not specify what that model is. The specific character of the model is spelled out in Spinoza's subsequent descriptions of "virtue" (defined at 4d8), of "the guidance of reason" (introduced at 4p18s), and, especially, of the "free man" (introduced at 4p66s); these more specific notions supplant the place-holder concept of "perfection."

In characterizing Spinoza's view of the meaning of ethical language, it is important to distinguish between the common usage of ethical terms and the philosophical extensions that he proposes. His remark at 3p9s that we call things "good" because we desire them, and not vice versa, suggests what would now be called "emotivism" about the common usage of "good" and "evil" – that is, the view that applications of these terms are neither true nor false, but rather are primarily *expressions* of desire, rather than, for example, descriptions of desires, or statements concerning objective features of the objects evaluated. Other remarks (E 1ap, E 4pr), however, suggest that he thinks the common usage of these terms may also involve a misconstrual of states of desire and aversion as expressing or representing intrinsic states of the objects desired. His remarks about the common usage of the terms "perfect" and "imperfect" also suggest that their application embodies a mistake. That is, uses of these latter terms typically assert (though perhaps only vaguely, at this point in their evolution) the existence of a correspondence or noncorrespondence between the thing evaluated and the purposes of Nature, with imaginative models serving as the criteria for judging this relation. Since Nature in fact has no purposes, all such evaluations are false. (A similar claim would apply to ethical uses of such legalistic terminology as "just" and "unjust," "sin" and "merit," because ethical evaluations in these terms assert relations between human actions and the commands of a divine law-giver. Since God does not literally give commands or laws, we may suppose that all such evaluations are also literally false.[29] It is, evidently, only ethical evaluations understood in their naturalistic Spinozistic senses that are clearly true.

What, then, are the relations among Spinoza's terms of positive ethical evaluation? At least three of them (or their grammatical variants) prove to be coextensive in their application to action or behavior. As already noted, he identifies acting from virtue with acting from the guidance of reason (E 4p24, E 4p37s1). At 4p66s, he also identifies being "led [i.e., guided] by reason" with being "a free man."[30] Whoever acts under the guidance of reason also acts from his own power to preserve himself, and vice versa; and whoever acts from power to preserve himself is to that extent the adequate cause of his own actions, and so is free.

This coextensivity suggests that Spinoza's choice of which evaluative term to use in a given context may be largely arbitrary. And indeed, to a large extent he does simply alternate the cognitive-advisory language of "guiding reason" with the character-centered language of "virtues," and also with the consequentialist language of "good and evil" – as if to imply that at least many of his ethical doctrines can be expressed equally well in any of these terms. As he does also in his metaphysics, he takes some pains to show that his system accommodates many of the formulae of his disparate predecessors, once those formulae are properly interpreted with Spinozistic definitions.

It is notable, however, that Spinoza saves his discussion of the free man for the conclusion of Part 4, and notable too that the propositions composing it are concerned primarily with evaluating ways of behaving. This contrasts with the immediately preceding propositions of Part 4, which are primarily (though not exclusively) concerned with evaluating affects, features of character, and external objects. This way of concluding Part 4 anticipates the fifth of the five "means leading to freedom" that he summarizes at 5p20 – that is, the technique of using one's understanding to produce ethical maxims, which one can then associate in the imagination with the circumstances in which they are needed. His discussion of the "free man" is concerned chiefly with maxims of action, and his expression of these maxims in terms of the actions of "the free man" is evidently calculated to appeal to, or exploit, the imagination. For unlike doctrines about virtue and reason, the description of the free man allows us to imagine, not merely faculties or states of power, but the behavior of a complete ideal human being, whom we may then seek to emulate. In the language of the preface to *Ethics* Part 4, it provides us with "an idea of man, as a model of human nature which we may look to." The vindication of his claim in the preface to *Ethics* Part 4 that it *is* actually useful to have such a model must be found precisely in his later doctrine that an imaginative association of maxims of conduct with appropriate circumstances constitutes one of the means to freedom.

Yet the idea of a perfectly free human being is, taken literally, inconsistent. For to be completely free, one must act from the necessity of one's nature alone, uninfluenced by external forces (E 1d7). But this cannot be entirely achieved by any human being, because: "It is impossible that a man should not be a part of Nature, and that he should be able to undergo no changes except those which can be understood through his own nature alone, of which he is the adequate cause" (E 4p4). Since the very hypothesis that someone is a (completely) free man is inconsistent, it is possible to derive directly contradictory conclusions about the conduct of such a person. To take only one of many possible examples, 4p69 states that "the virtue of a free man is seen to be as great in avoiding dangers as in overcoming them." Yet nothing can harm itself through its own nature alone (E 3p5), and a *completely* free man could not be affected – and *a fortiori* could not be harmed – by any external cause. It follows that nothing is dangerous to a free man, and hence also that he can neither avoid nor overcome any dangers, contrary to 4p69.

Nonetheless, Spinoza believes that sober, literal truths can be expressed in terms of idealizations – as he explains in the *Treatise on the Emendation of the Intellect* in connection with the example of a "candle burning ... where there are no bodies [i.e., in a vacuum]."[31] The literal truth expressed in the idealizing portrait of the free man is that certain kinds of behavior become *more prevalent* as one becomes *more free* – that is, they vary *proportionately* with freedom. They do so because they are products of human virtue and the use of reason, each of which renders us relatively more free, more able to act from our own nature rather than be determined by external causes.[32] To use one of Spinoza's most common expressions, the description of the free man is to be understood as a description of the condition and behavior human beings approach "insofar as" they are free.

The nature of the good

What is the nature of the good, in Spinoza's view? On the one hand, it seems to follow directly from his definition of the good (i.e., the advantageous) as what is conducive to perseverance in being that death is the greatest evil, and that whatever contributes to continued life is the good. This construal of the good is supported by 4p39, which holds that whatever is conducive to continued life is good. (See also 4p22c, which holds that self-preservation is the "first and only foundation of virtue.") Yet as we have seen, he also argues at 4pp26–28 that the mind's true good is understanding, or adequate knowledge, itself. R. J. Delahunty expresses the resulting apparent conflict well:

> The kind of power we must be after if we want to stay alive in a hostile world does not seem to be the power which consists in, or follows from, an enlarged understanding. A cool, controlling type of man, or a man who bows before every change in the wind, has at least as good a chance of survival as a dedicated thinker or scientist: who would reckon the odds on Spinoza to be better than those, say, on Cromwell? It is not so much that Spinoza goes wrong in saying that we must pursue more and more power in order to survive, as that he misdescribes the *sort* of power we must have more and more of. (Delahunty 1985: 227)

While knowledge is often an aid to continuing one's life, inadequate knowledge of the first kind is very often as advantageous, or more advantageous, for this purpose than most adequate knowledge of the second and third kinds. Adequate knowledge is not entirely correlated with long life. Spinoza himself, after all, lived only to the age of forty-five.

This conflict can be resolved only if understanding can *itself* constitute or guarantee a kind of perseverance in being. Spinoza's doctrine of the eternality of part of the human mind, however, provides him with just such a resolution. That doctrine is not, therefore, a mere failure of naturalistic resolve on Spinoza's part, and it is more than simply an indication of his ability to suit the language of religious aspiration to his own metaphysics. Rather, it is logically required to reconcile his twin conceptions of the good as perseverance in being and as adequate knowledge, respectively. Gaining adequate knowledge, according to this doctrine, does more than merely provide one with more cognitive resources for preserving one's life, while increasing the activity and perfection of the life that one leads. It also makes a greater part of the mind eternal, and so ensures that a larger part of the mind – though not the whole of the mind – is indeed something that has an *eternal* being. Because understanding allows one to participate in the eternal, it cannot help but constitute the most important kind of "perseverance in being," whether the actual *duration* of one's life is long or not.

The doctrine of the eternality of part of the human mind reconciles Spinoza's two conceptions of the good without denying the goodness of what is conducive to continued life. According to Spinoza, the more adequate knowledge one has, the less one is harmed by death, and the less one is disturbed by fear of death (E 5p38s). Nevertheless, it can never be to one's own positive advantage to die. Death is always the end of *some* part of the mind – namely, that part which is *not* eternal. Furthermore, it marks the end of any prospect of further understanding, and hence the end of any prospect for *increasing* the part of one's mind that is eternal. Although "the free man thinks of nothing less than of death," this is because the free man is motivated by direct pursuit of the good of continued life, and not because death is not always an evil for a human being. According to 4p39, "Those things are good which bring about the preservation of the proportion of motion and rest the human body's parts have to one another." And the preservation of this proportion is simply the preservation of one's life, as 4p39s makes explicit.

Since one's own death is always an evil, it must always be good, on Spinoza's view, to do whatever will prevent one's own death. Yet this may seem to conflict with 4p72, which states that, "A free man always acts honestly, not deceptively." The demonstration of 4p72 is as follows:

If a free man, insofar as he is free, did anything by deception, he would do it from the dictate of reason (for so far only do we call him free). And so it would be a virtue to act deceptively (by 4p24), and hence (by the same proposition), everyone would be better advised to act deceptively to preserve

his being. I.e., (as is known through itself), men would be better advised to
agree only in words, and be contrary to one another in fact. But this is absurd
(by 4p31c). Therefore, a free man, etc. q.e.d.

In other words, the free man seeks, through the guidance of reason,
to join in cooperative action with others, and honesty is necessary to
make genuine cooperation possible; honesty is therefore also a virtue. Accordingly, any failure of honesty may be ascribed to an individual's lack of freedom, inability to be completely guided by reason,
and lack of virtue. Yet it seems that it must, in at least some circumstances, be *good* to act deceptively. Suppose, for example, that one
could successfully compete with fellow castaways for a limited food
supply only by deception, or save oneself from certain death at the
hands of one's captors only by deceiving them. Because whatever
preserves one's life is good, and deception is required in this instance
to preserve life, it seems to follow that it will be good to deceive. But
how can it be good to deceive, when the free man always acts honestly, and not deceptively?[33]

The term "good" is the only one of Spinoza's four main terms of
positive ethical evaluation that he does not explicitly claim to be
coextensive with one or more of the others. And indeed "good" does
appear to have a somewhat different scope, in several respects. For
one thing, "virtue," "from the guidance of reason," "free," and their
variants or extensions apply at most to states of character, to behavior, and to persons themselves, whereas not only these but also
external objects may be characterized as "good." Even restricting
our attention to actions, however, it appears that what is *good* to do
may diverge from what it is virtuous, or in accordance with reason,
or like a free man, to do.

The reason for this is simple. Someone who acts from virtue,
reason, and freedom has, to that extent, *already* achieved a certain
mode of being. The good, in contrast, is what will *enable* one to
achieve a certain mode of being. And the kinds of actions that will
enable one to achieve a mode of being are not necessarily the same
kinds of actions that one will perform once one has achieved it. For
example, the diet needed by the unhealthy person in order to become healthy may not be the same diet he or she will eat once
health has been achieved. Since virtue, reason, and freedom aim at
their own self-maintenance, we can be confident that whatever an

individual does from virtue, reason, and freedom will be good. But it does not follow that whatever is good for some individual will be a characteristic act of the virtuous, reasonable, or free person.

Spinoza explicitly considers the choice between death and deception in the scholium to 4p72:

> Suppose someone now asks: What if a man could save himself from the present danger of death by treachery? Would not the principle of preserving his own being recommend, without qualification, that he be treacherous? . . . If reason should recommend that, it would recommend it to all men. And so reason would recommend, without qualification, that men should make agreements to join forces and to have common laws only by deception – that is, that really they should have no common laws. This is absurd.

Reason cannot recommend treachery "without qualification," in such a case, for reason always recommends most highly that human beings join forces through cooperation. And, no doubt, the perfectly free and virtuous man would always have sufficient means other than deceit available, or would successfully avoid situations in which a choice between death and deceit was inevitable in the first place. No actual human being, however, has enough freedom or virtue to ensure that a choice between death and deception need never be faced; as we have already seen, the life of "the free man" is an approachable but not a completely attainable model or limit.

Rule utilitarians argue that it can be more useful in the long run to adopt exceptionless rules than to try to act by evaluating utility in individual cases. It may be tempting to suppose that, in a somewhat similar way, Spinoza in 4p72d and 4p72s is arguing, or at least implying, that it will be advantageous for a person to adopt an exceptionless policy of honesty even if this policy sometimes requires one to choose one's own death over deception of others. In general, Spinoza might well admit that it *can* sometimes be advantageous to bind oneself to an exceptionless rule rather than to allow oneself to assess the merits of individual cases. Nevertheless, it is difficult to see where any Spinozistic advantage could lie in adopting a rule of honesty that forbade making an exception for a choice of deceit over one's own death, for none of the considerations usually employed to justify the adoption of exceptionless rules over examination of particular cases apply. For example, the consequences of the two choices in such a situation need not be at all difficult to calculate;

there can be no long-term gain for oneself in compensation for an immediate choice of death; and there is no reason to suppose that others could be motivated to govern themselves by such a rule even on the condition that one adopted it oneself. Indeed, it seems that only *perfectly* free men (who cannot be harmed) could adopt such a rule – and there are none. Thus, it is hard to avoid the conclusion that, for Spinoza, a forced choice between deceit and one's own death would be a situation in which it would be good for an actual human being to act in a way different from the way in which the ideal free man is said to act.

This conclusion receives partial confirmation from the fact that Spinoza grants, in other contexts, that something can be "good," at least to some extent or in some circumstances, even though it is not virtuous. For example, he holds that shame is a kind of sadness, and so is not a virtue. It is nevertheless "still good insofar as it indicates, in the man who blushes with Shame, a desire to live honorably" (E 4p58s). And more generally, he holds that "a lesser evil is really a good" in relation to a greater evil, since "good and evil are said of things insofar as we compare them to one another" (E 4p65d). When the only alternative is death, deceit may well be a "lesser evil," for Spinoza, and hence a good, even though it is not an action of a free man.

One possible strategy for denying this latter conclusion would be to emphasize the first-person plural in Spinoza's definition of the good as "what we certainly know to be useful to us." That is, the definition might be interpreted to mean that only things that are beneficial *to all* should be called "good." This interpretation is strengthened to some extent by the fact that Spinoza criticizes the common usage of the term "good" on the grounds that it makes what is good relative to each individual. On this interpretation, a situation in which no one could be benefited except at the expense of another would be a situation in which there would be *nothing* that it would be "good" to do. "Good" would thus be used to describe only the common human advantage, and not the conflicting advantages of individuals that (inevitably) arise when their interests diverge.

But while this interpretation has some textual basis, it cannot entirely resolve the divergence between good actions and the actions of the ideal free man. For there can clearly be circumstances in which deceit would be advantageous *to all*, and not merely to its perpetrator. For example, an entire community might perish unless one of its members deceived all the rest into taking action that they could not be induced to take otherwise. Hence, we are still obliged to recognize that, in Spinoza's ethical theory, a good action can *sometimes* differ from the action of a free man.[34]

The practicality of reason

Spinoza regards reason as a cognitive, inferential process by which adequate knowledge is derived from other adequate knowledge. Yet he also writes of reason as guiding action *(ex ducto rationis)*, and as offering counsels *(consilium rationis)*, precepts *(praeceptum rationis)*, rules *(praescriptum rationis)*, and "dictates" *(dictamen rationis)*. Writing seventy years after the publication of the *Ethics*, David Hume maintained that reason itself has no motivational force, so that it is only "the slave of the passions" (Hume 1978: 415). Immanuel Kant maintained, in response to Hume, that in morality reason must be practical and must have motivational force; but he also allowed that it is beyond our capacity to explain *how* it is that reason can have this motivating force. Can Spinoza explain how reason itself motivates?

The key to understanding how Spinozistic reason can motivate lies in the account of the relation between ideas and affects that he gives in his explanation of the causes of bondage to the passions, in 4pp1–18. Ideas, as they occur in human minds, are ideas that represent (are "of") modifications, or features, of the human body. They may also indirectly represent external objects whose natures are involved in the causation of those modifications of the body. But ideas are not *merely* representations, for Spinoza; at least many of them also have an affective aspect or character. For example, a desire is not – as Hume would later hold – merely a simple feeling that is caused by, or accompanied by, an idea of some state of affairs involving its object. Rather, the desire *is* the idea of this state of affairs, occurring under certain circumstances. For example, an idea representing some food as present, occurring in a normally functioning individual who needs food, will, in its affective aspect, *be* a desire to obtain and eat the food.

Reason, for Spinoza, is a cognitive process by which adequate ideas follow logically from, and are caused by, other adequate ideas. Many desires are, of course, merely passionate products of the imagination, with little or no involvement of reason. But it is also possible for an adequate idea, produced by reason, to constitute a desire. If, for example, one determines by reason that one's own advantage lies in the pursuit of knowledge, or in the institution of a well-ordered state, or in association with individuals like oneself, then the idea that constitutes this understanding will itself be a desire for the thing so conceived, in Spinoza's view. It will not merely direct or stimulate such a desire; it will *be* such a desire. This is not to say that the desire cannot be overwhelmed by other, more powerful, passionate affects – that, of course, is the primary moral of 4pp1-18 – but it is to say that reason itself has motivational force.

Spinoza is able to maintain this view of the practicality of reason because he identifies affects (emotions) with (representational) ideas. Whereas the common view, shared by Hume and Kant, treats affects and ideas as two classes of mental events or entities, Spinoza construes the affective and the representational as two aspects of the *same* mental events or entities. This ensures that, when reason produces the right kind of representation, it *ipso facto* produces a motivating affect. He is enabled to maintain this identity of affects and ideas, in turn, by the *conatus* doctrine that every individual, by its very essence, necessarily endeavors insofar as it can to persevere in its own existence. For it is the *conatus* doctrine that explains how, when an individual perceives an object as something advantageous or beneficial to it, that very perception can constitute a desire for it. Spinozistic desire is not something that must be *added* to a mind, conceived as a set of representational contents. On the contrary, it pertains to the very *essence* of minds to desire whatever they can perceive (adequately or inadequately) as conducive to their own advantage. There is no need for Spinoza to distinguish the perception and the desire as separate parts of the mind, for a mind that perceives something as advantageous and yet does not, at least to some extent, desire it, is a contradiction on his theory. Spinozistic reason, which can provide adequate perceptions of things and their uses, is inherently practical.

This inherent practicality of reason, in turn, explains how Spinoza can conceive of ethical knowledge as both naturalistic and intrinsically motivating. There is no need, and no purpose, for Spinoza to command, exhort, or entreat his readers – the reader's own reason effectively does this for him. If his readers grasp his demonstrations that certain behaviors, character traits, and human relations are conducive to the preservation of their being, they will *ipso facto* be motivated to pursue them. The question, "Why be moral?" has no more skeptical force, for Spinoza, than the question, "Why seek to achieve your own ends?" Each individual, by metaphysical necessity, seeks its own self-preservation. Ethics merely shows in what that self-preservation consists and what are the most effective means to it.

The role of virtue

On the one hand, Spinoza's ethics appear to be a version of what has come to be called "consequentialism." That is, he appears to regard the most important or fundamental ethical evaluations to be evaluations of actions in terms of their consequences. The foundation of virtue, he insists, is self-preservation; and it seems therefore that virtue must be desirable only instrumentally, as an aid to achieving self-preservation – and also, perhaps, as an aid to achieving the affective states of joy or blessedness. Yet Spinoza also seems to be a proponent of what has come to be called "virtue ethics," according to which the most important or fundamental ethical evaluations are evaluations of a person's character or virtue. In fact, he seems to deny that the value of virtue is instrumental at all, for he claims to demonstrate "that we ought to want virtue for its own sake, that there is not anything preferable to it, or more useful to us, for the sake of which we ought to want it" (E 4p18s). How can this conflict be resolved?

In fact, Spinoza is both a consequentialist *and* a virtue ethicist.[35] Although self-preservation first appears in the *Ethics* as a tendency towards continued temporal duration, we have seen that the achievement of adequate understanding – which is the highest virtue – brings a participation in the eternal that is *itself* a kind of perseverance in one's being. Accordingly, the highest virtue is not merely a *means* toward self-preservation; it is itself a *kind* of self-preservation. That is, the very consequence at which Spinoza's consequentialism aims is also, at least in its most important manifestation, a state of character.

The value of joy, in contrast, is instrumental in Spinoza's ethics. For it is only an indication of a transition to a greater state of perfection and capacity for action.[36] It is this state of greater perfection and capacity for action itself that Spinoza values for its own sake, as that which his – and each person's – *conatus* is necessarily seeking to produce.

This state of greater perfection is virtue; but it is *also* the affective state of blessedness. For Spinoza, blessedness, as an affective state of mind, is not merely a consequence – even an inevitable consequence – of a virtuous character. As we have seen, he identifies affects with ideas. Because the highest virtue is the continued possession of adequate ideas, and the affective side of this adequate knowledge is blessedness, it follows that the pursuit of blessedness *is* the pursuit of virtue. Virtue and blessedness are equally valuable and fundamental – for they prove in the end to be identical.[37] Thus Spinoza asserts in the last proposition of the *Ethics* that, "Blessedness is not the reward of virtue, but virtue itself" (E 5p42).[38] Blessedness is the actual and eternal possession of the virtue of which joy is merely a temporal indicator.[39]

The requirements for freedom and moral responsibility

Spinoza is not a fatalist. For although he holds that all volitions, behaviors, and other events are completely determined by their causes, he does not deny that volitions are among the causes of behavior, nor that behaviors are sometimes among the causes of other events. His view is not that the same events would occur whether we acted or not, but rather that the causal determination of what we do contributes to the causal determination of what events will occur.

Spinoza, is, however, a necessitarian; he does hold that everything true is true necessarily. One aspect of his necessitarianism is his determinism: that is, his acceptance of the doctrine that the total state of the universe at any given time plus the laws of nature jointly determine the total state of the universe at any future time. And it is often supposed that determinism is incompatible with moral freedom and moral responsibility. Again, Spinoza adopts an objective, scientific attitude towards human beings, human actions, and human emotions, writing for example that he will "consider human actions and appetites just as if it were a Question of lines, planes, and bodies" (E 3pr). And it is often supposed that this kind of objective attitude is incompatible with what P. F. Strawson has called the moral "reactive attitudes" that are essential to attributions of moral responsibility (Strawson 1974). So the question arises: Does Spinoza recognize moral freedom and moral responsibility?

Spinozistic freedom, defined at 1d7, does not demand an absence of causal determination. It requires only that the free thing be determined by its own nature, rather than by external causes. As we have already noted, God alone is perfectly free in this sense; nevertheless, human beings can achieve a measure of freedom to the extent that they *act* through their own endeavor to persevere in their being. There is no incompatibility in saying both that God freely causes human behavior and that human beings sometimes freely cause their own behavior, for human beings are modes of God. Insofar as they act freely, God produces effects by constituting their own natures; insofar as they do not act freely, God produces effects through other means.

But although Spinoza clearly allows a measure of freedom, it is unclear whether this will be a kind of *moral* freedom unless it bears some relation to moral responsibility. Since Spinoza does not use the term "moral responsibility," we must look for his attitude toward it in his discussion of affects and attitudes toward those who do good and those who do evil.

Spinoza does use the terms "praise" (*"laus"*) and "blame" (*"vituperium"*). As he defines them, however, they apply only to affects towards individuals who strive to benefit or harm the person who feels the affect. Thus, praise is "the Joy with which we imagine the action of another by which he has striven to please us," while blame is "the Sadness with which we are averse to his action" when the other strives to harm us (E 3p29s).

Of more interest for our purposes are "favor" (*"favor"*; sometimes translated as "approval" or "approbation") and "indignation" (*"indignatio"*). Favor is "a Love toward someone who has benefited another," while indignation is "a Hate toward someone who has done evil to another" (3da19,20). Favor and indignation differ from praise and blame in three ways: (i) they are instances of love or hate, rather than merely joy or sadness; (ii) they are not explicitly restricted to the imagination; and (iii) they are attitudes towards actions affecting human beings generally, and not merely oneself. I will assume that behavior toward "another" means behavior toward someone other than the author of the behavior, and hence can include behavior toward oneself. On this assumption one can feel favor or indignation for benefits or harms to oneself, as well as to others. Favor and indignation are Spinoza's primary moral "reactive attitudes."

Spinoza asserts at 4p51s that "indignation . . . is necessarily evil." As a form of hate, and hence of sadness, it is directly evil in itself. Moreover, it leads us to desire to harm or destroy the person we hate, which is contrary to reason's aim of uniting human beings in friendship. It is also inappropriate for another reason: As we become aware of the causes of someone's doing harm to another person, we will inevitably become aware that the perpetrator is not the adequate cause of his or her own behavior. For the free man seeks to benefit, not to harm, other human beings. Those who do evil are never free and, accordingly, indignation toward them is never in accordance with reason.⁴⁰ There is no need to disturb one's peace of mind through feelings of hatred or desires for vengeance.

In contrast, 4p51 affirms that "Favor is not contrary to reason, but can agree with it and arise from it." This is because it can arise from an adequate understanding of another's actions. This is not to say that *all* favor is in accordance with reason. If, for example, we feel favor toward someone who, from passion, has accidentally behaved in a way that has benefited others, that person is not the adequate cause of the benefit. Understanding this fact will result in a withdrawal of our favor or approval. When human beings benefit others out of nobility, however, seeking to unite others to themselves in friendship, they are the adequate causes of their actions; when we are guided by reason, therefore, we will feel favor toward them. That the beneficial acts flow from the necessity of the divine nature is no hindrance to our favor or approbation for the human agent. For as we have seen, God and the human agent are not competitors for the causation of the good; rather, God produces the benefit through the adequate causality of the human agent who is, of course, a mode of God, and whose own power is a share of God's power.

The two main parties in the so-called free-will debate are the compatibilists and the incompatibilists. The former hold that determinism is compatible with freedom and hence with moral responsibility for good and evil actions. The latter hold that determinism is incompatible with freedom, and hence also incompatible with moral responsibility for good and evil actions. These two parties thus share a common assumption that Spinoza denies: namely, that freedom to perform (and hence moral responsibility for) good actions and evil actions must go together. That is, the two parties agree that freedom and moral responsibility either apply to both good and evil actions, or they apply to neither. Spinoza denies this because he has a conception of "asymmetrical freedom."[41] By this I mean that he holds that we sometimes freely do good, but can never freely do evil. Evil is always the result of passion or lack of power, and hence not the result of one's own adequate causality – that is, not the result of freedom. Because freedom is asymmetrical in this way, so too are rational assignments of moral responsibility. Reason counsels (i.e., moves us to) love and favor for those who freely do good, without hate or indignation for those who do evil.

Spinoza emphasizes that a lack of indignation does not imply an unwillingness to engage in punitive action. But such action will be motivated entirely by an informed desire for self-protection; it will not be motivated by resentment, or a desire for retribution. Thus, for example, he writes: "But it should be noted that when the supreme power, bound by its desire to preserve peace, punishes a citizen who has wronged another, I do not say that it is indignant toward the citizen. For it punishes him not because it has been aroused by Hate to destroy him but because it is moved by duty" (E 4p51s).[42]

Indignation is evil and not in accordance with reason; and hence the free man does not feel indignation. However, absolute freedom is an approachable but unreachable ideal; and this is true not just in application to the free man's actions, but also in application to the free man's affective *reactions*. Spinoza would certainly admit that he was not, and could not be, the model free man; and his seemingly indignant reaction to the murder of his friends, the De Witt brothers (as described by Leibniz and by Lucas; see Freudenthal 1899: 19) is evidence that Spinoza's own affective reactions were sometimes passionate rather than determined entirely by reason. To the extent that one gains understanding, however, one's power over the passions will tend to increase, and the more free one is, the less indignation one will feel.

The possibility and moral significance of altruism

Spinoza holds that each thing's genuine activity consists entirely in endeavoring to achieve its own advantage, construed as self-preservation. Yet observation of human life suggests that human beings frequently seek to benefit one another independent of any prospect of advantage to themselves. Indeed, human beings often appear to sacrifice their own advantage for the welfare of others. Is Spinoza committed to denying these seemingly evident facts?

In his *Enquiry Concerning the Principles of Morals,* David Hume distinguishes two forms of psychological egoism:

> [i] There is a principle, supposed to prevail among many . . . that all *benevolence* is mere hypocrisy . . . and that while all of us, at bottom, pursue only our private interest, we wear these fair disguises, in order to put others off their guard, and expose them the more to our wiles and machinations. . . .
>
> [ii] There is another principle, somewhat resembling the former . . . that, whatever affection one may feel, or imagine he feels for others, no passion is, or can be disinterested; that the most generous friendship, however sincere, is a modification of self-love. . . .
>
> [One who holds this latter principle] readily allows, that there is such a thing as friendship in the world, without hypocrisy or disguise; though he may attempt, by a philosophical chymistry, to resolve the elements of this passion, if I may so speak, into those of another, and explain every affection to be self-love, twisted and moulded, by a particular turn of imagination, into a variety of appearances. (Hume 1975: 295–7)

Hume himself, although he regards the second form of psychological egoism as compatible with morality, rejects both forms in favor of a psychology that makes room for sympathetic benevolence as an original principle independent of "self-love." In terms of Hume's distinction, however, Spinoza clearly belongs, not with those who maintain that all apparent benevolence is hypocrisy and deceit, but rather with proponents of the "second principle" – that is, those who seek to apply a kind of "philosophical chymistry" to resolve all behavior into modifications of a single original force of self-interest, directed and redirected by circumstances.

Spinoza need not deny that human beings are sometimes motivated in their behavior by thoughts of the welfare or harm of others without thought or concern of themselves. He need not deny that individuals sometimes forego something that they desire for themselves for the sake of the happiness or welfare of another. He need not deny even that individuals sometimes sacrifice their lives for the well-being of others. Thus, he need not deny the *phenomena* of altruism. He is committed only to the view that the causal *origins* of these phenomena always lie in a single psychological force, which is the individual's own endeavor for his or her own self-preservation. This force can, through circumstance, come to be directed onto a variety of objects, objects which the agent may then experience himself or herself pursuing directly. As he emphasizes, we often know our desires while in ignorance of their causes (E 1ap and elsewhere).

In order to explain altruistic behavior, then, Spinoza must explain how this self-preservatory force or *conatus* comes to be directed onto the well-being of others. Hume mentions only one faculty by which his "philosophical chymists" might suppose an original egoistic force to be directed – namely, the imagination. This is understandable, since Hume does not recognize a separate representational faculty of intellect in addition to the imagination. Spinoza, in contrast, distinguishes intellect and imagination as two distinct representational faculties; and for him, the individual's endeavor for self-preservation may be directed by either.

The imagination can direct the *conatus* of an individual towards the well-being of another in many ways. For example, if we perceive another individual as the cause of imaginative ideas that affect us with joy, we will love that individual and thereby seek to benefit him or her. If we perceive that an individual hates another individual whom we also hate, we will seek to benefit the first individual in order to harm the object of our hate. If we perceive an individual to be like ourselves, our affects will imitate the affects of that individual, and we will be motivated to pursue the well-being of that individual as well as our own well-being. In each case, the well-being of another becomes one of the many objects onto which our fundamental self-preservatory endeavor becomes directed. To the extent that this direction occurs through the imagination, we are passive.

When the intellect, through the use of reason, directs the *conatus* of the individual toward the welfare of others, it does so through recognition that the true advantage of individuals largely coincides because "to man ... there is nothing more useful than man" (E 4p18s). Among human beings, the most useful are those who are guided by reason, for to the extent that human beings are guided by reason they share the same nature, so that whatever is beneficial to one is beneficial to all. The good that such individuals pursue – namely, knowledge – is not only shareable rather than limited; it is also a good that can best be pursued in company with others. As we have observed, Spinoza regards altruistic behavior in these circumstances with "favor" or approbation.

Nevertheless, as we have also seen (in connection with the choice between deceit and death, for example), a *complete* coincidence of human interests is not possible. Each individual necessarily endeavors to achieve his or her own advantage; and because individuals are finite beings who must maintain life in order to pursue even understanding, they may be in competition for limited resources. Hence, their interests can diverge. When such divergence occurs, a common cooperative course of conduct on which all can rationally agree is impossible. One may then be forced to choose between achieving one's own advantage at the expense of others, and aiding others through sacrificing oneself. What is Spinoza's assessment of such self-sacrificing altruism?

Although genuine self-sacrifice is *possible*, it cannot be *good* for the sacrificing individual, and it cannot be the result of reason or virtue. Accordingly, it must result from being overcome by passion. Since the self-sacrificing individual cannot be the adequate cause of his or her own action, favor is not a rational response. Neither, however, is indignation, since the individual has not harmed others. Hence, reason calls for neither favor nor indignation toward one who chooses self-sacrifice in order to benefit others.

On the other hand, an individual who refuses altruistic self-sacrifice cannot be the object of favor either, since he or she has not benefited others. Yet neither does reason counsel indignation toward such an individual, since indignation is never in accordance with reason. Hence, the rational affect toward any person faced with a choice between self-preservation at others' expense and self-sacrifice will be neither favor nor indignation, *regardless* of the person's ultimate choice. Such a situation calls only for understanding; it is entirely outside the reach of moral reactive attitudes or moral responsibility – at least, from the standpoint of reason.

However, just as a complete coincidence of interests is an ideal that no human community can entirely attain, so the affective standpoint of reason is an ideal that no actual human being can entirely maintain. If a self-sacrificing individual benefits individuals that we love, we – and Spinoza among us – are likely to feel at least some degree of favor, even if the ideally rational "free man" would feel none.

3. THE PLACE OF SPINOZA'S ETHICS IN MORAL THEORY

Spinoza's geometrical method of demonstration tends to obscure the historical context of his ethical theory. By way of conclusion, I will comment briefly on his ethical theory in relation to his Greek and Judeo-Christian predecessors, to his seventeenth- and eighteenth-century contemporaries (and near-contemporaries), and to more recent ethical theory.

Spinoza and his predecessors

A number of ancient influences are evident in Spinoza's ethical theory. From Plato, he accepts a conception of ethics as concerned with the conflict between reason and the passions, and the distinction between understanding the eternal, on the one hand, and sensing or imagining the merely durational, on the other. From Aristotle, he takes a conception of ethics as concerned with virtue and a kind of human flourishing whose highest expression lies in the life of active reason. From the Stoics, he appropriates the ideal of an internal freedom found in reconciling oneself to the necessities of nature. His own ethical theory, however, is distinctive, and not reducible to any of these influences.[43]

Spinoza's relation to the Judeo-Christian moral tradition is complex. He endorses the Christian view that hate is to be overcome by returning love to those who hate us (E 3pp43–44, E4ap11). However, he rejects Christian asceticism and guilt, and maintains that such central Christian "virtues" as humility, repentance, and pity are not virtues at all but evils, because they are all species of sadness and hence indications of lack of power.

Spinoza's God does not issue any commands, nor does his God desire that human beings should live well. Nevertheless, Spinoza believes, one can appeal to the popular imagination by describing the content of ethics *as though* it consisted of a set of commands promulgated, with promises of rewards and punishments, by a divine law-giver. As he writes to Willem van Blijenbergh:

When we say that we sin against god, we are speaking inaccurately, or in a human way, as we do when we say that men anger god. . . . [B]ecause God had revealed the means to salvation and destruction, which are nothing but effects which follow from the means, [the prophets] represented him as a king and lawgiver. The means, which are nothing but causes, they called laws and wrote in the manner of laws. Salvation and destruction, which are nothing but effects which follow from the means, they represented as reward and punishment. They have ordered all their words more according to this parable than according to the truth. Throughout they have represented god as a man, now angry, now merciful, now longing for the future, now seized by jealousy and suspicion, indeed even deceived by the devil. So the Philosophers, and with them all those who are above the law, i.e., who follow virtue not as a law, but from love, because it is the best thing, should not be shocked by such words. (Ep. 19)

Spinoza remarks at E2p7s, concerning the doctrine that a mode of extension and a mode of thought are the same thing expressed in two ways, that "the Hebrews seem to have seen this, as if through a cloud, when they maintained that God, God's intellect, and the things understood by him are one and the same." In a similar way, Spinoza holds, the Hebrew prophets captured some of the content of ethics, but represented it as though the beneficial and harmful consequences of natural laws governing humans and their well-being were instead freely chosen rewards and punishments of a passionate and purposeful God. Just as the religion of the philosophers has its imaginative reflection in the popular religion of the vulgar, so too the ethics of the philosophers has its imaginative reflection in the religious morality of the vulgar. As he makes clear in the *Theological-Political Treatise*, popular religion can be extremely dangerous; but in a state where not all human beings are philosophers, and so must be governed by hope and (especially) fear, the imaginative morality based on popular religion is nevertheless essential for many.

Spinoza and his contemporaries

Spinoza anticipates other modern ethical theorists in his effort to make ethics entirely independent of literal divine commands by locating ethical discernment, ethical authority, and the source of ethical motivation, entirely within the individual. The influence of Hobbes seems evident in Spinoza's egoistic moral psychology founded on a fundamental drive for self-preservation, and in his effort to reconcile freedom with the application of natural necessity to human beings. He differs from Hobbes, however, in his concurrent acceptance of Descartes's ethical project of training the imagination and empowering the intellect – the latter being a representational faculty for which Hobbes has no use. Indeed, more than any other single factor, it is his acceptance of the Cartesian distinction between intellect and imagination that separates Spinoza not only from the seventeenth-century Hobbes but also from such eighteenth-century British moral thinkers as Locke, Hutcheson, Shaftesbury, Butler, and Hume. It is only a mild over-simplification to say that Hume's sentimental, sympathy-based ethical judgments are what would remain of Spinoza's ethical theory were Spinoza obliged to give up the existence of the intellect and, along with it, the second and third kinds of knowledge.[44]

Many seventeenth-century philosophers undertook to adapt metaphysics to the content and methods of the New Science. Some, like Spinoza, sought also to render *ethics* scientific, by basing it on an entirely naturalistic and deterministic understanding of human beings, their passions, and their behavior. Spinoza stands alone, however, in aiming to marry science to ethics in a further respect as well. Unlike his contemporaries, he sought to construe natural scientific understanding itself (also describable, for him, as "knowledge of God") as the highest virtue and, indeed, as eternal blessedness. His is not merely a scientifically informed ethics; it is an ethics whose very centerpiece is the practice of science. His ethical vision is one in which scientific understanding allows us to participate in a peaceful and cooperative moral community with other co-inquirers, sharing and taking joy in one another's achievements without being disturbed by one another's human weaknesses.

Spinoza and his successors

The immediate reception of Spinoza's ethical theory was no more positive than was the reception of his metaphysics. Although German Romanticism rendered a more favorable verdict on Spinoza generally, it cannot be said that the romantic movement as a whole was deeply influenced by his ethical theory.

Readers often find echoes of Spinoza in Nietzsche's "will to power," with its concurrent naturalism and rejection of Christian ethics. Nietzsche himself saw a predecessor in Spinoza, although only relatively late in his life.[45] A Spinozist approach is also echoed in the work of another astute psychologist, Sigmund Freud. For Spinoza's is fundamentally an ethics of *mental health*, in which one achieves a healthy power to control the direction of one's affects through knowledge of their causes.

Spinoza's ethical theory has been historically less influential than the ethical theories of such other early modern philosophers as Hume and Kant. Nevertheless, in its naturalism, its practical rationalism, its asymmetrical conception of moral freedom and responsibility, its nonretributivism, its emphasis on virtue as well as consequences, and its close relation to social and political theory, it is a forerunner of, and of special relevance to, contemporary trends in ethical theorizing.

Because Spinoza derives his ethical theory in formal geometrical order from his metaphysics, anyone who rejects that metaphysics may also reject his demonstration of ethics. His necessitarian, monistic metaphysics, in turn, is based largely on a strong Principle of Sufficient Reason (see Bennett's discussion of "explanatory rationalism" in Chapter 1, and Garrett 1991). Few contemporary philosophers would accept his strong version of that principle, and few would accept his necessitarianism or his monism in the form in which he expressed them.[46] Most contemporary philosophers, however, would agree that the universe in general, and human behavior in particular, are at least approximately deterministic at a large-scale level (allowing for quantum indeterminacies), and that the human mind is a part of nature that is identical with some part of the human body. The most important aspects of Spinoza's ethical theory may well prove nearly as adaptable to this contemporary scientific metaphysics as they are to his own seventeenth-century scientific metaphysics.

NOTES

1 In his preface to the *Nagelate Schriften*, Spinoza's friend Jarig Jelles wrote:

He was driven by a burning desire for knowledge; but because he did not get full satisfaction either from his teachers or from those writing about these sciences, he decided to see what he himself could do in these areas. For that purpose he found the writings of the famous René Descartes, which he came upon at that time, very useful. (Akkerman 1980: 216–17, as cited in Spinoza 1994: x–xi).

2 For a fine accessible treatment of Spinoza's relation to both Descartes and Hobbes, see Curley 1988.

3 The phrase is from the first paragraph of the appendix to *Ethics* Part 4, and also occurs in the preface to Part 3. Spinoza uses the term "morality" not to designate a body of doctrine or knowledge, but as the name for a desire – specifically, "the desire to do good generated in us by our living according to the guidance of reason" (E 4p37s).

4 For a description of Descartes's distinction between the synthetic and analytic methods of demonstration, see the Introduction to this volume.

5 I have argued elsewhere that Spinoza was unable to finish the *Treatise on the Emendation of the Intellect* partly because, having arrived at his epistemology artificially, by reflection on Descartes and others, he was not able to show "how the thing in question was discovered methodically," which the analytic method requires (Garrett 1986).

6 See also Chapter 3, Section 1, and Chapter 10, Section 3 of this volume for further discussion of this passage, in connection with Spinoza's epistemology and Schopenhauer's interpretation of Spinoza, respectively.

7 As Edwin Curley wrote in 1973: "It is a rare book on ethics which does not have at least a passing reference to Spinoza. But it is an even rarer book which has more than a passing reference" (Curley 1973b). Curley mentions the exception of Broad 1930. Of recent works that have shed light on Spinoza's ethical theory, most are works devoted to multiple aspects of Spinoza's philosophy, including his ethical theory, rather than works devoted to ethical theory in Spinoza and others. Among the most stimulating recent treatments of Spinoza's ethical theory are those in Delahunty 1985, Donagan 1988, and, especially, Bennett 1984. My own account owes more to Bennett's incisive and uncompromising interrogation of Spinoza's ethical thought than to any other single source.

8 *Ethics* 5a1 states: "If two contrary actions are aroused in the same subject, a change will have to occur, either in both of them, or in one only, until they cease to be contrary." *Ethics* 5a2 states: "The power of an effect is defined by the power of its cause, insofar as its essence is explained or defined by the essence of its cause." *Ethics* 3p7 reads: "The striving by which each thing strives to persevere in its being is nothing but the actual essence of the thing."

9   "Strictly speaking, a *real* distinction exists only between two or more substances; and we can perceive that two substances are really distinct simply from the fact that we can clearly and distinctly understand one apart from the other" (*Principles of Philosophy* 2p60, in Descartes 1985 I,213).

10   See Garrett 1991 for a fuller discussion of the meaning and grounds of this doctrine. While I still believe it is correct to say that Spinoza's necessitarianism involves a kind of *logical* necessity, I would now emphasize that Spinoza's conception of logic – in contrast to Leibniz's, for example – makes logic a matter of content, rather than of form, and is closely related to conceptions of logic as "laws of thought," analogous to laws of physics.

11   Since things must be understood through their causes (E 1a4), and these causes necessitate (E 1a3), the good of knowledge is achievable only to the extent that things are necessitated.

12   For extended discussion of this proposition and its demonstration, see Chapter 5, Section 1.

13   See Garrett 1994 and Chapter 5, Section 1 of this volume.

14   What we would call human psychology is, for Spinoza, a branch of the science of the attribute of thought in general. It is distinguished from other branches by its taking as its primary objects human beings, who are capable of reasoning, of having their power of acting increase and decrease, and of forming and retaining complex images of external things. (See the postulates at the beginning of Part 3.)

15   For another, somewhat different account of these definitions, see Curley 1973b. Remarkably, Broad 1930: 44–7 reports that Spinoza himself uses "good" as a measure of each thing's powers within its own species, and that Spinoza restricts the use of the term "perfect" to products of deliberate human design. Broad's description of "good" is evidently influenced by *Short Treatise* I.x. However, Spinoza's definitions of "good" and "perfect" in the preface to Part 4 (as well as 4d1) show both of Broad's claims to be incorrect.

16   *Ethics* 4d3 and 4d4 concern the "contingent" and the "possible" respectively: Singular things are conceived as contingent insofar as we attend only to their essences and find them to involve neither existence nor nonexistence. (This is in contrast, on the one hand, to God, whose essence involves existence and so necessitates his existence; and on the other hand, to contradictory things, whose essences involve nonexistence and so necessitate their nonexistence.) Things are called "possible" when we attend to the causes which would produce them, without knowing whether those causes are actually determined to produce them or not. Conceiving of something as contingent and conceiving of some-

thing as possible both involve ignorance of the thing's actual existence; however, the latter requires a knowledge of and an attention to the thing's manner of production that are lacking in the former. *Ethics* 4d5 defines "opposite affects" as those that "pull a man differently," even if the affects themselves happen to be of the same genus. *Ethics* 4d6 refers the reader to 3p18s1 and 3p18s2 for explanation of affects toward "a future thing, a present one, and a past" (although these scholia are not very helpful in understanding *how* the mind represents things as future, present, or past, which is explained more fully at 2p44c1s). *Ethics* 4d7 states: "By the end for the sake of which we do something I understand appetite." This definition reinforces Spinoza's earlier claim (E 1ap) that "action for the sake of an end" is to be understood as the efficient causation of a present desire, and not as a species of final causation to be contrasted with efficient causation.

17 For more extensive discussion of the line of argument contained in 4pp29–36, see Steinberg 1984.

18 As Bennett rightly observes, this leaves open the possibility that a passion of hate will remain as powerful as before, but will no longer constitute hate – for example, it might simply become ordinary sadness (Bennett 1984: 333). Spinoza might reply that separating the affect from the idea of a cause can at least prevent the idea of the hated object from arousing or reinvigorating the affect.

19 Bennett discusses Spinoza's treatment of this source of power over the affects, and notes Spinoza's failure to include it in his summary (Bennett 1984: 337).

20 Bennett 1984: 345, for example, notes that not all the items on the list of 5p20s are techniques, and implies that this fact is an objection to Spinoza's procedure.

21 In the *Treatise on the Emendation of the Intellect,* Spinoza writes concerning his endeavor to replace "greed, desire for sensual pleasure and love of esteem" with love of something eternal:

I saw this, however: that so long as the mind was turned toward these thoughts, it was turned away from those things, and was thinking seriously about the new goal. That was a comfort to me. For I saw that those evils would not refuse to yield to remedies. And although in the beginning those intervals were rare, and lasted a very short time, nevertheless, after the true good became more and more known to me, the intervals became more frequent and longer. (TdIE 10–11)

The purpose of Spinoza's discussion of the five (or six) "means to freedom" is to show his readers that, and how, a similar change can occur in them.

22 Margaret Wilson convincingly suggests (in Chapter 3, Section 14 of this volume) that the final line results from a simple mistake on Spinoza's part, and should have read: "Now it is time to pass on to those matters that concern the reality of the mind without respect to the duration of the body."

23 For its metaphysical, epistemological, and theological dimensions, respectively, see Chapter 1, Chapter 3, and Chapter 8.

24 Certainly, the doctrine of the eternity of the mind stands in some *prima facie* tension with the parallelism of mind and body. This tension can, I believe, be removed by granting that a part of the human body – its formal essence – is also eternal for Spinoza.

25 At 5p36cs, Spinoza refers to this affect as "Joy (if I may still be permitted to use this term)."

26 There is an obvious parallel between this doctrine of blessedness or peace of mind (which implies lack of disturbance) as the highest affect which is at the same time literally no affect at all, and some forms of Buddhism. There is no evidence, however, of any direct causal connection.

27 For more on Spinoza's conception of "right," see Chapter 7 of this volume.

28 The terms "perfect" and "imperfect" do not occur in any of the definitions, axioms, propositions, corollaries, or demonstrations of Part 4, although "perfect" occurs in several scholia (twice in 4p18s, and once each in 4p45s and 4p58s). "Perfect" and related terms recur several times, in application both to God and to man, in Part 5, where they are connected especially with the third kind of knowledge. They also occur in ethical application in the *Short Treatise* and the *Treatise on the Emendation of the Intellect.*

29 Despite the literal falsity of these evaluations, Spinoza grants that thinking of God as a law-giver is in many ways a good imaginative representation of the fact that the laws of nature involve necessary causal relations between particular ways of life and particular outcomes.

30 Spinoza writes:

[W]e shall easily see what the difference is between a man who is led only by an affect, or by opinion, and one who is led by reason. For the former, whether he will or not, does those things he is most ignorant of, whereas the latter complies with no one's wishes but his own, and does only those things he knows to be the most important in life, and therefore desires very greatly. Hence, I call the former a slave, but the latter, a free man. (E 4p66s)

31 Spinoza's explanation is as follows:

[W]e say "Let us suppose that this burning candle is not now burning, or let us suppose that it is burning in some imaginary space, *or* where there are no bodies." Things like this are sometimes supposed, although *this last is clearly understood to be impossible*. But when this happens, nothing at all is feigned [i.e., we are not guilty of "fictitious ideas"]. For in the first case I have done nothing but recall to memory another candle that was not burning (or I have conceived this candle without the flame), and what I think about that candle, I understand concerning this one, so long as I do not attend to the flame. In the second case, nothing is done except to abstract the thoughts from the surrounding bodies so that the mind directs itself toward the sole contemplation of the candle, considered in itself alone, so that afterwards it infers that the candle has no cause for its destruction. So if there were no surrounding bodies, this candle, and its flame, would remain immutable, or the like. *Here, then, there is no fiction, but true and sheer assertions*. (TdIE 57; emphasis added)

As Bennett puts it, "we might see the concept of 'the free man' as a theoretically convenient limiting case, like the concept of an 'ideal gas' – one whose molecules have zero volume" (Bennett 1984: 317). And, in the light of the fifth of Spinoza's five "means" to freedom (E 5p20s), we might add that it is not only *theoretically convenient* for him, but also *ethically efficacious*. The idea of a human being who could be entirely and completely guided by reason, or entirely and completely virtuous (i.e., powerful) would be another literally-contradictory idealized limiting case.

32 For further discussion of this topic, see Garrett 1990a.

33 What follows draws on the more detailed discussion of this problem in Garrett 1990a.

34 Nor would it alter the situation materially to emphasize the "knowledge" or "certainty" requirement of Spinoza's definition; for one could also *know with certainty* that it would be good to deceive whenever doing so was the only way to save an entire community.

35 A third approach to ethical theory, in addition to consequentialism and virtue ethics, is of course deontology, which regards the most fundamental ethical evaluations as evaluations of actions for their conformity to duty or moral law. Although Spinoza makes little use of such concepts as "duty," "obligation," and "right," his description of reason as providing "counsels," "rules," "precepts," and "dictates" may be seen as also aligning him to some extent with the deontological approach to ethics. Certainly, he locates the source of these "rules" and "dictates" in the same faculty in which Kant locates the source of his moral imperatives – namely, practical reason.

36 This point is made in Broad 1930: 51–2.

37 Spinoza's view of virtue may be profitably compared with Hume's. Although the primary objects of ethical evaluation in Hume's moral theory are features of character, and the fundamental term of ethical evaluation is "virtue," the virtuousness of a feature of character is itself a consequence of its typical hedonic consequences. A Humean virtue's *source* of value is therefore not intrinsic to it, as is the case with a Spinozistic virtue.

38 See also 2p49s: "Virtue itself [is] happiness itself, and the greatest freedom."

39 I am grateful to Michael Slote, whose questions helped me to formulate this interpretation of the role of virtue in Spinoza's ethical theory.

40 As Spinoza emphasizes in 4p51s, "when the supreme power, bound by its desire to preserve peace, punishes a citizen who has wronged another, I do not say that it is indignant toward the citizen. For it punishes him, not because it has been aroused by Hate to destroy him, but because it is moved by duty."

41 The memorable phrase is Susan Wolf's (Wolf 1979). She does not use the term in connection with Spinoza, however, but in connection with Kant.

42 It is also worth noting Spinoza's willingness, in this passage, to refer to the affects of the State. The State is itself an individual thing, composed of human parts, that naturally endeavors to preserve its being. Although only human beings have *human* affects, just as only horses have equine affects (3p57s), it is no mere metaphor, for Spinoza, to speak of the desires and other affects of the state.

43 For discussion of the relation of Spinoza's ethical theory to Aristotle and Seneca, see Wolfson 1934, Chapter xix. Wolfson notes the similarity between Spinoza's portrait of the "free man" and Stoic descriptions of the "wise man."

44 It may also be said that Humean epistemology is what would remain of Spinoza's epistemology were Spinoza obliged to give up the intellect and, with it, the second and third kinds of knowledge.

45 The episode, reported by Nietzsche in a postcard to Overbeck in 1881, is described in Curley 1988: 128. P.-F. Moreau mentions this episode as well, in Chapter 10, Section 3.

46 However, Bennett 1984, Chapter 4 makes a strong case for interpreting Spinoza's monism in line with a contemporary "field metaphysics."

7 Kissinger, Spinoza, and Genghis Khan

In an interview with Oriana Fallaci in 1972, Henry Kissinger, asked about the influence of Machiavelli on his thought, denied that the Florentine adviser of princes had had any influence on him at all:

There is really very little of Machiavelli's one can accept or use in the contemporary world. . . . If you want to know who has influenced me most, I'll answer with two philosophers' names: Spinoza and Kant. Which makes it all the more peculiar that you choose to associate me with Machiavelli. (*The New Republic*, 16 December 1972, page 21)[1]

We may suspect, of course, that if Kissinger had learned anything at all from Machiavelli, the last thing he would want to do, given Machiavelli's reputation as a teacher of evil, would be to admit it. If a leader cannot actually *be* virtuous, Machiavelli tells us, he must at least try to *seem* virtuous (unless, in the particular circumstances, seeming vicious will be more helpful in maintaining his position).

So far as I can discover, however, no one seems to have noted the irony involved in Kissinger's combining his disavowal of Machiavelli with an embrace of Spinoza. Spinoza is arguably the most Machiavellian of the great modern political philosophers.[2] We do not know Spinoza,[3] and so we do not notice the irony. Let us try to repair our ignorance.

I. SPINOZA AS AN ECCENTRIC HOBBESIAN

At first glance Spinoza may appear, in his political philosophy, to be more an eccentric Hobbesian than a Machiavellian. He imagines a state of nature in which men's natural egoism and hostility to one another make their lives insecure, wretched, and brutal (TTP iv.18–

25).[4] This state of nature is completely amoral. Each individual in it has a perfect right to do whatever he is capable of doing, in the sense that he cannot be criticized on grounds of justice for pursuing his own self-interest in any way.[5] The concepts of justice and injustice make sense only in civil society, and there they are to be defined in terms of obedience or disobedience to the civil law (TTP xvi.42; cf. Hobbes, L xv.3, xxiv.5, xxvi.4,8). But because men live miserably in the state of nature, rational pursuit of their self-interest leads them to contract to form a state which will restrain their behavior (TTP xvi.12–14; cf. L xvii.1,13). They come to see that less really is more, that if they give up the right they have in the state of nature to take whatever they can, and transfer it to a state which will have the power to make and enforce rules about property, they will be more secure in the possession of what they have acquired in the past or might acquire in the future. Not only will they be better off economically, since enterprise can flourish only where possessions are secured by law, they will also be better off in terms of less mundane goods, like knowledge, since cultural pursuits can flourish only when not all of our waking hours are consumed in attending to basic needs. The state men form to provide these goods will have absolute authority over its citizens, the supreme right to compel them by force in all matters, including matters of religion (TTP xvi.24–25, and TTP xix; cf. L xvii.13, xviii, xxxi.37).

So far this all sounds very Hobbesian, and to the extent that there is little or no talk in Machiavelli about the state of nature or natural rights or a social contract, nor much concern with the question whether there might legitimately be limits on the authority of the state, not very Machiavellian. No doubt Machiavelli would agree with the Hobbesian claim about what life would be like without an effective government,[6] but the passages in his work which come closest to discussing a state of nature (*The Discourses* I.i–ii) seem to be more speculative history than a thought experiment. Though he cites the need for security as a motivation for the founding of cities, he does not develop a theory of human nature to explain that need. Very likely if Machiavelli were operating with the concept of a state of nature, he would agree with the Hobbesian contention that in the state of nature utility is the measure of right (DCv i.10).[7] But the fact is that he does not seem much interested in the concept of right (or rights). Perhaps there is a slight hint of a social contract where Machiavelli writes, regarding cities built by natives of the place where they are built, that the people "undertake to live together in some place they have chosen in order to live more conveniently and the more easily to defend themselves" (Machiavelli 1975: 100–1). But there seems here to be only the vague notion of an agreement to live together, with no notion of a transfer of rights, or of the establishment of a power possessing rights. Since Machiavelli is not interested in issues about the rights of the state, he does not discuss the right of the state in matters of religion (although his discussion of Roman religion in *Discourses* I.xi–xv certainly assumes that it is legitimate for the state to encourage such forms of religion as the rulers find useful for their secular purposes).[8] So Machiavelli's conceptual framework is very different from that of Hobbes and Spinoza.

Nevertheless, when we consider what kind of state is supposed to emerge from the contractual process in Spinoza, we see that he is an eccentric Hobbesian at best. Unlike Hobbes, he has a marked preference for democracy, characterizing it as the most natural form of government, because in it everyone remains equal, as they were in the state of nature, and because democracy approaches most nearly to the freedom of the state of nature. In a democracy, "no one so transfers his natural right to another that in the future there is no consultation with him; instead he transfers it to the greater part of the whole society, of which he makes one part" (TTP xvi.36). This may make us think more of Rousseau than of Machiavelli,[9] but it is clearly a perspective Hobbes is very anxious to argue against.[10]

Spinoza's preference for democracy is also grounded on the very un-Hobbesian assumption that in a democratic state, "there is less reason to fear absurdities. For if the assembly is large, it is almost impossible that the majority of its members should agree on one absurd action" (TTP xvi.30). The reasons for this confidence in the decisions of large assemblies are unclear. Surely Spinoza was familiar with Hobbes's argument that in a large assembly very few people would have the understanding of foreign and domestic affairs to judge wisely what is conducive to the common good, that the great majority would therefore be prey to orators who knew how to make the worse appear the better cause, appealing to popular prejudice rather than reason, and that the influence of passion on these decisions would frequently lead to faction, inconstancy, and in the worst case, civil war (cf. DCv x.9–15). And Spinoza's own view of the masses' capacity for rational choice does not, on the whole, seem to be more favorable than that of Hobbes.[11] So it is a puzzle, which for now I leave to be discussed later, why Spinoza should think there is less danger of absurdity in a democracy. But that he does think this, and that it is a very un-Hobbesian view, is clear.

Perhaps the strongest indication that Spinoza is at best a very revisionist Hobbesian, though, lies in the fundamental purpose of his main political work: to argue that, however absolute the sovereign's right may be to do as he pleases, even in sacred matters (TTP xix, title), nevertheless, "in a free state everyone is permitted to think what he wishes and to say what he thinks" (TTP xx, title). Hobbes, on the other hand, argues that the sovereign must have absolute control over what doctrines may be published in books, taught in the schools or preached in the churches (L xviii.9; Review and Conclusion, 16; xlii.68), and that this control is consistent with the freedom of his subjects (L xxi.7). And though Hobbes may be more concerned to defend the sovereign's right of control over the external expression of belief than he is to license attempts to control "the inward thought and belief of men" (L xl.2; cf. xxxii.4–5, xlii.11), still, so long as he holds that "the actions of men proceed from opinions, and in the well-governing of opinions consisteth the well-governing of actions, in order to their peace and concord" (L xviii.9), he cannot leave opinions alone for long.[12] However similar the foundations of their political philosophies may be, Spinoza somehow manages to reach very different conclusions than Hobbes does.

2. THE COEXTENSIVENESS OF RIGHT AND POWER

Sometimes comparisons are odious; sometimes they help us to understand by making the unfamiliar seem more familiar. But in the end Spinoza is Spinoza, not Hobbes (or Machiavelli either). He is, as one recent writer puts it, an anomaly.[13] To understand the anomaly we need to try to probe more deeply into the logic of the system. We may begin by considering why Spinoza holds that the right of each thing extends as far as its power does (TTP xvi.4).

I find this a disturbing thesis, and I imagine that most readers of Spinoza share that reaction. Perhaps the fact that this thesis is so central to Spinoza's political theory, and has often seemed not to be persuasively argued, helps explain why historians of political thought have often neglected him. The thesis is reminiscent of Hobbes's claim, already disturbing enough, that in the state of nature every man has a right to every thing (L xiv.4), but it is a stronger statement in at least two respects: Spinoza applies it to all individuals (and not only to human beings), and he does not qualify it by saying that it applies only to individuals in the state of nature.[14]

In Hobbes we can construct at least two paths to the more restricted claim,[15] and at least one of these may have exercised some influence on Spinoza. The more familiar line of argument proceeds as follows: In war it is permissible to do whatever is necessary to preserve yourself; but the state of nature is a state of war; therefore, in the state of nature it is permissible to do whatever is necessary to preserve yourself; but anything at all might turn out to be necessary for self-preservation; therefore, there is nothing which is absolutely impermissible in the state of nature; in that state, you may do whatever you can do.

This can seem at least to be the argument running from the beginning of *Leviathan* xiii through *Leviathan* xiv.4, and perhaps it does represent the best way to understand that argument. It has the virtue of relying on a moral intuition – the permissibility of self-preservation in extreme situations – which seems to be deeply rooted in people and might be granted even by people who are otherwise quite skeptical of morality. It has the virtue that Hobbes can and does make a strong case for the assumption that in the state of nature (understood as a state in which there is no effective government) there would be enough actual conflict (or well-founded fear of conflict) to make everyone's life intolerably insecure. It has the weakness (from the standpoint of justifying a conclusion as strong as the one Hobbes seems to want) that it seems to license behavior contrary to conventional morality only where you can make a plausible case that the behavior really is necessary for self-preservation.[16]

In some passages of *De Cive* there may be a different, more theological route to the conclusion that right is identical with power, and one which gets us closer to Spinoza's argument in the *Theological-Political Treatise*. Suppose we begin with the proposition that God's right of sovereignty over man derives from his omnipotence (DCv xv.5). This seems a plausible reading of the book of *Job*, where God defends the justice of his afflicting Job, not by pointing to any sin Job has committed, but by affirming his own power (cf. *Job* 38:4, cited by

Hobbes in DCv xv.6). We then contend that if it is the irresistibility of God's power which confers on him a right to behave in whatever way he pleases, similar power in man must confer a similar right on the man who possesses it. Under pressure from theological opponents Hobbes may deny that any man could have irresistible power, but that does not appear to be his position in *De Cive* i.14, where, in virtue of the maxim that irresistible power confers a right of ruling, conquest is held to confer a right to the obedience of the vanquished without the need to argue that the vanquished consent by their submission.[17]

The argument in *Theological-Political Treatise* xvi.3–4, seems to follow a similar pattern, except insofar as it apparently involves at least one thesis peculiar to Spinoza's metaphysic: God has absolute sovereignty, that is, the supreme right to do all things, that is, whatever he can do; but the power of nature (considered absolutely) simply is the power of God; therefore, nature (considered absolutely) has the right to do whatever it can do; but the power of the whole of nature is nothing but the power of all the individuals in nature; therefore, everything in nature has a right to do what it can do. Right is coextensive with power.

You can understand why some people might find this argument unpersuasive. Insofar as it relies on traditional assumptions about God's sovereignty, it is an argument we might expect to be persuasive to Spinoza's audience. Insofar as it relies on the doctrine that the power of God may be identified with the power of nature (where that notion in turn is identified with the power of all the individuals in nature), it is not. Some have suggested that this is not a peculiarly Spinozistic assumption, and hence is an assumption one would not have to be a Spinozist to grant,[18] but this seems to me to be wrong. Spinoza's critique of the common understanding of miracles proceeds very much on the assumption that people ordinarily make a (mistaken) distinction between the power of nature and the power of God (cf. TTP vi.1–2). Moreover, if we compare the version of Spinoza's argument in *Theological-Political Treatise* xvi.3–4 with the reprise in the *Political Treatise* ii.2–3, we can see that in his later work Spinoza is trying to provide an alternative version of the argument which avoids simply assuming an identity between the power of nature and the power of God.[19]

Whether or not that attempt is successful, there will, I think, be a problem with any argument for the coextensiveness of right and power which proceeds on the assumption that God's right is based on his power (as the argument of the *Political Treatise* does explicitly, and the argument of the *Theological-Political Treatise* does implicitly). Some theists will grant this; others will not. I suggest that Spinoza has a more effective argument for the coextensiveness of right and power, which does not presuppose this assumption, to be found not in the overtly political chapters of the *Theological-Political Treatise*, but in Chapter iv.

We might reconstruct the argument of Chapter iv in the following way: Suppose there is a law which imposes an obligation on us, and hence limits what we are permitted to do; if this law is to impose an obligation on us, we must conceive it as a command, and not merely as a statement about how, in virtue of their nature, some or all members of some species act;[20] a law in the proper sense must be, not only a command, but a command which it is possible for the person commanded to disobey (not only does "ought" imply "can," it also implies "cannot"); but a command which it is possible for the person commanded to disobey must be a human command; for if God commands something, then obedience must follow, else he would not be omnipotent (we assume here that to command an act is to will that it occur, and that God's omnipotence implies that what he wills to occur occurs); therefore, any law which imposes an obligation on us must be a human law; God cannot be a law-giver. This conclusion of reason is confirmed by what we find in experience; for a law-giver rewards obedience and punishes disobedience; but experience teaches us, as Solomon puts it, that "the same fate comes to all, to the righteous and the wicked, to the good and the evil."[21] As far as God or nature is concerned, what we can do, we may do.

It is sometimes said that Spinoza's theory of natural right is "without normative content,"[22] and it is sometimes suggested that in this way he avoids the objection Rousseau made against those who base right on power (*Social Contract* I.iii). Spinoza, the idea is, grants that might gives you a right, but because he simply identifies the notion of right with that of physical power, this doctrine has no justificatory implications:

If a new Genghis Khan invaded a small Spinozist republic with crushing forces, he would have the right to invade it, then the right to oppress its inhabitants, as long as they remained too frightened to resist him. Not that Spinoza intends by that to justify whatever tyranny may be, nor to justify anything in general. (Matheron 1985: 176)

Certainly Spinoza does not intend to justify such an invasion or oppression, if justifying it implies that the people invaded have a moral duty to submit to their new master (as it seems to in Rousseau's critique of this doctrine). To point this out is useful. But I think the doctrine that right is coextensive with power should not be thought of as a doctrine which *identifies* right with power if that implies that, when Spinoza says this "new Genghis Khan" (Louis XIV, perhaps) has the *right* to invade "a small spinozistic republic" (the Dutch Republic of 1672, perhaps), all he *means* is (what we already knew) that Genghis Khan has the *power*.

Generally Spinoza will express his thesis about the relation between right and power by saying that right *extends as far as* power does. He does not identify the two concepts. And if he did, the thesis would lose interest. As things stand, though, Spinoza is using normative language with normative implications here: He is saying that there is no transcendental standard of justice by which Genghis Khan's actions can be judged to be unjust (cf. note 5). And this (challenging) normative disclaimer does not imply that there is no other standard by which his actions may be judged. For to say that Genghis Khan acts in accordance with natural right is compatible with saying that he acts contrary to the law of reason (cf. TTP xvi.5– 6), and I take this also to be a genuinely normative claim.[23]

3. SPINOZA AS A SOCIAL CONTRACT THEORIST

To say that it is not unjust for us to do, because no transcendent law forbids us to do, what we have the power to do, is to make a disturbing, normative, perhaps Machiavellian claim. It is also to make trouble for the idea that the right of the state is founded on a social contract.

This idea was already in trouble in Hobbes. For although it is a law of nature, according to Hobbes, that we should keep covenants we have made (L xv.1), it is unclear what the status of the laws of nature is in Hobbes. In the final paragraph of *Leviathan* xv Hobbes will say that these "laws" cannot be regarded as laws in the strict sense of the term unless we think of them as divine commands; his own commitment to theism is questionable enough that we do not know what to make of this escape clause. Elsewhere (Curley 1992) I have argued that Hobbes was probably (as many of his contemporaries thought) an atheist. If that is correct, the escape clause implies that the laws of nature do not bind us (since the condition for their being binding cannot be satisfied).[24] So we would be left with the conclusion that the laws of nature are simply theorems about what conduces to our self-preservation, and do not impose any obligations on us. On this view, the imperative "keep covenants you have made" looks like no more than good general advice about how to conduct your life, advice you would be free to disregard if special circumstances made it seem not to be good advice – as, for example, when there is no sovereign to make sure that the other party reciprocates your honesty (L xvii.2).

I do not think Hobbes was happy to settle for viewing his laws of nature in that way. He seems, for example, to have a very deep attachment to the value of promise keeping, arguing repeatedly that we are bound to keep promises even in the state of nature, provided the other party has already performed first (L xiv.27; cf. DCv ii.16, and *Elements of Law* I.xv.13). In his famous "reply to the fool" (L xv.5), he goes to some lengths to persuade us that, appearances to the contrary notwithstanding, this really is the prudent thing to do. But his indignation against Wallis for betraying the King during the Civil War (*English Works* IV: 416–19) seems evidence of moral intuitions which it is hard for prudential considerations of the normal sort to justify.

Spinoza seems to lack those intuitions entirely. As we might expect, given the argument of the preceding section, that right is coextensive with power, he holds that "no contract can have any force except by reason of its utility. If the utility is taken away, the contract is taken away with it, and is null and void" (TTP xvi.20). This conclusion is also derived in part from an egoistic psychology which seems to make any contractarian theory of the state hopeless: "The universal law of human nature is that no one fails to pursue anything which he judges to be good, unless he hopes for a greater good, or fears a greater harm, nor does he submit to any evil, except to avoid a greater one, or because he hopes for a greater good" (TTP xvi.15). From this it follows, Spinoza says, that "no one will promise to give up the right he has to all things except with intent to deceive, and absolutely, that no one will stand by his promises unless he fears a greater evil or hopes for a greater good" (TTP xvi.16).[25] There are two strange things here: one is that Hobbes, whose psychology generally seems to be no less egoistic than Spinoza's, should present people as sincerely making, in the social contract, an irrevocable commitment to obey the commands of the sovereign (or his heirs) in perpetuity (L xviii.3); the other is that Spinoza, who has no such expectations of people, should nevertheless couch his political theory in terms of a social contract.

Commentators frequently point out that talk of a social contract is prominent in Spinoza's earlier political work, the *Theological-Political Treatise*, and absent in his later work, the *Political Treatise*, from which we might infer that Spinoza abandoned social contract theory because he recognized that the contract was superfluous.[26] If no contract is binding unless it is useful, then the supposed social contract can play no real part in founding the sovereign's right to command. The sovereign's right will depend on his power to persuade his subjects (in one way or another) that it is in their interest to obey. If they believe that, they will obey (and the sovereign, in virtue of his power, will command with right). If they do not, then no matter what promises they may have made, they will not obey (and he, in virtue of his lack of power, will cease to be the sovereign).

Now there is much that is right about the discussion summarized in the preceding paragraph, but I think we should not infer from it that Spinoza changed his mind, in any fundamental way, about the issue of political legitimacy, between the *Theological-Political Treatise* and the *Political Treatise*. Even in the *Theological-Political Treatise*, where Spinoza seems to be most contractarian, there is something distinctly odd about his contractarianism. Given his views about the moral and psychological force of the act of making a promise, Spinoza simply cannot regard that act by itself as endowing the sovereign with the moral authority to command his subjects. If all people were rational, he thinks, it would be rational for all people to keep their promises; but most of the time people are not rational, and no natural law obliges them to behave rationally (TTP xvi.21–22). That is why, he says,

though men may promise with definite signs of an ingenuous intention, and contract to maintain trust, still, no one can be certain of another's reliability *unless something else is added to the promise.* For by natural right each person can act deceptively, and is bound to stand by the contract only by the hope of a greater good or fear of a lesser evil. (TTP xvi.23; emphasis added)

What must be added, I take it, is the existence of a sovereign with the power (and the will) to enforce contracts. If such a sovereign exists, then we will be able to rely on others to perform what they have promised and we will be bound to do the same.

But what does it take to bring such a sovereign into existence if the act of promising in a social contract is not enough? Here I think Spinoza's answer is that we must reconceive the social contract, not (as in Hobbes) as a transfer of right, but (in accordance with Spinoza's theory about the relation between right and power) as a transfer of power (cf. TTP xvi.24–25). It is the transfer of power which generates the sovereign, not the utterance of any magic formulas.

But how can power be transferred? The best way to approach this, I think, will be to consider what the social contract ultimately comes to in Hobbes. Hobbes does not always write as though what bound us to obey the government in power was a promise we (or our ancestors) made in the past. He knows that the actual origins of many, if not most, political orders are lost in the mists of history, and that if we knew what they were, we might not find them pretty. "There is scarce a commonwealth in the world whose beginnings can in conscience be justified" (L "Review and Conclusion," 8). What matters, in the end, is not whether promises were made, but whether the government has the power to provide us with the security which was our end when we agreed to obey its commands. This strain of thought is strongest in Hobbes in the "Review and Conclusion" of *Leviathan*, where he is explicitly concerned to settle a problem of conscience for those who had supported the late king in the Civil War: At what point may they, consistently with any oaths of loyalty they may have taken, transfer their allegiance to the new government? But it is present earlier in *Leviathan*, and even in Hobbes's earlier works (cf. DCv vi.3; *Elements of Law* II.i.5), so we cannot in fairness accuse Hobbes of having written *Leviathan* "to secure Oliver's title." And in any case, from this point of view what matters is not the person who holds power, but the power he holds. "The obligation of subjects to the sovereign is understood to last as long, and no longer than, the power lasteth by which he is able to protect them" (L xxi.21).[27]

When Hobbes is in this mode, the fundamental question is "what are the conditions for the preservation of political power?" Having lived through a civil war in which the rebels won, Hobbes is acutely conscious of the fragility of political power. One of the fundamental propositions of his political theory is that individuals are approximately equal in mental and physical power. Whatever differences may exist between them are not sufficient to provide the basis for a lasting relationship of dominion based on power alone (L xiii.1). It is a consequence of this that a ruler cannot dominate a multitude of subjects unless many of those subjects are willing to help him enforce his commands. It need not be the case that the majority of the people obey all of his commands willingly, but there must be at least a substantial number who willingly obey enforcement commands, and the enforcement cadre must be larger and more dedicated just in proportion as people in general are more hostile to the regime. Enforcing the law is risky business and Hobbesian man is highly risk averse.[28]

Hobbes puts this most sharply in *Behemoth*, his history of the English Civil War, where he writes: "The power of the mighty hath no foundation but in the opinion and belief of the people. . . . If men know not their duty, what is there that can force them to obey the laws? An army, you will say? But what shall force the army?" (*English Works* VI,184,237). Spinoza could not have known *Behemoth*, but he might have found similar reflections in *Leviathan* itself, for example, in the analysis of power in the opening sections (1–15) of Chapter x, or in Chapter xxx, which reminds sovereigns that they were entrusted with power to procure the safety of the people (L xxx.1) and that they need to be both loved and feared by the people if they are to perform their office with good success (L xxx.28–29). It is not enough, *pace* Machiavelli, for the ruler to be feared.[29]

If we apply these reflections on the conditions of power to the question of political legitimacy, in the context of a political philosophy where it is understood that right is coextensive with power, the result we get is that rulers govern with right just to the extent that their subjects consent to their rule by obeying their commands. What matters is not an oath of loyalty to the state, but a willingness in the enforcement cadre to see that the laws are obeyed, and a willingness in the general population at least not to forcibly resist the enforcement cadre.[30] As we shall see in the next section, this perspective yields limits on the right of the sovereign which one might not have expected from Spinoza's initial characterization of the social contract.

4. SPINOZA AS A MACHIAVELLIAN

I began this essay by suggesting that in some important sense Spinoza was a Machiavellian in political theory. You may feel that I have already identified one important sense in which that is true: Spinoza holds that it is never unjust to do what your power permits you to do. Given this doctrine, we would expect a Spinozistic political leader to behave like Kissinger's Bismarck: pursuing "political utility unencumbered by moral scruples" (Kissinger 1968: 916).[31] If Machiavelli were to agree that right and power are coextensive, then he would agree with one of the most central tenets of Spinoza's political theory. But I am not sure he would agree with Spinoza about that.

The question of Machiavelli's amoralism is often framed in terms of the question whether the end justifies the means. We might better ask, I think, whether there are certain ends (such as the establishment or preservation of a political community) so good that they justify the use of any means whatever. The most instructive passage I find on this occurs in Machiavelli's discussion of Romulus's murder of Remus, where his consequentialism falls somewhere in between the extreme individualism of the egoist and the extreme universalism of the utilitarian:

A prudent founder of a republic, one whose intention is to govern for the common good, and not in his own interest, not for his heirs, but for the sake of the fatherland, should try to have the authority all to himself; nor will a wise mind ever reproach anyone for some extraordinary action performed in order to found a kingdom or institute a republic. It is, indeed, fitting that while the action accuses him, the result excuses him; and when the result is good, as it was with Romulus, it will always excuse him; for one should reproach a man who is violent in order to destroy, not one who is violent in order to mend things. (*The Discourses* I.ix in Machiavelli 1979: 200–1)

In this passage Machiavelli does concede that in some sense an act like that of Romulus is reprehensible; the fact that it leads to a good result does not *justify* the action, it *excuses* it. But I think we should not put too much weight on this distinction in this context. On some readings of Machiavelli, he remains committed to the moral standards which would judge the actions of a Romulus to be evil at the same time that he is recommending that political actors disregard those standards.[32] I find this not merely paradoxical, but incoherent. If "good" really is the most general adjective of commendation (as the Oxford English Dictionary tells us, and as I believe), then there is a kind of contradiction in recommending conduct you go on to call evil. I think we must take Machiavelli to be using the term "good" ironically when he urges rulers to learn how not to be good.[33] In the passage under discussion here, he talks about excuses only because he wants to allow for the condemnation of such actions when they are not aimed at (and do not lead to) results of the kind Romulus's did. We should still reproach the man "who is violent in order to destroy."

It is not just any good result which will "excuse" an action of this character. It takes a very significant result, affecting a large number of people, not merely the agent and those who are close to him. As Bondanella and Musa point out, the result in this case was "the establishment of the most durable and powerful republican government in human history" (Machiavelli 1979: 22, editors' introduction). It may be that "patriotism, as Machiavelli understood it, is collective selfishness,"[34] but Machiavelli's "patriotic consequentialism," as I am inclined to call it, falls short of saying that whatever you can do, you may do. What it does hold is that a ruler is to be praised, not blamed, even though he does things which might otherwise be highly reprehensible, provided he acts with a prudent regard for the well-being of the community he is ruling. So I do not call Spinoza a Machiavellian because he believes that right is coextensive with power, since I do not think Machiavelli himself believed that. As Spinoza is sometimes more Hobbesian than Hobbes himself, sometimes he is more Machiavellian than Machiavelli himself.

A much more fundamental point of similarity, I believe, lies in Spinoza's pragmatic attitude toward politics, exemplified in the opening paragraph of the *Political Treatise*, where he writes that

Philosophers . . . think they perform a godly act and reach the pinnacle of wisdom when they have learned how to praise a human nature which exists nowhere, and how to assail in words the human nature which really exists. For they conceive men not as they are, but as they wish them to be. That's why for the most part they have written satire instead of ethics, and why they have never conceived a politics which can be put to any practical application. The politics they have conceived would be considered a chimæra, and could be set up only in utopia, or in the golden age of the poets, i.e., where there was no need for it at all. In all the sciences which have a practical application, theory is believed to be out of harmony with practice, but this is most true of politics. (TP I.1)

This critique of utopian political theorizing naturally makes us think of the similar critique Machiavelli makes at the beginning of Chapter xv of *The Prince*, and on the other side, of Thomas More's *Utopia* or Plato's *Republic*. But in a fascinating article (Matheron 1986) Matheron has argued that we need not imagine that Spinoza meant to criticize only such thinkers as Plato and More, that the less obviously utopian political theory of Thomas Aquinas is also subject to these strictures, and that if we take what Spinoza said strictly he must have had Hobbes in his sights as well. For Spinoza does not say merely that *some* or *many* philosophers who have written on politics have erred by conceiving men not as they are but as they wish them to be; he says *philosophers* have done this, that is, that this is what philosophers generally do when they write about politics. Machiavelli will escape criticism, because it is clear that Spinoza classes him, not with the philosophers attacked in *Political Treatise* i.1, but with the politicians, who are praised in *Political Treatise* i.2, for having learned from experience to anticipate the wicked conduct of men, and for having, as a result, written successfully about human affairs. But there is no denying that Hobbes is a philosopher, and that his work was too prominent in Spinoza's field of vision for Spinoza to have ignored it when he made his generalization about philosophers.

Now if we must include Hobbes among the targets of Spinoza's critique, that really is a paradox. Who would have thought that Hobbes, of all people, would be criticized for conceiving men not as they are, but as he wished them to be? Can Spinoza fairly charge Hobbes with taking an overly optimistic view of man, when Hobbes wrote that, because of man's natural propensity to competition, mistrust, and glory-seeking, the life of man in the state of nature would be "solitary, poor, nasty, brutish and short"? Can we really class Hobbes with Plato, Aquinas, and More?[35]

And yet, from what we have said above, we can see that there would be some justice in that criticism. Hobbes does (in some moods, at least) found the legitimacy of the sovereign on men's willingness to surrender all their natural rights to him, and the sovereign's power on their willingness to stand by that promise come what may. And this is arguably an abandonment of his otherwise realistic psychology.[36] So we find Spinoza, after defending a broadly Hobbesian theory of sovereignty in Chapter xvi of the *Theological-Political Treatise*, taking much of it back in Chapter xvii, which begins with the following warning:

In the last chapter we contemplated the right of the supreme powers to do everything, and the natural right which each person has transferred to them. But though the view expressed there agrees in no small measure with practice, and a practice could be established so that it approached more and more closely to the condition contemplated, still, it will never happen that this view should not remain, in many respects, merely theoretical. For no one will ever be able to so transfer his power, and hence, his right, to another that he ceases to be a man, nor will there ever be any supreme power which can carry out everything it wishes. (TTP xvii.1–2)

There are some things a sovereign cannot effectively command a subject to do – hate someone who has benefited him, love someone who has harmed him, not be offended by insults, and so forth. And since the sovereign's right can be no more extensive than his power, these matters to which the sovereign's power cannot reach are also matters to which his right does not extend.

Men have never surrendered their right and transferred their power to another in such a way that they were not feared by the very persons who had received the right and power from them, and that the state was not in greater danger from its own citizens . . . than from enemies. . . . It must be granted that each person reserves many things to himself, that he is his own master *(sui juris)* in many things, which depend on no one's decision but his own. (TTP xvii.3–4)

Spinoza concludes from this that a violent rule never lasts long, that it is incumbent on the supreme powers to consult the common good (to maintain their own power, if for no other reason – cf. TTP xvi.16). The most stable state will be one in which the constitutional arrangements decentralize the decision making.

In the *Theological-Political Treatise* Spinoza makes his argument for this, paradoxically, in a lengthy analysis of the political history of the Hebrew state. It is a mistake to regard this apparent digression, which begins at *Theological-Political Treatise* xvii.25, and runs to the end of Chapter xviii, as mere "aimless wandering," and as a place where the "progressive tendencies" of Spinoza's thought are not visible.[37] For its point is to argue that after the death of Moses

No one had all the functions of the supreme commander. These things did not all depend on the decision of one man, nor of one council, nor of the people, but some were administered by one tribe, and others by the other tribes, with equal right for each one. From this it follows most evidently that after Moses' death the state was neither monarchical, nor aristocratic, nor popular. (TTP xvii.60)

In the continuation of the passage quoted, Spinoza will characterize this state as a theocracy, because of the central place which religion held in it, but his political message appears more clearly in an earlier passage in which he argues that, though from a religious point of view the people of Israel were fellow citizens, "in relation to the right they had against one another, they were only allies, *in almost the same way as the Federated States of the Netherlands are* ...." (TTP xvii.54; emphasis added). The path to political stability lies in constitutional arrangements which "contain both the rulers and the ruled so that the ruled [do] not become rebels and the rulers [do] not become tyrants" (TTP xvii.62; cf. TP vi.3).

There is a similar movement of thought in the final two chapters of the *Theological-Political Treatise*. Chapter xix argues for a strongly Hobbesian juridical position regarding the rights of the state concerning religion:

[S]acred matters ... are subject only to the control of the supreme [secular] powers. Without their authority or permission no one has the right or power to administer these things, to choose their ministers, to determine ... the foundations of the Church and its doctrine, to judge concerning customs and the actions of religious duty, to excommunicate someone or to receive someone into the Church, nor even, finally, to provide for the poor. (TTP xix.39)

But Chapter xx undermines that Hobbesian position by arguing that there are necessary limits on the sovereign's power to control people's minds (TTP xx.1- 6), and hence on his right to do so (TTP xx.7). Even Moses, who was able to persuade most of his people that he spoke by divine inspiration, was not able to entirely avoid dissent and rebellion (TTP xx.5). Less charismatic leaders must beware of trying for too much control over their subjects' minds and tongues, lest they alienate their subjects and consequently destroy the power they have, which depends on the willing obedience of their subjects. The best state, judged purely by the criterion of stability, will be one which permits its citizens a broad freedom to think as they like and to say what they think. Though Spinoza often seems to be an extremely conservative political thinker,[38] the emphasis he places on freedom is an important liberal element in his thought.

The most important point of similarity between Spinoza and Machiavelli, however, lies in the preference they both have for a form of republican government in which the people act as a check on their leaders, a preference which readers of Machiavelli will not learn about if they read only *The Prince*. As I noted above, Spinoza claims that there is less reason to fear absurdities in a democratic state. This is reminiscent of Machiavelli's claim that, although the people are apt to be unstable, ungrateful, and unwise, princes are even more liable to these faults: A prince who is able to do what he wishes, that is, who is unrestrained by laws, is apt to behave like a madman, whereas a people which can do what it wishes is apt merely to act unwisely (*Discourses* I.lviii). In Spinoza's case part of the explanation for this somewhat unexpected optimism about the decisions of popular assemblies seems to be that in a large population true madness is likely to be found only among a minority, who will find it difficult to persuade the majority to behave as the minority would (TTP xvi.30). But where power is concentrated in the hands of one person, if that one person is mad, the consequences can be disastrous.

But I suspect that Spinoza also felt that a reading of history would show that if a ruler was not mad when he assumed power, his possession of absolute power was very apt to drive him mad. This certainly seems to be an important theme in one of his favorite Roman historians. Consider the speech Tacitus puts in the mouth of Lucius Arruntius, as he is about to commit suicide, to escape punishment on trumped-up charges of adultery and disloyalty to Tiberius:

I have lived long enough . . . I only regret that between insults and dangers I have endured an anxious old age. . . . Certainly I might survive the few days before Tiberius dies, but how will I avoid the youth of his successor? *If Tiberius, with all his experience of affairs, has been subverted and transformed by the power of domination*, will Gaius Caesar [Caligula] take a better course, when he is hardly out of his boyhood, knows nothing, and has been trained by the worst people . . . ? I foresee an even more bitter bondage, and so flee both evils past and those to come. (Tacitus, *Annals* VI.xlviii; emphasis added)[39]

We lack Tacitus's account of the reign of Caligula, but the corrupting effect of power is a central theme in his work.[40]

Nero provides another example of the same phenomenon, as Spinoza's contemporary, Racine, saw. Defending himself against the conflicting accusations that in his *Britannicus* he had made Nero both too cruel and too good, he wrote: "It is necessary only to have read Tacitus to know that, if he was for a while a good emperor, he was always a very wicked man. . . . I have always regarded him as a monster, but here he is a nascent monster."[41] Racine's play can be read as a case study in the effects of power on personality: how the subservience of his subjects permits an autocratic ruler to act on desires others must repress, but how, in spite of his power, he must nevertheless be tormented by continual fear of rivals and assassins.[42] Spinoza too is acutely aware of the dangers, both to the ruler and to the ruled, when one man possesses "absolute" power, though in his case they are articulated in the abstractions of political theory, not in the concreteness of historical drama (cf. TP vi.3, vii.1,14,27).

5. CONCLUSION

The fundamental question I have about Spinoza's political philosophy is whether he is not too complacent about the limits of state power. Alexandre Matheron seems to sum up Spinoza's position very well when he writes: "If the people acquiesces in obeying a tyrant, whatever its reasons, so much the worse for it. And so much the worse for the tyrant, if the people awakes, for a small minority, even well armed, can no longer do anything, and hence has no right against a multitude unified by a common desire and no longer restrained by fear."[43] In our own time we might illustrate this proposition by citing the breakup of the Soviet Union and the end of its domination of Eastern Europe, or the rapid rise and fall of Nazi Germany. Spinoza, lacking these examples, is fond of quoting Seneca's observation that "no one has ever maintained a violent rule for long."[44]

Perhaps tyrannical governments do inevitably destroy themselves. If the power of autocratic rulers is as fragile as Spinoza seems to think,[45] this would seem likely. The question I have is whether such a dispassionate view of tyranny is acceptable. A tyrant can do a great deal of harm even if his tyranny lasts only a relatively short time, as the history of the Third Reich illustrates. And Stalin's rule was not so very short. Does viewing things *sub specie aeternitatis* require us to accept the success of such governments so long as they are able to maintain their power? If so, does being a good Spinozist not require a level of detachment from individual human suffering which is either superhuman or subhuman?[46]

In the *Political Treatise* Spinoza recognizes that a tyrannical government can be quite stable and long-lasting, and he is apparently not so preoccupied with security that he is prepared to approve of such a government simply for that reason. He writes:

No state has stood so long without any notable change as that of the Turks, and, conversely, none has been less lasting or more liable to civil strife than democratic or popular states. But if slavery, barbarism, and desolation *(solitudinem)* are to be called peace, nothing is more miserable for men than peace . . . peace consists not merely in the absence of war, but in a union or harmony of minds. (TP vi.4)

This eloquently expresses a sentiment which I believe many of us share. But does Spinoza's philosophy possess the theoretical resources to condemn tyrannical governments as strongly as we would wish to?

Consider the classical passage to which Spinoza is alluding here. The *Agricola* is Tacitus's homage to his father-in-law, the general who completed the Roman conquest of Britain. It is a tribute to Tacitus's objectivity that, in the course of celebrating the imperialist, he composes for the British leader, Calgacus, a biting condemnation of the imperialism, culminating in the famous lines: "If the enemy is rich, they [the Romans] are greedy; if he is poor, they are ambitious [for power] . . . alone of all people they lust equally after both poverty and riches. To robbery, slaughter and rapine they give the lying name of 'empire.' They make a wasteland *(solitudinem)*, and call it peace" *(Agricola* 30).[47] Part of what gives this passage its force is the use of language which implies, not merely that the Romans are making life miserable for the Britons, which would no doubt be bad enough, but that they are doing something even worse: violating their rights by taking from them what is properly theirs, their lives, their property, and their honor. If we cannot make sense of the idea that people have a natural right to such things, then we seem to be handicapped in the criticism we want to make of the Roman conduct (or of a tyrant's treatment of his own people). That the notion of natural right (not coextensive with power) disappears in Spinoza seems to me still to be a defect in his political philosophy, sympathetic though I may be to the arguments which lead to that result.

NOTES

1 Regrettably Ms. Fallaci did not follow up by asking Dr. Kissinger which aspects of Spinoza's (or Kant's) thought had influenced him. There is, of course, some question as to whether the printed interview corresponds to what Kissinger actually said on the occasion. See Walter Isaacson, *Kissinger*, Simon and Schuster, 1992, page 478. But I see no reason to question this part of the interview.

2 Machiavelli's influence on Spinoza has been emphasized both in McShea 1968, and Stanley Rosen, in his contribution to Cropsey and Strauss 1981. The most thorough study is Calvetti 1972.

3 I.e., Anglo-American philosophers do not know Spinoza as a political thinker, particularly if their knowledge of the history of political thought is derived from works like Sabine's influential *A History of Political Theory* (4th edition, rev. by T. L. Thorson, Dryden Press, 1973), where he is barely mentioned.

4 The *Theological-Political Treatise* (TTP) was Spinoza's first political work, published anonymously in 1670, with false information about the publisher and the place of publication. It aroused a great storm of protest, mainly because of the theological portions of the work, which encouraged skepticism about miracles, prophecy, and the authority of scripture. At his death Spinoza was at work on a purely political treatise, the *Tractatus politicus* (TP), which was published in an unfinished state in his *Opera Posthuma* (1677). Translations from Spinoza's political works are mine, from the forthcoming second volume of my *Collected*

Works of Spinoza, Princeton University Press. I use the Bruder section numbers for references to the *Theological-Political Treatise*.

For a comparable passage in Hobbes, see *Leviathan* xiii. In comparisons with Hobbes I will cite either *De Cive* (which we know Spinoza owned a copy of) or *Leviathan* (which some scholars think he never read), as convenience dictates. *Leviathan* was translated into Dutch in 1667, by Abraham van Berkel, a member of the "Spinoza circle" who saw its argument for the indivisibility of sovereignty as supporting the De Witts in their controversy with the House of Orange, which had traditionally claimed executive and military power (see Secretan 1987). It was available in Latin by 1668. I think it virtually certain that Spinoza knew *Leviathan* at least by the time he was composing the final draft of the *Theological-Political Treatise*. I abbreviate *Leviathan* as L, and cite it by chapter and paragraph. I abbreviate *De Cive* as DCv, and cite by chapter and section. The edition of *Leviathan* which I recently published with Hackett (1994) indicates the major differences between the English and Latin editions of *Leviathan*.

5 Cf. *Theological-Political Treatise* xvi.2–4. For the distinction between weaker and stronger senses of right *(jus)*, cf. Grotius, *De jure belli ac pacis*, I.i.3–4. Comparable passages in Hobbes would be L xiii.13, xiv.4, though Hobbes does not use the language of natural rights in connection with animals, and apparently grounds the natural right of every man to every thing on the right of self-preservation (L xiv.1). There will be more on this below.

6 This seems a reasonable inference from his account of what people are like in civil society. See particularly Chapters xv–xix of *The Prince* (Machiavelli). I have discussed this in Curley 1991a.

7 Relevant here is a controversial sentence in the final paragraph of Chapter xviii of Machiavelli's *Prince*: "In the actions of all men, and especially of princes, who are not subject to a court of appeal, always look to the end" (Machiavelli 1992: 49). I take this to imply: (a) that whatever standards of behavior apply to princes apply to anyone similarly situated, i.e., to anyone not subject to a sovereign capable of adjudicating disputes, and hence, to human beings in a state of nature; (b) that although the sentence is descriptive, not prescriptive, it does indicate that Machiavelli believes that people will generally apply a consequentialist standard to human behavior. That Machiavelli would endorse the use of such consequentialist standards seems clear from *Discourses* I.ix (to be discussed below).

8 Presumably his consequentialism would also imply the legitimacy of discouraging forms of religion which may be harmful to the state (as he appears to think that Christianity is, in *Discourses* II.ii).

9 Cf. *Social Contract* I.viii: "freedom is obedience to a law one prescribes to oneself." But in Rousseau this freedom appears to be consequent on membership in any legitimate civil society, whether the form of government is democratic or not. In fact Rousseau seems to have thought that as a form of government democracy was fit only for gods, not for men (cf. the *Social Contract* III.iv) and that the best form of government was an aristocracy (*Lettres écrites de la montagne* vi; III,808–9 of the Pléiade edition). It is against the natural order that the greater number should govern and the smaller number be governed. In Machiavelli the contrast is not democracy vs. monarchy or aristocracy, but republican or popular government vs. princely rule, and the assumption is that there is more freedom in republican government. Cf. *Discourses* I.iv–v, I.xvi–xviii, and II.ii.

10 Cf. DCv x.8, for an attack on the view that there is more liberty in a democracy than in a monarchy.

11 Cf., for example, *Theological-Political Treatise* xvii.13–16, or *Political Treatise* i.5.

12 For a suggestive treatment of these issues, see Ryan 1983.

13 Cf. Negri 1991. Though I accept Negri's phrase, I reject what he seems to mean by it: "that in posing *spes* against *metus*, *libertas* against *superstitio*, the republic against the monarchical absolute, Spinoza proposes and renews concepts that the entire century is moving against" (page 122). To see Spinoza as standing in romantic isolation against the dominant intellectual tendencies of his century is to neglect the strength of the contemporary republican tradition (here see Mulier 1980) and to ignore the extent to which Hobbes anticipates Spinoza's critique of revelation (on which, see Curley 1992).

14 Cf. the famous statement in Letter 50:

As far as politics is concerned, the difference between myself and Hobbes, which you ask about, consists in this: that I always keep natural right intact, and that I maintain that in any state whatever, the supreme magistrate has no more right over his subjects than he has an excess of power over them, which is always the situation in the state of nature.

Similarly in the *Political Treatise* iii.3: "the right of nature does not cease in the civil order."

15 In what follows I partly rely on (and partly, I hope, improve on) things I have said in more detail in two recent articles: Curley 1990, and Curley 1991b.

16 In the comparable passage in *De Cive* (DCv i.7–10) Hobbes deals with this by arguing that the right to preserve yourself entails a right to judge what means are necessary to self-preservation. But even this seems to

require, as a condition for my rightfully taking, say, the life of an un-
armed prisoner, that I believe, in good faith, that he is a danger to my
preservation. Perhaps that is why Hobbes drops this line of defense in
Leviathan. Cf. Hobbes's *Elements of Law* I.xix.2, and my discussion of
this and other passages in Curley 1991b. See also the useful discussions
in Spinoza 1958: 13–14 and Den Uyl 1983: 11–14.

17 As Hobbes will argue in L xx.11. In "Of Liberty and Necessity" Hobbes
says that *"Power irresistible justifies all actions, really and properly,* in
whomsoever it be found; less power does not, and because such power is
in God only, he must needs be just in all actions, and we, that not
comprehending his counsels, call him to the bar, commit injustice in it"
(*English Works* IV,250). In *Leviathan* (xxxi.5) Hobbes does not explicitly
deny that any man's power can be irresistible, but he does treat the
hypothesis as counterfactual ("if there had been any man of power irresistible . . . "). By contrast, in DCv i.14 and in the *Elements of Law*
(I.xiv.13), Hobbes understands the notion of irresistible power in such a
way that a man can possess it (e.g., when the other person is an infant or
temporarily indisposed). I think, then, that Matheron is wrong to say
that Hobbes does not make any use, even surreptitiously, of the maxim
that might makes right (Matheron 1985, see particularly page 151).

18 Cf. Alexandre Matheron in Matheron 1969: 290.

19 I have discussed this in much more detail in Curley 1991b. Also interesting in this connection is Pufendorf's critique of Spinoza in *De jure
naturae et gentium* (II.ii.3, and III.iv.4), which I have discussed in an
article to appear in the proceedings of the Cortona conference on the
reception of the *Theological-Political Treatise,* edited by Paolo Cristof-
olini. One point Pufendorf sharply criticizes is Spinoza's identification
of the power of nature with the power of God.

20 Note that Spinoza begins Chapter iv by distinguishing between laws
which describe how all or some members of a species act and laws
which prescribe a certain kind of conduct. Only the latter are properly
called laws. It is an interesting question how far the assumption that
only commands are properly called laws was common in the natural law
tradition. Certainly Hobbes and Suárez make this assumption (cf. *Leviathan* xxvi.2 and xv.41; and *De legibus* II.vi). And Suárez claims to be
following Aquinas, who had defined law as "a rule and measure of acts,
whereby man is induced to act or is restrained from acting" (*Summa
theologiae* I-II.xc.1 [Aquinas 1964–6]). This suggests a prescription of
some kind (if not a command, then a counsel). But by using the natural
inclinations of creatures as a guide to what they ought to do, Aquinas
arguably confuses the descriptive with the prescriptive (cf. *Summa,* I-
II.94.2). This may be why Spinoza insists so strongly on distinguishing

them. Again, if a command must proceed from a superior to an inferior (as Suárez argues, *De legibus* I.xxi.4), and if natural law is binding on God (as Grotius contends, in *De jure belli ac pacis* I.i.10), presumably it cannot be essential to natural law that it be a command. So far as I can see, the tradition does not speak with one voice on this issue, which may limit the effectiveness of Spinoza's argument.

21 *Ecclesiastes* 9:1–3, cited twice in the *Theological-Political Treatise*, at vi.32, and in xix.7.

22 The phrase is Douglas Den Uyl's, in Den Uyl 1983: 7.

23 See Curley 1973.

24 I take it to be significant that the escape clause is omitted in the Latin *Leviathan* and even in a subsequent reference back to this passage in the English *Leviathan* (L xxvi.8).

25 McShea is right to point out (McShea 1968: 167), however, that this statement about promises occurs in the context of a philosophy which makes the knowledge and love of God the highest good. (Cf. *Ethics* 4p28 and *Theological-Political Treatise* iv.9–16.)

26 See, for example, Spinoza 1958: 25–7. We might also class Alexandre Matheron with Wernham, on the strength of his discussion in Matheron 1969: 307–30. But a subsequent article on this topic makes it clear that Matheron does not intend his theory to address the issue of the legitimacy of the state, but only the issue of its historical origin. See Matheron 1990.

27 My interpretation of Hobbes here is much influenced by the work of Quentin Skinner, e.g., Skinner 1974.

28 I have discussed these issues in more detail in Curley 1990, Section 4.

29 This may be unfair to Machiavelli. Chapter xvii of *The Prince* advises that it is hard to be both loved and feared, and that if forced to choose, a prince should prefer being feared to being loved. But Chapter xix counterbalances this with the advice that a prince need not worry too much about conspiracies "as long as his people are devoted to him; but when they are hostile, and feel hatred toward him, he should fear everything and everybody." Machiavelli concludes that one of the most important of a prince's concerns is "to keep the aristocracy from desperation and to satisfy the populace by making them happy" (Machiavelli 1992: 51; cf. TP vii.12,14 – passages which contain several allusions to Tacitus).

30 So I agree with Matheron when he writes "Spinoza always thought that the existence and legitimacy of political society derive, ultimately, from the consent of the subjects; if you wish to call that 'contract,' he was always a contractualist [not only in the *Theological-Political Treatise*, but even in the *Political Treatise*] ... if you wish to

call 'contractualism' the doctrine according to which the conclusion of an agreement would give rise, by itself alone, independently of any subsequent variation in the relations of forces, to an irreversible obligation, he was never a contractualist [not only in the *Political Treatise*, but even in the *Theological-Political Treatise*]" (Matheron 1990: 258). The contractualism Matheron is interested in is a theory according to which (questions of legitimacy to one side) political society is in fact founded in a historically actual state of nature, by a deliberate, rational, collective decision, and not by a dynamic process involving the interplay of the passions, in which the imitation of the affects plays a key role. This is the contractualism he finds in the *Theological-Political Treatise*, and not in the *Political Treatise*. At the moment I am not persuaded that Matheron is right to find the evolution he claims, since it seems to me that Spinoza is quite pessimistic about human rationality even in the *Theological-Political Treatise* (cf. TTP xvii.14–16). My main point is that Hobbes sometimes inclines toward a contractualism of the kind which (according to Matheron) Spinoza always embraced. Hobbes is not always a contractualist of the kind Spinoza never was.

31 Kissinger does not hesitate to characterize Bismarck's approach to politics as Machiavellian (page 906), though he also reports that Bismarck was a great reader of Spinoza (page 894). Did the influence of Spinoza on Kissinger really make it "peculiar" for Ms. Fallaci to associate him with Machiavelli?

32 An example is the interpretation of Walzer 1973 (specifically, pages 175–6). Cf. Isaiah Berlin: "It is important to realise that Machiavelli does not wish to deny that what Christians call good is, in fact, good, that what they call virtue and vice are in fact virtue and vice" (Berlin 1982: 46). Berlin's Machiavelli does, nevertheless, reject Christian ethics in favor of a rival ("Roman or classical") morality (page 54).

33 Berlin tacitly recognizes this when, in paraphrasing this passage, he consistently puts the term "excuse" in single quotes: "The end 'excuses' the means, however horrible these may be in terms of even pagan ethics, if it is (in terms of the ideals of Thucydides or Polybius, Cicero or Livy) lofty enough. Brutus was right to kill his children: he saved Rome" (Berlin 1982: 64; cf. page 62). Another symptom of this is the fact that Walker feels obliged to use the term "justify" for "*scusare*" in this passage (Machiavelli 1975: 132).

34 As Leo Strauss argued, in Strauss 1984: 11.

35 It seems a curious fact that Hobbes never mentions Machiavelli. (At any rate, there is no entry for Machiavelli in Molesworth's indices of either the English or the Latin works.) We might suppose that this was because

of Machiavelli's reputation. But Francis Bacon (whom Hobbes served for a while as secretary) was not afraid to praise Machiavelli:

We are much beholden to Machiavelli and other writers of that class, who openly and unfeignedly declare or describe what men do, and not what they ought to do. For it is not possible to join the wisdom of the serpent with the innocence of the dove, except men be perfectly acquainted with the nature of evil itself. (From *De augmentis scientiarum* VII.ii, translated by F. R. Headlam, cited by Adams in the Norton Critical Edition of *The Prince*, page 270)

Spinoza is generous in his praise of Machiavelli (TP v.7, x.1).

36 Cf. Hampton 1986 Chapters vii–viii, and my discussion of her book in Curley 1990: 205–11.

37 The phrases are Negri's, Negri 1991: 116–17. Haitsma Mulier is very helpful on this theme. Cf. Mulier 1980: 181–5.

38 As when he argues in *Theological-Political Treatise* xviii.28–37 (in the manner of Machiavelli) that it is extremely dangerous for any state to attempt a fundamental change in its form of government, moving either from a republican form of government to a monarchy or vice versa. Cf. *The Prince*, Chapter v.

39 I have given a conservative, literal translation of this passage, but Michael Grant's freer translation of the italicized clause would suit my purposes even better: "If Tiberius, in spite of all his experience, has been transformed and deranged by absolute power . . ." (Tacitus 1989: 225). On Tacitus's overall influence on Spinoza, see Wirszubski 1955. I am indebted for this reference to F. Akkerman, "Spinozas Tekort aan Woorden," in Akkerman 1980.

40 Cf. his comment on Vespasian in *The Histories* I.l: "He alone, unlike all the emperors before him, was changed for the better [by his office]."

41 Preface to the first edition, 1670, *Théâtre complet*, Garnier, page 254.

42 I suggest that Racine believes Nero's decline to be inevitable, once he takes the fatal step of murdering his half-brother (and potential rival for power), Britannicus. He conveys this by presenting Nero at an early, comparatively innocent stage of his reign, and having both Burrus and Agrippina predict, with prophetic accuracy, his future crimes and ultimate suicide. Cf. ll.1337–76,1673–94. This is similar to the effect of the speech Tacitus composes for Lucius Arruntius, predicting the corruption of Caligula.

43 Matheron 1985: 176. I note that Kissinger expressed a similar view in his analysis of the situation in Europe in the early nineteenth century: "The Napoleonic Empire for all its extent demonstrated . . . the tenuousness of a conquest not accepted by the subjugated people" (*A World Restored:*

Metternich, Castlereagh and the Problems of Peace, 1812–1822, Houghton Mifflin, page 4; cf. page 21). In Kissinger 1968, Kissinger makes an analogous point at the level of international relations: "The stability of any international system depends on at least two factors: the degree to which its components feel secure and the extent to which they agree on the 'justice' or 'fairness' of existing arrangements" (pages 899–900).

44 The quotation is from the *Troades* 258–9, and is used by Spinoza in *Theological-Political Treatise* v.22, and xvi.29.

45 Cf. particularly *Theological-Political Treatise* vii.12,14. The latter passage is particularly interesting for its use of Tacitus (*Histories* I.xxv) to illustrate the proposition that once political power has been vested entirely in one man, it is all the easier to transfer it to another. Spinoza cites the same passage in a note he added to *Theological-Political Treatise* xvii.3.

46 As Aristotle says that any man must be who is capable by nature of living outside any political community (*Politics* 1253a1–3).

47 Spinoza also alludes to this passage in *Political Treatise* v.4. Stanley Karnow took the famous line *"solitudinem faciunt, pacem appellant"* as the motto for his history of Vietnam (*Vietnam, a History,* New York: Viking Press, 1983).

8 Spinoza's theology

Spinoza's theology, although original, owes much to the cultural soil that nourished it. His parents were among the many "Marranos" – Portuguese Jews who in their native country had been compelled outwardly to embrace Roman Catholicism – who had emigrated to Amsterdam in the early seventeenth century. In the freedom of their new country, the immigrant Marrano community set out to recover its full religious heritage, and to shed beliefs and practices contrary to it. However, some of its members, of whom Spinoza was one, not only remained attached to non-Jewish elements in their Marrano culture, but, having embraced the revolution in the physical sciences associated with Galileo, Bacon, and Descartes, wished to pursue its implications for religion.[1] When he was twenty-three, partly because he would not renounce these non-Jewish interests, the Amsterdam synagogue expelled and cursed him. Yet even among the radical Christians who befriended him, and who repudiated the trinitarian and Christological doctrines he found absurd, only a small circle of intimates were prepared to follow him when he jettisoned the conception of God as a supernatural creator of the natural universe, and developed a "naturalized" theology, in which the natural universe, as conceived in Baconian-Cartesian natural science, derives its existence from nothing above and beyond it.

Despite its radical naturalism, Spinoza's theology is articulated much as are the supernaturalist ones he rejected. It has two major divisions, speculative and practical. Speculative theology treats of God's existence and nature, and of his relation to the natural world and the human beings in it. Practical theology treats of how human beings are to live, given God's nature and their relation to him; and it subdivides into a natural (or philosophical) part, which treats of what can be established by reason in the light of human experience, and a revealed part, which treats of what God has communicated to individual human beings.[2] While traditional speculative theology likewise had a revealed as well as a natural part, Spinoza's does not. On both historical and philosophical grounds he contended that all divine revelation to individuals is practical. It follows that little can be learned from revelation about the nature of God and his relation to the world: What is known of them that matters is philosophical. It also follows that the nature of revelation is not itself revealed: Knowledge of it is derived partly from historical reports of alleged revelations, some of them spurious, and partly from philosophical considerations.

Spinoza expounded the various parts of his theology in the following writings: his speculative theology in his posthumously published *Ethics* Parts 1 and 2 (the first half); his historical-philosophical theory of divine revelation and of the limits of revealed theology in the *Theological-Political Treatise*, which he published anonymously in 1670; and his practical theology in the *Theological-Political Treatise* and in *Ethics* Parts 4 and 5. In what follows, I take my primary task to be to establish the sense of what he wrote, never forgetting that, consistently with his motto "*Caute,*" he was reserved, especially in the *Theological-Political Treatise*, which he published during his lifetime, and in letters to correspondents who had not proved themselves friends; and that he made free use of recognized literary devices such as irony.

The chief obstacles to understanding these writings are two: one internal, and one external. The internal one is that the diction of his *Ethics* is apt to mislead readers who are not vigilant, especially if they neglect the *Theological-Political Treatise*, the Dutch version of his *Short Treatise on God, Man, and his Well-Being*, and his *Correspondence*, above all his letters to and from Oldenburg. That diction is scholastic-Cartesian; and, as he must have been aware, much of what he wrote, although not all, makes sense if his words are taken in their scholastic-Cartesian senses. However, he assigns new senses to many of the expressions he uses, sometimes explicitly, and sometimes implicitly by the structure of his reasoning or by his examples. Readers who have persuaded themselves that Spinoza is the last of the medievals or the first of the absolute idealists are apt to overlook the passages in which he does so.

The chief external obstacle to understanding Spinoza's theological writings is the notion that they are esoteric, which Leo Strauss has made fashionable.[3] According to Strauss, Spinoza's *Theological-Political Treatise*, like the writings of Plato, and of medieval Muslim and Jewish philosophers menaced by orthodox persecution, has a double meaning: the "exoteric" or surface meaning unintelligent readers like censors will take it to have, and the "esoteric" or hidden meaning intelligent readers, alert to signs such as deliberate contradictions and inapposite examples, will detect in it. The esoteric meaning may not only go far beyond the exoteric one, but may even contradict it. While I have no space to examine Strauss's case thoroughly,[4] I shall not be able wholly to avoid examining his interpretation of Spinoza's view of Jesus, "whom he regularly calls Christ," as sinister (Strauss 1988: 171).

I. NATURAL THEOLOGY

In natural theology, Spinoza in *Ethics* Part 1 breaks with Judaeo-Christian orthodoxy by conceiving God, not as the creator of human beings and of the world they inhabit, but as an infinite being "in" which they exist as finite modes (E 1p15). No substance except God, he contends, can be, or be conceived; and he draws the inevitable inference that the extended and thinking things of everyday experience "are either attributes of God, or affections [i.e., modes] of God's attributes" (E 1p14c2). God, he concludes, cannot create anything outside himself. He is "the immanent, not the transient, cause of all things," and not of their existence only, but also of their essence, which cannot be identical with their existence (E 1p18,24,25).

Notwithstanding these heresies, he implies that two of his three proofs of God's existence in *Ethics* 1p11d, as well as an additional one in its scholium, are a priori; and of these four, two not only look like the "ontological" proofs offered by Descartes and Leibniz, but one is reminiscent of those of Anselm and of Duns Scotus (E 1p11d,s). Since he also follows many orthodox theologians in deducing from God's infinity the negative "attributes" they ascribed to him, which he denied to be genuine attributes – namely, indivisibility, uniqueness, causal independence, eternity, immutability and the indistinguishability of his existence from his essence – (E 1p13, 14c1,17c1,20,20c2), many commentators have reduced Spinoza's natural theology to a stage in the supposed advance from scholasticism to Hegelian idealism. As they read him, he conceived the infinite positive attributes which he ascribed to God, such as extension, thought, and others to which human beings have no access, as attributes only in the sense that they each appear to some finite beings, human or nonhuman, to constitute God's essence, even though they do not in fact constitute it.[5] Extension, for example, is no more than a *phenomenon bene fundatum* ("well-founded phenomenon"), in the terminology Leibniz was to introduce.

While such readings will always captivate those attracted by Hegelian history of philosophy, they are incompatible not only with the great scholium to *Ethics* 1p15, but also with what Spinoza discloses in his early *Short Treatise on God, Man, and His Well-Being*[6] about the reflections on his predecessors that led him to the natural theology of the *Ethics*.

In the "Short Outline" preceding the text of the *Short Treatise*,[7] Spinoza's editor describes him as having "an idea of God" according to which: "he defines God as a being consisting of infinite Attributes, of which each is infinitely perfect in its kind. From this he then infers that existence belongs to [God's] essence, or that God necessarily exists." This reverses the order in which most medieval theologians – Muslim, Jewish, and Christian – derived the divine attributes. Both Maimonides and Aquinas, for example, begin with the identity of God's essence with his existence (*esse*), and infer, first, that God exists necessarily and not contingently, and then that his existence cannot be limited by his essence, that is, cannot be limited to the power of any given kind of thing as opposed to that of any other. They then conclude, in Maimonides's words, that while we can know that God is infinite in the sense that "all deficiencies are negated" with respect to his essence, this knowledge is merely negative: We "cannot apprehend his quiddity" – what he is (Maimonides 1963: 132–137 [I.57–58]; Aquinas 1964–6: I.xii.11–12).

Maimonides confined nonnegative human knowledge of God to his existence and to his works – his creation of the world and to his interventions in it, as revealed in the Scriptures (Maimonides 1963: 280–359 [II.13–31]; 502–10 [III.25–26]; and 618–28 [III.51]). Aquinas was only slightly less restrictive. He asserted that human beings can demonstrate that nonnegative terms standing for pure perfections (such as wisdom) are true of God, although the only senses they can attach to those terms when applied to God are analogical. Thus they can know that God is wise, not in the only way that human experience enables them to understand positively – the imperfect and derivative one in which human beings are wise – but in a perfect way which they can only understand as not imperfect: the way in which the first cause of all wisdom is wise (Aquinas 1964–6: I.13.1–3). Yet Maimonides and Aquinas were both agreed that, since God cannot be composed of elements, he must, in the technical language of scholasticism, be "simple," and hence that the many "attributes" he can be shown to possess cannot be really distinct. In predicating different perfections of God, whether negatively or analogically, human beings do no more than ascribe to him, in different imperfect ways, a simple perfection they cannot comprehend (Maimonides 1963: 235–41 [II.Introduction.1]; 249–52 [II.9b–10b]; Aquinas 1964–6: I.13.4ad3).

A caustic remark in the *Short Treatise* shows that Spinoza derided this medieval consensus at a very early stage in his thinking. "[T]he philosophers," he wrote, meaning the medieval natural theologians, "sufficiently conceded . . . that they have a very slight and inconsiderable knowledge of God" when they denied that a "legitimate definition of God can be given," giving as their ground that such a definition "must represent the thing absolutely and affirmatively, and . . . [that] one cannot know God affirmatively, but only negatively" (ST I.7). And he went on to attribute their complacency in ignorance to their Aristotelian mistake that legitimate definitions of substances – that is, of beings neither predicated of nor present in another – or of accidents, of which there are nine fundamental categories,[8] *must be by genus and difference.* Descartes had corrected this mistake by showing that the essences of created substances are only two, each constituted by a single principal attribute that is the subject-matter of a fundamental science, and that Aristotelian accidents of a substance – beings that exist only as "present in" it – are each no more than modifications, or "modes," of the attribute constituting its essence. Thus a noncomplex body, or corporeal substance, is constituted by the attribute of extension (i.e., spatial three-dimensionality); and its modes at any given time are its shape, size, and state of motion or rest relative to other bodies. Aristotelian accidents of a complex body that are not reducible to modes of extension – for example, its hue as seen – are not present in it at all, but are propensities of the modes of the bodies composing it to cause certain modes of thinking in embodied thinkers.

From the beginning, as his *Short Treatise* shows, Spinoza saw Descartes's scheme as the foundation of a new theology as well as of a new physics. A definition in Cartesian science is not by *genus* and *differentia*; and that of a substance simply states what its Cartesian principal attribute is. Such attributes "require no genus, or anything else through which they are better understood or explained; for since they, as attributes of a being existing through itself, exist through themselves, they are also known through themselves" (ST I.7). Definitions of modes, by contrast, specify in what modifications of the principal attribute of their substances they consist, and exist wholly "through" those attributes (ST I.7). Like most of his scientifically-minded contemporaries, Spinoza believed that Descartes had shown that the physical universe is an unbounded extended plenum, in which bounded or finite things exist as modifications by virtue of internal motions the quantity of which is conserved. Empty space is a nonthing; for an attribute must be an attribute of something, and the extension of an empty space would be an attribute of nothing. Since a vessel emptied of everything extended must collapse, one that seems to be empty, for example, a glass jar emptied by an air-pump, can have been emptied only of whatever stuff (air) an air-pump pumps, not of the finer stuff it cannot pump. And since no extended body can move from the place it occupies unless some other extended body or bodies replace it, all motion in the infinite plenum must be vortical, like the motion that goldfish swimming in a bowl produce in the water in it. The infinite plenum, however, is not absolutely infinite; for it has no modes that are not modes of extension. It cannot, for example, think. But in its kind – *res extensa* – it is infinite.

Rightly apprehensive that his physics would prompt heretical theological speculation, Descartes himself protested that the extended corporeal plenum is *not* infinite in any legitimate sense, but merely "indefinite":

[I]n the case of God alone, not only do we fail to recognize any limits in any respect, but our understanding positively tells us that there are none. [But] . . . in the case of other things, our understanding does not in the same way tell us that they lack limits in some respect; we merely acknowledge in a negative way that the limits they have cannot be discovered by us. (*Principles of Philosophy* 1.27)

This, however, obfuscates a distinction that Spinoza saw, and is there for anybody to see: that between infinity in a kind and absolute infinity, or infinity in every kind. In discussing the corporeal universe in its kind, that is, as an extended substance, Descartes wrote:

[T]his world, that is, the whole universe of corporeal substance, has no limits to its extension. For no matter where we imagine the boundaries to be, there are also some indefinitely extended spaces beyond them, which we not only imagine *but also perceive to be imaginable in a true fashion, that is, real.* (*Principles of Philosophy* 2.21; emphasis added)

This implies, not only that "we merely acknowledge . . . that the limits [this world has] cannot be discovered by us," but that there are no such real limits, because beyond any finite extended thing there are real extended spaces.

What of the scholastic objection[9] that, since what is extended is divisible, it must be made up of finite parts, and so cannot be an infinite *substance*? Spinoza had found its refutation as early as when he wrote the *Short Treatise*, and repeated it in Letter 12 and *Ethics* 1p15s. Neither the parts human beings distinguish in extended space, nor the whole considered as composed of those parts are "true or actual beings, but only beings of reason" (ST I.2). The extended universe is in fact indivisible, although for some practical purposes we must think of it as divided into parts; but the parts into which we mentally divide it are not true and actual beings, but mere *entia rationis*, like the hours into which we divide the day. Not only is this infinite extended plenum not created, as Descartes had mistakenly believed, but two predicates are true of it which traditional theology held to be true only of God: namely, "exists in itself" and "is conceived through itself." In other words, like all infinites, it is a substance.

By saying that the infinite extended plenum "exists in itself" Spinoza meant that it is its own immanent cause, that is, it depends on itself for its existence. Immanent causation is the self-dependence of an independent existent, and the other-dependence, or dependence on an independent existent, of any dependent existent or mode. Although the only laws of immanent causation discovered by human beings about the extended plenum are laws of conservation – that both its infinite quantity and the proportion of motion to rest in it are always the same – it can be inferred from the nature of substance in general that there must be others by which it immanently causes the changing states of motion and rest that occur in it. That inference is confirmed by the discovery of laws of transient causation according to which one state of motion and rest is succeeded by another. When E. W. von Tschirnhaus suggested in a letter that of itself the infinite extended substance must be an inert mass, Spinoza flatly denied it, and declared that the nature of the actual infinite extended substance – that is, the laws by which it immanently causes whatever it does – must determine not only whatever motion and rest occur in it, but also what unchanging laws of transient causation govern the continual changes in the motion and rest of finite bodies in it.[10]

Having affirmed what Descartes had denied, that extension is an attribute expressing an essence that is infinite in the strict sense, and that the medieval objections to the infinity of the extended universe are unsound, Spinoza naturally proceeded to inquire whether thought (*cogitatio*), the second of the really distinct attributes that constitute Cartesian created substances, also expresses an infinite essence.

Jewish and Christian theologians, while speaking with the vulgar in referring to God's intellect and in ascribing infinite knowledge to it, at the same time endorsed a principle which Maimonides had said "should be established in everybody's mind," namely,

that our knowledge or our power does not differ from [God's] knowledge or His power in the latter being greater and stronger, the former less and weaker, or in other similar respects, inasmuch as the strong and the weak are necessarily alike with respect to their species, and one definition comprehends both of them. . . . [E]verything that can be ascribed to God, may He be exalted, differs in every respect from our attributes, so that no definition can comprehend the one thing and the other. (Maimonides 1963: 80 [I.35,42a])

According to that principle, thought, so far as it expresses either the essence of any individual human mind (as Descartes believed) or that of a substance of which individual human minds are modes (as Spinoza believed), neither can be an attribute of God nor can express an infinite essence. Here too, Spinoza boldly rejected both the principle and its implications. Just as he had maintained that a finite extended thing must be a mode of an infinite extended substance through the attribute of which, namely extension, it is conceived, so he urged that a finite set of ideas, which is what a human mind at bottom is, must be a mode of an infinite substance through the attribute of which, namely thought, it is likewise conceived (E 2p1 and E 2p2d). Nothing in any human idea, however inadequate, forbids that it be part of the complex infinite adequate idea that is an infinite mode of such an infinite thinking substance.

Yet even if Spinoza were right – even if all finite bodies and their states were modes of an infinite corporeal substance, and all finite minds and their thoughts were modes of an infinite thinking substance – Descartes's doctrine that essences expressed by really distinct attributes must be of really distinct substances would not be impugned. And if it were true, Spinoza's infinite extended substance and an infinite thinking substance would each be a really distinct substance of one attribute. No infinite thinker who was infinitely extended could be more than a *union* of two distinct substances, as Descartes believed a human being is. Nor could any such substantial union be a substance, because it would need an external cause.

Spinoza would have nothing to do with this line of thought. "[T]he more reality or being a thing has," he declared, not only do "the more attributes belong to it," but each of these attributes "must be conceived through itself" – that is, must express an infinite essence by itself, and not merely in conjunction with the others (E 1p9–10). This doctrine raises two questions that go to the heart of Spinoza's metaphysics and continue to be disputed by commentators on it. First, how can really distinct attributes, which express really distinct essences, each infinite in its kind, constitute the essence of one and the same substance? And secondly, even if an infinite substance consisting of really distinct attributes *can* exist, is there any good reason to believe that one *does*?

In *Ethics* 2p7 – "The order and connection of ideas is the same as the order and connection of things" – Spinoza furnishes a clue to how he conceives the unity of a substance that is both extended and thinking. It suggests that the unity of any substance consisting of really distinct attributes is the *necessary* identity, under each of those attributes, of the order and connection of its modes. But what are order and connection? Presumably, the order of a thing's modes as constituted by really distinct attributes is the same if and only if, considered in their causal order – both immanent and transient – those constituted by any one attribute correspond one to one with those constituted by any other. Sameness of connection is more obscure. It cannot be determination by the same causal laws, because the causal laws determining the order of the modes under any one attribute must be conceived through that attribute. I conjecture that Spinoza thought that there must be transattribute laws of nature determining, for a substance's modes as constituted by any one attribute, how they are constituted by any other. Given what those laws of nature are, and how the totality of the substance's modes are constituted under any one attribute, it would follow, for any mode as constituted under one, how it is correspondingly constituted under any other. If that is so, and I know of no coherent alternative that does not contradict his text, Spinoza conceived God as a substance consisting of every one of the infinite attributes that constitute an infinite essence, the constitutive laws of whose nature determine, for any mode constituted by any of its attributes, both that it will also be constituted by every other, and how it will be so constituted.

Why believe that God, so conceived, exists? This question reduces to, "Does each of the various attributes that express an infinite essence express the essence of a unique being consisting of infinite attributes, or are those attributes distributed among more than one being?" If the former, Spinoza's God exists; if the latter, he does not. The fundamental argument Spinoza offers for the former runs: "[s]ince being able to exist is power, it follows that the more reality belongs to the nature of a thing, the more powers it has, of itself, to exist. Therefore, an absolutely infinite Being, or God, has, of himself, an absolutely infinite power of existing. For that reason, he exists absolutely" (E 1p11s; cf. ST I.2). This amounts to a principle of plenitude: that the possible substance that has most reality must exist. Unfortunately, Spinoza's argument for it is unsound; for, as Leibniz was to show, possible independent existents are possible worlds rather than possible substances. Spinoza himself recognized that how much reality a substance has is determined by how many attributes it has. If so, as long as all the attributes there are are somehow distributed over substances in a possible world, how much reality it has cannot be increased or decreased by distributing them differently: it must remain the same, whether they all constitute a single substance, or each a different one. Hence an argument on Spinoza's lines can at best show that every attribute expressing an infinite essence must be instantiated in some set of substances, not that they must all be instantiated in a single one.

Although Spinoza presumably never perceived that his form of the principle of plenitude is flawed, in his *Short Treatise* he supplemented it by arguing a posteriori that the attributes Extension and Thought must both belong to the same substance, "because of the unity which we see everywhere in Nature; if there were different beings in Nature, the one could not possibly unite with the other" (ST I.2). Since the only attributes "we," that is, human beings, cognize are Extension and Thought, the only attributes we can in any sense "see" united everywhere in Nature are Extension and Thought. But, since we cannot see Thought, how can we see that? Presumably by experiencing in ourselves that the primary object of human thought is the corporeal universe, as mediated through the changing states of particular human bodies. While it does not strictly follow that all the primary finite modes of thinking in the infinite thinking substance have modes of the corporeal universe for objects, if the ones we immediately cognize do, and if there is no reason to believe them unique, then it is at least a reasonable conjecture that the infinite thinking being of which our minds are complex finite modes has for its primary object the infinite extended thing of which our bodies are complex finite modes, and that it truly represents that primary object because the causal order of the modes of that thinking thing and that of the modes of that extended thing are one and the same.

A further conjecture seems natural, although Spinoza explicitly stated it only in a letter. Given that the absolutely infinite divine substance consists of infinite attributes besides extension and thought, and that, as thinking, it cognizes all its modes under all of them, his correspondent Tschirnhaus inquired why human beings, who are modes of the divine substance, cognize only one attribute besides thought, namely extension (Ep 63). Spinoza answered that since, as thinking, God must adequately cognize every one of his attributes, and since each complex idea in him that adequately represents him under a given attribute must be infinite, God as thinking must consist of an infinity of minds, each primarily representing him as infinite in one of his kinds (Ep 66). Human minds are finite modes only of one of the infinite minds in the infinite idea that is an eternal mode of God as thinking, namely, that mind whose primary object is God as extended. God as thinking cognizes all his infinite attributes; but just as each infinite attribute is really distinct from every other, so is the idea of each in the infinite idea of God really distinct from the idea of every other. Accordingly, each finite mind is a mode of the idea that is God's self-cognition of one of his infinite attributes, and of himself as cognizing it. Each human being is both a human body, a finite mode of God constituted by the attribute Extension, and a human mind, the finite mode of God as thinking that is primarily constituted by an idea of that body *and of nothing else;* and for each further attribute of God, A_i, that same finite mode will also be constituted by A_i and by a mind that is primarily constituted solely by the idea of that mode as constituted by A_i. Hence God, so far as he constitutes the idea of that finite mode, will be a series of ideas, each primarily constituted by an idea of it under a different attribute other than Thought. Not only is the finite mode that as extended and thinking is a human being much more than a human being; but, as thinking, it is much more than a human mind.

In writing the *Theological-Political Treatise,* Spinoza thought it prudent to explain to his readers what he meant both by the word "God" and by the traditional theological terms he applied to God. By "God" he meant the absolutely infinite substance, which he identified with Nature, considered as an infinite all-embracing immanent cause, and not simply as the corporeal universe. He wrote:

[S]ince nothing can be or be conceived without God, it is certain that all those things which are in nature involve and express the concept of God, in proportion to their essence and perfection. Hence the more we cognize natural things, the greater and more perfect is the cognition of God we acquire, or, (since cognition of an effect through its cause is nothing but cognizing some property of that cause) the more we cognize natural things, the more perfectly do we cognize the essence of God, which is the cause of all things. So all our cognition, that is our greatest good, not only depends on the cognition of God but consists entirely in it. (TTP iv.11)[11]

It follows that to happen according to the laws of Nature and to happen according to the knowledge and will of God are one and the same. Spinoza makes this point with an example from geometry, but he would certainly have accepted one from physics.

[W]hen we attend only to the fact that the nature of a triangle is contained in the divine nature from eternity, as an eternal truth, then we say that God has the idea of the triangle, or understands the nature of the triangle. But when we attend afterwards to the fact that the nature of the triangle is contained in the divine nature in this way, solely from the necessity of the divine nature, . . . then that very thing which we called God's intellect we call God's will or decree. (TTP iv.24)

In a later chapter he sums up his doctrine of the identity of Nature, the absolutely infinite substance, with God:

[S]ince nothing is necessarily true except by the divine decree alone, it follows quite clearly from this that the universal laws of Nature are nothing but decrees of God, which follow from the necessity and perfection of the divine nature. Therefore, if anything were to happen in Nature contrary to her universal laws, it would also necessarily be contrary to the divine decree, intellect and nature. . . . We could also show the same thing from the fact that *the power of nature is the divine power and virtue itself*. Moreover, the divine power is the very essence of God. (TTP vi.8–9; emphasis added)

Spinoza's theology, in short, naturalizes God.

This naturalization transforms the sense of two terms which Spinoza continued to apply to God: the predicates "eternal" and "perfect." Following Boethius, both medieval and Cartesian theologians had conceived eternity as timeless existence. Spinoza redefined it as "existence itself, insofar as it is conceived to follow necessarily from the definition alone of the eternal thing" (E 1d8). The existence of an absolutely infinite being, as Spinoza describes it, follows necessarily from its definition because it is defined as immanently causing its own existence;[12] and a thing immanently causes its own existence if and only if it is such that it is a law of nature that it is conserved, that is, can neither be created nor destroyed. Eternity so understood does not exclude the passage of time in the everyday sense;[13] for motion and rest is an eternal mode of infinite extended substance, and motion is relative change of position in time.[14]

Again, both medieval and Cartesian theologians conceived "perfection" a priori, as a standard by which Nature and everything in it can be judged imperfect. Spinoza, without redefining it, treats it as equivalent to "infinite." Hence, since the extended corporeal universe is infinite in its kind, it is perfect in its kind too, not because it satisfies some a priori standard of perfection, but because, as far as extension is concerned, it is itself the only rational standard of perfection. God, as absolutely infinite being, is likewise absolutely perfect, not as satisfying some a priori human standard, but as providing the only ultimate standard by which human beings can judge anything as imperfect. As Spinoza put it, "[T]he perfection of things is to be judged solely from their nature and power; things are not more or less perfect because they delight or offend men's senses, or because they agree with human nature or are repugnant to it" (E 1ap).

In declaring that the absolutely infinite being whose existence he claimed to demonstrate is the true God whom orthodox Jews and Christians ignorantly worship, was Spinoza concealing his atheism from himself by a play upon words? Maimonides would have thought so:

I shall not say that he who affirms that God, may He be exalted, has positive attributes either falls short of apprehending Him or . . . has an apprehension of him that is different from what He really is, but I shall say that he has abolished his belief in the existence of the deity without being aware of it. (Maimonides 1963: 145 [I,60,76b])

When confronted with a letter in which Lambertus van Velthuysen reprobated the author of the *Theological-Political Treatise* (not knowing who he was) for "teaching pure Atheism with hidden and disguised arguments" (Ep 42), Spinoza indignantly asked, "Does that man . . . cast aside all religion who declares that God must be recognized as the highest good, and that he must be loved as such with a free spirit?" (Ep 43).[15] But, as Maimonides would properly have answered, anybody who identifies God with Nature confounds the highest good with a being who is nothing like the God of Abraham, Isaac, and Jacob. He did not make the heavens and the earth, he did not create our ancestors and place them on earth, and he is not, through the calling of the Jews, engaged in blessing all the nations of the earth. Spinoza's God cannot rationally be worshiped as the God of orthodox Judaism and Christianity can: Human beings are not made in his image, and their relations with him are not those of like with like in any sense at all. And yet human beings would have to Spinoza's God, if he existed, something not wholly unlike the relations they would have with the God of Judaism and Christianity, if he existed. They are causally totally dependent on him for their existence. Nobody who is not so insane as to hate his own existence

can, as Spinoza pointed out, hate Spinoza's God (E 5p18). Our attitude to him will, however, be one of "intellectual love" in a sense to
be defined, which is identical with an attitude Spinoza called "*acquiescentia.*" If God is conceived as traditionally minded Jews and
Christians conceive him, Spinoza denies his existence, and can legitimately be accused of atheism. Not of idolatry; for he does not offer
to his "God" the sort of worship that pagan polytheists offered to
theirs. Spinoza's God, however, is more like the Jewish and Christian one than like those of paganism; and the intellectual love Spinoza thinks due to his God, while unlike monotheistic worship, has
some analogy to it. Spinoza can legitimately claim that his absolutely infinite being is sufficiently like the Jewish and Christian
God, and the attitude it would be rational to take to such a being
sufficiently like worship, for it to be proper to describe it as "God."

2. REVELATION, IMAGINATION, AND UNIVERSAL RELIGIOUS FAITH

Those who identify God with Nature, if they have a theology at all,
usually confine it to natural theology, and dismiss divine revelation
as a superstition. In the *Theological-Political Treatise*, Spinoza
does neither. Defining revelation (or, from its recipient's point of
view, prophecy), as "certain (*certa*) cognition of some thing revealed
by God to men" (TTP i.1), he accepts the Jewish and Christian
scriptures as records of a long tradition of divine revelation, and
economically investigating that tradition, develops a general theory
of revelation, and deduces from it the tenets of a universal religious
faith.

Spinoza recognized that his definition of revelation is satisfied by
natural cognition, or cognition of the second and third kinds as
defined in *Ethics* 2p40s2; for such cognition is both certain and
immanently caused by God. However, he also recognized that, while
what God certainly reveals through science is in no way inferior to
what he certainly reveals in other ways, Europeans generally (the
vulgus among whom the *Theological-Political Treatise* was published) take revealed cognition to exclude the scientific, and recognize as revelation only the specimens of it recorded in the Jewish and
Christian scriptures. He himself was no bigot: While accepting the
Jewish-Christian revelation as authentic, he took care to point out

that the Jewish scriptures attest that "the other nations had their own prophets also, who prophesied to them and to the Jews" (TTP iii.35).

Spinoza's philological principles for studying the Jewish and Christian scriptures were not original. Among philologists in the Netherlands, especially after J. J. Scaliger's appointment to a chair at Leiden in 1594, they were regularly followed in studying nonscriptural texts.[16] As Richard H. Popkin shows in Chapter 9 of the present volume, they had been stated and employed by a succession of Biblical scholars, both Jewish and Christian, most of whom were perfectly orthodox, like the medieval rabbi Abraham ibn Ezra,[17] whose commentary on the Pentateuch was printed alongside the Hebrew text of the Venetian Bomberg edition of the Jewish Scriptures. (A few others were not, like Spinoza's friend and correspondent Lodewijk Meyer.) However, classical philologists tended to leave Biblical studies to theologians,[18] with the result, as Popkin also shows, that nobody before Spinoza explored what would follow from combining good philology with his naturalized theology.

This is how Spinoza states and defends his philological principles for studying scripture:

[J]ust as the method of interpreting nature consists above all in putting together a history of nature, from which, as from certain data, we infer the definitions of natural things, so to interpret Scripture it is necessary to prepare a straightforward history of Scripture and to infer the mind of the authors of Scripture from it, by legitimate reasonings, as from certain data and principles. For if somebody has admitted as principles or data for interpreting Scripture and discussing the things contained in it only those drawn from Scripture itself *and its history*, he will always proceed without any danger of error. (TTP vii.8; emphasis added)

Spinoza makes two general claims about what can be established by following these principles. First, it can often be shown whether a sacred text has in fact been transmitted from antiquity or has been interpolated or added to out of "the blind and reckless desire to interpret Scripture and to think up new doctrines in religion" (TTP vii.3). Secondly, it can often be demonstrated that a report of an alleged revelation is a mere fabrication – whether by the alleged prophet himself, or by somebody in a position to ascertain whether or not he claimed to have had this or that revealed to him. By contrast, invalidating the reasons offered for interpolation or addition can approach a proof of authenticity.

Both the Jewish scriptures and the nonepistolary part of the Christian ones largely consist of historical narratives: some of divine revelations to individuals, of the actions they prompted, and of reactions to them; others simply of revelations and of the situations in which they were vouchsafed. Of those narratives, some purport to have been written by those who received the revelations they record, but most do not. Spinoza argues that the Pentateuch, *Judges, Ruth, I* and *II Samuel,* and *I* and *II Kings,* "were all written by one and the same Historian, who wanted to write about the past history of the Jews from their first origin up to the first destruction of the City" (TTP viii.42). Who that historian was, he does not claim to be able to prove, but he suspects that it was Ezra (TTP viii.48), and thereafter refers to him, whoever he was, by that name (TTP ix.2). Ezra, however, left his work incomplete. In parts, it is incoherent, although later editors have removed some of its gaps and incoherencies by additions and interpolations of more doubtful authority (TTP ix passim).

Since it can be inferred from the Jewish scriptures themselves that "before the time of the Maccabees there was no canon of the Sacred Books, but the ones we now have were selected from many others by the Pharisees of the second temple, . . . and those books were accepted only because of their decision" – which neither was divinely inspired nor was claimed to be – Spinoza declares that "those who want to demonstrate the authority of Holy Scripture are bound to show the authority of each separate book," and the authenticity of any given passage in it (TTP x.43). Yet he doubts neither that Ezra had honestly used authentic materials, nor that his work can usually be distinguished from that of later editors. Hence he does not impugn the authority of most of the scriptures as edited, even though little in them had been written by the prophets whose thoughts or deeds they report. Even less does he impugn the authority of the Pentateuch because of such trifles as that Moses could not have written the whole of it: for example, the preface to *Deuteronomy,* which implies that it was written after the Jews had crossed the Jordan, which they did not do until after Moses' death (TTP viii.6).

Despite the weight he attaches to philological evidence, Spinoza could not have arrived at his more important conclusions about revelation from it alone. He acknowledges that two philosophical principles are needed as well.

The first is a corollary of his naturalism: namely, that, although the specific causes of nonscientific revelations are usually beyond human knowledge, they fall wholly within the natural causal order, and are not supernatural interventions in it. According to *Ethics* 1p29, "in nature there is nothing contingent, but all things have been determined from the necessity of the divine nature to exist and produce an effect in a certain way." In his discussion of miracles in the *Theological-Political Treatise*, Spinoza points out what this implies for revelation: namely, "that nothing happens in nature that does not follow from her laws, that her laws extend to all things that are conceived by the Divine intellect itself, and finally, that nature maintains a fixed and immutable order," and hence that "the term 'miracle' cannot be understood except in relation to men's opinions, and means nothing but a work (*opus*) whose natural cause we cannot explain by the example of some other [to which we are] accustomed, or at least which cannot be so explained by the one who writes or relates the miracle" (TTP vi.13). Far from helping us to understand God's true nature, miracles distract us from it; for "those who run back to the will of God when they are ignorant of something are just silly; it is a ridiculous way of professing ignorance" (TTP vi.23).

The second philosophical principle on which Spinoza's revealed theology rests has to do with cognition. According to *Ethics* 2pp32–43, to cognize is to have an idea. Cognition is imaginative (of the first kind) if it consists partly of inadequate ideas; it is properly intellectual (of the second or third kinds) if it consists wholly of adequate ones. Adequate ideas are either "of things that are common to all, and are equally in the part and in the whole" (E 2p38), or of what is common and proper both to the human body and to an external thing customarily affecting it, and is in the whole of each and in every part (E 2p39). Cognition by adequate ideas is either (i) discursive – by "reason (*ratio*) or cognition of the second kind" – in which an effect is cognized by deriving its idea from the idea of its cause, or (ii) intuitive – "*scientia intuitiva* or cognition of the third kind" – in which the essence of a thing is cognized by forming an idea that presents it as immanently caused by God, the absolutely infinite substance (E 2p40s2). Spinoza also believes that, in *Ethics* Parts 3 and 4, he has shown how, by analyzing the affects of the human mind functionally, to develop a theory of them that is intuitive in this sense.[19]

As he himself observes (TTP i.2), natural intellectual cognition of either kind satisfies his formal definition of revelation or prophecy, that is, "certain cognition of some thing, revealed by God to man"; for "the things we cognize by the natural light depend solely on the cognition of God and his eternal decrees" (TTP i.2). But, as he also observes, most people do not speak strictly. Partly because they spurn their natural gifts, and partly because they thirst for things that are rare and foreign to their nature, they call no cognition revelation or prophecy unless it "extends beyond the limits of [natural cognition] and . . . the laws of human nature, considered in themselves, cannot be its cause" (TTP i.3).

After examining, in the light of his naturalism and his theory of cognition, the parts of the Jewish scriptures that he considers Ezra to have edited, Spinoza concludes that:

all those things God revealed to the prophets were revealed to them either in words, or in visible forms (figurae), or in both words and visible forms. The words and visible forms were either true, and outside the imagination of the prophet who heard or saw them, or else imaginary, [occurring] because evidently the imagination of the prophet was so disposed, even while he was awake, that he clearly seemed to himself to hear words or to see something. (TTP i.9)

He also infers, from the report in *Numbers* 12:6–7, that God made the following declaration to Aaron and Miriam in Moses' presence and by an actual voice: "If there be a prophet among you [i.e., the Jews], I the Lord will make myself known unto him in a vision, and will speak unto him in a dream. My servant Moses is not so, who is faithful in all mine house. With him I will speak mouth to mouth" (TTP i.21). And finally, he endorses the Jewish belief that Moses was unique among the Jewish prophets: All the others received their revelations through imaginary words and visible forms which only they cognized, but Moses received his through real sounds, which bystanders could hear (TTP i.10–13,19–22).

Here, if anywhere, a doubt intrudes whether Spinoza believed what he wrote; although if he did not, he betrays it neither by exaggeration nor by any other turn of style. If Moses received his revelations from God by a real voice, that voice would have been a miracle, according to his own definition: "a work [of God] whose natural cause we cannot explain by the example of another customary thing, or at least which cannot be so explained by the one who writes or relates the miracle" (TTP vi.13). This conception of a miracle implies, of any reported miracle, either that it really occurred and has a natural cause, or that it lacks a natural cause and did not really occur. If Spinoza had believed that the former is true of the scriptural reports of the real voice through which God revealed to Moses what he did, would not he have speculated about what the natural cause of that voice was?

His treatment of the miracle which the Roman Holy Office adduced as evidence against Galileo's Copernicanism suggests that he would have. That miracle is reported in *Joshua* 10:12–14:

Then spake Joshua to the Lord in the day when the Lord delivered up the Amorites before the children of Israel, and he said in the sight of Israel, Sun, stand thou still upon Gibeon; and thou, Moon, in the valley of Ajalon. And the sun stood still, and the moon stayed, until the people had avenged themselves upon their enemies. Is not this written in the book of Jasher? So the sun stood still in the midst of heaven, and hasted not to go down about a whole day. And there was no day like that before it or after it, that the Lord hearkened unto the voice of a man.

Spinoza acknowledges that, when Joshua said, "Sun stand thou still," he believed that God would arrest the sun's rotation about the earth long enough for his victory to be decisive, and later, that God had so arrested it; and that Joshua's belief was so far false, because, according to the new physics, the earth is a planet rotating about the sun, and the appearance of sunrise and sunset is not produced by the sun's motion (TTP ii.26). But he denies it to follow either that there was no miracle, or that, since Joshua's cognition of it was false, and hence not certain, it was not prophetic.

Are we [he asked] bound to believe that Joshua, a soldier, was skilled in astronomy? and that the miracle could not be revealed to him, or that the light of the sun could not remain longer than usual above the horizon unless Joshua understood the cause of this? . . . I prefer to say openly that Joshua did not know the cause of the greater duration of that light. . . . [He] did not allow for the fact that a refraction greater than usual could arise from the great amount of ice which was then in that part of the air (see *Joshua* 10:11), or from something else like that, which we do not inquire into now. (TTP ii.27)

However absurd his scientific speculation appears today, when much more is known about refraction, it was not excluded by the state of physics when he wrote.

Would not Spinoza have offered a similar speculation about the natural causes of the voice by which Moses received his revelations if he had believed it to be real? A parallel should be considered. Just as the reality of Moses' voices is crucial to orthodox Judaism, so that of Jesus' bodily resurrection is crucial to orthodox Christianity. How does Spinoza treat the reports of resurrections of the dead in *II Kings* 4:31–37 (the Shunammite's son), and in all four gospels (Jesus)?

In the former case, by offering a natural explanation of it, he has no difficulty in accepting that the revival of the Shunammite's son really occurred (TTP vi.47). In the latter, by his striking silence, when expounding the true nature of Jesus' teaching, about his reported resurrection, he plainly implies that Jesus' body did not return to life – an implication which he expressly confirms in a letter to Oldenburg (Ep 75). Presumably part of the reason why he accepts the former and not the latter is that he does not think the restoration to life of the Shunammite's son to be a genuine resurrection: He was merely revived by the warmth of the prophet's body, and so was only apparently dead. By contrast, on the evidence of the gospels, he accepts that Jesus really died on the cross, but maintained to Oldenburg that the reported appearances of his resurrected body, contrary to the Apostles' sincere belief, were imaginary – "not unlike the appearance by which God appeared to Abraham, when he saw three men whom he invited to dine with him" (Ep 75). Oldenburg expostulated that "in the gospels, Christ's resurrection seems to be reported (*tradi*) equally literally with [his passion and death]" (Ep 79), presumably having in mind the story of doubting Thomas (*John* 20:24–8); but unfortunately no answer to his letter, dated only a year before Spinoza's death, has been preserved.

Spinoza asserts, as his general conclusion about scriptural reports of miracles,

that everything that is truly narrated in Scripture to have happened necessarily happened, as all things do, according to the laws of nature. And *if anything can be found which can be conclusively demonstrated to be contrary to the laws of nature, or not to have been able to follow from them*, it should simply be believed that it has been added to the Sacred Texts by sacrilegious men. (TTP vi.51; emphasis added)

This, however, is far from Hume's doctrine in his essay "Of Miracles" that all reports of phenomena are suspect that are not of kinds customarily observed. By defining a miracle as "a work whose natural cause we cannot explain by the example of another customary thing" (TTP vi.13), Spinoza implies both that phenomena that are not of kinds customarily observed really do occur, and that they are naturally caused. He makes that implication explicit by declaring that, "if we find in the Sacred Texts certain things whose causes we do not know how to give an account of, and which seem to have happened beyond, indeed contrary to, the order of nature, that ought not to cause us to hesitate to believe unreservedly that what has really and truly happened has happened naturally" (TTP vi.45). It is, also, confirmed by his examples. Daylight is not customarily prolonged, even when there is a great amount of ice in the air, as reported in *Joshua* 10; nor are those whose observable vital functions have ceased after suffering severe pains in the head customarily restored to life after somebody has lain on their apparently dead bodies, as reported in *II Kings* 4. A consistent Humean would be obliged to reject both reports as fabrications. A consistent Spinozist, however, is obliged only to reject philologically authenticated reports (as Spinoza took these to be) if they are excluded by Cartesian physics; and Cartesian physics, as Newton was later to complain, is licentious in the speculative hypotheses it sanctions.[20] With respect to these reports, if it does not exclude those Spinoza accepted, I do not see how it excludes those he did not.

That Moses' voices and Jesus' resurrection were real are each believed, by those who believe them, on the ground of scriptural reports which Spinoza accepts as based on reliably transmitted oral or written records of original observations. If either in the *Theological-Political Treatise* or in his correspondence Spinoza gives a defensible reason for accepting the former but not the latter I have not found it. The evidence for the latter, while far from conclusive, is stronger. Although some Jewish commentators have accused Spinoza of tendentiously preferring to attack Judaism rather than Christianity,[21] in the *Theological-Political Treatise* he chose to accept the miracle crucial to orthodox Judaism while conspicuously refraining from accepting the one crucial to orthodox Christianity. Apart from this, his theoretical treatment of both is even-handed, although some of his remarks about Judaism are not.[22]

He endorses as authentic the bulk of the revelations reported in the Jewish scriptures from *Genesis* to *II Kings*. He then argues that, when studied according to correct philological and philosophical principles, those scriptures show that the Jewish prophets, even Moses, received their revelations wholly through cognition of the first kind, namely imagination: Moses receiving it through a real voice, and the rest through purely imaginary words and visible forms. That the medium of revelation is imagination supplies a principle for interpreting the scriptural record. The case of Moses shows that the greatest of the prophets was not the one who knew the most. As a man of his time, he was ignorant of much that became commonplace to rabbinical students: for example, "he taught that . . . [Yahweh] chose, for himself alone, the Hebrew nation and a certain region of the world (see *Deuteronomy* 4:19, 32:8– 9), but that he left other nations and regions to the care of the other gods substituted by him" (TTP ii.38). The same holds for the lesser Jewish prophets. What was revealed to them was "accommodated" to the speculative beliefs about God and his relation to the world they already had, and so did not derive from revelation (TTP ii.41). Since many have been deluded that they were receiving revelations but were not, how does God make a prophet certain that a cognition vouchsafed him is a revelation? Spinoza's answer is that every prophet who receives a new revelation both "has a heart inclined only to the right and the good," and imagines what is revealed "very vividly" and with "signs" accommodated to his imagination – they differ from prophet to prophet – that render him totally certain of it (TTP ii.10–12). This answer unfortunately fails to tell those who are deluded into thinking that they are prophets how to find that out.

Cognition is either speculative (of what is the case) or practical (of what to do). Hence, if no revealed cognition is theoretical, it must all be practical. Practical cognition, in turn, is either general or particular. The general practical cognition revealed to Moses is the Jewish Law which he promulgated only to the Jewish people, and which therefore only they were bound to observe. It includes, besides general rules of individual conduct (summed up in the Decalogue), ceremonial rules for divine worship, among them rules for instituting a hereditary priesthood and offering various forms of sacrifice, and judicial rules for adjudicating disputes, trying charges of criminality, and punishing those found guilty. Later prophets added other provisions, as when the prophet Samuel anointed first Saul and later David as king. Particular revelations were accorded to political leaders (judges and then kings) as well as to private individuals (those usually referred to as "prophets"), about what should be done, by given individuals (not necessarily the prophet) or by the state, in individual situations.

Spinoza expressed the greatest admiration for "the extent to which [Moses'] way of constituting a government (*imperium*)" – that is, the way it was constituted before the kings – "was able to moderate spirits (*animos*), and to restrict those who ruled equally with those who were ruled so that the latter neither became rebels nor the former Tyrants" (TTP xvii.62). He conceded only one defect in it: that the sacred ministry was reserved to the tribe of Levi, although, before the brief apostasy in which everybody except the Levites worshipped the golden calf, it was to have consisted of the first-born in each family (TTP xvii.96–97). The new arrangement caused dissension between people and sacred ministry which repeatedly tempted the political leaders to introduce forbidden forms of worship, which in turn caused the prophets to denounce them. While suggesting that the character of the people made it inevitable that their sacred ministry would either apostatize or cause dissension, Spinoza somberly described the situation in prophetic terms: "At that time, the security [of the Jewish people] was not the concern of God, but vengeance" (TTP xvii.97).[23] Had it not been for this causally intelligible defect, "in the state (*republicam*) of the Hebrews . . . the government (*imperium*) would have been everlasting" (TTP xvii.112). Even as it was, it repeatedly overcame great dangers, but sometimes only because of "God's external aid" through individual prophets (TTP iii.17).

Spinoza offers his conclusion that the nearly flawless constitution of the Hebrew state was the work of prophets and not of political theorists as a matter of historical fact, which, like facts of any kind, theorists ignore at their peril. He recognized that the kind of cognition most needed for competence in practical affairs is the first – imagination; it is not the second and third – reason and *scientia intuitiva* – although the latter are needed for explaining that competence ex post facto. Here it must not be forgotten that Spinoza uses the words "imagination" and "reason" in connection with prophecy in senses he carefully defines in the second scholium of *Ethics* 2p40.

Executive power accomplishes its particular purposes only by correctly perceiving the individual situations in which it is exercised. Such situations are "sized up" imaginatively, and possession of correct theories does not ensure that they will be sized up well. Spinoza saw clearly that those whose powers of imaginative perception are extraordinary and whose rational attainments moderate often do better in constitution-making and legislation, in establishing creeds and forms of worship, and even in formulating moral codes, than those whose rational attainments are extraordinary and whose powers of imaginative perception moderate. And when somebody of strong imaginative power founds an enduring constitution, although the power by which he does it is natural, he and his followers, believing that nobody could have done it without supernatural help, may well ascribe his doing it to such help.

Because Spinoza finds Christian teaching to be directed to the whole world and Jewish only to the Jewish people, and explains this partly by the mode in which Jesus received the revelation he did, some commentators have imputed to him a prejudice against Judaism. But he is usually even-handed. Just as he dismissed the speculative doctrines of orthodox Judaism as not part of what was revealed to the Jewish prophets, so he dismisses those of orthodox Christianity, which he professes not to grasp (*capere*) (TTP i.24), as not part of what was revealed to Jesus or to the Apostles. The revelation to Jesus, he wrote, "as the apostles preached it, doubtless by relating the simple story of Christ, does not fall under reason, yet everyone can easily appreciate by the natural light that, like the whole of Christ's teaching, it consists chiefly of moral lessons" (TTP xi.15). And he finds it to differ from the Jewish revelation only in this: "before the coming of Christ the Prophets were accustomed to preach religion as the law of their own Fatherland (*Patriae*) and by the force of the covenant entered into in the time of Moses; but after the coming of Christ the Apostles preached *the same religion* to everyone as a universal law, solely by the force of the passion of Christ" (TTP xii.24; emphasis added). The Christianity of Jesus and the early Church was therefore a reduced rather than an augmented Judaism: for example, it lacked laws for a state, for a sacerdotal system, or for religious rites.[24] Substantially, it taught what Spinoza called "the tenets of the universal faith, or the fundamental principles of the whole of Scripture," which are seven: (1) that there is a supreme being, supremely just and merciful; (2) that the supreme being is unique; (3) that the supreme being is omnipresent; (4) that the supreme being has the supreme right and dominion (*dominium*) over all things; (5) that the supreme being is worshipped and obeyed only by justice and charity, or love of one's neighbor; (6) that only those who obey the supreme being by living in the way prescribed in (5) are saved (*salvos*); and (7) that the supreme being pardons all who repent. This was the substance of Moses' religious teaching of the Jewish people; the primary function of the Christian revelation was to teach it to all people (TTP xiv.24–28).[25]

These fundamental principles not only leave it open whether God is identical with Nature or is its supernatural creator, but they also describe God as just, merciful, and forgiving. It therefore falls short of the theology Spinoza expounds in the *Theological-Political Treatise* in failing to make plain either that God is identical with Nature (TTP vi.7–22), or that it is only because of "a defect in [the multitude's] thinking" that God "is described as a lawgiver or prince, and called just, merciful &c." (TTP iv.37). In itself, this should not trouble readers. If, as Spinoza has maintained, prophets characteristically receive their revelations through their imaginations, and interpret them according to their antecedent beliefs, Jesus, who had been taught the speculative beliefs of the early rabbinic Judaism, would have interpreted whatever was revealed to him compatibly with those beliefs.

This explanation, however, is excluded by a series of passages in Chapter i of the *Theological-Political Treatise*. First of all, Spinoza confesses that he believes nobody but Jesus to have arrived at "so great a perfection above others" that it enabled him "to perceive by the mind alone certain things that are not contained in the first foundations of our cognition, nor can be deduced from them" (TTP i.22). He then proceeds to acknowledge that, according to the reports in the Christian scriptures, God did not reveal things to Jesus by appearing to him, or through angels: "if Moses spoke with God face to face, . . . Christ communicated with God mind to mind" (TTP i.24). To Jesus alone

God immediately revealed – without words or visions, God's appointed conditions (*placita*), which lead men to salvation. So God revealed himself to the Apostles through Christ's mind, as formerly he had revealed himself to

Moses by means of a heavenly voice. And therefore Christ's voice, like the
one Moses heard, can be called the voice of God. And in this sense we can
also say that God's Wisdom, that is, a Wisdom surpassing human wisdom,
assumed a human nature in Christ. (TTP i.23)

Hence Jesus, and he alone, received God's revelations without the
aid of imagination, that is, without the aid of words or of images.[26]

Finally, in *Theological-Political Treatise* iv.29–32, Spinoza asserts
that, unlike Moses and the Jewish prophets, who "did not perceive
God's decrees adequately, as eternal truths," Jesus "perceived things
truly and adequately"; and that therefore "it would be as contrary to
reason to maintain that God accommodated his revelations to the
opinions of Christ as to maintain that God previously accommodated his revelations to the opinions of the angels [through whom he
revealed them], that is [to the opinions] of a created voice and of
visions"[27] (TTP iv.29–31). And he adds,

from the fact that God revealed himself immediately to Christ, or to his
mind, and not, as he did to the Prophets, through words and images, we can
understand nothing but that Christ perceived or understood truly the things
revealed; for a thing is understood when it is perceived with a pure mind,
without words and images. And so Christ perceived the things revealed
truly and adequately. (TTP iv.32)

As a result, Jesus was able to teach human beings how to live, not
merely by promulgating a law to be obeyed, but by revealing the eternal causal truths by virtue of which that law is not simply a command
to be obeyed, but a dictate of reason, which only prescribes what is for
their advantage (*utile*). Spinoza did not deny that, when speaking to
those who did not understand the kingdom of heaven, Jesus may have
taught what was revealed to him as law; but he inferred from Paul's
epistles that, when speaking to those who did understand, Jesus
taught it as eternal truth, and not as law. By thus writing it in their
hearts, he paradoxically both confirmed and stabilized it as law, and
freed them from a servile relation to it (TTP iv.33–34).

That these passages are difficult does not excuse the license with
which Strauss has interpreted them. According to Strauss,

Spinoza asserts first that no one except Jesus (whom he regularly calls
Christ) has reached the superhuman excellence sufficient for receiving,
without the aid of the imagination, revelations of supra-rational content; or

that he alone – in contradistinction to the Old Testament prophets in particular – truly and adequately understood what was revealed to him. (Strauss 1988: 171)

As we have seen, Spinoza did assert that nobody but Jesus arrived at "so great a perfection above others" (*"ad tantam perfectionem supra alios pervenisse"*) that God revealed to him things he did not reveal even to Moses. But that implies, not that his perfection was "superhuman," but that it excelled that of *other* human beings like himself. Again, Spinoza did assert that Jesus perceived what was revealed to him "adequately, as eternal truths," and not "as precepts and things instituted," as Moses perceived what was revealed to him (TTP iv.29). But far from implying that the content of what was revealed to Jesus was "supra-rational," adequate perception is necessarily rational. Finally, Spinoza did assert that what was revealed to the Jewish prophets was accommodated to their opinions, and that they interpreted it in the light of their opinions. But that does not imply that there was any defect in how they understood what it was revealed to them that they should do. Since nothing speculative was revealed to them, their speculative mistakes were not revelations inadequately understood.

Strauss's misunderstanding of what Spinoza writes in these passages is of a piece with his radical misunderstanding that, in implicitly asserting in some passages that "revelation or prophecy as certain knowledge of truths which surpass the capacity of human reason is possible," and explicitly denying in others "the possibility of any supra-rational knowledge," Spinoza "contradicts himself . . . regarding what may be called the central subject of his book" (Strauss 1988: 169).[28] The "certain knowledge" he ascribes to the Jewish prophets is (extrinsically) true cognition of the first kind – imagination – which the prophet is unable to doubt. As cognition, it is subrational rather than superrational, and the cause of the prophet's certainty is natural. It surpasses the capacity of the higher forms of cognition (reason and *scientia intuitiva*) because, while they can supply the general dictates of reason (roughly, the moral law, and the general principles of politics), they cannot supply certain cognition of how to act to advantage in particular situations. There is no contradiction whatever in asserting that, although the provisions of the Jewish law divinely revealed to Moses through a voice included the moral dictates of reason that apply to all human beings, it was not revealed to Moses *that* it did include them. Nor is there any contradiction in asserting that, although reason and *scientia intuitiva* are higher forms of cognition than imaginative insight into particular situations, one variety of which is prophecy, there are many practical problems that can only be solved by recourse to the latter.

Yet a problem of consistency remains after the fogs of Straussian misreading have been dispersed. Spinoza depicts Jesus not as a philosopher, but as a prophet in the colloquial sense: as receiving sure cognition from God, not as philosophers do, "from the first foundations of our cognition" (TTP i.22), that is, from the principles laid down in *Ethics* Part 1, but in a way that, although natural, nobody yet understands. He is a greater prophet even than Moses; but he *is* a prophet, not a philosopher. Yet if Jesus understood what he taught "truly and adequately," must his cognition of it not have been of the second or third kind, and hence philosophical? And in that case, how could he have been a prophet?

Closer scrutiny of what Spinoza wrote in the crucial passages of the first and fourth chapters of the *Theological-Political Treatise* shows that this difficulty too springs from misreading. What was revealed to Jesus? Presumably, the tenets of the universal faith, various applications of those tenets, and many of the theorems in *Ethics* Part 4 about the effects of various dispositions to act, both virtuous and vicious, together with solutions, according to those theorems, of many practical problems that confronted him during his ministry. Let us assume that Jesus understood what was revealed to him "truly and adequately." What would that involve? An adequate idea is one that has all the intrinsic properties of a true idea, as distinct from the extrinsic property of agreement with its object (E 2d4); and this is to be understood in the light of the axiom that "Cognition of an effect depends on, and involves, cognition of its cause" (E 1a4). Because everything is an effect, including God or Nature, which as cause of itself is also effect of itself, adequate cognition of anything whatever is cognition of its cause. Thus adequate cognition that it is advantageous to accept and observe the tenets of the universal faith, or to observe certain rules of conduct, or to adopt a particular course of action, is cognition of such practices and actions as causing advantage. Yet although such causal cognition is attainable by anybody capable of studying the *Theological-Political Treatise* thoroughly,

Spinoza did not think it can be deduced from the first foundations of our cognition, and in the *Ethics* he showed why it cannot. In advancing to the theories of the affects and of servile and free action in *Ethics* Parts 3 and 4, from the fundamental metaphysics and theory of mind in *Ethics* Parts 1 and 2, he makes it plain that six postulates in *Ethics* Part 2 (stated after 2p13) and two in *Ethics* Part 3 are indispensable, none of which is deduced from "the first foundations of our cognition" as laid down earlier. They are derived according to the theorem that "if something is common to, and peculiar to, the human Body and certain bodies by which the human body is affected, and is equally in the part and in the whole of each of them, its idea will also be adequate in the Mind" (E 2p39). The practical cognition imparted in *Ethics* Parts 3 and 4 is all attainable by what Spinoza called "cognition of the second kind" – by certain "common notions," and by adequate ideas of what is common and peculiar to the human body and to certain bodies that affect it. Such practical cognition is not in itself philosophical; that is, it is not the *scientia intuitiva* attainable only when its principles as set out in *Ethics* Parts 1 and 2 have been mastered. What can be adequately cognized ("perceived") by the mind alone is not the same as what can be deduced from the first foundations of our cognition. The mind alone adequately cognizes certain things from common experience which it cannot deduce from the first foundations of our cognition – even though those foundations determine when common experience yields adequate cognition and when it does not. Adequate cognition remains adequate even though the principles determining its adequacy have not even been thought of.

Jesus' adequate cognition, as Spinoza conceived it, was not accompanied by cognition of the principles determining its adequacy. His perfection exceeded that of his fellow men because he "perceive[d] by the mind alone things that are not contained in the first foundations of our cognition, and cannot be deduced from them," even though he did not perceive by the mind alone the metaphysical and epistemological principles according to which his perceptions or cognitions were adequate. Jesus' mind, Spinoza declared, "would necessarily have to be more outstanding and far more excellent than the human mind is" (TTP i.22–23); but that does not imply that his mind was raised to that level of excellency by external causes of a kind that do not operate on other human minds, or that it was

superhuman by nature, much less divine. No mind, according to
Spinoza, is anything but a complex idea; and to act on a mind is to
cause the ideas that compose it to be other than they would have
been but for that action. Hence God could externally cause Jesus to
perceive something by the mind alone only if he *directly* – without
imaginative mediation – caused certain ideas to be among those
composing his mind that otherwise would not have been among
them. It is not contrary to Spinoza's theory of mind, as far as I can
tell, that natural causes might directly introduce into the ideas composing Jesus' mind either the partly inadequate ideas expressed in
the tenets of the universal faith, or the adequate ideas set out in
Ethics Parts 3 and 4 of the advantage or disadvantage actions of this
or that kind tend to cause; and no matter what those natural causes
might be, they would be God or Nature acting.

Spinoza's position, in short, is that God introduced into Jesus'
mind both the tenets of the universal faith and the dictates of reason
stated in *Ethics* Parts 3 and 4. Jesus' cognition of the latter was
adequate, even though he had no notion either of the metaphysical
propositions from which a philosopher would derive those theorems, or of their proofs. The difference between Jesus' moral and
religious teaching and Spinoza's is that between the conception of
God expressed in the first four tenets of the universal faith and that
expressed in *Ethics* Part 1 and the latter half of Part 5; and that
difference explains why to Spinoza Jesus is a prophet in the colloquial sense, not a philosopher. Since he lacks cognition of the principles by which his prophetic cognition can be shown to be adequate,
he cannot demonstrate its adequacy, as a philosopher must, from
"the first foundations of our cognition."

Spinoza's theory of divine revelation is therefore consistent both
with itself and with his natural theology. Yet to most who follow his
philological treatment of scripture, his explanatory theory is much
more persuasive than his religious conclusions. Given his naturalized theology, not only his explanation of the phenomena of Jewish
and Christian prophecy, but his extraction of the tenets of his universal faith as the rational core of both Judaism and Christianity, are
alike defensible. True, his universal faith was still-born as a religion,
and was not, as a matter of history, the essence of either Judaism or
Christianity. But Spinoza's deficiencies as a religious teacher do not
show that his theology was defective.

One of the attractions of Spinoza's theory of prophecy is that it explains why this is so. Even the ablest theorists have shown themselves poor at designing institutions, whether religious or political, that work at all, much less that go on working. Spinoza's universal religion, like Hobbes's state Christianity, is designed to subserve political rather than religious needs. Adopting it would certainly curb the persecuting clergy whom Spinoza detested; but it does not satisfy the religious needs that the faiths proclaimed by Moses and Jesus did. In his theory of prophecy Spinoza not only recognized that the two religious faiths embraced by most of his contemporaries were instituted not by philosophers but by prophets, but began to explain why. To complete his explanation, the histories of both faiths must be investigated more thoroughly than he investigated them. Just because he does not try to make the Jewish prophets respectable from the point of view of his naturalist philosophy, his depiction of them is nearer to the truth than his depiction of Jesus and the Apostles.

If Spinoza's naturalist theology is true, then the claims of Judaism and Christianity to revealed truth are false. However, his theory of Judaism as founded on imaginative cognition would remain plausible in itself, and extensible to Christianity. The source of their power as faiths would have to be sought in a theory explaining how certain kinds of error about ultimate questions can become foundations of shared ways of living. There is no obvious reason why the *Theological-Political Treatise* could not be revised along these Spinozist lines. And even if Spinoza's naturalist theology is not true, at least he saw, what few theologians and fewer philosophers see, that religions are sustained by prophecy, not by philosophy or theology.

3. PRACTICAL THEOLOGY

Spinoza's revealed practical theology is that of "the universal faith" which he believed to be the true core both of Judaism and Christianity. It is, like all revealed theology, practical. However, its practical directions are expressed by imagining God as the perfect model for human conduct; and, so far, its expression is false. Spinoza's definitive practical theology is the natural one found in *Ethics* Parts 4 and 5. Its practical content is summed up in the "dictates of reason" for human life there expounded. It is therefore identical with his ethics as ordinarily understood, which Don Garrett studies in Chapter 6 of this volume. What it signifies theologically is found by examining the dictates of reason from the point of view of the relation of human beings to God.

Everything human beings do or undergo – all their actions and "passions" – are done or undergone according to the laws of immanent causation that constitute God's or Nature's essence. Since God's essence is perfect, it is absurd to wish that anything that happens should happen otherwise. From God's point of view, human violations of the dictates of reason are as necessary to his perfection as human observances of them. As Spinoza explained to his correspondent Willem van Blijenbergh,

> if *good in relation to God* implies that the just man does some good to God, and the thief some evil, I answer that neither the just man nor the thief can cause either delight or disgust (*taedium*) in God. If it is then asked whether each of those actions, so far as it is something real and caused by God, is equally perfect, I say that if we attend to the actions alone, and in the way proposed, then it can turn out that each is equally perfect. (Ep 23)

Since God, as even traditional theology had taught, is wholly active, and so without passions, "strictly speaking, [he] loves no one, and hates no one" (E 5p17c). Hence to God, considered as he is in himself, and not as he constitutes this or that individual finite mind, nothing any human being does or undergoes is good or bad, just or unjust. It is irrational even to ask whether anything whatever might be better than it is, because nothing can happen except as it does in God – the absolutely infinite substance that is the only being that can exist.

It follows that, although human beings can and should inquire what is the best way for human beings to act, and what is the best attitude for them to take to God or Nature, and to Nature's course, they should not delude themselves that what is best for them is more than that. Since the nature of everything is a *conatus* to persevere in being what it is, what is good for a thing is what promotes its perseverance in being – what is advantageous (*utile*) for it; and what is bad for it is what hinders its perseverance in being. However, a human being does not persevere in being simply because his or her vital functions, such as breathing, continue. The highest good to which any human being can aspire is to be as free as a human being can be; that is, to be able to take advantage of every opportunity to increase his or her power to act that circumstances can make possible. The greatest opportunity anybody can have is to live in a free society as one among many who are fully capable of taking advantage of its freedom; but to take advantage of that opportunity, each must develop the cooperative virtues of good faith and benevolence. Spinoza contemptuously dismissed the objection that the virtues necessary for making the most of the greatest opportunity are not unqualified advantages, because they unfit human beings for saving their lives in circumstances in which they can only be saved by servility, treachery, or cowardice (E 4p72d). If you cannot survive without servile complicity in crime, the lesser evil, that is, what is advantageous (*utile*), is to refuse and die, as Seneca did (E 4p20s); for nobody capable of saving his life by such complicity can thrive in the only circumstances in which a rational human being can: those in which one can live without violating the dictates of reason.

While he forcibly asserts that reason imposes on the rational a set of dictates very like those of traditional Judaism and Christianity, Spinoza as forcibly denies that it permits them to reprobate those who violate those dictates as both Jewish and Christian preachers have done. He writes of them:

They seem to conceive man in nature as a government (*imperium*) within a government. For they believe that man disturbs, rather than follows, the order of nature, that he has absolute power over his actions, and that he is determined only by himself. And they attribute the cause of human impotence, not to the common power of nature, but to I know not what vice of human nature, which they therefore bewail, or laugh at, or (as usually happens) curse. And the more he knows how eloquently and bitingly to rail at the impotence of the human Mind, the more he is held to be Godly. (E 3pr)

Such denunciations are in fact more blasphemous than godly. The dictates of reason require every human being to produce as much good as he can, and to reduce evil as much as he can; but how much of either he can do depends not on him, but on how things necessarily are. To the extent he can do neither, he should neither decry the state of the world as evil, nor heap contumely on those whose wrong actions he cannot prevent. "He who rightly knows (*novit*) that all things follow necessarily from the necessity of the divine nature ... will certainly find nothing worthy of Hate, Derision, or Contempt, *nor anyone whom he will pity* (*miserebitur*)" (E 4p50s; emphasis added). He will try to have only affects that prompt him to benevolent action, which pity, or "sadness, accompanied by the idea of an evil that has happened to somebody we imagine to be like ourselves" (E 3da18), will not. To one already committed to active benevolence, sadness at what he cannot do can only distract him from what he can, and at the same time impair his love of God. Spinoza, however, scrupulously added that "one who is moved to help others *neither* by reason *nor* by pity is rightly called inhuman" (E 4p50s; emphasis added).

The love Spinoza's God attracts from those who rightly know him is described by Spinoza as "intellectual." That love is an action, not a passion: the action of a rational finite being whose essence is a *conatus* to persevere in being, and who adequately cognizes that, since God is the substance of which he is a finite mode, his own existence would be unthinkable unless God were exactly as he is. Unlike the love of God preached by Moses and Jesus, gratitude for benefits received, whether in answer to prayer or as a reward for worship, has no part in it. Nor is it a due return for God's love to us. It is our participation in "the very Love of God by which God loves himself" (E 5p36); and nobody who so loves God can "strive that God should love him in return" (E 5p19). To love God intellectually is to be intellectually at peace (*quies*) with how things are: ourselves, and the absolutely infinite substance of which we are finite modes. The highest blessedness (*beatitudo*) is true acquiescence of spirit (*vera animi acquiescentia*) (E 5p42s).

Spinoza argues that nobody can hate God, because to the extent that we consider God as immanent cause of all that exists we are active, and so not sad – hate being the passive affect of sadness, accompanied by the idea of an external cause (E 5p18). His premise, however, seems to me false. Considering God as the immanent cause of all that exists is an action so far as one strives to exist oneself, for it contributes to directing that active striving rationally; but it is not an action if external causes so overwhelm one's *conatus* to persevere in existence that one wishes never to have existed at all.

Spinoza might, indeed, save his proof if he could show that extreme pain could not overwhelm one's *conatus* to persevere in existence without obliterating our power to consider God as immanent cause of all that exists. But he did not show it, and I do not believe he could have. Of course, even if he could not, it would not follow that it can be rational to hate God: that some finite mode in the absolutely infinite being wishes that it had never been does not show that it is irrational for the infinite being itself to will to exist.

Notoriously, Spinoza has embarrassed many of his admirers by claiming to demonstrate that "the human Mind cannot be absolutely destroyed with the Body, but something of it remains which is eternal" (E 5p23). Most recent commentators have rejected his proof as either fallacious or sheerly unintelligible. It is, however, a natural development of his conception of the human mind as a subset of the ideas that are modes of the eternal mode he refers to as the infinite idea of God, when taken together with his doctrine that a human individual's adequate idea of itself, if that individual has one, is a functional idea of its existence as caused at a certain stage in the course of nature. Given that all adequate ideas are eternal elements in the infinite idea of God, it appears to follow that if an adequate idea of itself is part of an individual human mind, that part of it not only will remain eternally after the individual body that is the primary object of that mind has been destroyed, but has eternally pre-existed the coming into existence of that body.[29]

Theologically, the question raised by Spinoza's doctrine that part of the human mind remains after the dissolution of the body that is its primary object, is what bearing it has on how human beings should live. I think the answer is that the eternal continuance of part of one's own mind in the mind of God cannot but be something a mind that wills to persevere in existence must will. However, it does not have the place in the lives of Spinozists that the hope of resurrection has in the lives of many Jews and Christians. What exists eternally is part of what exists during life, and is neither better nor worse than it is then. If we (that is, God, so far as he constitutes our minds) adequately cognize our lives as worth living, then we (i.e., he, so far as he is us) shall so cognize them forever. Our deaths will not be followed by divine judgment, and our continuation after death will be neither glorification in heaven nor damnation in hell. But neither will our deaths be wholly the end of us.

NOTES

1 Yovel 1989 is the best comprehensive treatment of Spinoza as a dissident Marrano. It draws on a large and growing body of studies of the Amsterdam Jewish community and his relations with it. His relations with Protestant groups were authoritatively examined by K. O. Meinsma in 1896, in a book now most accessible in Henri Mechoulan and Pierre-François Moreau's French edition of it (Meinsma 1983), with appendices, entitled *Spinoza et son cercle* (Paris: J. Vrin, 1983), and they continue to be closely investigated by many scholars. The influence of Franciscus van den Enden, an ex-Jesuit with whom Spinoza studied as a young man, remained largely unexplored until the recent investigations of Wim Klever, who has announced his discovery of a number of van den Enden's writings, which he plans to present in a forthcoming book, *Van den Enden, Biographical Documents and Works.*

2 Spinoza's Latin name for God, *"Deus,"* is masculine; and his name for an infinite being he held to be identical with God, *"Natura,"* is feminine. He sometimes refers to this individual as *"Deus sive Natura"* – "God or Nature." In the genders of the pronouns I use in place of these names, I follow Spinoza for the first two: "he" for "God" and "she" for "nature." For "God or Nature" I use "it."

3 See Strauss 1988, Chapter 5. (This book was originally published in 1952.)

4 Only a thorough examination could convince. Errol E. Harris in Harris 1978 has done much of what is needed by showing that what Strauss considers the eight chief signs by which Spinoza indicates the esoteric sense of the *Theological-Political Treatise* are nothing of the sort.

5 The "subjective" interpretation of what Spinoza meant by *"attributum"* is sometimes supported by translating *"tanquam"* in Spinoza's definition of an attribute, namely, *"id, quod intellectus de substantia percipit, tanquam ejusdem essentiam constituens"* (E 1d4), as "as if" rather than as "as." The decisive examination of the question of the objectivity of Spinoza's attributes is Gueroult 1968–74: I,428–61 (Appendix 3, *"La Controverse sur l'Attribut"*).

6 Mignini (in Spinoza 1986) has persuasively argued that Spinoza wrote the first half of this work in Latin in the middle of 1660, and amplified it as objections were made or occurred to him. According to Mignini, he permitted a friend to translate it, with additional notes, into Dutch; after which he revised the translation and added to the text. By early 1662, having decided to restate his conclusions *more geometrico* (in the geometrical manner), he began to rework it into what became the *Ethics.*

Edwin Curley judiciously surveys the theories that have been offered of the composition of the *Short Treatise* in Spinoza 1985a: 50–3.

7 The author of this outline has usually been thought to be the Amsterdam philosopher, Willem Deurhoff. Some, however, attribute it to Monnikhoff. Cf. Spinoza 1925: 436, and Spinoza 1985a: 53n1.

8 Aristotle, *Categories* 1a16–2b7; cf. *Metaphysics* VII.1028a8–1028b8.

9 Cf. Maimonides 1963: 249–52 [II.1.9b–10b]; cf. Aquinas 1964–66: I.3.1 (*secundo*).

10 Part of this correspondence was conducted through an intermediary, G. H. Schuller. The relevant passages in Spinoza's letters are Letter 64, where he referred Tschirnhaus to E 1p25c,s and to E 2p13le7s; and Letter 83. My disagreements both with Abraham Wolf's translation of Spinoza 1925: IV.334/24–5 in Letter 83, and with his commentary on the passage cited (Spinoza 1928: 61–62,365) are explained in Donagan 1988: 100,120.

11 Here as elsewhere my translation closely follows Edwin Curley's draft of a translation that will appear in the second volume of his *The Collected Works of Spinoza* (forthcoming from the Princeton University Press). I thank Professor Curley for his kindness in providing me with a copy of his draft, and for permitting me to use it. I have also consulted Samuel Shirley's excellent translation in Spinoza 1989. While I do not record minor divergences from Curley's renderings (mostly intended to be more literal if less elegant), readers should take note that I always render Spinoza's "*cognoscere*" and "*cognitio*" as "cognize" and "cognition," and not as "know" and "knowledge." My chief reason is that Spinoza held that human beings often cognize falsely.

12 That "necessarily" in Spinoza's definition means "by (immanently) causal necessity" and not "by logical necessity" is plain from the structure of *Ethics* Part 1. See Donagan 1988: 60–4,73–5.

13 He does deny it in a technical sense. See Donagan 1988: 109–13.

14 This has been denied by some, on the ground of some passages in which Spinoza uses the word "*tempus*" in a technical sense. See Bennett 1984: 202–3.

15 I have falsely asserted that Spinoza's contemporaries accused him "not of disbelieving what he professed to believe, but of concealing the heretical implications of what he professed" (Donagan 1988: 15). In "Van Velthuysen, Batelier and Bredenburg on Spinoza's Interpretation of the Scriptures," a paper presented in April 1991 to a conference at Cortona organized by the Scuola Normale Superiore di Pisa, Dr. Wiep van Bunge has shown that van Velthuysen did what I denied any of Spinoza's contemporaries did. The distinction I drew is philosophically suspect as well as historically false, because the distinction between difference in meaning and difference of belief is (as Quine has shown) indeterminate.

16 For the development of philology in the Netherlands see Wilamowitz-Moellendorff 1982: 50–3,65–76.

17 Born *c.* 1090 in Tudela, Spain, died 1164. Cited by Spinoza as "Aben Ezra."

18

> No other text [than that of the New Testament] posed the problem of the Textus Receptus . . . in so stark a form; and no other text was necessary to salvation. The character of the Vulgate established by Erasmus, Beza and Stephanus was so obviously haphazard that thoughtful critics, in countries where it was allowable to do so, had the strongest motives for questioning its authenticity. (Kenny 1974: 99)

Even though, as Kenny adds in a footnote on the same page, "there are almost no doctrinal issues of any significance which turn on the criticism of the text, as was remarked by Bentley" – but thirty years after Spinoza's death.

19 Spinoza's theory of the three kinds of cognition is discussed in Chapter 3 by Margaret Wilson. My own treatment, which is largely derived from Matheron 1969 and Matheron 1986a, may be found in Donagan 1988: 135–40.

20 For a scientific example of Spinoza's licentiousness in hypothesis, see his controversy with Boyle (with Oldenburg as intermediary) about the reconstitution of nitre (Ep 6,11,13). For why Newton found it necessary to formulate a principle limiting what hypotheses scientists should consider, see Hall and Hall 1964.

21 E.g., Hermann Cohen in the nineteenth century, and (less vehemently) Leo Strauss in this. See Strauss 1965: 19–20; and Strauss 1988: 190–1.

22 I say what I think necessary about his offensive incidental remarks about Judaism in Donagan 1988: 26–7.

23 As he acknowledged, he took his words from Tacitus: "[Nec] enim umquam atrocioribus populi Romani cladibus magisve iustis indiciis adprobatum est non esse curae deis securitatem nostram, sed ultionem" (*Historiae* I.3).

24

> As for the ceremonies of the Christians, viz. Baptism, the Lord's Supper, feasts, liturgies (*orationes externas*), and whatever others there may be in addition which are and always have been common to all Christianity, if Christ or the Apostles ever instituted these (which so far I do not find to be sufficiently established), they were instituted only as external signs of the universal Church, but not as things which contribute to blessedness or have any Holiness in them. (TTP v.32)

As philology, this is fantastic with respect to the Eucharist (the Lord's Supper).

25 The most illuminating treatment of Spinoza's project for a universal faith, and of its relation to Christianity, is Matheron 1971.

26 "Except for Christ, nobody received revelations from God unless by the help of imagination, that is, by the help of words or of images" (TTP i.25).

27 Spinoza's point seems to be that just as God, in causing a voice or an image that conveys a revelation, does not accommodate the revelation to the (nonexistent) opinions of that voice, so, in causing an idea in Jesus' mind, he does not accommodate himself to the other ideas in that mind. Angels, it must be remembered, are not real, but figments of the imaginations of the prophets who ascribe to them the voices they hear or the visual appearances they see.

28 The passages Strauss cites for the former of the two allegedly contradictory propositions are: TTP i.1–4,6–7,22–23,25; and xv.22,26–27,44 (with vi.65, vii.8–10,78, xi.14–15; xii.21–22, xiii.6–8,20, xvi.53–56, 61,64 for comparison); and those cited for the latter are TTP v.49; xiii.17, xiv.38; and xv.21,23,42 (with iv.20 and vii.72 for comparison).

29 I have examined elsewhere how Spinoza derives *Ethics* 5p23, and defended its validity, given his axioms, in Donagan 1988: 191–200. Strictly, it is not part of his theology.

9 Spinoza and Bible scholarship

Spinoza is usually considered one of the creators of modern Biblical scholarship and Biblical criticism because of the views about the Bible that he expressed in the *Theological-Political Treatise* and in some of his letters. In this chapter I shall briefly indicate a way in which Spinoza's views might have developed, then present what his views are, and compare and contrast them with those of some of his contemporaries. Finally I will try to evaluate the extent of his originality.

The usual picture of Spinoza's development is taken from what appears in "the oldest biography," attributed to one Jean-Maximillien Lucas; in the *Life of Spinoza* by Johann Colerus; and from occasional remarks by Spinoza. Spinoza is seen as being born into, and growing up in, a rigid orthodox Jewish community in Amsterdam. He studied in the school of the Portuguese Jewish Synagogue. As a youth he began questioning some of what he was being taught, and by 1655 was rejecting the theological assumptions of the Jewish community, and the views of his teachers, the rabbis of Amsterdam. In July 1656 he was excommunicated, charged with holding outrageous beliefs and execrable practices.[1]

From what we now know about the community, the traditional account has to be taken with many grains of salt. The community was not a typical orthodox Jewish one, but rather an amazingly atypical one. Most of its members had been raised in Spain and Portugal as Catholics, and fled to Amsterdam because of persecution by the Inquisition. They were originally *Marranos*, so-called secret Jews, the descendants of forced converts who secretly maintained some aspects of Judaism, usually just a spiritualized Judaism with minimal practices (since any overt practices could lead to Inquisi-

383

tion punishment). The community at the time of Spinoza had unified into one group with its own school to teach the young, the
adult, and the old the rudiments of Judaism. Since almost all of the
members of the community had been raised in Christian countries,
and were educated in Christian schools, many had a minimal knowledge of Judaism and its practices. Very, very few of the group knew
any Hebrew.[2]

From records of the Synagogue, which only became available after
World War II, after they were recovered by the Dutch government
from enormous thefts by the Nazis, we now know that the school
tried to teach the Bible, some rudimentary Hebrew, Jewish history
and beliefs, and Jewish answers to Christian conversionist arguments. Some of its leading teachers, Menasseh ben Israel, Judah
Leon, and Isaac Aboab, translated prayers, prayer books, parts of the
Bible, and other essential items into Spanish, the learned language of
most of the members.

Because few members had really carried on many Jewish practices
in Spain and Portugal, and knew only fragmentarily about what the
practices were, people had to be taught them. When the practices
were too arduous (such as adult circumcision) or in conflict with
people's beliefs, some kind of explanation had to be offered.
Menasseh ben Israel's first great work, *The Conciliator*, which appeared in Spanish and Latin in 1633, attempted to show how to
explain apparent conflicts of passages in the Bible using Jewish,
Christian, and ancient Greek philosophical materials. The work is
not a typical work of Jewish apologetics. There is not much like it in
Jewish literature, because it is written in the special context of Amsterdam, where people had no Jewish background, and found all
kinds of difficulties in understanding what they were supposed to
do, and what they were supposed to believe.

We know that from at least 1617 onward there were troublemak-
ers in the community, people who refused to accept the views of the
rabbis as to what constituted Judaism or its practices. First one David Farrar, and then Uriel da Costa, challenged the official views.
They were both excommunicated from the Amsterdam Synagogue.
Without going into their cases, what is of interest is that especially
in Da Costa's case, he appealed to literalism about the Biblical text,
and to a rational reading of the text, against the rabbinical readings.[3]

The usual and traditional body of learning that Jewish children acquire, studying the Bible and the Talmud in the original languages, was beyond what was carried on in Amsterdam. Neither the teachers nor the students knew enough Hebrew or Aramaic. The main texts had first to be translated into Spanish. The traditional Bible interpreters, Rashi, Kimchi, Abarbenel, Aben Ezra, and so forth, were usually known only in fragments at best, by those who did not know enough Hebrew. And the rabbis, except for Menasseh and chief rabbi Morteira, did not know enough about traditional Judaism to answer complex and deep questions.[4]

In this milieu, young Spinoza, of the first generation of students born as Jews (not as secret Jews, Marranos) in Amsterdam, attended school. Spinoza knew Hebrew. He seems to have been a star student. At some time, undatable, he began to have questions about what he was being taught, questions about the content of the Bible, about the status of the Bible, and about Jewish explanations. In the *Theological-Political Treatise* he says that "I have been educated from boyhood in the accepted beliefs concerning the Bible," namely that Moses was the author of the Pentateuch, and that the Bible is the Word of God.[5] By 1655 there are indications that Spinoza, and some others (Juan de Prado and Daniel Ribera) were raising questions about the status of the Bible and its contents.[6] When requested to apologize, and be quiet, Spinoza refused. He was apparently offered a large sum of money just to keep his views to himself, and to appear a few times a year at the Synagogue. By the time of the excommunication he had moved out of the Jewish community, and into the world of the radical nondenominational Protestants. When and how he met them, whether through his Latin teacher, van den Enden, through the business he and his brother were engaged in, or through the presence of these Protestants, including Quakers, in the Synagogue, we do not know.[7]

The excommunication statement accuses Spinoza of holding to abominable heresies, but does not name any. Spinoza apparently wrote an answer in Spanish, that existed at the time of his death in 1677. This may have included the basis of the analysis of the Bible that appeared in the *Theological-Political Treatise*.

In terms of the history of Bible scholarship and Biblical criticism, one of Spinoza's main points, that Moses is not the author of the Pentateuch, is central in the reconsideration of what the Bible is, and how it should be read and interpreted.

Spinoza said, "To treat the matter in logical order, I shall first deal with misconceptions regarding the true authorship of the Sacred Books, beginning with the Pentateuch. The author is almost universally believed to be Moses, a view so obstinately defended by the Pharisees that they have regarded any other view as a heresy" (TTP viii.161).

Spinoza then mentioned that Aben Ezra, a medieval Spanish rabbi (1092–1167) who wrote an important commentary on the Bible, "a man of enlightened mind and considerable learning . . . was the first, as far as I know, to call attention to this misconception." He "did not venture to explain his meaning openly, and expressed himself somewhat obscurely" (TTP viii.161–2). Spinoza's evidence for denying the Mosaic authorship is a version of what Aben Ezra had offered.

To appreciate what Spinoza was stating, it may help to review the state of the question in the mid–seventeenth century. There had been an immense amount of scholarship regarding the Bible in the two hundred years before Spinoza. The Jewish Bible commentators were discovered by Christian scholars and were edited and studied, and used in Christian commentaries. The existing manuscripts of the Bible in many languages were carefully examined and studied. New editions of the Bible occurred, sometimes offering very important textual changes (as in Erasmus's edition of the New Testament, omitting the line stating the doctrine of the Trinity).

Aben Ezra was recognized as an important commentator by Christian and Jewish scholars. In fact he was the favorite Jewish commentator, the one who was studied most, for Christian exegetes.[8] In his commentary on *Deuteronomy*, he had pointed out that Moses could not have written the passage in *Deuteronomy* 33 about the death of Moses, and what happened thereafter. Aben Ezra did not make any drastic claims about what this indicated about the authorship question. Rather he suggested that the post-Mosaic and non-Mosaic verses probably had some special status and meaning. (There is nothing to suggest Spinoza's view that he was a pre-Spinoza Spinozist.)[9] His commentary on the Pentateuch was one of the major ones read during the late Middle Ages and thereafter. It was first published in the late fifteenth century. It also appears alongside the Hebrew text in the Venetian Bomberg edition of the Old Testament, published first in 1546, and reprinted a few times thereafter. His views were known to Christian and Jewish Scripture scholars. They are cited in the very widely read *Scrutiny of the Scriptures*, by Pablo de Santa

Maria, Bishop of Burgos, and formerly rabbi of Burgos (Paulus Burgensis). The work was of great importance in making Jewish exegesis known to Christian readers, and was a much studied controversial work by both Christians and Jews.[10]

In Reformation literature about the Old Testament, the news that Moses did not write the passage about his own death was accepted by Andraes von Karlstadt. Martin Luther agreed that this portion of the text had been added by another hand. But he held that Moses was the author of the material up to that point. Luther dismissed incipient skepticism about the Mosaic authorship by saying "it does no harm to say that the Pentateuch could not have been written by Moses" (Greenslade 1963: 7,87). Various late-sixteenth-century commentaries, using Aben Ezra, showed that there were difficulties in assuming the Mosaic authorship of the Pentateuch (Greenslade 1963: 92).

One finds in various Christian commentaries of the seventeenth century, that when the author got to the passage about the death of Moses, the commentator just said that this passage was not written by Moses, but probably by Joshua. And then, we are told, the passage about the death of Joshua was also written by somebody else. The commentators did not seem to see this as a special or difficult problem, even though it was accepted by them that Moses was the author of the Pentateuch.

To indicate how accepted the view was that Moses did not write the Moses death scene, I will cite from standard commentaries. The great English Hebraist, John Lightfoot, said in 1647, "The last Chapter of the Booke was written by some other than *Moses*; for it retaleth his death and, and how he was buryed by the Lord" (Lightfoot 1647: 79); John Richardson, Bishop of Ardagh in Ireland said in 1655, "The last Chapter of Deuteronomie was written after *Moses'* death. As likewise the Conclusion of the Book of *Jeremie* was written after his death" (Richardson 1655).[11]

There were some efforts to offer a way in which Moses could have written the passage about his own death. God could have told him what was going to happen. A medieval *Midrash* even has Moses weeping about what God had told him, and writing these lines in his own tears.[12] However, Simon Patrick, Bishop of Ely, in his *A Commentary upon the Fifth Book of Moses, called Deuteronomy*, in his note to Chapter 4, says that the verses were "not written at the same time with the rest of the Book," because of the account of Moses' death and burial, "unless we suppose *Moses* to have given an account of his own Death and Burial by the Spirit of Prophecy, which is not probable." So Bishop Patrick calmly offered the possibility that the passage was most likely by Samuel, "who was a Prophet and wrote by Divine Authority, what he found in the Records which were left by Joshua" (Patrick 1700: 678–9).

The importance of maintaining the Mosaic authorship is that it was the supposed guarantee of the truth of the text. Moses received the text directly from God. According to the Westminster Confession of 1658 (a statement of the leading English Protestants), God guaranteed the transmission of His Message to Moses and preserved the Mosaic text perfectly in all transmissions from then on.[13] A recent review in the *New York Times* of Harold Bloom's *The Book of J* states, "Strict religious tradition, of course, states that the Hebrew Pentateuch was given directly by God to Moses. In this sense, any notion that the first five books of the Bible were written and revised by men or women over the centuries is heretical to strict believers, as much biblical scholarship is."[14]

From what appears in various commentaries, the recognition that Moses was not the author of a few lines in *Deuteronomy* did not constitute much of a problem for believers. They accepted the text as Divine Revelation, the Word of God, given in most part to Moses by God. The recognition of non-Mosaic lines only began to have serious and severe repercussions in the 1650s, in the writings of Thomas Hobbes, Isaac La Peyrère, Samuel Fisher, and then Spinoza. All seem to have gotten their view about the lines directly or indirectly from Aben Ezra.

There was also a low-brow rabble-rousing kind of Bible criticism offered by untutored people during the Puritan Revolution. There were Ranters and Levellers and Seekers who rejected the Bible as the work of nasty oppressive priests. These radicals looked for all sorts of reasons to justify rejecting the Bible, and found all of the obvious problems that learned Bible scholars were to dwell upon, including the claim that Moses could not have written about his own death.[15]

What has been taken as the first intellectual statement of the questioning of the Mosaic authorship of Scripture is in Thomas Hobbes's *Leviathan*, Book III, Chapter xxxiii. Hobbes pointed out that there is no sufficient testimony in Holy Scripture or elsewhere to assure us about who were the writers of the various books. "[F]or the *Pentateuch*, it is not argument enough that they were written by Moses, because they are called the five Books of *Moses*" (Hobbes 1947: 247–8). He then pointed out the problem in the last chapter of *Deuteronomy* about Moses' death. First Hobbes considered the minimal interpretation of this, namely that everything in the *Pentateuch* was written by Moses except for this chapter. He concluded that this would not work because *Genesis* 12:6, and *Numbers* 21:14, refer to events after the time of Moses. From this Hobbes made the sweeping judgment that "It is therefore sufficiently evident, that the five Books of Moses were written after his time, though how long after it be not so manifest" (Hobbes 1947: 248).

Hobbes then settled for a modest revisionist view. "But though Moses did not compile those books entirely, and in the form we have them; yet he wrote all that which he is there said to have written" (Hobbes 1947: 248). So, Hobbes retained the Mosaic authorship of some of Scripture. He applied his analysis to other books of the Bible, and questioned the usual authorship attributions.

What gave the whole text its guarantee and authority? If it has not been revealed to us that the text is God's word, then the acceptance of the text, and the acquiescence to it, is from the authority of the commonwealth. Hobbes made the question a political one for those who have not had a personal supernatural revelation. And for Hobbes it was the sovereign church, the Church of England, that then declared what was Scripture, and what one should do about it. It is obvious in the chapter that Hobbes was concerned to rule out the disruptive force of private interpreters, such as those who had taken over England, and to reinforce the role of the state's political Church as the arbiter, even of the question of what book is Scripture, and who wrote it.

A contemporary, who was probably an acquaintance of Hobbes, presented a more far-reaching examination of the problem of the Mosaic authorship. Isaac La Peyrère, 1596–1677, the secretary of the Prince of Condé, composed a work in 1640–1 justifying his French Messianic expectation that the King of France would rule the world with the Messiah, who would appear at any moment. Most of La Peyrère's book was suppressed, and only known in manuscript until it was published in Amsterdam in 1655, under the title *Prae-Adamitae* (*Men before Adam*). La Peyrère was a Calvinist from Bor-

deaux, probably of Marrano background. In Paris he was part of the
Mersenne circle (which Hobbes also belonged to) and was known to
many *érudits*. He traveled on business to the Netherlands, to Scandi-
navia, Spain, and England. He was friendly with many of Hobbes's
associates. In 1654 the recently abdicated Queen Christina of Sweden persuaded La Peyrère to publish his manuscript in Holland, and
she probably paid for the printing of it. It quickly appeared in five
Latin editions in the Netherlands and Switzerland, an English edition, and a Dutch one. The work was soon banned and burned all
over Europe, as scandalous, blasphemous, and Godless, and the author was incarcerated in Belgium until he agreed to apologize personally to the Pope, and to become a Catholic.[16]

In order to justify his revised reading of the Bible, La Peyrère
questioned whether we have an accurate copy, and whether we can
be sure who wrote the document we have. After discussing the passage about Moses' death, plus quite a few other passages that appeared to relate to events after Moses, La Peyrère pointed out that
some other books are mentioned in the Bible, which were apparently
the sources of the surviving text. He hypothesized that Moses may
have kept a diary, and that that was one of the several sources.
However, what has come down to us is a compilation of diverse
materials, a "heap of copie of copie" (La Peyrère 1656: 204–5). La
Peyrère did not question whether the "real" Bible was the Word of
God. But he did question whether the confused and mixed-up text
that we now have, with thousands of variants in the different manuscripts, was accurate. He learned personally from experts such as
Louis Cappel, Andre Rivet, Claude Saumaise, and Isaac Vossius
what the problems were in deciding what was the correct text. What
was needed was to reconstruct the actual original message from
what we now possess.

A further heretical claim of La Peyrère was that the Bible is not
the history of mankind, but is just the history of the Jews. All sorts
of evidence indicated that there were men before Adam. Some of the
evidence was found in the Bible. Who was Cain's wife? The only
people mentioned in the Bible up to the point where Cain took a
wife were Adam, Eve, and their sons, Abel and Cain. Cain killed
Abel, was driven out of Eden, and then married. But married whom?
La Peyrère said the wife must have been a pre-Adamite, whose lin-
eage was outside the Adamic framework. (Commentaries of the

time take note of the question, and offer the answer that Cain married a sister, who had not been named in the text.[17]) Some of the evidence came from ancient history, some from the Voyages of Discovery. According to La Peyrère, mankind has existed for an indefinite length of time, living in a state of nature that was nasty, brutish, and short. (His description is almost the same as Hobbes's.) God, to improve the situation, created Adam, and through him, the Jews, who had a Providential destiny, that was about to be fulfilled with the coming of the Jewish Messiah, who would rule the world with the King of France, and save everyone, Adamite, and pre-Adamite.

La Peyrère made radical suggestions about the Biblical message, but still seemed to insist that there was a most important supernatural message. He said he was only offering a hypothesis that reconciled the text with all of the other known information. One of his last efforts was the preparation of a French Bible with notes, a text that was suppressed before publication. It has a long footnote when Adam is first mentioned in *Genesis* to the effect that there is a theory that has been declared heretical by the Pope, but which says . . . , and the evidence for it is. . . .[18]

La Peyrère was not just a nut-case. He was known to many of the leading Bible scholars of the time. His book was very widely read. Spinoza had a copy and used it extensively in his own presentation in the *Theological-Political Treatise*.[19] Rabbi Menasseh ben Israel knew La Peyrère personally (and became a supporter of his French Messianism).[20] He was planning to debate him in Amsterdam, and he wrote an answer which has disappeared. La Peyrère was in Amsterdam for six months in 1655 while his book was being published. The book is dedicated to all the synagogues of the world. He was there during the period when Spinoza seems to have become disillusioned with the views of the Synagogue. Some of La Peyrère's views appear in the charges against Spinoza's associates of the time, Juan de Prado and Daniel Ribera. It is claimed by one of La Peyrère's opponents that he established a sect of "pre-Adamites" in Amsterdam in 1655. Nobody has been able to find who this group was, but it may have included Spinoza and his friends.[21]

From Hobbes to La Peyrère there is an increasingly forceful questioning of whether Moses can have been the author of all of Scripture, and whether we have an accurate text. A further strong challenge appeared in the work of the Quaker Bible scholar, Samuel

Fisher, 1605–65. Fisher was one of the few early Quakers who had a university background. He had graduated from Oxford, where he learned Hebrew. Then he became a Baptist minister. In 1654 he became a Quaker. He took the message of the Quakers to Jewish communities in Amsterdam, Germany, and Italy, and held long discussions with Jewish leaders wherever he went.

When he returned to England in 1660, he wrote his 900-page answer to the Puritan contention that Scripture is the Word of God, *The Rustic's Alarm to the Rabbies,* combining the popular English Bible criticism with his own learned case (Fisher 1660). Christopher Hill has called Fisher "the most radical Bible critic of the time" (Hill 1980: 259–68).

The question of the Mosaic authorship comes up in a marginal note questioning whether Moses could have written the passage about his own death. But for Fisher there are two central questions, one whether the text that we possess is an accurate version of the ancient Hebrew or Greek text, and the other, whether a written document, written sometime in human history, can be the Word of God.

On the first point Fisher brought up two central problems. One was that of whether there is any basis for calling the particular collection of documents that have come down to us "Scripture," and the other whether these documents have been passed down to us in exact copies of the originals. Scholars knew the history of the Old Testament canon, as reported in Josephus's *History of the Jews,* and in the Talmud, namely that a rabbinical council, either in Ezra's time, or around 300 B.C., decided which texts were canonical. Fisher challenged the reliability of such a human decision to have determined which texts were revealed ones, and stressed that there were more books available than those now bound in the Bible. Why are only the included books "Scripture"?

Fisher spent an inordinate amount of time on the second point, the transmission problem. The Westminster Confession of 1658 had declared that the text had been transmitted exactly and that God had guaranteed and protected the text. But then what about all of the thousands of variants in different manuscripts? Fisher learned from various Jewish and Christian authorities, including Elias Levita, Louis Cappel, Christian Ravius, and the Buxtorfs, that Hebrew vowel markings did not exist in the original Bible, and were introduced much later. Therefore the text has changed, and we do not possess an exact fixed text of God's Word. None of the manuscripts now existing is a holograph manuscript written by Moses, by any of the Prophets, or by Ezra. The manuscripts we have are copies of copies of copies, made by fallible human beings. And they are not only fallible, they are also people of dubious reliability. The earliest manuscripts were made by stiff-necked Jews who refused to see the Light, and the later ones were made by corrupt Catholic monks. Now what we have is what greedy printers decide is the text. (All of these points can be raised as well about New Testament texts.)

The upshot for Fisher is that one cannot tell whether a given manuscript or book contains the Word of God exact and entire, unless one knows *independently* what the Word of God is. The Word of God presumably existed before any attempt was made to write it down. It was known before Moses by Adam, Noah, Abraham, Isaac, Jacob, and so forth, none of whom had a copy. It was even known to Moses *before* he supposedly wrote it down. Fisher rushed further to a form of Quaker universalism. The Word of God can be known anywhere at any time in any language – why should it only be stateable in Hebrew and Greek?[22]

Fisher was in Amsterdam for around six months in 1657–8, before he left for Rome and Constantinople to try to convert the Pope and the Sultan. He attended Synagogue services, and spent lots of time trying to convince members of the community of the Quaker message. He was then also translating two pamphlets by Margaret Fell, the mother of the Quakers, into Hebrew, to try to convert the Jews. I have offered evidence elsewhere that Spinoza, after his excommunication, became involved with the Quakers, and that he joined with Samuel Fisher in translating the pamphlets.[23] If this was the case, Fisher and Spinoza could easily have shared their views about the Biblical text. Spinoza, in the *Theological-Political Treatise*, expressly set forth the thesis that the Word of God is not a physical object. The Word of God would remain and be recognizable even if all physical books disappeared. For Fisher the Word would be recognized by the Spirit or Light within, for Spinoza by reason.

This leads to the last antecedent Biblical theory leading up to Spinoza's, that of the Socinians and rationalists. Spinoza's close friend and doctor, Lodewijk Meyer, published a work shortly before the *Theological-Political Treatise* on the philosophical reading of the Scripture, in which he advocated the need to employ reason as the judge of what Scripture said and meant (Meyer 1666).[24] A view like this had been developing for a century from the skeptical reformer, Sebastian Castellio, and from Faustus Socinus. The latter, whose followers were the Socinians or Unitarians of the seventeenth century, insisted on a literal reading of Scripture, and a rational assessment of what it said. The Socinians' great heresy was to contend that Scripture does not state the doctrine of the Trinity, and that a rational reading of the text denies that Jesus is of the same substance as God the Father. But the Socinians up to Spinoza's time insisted that they recognized Jesus as central to their religion, as the Lamb of God, as God's messenger to man, the most special member of the human race, and that their religion was based on Scripture taken in its most literal sense. It was only at the same time as the *Theological-Political Treatise* appeared that the Socinian leader, Wiszowaty (Socinus's grandson), offered the most radical view that reason should not only be the measure of one's religious belief, but should be the source of it.[25] Spinoza knew Socinians, must have mingled with them at Collegiant gatherings, and he had some of their literature in his library.[26]

To examine Spinoza's own statement of his views about the Bible in the *Theological-Political Treatise*, let us start with what he said about the authorship of the text. Chapter viii has the title, "*In which it is shown that the Pentateuch and the Books of Joshua, Judges, Ruth, Samuel and Kings were not written by themselves. The question of their authorship is considered. Was there one author, or several, and who were they.*" Spinoza stated that to treat the matter in a logical order, he began with the views of Aben Ezra about the Mosaic authorship. He quoted from Aben Ezra's commentary on *Deuteronomy* (which appears in the Bomberg Bible, to which Spinoza specifically refers in Chapter ix). Then Spinoza said, "In these few words he [Aben Ezra] gives a clear indication that it was not Moses who wrote the Pentateuch but someone else who lived long after him, and that it was a different book that Moses wrote" (TTP viii.162). Next Spinoza broke down Aben Ezra's case to six points: (1) the preface to Deuteronomy could not have been written by Moses; (2) the *Book of Moses* must have been much smaller than the Pentateuch; (3) where Moses is talked of in the third person, as in *Deuteronomy* 31:9, the words "must be those of another writer narrating the deeds and writings of Moses"; (4) *Genesis* 12:6, about the land of Canaan, must have been written after the death of Moses; (5) *Genesis* 22:14, about where the Temple was to be built, must be post-Moses, for Moses does not indicate any position as chosen by God, but just foretells that God will sometime choose the place; and (6) in *Deuteronomy* 3 some texts have been added long after the time of Moses.

Spinoza then added a list of other texts which he contended also could not be by Moses. His list contains many that appear in La Peyrère and in Fisher as well. From texts in *Deuteronomy* 29 and 31, Spinoza (and La Peyrère) claimed that Moses actually wrote a small book explaining the Mosaic laws, called the *Book of the Law of God*, to which Joshua later added an account of the covenant by which his contemporaries bound themselves (*Joshua* 24:25–26). No book now exists that looks like this. "We may therefore conclude that the book of the Law of God which Moses wrote was not the Pentateuch, but a quite different book which the author of the Pentateuch inserted in proper order in his own work, and this conclusion follows on the clearest evidence" (TTP viii.166). On the next page, Spinoza announced that "since there are many passages in the Pentateuch that could not have been written by Moses, it follows that there are no grounds for holding Moses to be the author of the Pentateuch, and that such an opinion is quite contrary to reason" (TTP viii.167). Spinoza then examined the text and offered a theory of how the work could have been put together by a historian post-Moses.

All of this might make Spinoza just a more extreme evaluator of the Biblical text. Aben Ezra had just said that Moses did not write the entire Pentateuch, and gave some texts that he suggested were not by Moses. Various commentators have pointed out that Aben Ezra did not draw any heretical conclusions from this.[27] Hobbes extended this and said that Moses should only be considered the author of the texts which are said to be by him. La Peyrère separated the finished text from a possible Mosaic text. Fisher cast more doubts on the authorship. But all of them held in some sense that the text, regardless of how it came to be, should be taken as the Word of God. (Fisher would require that it be recognized as such by the Spirit or Light.) Other commentators who noticed some of the problems cited by these critics, and who shrugged them off by saying Joshua wrote that, and Samuel wrote that, and so forth, were convinced that the entire text was inspired and written by men who were inspired by God. Hence the petty difficulty that Moses could not have written line x did not matter, if the author was also in contact with God.

Hobbes began the next line of Biblical criticism by asking "from whence the Scriptures derive their authority?" It is believed, he said, "on all hands, that the first and original *author* of them is God." This is not what is in dispute. One can only know what is God's word if God has revealed this supernaturally. Where this has not occurred, as in the case of most people, then a political authority has to settle this question for people. And so Hobbes, not denying the Divine status of Scripture, lets the Church of England decide what text is Scripture (Hobbes 1947: 245–55).

La Peyrère, in apologizing to the Pope, said he was led to his heresies by his Calvinist upbringing. He had been taught that where there were conflicting views, he was to appeal to his own reason to decide. Since he found Scripture to be a mass of conflicting texts, he felt free to offer his own hypothesis about how the text came to be what it is. He said that he was like Copernicus. He was not changing anything in nature, but just offering a different way of looking at it (La Peyrère 1663).[28] In his novel hypothesis, the present Scriptural text was seen as a mess that needed to be reconstructed and deciphered. The messy aspect could be explained by human history, but behind it was a divine message.

Spinoza said, as he began his examination of Scripture, that to avoid confusion, theological prejudice and "the hasty acceptance of human fabrications as divine teachings," we need the true method of Scriptural interpretation. "Now to put it briefly, I hold that the method of interpreting Scripture is no different from the method of interpreting Nature, and is in fact in complete accord with it." We should allow "no other principles or data for the interpretation of Scripture and study of its contents except those that can be gathered only from Scripture itself and from a historical study of Scripture" (TTP, vii.141). In saying this, Spinoza began a quite different way of examining and evaluating Scriptural texts than his predecessors employed. The literalism and the contextualism led to a completely secular reading of the Bible. For Spinoza, one had to examine and study the language of the Biblical authors: the way the language was used, the circumstances under which the books were written, including the intentions of the authors. This kind of study, as conceived by Spinoza, placed the Scripture clearly inside human history.

Even in this Spinoza was not completely original. As a result of all the discoveries of different kinds of religions all over the planet, and of the myriad varieties of ancient religions, a kind of anthropology of religion began to be developed in the seventeenth century. Its form, pre-Spinoza, as stated at great length by such eminent scholars as Gerard Vossius of Leiden and Amsterdam in his *Origins of Gentile Theology*, of 1641 (reprinted several times in the seventeenth century, and studied and used by Hugo Grotius, Herbert of Cherbury, Ralph Cudworth, and Isaac Newton), was to account for polytheism as a historical development from an original natural and revealed religion. The ancient Hebrews first presented a natural religion in the form of the several principles of Noah (the Noachide laws), and later, with Moses, presented a revealed religion as well. All other religions, according to Vossius, derive from, and are degenerate forms of, this Ur-religion. Some of the degenerate elements got into later Judaism and Christianity (and account for some of the corruptions in Scripture). Through most careful philological and historical studies, scholars can reconstruct the development of religion from its natural beginning to its many manifestations today. This historical reconstruction places most religious developments in historical human contexts, political, social, economic, military, and so on.

Spinoza went somewhat further, in assessing the first alleged inspired religious teachers, the prophets of ancient Israel. Crucial reasons for this appear in the earlier chapters of the *Theological-Political Treatise*, in which so-called divine inspiration is analyzed into a form of strictly human manic-depression, and so-called divine history, or Providential history, is analyzed into local political history of the early Hebrews. Their peculiar situation after the escape from Egypt put them into a situation where they were without laws. Moses gave them laws, and called them God's laws to make sure that the early Hebrews would obey them.

The *Theological-Political Treatise* begins with an examination of what prophecy and prophetic inspiration can mean. Spinoza questioned whether the prophets could have known something different from what can be known by ordinary persons through reason and experience. It could not be mathematical knowledge, or knowledge of empirical facts. As Spinoza examined the matter, he decided that there is no special knowledge that the prophets possessed, but rather that the prophets had a more vivid imagination than ordinary people.

The Cambridge Platonists in England, just before Spinoza, had been attempting to define "divine inspiration" clearly and carefully, so that it could be completely distinguished from "enthusiasm," which Henry More defined as a belief that one is divinely inspired when one is in fact not so.[29] The Quakers, whom the Cambridge Platonists considered the worst kind of enthusiasts, had to try to explain how they could be sure they were expressing the Word of God, and others were not.

Whether Spinoza knew of these discussions (and some evidence suggests he did),[30] he contended that the prophets did not offer special knowledge claims that other people could not know by other means, but offered vivid accounts of their imaginings. To understand what prophets were saying and why they were saying it in the way that they did, one had to employ Spinoza's contextualistic method of reading the Bible.

Spinoza claimed that there were some works which were self-explanatory. The concepts employed were clear, the reasoning obvious, so that no more information was needed to understand them. The example offered of such a work was Euclid's *Elements*. Spinoza declared that the reader did not need to know Greek, did not need to know Euclid's personal autobiography, did not need to know the state of affairs under which he wrote:

Euclid, whose writings are concerned only with things exceedingly simple and perfectly intelligible, is easily made clear by anyone in any language; for in order to grasp his thought and be assured of his true meaning there is no need to have a thorough knowledge of the language in which he wrote. A superficial and rudimentary knowledge is enough. Nor need we enquire into the author's life, pursuits, and character, the language in which he wrote, and for whom and when; nor what happened to his book, nor its different readings, nor how it came to be accepted and by what council. And what we here say of Euclid can be said of all who have written of matters which of their nature are capable of intellectual apprehension. (TTP vii.154)

In contrast "Scripture does not provide us with definitions of the things of which it speaks" (TTP vii.142). In order for us to figure out what is being said, we have to look into the nature and properties of the language in which the Bible is written. We have to see how the Biblical authors use this language. And we have to find out the circumstances relevant to all of the books of the prophets that have come down to us, including knowledge of the life, character, and pursuits of the author of each book. This includes finding out who each author was, when and for whom he wrote the book, how the book was revised, and who decided that it is sacred.

All of this contextualism could be compatible with traditional orthodoxy if one regarded the Biblical texts as divinely inspired. Spinoza insisted that those who contend that the light of reason is inadequate to interpret Scripture, and that a supernatural light is absolutely essential, cannot explain what this supernatural light is (TTP vii.155). They cannot make clear what this supposed supernatural light is supposed to be. The explanations that they offer are remarkably similar to natural ones, "their explanations are human, the fruit of long thought, and elaborately devised" (TTP vii.155). If the supernatural light is known only to the faithful, then what about the fact that the prophets were also preaching to the unbelievers and the impious? Could the audience have understood what was being said, if they did not have any supernatural light? Spinoza concluded his discussion by saying "those who look to a supernatural light to understand the meaning of the prophets and the apostles are sadly in need of the natural light, and so I can hardly think that such men possess a divine supernatural gift" (TTP vii.155).

Thus, having excluded any supernatural or divine element in the Biblical text, Spinoza's contextualism took on a radically different form than those before and after him who used similar materials to elucidate what they took to be a divinely inspired text. For Spinoza the meaning of what was related in Scripture was to be found, and exhausted, in elucidating the linguistic formulation, the historical context, and the personality of the Biblical author.

In terms of this, Spinoza saw that the central part of the Pentateuch, the receiving and acceptance of the Ten Commandments and the Mosaic law by the Jews, was to be understood in terms of the circumstances of the time. The ancient Hebrews had just escaped from Egypt, and from Egyptian law. They were then in a lawless world, a state of nature. Moses fortunately rescued them from that state of affairs by giving them new laws, and making them accept the laws by clothing them in divine terms. Thus the ancient Hebrew theocracy was established. This explains what happened at the great episode at Mount Sinai, and accounts for the Jews setting up a new state under these laws.

On Spinoza's reading, the ceremonial laws of this theocracy can be understood in terms of the conditions of the time, and the beliefs of the time. But these laws are not binding in different times and different conditions. The only universally binding law is the moral law, binding because it is rationally derived rather than historically accepted.

Spinoza's explanation is like that offered by Machiavelli and Hobbes of how pagan religions developed, and gained their authority. The political explanation of religion was being offered in the mid–seventeenth century for all cases other than Judaism and true Christianity. (Reformers explained the rise and power of Roman Catholicism in political terms, and some Catholics did the same for the Reformation.) In 1656, Henry Oldenburg, who was to become Spinoza's most important friend outside of the Netherlands, wrote from Oxford to Adam Boreel, the leader of the Collegiants, the group Spinoza joined after his excommunication in the same year, to tell Boreel that a theory was being offered to the effect that Moses, Jesus, and Mahomet were impostors, political intriguers, who gained power by foisting a new religion on people. (This is, of course, the thesis of the notorious clandestine work, *Les Trois Imposteurs, ou l'Esprit de M/ Spinosa*, published in the early eighteenth century, but written in the latter part of the seventeenth century.)[31]

Oldenburg did not identify who was offering this theory. But he beseeched Boreel to write an answer in order to save religion. Boreel over the next several years wrote an as-yet-unpublished response entitled *Jesus Christ Legislator of the Human Race.*[32]

It seems likely that this project – the largest undertaking in Boreel's career, his answer to unbelievers as well as to Jews and Moslems – would be known to those in the Collegiant movement that he headed, including Spinoza. I think that some of Spinoza's remarks about Jesus in the *Theological-Political Treatise* make sense as an alternative to Boreel's thesis that Jesus is the universal law-giver.[33]

In Chapter iv, Spinoza said that,

With regard to Christ, although he also appears to have laid down laws in God's name, we must maintain that he perceived things truly and adequately; for Christ was not so much the prophet as the mouthpiece of God. It was through the mind of Christ . . . that God made revelations to mankind just as he once did through angels . . . Christ was sent to teach not only the Jews but the entire human race . . . God revealed himself to Christ, or to Christ's mind, directly, and not through words and images as in the case of the prophets. . . . Christ perceived truly, or understood, what was revealed.

Christ, then, perceived truly and adequately the things revealed to him; so if ever he proclaimed these things as law, he did so because of people's ignorance and obstinacy. (TTP iv.108–109)

Spinoza insisted that Christ did not introduce any new laws, and even doubted that Christ introduced any ceremonies (TTP v.119).[34] He pronounced the divine moral law. And, "He who firmly believes that God, out of the mercy and grace with which He directs all things, forgives men's sins, from the mercy and grace whereby he directs all things, and whose heart is thereby more inspired by love of God, that man verily knows Christ according to the spirit and Christ is in him" (TTP xiv.225).

These, and many other passages about Jesus Christ in Spinoza have provoked much discussion, even learned tomes.[35] If Spinoza was supposed to be an atheist, could these express a serious view? If Spinoza had a Jewish upbringing, could he ever have strayed so far as to be a believing Christian? (We know he never joined any Christian organization, though he was buried in the yard of a Christian church.)

Jewish readers often ask me: Why? Who is he trying to kid? Did he have to say such things to please the censor, or the audience? They assume that he could not have been serious or sincere.

I cannot here prove the opposite, but I will suggest that what Spinoza said about Christ makes sense as an alternative to Boreel's view, and as an expression of Socinian and Quaker views about Christ that Spinoza could have accepted without committing himself to any supernatural view. For Spinoza, unlike Boreel, Christ was not a law-giver, nor was he an impostor, but was God's spokesperson. In this he offered a view close to that of the Socinians in Holland of the time, and a Christology like theirs, in making Christ of a different order than Moses and the prophets in relation to God, *without* attributing any Divine substance or features to Christ. To "know Christ according to the spirit, and to have Christ within oneself" was a Quaker expression, in which anyone, Christian, Jew, Moslem, pagan, could have Christ within themselves. Spinoza's patron, Peter Serrarius, said he was sure that the spirit of Christ was within Rabbi Nathan Shapira of Jerusalem, when the rabbi said that he found the Sermon on the Mount was the fount of all wisdom and the expression of the teaching of our greatest rabbis.[36] The Quakers were accused of being non-Christian because of their universalism, and their nonhistorical conception of Christ as the Spirit of God.

Spinoza made it clear that he was not a Christian in many senses in his late correspondence with Oldenburg, when Spinoza said he was willing to accept the historical account in the Gospels except for the Resurrection. Oldenburg told his friend that that tears up Christianity by its roots (Ep 79, 11 February 1676). Spinoza was unimpressed, since for him the essence of Christianity was the golden rule, not the activities of a supernatural being. He, like the Socinians, was willing to accept a superhuman role for Jesus, and like the Quakers saw Christ as the name of the spirit within that made men moral.[37]

Turning now to the larger picture of Spinoza's view of the Bible, what is original and *really* significant? In detail, I have suggested Spinoza was reiterating what both orthodox Bible scholars, and radical ones like Hobbes, La Peyrère, and Samuel Fisher, had already said. His startling examples appear in early writers, and did not lead everyone to see that the Bible was just a human document. As I have indicated, Hobbes and La Peyrère said they believed that there was a Divine Message in the Book, but that it might be harder to find than people expected because of the state of the evidence and the state of the text. Fisher believed one could experience the Word of God, and use it as a measure of the texts presented as Scripture.

Spinoza indicated the crucial new step he had taken in his summation of his evaluation of the Bible in Chapter xii of the *Theological-Political Treatise*. He said, "In the case of both Testaments, the books were not written by express command at one and the same time for all ages" (TTP xii.210). Hobbes, La Peyrère, and Fisher would all agree, as would many orthodox scholars.[38] He went on, "They were the fortuitous work of certain men who wrote according to the requirements of their age and of their own particular character," again a view held by many.

Spinoza began to strike out originally when he next stated that understanding Scripture and the mind of the prophets is "by no means the same thing as to understand the mind of God, that is, to understand truth itself" (TTP xii.210). Understanding Scripture then became a strictly historical enterprise. One had to understand that the books of the Old and New Testaments were selected by groups of men. "But the membership of these councils (both of Pharisees and of Christians) did not consist of prophets, but only of teachers and scholars" (TTP xii.210). Spinoza was willing to put forth a Quakerish sentiment, that these teachers or scholars took the Word of God as their standard, in making their selection. Hence they must have had some idea of the Word of God before they approved the books that went into the canon.

However, and this is all-important, "We have thus shown that it is only in respect of religion – i.e. in respect of the universal divine law – that Scripture can properly be called the Word of God." The rest is historical, to be understood in terms of human causes, psychological, sociological, political, economic, and so forth. In separating the Message – the Word of God, the Divine Law, and the historical Scriptures – Spinoza made the documents themselves of interest only in human terms, and to be explained in human terms. In this he diverged even from the anti-Scripturalism of the Quakers, who lived and breathed the Bible, and spoke through it. They did not take it as the Word of God, but the Word for them was expressed often within it. For Spinoza, the voice of reason, the Word of God, was expressed in it only in the Divine Law.

Looked at from a different angle, Spinoza totally secularized the Bible as a historical document. He could do this because he had a radically different metaphysics, more radical than that of even his most radical contemporaries, a metaphysics for a world without any supernatural dimension. But what he said as a historical scholar (and he really was not much of one, compared to some of his contemporaries)[39] did not imply or prove his naturalist stance. What he said as a historical scholar was interpreted in terms of his historical stance, and became the new Enlightened way of seeing the religious world as a human creation. His immediate successor Father Richard Simon said that he agreed with Spinoza's method but not with his conclusions. Father Simon used inordinate historical researches to try to get to the ur-text, and spawned the industry now known as Higher Criticism. (And perhaps it was Simon's historical and philological details that made Spinoza's claims plausible at the time.) Its practitioners contend that they are still in a supernaturalism of sorts,[40] seeking in scraps of Dead Sea Scrolls, in Gnostic texts, for God's Message to man. Spinoza was baldly willing to claim that the historical scriptures are some men's messages to man. And the worthwhile messages are those that follow from unfettered, unprejudiced reasoning. This rational secularism based on a naturalistic metaphysics is reinforced by the historical analysis of religious writings, rather than based upon them. And it is this new metaphysics (or revived Greek naturalism) that is Spinoza's great contribution, for better or worse, to the making of the modern mind. One may wonder, as I do, why it was so acceptable to a world of thinkers raised on taking supernaturalism seriously. But that is another long, long story.[41]

NOTES

1 See Popkin 1990b, and Biderman and Kasher 1990.

2 The best picture of the community and the background of its members appears in Kaplan 1989.

3 Uriel da Costa wrote a response in Portuguese in 1623 stating his views. It was believed that all copies of this work had been destroyed by the Synagogue at the time of his excommunication. However, Prof. H. P. Salomon has discovered a copy, and has published an edition of it as Da Costa 1993.

4 Little is known of Menasseh's training. He was born in La Rochelle, France, raised in Lisbon, turned up in Amsterdam as a teenager, and was teaching in the synagogue school when he was eighteen. He and rabbi Aboab apparently learned much privately from the Cabbalist, Abraham Cohen Herrera, who lived in Amsterdam but played no role in the community. Menasseh published only one work in Hebrew, and there is some question as to whether it was translated for him.

Morteira was born and raised in the Jewish community in Venice. He left at age thirteen, and went to Paris as secretary to Queen Marie de Medici's doctor, Elijah de Montalto. He was at the Louvre until 1617, when he went to Amsterdam to bury Dr. Montalto, and stayed there.

5 Spinoza, TTP ix.179. All quotations are taken from the translation of Samuel Shirley (Spinoza 1989).

6 See Révah 1964, 1959, 1970–2.

7 There has been a recent discovery of the writings of van den Enden. The texts will be published by Professor Wim Klever of Erasmus University, Rotterdam. He has told me that the texts will show the source of Spinoza's views. The texts postdate Spinoza's excommunication and, Klever tells me, do not deal with Judaism.

8 See Goshen-Gottstein 1989: 34.

9 Zac 1965: 37–9, shows that there is no reason to suspect any heterodoxy in Aben Ezra's views.

10 Some of the answers to Christianity written in Amsterdam specifically direct their attack against claims made by Pablo de Santa Maria.

11 The work says it was perused and attested by the Bishop of Armagh, who was Archbishop Ussher.

12 Amos Funkenstein has pointed out to me that even as far back as the Babylonian Talmud, *Baba Bahia*, mention is made that Moses could not have written about his own death.

13 *Westminster Confession*, London 1658, Chapter 1, page 6: "The Old Testament in Hebrew (which was the Native Language of the People of GOD of old) and the New Testament in Greek (which at the time of the writing of it was generally known to the Nations) being immediately inspired by God, and by his singular care and Providence kept pure in all Ages, are therefore Authentical."

14 Richard Bernstein, in *New York Times*, October 24, 1990, Section C, page 11. Modern commentaries just take it for granted that Joshua or somebody else wrote the lines about Moses' death and what happened thereafter. See Reider 1937: 342; Driver 1973: 417, 535; and Buttrick 1952–7: 535. The latter gives a full "higher critical" gloss. *Deuteronomy* 34: 1–12 is a final appendix to the book in narrative form. "Scholars have long agreed that it was taken from a priestly editor's edition of the old historical sources, JE, which perhaps had been expanded by a Deuteronomic writer, presumably the historian responsible for the books of *Joshua-II Kings*."

15 See Hill 1980.

16 On La Peyrère, see my book, Popkin 1987a.

17 For instance there is a text by George Hughes, a minister at Plymouth, *An Analytical Exposition of the Whole First Book of Moses called Genesis*, 1672, where the answer to the question who was Cain's wife is, "It must surely be one of Adam's daughters; many vain conceits there are that she was a twin born with him, that her name was *Schave*, other *Calmana*; but the scripture is silent of these, therefore no faith can be on them."

18 Copies of this, entitled Michel de Marolles, *Le Livre de Genese*, are in the British Library and the Bibliothèque Nationale.

19 A quite incomplete list of borrowings appears in Strauss 1965.

20 See Popkin 1984a.

21 See Popkin 1987a for details on these matters.

22 On Fisher, see Popkin 1985.

23 See Popkin 1984c, 1987b.

24 A French translation of this work with an important introduction has recently appeared (Meyer 1988) with introduction and notes by Jacqueline Lagrée and Pierre-François Moreau.

25 See Wiszowaty 1980 (published originally in 1685).

26 The Socinian, Christopher Sand, gave him a copy of his work.

27 See, for instance, the discussion in Zac 1965: 37–9.

28 See Popkin 1987a: 15–16.

29 On this, and the view of the Cambridge Platonists about Spinoza, see Hutton 1984.

30 See Hutton 1984.

31 Oldenburg wrote that, according to this horrendous view:

> . . . the whole story of the Creation seems to have been composed in order to introduce the Sabbath, and that from motives of merely political prudence. For to what purpose . . . is the fatiguing labor of so many days assigned to Almighty God, when all things submit to his bidding in a single instant? It seems that that very prudent legislator and ruler, Moses, concocted the whole story on purpose, so that (when he had gained acceptance of it in the minds of his people) one certain day should be set aside on which they should solemnly and publicly worship that invisible Deity; and so that whatever Moses himself should say proceeded from that same Deity they would observe with great humility and reverence. The other problem is that Moses certainly encouraged and excited his people to obey him and to be brave in war by hopes and promises of acquiring rich booty, and ample possessions, and that the man Christ, being more prudent than Moses, enticed his people by the hope of eternal life and happiness though aware that the soul seriously contemplating eternity would scarcely savor what is vile and low. But, Mahommed, cunning in all things, enlisted all men with the good things of this world as well as of the next, and so became their master, and extended the limits of his empire much more widely than did any legislator before or after him. You see what license this critic adopts out of love of reasoning. (Oldenburg 1965–86: 89–92)

32 The manuscript, in confused order, is in the Boyle Papers in the Royal Society of England, Volumes 12, 13, and 15. Henry More knew of the text, from a copy that belonged to Francis Van Helmont.

33 See Popkin 1991.

34 Spinoza's view is like that of some of the Judaizing Socinians, who denied that any religious laws had been changed by Jesus' appearance in the first century. Some of these Judaizers, unlike Spinoza, then kept all the Mosaic laws while being "Christians" of sorts.

35 Such as Matheron 1971.

36 See Popkin 1984b.

37 The early Quakers saw themselves as the Second Coming, the second expression of the Spirit of God on earth. See, for instance, William Penn's *Visitation to the Jews*.

38 For instance, Edward Stillingfleet, Bishop of Worcester, after reading Spinoza's *Theological-Political Treatise* and Richard Simon's *Critical History of the Old Testament*, said:

> The Question is not, whether the Books of Moses were written by himself, or by others according to his Appointments or Direction. It is not, whether the Writings of Moses were preserved free for all literal mistakes, or varieties of Readings in matters of no great consequence. . . . But it is a Question of great weight & moment, & whereon very much depends, whether the Books of Moses contain the genuine Writings or only some Abstracts & Abridgements of them. . . . For then the Certainty of our Faith doth not depend on the Authority of Moses or the Prophets, but on the Credibility of those Persons, who have taken upon them to give out these Abridgements in stead of their Original Writings. (Stillingfleet's notes for a Sermon, 1682/3, published in Reedy 1985: 147)

39 Spinoza cited none of the standard commentaries by Christian scholars that were read by almost everyone in the republic of letters. In his library he had grammars and dictionaries by the Christian Hebraists, but not their expositions or explanations of Scripture. The first to write an answer to the *Theological-Political Treatise*, Regneri à Mansvelt (Mansvelt 1674; written by 1672), lists many experts who worked diligently and carefully on the problems of the Hebrew text but are not mentioned by Spinoza – Drusius, Buxtorf, Fagius, Bochart, Coccocieus, Capell, Selden, Munster, Hottinger, and Scaliger.

40 Consider Bultmann, for example, about what is left of the message when all of the aspects of the text have been demythologized.

41 A version of this paper has also appeared in Force, James and R. H. Popkin, eds., *The Books of Nature and Scripture* (Dordrecht: Kluwer, 1994).

10 Spinoza's reception and influence

Investigating "Spinozism" teaches at least as much about interpretations of Spinoza by other movements – both those approving him and (more often) opposing him – as it does about Spinoza's thought itself. More than other philosophies, Spinoza's has been held up like a mirror to the great currents of thought, a mirror in which their distorted images can be seen. Its first reception was accomplished in the midst of polemics; the modalities of its influence have always suffered from this, so that, at every period, the recovery of the exact situation of Spinozism from under the accumulation of abuses and misunderstandings is an effective intellectual instrument for analyzing the disposition of forces within the domain of ideas, its dominant and dominated ideas, and the battle they wage against one another. In this way one can see Calvinism, Cartesianism, the Enlightenment, and other movements, look upon their reflections, and see their own contradictions revealed in it.

I. THE SEVENTEENTH CENTURY

For a century and a half after his life, the first figure Spinoza assumed was that of the atheist or impious person. Leo Bäck (1895), P. Vernière (1954), and W. Schröder (1987) have studied the formation of this image. For many years, Spinoza was discussed primarily for refutation; it was even asserted that he must be read only with that intention.[1] Alternatively, if he awakened some positive interest, it was with thinkers who already looked upon official religion with a

408

critical eye. Both the orthodox and the libertine, however, concurred in conceiving him as atheistic or impious.

The critique of the Theological-Political Treatise

The publication of the *Theological-Political Treatise* in 1670 had the effect of a lightning bolt. The first public attack came from Leibniz's teacher, Thomasius, and soon a whole series of clergy and university people – German, Dutch, and even French Huguenots who had taken refuge in the United Provinces – denounced the work. Yet it was not the first time that official certainties about the Bible were put into question: Lorenzo Valla, Erasmus, and the Protestant exegetes of the school of Saumur had submitted the sacred text to philological critique. It was not the first time that this critique was combined with political theses, either: Thomas Hobbes had done so in the third part of the *Leviathan*. But it was perhaps the first time that it was done so radically. The critique of superstition and miracles took a more coherent turn, and the relation between prophecy and imagination founded the whole on a rigorous anthropology. The polemical dimension of most of the responses arose from this.

What was it about the *Theological-Political Treatise* that made such an impression? On the one hand, there was the apology for freedom of conscience, that is, of the claimed right to choose one's religion (understood as: the right to have none), which critics asserted would lead to anarchy – especially if one adds to it the relativity of good and evil (which one finds systematized in the fourth part of the *Ethics*). On the other hand, there was the critique of the Bible – and in particular the demonstration of the non-Mosaic provenance of the Pentateuch (which, however, takes only a chapter of the *Theological-Political Treatise*) and of the late character of the Hebrew vowel points – which disturbed traditional exegesis and unleashed the furor of the apologists. Why? Because Spinoza's era grounds the authority of the sacred books with their authenticity; to refuse them their traditional authors is to break the continuity of revelation, and therefore to withdraw from the Scriptures their claim to legitimacy. Moreover, with Protestants, who were among the first critics and the most numerous, the constancy of Biblical text is one of the conditions of the principle of "*Scriptura sola*" on

which they support their Churches. But we must go further to understand their difficulty. The Calvinists themselves had developed a
reading of the Bible that was most critical with respect to idolatry
and superstition; by insisting on the immutability of the laws of
nature, Spinoza seems to be using their argument to push it beyond
what is acceptable. They had insisted on the continuity of the two
Testaments, to the point of sometimes making the Hebrew State a
model for thinking about politics; Spinoza presupposes this continuity, but pushes it to the point of refusing the divinity of Christ and,
symmetrically, any present-day validity to the Mosaic laws of the
state.

The critique of Spinoza by such writers as Richard Simon (Simon
1687) or Jean Le Clerc relates to questions of method. Although
Spinoza is content to note the alteration of sacred texts after their
determination, Simon for his part undertakes the history of their
subsequent reception to guarantee their authority, by means of more
complex methods than those of traditional exegesis. As for what
concerns, on the other hand, the first *constitution* of the text (which
is Spinoza's principal object), he saves it at little cost by a theory of
"inspired scribes," which preserves the classical thesis of inspiration
while correcting it on the points where it has become untenable.
Spinoza's victory can, however, be measured by the fact that
Bossuet, in his *Discours sur l'Histoire Universelle*, although he does
not name Spinoza, is forced to admit the existence of distortions in
the Biblical text (in order to deny their importance). Thus, even
orthodoxy is forced to register its retreat on the specific points where
it articulated its authority and legitimacy.

The unity of substance

The second great controversial theme concerns metaphysics, notably, the unity of substance and determinism. It can be illustrated by
two figures: Bayle and Leibniz. Pierre Bayle devoted an article of the
Dictionnaire historique et critique (Bayle 1697) to Spinoza; and
many readers came to know Spinozism through the summary he
gave of it, which is more easily accessible than the *Opera Posthuma*.
There he gives an *éloge* of Spinoza's life, who is, for him, the model
of the virtuous atheist. (It is known that for Bayle – pushing a Calvinist theme to its extreme – atheism is no more dangerous than idola-

try.) But he caricatures the doctrine by not distinguishing between *natura naturans* ("nature naturing") and *natura naturata* ("nature natured"), and by treating the relation of modes to substance as a mechanical identity. Spinozism thus appears as a gigantic fusion of God and the world, which therefore renders the world's contradictions incomprehensible. Here, still, the limit of acceptability is furnished by Bayle's particular Calvinism: The thought of the one substance suppresses transcendence and shows the contradictions of a reason given to its own excesses without the barrier of dogma. Logically, such a paradigmatic role should exceed the frame of any particular era and manifest itself wherever Reason seems to act on itself; and in fact, Bayle discovers a kind of pan-Spinozism – ready to rise again at the edge of each controversy – in the Presocratics, the Orientals, and the Averroists. This transformation of Spinoza's philosophy into a transhistorical conceptual category will make up a school: We will rediscover it with Hegel and with Victor Cousin.

As for Leibniz, he was attracted by the philosopher of The Hague; he corresponded with him, met him, and attempted to know more of him through the intermediary of Tschirnhaus, their common friend. This did not, however, prevent him from denouncing Spinoza every time it was useful for him to do so – notably in his polemics with the Cartesians, where he displayed the roots of Spinozism in Cartesianism. But the essentials of his metaphysics seem sometimes to issue wholly from a dialogue with the *Ethics*, or, more precisely, from a willingness to reply otherwise to the questions that Spinoza takes up from Descartes's philosophy. The monad seems truly to inherit the spontaneity of the one substance by multiplying it; the theory of preestablished harmony seeks to resolve the difficulty of Cartesianism (namely, the relation of mind and body) to which Spinoza replied with his "parallelism" of thought and extension. As for the theory of determination in the *Theodicy*, it appears to harness the idea of the law of nature, to give a role to determinism without accepting the universal rule of a necessity conceived as constrained.[2]

The Spinozist circles

However, Spinoza did not have only detractors. There were also some Spinozist circles, initially those of his close friends during his life. Their members can be reduced to two kinds: (i) savants such as

Tschirnhaus, whose *Medicina mentis* (Tschirnhaus 1686; translated into French as *Médecine de l'esprit*, Tschirnhaus 1980) is in many respects a synthesis of the doctrines of the *Treatise on the Emendation of the Intellect* with Cartesian and Leibnizian methodologies; and (ii) Christians of the Second Reform, such as Meyer and Balling, and later Van Hattem and Leenhof. The existence of these Spinozist circles is well attested by two *romans à clef*, *The Life of Philopater* and *The Continuation of the Life of Philopater* (Duijkerius 1991), which illustrate doctrinal discussions in the Dutch intellectual atmosphere at the end of the seventeenth century. The hero (like the author) goes from being an orthodox Calvinist to being a convinced Spinozist in the midst of discussions with Voetians, Cocceians, and Cartesians. The books' publisher was jailed. It is not accidental that, in the most tolerant country of the seventeenth century, two of the rare condemnations concerning intellectual matters – resulting in detention – were aimed against Spinozists.[3]

All of this also shows that one did not become a Spinozist accidentally; often, Spinozism was the result of departing from certain heterodox Cartesian foundations. From this arises the care taken by certain Cartesian circles to refute Spinozism, to separate themselves from it;[4] from this also arises the refutation of these refutations, coming from orthodox quarters, to show that the Cartesian refutations are insufficient and hardly better than covert apologetics. Thus arises a polemic whose aim is to reveal whether Descartes is *"architectus"* or *"eversor spinozismi"* (the architect or the destroyer of Spinozism). In sum, the reception of Spinozism here is at the same time witness to, and element in, the disintegration of the determinant philosophy of the century – Cartesianism – and, in some Protestant countries, of its relations with Calvinism. In fact, in the Low Countries and in certain German universities, Reformation theology had quickly adopted a "Cartesian scholasticism." It is this alliance that the first debates on Spinozism dissolved. They showed, in effect, that the first attempt rationally to justify revealed religion through the metaphysics of *ego cogito*, which establishes the discovery of the transcendent God and creation *ex nihilo*, clashes head-on with the developments Spinoza gave to Cartesian reason conceived as power of thought:[5] the one substance, immanent God, and thought as an attribute of God exceeding human consciousness.

Rarely was Spinoza's thought known directly at the beginning of the eighteenth century. Of course, the *Opera Posthuma* and the *Theological-Political Treatise* were found in many libraries and some authors of refutations knew and cited them; but most often, as Paul Vernière showed in his classical work, *Spinoza et la Pensée française avant la Révolution* (Vernière 1954), Spinozist ideas were known indirectly: through Pierre Bayle's article in the *Dictionnaire historique et critique* (Bayle 1697; cf. Bayle 1984); through Boulainvilliers's texts; through the French translation of the *Theological-Political Treatise* (*La Clef du Sanctuaire* [Spinoza] 1678); and finally, often, through refutations or adaptations.

This indirect character concerns not only knowledge about Spinozism, but also its comprehension and use. The great theses of the Spinozist system were transformed and used in several different ways. Whether one reads the underground texts or those of the great Enlightenment authors, one has the impression that Spinozism was everywhere; but at the same time, it can be said that, strictly speaking, there were no Spinozists (except as convenient phantoms for apologists); there were only thinkers who make use of Spinoza. Naturally, they could do so with more or less creativity, style, and depth.

Pantheism and Cabbalism

Two new interpretations with great promise were born at the beginning of the eighteenth century. Toland, who was first Locke's disciple, invented the term "pantheism" (in his 1705 *Socinianism Truly Stated*) in order to refer to a doctrine in which God is identified with the whole of nature. According to him, it was Moses' thought as well as Spinoza's, and it is the true common basis of all revealed religions. From then on Spinozist doctrine was often called "pantheism," and most often seen (*contra* Toland) as evidence of hypocrisy: God is put everywhere so that he subsists nowhere.

As for Wachter, he reads Spinozism within the framework of Cabbalism, by condemning both doctrines with the charge that they deify the world (Wachter 1699).[6] Thus, he shows a way of linking Spinoza with Jewish tradition, one more serious than the anti-

Semitic abuses scattered in the polemics ("*Judaeus et atheista*") and more original than the classical comparison with Maimonides. This idea runs counter to the fact that, on the one occasion on which Spinoza mentions the Cabala, he does so in rather scornful terms. But this does not invalidate Wachter's idea. It is important to remember that in the heritage of the Jewish culture of Amsterdam, one does not find merely the different versions of medieval Aristotelianism. We will see this reading reappear again almost two centuries later, when Victor Cousin will use the materials put at his disposal by Franck and Munk. It will reappear at regular intervals, without ever finding the analytic interpreters it deserves.

The Underground Militant Literature

In the first half of the eighteenth century there appeared a whole literature directed against revealed religion, and sometimes against all religion. This tendency, often present in the texts propagated underground, is well illustrated by the *Traité des Trois Imposteurs* (Charles-Daubert 1994). In this work, the classical idea that the three great monotheist religions are in fact the product of three political impostors was articulated with numerous borrowings from Spinoza's texts, judiciously edited to accentuate their anti-Christian spirit. It is also illustrated by the *Lettre de Thrasybule à Leucippe*, attributed to Nicolas Fréret (Fréret 1986, a remarkable edition), a classical text of underground literature, composed no doubt about 1722. The latter is more interesting for the history of the reception of Spinozism, in that Spinozism is more diffused in it, and thus it better testifies to a presence detached from the direct influence of the system. The author of the letter is supposed to be writing, at the time of the Roman Empire, to a friend who is falling into devotion. He explains to her the various religions and their rites, in what they resemble each other, and why they deviate from the true comprehension of nature and ourselves. One discovers three great Spinozistic themes in it:

(i) Struggle against superstition:
They vary endlessly, agree about nothing, accuse each other of error, and do no more than accumulate absurdity upon absurdity, when they undertake to illuminate, or even to develop, the ideas they claim to have . . . the people

beset with this kind of delirium go further . . . they wish to force other people to see these nonexistent objects and constrain them to conform to their own conduct and to follow the examples they give them. (Fréret 1986: 252–3)

The important thing here is not the accusation of absurdity and persecution brought against religions (at least in their extreme form) – that is a theme common to all this literature. Rather, what is more remarkable is the work's indication of ideological variation as essential to religious delirium and as the root of theological hatred, and its explanation of violence through the desire to have the other conform to oneself. Here we are closer to the Preface of the *Theological-Political Treatise* than to other sources. However, Spinoza develops this theme as an application of a universal law of human nature: the tendency of everyone (including the philosopher) to want others to live according to his own mind (*ingenium*);[7] this universalization is absent in the *Lettre*.

(ii) Critical reading of the Bible:
[Christians] say that the author of their sect was not a simple man, that he was God himself having taken a body, and that, although he lost his life in pain, they are no more embarrassed about it than are the Egyptians of Osiris's cruel death; they claim to secure the honor of his divinity by I know not how many miracles that followed him, according to them, and about which they claim his followers have been witness, even though they are the only ones who talk about them.

We must note that Fréret formulates a rule of comprehension of the Old Testament that seems directly borrowed from Spinoza's methodological precautions: "it is to God alone that one refers all events, without paying any attention to proximate or sensible causes or to the corporeal means he has used" (Fréret 1986: 274–5).

(iii) Comparison of religions:
Here are, my dear Leucippe, all the essentially different religious sects that we know among men. All the others are only modifications, most often formed by the assemblage of diverse opinions taken from opposed systems. (Fréret 1986: 281)

This same theme is also applied to the means by which religions win over and preserve their adherents:

I have already told you several times: all these religions use proofs of the same kind to demonstrate the truth of what is contained in them. I see equal persuasion on all sides, equal zeal, equal devotion for the dogmas whose truth one is said to be ready to seal with one's blood. (Fréret 1986: 316)

Where do these analyses come from? In part from Spinoza, in part from Hobbes, and, finally, in part from the tradition of *libertinage érudit*, whose erudition is amplified here by the development of Fréret's real science of comparative religion. One can detect the difference from seventeenth-century *libertinage érudit*, which was based on the repetition, in a closed circle, of a certain number of observations borrowed from the ancients or from the repertory of Renaissance discoveries. Here, on the contrary, the comparison is supported and supplemented by the real process of a discipline being constituted, as influenced by the contributions of a growing orientalism. No doubt, it is because Fréret has received a portion of the heritage of the *Theological-Political Treatise* through this discipline that he is able to remain above the level of simple anti-Biblical polemics, as do many of the underground manuscripts.

We must now address the lines of demarcation between the two problematics. Fréret takes up certain psychological characteristics that support religious practice, but they are never themselves made into a theme; the theory of human behavior of *Ethics*, Parts 3 and 4, which underlies the *Theological-Political Treatise* and which the *Theological-Political Treatise* has no doubt transformed (by accentuating the theory of the individual) is resolutely absent in Fréret. It has been replaced by a theory of knowledge, one that owes much to Locke, connected to a theory of pleasure. In Spinoza, on the other hand, the anthropology of the *Theological-Political Treatise* is extremely complex and presupposes a theory of the imagination, the passions, and individual identity, one almost always unperceived by the authors of the underground literature. Furthermore, there is in Fréret a characteristic that openly contradicts Spinoza: the attack on the effectiveness of the Hebrew State. Fréret considers that, in fact, the more the Hebrews are faithful to the Law, the more their fate overwhelms them. "According to the positive promises of their God, they must be happy and flourishing while they are faithful to his law. They have never been more so since their return from Babylon; and never have they been more unhappy" (Fréret 1986: 311). In contrast, Spinoza considers that the Hebrew State was well-fashioned (except for the institution of the priesthood of the Levites, but that took some time to be felt) and that it brought peace and prosperity to the Hebrews for some centuries.

In sum, Fréret's *Lettre* amounts to an antitheological politics in which Spinoza's anthropology remains absent, and in which, in addition, the first part of the *Ethics* is hardly referred to. We could characterize this reading as typical of a militant attitude for which the *Theological-Political Treatise* appears rather like a reservoir of antisuperstitious arguments, and which abandons Spinoza's theory of substance for a polemic against orthodoxy.

All of these texts, the *Traité des Trois Imposteurs*, *Lettre de Thrasybule*, and many others still, whether underground or published, are representative of an anonymous Spinozism (even when we happen to know the name of a writer). They exemplify a conception of writing in which it is not systematic power that counts, but rather repetitive force and (paradoxically) the multiplicity of juxtaposed arguments. There is truly a coherence in these texts, but it is a coherence of intensity, of argumentative atmosphere, and not a conceptual coherence linked to the articulation of arguments. The authors of these authorless texts therefore take their goods where they find them: in Spinoza, but also in Hobbes, in ancient skepticism but also in Gassendi. In other words, we are dealing with an aesthetics of compilation, and even with a politics of compilation. Of course, there is still a place for the originality of an individual writer; it is not found in invention, but in its own form obtained by a certain intonation and in the choice of sources. Two blows with a differently situated chisel do not produce the same result. The *Traité des Trois Imposteurs* has revolutionary accents; the *Lettre de Thrasybule* resembles more an adjustment based on the growing science of comparative religions. There are as many Spinozisms (or Spinozist dimensions in composite texts) as there are different writers of these texts. But all these Spinozisms have a familial air, which arises from the fact that they are produced by mixing almost the same ingredients.

Neo-Spinozism

The seventeenth century was not a great century for the life sciences. Of course, important discoveries were made in it, such as Harvey's circulation of the blood; but the latter was too easily interpretable in mechanistic terms to allow by itself the development of a consciousness about vital motions. On the contrary, Cartesian emphasis on shape and motion would produce a will to reduce all the phenomena of life to those of extension. Even though iatromechanism was not alone at the forefront of the intellectual scene, discoveries in the life sciences did not have any direct influence on the interpretation of Cartesianism.

In contrast, a new version of the Spinozist heritage was developed in the eighteenth century, especially during the second half, one that restored meaning to the theory of the one substance by linking it with new developments in the sciences of nature.[8] Diderot's evolution can provide a good example.

(i) Diderot begins by confronting Spinozism with deism and atheism; he is then already interested in going beyond the purely militant uses of Spinoza. In *La promenade du sceptique* (1747), he constructs a dialogue between a Spinozist and representatives of different philosophical positions; this Spinozist seems to triumph in the end by teaching a synthesis of necessitarianism and divine omnipotence. He declares:

Thinking being, according to him [that is, the deist], is not a mode of corporeal being. According to me, there is no reason to believe that corporeal being is an effect of thinking being. It therefore follows from his admission and my argument that thinking being and corporeal being are eternal, that these two substances make up the universe, and that the universe is God.

He then puts forward a critique of the deist who would say to him "you deify the butterflies, insects, flies, drops of water, and all the molecules of matter" by affirming that what counts is the side one takes, rather than the content of the propositions: "I do not deify anything, I would reply to him. If you understand me a little, you will see on the contrary that I work toward banishing presumption, lies, and gods from the world" (Diderot 1747: I,233–4). This is a way of saying that the interest of Spinozism lies less in its assertion of a certain number of propositions than in putting a dynamic of battle into place.

(ii) On the other hand, this is the set of propositions that Diderot critiques in the *Encyclopédie* (circa 1750–65) when giving an exposition of Spinoza's system; this exposition owes much to Bayle and Brucker, and doubtless does not presuppose a direct reading of Spinoza's work. As for the critique, it resembles that of many philosophical articles of the *Encyclopédie*; it implies an orthodox rhetoric that does not fully engage the personal judgment of the author.

(iii) Finally, Diderot elaborates a metaphysics of sensible matter in which "neo-Spinozism" is renewed by the lessons of the sciences of nature (in *Le Rêve de d'Alembert* and the other dialogues from the end of the 1760s). The argument is based on two observations: the development of the egg, and the growth of the animal. "There is not more than one substance in the universe, in man, in animals" (*Entretien entre d'Alembert et Diderot*, Diderot 1747: II,117); "there is only one individual; it is the totality" (*Le Rêve de d'Alembert*, Diderot 1747: II,139). This one substance is matter, but a living, dynamic, matter in perpetual flux. We find ourselves here in the domain of discussions about the necessity of matter for life, and of life for thought. Such a renewal of Spinozism through a dynamic conception of matter and the rejection of the mechanism of the attribute of extension, considered as overly Cartesian, can already be found in Toland's *Letters to Serena*. One can find other such examples in La Mettrie, and similar ideas, from other lines, in Maupertuis or in the *Telliamed* of Benoit de Maillet. It is truly a characteristic of the period.

In sum, this evolution testifies to a wish to let Spinozism break out of the specifically antireligious classification in which a whole current of the Enlightenment wanted to maintain and reduce it. It testifies to an effort to think of its metaphysical core as a metaphysics of power and becoming. The letter of the text and its mathematical structure must be abandoned in order for its necessitarianism to be renewed by another model, that of biology.

The pantheism conflict ("Pantheismusstreit")

Spinozism was introduced very early in Germany by being mixed with atomism and Socinianism. It was not so much read for itself as it was used as a component for constructing heterodox theses in which God was identified with a world constituted, in other respects, by eternal particles. That is what one finds in Stosch and Lau.[9] One sees in such a reception how a philosophy can lose its systematic coherence in order to become merely a power of heterodoxy. It does not necessarily lose its force in other respects. But it loses some of the aspects in which its author might recognize himself. Thus German materialists finally have in common with their orthodox adversaries that they lost sight of the fact that Spinozist thought is first of all a meditation on God. This is not too troublesome for that part of the eighteenth century which perceived Spinozism only under very weak or conventional characteristics, thinking, on the whole, more about attacking it or defending it than about renewing it. Besides, Edelmann had introduced the Spinozist reading of the Bible into the domain of theology, radicalizing its results even more (Edelmann 1756) and setting off a series of persecutions against him.

But the conflict over Spinozism bears on more than Biblical interpretation, since the development of Biblical science in Germany during the second half of the century rendered common some otherwise perfectly heterodox theses.[10] "*Pantheismusstreit*" (the "pantheism conflict") was born after the death of Lessing, following the latter's beliefs. He had defended tolerance and had published the *Fragments* of Reimarus; with Mendelssohn, he represented the highest point of the Enlightenment, that is, of a critique of tradition, careful however to justify revealed religion by purging it of superstitions, making it tolerant, and giving it a place in the system of Reason – a program which would displease the most zealous orthodox, but to which a number of enlightened believers rallied. Now, Jacobi published a work (Jacobi 1785) in which he revealed that Lessing had told him he was a Spinozist, meaning by "Spinozism" the doctrine of the world's unity of principle, over and above its modifications, and against all revealed theology. Mendelssohn became incensed and defended the memory of his friend against this reproach; others responded. Nearly everyone who mattered in the intellectual world entered into the conflict, reread Spinoza, reevaluated his doctrine, and put into question the simple concept of the Enlightenment. In fact, the conflict terminated the Enlightenment by making its contradictions appear, in the same way that, a century earlier, another conflict had caused the contradictions of Cartesianism to emerge. At the same time, Jacobi had announced that Spinozism could not be refuted by reason – from which arose the necessity of a "*salto mortale*" to overcome it. This legitimated Spinozism in metaphysics for those who wanted to establish an independent philosophical thought. From then on, Spinoza no longer appeared as dangerous for revelation because of his impiety, but rather because he was potentially the carrier of a rival doctrine of Divinity, attributing both philosophy and religion to Mind. That would be precisely the conception of Romanticism and then of the great systems of German idealism. The times were ripe for Spinoza henceforth to change his appearance.

Right and politics

But first we must note another important part of the Spinozist inheritance: its conception of natural right and the State. It has been noted that Rousseau (who hardly refers to Spinoza) has in common with him a conception of the total alienation of the individual, articulated with the intent to establish the freedom of citizens in spite of it.[11] During the French revolution, Abbé Sieyès constructed an equilibrium of powers that seems to come directly from the *Political Treatise*.[12] We must underscore these developments, for beginning with the nineteenth century, Spinoza's political doctrine receives less and less interest, until this trend is reversed and his political theory becomes a center of essential interest during the last twenty years.[13]

3. THE NINETEENTH CENTURY

German idealism

The Romantics had derived a new reading of Spinoza from the *Pantheismusstreit*, one in which the traditional figure of the atheist disappeared in order to make room for its opposite: a "God-intoxicated man" (Novalis). At the same time, they brought the *amor intellectualis Dei* (intellectual love of God) closer to the *logos* of the Gospel of John. For his part, Goethe defined Spinoza as "*christianissimus.*" We are therefore far, henceforth, from the abuses of orthodoxy and the anti-Christian arguments of the libertines, Spinozism having gained metaphysical respectability. Hegel articulated the choice imposed upon any philosopher thus: either Spinozism or no philosophy at all. This does not mean that one must remain within Spinozism. Rather, the latter is a required point of departure, for Hegel, because of its affirmation of Sub-

stance; but it is reserved to dialectics to think of this Substance as
Subject, that is, as having self-motion, while in Spinoza it allegedly
remains inert, empty, and tautological. That is why, instead of ac-
cusing him of atheism, he must be charged with a-cosmism, according to Hegel, since he does not give any means of justifying the real
and multiple existence of the world after positing its point of departure. Hegel understands the attributes as points of view about substance and indicates how to correct Spinozist inertia, by thinking
of extension from thought, that is, by introducing the motion of
Mind into the exercise. In other words, it is the definition of his
own philosophy and the stripping bare of its roots that Hegel
makes manifest in his critical appreciation of Spinozism.[14]

Eclecticism and positivism in France

During the period 1815–48 that marked the apogee, under various
regimes, of bourgeois domination of the "middle classes," there was
a battle on two fronts: on the one side, the legitimist reactionaries,
supported by the aristocracy and the clergy, and on the other, the
petite bourgeoisie and the proletariat, with whom democratic and
socialist ideas were being debated. On the philosophical plane, Victor Cousin, master of the eclectic school and of the institution of the
university, represented to himself a field of battle with three elements: *political traditionalism*, rejecting indifferently as impious
both moderate liberalism and extremist tendencies; *sensualist tradition*, still lively in democratic circles, finding some new support
with physicians; and finally the *"proper middle"* represented by
Cousin himself. Initially, he made use of Hegel and Spinoza; criticized as a pantheist by the right wing, he then abandoned these
bothersome references to make use of Descartes, the "first French
psychologist," and to establish metaphysics on the analysis of consciousness. What then is Spinoza's place in this configuration?
Cousin and his followers accuse him of having overwhelmed Cartesianism by disregarding the teachings of consciousness and experience, and by letting himself be pushed by the spirit of mathematics
to the point of accepting absolute necessity. Spinoza has therefore
entered into pantheism – or rather into one of the two forms of
pantheism, the one that absorbs the world into God and not the
inverse (one sees that Hegel's lesson had been understood); he can-

not therefore be classified with materialists, but rather as a kind of mystical deviation of Cartesianism (analogous to the Hindu Munis and to the Persian Sufis). Cousin's school thus fabricated some stereotypes that were to last for a long time in French universities and those influenced by them. However, this did not prevent it from producing some respectable tools of research.[15]

This construction became the object of two kinds of attacks. First, a more radical idealism than Cousin's attacked Descartes as being compromised because of Spinoza (one recognizes here Leibniz's tactic; moreover the main proponent of this thesis was Foucher de Careil, the editor of Leibniz's previously unedited works). Cousin defended himself, in his later years, by trying to eliminate still more of Descartes's Spinozism, as one would rid oneself of a burdensome package. He then stated that pantheism came to Spinoza through the Jewish tradition, notably through the Cabala; henceforth it no longer owed anything to Cartesian science, even by amplification.[16]

Then came the critique of the positivists, who reproached the followers of Cousin with the claim that their rhetoric was incapable of explaining the real laws of the development of mankind. A good example might be Taine, who referred to Spinoza precisely because he read in him the determinism which, until now, had been so abhorred. All of our actions are determined by laws as explicable as those that govern the objects of nature. La Fontaine and Titus Livy can be explained, as can the passions of a man and the temperament of a people, on the model of Parts 3 and 4 of the *Ethics*. In Taine's writings, Spinoza thus appeared as the precursor of the most objectivist version of the social sciences.

Schopenhauer and Nietzsche

Schopenhauer was highly critical of Spinoza's thought. He reproached him for having identified *"causa"* and *"ratio"* and for his "metaphysical optimism." However, he played an important role in the transformation of the image of Spinozism by proposing a new vision of the man Spinoza. This is not the place to summarize everything Schopenhauer said about Spinoza. Still, we can note, in spite of the theoretical divergence, the hagiographic tone of the reference to Spinoza in the conclusion of *Of the Will in Nature*: Like the Stoic Cleanthes, Spinoza preferred truth to institutions, and needed to earn his bread by the sweat of his brow. This is a way of opposing the authenticity of Spinoza's life to the nonauthenticity of the life of anti-Schopenhauerian professors: "For assuredly, whoever seeks this naked beauty, this alluring siren, this bride without dowry, must renounce the happiness connected with being a philosopher of the State and of the university . . . we would rather polish lenses like Spinoza or dig for water like Cleanthes." But it is in *The World as Will and Representation* that one finds the most original pages: Schopenhauer emphasizes the extraordinary character of the first pages of the *Treatise on the Emendation of the Intellect*.[17] At the end of the fourth part of his work, Schopenhauer states that he believes that Spinoza has shown for the first time in an abstract manner the essence of renunciation and voluntary mortification. But, he adds, this essence was already grasped intuitively and expressed in the actions of saints and ascetics; whoever would want to understand it completely would have to learn to understand it by means of examples derived from experience and reality (extremely rare examples, he specifies, citing the last phrase of the *Ethics*).[18] He then refers to some such examples, and among them – between Madame Guyon and the *Confessions of a Beautiful Soul* inserted in *Wilhelm Meister* – is the life of Spinoza.[19] But to understand this biography, we must use the introduction to the *Treatise on the Emendation of the Intellect* as its key; he recommends the latter as "the strongest means" he knows to "appease the storm of passions."[20] The beginning of the treatise is praised, proposed for philosophical meditation, and put forward as "sublime," but less for its systematic virtue than for its value in communicating with a vital threshold of engagement with suffering. Schopenhauer therefore invents here a new approach to Spinoza, consisting in reading the intensity of the *Treatise on the Emendation of the Intellect* in the light of the authenticity of its author.

Schopenhauer thus gave a point of departure to a new image in the history of the reception of Spinoza: that of Spinoza as sufferer. The great philological explanations and commentaries on the *Treatise on the Emendation of the Intellect* would henceforth be aligned with that thesis,[21] and all of them, in one way or another, even if they did not share Schopenhauer's opposition to the rest of the system, would reread the first pages into the thus delimited "passionate" account. Thus Freudenthal, after having noted that "the *Tractatus de Intellectus Emendatione* is not among the most important of Spinoza's works" (because almost everything it contains is found elsewhere, sometimes under some other form), adds that it is one of the most moving and that it allows us "an in-depth glimpse into his soul and into the motives of his action" (Freudenthal 1927: 96). Gebhardt writes that "nowhere in Spinoza's works do we encounter so immediately the philosopher in all the sublimity and purity of his sentiments" (Gebhardt 1905: 54), and follows up by citing Schopenhauer's formula. We are truly here within an account that directly communicates its thought and its rootedness in what is most intimate and painful in life, since a certain quality of living and of its transcription is supposed to establish the truth of what is later asserted theoretically and, at the same time, to speak to the soul of the reader more directly than geometry. The historiographers will therefore continue in the direction that makes the prologue an immediate and authentic testimony of human suffering; they will simply add to it what can be produced through the machinery of erudition.

It is not idle to spend a little time on the meaning of Schopenhauer's discovery. We can think that it is not by accident that a philosophy which grants so decisive a place to suffering and the problem of overcoming it would point out the text that makes Spinozism incapable of reduction to intellectual pantheism.[22] The text was available before, but it remained literally unreadable for the interpretations which posited in principle that Spinozism reduced creatures to illusions drowning in the one substance. From then on, Spinozist philosophy would itself produce the means for its reception. But there was a price to pay; it is that the reclaimed intensity seems to require an explanation: either communicate directly with the life of the author[23] or with the consciousness of the reader.

Nietzsche wrote to Overbeck on 30 July 1881: "*Ich habe einen Vorganger, und was für einen!*" ("I have a forerunner, and what a forerunner!"); in August 1881 he elaborated the great concepts that would henceforth animate his thought. The style of Nietzsche's philosophy, based on aphorism and paradox, at times masked its continuity; moreover, to recognize a precursor does not mean to see oneself as an imitator. But one can show the proximity between Spinoza's opposition *Laetitia/tristitia* and Nietzsche's opposition *Wille zur Macht/Wille zum Nichts*; between *amor Dei* and *amor fati*; between necessity and the eternal recurrence of the same.[24]

Marx and Marxism

In 1841, the young Marx read Spinoza's writings (the letters and the *Theological-Political Treatise*), pen in hand, into a montage that ultimately rigidifies the division between philosophy and religion, so that they are no longer related in any way. In the former, a universal determinism excludes the supernatural; in the latter, a series of opinions incites obedience. Hence there is no interest either for Biblical exegesis or for minimal faith.[25] In the *Holy Family*, on the other hand, Marx ranked Spinoza among the metaphysicians, being inspired by a Renouvier textbook (as O. Bloch has shown). But it was Engels who defined Spinoza as "the splendid representative of dialectics" (in the *Anti-Dühring*) and who responded to a question by Plekhanov – was Spinoza right to say that thought and extension are but two attributes of a single and identical substance? – "Naturally the old Spinoza was completely right." From then on, Spinoza would reappear at regular intervals in the history of Marxism, notably in moments of crisis, where he usually served as a revealer of conflicts between various tendencies. Plekhanov referred to Spinozist "materialism" to affirm the rigor of objective laws that govern nature and society, against Bernstein, who used Kant to return socialism to a moral attitude. Similarly, in the USSR of the twenties, the different philosophical camps (mechanists and dialecticians) each constructed an image of Spinozism and its place in the history of thought that brought comfort to their own positions.[26]

Literary readings

In the nineteenth century, Spinoza became temporally distant enough to be viewed as a literary figure or reference.[27] The first who risked this was Spinoza's German translator and biographer, Berthold Auerbach (Auerbach 1837). A writer of note, author of novels about Black Forest villages, Auerbach was a liberal Jew whose life was connected to the battles for democracy and progress. His ideas were revealed in his book, which opens with the burial of Uriel da Costa[28] so as first to evoke the power of a thought exempt from tradition, which Spinoza was to carry forward in spite of prejudices and difficulties. This "novel of moral edification"[29] imposes the image of Spinoza as a genius who has it as his mission to guide men on the path of progress, but is blocked by superstition and irrationality.

With respect to English literature, we must remember that George Eliot had translated the *Ethics* and *Theological-Political Treatise*. Her novels attempt to broadcast Spinozist morality under a practical form adapted to the masses of readers, through characters who illustrate the opposition between servitude and freedom, adequate and inadequate ideas, desire for finite goods, and search for true freedom. Thus *Adam Bede* and *Middlemarch* allow the penetration into English thought of a Spinozism stripped of its geometric form; it is the behaviors of heroes and their consequences that exemplify the different kinds of knowledge and the happiness or unhappiness to which they lead.[30]

Finally, in France, Spinoza played the role of the bad teacher – or rather, of one of the bad teachers (with Taine) – in *Le Disciple* (1889), the novel of the traditionalist Paul Bourget, inspired by a contemporary news item. The hero is a modern philosopher whose whole life consists in one word: thought. He systematically prohibits charity to himself because he believes, like Spinoza, that "pity in a wise man who lives by reason is bad and useless." He detests Christianity as an illness brought on by humility. He relies on Darwin (but with reference to Spinoza) for the idea that "the moral universe reproduces exactly the physical universe and that the former is only the painful and ecstatic consciousness of the latter." We can surmise the morality of the tale: Such a philosophy leads to assassination on the part of the student who applies too well the teacher's maxims. That the teacher is elsewhere described as someone "very sweet" is not an extenuating circumstance; Bourget is concerned with showing that even virtuous atheists are still worse than other individuals.

4. THE TWENTIETH CENTURY

German scholarship

The end of the nineteenth and the first thirty years of the twentieth century were witness to a formidable development in Spinoza scholarship. Henceforth, before interpreting the doctrine, there is an attempt to know it, to reject the tales of the author's life, and to fix its contexts and influences. The essentials of this scholarly movement are German and, in part, Dutch. Researchers delved into biography (Meinsma), published archival documents (Freudenthal), and established the text of the complete works (Van Vloten and Land, then Gebhardt). The journal *Chronicon Spinozanum* collected articles that illuminated specific points, researched influences, and informed contemporary interpretations; it also led to the reading of Steno's *Epistola*, Peiter Balling's book, and Van den Enden's three letters to Jan de Witt.

This enormous work was incontestably useful; this was the period that constructed most of the tools of research still in use today. On the other hand, Spinoza interpretation did not make great progress. Knowledge of Spinoza's system became more exact without becoming deeper. Gebhardt defended a rather weak *religio philosophica*. Finally, we should mention the most ambitious of these workers, Dunin-Borkowski, the author of a gigantic *summa* on the history of ideas,[31] in which, unfortunately, Spinoza's thought loses its specificity.

All of this great research was rudely interrupted in Germany by the victory of the Nazis within the framework of anti-Semitism, of the reordering of the universities, and of the battle against rationalist doctrines.

The echoes of Spinozism

Outside philosophy, properly speaking, one may seek, if not living interpretations, at least ideas that recognize vague paternity with Spinoza or thinkers who believe themselves to have been influenced by him.

(i) Freud rarely refers to Spinoza, but in one of his interjections, he asserts that he has always lived "in a Spinozist environment," whatever that might have meant. Several of his associates (Lou Andras Salomè, Viktor Tausk) knew the doctrines and figure of Spinoza well.[32] Moreover, a certain number of Freudian motifs recall the great themes of the *Ethics*, without ever repeating them: first of all, the idea that the psychological does not reduce to the conscious, and that events occurring in the psychological realm manifest themselves in the body. Often, Spinoza's ghost came to haunt the history of psychoanalysis. When Jacques Lacan broke with the official psychoanalytic institution to defend alone some theses which in his view were more in conformity with Freudian truth, he evoked the exclusion of Spinoza from the Amsterdam synagogue.[33]

(ii) Reference to Spinoza had played a role in the movement of the Jewish Lights (the *Haskalah*); it was considered a precursor to the coming out from the ghetto and to the movement of emancipation of a Judaism liberated from religious tradition. In turn, some Zionists saw in Spinoza the witness to an attitude that they would take up as their own; that was the case with Moses Hess in the nineteenth century, and also with Joseph Klausner, historian of Judaism and one of the founders of the Hebrew University of Jerusalem, as well as with Ben Gurion himself.[34]

(iii) Finally, Albert Einstein referred to Spinoza on many occasions, although one cannot assign any specific content to the doctrinal comparison.[35]

Literature

One would not expect to find a writer connected with Nazism among Spinoza's admirers. That is, however, the case of E. G. Kolbenheyer.[36] It is true that his novel *Amor Dei* was very early relative to the National-Socialist dictatorship (1908), but the ideas with which it is imbued are truly marked by an irrationalism and a cult of the great individuals that allow one to foresee the later evolution of its author: The mob is only the incarnation of a vital force that contains the seeds of its own destruction; the people are born for servitude; the exceptional individual (Spinoza, under the circumstances) is fascinated by the force of the mob, but rejects this animal brutality.

In *The Fixer* of Bernard Malamud, the hero, a poor Jew, persecuted at the renewed outbreak of anti-Semitism in Russia at the start of the century, appears to his surprised lawyer as a reader of the *Ethics*.

Finally, Jorge-Luis Borgès,[37] who has devoted several writings to Spinoza, has confessed his fascination for a philosopher who "constructs God in the shadows." He never enters into the details of the system, but when he assimilates metaphysics to a branch of fantastic literature, one can glimpse why this specific metaphysics pleases him particularly – perhaps precisely because of the aspects that seemed the most strange, indeed the most repugnant, to the critics of the classical age, or the farthest from experience to the sober disciples of Victor Cousin. The infinity of divine attributes, of which we know only two, but in which phenomena corresponding in some way to body and soul must exist, in virtue of the unity of substantial causality, is an idea that cannot but evoke the theme of the double and the theme of parallel universes that are at the base of fantastic literature as conceived by Borgès.

The renewal of Spinozism after 1945

After long years of relative inactivity (in which, however, some meritorious works can be distinguished), the end of the 1960s saw a sharp renewal of Spinozistic studies, along several directions. On the one hand, there were works devoted to studying the logical order of reasons of the system, the architectonic within which every element derives its meaning. Such a tendency is clearly illustrated at the highest level by the work of Martial Gueroult,[38] but one should also mention the whole school he inspired in France, most notably Alexandre Matheron;[39] and one can mention Edwin Curley's work in the English-speaking world.[40] On the other hand, there are interpretations that see in Spinozism a philosophy of power (Deleuze)[41] or constitutive thought (Negri);[42] and finally, other readings, careful to compare Spinozism with non-Western traditions, Buddhism, for example (Wetlesen).[43] In addition we must mention historiographical studies (Mignini, Proietti, Popkin, Yovel) and the construction of research tools (at the highest level of which is the *Lexicon Spinozanum* of Emilia Giancotti). Further proof of the rebirth of Spinozist studies is provided, half a century after the disappearance of the *Chronicon Spinozanum*, by the appearance of two journals devoted entirely to Spinoza: *Studia Spinozana* (under the editorship of Manfred Walther) and *Cahiers Spinoza*. It is clear that Spinoza, and Spinozism, will continue to be a powerful force in the intellectual and cultural world.

Translated by Roger Ariew.[44]

NOTES

1 "It pertains to the natural right not to read such books, unless one wishes to refute them and one has enough talent for that," Arnauld, quoted in Vernière 1954: I,116.

2 "We are always more inclined and consequently more determined on one side than on another, but we are never necessitated with respect to the choices we make," (*Théodicée* II, section 132).

3 The other was that of Adriaan Koerbagh, discussed at greater length in Chapter 1 of this volume.

4 This is the case, for example, with Wittichius.

5 Cf. Schmidt-Biggemann 1992 and Scribano 1988.

6 Wachter 1706 gives a more favorable slant to Spinoza.

7 See Moreau 1994.

8 Here we follow essentially Vernière's conclusions (Vernière 1954: 555–611).

9 Let us cite, for example, some of Theodor Ludwig Lau's phrases from Lau 1992. "*Deus Natura naturans: ego natura naturata. . . . Materia simplex: ego materia modificata. Oceanus: ego fluvius. Aqua: ego gutta. . . .*" (I,4); "*Est totum navis: Deus nauclerus. Currus: Deus auriga. Horologium Deus aequilibrium inquies. Machina: Deus rota. Automaton: Deus loco-motiva*" (II,17).

10 We must note, however, that the Old Testament science differs in its approach from that of the *Theological-Political Treatise*; it tends, following the Frenchman, Astruc, to dissect each sacred book in order to recover in it a plurality of documents; Spinoza, on the other hand, preserved the unity of these books and reasoned on them as on a totality.

11 See Eckstein 1944 and Vernière 1954: 475–94.

12 See Pariset 1906 and Vernière 1954: 684–7.

13 One exception is the Italian historiographical tradition, which has always attached much importance to Spinoza's politics, and especially to the problems of the relations between the doctrines of Hobbes and Spinoza.

14 See Macherey 1979.

15 The first complete French translation of Spinoza by Emile Saisset, for example.

16 We must note that this new interpretation was not unanimous in his own school: Saisset, for example, maintained the earlier positions.

17 By opposition to what follows, in any case: "*in jenem herrlichen Eingang zu seiner ungenügenden Abhandlung*" (*Die Welt als Wille und Vorstellung* I.iv.68, in Schopenhauer 1960: I,523).

18 "But all things excellent are as difficult as they are rare" (E 5p42s).

19 "*Gewissermaßen könnte man als ein hierhergehöriges Beispiel sogar die bekannte französische Biographie Spinozas betrachen*" (*Die Welt als Wille und Vorstellung* I.iv.68, in Schopenhauer 1960: I,523). Similarly, Goethe's text is mentioned only by reference to the life which he took as model, that of Susanna von Klettenberg, and of which he speaks directly in *Dichtung und Wahrheit*.

20 ". . . das wirksamste, mir bekannt gewordene Besänftigungsmittel des Sturms der Leidenschaften" (Die Welt als Wille und Vorstellung I.iv.68, in Schopenhauer 1960: I,523).

21 The first work completely devoted to the Treatise on the Emendation of the Intellect was Elbogen 1898, but all the great Spinoza scholars of the end of the nineteenth and beginning of the twentieth century devoted a chapter to it.

22 On Schopenhauer and Spinoza, see the selection of main texts in Grunwald 1897: V,109, pages 247–53, as well as Rappaport 1899. Italian commentators have often developed useful detailed comparisons between Spinozistic and Schopenhauerian motifs, notably Moretti-Constanzi 1946: 173ff. and Semerari 1952: 94,103,109–10.

23 With respect to Giordano Bruno and Spinoza, Schopenhauer speaks of their "kümmerliches Daseyn und Sterben" (Die Welt als Wille und Vorstelling, "Anhang: Kritik der Kantischen Philosophie" Schopenhauer 1960: I,571).

24 See Snel n.d. See also Wurzer 1975.

25 See the analysis given in Matheron 1977.

26 See Kline 1952.

27 On this general theme, see volume 5 of Studia Spinozana, "Spinoza and Literature" (Königshausen and Neumann, 1989).

28 See Chapter 1 of this volume.

29 See Lagny 1993.

30 See Atkins 1985.

31 See Dunin-Borkowski 1910; and Dunin-Borkowski 1933–36 (vol. 1: Der junge de Spinoza [which takes up again the 1910 work]; vol. 2: Aus den Tagen Spinozas, Das Entscheidungsjahr 1657; vol. 3: Aus den Tagen Spinozas: Das neue Leben; vol. 4: Aus den Tagen Spinozas: Das Lebenswerk).

32 Tausk had written a poem about wisdom that consisted in a dialogue between Spinoza and himself.

33 One would need also to evoke the figure of Constantin Brunner, a Jewish philosopher from Berlin, who counted Spinoza among his inspirations; his doctrines had little success with professional philosophers in the twenties, but had considerable influence among the various circles of biologists and physicians; one finds there a reading of Spinozism particularly insistent about the relations between soul and body.

34 See Yakira 1993.

35 See, however, Paty 1985.

36 See Lagny 1993.

37 See Damade 1993.

38 See Gueroult 1968–74, 2 vols.: vol. 1: *Dieu* (*Ethique, 1*), 1968; vol. 2: *L'âme* (*Ethique, 2*), 1974.
39 See Matheron 1969.
40 See Curley 1969, 1988.
41 See Deleuze 1970, 1969.
42 See Negri 1981.
43 See Wetlesen 1979.
44 English translation by Roger Ariew, Department of Philosophy, Virginia Polytechnic Institute and State University, Blacksburg, Virginia, USA.

BIBLIOGRAPHY

Akkerman, F. 1980. *Studies in the Posthumous Works of Spinoza: On Style, Earliest Translation and Reception, Earliest and Modern Edition of Some Texts.* Reprint of a monograph which originally appeared in the Mededelingen vanwege het Spinozahuis. Krips Repro Meppel.

Akkerman, F., and H. G. Hubbeling. 1979. "The Preface to Spinoza's Posthumous Works, 1677, and its Author Jarig Jelles (c. 1619–1683)." *LIAS* 6: 103–73.

Albiac, G. 1987. *La sinagoga vacía. Un estudio de las fuentes marranas del espinosismo.* Libros Hiperion.

Allison, Henry E. 1987. *Benedictus de Spinoza: an Introduction.* Revised ed., New Haven: Yale University Press.

1992. "Spinoza and the Philosophy of Immanence: Reflections on Yovel's The Adventure of Immanence." *Inquiry* 35 (1): 55–67.

Alsted, Johann-Heinrich. 1649. *Encyclopedia.* (first ed. Herborn, 1630) 4 Vols. Lyons.

Altkirch, E. 1912. *Spinoza im Porträt.* Leipzig.

[Anonymous]. 1977. *Spinoza. Troisième centenaire de la mort du philosophie.* (Catalog) Paris: Institut Néerlandais.

[Anonymous], ed. 1965. *Catalogus van de bibliotheek der Vereniging 'Het Spinozahuis' te Rijnsburg.* (Catalog) Leiden: Brill.

Aquila, Richard. 1978. "The Identity of Thought and Object in Spinoza." *Journal of the History of Philosophy* 16: 271–88.

Aquinas, St. Thomas. 1964–6. *Summa Theologiae.* 60 Vols. London: Eyre and Spottiswoode.

Ariew, Roger. 1987. Review of Jonathan Bennett's A Study of Spinoza's Ethics. In *Philosophy and Phenomenological Research* 47: 649–54.

Atkins, Dorothy. 1985. "La philosophie de Spinoza selon George Eliot." *Spinoza entre Lumières et Romantisme, Cahiers de Fontenay* 36–8: 349–58.

Auerbach, Berthold. 1837. *Spinoza, ein historischer Roman.*

435

Bäck, Leo. 1895. *Spinozas erste Enwirkungen auf Deutschland*. Berlin.

Bacon, Francis. 1857–74. *The Works of Francis Bacon*. eds. J. Spedding, R. L. Ellis, and D. D. Heath. 15 Vols. London: Longmans and Co.

Baier, Annette. 1993. "David Hume, Spinozist." *Hume Studies* 19: 237–52.

Balibar, Etienne. 1990. "Ultimi Barbarorum – Espinoza: o temor das massas." *Discurso* 18: 7–35.

Barbone, Steven L. 1993. "Virtue and Sociality in Spinoza." *Iyyun* 42 (3): 383–95.

Barker, H. 1972. "Notes on the Second Part of Spinoza's Ethics (I)." In *Studies in Spinoza*, ed. Paul Kashap, 101–22. Berkeley: University of California Press.

Bar-On, A. Z. 1983. "The Ontological Proof – Spinoza's Version in Comparison with Those of Anselm and Descartes." In *Spinoza: His Thought and Work*, eds. Nathan Rotenstreich and Norma Schneider, Jerusalem: The Israel Academy of Arts and Sciences.

Bartuschat, Wolfgang. 1991. "Metaphysik und Ethik in Spinoza's 'Ethica.' " *Studia Spinozana* 7: 15–37.

Batalier, J. 1674. *Vindicia miraculorum*. Amsterdam.

Bayle, Pierre. 1697. Dictionnaire historique et critique. Paris.

   1984. *Ecrits sur Spinoza*. eds. F. Charles-Daubert and P.-F. Moreau. Paris: Berg.

Bedjai, M. 1990. "Métaphysique, éthique et politique dans l'oeuvre du docteur Franciscus van den Enden (1602–1674): contribution à l'étude des sources des écrits de B. de Spinoza." Dactylographié, Leiden (thesis).

Bennett, Jonathan. 1980. "Spinoza's Vacuum Argument." *Midwest Studies in Philosophy* 5: 391–9.

   1981. "Spinoza's Mind–Body Identity Thesis." *Journal of Philosophy* 78: 573–84.

   1983. "Teleology and Spinoza's Conatus." *Midwest Studies in Philosophy* 8: 143–60.

   1984. *A Study of Spinoza's "Ethics."* Indianapolis: Hackett.

   1986. "Spinoza on Error." *Philosophical Papers* 15: 59–73.

   1990. "Spinoza and Teleology: A Reply to Curley." In *Spinoza: Issues and Directions*, eds. Edwin Curley and Pierre-François Moreau, 53–7. Leiden: Brill.

   1991. "Spinoza's Monism: A Reply to Curley." In *God and Nature: Spinoza's Metaphysics*, ed. Yirmiyahu Yovel, Spinoza by 2000: The Jerusalem Conferences, 53–9. Leiden: Brill.

Berlin, Isaiah. 1982. *Against the Current*. New York: Penguin.

Bernadete, José. 1980. "Spinozistic Anomalies." In *The Philosophy of Baruch Spinoza*, ed. Richard Kennington, 53–71. Washington, D.C.: Catholic University of America Press.

Biasutti, Franco. 1979. *La dottrina della scienza in Spinoza. Scienze Filosofiche*, 23. Bologna: Pàtron Editore.

Biderman, S., and A. Kasher. 1990. "Why was Spinoza Excommunicated?" In *Sceptics, Millenarians and Jews*, eds. D. S. Katz and J. Israel, 98–141. Leiden: Brill.

Bidney, David. 1940. *The Psychology and Ethics of Spinoza: A Study in the History and Logic of Ideas*. New Haven: Yale University Press.

Bos, E. P., and H. A. Krop, eds. 1993. *Franco Burgersdijk (1590–1635)*. Studies in the History of Ideas in the Low Countries. Amsterdam: Rodopi.

Bos, H. J. M. et al., ed. 1980. *Studies on Christiaan Huygens: Invited Papers from the Symposium on the Life and Work of Christiaan Huygens, Amsterdam, 22–25 August 1979*. Lisse: Swets and Zeitlinger B. V.

Bourget, Paul. 1889. *Le Disciple*. Paris.

Boyle, Robert. 1661. *Tentamina quaedam physiologica, diversis temporibus et occasionibus conscripta. A Latin translation of Certain Physiological Essays, Written at Distant Times, and on Several Occasions*. London.

Brett, G. S. 1965. *Brett's History of Psychology*. revised edition, ed. R. S. Peters. Cambridge, Mass.: MIT Press.

Broad, C. D. 1930. *Five Types of Ethical Theory*. London: Routledge and Kegan Paul.

Brunschvicg, Léon. 1951. *Spinoza et ses contemporains*. 4th ed., Paris: Presses Universitaires de France.

Burgersdijk, Frank. 1651. *Institutionum logicarum libri duo. Accedit Adriani Heerboord Synopseos logicae Burgersdicianae explicatio: unà cum ejusdem autoris Praxi logica*. London: Roger Daniels.

Buttrick, George Arthur, ed. 1952–7. *The Interpreter's Bible*. New York: Abingdon-Cokesbury.

Caird, E. 1910. *Spinoza*. Edinburgh.

Calvetti, Carla Gallicet. 1972. *Spinoza lettore del Machiavelli*. Milan: Università Cattolica del Sacro Cuore.

Carr, Spencer. 1978. "Spinoza's Distinction Between Rational and Intuitive Knowledge." *The Philosophical Review* 87: 241–52.

Carriero, John P. 1991. "Spinoza's Views on Necessity in Historical Perspective." *Philosophical Topics* 19: 47–96.

Chappell, Vere, ed. 1992. *Essays on Early Modern Philosophers*, Volume 10: Baruch de Spinoza. Hamden: Garland.

Charles-Daubert, F., ed. 1994. *Le Traité des Trois imposteurs*. Universitas.

Clericuzio, Antonio. 1990. "A Redefinition of Boyle's Chemistry and Corpuscular Philosophy." *Annals of Science* 47: 561–89.

Cohen, I. B. 1964. " 'Quantum in se est': Newton's Concept of Inertia in Relation to Descartes and Lucretius." *Notes and Records of the Royal Society of London* 19: 131–55.

Colerus, John. 1705. *Korte, dog waaragtige Levens-Beschrijving van Bene-dictus de Spinosa, uit Autentique Stukken en mondeling getuigenis van nog levende Personen, opgestelt*. Amsterdam.

——— 1899. "The Life of Benedictus de Spinoza." In *Spinoza: His Life and Phi-losophy*, ed. Frederick Pollock, 386–418. London: Duckworth.

Cover, J. A., and Mark Kulstad, eds. 1990. *Central Themes in Early Mod-ern Philosophy: Essays Presented to Jonathan Bennett*. Indianapolis: Hackett.

Cropsey, Joseph, and Leo Strauss, eds. 1981. *History of Political Philosophy*. Chicago: University of Chicago Press.

Cuper, Franciscus. 1676. *Arcana atheismi revelata*. Rotterdam: Naeranus.

Curley, Edwin. 1969. *Spinoza's Metaphysics: An Essay in Interpretation*. Cambridge, Mass.: Harvard University Press.

——— 1973a. "Experience in Spinoza's Theory of Knowledge." In *Spinoza: A Collection of Critical Essays*, ed. Marjorie Grene, 25–59. Garden City: Doubleday/Anchor Press.

——— 1973b. "Spinoza's Moral Philosophy." In *Spinoza: A Collection of Critical Essays*, ed. Marjorie Grene, 354–76. Garden City: Doubleday/Anchor.

——— 1975. "Descartes, Spinoza, and the Ethics of Belief." In *Spinoza: Essays in Interpretation*, eds. Eugene Freeman and Maurice Mandelbaum, LaSalle: Open Court.

——— 1977. "Spinoza – as an Expositor of Descartes." In *Speculum Spinozanum 1677–1977*, ed. Siegfried Hessing, 133–42. London: Routledge and Ke-gan Paul.

——— 1978. "Man and Nature in Spinoza." In *Spinoza's Philosophy of Man: The Scandinavian Spinoza Symposium, 1977*, ed. J. Wetlesen, 19–26. Olso: Universitetsforlaget.

——— 1986. "Spinoza's Geometric Method." *Studia Spinozana* 2: 151–69.

——— 1988. *Behind the Geometrical Method*. Princeton: Princeton University Press.

——— 1990a. "Notes on a Neglected Masterpiece, II: The Theological-Political Treatise as a Prolegomenon to the Ethics." In *Central Themes in Early Modern Philosophy*, eds. J. A. Cover and Mark Kulstad, 109–59. India-napolis: Hackett.

——— 1990b. "On Bennett's Spinoza: The Issue of Teleology." In *Spinoza: Issues and Directions*, eds. Edwin Curley and Pierre-François Moreau, 39–52. Leiden: Brill.

——— 1990c. "Reflections on Hobbes: Recent Work on his Moral and Political Philosophy." *Journal of Philosophical Research* 15: 169–250.

——— 1991a. "A Good Man is Hard to Find." *Proceedings and Addresses of the American Philosophical Association* 65: 29–45.

——— 1991b. "On Bennett's Interpretation of Spinoza's Monism." In *God and*

Nature: Spinoza's Metaphysics, ed. Yirmiyahu Yovel, Spinoza by 2000: The Jerusalem Conferences, 35–51. Leiden: Brill.

1991c. "The State of Nature and its Law in Hobbes and Spinoza." *Philosophical Topics* 19: 91–117.

1992. " 'I Durst Not Write So Boldly'; or, How to Read Hobbes Theological-Political Treatise." In *Hobbes e Spinoza*, ed. Daniela Bostrenghi, Naples: Bibliopolis.

1994a. "Spinoza and the Science of Hermeneutics." In *Spinoza: The Enduring Question*, ed. Graeme Hunter, Toronto: University of Toronto Press.

1994b. "Spinoza on Truth." *Australian Journal of Philosophy* 72: 1–16.

Curley, Edwin, and Pierre-François Moreau, eds. 1990. *Spinoza: Issues and Directions*. Brill's Studies in Intellectual History, vol. 14. Leiden: Brill.

1995. "Spinoza and the Science of Hermeneutics." In *Spinoza: The Enduring Questions*, ed. Graeme Hunter, Toronto: University of Toronto Press.

Da Costa, Uriel. 1993. *Examination of Pharisaic Traditions*. ed. H. P. Salomon. Leiden: E. J. Brill.

Damade, Jacques. 1993. "Le Saint et l'Herétique. Borgès et Spinoza." In *Spinoza au XXe siècle*, ed. O. Bloch, 483–92. Paris: PUF.

Daudin, Henri. 1948. "Spinoza et la science expérimentale: sa discussion de l'expérience de Boyle." *Revue d'Histoire des Sciences* 2: 179–90.

Davidson, Donald. 1980. *Essays on Actions and Events*. Oxford: Clarendon Press.

1982. "Paradoxes of Irrationality." In *Philosophical Essays on Freud*, eds. R. A. Wollheim and J. Hopkins, 289–305. Cambridge: Cambridge University Press.

1985. "Incoherence and Irrationality."*Dialectica* 39: 345–54.

De Deugd, C. D. 1966. *The Significance of Spinoza's First Kind of Knowledge*. Assen: Van Gorcum.

De Dijn, Hermann. 1986. "Spinoza's Logic or Art of Perfect Thinking." *Studia Spinozana* 2: 15–25.

De Murr, C. T. 1802. *Adnotationes ad tratatum theologico politicum. Ex autographo . . .* The Hague.

De Vet, Joannes J. V. M. 1983. "Was Spinoza de Auteur van Stelkonstige Reeckening van den Regenboog en Reeckening van Kanssen?" *Tijdschrift voor Filosofie* 45: 602–39.

1986. "Spinoza's Authorship of the 'Algebraic Calculation of the Rainbow' and of 'Calculation of Chances' Once More Doubtful." *Studia Spinozana* 2: 267–309.

Delahunty, R. J. 1985. *Spinoza*. London: Routledge and Kegan Paul.

Delbos, Victor. 1968. *Le Spinozisme*. Paris: Librarie Philosophique J. Vrin.

Deleuze, Gilles. 1970. *Spinoza. Philosophie pratique*. Paris: Editions de Minuit.

1978. *Spinoza et le problème de l'expression*. Second edition, 1978 Paris: Edition de Minuit, 1969.

1992. *Expressionism in Spinoza*, ed. and trans. Martin Joughin. Cambridge: MIT Press.

Della Rocca, Michael. 1991. "Causation and Spinoza's Claim of Identity." *History of Philosophy Quarterly* 8: 265–76.

1993. "Spinoza's Argument for the Identity Theory." *The Philosophical Review* 102: 183–213.

n.d. "Egoism and the Imitation of Affects in Spinoza." In *Spinoza on Reason and the Free Man*, ed. Yirmiyahu Yovel, Spinoza by 2000: The Jerusalem Conferences, Leiden: Brill, forthcoming.

1996. *Representation and the Mind-Body Problem in Spinoza*. New York: Oxford University Press, forthcoming, 1996.

den Uyl, Douglas. 1983. *Power, State and Freedom*. Assen: Van Gorcum.

Descartes, René. 1964–74. *Oeuvres de Descartes*, eds. Charles Adam and Paul Tannery. 13 Vols. Paris: Cerf, 1897–1913, New edition eds. P. Costabel, J. Beaude, and B. Rochot. 11 Vols. Paris: Vrin.

1985. *The Philosophical Writings of Descartes*, ed. and trans. John Cottingham, Robert Stoothoff, and Dugald Murdoch. 3 Vols. Cambridge: Cambridge University Press.

Dibon, Paul. 1954. *La philosophie néerlandaise au Siècle d'Or. Tome I: L'enseignement philosophique dans les universités à l'époque précarté-sienne (1575–1650)*. Publications de l'Institut Français d'Amsterdam, Maison Descartes, no. 21. Paris: Elsevier Publishing Company.

Diderot, Denis. 1747. *Oeuvres complètes*. Assézat.

Donagan, Alan. 1973a. "Essence and the Distinction of Attributes in Spinoza's Metaphysics." In *Spinoza: A Collection of Critical Essays*, ed. Marjorie Grene, 164–81. Garden City: Doubleday/Anchor.

1973b. "Spinoza's Proof of Immortality." In *Spinoza: A Collection of Critical Essays*, ed. Marjorie Grene, 241–58. Garden City: Doubleday/Anchor.

1980. "Spinoza's Dualism." In *The Philosophy of Baruch Spinoza*, ed. Richard Kennington, 89–102. Washington, D.C.: Catholic University of America Press.

1988. *Spinoza*. Chicago: University of Chicago Press.

Doney, W. 1971. "Spinoza on Philosophical Skepticism." *Monist* 55: 617–35.

Driver, S. C. 1973. "A Critical and Exegetical Commentary on Deuteronomy." In *International Critical Commentary*, 3rd ed., Edinburgh: T. and T. Clark.

Duchesneau, François. 1974. "Du modèle cartésien au modèle spinozist e de l'être vivant." *Canadian Journal of Philosophy* 3: 539–62.

Duff, R. A. 1970. *Spinoza's Political and Ethical Philosophy*. First edition, Glasglow: James Maclohose and Sons, 1903. Reprinted, New York: Augustus M. Kelly.

Duijkerius, Johannes. 1991. *Het leven van Philopater. Verlog van't leven van Philopater. Een spinozistiche sleutelroman uit 1691–1697.* Edited and annotated by Géraldine Marechal. Amsterdam: Rodopi.

Dunin-Borkowski, Stanislaus von. 1910. *Der junge de Spinoza. Leben und Werdegang im Lichte der Weltphilosophie.* Münster: Aschendorf.

 1933. "Die Physik Spinozas." In *Septimana Spinozana: Acta conventus oecumenici in memoriam Bendicti de Spinoza diei natalis trecentissimi Hagae Comitis habiti, curis Societatis Spinozanae edita*, 85–101. The Hague: Societas Spinozana.

 1933–6. *Spinoza.* 4 Vols. Münster: Aschendorf.

Dunner, Joseph. 1955. *Baruch Spinoza and Western Democracy.* New York: Philosophical Library.

Dutka, Jacques. 1953. "Spinoza and the Theory of Probability." *Scripta Mathematica* 19: 24–33.

Earman, John. 1989. *World Enough and Space-Time: Absolute versus Relational Theories of Space and Time.* Cambridge, Mass.: MIT Press.

Eckstein, W. 1944. "Rousseau and Spinoza." *Journal of the History of Ideas,* 259–91.

Edelmann, Johann Christian. 1756. *Moses.*

Eisenberg, Paul. 1977. "Is Spinoza an Ethical Naturalist?" In *Speculum Spinozanum 1677–1977,* ed. Siegfried Hessing, 145–64. London: Routledge and Kegan Paul.

Elbogen, Ismar. 1898. *Der Tractatus de Intellectus Emendation und seine Stellung in der Philosophie Spinozas.* Breslau.

Evenhuis, R. B. 1971. *Ook dat was Amsterdam.* Baarn.

Feuer, Lewis Samuel. 1964. *Spinoza and the Rise of Liberalism.* Boston: Beacon Press. Originally published in 1958.

Fisher, Samuel. 1660. *The Rustick Alarm to the Rabbies.* London: Robert Wilson.

Floistad, Guttorm. 1973. "Spinoza's Theory of Knowledge in the Ethics." In *Spinoza: A Collection of Critical Essays,* ed. Marjorie Grene, Garden City: Doubleday/Anchor.

Force, James, and R. H. Popkin, eds. 1994. *The Books of Nature and Scripture.* Dordrecht: Kluwer.

Francès, M. 1937. *Spinoza dans les Pays Nerlandais de la seconde moitié du XVIIe siècle.* Paris.

Francks, Richard. 1985. "Caricatures in the History of Philosophy: The Case of Spinoza." In *Philosophy, its History and Historiography*, ed. A. J. Holland, Royal Institute of Philosophy Conferences, Vol. 1983, 179–94. Dordrecht: Reidel.

Frankena, William K. 1975. "Spinoza's 'New Morality': Notes on Book IV." In *Spinoza, Essays in Interpretation*, eds. Eugene Freeman and Maurice Mandelbaum, 85–100. La Salle: Open Court.

Freeman, Eugene, and Mandelbaum, Maurice, eds. 1975. *Spinoza: Essays in Interpretation*. La Salle: Open Court.

Freudenthal, J. 1904. *Spinoza: sein Leben und seine Lehre, Band I: Das Leben Spinozas*. Stuttgart: Frommann.

1927. *Spinoza Leben und Lehre. Zweiter Teil: Die Lehre Spinozas auf Grund des Nachlasses von Freudenthal bearbeitet von Carl Gebhardt*. Heidelberg: Carl Winter Verlag.

Freudenthal, J., ed. 1899. *Die Lebensgeschichte Spinoza's Quellenschriften, Urkunden, und nichtnamlichen Nachrichten*. Leipzig.

Fréret, Nicholas. 1986. *Lettre de Thrasybule à Leucippe*. ed. Sergio Landucci. Florence: Olschki.

Friedman, Joel I. 1978. "An Overview of Spinoza's Ethics." *Synthèse* 37: 67–106.

1983. "Spinoza's Problem of 'Other Minds'." *Synthèse* 57: 99–126.

1986. "How the Finite Follows from the Infinite in Spinoza's Metaphysical System." *Synthèse* 69: 371–407.

Friedmann, George. 1962. *Leibniz et Spinoza*. 2nd ed., Paris: Gallimard.

Fuks-Mansfeld, R. G. 1989. *De Sefardim in Amsterdam tot 1795. Aspecten van een joodse minderheid in een Hollandse stad*. Hilversum.

Gabbey, Alan. 1973. Review of W. L. Scott, The Conflict Between Atomism and Conservation Theory 1644–1860. In *Studies in History and Philosophy of Science*, 373–85. 4.

1980. "Force and Inertia in the Seventeenth Century: Descartes and Newton." In *Descartes: Philosophy, Mathematics and Physics*, ed. Stephen Gaukroger, 230–320. Sussex: Harvester Press.

1992. "Newton's Mathematical Principles of Natural Philosophy: a Treatise on 'Mechanics'?" In *An Investigation of Difficult Things: Essays on Newton and the History of the Exact Sciences in Honour of D. T. Whiteside*, eds. P. M. Harman and Alan E. Shapiro, 305–22. Cambridge: Cambridge University Press.

Garber, Daniel. 1992. *Descartes' Metaphysical Physics*. Chicago: University of Chicago Press.

Garber, Daniel, and Lesley Cohen. 1982. "A Point of Order: Analysis, Synthesis and Descartes's Principles." *Archiv für Geschichte der Philosophie* 64: 136–47.

Garrett, Don. 1979. "Spinoza's 'Ontological' Argument." *The Philosophical Review* 88: 198–223.

1986. "Truth and Ideas of Imagination in the Tractatus de Intellectus Emendatione." *Studia Spinozana* 2: 56–86.

1990a. " 'A Free Man Always Acts Honestly, Not Deceptively': Freedom and the Good in Spinoza's Ethics." In *Spinoza: Issues and Directions*, eds. Edwin Curley and Pierre-François Moreau, 221–38. Leiden: Brill.

1990b. "Ethics Ip5: Shared Attributes and the Basis of Spinoza's Monism." In *Central Themes in Early Modern Philosophy: Essays Presented to Jonathan Bennett*, eds. J. A. Cover and Mark Kulstad, 69–107. Indianapolis: Hackett.

1990c. "Truth, Method, and Correspondence in Spinoza and Leibniz." *Studia Spinozana* 6: 13–43.

1991. "Spinoza's Necessitarianism." In *God and Nature: Spinoza's Metaphysics*, ed. Yirmiyahu Yovel, Spinoza by 2000: The Jerusalem Conferences, 191–218. Leiden: Brill.

1994. "Spinoza's Theory of Metaphysical Individuation." In *Individuation in Early Modern Philosophy*, eds. Kenneth F. Barber and Jorge J. E. Gracia, 73–101. Albany: State University of New York Press.

Gebhardt, Carl. 1905. *Abhandlung über die Verbesserung des Verstandes. Eine entwicklungsgeschichtliche Untersuchung.* Heidelberg. 1905.

1923. "Juan de Prado." *Chronicon Spinozanum* 3: 269–91.

1987. *Supplementa [to Spinoza: Opera].* Heidelberg: Winter.

Giancotti Boscherini, E. 1970. *Lexicon spinozanum.* 2 Vols. The Hague: M. Nijhoff.

Gildin, H. 1973. "Spinoza and the Political Problem." In *Spinoza: A Collection of Critical Essays*, ed. Marjorie Grene, 377–87. Garden City: Doubleday/Anchor.

1980. "Notes on Spinoza's Critique of Religion." In *The Philosophy of Baruch Spinoza*, ed. Richard Kennington, 155–71. Washington, D.C.: Catholic University of America Press.

Gillispie, Charles Couston, ed. 1970–80. *Dictionary of Scientific Biography.* 16 Vols. New York: Charles Scribner's Sons.

Goclenius, Rodolphus. 1964. *Lexicon philosophicum, quo tanquam clave philosophiae fores aperiuntur, informatum opera & studio Rodolphi Goclenii senioris, in Academia Mauritania, quae est Marchioburgi, Philosophiae Professoris primarii.* Reprint, Hildesheim: Georg Olms (in same volume: Goclenius's Lexicon philosophicum Graecum, 1615). Frankfurt: Matthias Becker, 1613.

Goshen-Gottstein, Moshe. 1989. "Bible et judaisme." In *Le grand siècle et la Bible*, ed. J.-R. Armogathe, 33–9. Paris: Beauchesne.

Graeser, Andreas. 1991. "Stoische Philosophie bei Spinoza." *Revue Internationale de Philosophie* 45 (178): 336–46.

Gram, Moltke S. 1968. "Spinoza, Substance, and Predication." *Theoria* 3: 222–44.

Greenslade, S., ed. 1963. *Cambridge History of the Bible*. Cambridge: Cambridge University Press.

Grene, Marjorie, ed. 1973. *Spinoza: A Collection of Critical Essays*. Modern Studies in Philosophy. Garden City: Doubleday/Anchor Press.

Grene, Marjorie, and Debra Nails, eds. 1986. *Spinoza and the Sciences*. Boston Studies in the Philosophy of Science, vol. 91. Dordrecht: Reidel.

Grunwald, Max. 1986. *Spinoza in Deutschland*. Reprinted by Neudruck Scientia Verlag Aalen. Berlin: S. Calvary, 1897.

Gueroult, Martial. 1968–74. *Spinoza*. Vol. 1: *Dieu (Ethique 1)*; Vol. 2: *L'âme (Ethique 2)* 2 Vols. Paris: Aubier.

   1970. *Etudes sur Descartes, Spinoza, Malebranche et Leibniz*. Vol. 1970. Hildesheim: Georg Olms.

Hall, A. Rupert, and Marie Boas Hall. 1964. "Philosophy and Natural Philosophy: Boyle and Spinoza." In *Mélanges Alexandre Koyré II: l'Aventure de l'Esprit*, 241–56. Paris: Hermann.

Hallett, H. F. 1957. *Benedictus de Spinoza: The Elements of his Philosophy*. London: Athlone Press.

   1962. *Creation, Emanation, Salvation: A Spinozistic Study*. The Hague: M. Nijhoff.

Hampshire, Stuart. 1951. *Spinoza*. New York: Penguin.

   1971. "Spinoza's Theory of Human Freedom." *Monist* 55: 554–66.

   1972. "Spinoza and the Idea of Freedom." In *Studies in Spinoza*, ed. Paul Kashap, 310–31. Berkeley: University of California Press.

   1977. *Two Theories of Morality*. Oxford: Oxford University Press (for the British Academy).

Hampton, Jean. 1986. *Hobbes and the Social Contract Tradition*. Cambridge: Cambridge University Press.

Harris, Errol E. 1973. *Salvation from Despair: A Reappraisal of Spinoza's Philosophy*. The Hague: Martinus Nijhoff.

   1978. *Is There an Esoteric Doctrine in the Tractatus Theologico-Politicus?* Leiden: Vanwege het Spinozahuis, Brill.

   1992. *Spinoza's Philosophy: An Outline*. Atlantic Highlands: Humanities Press.

Heereboord, Adriaan. 1659. *Meletemata philosophica*. Leiden: Fr. Moyard.

Herrnstein, Richard J. and Edwin G. Boring, eds. 1965. *A Source Book in the History of Psychology*. Source Books in the History of the Sciences. Cambridge, Mass.: Harvard University Press.

Hessing, Siegfried, ed. 1977. *Speculum Spinozanum 1677–1977*. London: Routledge and Kegan Paul.

Hill, Christopher. 1980. *The World Turned Upside Down*. New York: Penguin.

Hobbes, Thomas. 1947. *Leviathan*. ed. Oakeshott. Oxford: Basil Blackwell.

1994. *Leviathan*, ed. and trans. Edwin Curley. (With variants from the Latin edition.) Indianapolis: Hackett.

Hoffman, Paul. 1991. "Three Dualist Theories of the Passions." *Philosophical Topics* 19: 153–200.

Hubbeling, H. G. 1964. *Spinoza's Methodology*. Assen: van Gorcum.

1986. "The Third Way of Knowledge (Intuition) in Spinoza." *Studia Spinozana* 2: 219–31.

Hume, David. 1975. *Enquiries concerning Human Understanding and concerning the Principles of Morals*. 3rd ed., ed. P. H. Nidditch. Oxford: Clarendon Press.

1978. *A Treatise of Human Nature*. 2nd ed., ed. P. H. Nidditch. Oxford: Clarendon Press.

Hutton, Sarah. 1984. "Reason and Revelation in the Cambridge Platonists and their Reception of Spinoza." In *Spinoza in den Frühzeit seiner religiosen Wirkung*, eds. K. Grunder and Schmidt-Biggeman, Wolfenbutteler Studien zur Aufklärung, Vol. 12, 181–200. Heidelberg.

Huygens, Christiaan. 1888–1950. *Oeuvres complètes de Christiaan Huygens, publiées par la Société hollandaise des sciences*. eds. D. Bierans de Haan, J. Bosscha, D. J. Kortweg, and J. Vollgraff. 22 Vols. La Haye: Martinus Nijhoff.

Jacobi, Friedrich Heinrich. 1785. *Ueber die Lehre des Spinoza in Briefen an den Herrn Moses Mendelssohn*.

Jarrett, Charles E. 1976. "Spinoza's Ontological Argument." *Canadian Journal of Philosophy* 6: 685–92.

1991. "Spinoza's Denial of the Mind-Body Interaction and the Explanation of Human Action." *Southern Journal of Philosophy* 29: 465–85.

Joachim, Harold H. 1901. *A Study of the Ethics of Spinoza*. Oxford: Clarendon Press.

1940. *Spinoza's Tractatus de Intellectus Emendatione: A Commentary*. Oxford: Clarendon Press.

Jonas, Hans. 1973. "Spinoza and the Theory of the Organism." In *Spinoza: A Collection of Critical Essays*, ed. Marjorie Grene, 259–78. Garden City: Doubleday/Anchor Press.

Kaplan, Yosef. 1989. *From Christianity to Judaism: The Life of Isaac Orobio de Castro*. Oxford: Oxford University Press.

Kashap, S. Paul, ed. 1972. *Studies in Spinoza: Critical and Interpretive Essays*. Berkeley: University of California Press.

Keckermann, Bartholomew. 1614. *Operum omnium quae extant tomus primus*. Geneva: Pierre Aubert.

Kennington, Richard, ed. 1980. *The Philosophy of Baruch Spinoza*. Studies in Philosophy and the History of Philosophy, vol. 7. Washington, D.C.: Catholic University of America Press.

Kenny, E. J. 1974. *The Classical Text*. Berkeley: University of California Press.

Kerckringh, Theodor. 1670. *Opera anatomica, continentia Spicilegium anatomicum*. Leiden: Boutesteyn.

Kingma, J., and A. K. Offenberg. 1985. *Bibliography of Spinoza's Works up to 1800*. Amsterdam: Amsterdam University Press, 1977. Corrected and annotated edition, 1985.

Kissinger, Henry A. 1968. "The White Revolutionary: Reflections on Bismarck." *Daedalus* 97: 888–924.

Klein, D. B. 1970. *A History of Scientific Psychology: Its Origins and Philosophical Backgrounds*. New York, London: Basic Books, Routledge and Kegan Paul.

Klever, W. N. A. 1983. "Nieuwe argumenten tegen de toeschrijving van het auteurschap van de SRR en RK aan Spinoza." *Tijdschrift voor Filosofie* 47: 493–502.

1986. "Axioms in Spinoza's Science and Philosophy of Science." *Studia Spinozana* 2: 171–95.

1987. "The Helvetius Affair, or, Spinoza and the Philosopher's Stone." *Studia Spinozana* 3: 439–50.

1988a. "Burchard De Volder (1643–1709): A Crypto-Spinozist on a Leiden Cathedra." *LIAS* 15: 191–241.

1988b. "De Spinozistische prediking van Pieter Balling. Uitgave van 'Het licht op den kandelaar' met biografische inleiding en commentaar." *Doopsgezinde Bijdragen; Nieuwe Reeks* 14: 55–85.

1988c. "Letters to and from Neercassel about Spinoza and Rieuwertsz." *Studia Spinozana* 4: 329–38.

1988d. "Moles in Motu: Principles of Spinoza's Physics." *Studia Spinozana* 4: 165–95.

1989a. "Hudde's Question on God's Uniqueness: A Reconstruction on the Basis of Van Limborch's Correspondence with John Locke." *Studia Spinozana* 5: 327–59.

1989b. "Spinoza and Van den Enden in Borch's Diary in 1661 and 1662." *Studia Spinozana* 5: 311–27.

1989c. "Spinoza's fame in 1667." *Studia Spinozana* 5: 359–65.

1990a. "Anti-falsificationism: Spinoza's Theory of Experience and Experiments." In *Spinoza: Issues and Directions*, eds. Edwin Curley and Pierre-François Moreau, 124–35. Leiden: Brill.

1990b. "Hume Contra Spinoza?" *Hume Studies* 16: 89–105.

1990c. "Schrift en rede, of De vermeende tegenstelling tussen Spinoza en Meyer." *Nederlands Theologisch Tijdschrift* 44: 223–41.

1990d. *Verba et sententiae, or Lambert van Velthuysen on Words and Conceptions of Spinoza*. Maarssen: APA.

1991a. "La Clé d'un nom: Petrus van Gent à partir d'une correspondance." *Cahiers Spinoza* (Éditions Réplique) 6: 169–202.

1991b. "A New Source of Spinozism: Franciscus van den Enden." *Journal of the History of Philosophy* 29: 613–31.

1993. "More About Hume's Debt to Spinoza." *Hume Studies* 19: 55–74.

1994. "Spinoza's 'corruptor' de Prado, o la Acoría de Gebhardt y Révah invertida." In *Spinoza y España*, ed. A. Dominguez, 217–29. Cuidad Real: Castilla- La Mancha.

Klever, W. N. A., and J. van Zuylen. 1990. "Insignis opticus. Spinoza in de geschiedenis van de optica." *De Zeventiende Eeuw* 6: 47–63.

Klijnsmit, A. J. 1986. *Spinoza and Grammatical Tradition*. Leiden: Brill.

Kline, George L. 1952. *Spinoza in Soviet Philosophy*.

Koerbagh, Adriaan. 1974. *Een ligt schijnende in duystere plaatsen / om te verligten de voornaamste saaken der Gods-geleertheyd en Gods-dienst / ontsteeken door Vreederijk Waarmond / ondersoeker der Waarheyd. Anders Adr. Koerbagh.* ed. H. Vandenhossche. Brussels.

Kortholt, Christian. 1700. *De tribus impostoribus*. Hamburg.

La Peyrère, Isaac. 1656. *Men before Adam*. London.

1663. *Apologie de la Peyrère*. Paris.

Lachterman, David R. 1978. "The Physics of Spinoza's Ethics." In *Spinoza: New Perspectives*, eds. Robert W. Shahan and John Biro, 77–111. Norman: University of Oklahoma Press.

Lagny, A. 1993. "Spinoza personnage de roman." In *Spinoza au XXe siècle*, ed. O. Bloch, Paris: PUF.

Lau, Theodor Ludwig. 1992. *Meditationes philosophicae de Deo, Mundo, Homine (1717) Meditationes. Theses, Dubia philosophico-theologica (1719). Dokumente. Mit einer Einleitung herausgegeben von Martin Pott.* Stuttgart-Bad Cansatt: Frommann-Holzboog.

Lecrivain, André. 1986. "Spinoza and Cartesian Mechanics." In *Spinoza and the Sciences*, eds. Marjorie Grene and Debra Nails, 15–60. Dordrecht: Reidel.

Leibniz, Gottfried Wilhelm. 1710. *Théodicée*. Amsterdam.

1980. *Sämtliche Schriften und Briefe*. Berlin: Akademie-Verlag.

1989. *Philosophical Essays*, ed. and trans. Roger Ariew and Daniel Garber. Indianapolis: Hackett.

Leopold, J. H. 1902. *Ad Spinozae Opera Posthuma*. The Hague.

LePore, Ernest, and Barry Loewer. 1987. "Mind Matters." *Journal of Philosophy* 84: 630–42.

Levi, Ze'ev. 1987. "The Problem of Normativity in Spinoza's Hebrew Grammar." *Studia Spinozana* 3: 351–90.

Lightfoot, John. 1647. *The Harmony of the Four Evangelists, Among themselves, and with the Old Testament.*

Loeb, Louis. 1981. *From Descartes to Hume*. Ithaca: Cornell University Press.

Lowinan, Moses. 1756. *Three Tracts*. London.

[Lucas, Jean Maximilien]. 1927. *The Oldest Biography of Spinoza*, ed. and trans. A. Wolf. London: George Allen and Unwin.

Macherey, P. 1990. *Hegel ou Spinoza*. Paris: Maspero, 1979. Second edition, La Découverte.

Machiavelli, Niccolò. 1975. *The Discourses of Niccolo Machiavelli*, ed. Bernard Crich and trans. Leslie Walker. London: Routledge and Paul.

   1979. *The Portable Machiavelli*, ed. and trans. Peter Bondanella and Mark Musa. New York: Viking Press.

   1992. *The Prince*. 2nd ed., ed. and trans. Robert Adams. New York: Norton.

Madanes, Leiser. 1992. "How to Undo Things with Words: Spinoza's Criterion for Limiting Freedom of Expression." *History of Philosophy Quarterly* 9: 401–8.

Maimonides, Moses. 1963. *The Guide of the Perplexed*, ed. and trans. Shlomo Pines. Chicago: University of Chicago Press.

Mansvelt, Regnerus à. 1674. *Adversus anonymum theologico-politicum*. Amsterdam: Wolfgang.

Marcus, Ruth Barcan. 1983. "Bar-On on Spinoza's Ontological Proof." In *Spinoza: His Thought and Work*, eds. Nathan Rotenstreich and Norma Schneider, 110–20. Jerusalem: The Israel Academy of Arts and Sciences.

   1986. "Spinoza and the Ontological Proof." In *Human Nature and Natural Knowledge*, eds. A. Donagan, A. N. Perovich, and M. V. Wedin, 153–66. Dordrecht: Reidel.

Mark, Thomas Carson. 1972. *Spinoza's Theory of Truth*. New York: Columbia University Press.

   1978. "Truth and Adequacy in Spinozistic Ideas." In *Spinoza: New Perspectives*, eds. R. W. Shahan and J. I. Biro, 11–34. Norman: University of Oklahoma Press.

Martineau, James. 1882. *A Study of Spinoza*. London: Macmillan.

Mason, Richard V. 1986. "Spinoza on Modality." *Philosophical Quarterly* 36: 313–42.

   1993. "Ignoring the Demon? Spinoza's Way with Doubt." *Journal of the History of Philosophy* 31: 545–64.

Matheron, Alexandre. 1969. *Individu et Communauté chez Spinoza*. Paris: Les Editions de Minuit.

   1971. *Le Christ et le salut des ignorants chez Spinoza*. Paris: Aubier.

   1977. "Le traité théologico-politique vu par le jeune Marx." *Cahiers Spinoza* 1: 159–212.

   1985. "Le 'droit du plus fort': Hobbes contre Spinoza." *Revue philosophique* 110: 149–76.

1986a. "Spinoza and Euclidean Arithmetic: the Example of the Fourth Proportional." In *Spinoza and the Sciences*, eds. Marjorie Grene and Deborah Nails, Boston Studies in the Philosophy of Science, Dordrecht: Reidel.

1986b. "Spinoza et la décomposition de la politique thomiste: machiavélisme et utopie." In *Anthropologie et politique au xviie siècle*, Paris: Vrin, 1986.

1990. "Le problème de l'évolution de Spinoza du Traité théologico-politique au Traité politique." In *Spinoza: Issues and Directions*, eds. Edwin Curley and Pierre-François Moreau, 258–70. Leiden: Brill.

Matson, Wallace. 1971. "Spinoza's Theory of Mind." *Monist* 55: 567–78.

1977a. "Death and Destruction in Spinoza's Ethics." *Inquiry* 20: 403–17.

1977b. "Steps Towards Spinozism." *Revue internationale de philosophie* 119–20: 69–83.

Mattern, Ruth. 1979. "An Index of References to Claims in Spinoza's Ethics." *Philosophy Research Archives* 5: 1358.

Maull, Nancy. 1986. "Spinoza in the Century of Science." In *Spinoza and the Sciences*, eds. Marjorie Grene and Debra Nails, 3–13. Dordrecht: Reidel.

McKeon, Richard. 1928. *The Philosophy of Spinoza: The Unity of his Thought*. London: Longmans, Green, and Co.

1965. "Spinoza on the Rainbow and on Probability." In *Harry Austryn Wolfson Jubilee Volume on the Occasion of his Seventy-Fifth Birthday*, ed. Leo W. Schwartz and others, Vol. 1, 533–59. Jerusalem: The American Academy for Jewish Research, 2 Vols.

McShea, Robert. 1968. *The Political Philosophy of Spinoza*. New York: Columbia University Press.

Méchoulan, H. 1990. *Amsterdam au temps de Spinoza*. Paris: Presses Universitaires de France.

Méchoulan, H. and G. Nahon. 1979. *Menasseh Ben Israel, Espérance d'Israel*. Paris: Vrin.

Meinel, Christoph. 1988. "Early Seventeenth-Century Atomism: Theory, Epistemology and the Insufficiency of Experiment." *Isis* 79: 68–103.

Meininger, J. V., and Guido van Suchtelen. 1980. *Liever met wercken als met woorden. De levensreis van doctor Franciscus van den Enden, leermeester van Spinoza, complotteur tegen Lodewijk de Veertiende*. Weesp: Heureka.

Meinsma, K. O. 1980. *Spinoza en zijn kring. Historisch-kritische studiën over Hollandsche vrijgeesten*. The Hague: Gravenhage 1896. Reprinted, Utrecht: M. Nijhoff.

1983. *Spinoza et son cercle*. eds. Henri Mechoulan and Pierre-François Moreau. Paris: Vrin.

Melchior, J. 1671. *Epistola ad amicum, continens censuram libri.* Utrecht: Noenaert.

Meyer, Lodewijk. 1666. *Philosophia s. scripturae intepres.* Eleutheropoli (=Amsterdam).

　1988. *La philosophie interprète de l'Ecriture Sainte,* ed. and trans. Lagrée, J. and Moreau, P.-F. Paris: Intertextes éditeur.

Mignini, Filippo. 1986b. "Spinoza's Theory on the Active and Passive Nature of Knowledge." *Studia Spinozana* 2: 27–58.

　1990. "In Order to Interpret Spinoza's Theory of the Third Kind of Knowledge: Should Intuitive Science be Considered per causam proximam Knowledge?" In *Spinoza: Issues and Directions,* eds. Edwin Curley and Pierre-François Moreau, 136–46. Leiden: Brill.

Miller, David, ed. 1987. *The Blackwell Encyclopedia of Political Thought.* Oxford: Basil Blackwell.

Moreau, Pierre-François. 1971. *Spinoza et spinozisme.* Paris.

　1975. *Spinoza.* Paris.

　1994. *L'Expérience et l'Eternité. Recherches sur la constitution du système spinoziste.* Paris: PUF.

Moretti-Constanzi, T. 1946. *Spinoza.* Rome: Editrice Universitas.

Mulier, Eco Haitsma. 1980. *The Myth of Venice and Dutch Republican Thought in the Seventeenth Century.* Assen: Van Gorcum.

Musaeus, J. 1674. *Tractatus Theologico-politicus ad veritatis lumen examinatus.* Jena.

Naess, Arne. 1975. *Freedom, Emotion, and Self-Subsistence: The Structure of a Central Part of Spinoza's Ethics.* Oslo: Universitetsvorlaget.

Nagel, Thomas. 1986. *The View From Nowhere.* New York: Oxford University Press.

Nails, Debra. 1986. "Annotated Bibliography of Spinoza and the Sciences." In *Spinoza and the Sciences,* eds. Marjorie Grene and Debra Nails, 305–14. Dordrecht: Reidel.

Negri, Antonio. 1981. *L'anomalia selvaggia. Saggio su potere e potenza in Baruch Spinoza.* Translated into French as *L'anomalie sauvage. Puissance et pouvoir chez Spinoza.* Milan: Felltrinelli, 1981, Paris, 1982.

　1991. *The Savage Anomaly,* ed. and trans. Hardt, Michael. Translation of *L'anomolia selvaggia,* Giangriacomo Feltrinelli Editore, 1981. Minneapolis: University of Minnesota Press.

Neu, Jerome. 1977. *Emotion, Thought and Therapy.* Berkeley: University of California Press.

Nil Volentibus Arduum (NVA). 1989. *Onderwijs in de tooneelpoëzy.* ed. A. J. E. Harmsen. Rotterdam: Ordeman.

Odegard, Douglas. 1975. "The Body Identical with the Human Mind: A Problem in Spinoza's Philosophy." In *Spinoza, Essays in Interpretation,* eds. Eugene Freeman and Maurice Mandelbaum, 61–83. La Salle: Open Court.

Oldenburg, Henry. 1965–86. *The Correspondence of Henry Oldenburg*, ed. and trans. A. Rupert Hall and Marie Boas Hall. 13 Vols. Madison: University of Wisconsin Press, London: Mansell, Taylor, and Francis.

Osier, J. P. 1983. *D'Uriel da Costa à Spinoza*. Berg International.

Parfit, Derek. 1984. *Reasons and Persons*. New York: Oxford University Press.

Pariset. 1906. "Sieyès et Spinoza." *Revue de synthèse historique* 12: 309–20.

Parkinson, G. H. R. 1954. *Spinoza's Theory of Knowledge*. Oxford: Clarendon Press.

1971. "Spinoza on the Power and Freedom of Man." *Monist* 55: 527–53.

1990. "Definition, Essence, and Understanding in Spinoza." In *Central Themes in Early Modern Philosophy*, eds. J. A. Cover and Mark Kulstad, 49–67. Indianapolis: Hackett.

Pascal, Blaise. 1663. *Traité de l'équilibre des liueurs et de la pesanteur de la masse de l'air*. Paris: Desprez.

Patrick, Simon. 1700. *A Commentary upon the Fifth Book of Moses, called Deuteronomy*. London.

Paty, Michel. 1985. "La doctrine du parallélisme de Spinoza et le programme épistémologique d'Einstein." *Cahiers Spinoza* 5: 93–108.

Petry, M. J. 1994. "Algebra, Chances and the Rainbow." In *Les textes de Spinoza. Etudes sur les mots, les phrases, les livres*, eds. Fokke Akkerman and Piet Steenbakkers, Philosophia Spinozae Perennis: Spinoza's Philosophy and its Relevance, Vol. 9, Assen: Van Gorcum, 1994; Naples: Bibliopolis, 1994.

Pollock, Frederick. 1912. *Spinoza: His Life and Philosophy*. Corrected reissue of the 2nd edition (1899) ed., London: Duckworth.

Popkin, Richard H. 1979a. "Hume and Spinoza." *Hume Studies* 5: 65–93.

1979b. *The History of Scepticism from Erasmus to Spinoza*. Berkeley: University of California Press.

1984a. "Menasseh ben Israel and La Peyrère." *Studia Rosenthaliana* 18: 12–20.

1984b. "Rabbi Nathan Shapira's Visit to Amsterdam." In *Dutch Jewish History*, ed. Michman, 185–205. Jerusalem: Tel-Aviv University.

1984c. "Spinoza's Relations with the Quakers." *Quaker History* 73: 14–28.

1985. "Spinoza and Samuel Fisher." *Philosophia* 15: 219–36.

1986. "Some New Light on the Roots of Spinoza's Science of Bible Study." In *Spinoza and the Sciences*, eds. Marjorie Grene and Debra Nails, 171–88. Dordrecht: Reidel.

1987a. *Isaac La Peyrère (1596–1676): His Life, Work and Influence.* Leiden: Brill.

1987b. *Spinoza's Earliest Publication? The Hebrew Translation of Margaret Fell's Loving Salutation.* Assen: Van Gorcum.

1987c. "The Religious Background of Seventeenth-Century Philosophy." *Journal of the History of Philosophy* 25: 35–50.

1990a. "Notes from the Underground." *New Republic,* May 21, 35–41.

1990b. "Was Spinoza a Marrano of Reason?" *Philosophia* (Israel) 20: 243–6.

1991. "Spinoza and The Three Impostors." In *Spinoza: Issues and Directions,* eds. Edwin Curley and Pierre-François Moreau, 347–58. Leiden: Brill.

Porges, N. 1924–6. "Spinoza's Compendium der Hebräischen Grammatik." *Chronicon Spinozanum* 4: 123–59.

Powell, Elmer Ellsworth. 1906. *Spinoza and Religion.* Chicago: Open Court.

Préposiet, J. n.d. *Bibliographie spinoziste.* Besançon: Centre de Documentation.

Proietti, O. 1985. "Adulescens luxu perditus; classici latini nell'opera di Spinoza." *Rivista di Filosofia Neo-Scolastica* 77: 210–57.

1989a. "Il 'Satyricon' di Petronio et la datazione della 'Grammatica ebraica'." *Studia Spinozana* 5: 253–72.

1989b. "Lettres à Lucilius, une source du 'De Intellectus Emendatione' de Spinoza." In *Lire et Traduire Spinoza. Travaux et Documents [du] Groupe de Recherches Spinozistes,* Vol. I, Paris.

1989c. "Petronius and Spinoza's Hebrew Grammar." *Studia Spinozana* 5: 253–72.

Radner, Daisie. 1971. "Spinoza's Theory of Ideas." *The Philosophical Review* 80: 338–59.

Rappaport, Samuel. 1899. *Schopenhauer und Spinoza.* Halle/Wittemberg (thesis).

Reedy, Gerard. 1985. *The Bible and Reason: Anglicans and Scripture in Late Seventeenth-Century England.* Philadelphia: University of Pennsylvania.

Reider, Joseph. 1937. *Deuteronomy with Commentary.* Philadelphia: The Jewish Publication Society of America.

Révah, I. S. 1959. *Spinoza et le docteur Juan de Prado.* The Hague: Moputon.

1964. "Aux origines de la rupture spinozienne: nouveaux documents sur l'incroyance dans la communauté judéo-portugaise d'Amsterdam à l'époque de l'excommunication de Spinoza." *Revue des Etudes Juives* 123: 359–431.

1970–2. "Aux origines de la rupture spinozienne: nouvel examen des origines du déroulement et des consequences de l'affaire Spinoza-Prado-Ribera." *Annuaire du Collège de France* 70–2: 562–8, 574–87, 641–53.

Rice, Lee C. 1971. "Spinoza on Individuation." *Monist* 55: 640–59.

Richardson, John. 1655. *Choice Observations and Explanation upon the Old Testament*. London.

Rivaud, Albert. 1924–6. "La physique de Spinoza." *Chronicon Spinozanum* 4: 24–57.

Robinson, Amy. 1991. *Two Problems in Spinoza's Theory of Sense Perception*. Princeton University (dissertation).

Roth, Leon. 1924. *Spinoza, Descartes, Maimonides*. Oxford: Clarendon Press.

1929. *Spinoza*. London: E. Benn.

Rovane, Carol. n.d. "Charity and Identity." *Forum für Philosophie* (forthcoming).

Ryan, Alan. 1983. "Hobbes, Toleration and the Inner Life." In *The Nature of Political Theory*, eds. David Miller and Larry Seidentop, Oxford: Clarendon Press.

Sahakian, William S., ed. 1970. *History of Psychology: A Source Book in Systematic Psychology*. Itasca, Illinois: F. E. Peacock Publishers.

Salomon, H. P. 1988. *Saul Levi Mortera en zijn "Traktaat betreffende de waarheid van de wet van Mozes."* Braga.

Santayana, G. 1886. "The Ethical Doctrine of Spinoza." *The Harvard Monthly*: 144–52.

Savan, David. 1973. "Spinoza and Language." In *Spinoza: A Collection of Critical Essays*, ed. Marjorie Grene, Garden City: Doubleday/Anchor.

1986. "Spinoza: Scientist and Theorist of Scientific Method." In *Spinoza and the Sciences*, eds. Marjorie Grene and Debra Nails, 95–123. Dordrecht: Reidel.

Schmidt-Biggemann, W. 1992. "Spinoza dans le cartésianisme." In *Travaux et Documents du Groupe de recherches spinozistes*.

Schopenhauer, Arthur. 1960. *Sämtliche Werke*. ed. Wolfgang Löhneysen. Frankfurt: Insel-Cotta.

Schröder, Winfried. 1987. *Spinoza in der deutschen Frühaufklärung*. Wurzburg: Königshausen und Neumann.

Scribano, M. E. 1988. *Da Descartes a Spinoza. Percosi della teologia razionale nel Seicento*. Milan: Franco Angeli.

Secretan, Catherin. 1987. "La reception de Hobbes aux Pays-Bas au xviie siècle." *Studia Spinozana* 3: 27–46.

Seligman, Edwin R. A., and Alvin Johnson, eds. 1930–5. *Encyclopedia of the Social Sciences*. 15 Vols. New York: MacMillan.

Semerari, G. 1952. *I Problemi dello Spinozismo*. Vecchi: Trani.

454   Bibliography

Shahan, Robert W., and J. I. Biro, eds. 1978. *Spinoza: New Perspectives.* Norman: University of Oklahoma Press.

Sherwood, William of. 1966. *William of Sherwood's Introduction to Logic,* ed. and trans. Norman Kretzmann. Minneapolis: University of Minnesota Press.

Siebrand, Heine. 1986. "Spinoza and the Rise of Modern Science in the Netherlands." In *Spinoza and the Sciences,* eds. Marjorie Grene and Debra Nails, 61–91. Dordrecht: Reidel.

Sills, David L., ed. 1968–79. *International Encyclopedia of the Social Sciences.* 18 Vols. New York: MacMillan, Free Press.

Simon, Richard. 1687. *De l'Inspiration des livres sacrés.* Rotterdam.

Skinner, Quentin. 1974. "Conquest and Consent: Thomas Hobbes and the Engagement Controversy." In *The Interregnum: the Quest for Settlement,* ed. G. E. Alymer, 79–98. New York: MacMillan.

Snel, Robert. n.d. *Het hermetisch universum. Nietzsches verhouding tot Spinoza en de moderne ontologie.* Mededelingen vanwege het Spinozahuis 60. Delft: Eburon.

Sosa, Ernest. 1984. "Mind–Body Interaction and Supervenient Causation." *Midwest Studies in Philosophy* 9: 271–81.

Spinoza, Benedictus de. 1663. *Renati Des Cartes Principiorum Philosophiae Pars I, & II, more geometrico demonstratae per Benedictum de Spinoza Amstelodamensem. Accesserunt ejusdem Cogitata Metaphysica . . .* Amsterdam: Jan Rieuwertsz.

   1664. *Renatus Des Cartes Beginzelen der Wysbegeerte, I en II Deel, Na de Meetkonstige wijze door Benedictus de Spinoza Amsterdammer. Mitsgaders des zelfs overnatuurkundige Gedachten . . . Alles uit 't Latijn vertaalt door P. B.* Amsterdam: Jan Rieuwertsz.

[Spinoza, Baruch]. 1678. *La clef du Sanctuaire.* Translated by Saint-Glain. Leyde: Warnaer.

   1910. *Short Treatise on God, Man, and His Well-Being, and a Life of Spinoza,* ed. and trans. A. Wolf. London: Adam and Charles Black.

   1925. *Spinoza Opera.* ed. Carl Gebhardt. 4 Vols. Heidelberg: Carl Winter.

   1966. *The Correspondence of Spinoza,* ed. and trans. A. Wolf. London: Allen & Unwin, 1928. Reprinted, London, Frank Cass.

   1954. *Oeuvres complètes,* ed. and trans. Roland Caillois, Madeleine Francès, and Robert Misrahi. Paris: Gallimard.

   1958. *Political Works.* ed. A. G. Wernham. Oxford: Clarendon Press.

   1968. *Abrégé de Grammaire Hébraique.* Introduction, traduction française et notes, ed. and trans. J. Askenazi and J. Gerson, Paris: Vrin.

   1974. *The Principles of Descartes' Philosophy [and the Cogitata Metaphysica],* ed. and trans. Halbert Hains Britan. first edition 1905 La Salle, Illinois: Open Court.

(Spinoza, Baruch). 1982. *The Ethics, and Selected Letters*, ed. and trans. Samuel Shirley. Indianapolis: Hackett.

(attributed). 1984–5. "Calcul algébrique de l'arc-en-ciel, Calcul des chances." Translated by P.-F. Moreau. *Cahiers Spinoza* 5: 7–69.

1985a. *The Collected Works of Spinoza*. Vol. 1, ed. and trans. Edwin Curley. Princeton: Princeton University Press.

(attributed). 1985b. *Spinoza's Algebraic Calculation of the Rainbow; and, Calculation of Chances*. ed. M. J. Petry. The Hague: M. Nijhoff.

1986. *Korte Verhandeling van God, de Mensch en deszelvs Welstand/ Breve Trattato su Dio, l'Uomo e il suo Bene*, ed. and trans. Filippo Mignini. L'Aquila: L. U. Japadre Editore.

1989. *Tractatus Theologico-Politicus*, ed. and trans. Samuel Shirley. Leiden: Brill.

1994. *A Spinoza Reader*. ed. Edwin Curley. Princeton: Princeton University Press.

Spizelius, T. 1675. *Infelix litterator*. Rotterdam.

Sprigge, Timothy. 1977. "Spinoza's Identity Theory." *Inquiry* 20: 419–45.

Steinberg, Diane. 1981. "Spinoza's Theory of the Eternity of Mind." *Canadian Journal of Philosophy* 11: 35–68.

1984. "Spinoza's Ethical Doctrine and the Unity of Human Nature." *Journal of the History of Philosophy* 22: 303–24.

1993. "Spinoza, Method, and Doubt." History of *Philosophy Quarterly* 10: 211–24.

Stenonis, Nicolai. 1952. *Epistolae et epistolae ad eum datae*. Vol. 1. ed. G. Sherz. Hafnia.

Strauss, Leo. 1965. *Spinoza's Critique of Religion*, ed. and trans. E. M. Sinclair. New York: Schocken Books.

1984. *Thoughts on Machiavelli*. Chicago: University of Chicago Press.

1988. *Persecution and the Art of Writing*. Chicago: University of Chicago Press.

Strawson, P. F. 1974. *Freedom and Resentment and Other Essays*. London: Methuen.

Tacitus. 1989. *The Annals of Imperial Rome*. New York: Penguin.

Thijssen-Schoute, Louise. 1989. *Nederlands Cartesianisme*. Utrecht.

Toland, John. 1705. *Socinianism Truly Stated*. London.

Totaro, G. 1989. "Un manoscritto inedito delle 'Adnotationes' al 'Tractatus Theologico-politicus' di Spinoza." *Studia Spinozana* 5: 205–24.

Tschirnhaus, Ehrenfried Wilhelm von. 1686. *Medicina mentis sive Artis inveniendi praecepta generalia*. Amsterdam: Jan Rieuwertsz.

1980. *Médecine de l'esprit*, ed. and trans. Jean-Paul Wurtz. Paris: Ophrys.

Van Balen, Dr. P. 1988. *De verbetering der gedachten*. ed. M. J. Van Hoven. Utrecht: Ambo.

Van Blijenbergh, Willem. 1674. *De waerheyt van de christelijcke godtsdienst*. Leiden: Van Gaesbeeck.

Van Bunge, Wiep. 1989. "On the Early Dutch Receptions of the Tractatus Theologico-Politicus." *Studia Spinozana* 5: 225–53.

Van Bunge, Louis. 1990. *Joannes Bredenburg (1643–1691). Een Rotterdamse collegiant in de ban van Spinoza*. Erasmus Universiteit (thesis).

Van der Bend, J. G., ed. 1974. *Spinoza on Knowing, Being and Freedom*. Assen: van Gorcum.

Van der Hoeven, P. 1973a. *De Cartesiaanse Fysica in het Denken van Spinoza*. Mededelingen Vanwege het Spinozahuis 30. Leiden: Brill.

1973b. "Over Spinoza's Interpretatie van de Cartesiaanse fysicaen Betekenis daarvan voor het System der Ethica." *Tijdschrift voor Filosofie* 35: 27–86.

Van Peursen, C. A. 1993. "E. W. Von Tschirnhaus and the Ars Inveniendi." *Journal of the History of Ideas* 54: 395–410.

Van Rooijen, A. J. Servaas. 1888. *Inventaire des livres formant la bibliothèque de Bénédict Spinoza*. The Hague, Paris: W. C. Tengeler, Paul Monnerat.

Van Schooten, Francis. 1657. "Tractatus de ratiociniis in aleae ludo." In *Exercitationum mathematicarum, libri quinque*, ed., Leiden: Johann Elsevier, 1657. Original Dutch text and facing French trans. in Huygens 1888–1950: XIV,50–91.

Van Suchtelen, Guido. 1987. "Nil Volentibus Arduum. Les amis de Spinoza au travail." *Studia Spinozana* 3: 391–404.

Van Til, Salomon. 1694. *Het Voor-Hof der Heydenen, voor alle Ongeloovigen geopent*. Dordrecht.

Vandenbossche, H. 1978. *Adriaan Koerbagh en Spinoza*. Leiden: Brill.

Vaz Diaz, A. M., and W. G. van der Tak. 1982. "Spinoza, Merchant and Autodidact." *Studia Rosenthaliana* 16: 105–48.

Verbeek, T. 1988. *La querelle d'Utrecht*. Paris: Impressions Nouvelles.

Vermij, R. H. 1988. "De Nederlandse vriendenkring van E. W. von Tschirnhaus." *Tijdschrift voor de geschiedenis der geneeskunde, natuurwetenschappen, wiskunde en techniek* 11: 153–78.

Vernière, Paul. 1982. *Spinoza et la pensée française avant la Révolution*. Paris: PUF 1954. Second edition 1982.

Versé, Noël Aubert de. 1684. *L'impie convaincu, ou dissertation contre Spinosa*. Amsterdam.

Voss, Stephen. 1981. "How Spinoza Enumerated the Affects." *Archiv für Geschichte der Philosophie* 63: 167–79.

Vries, Theun de. 1985. *De gezegende. Het leven van Spinoza in honderdzeven scènes*. Amsterdam: Querido.

Vulliaud, Paul. 1934. *Spinoza d'après les livres de sa bibliothèque*. Paris: Chacornac.

Wachter, Johann Georg. 1699. *Der spinozismus im Judentum*. Amsterdam. 1706. *Elucidarius Cabalisticus*. Amsterdam.

Walker, Ralph C. S. 1989. *The Coherence Theory of Truth*. London: Routledge.

Walther, Mannfred. 1971. *Metaphysik als Anti-Theologie. Die Philosophie Spinozas im Zusammenhang der religionsphilosophischen Problematik*. Hamburg.

Walzer, Michael. 1973. "The Problem of Dirty Hands." *Philosophy and Public Affairs* 2: 160–80.

Wetlesen, Jon. 1979. *The Sage and the Way: Spinoza's Ethics of Freedom*. Assen.

Wetlesen, Jon, ed. 1978. *Spinoza's Philosophy of Man: The Scandinavian Spinoza Symposium, 1977*. Oslo: Universitetsvorlaget.

Wilamowitz-Moellendorff, U. von. 1982. *History of Classical Scholarship*, ed. and trans. Alan Harris. Baltimore: Johns Hopkins University Press.

Williams, Bernard. 1978. *Descartes: The Project of Pure Inquiry*. Harmondsworth, England: Pelican.

Wilson, Margaret. D. 1978. *Descartes*. London: Routledge.

1980. "Objects, Ideas, and 'Minds': Comments on Spinoza's Theory of Mind." In *The Philosophy of Baruch Spinoza*, ed. R. Kennington, 103–20. Washington, D. C.: The Catholic University of America Press.

1983. "Infinite Understanding, Scientia Intuitiva, and Ethics I.16." *Midwest Studies in Philosophy* 8: 181–91.

1991. "Spinoza's Causal Axiom (Ethics 1, Axiom 4)." In *God and Nature: Spinoza's Metaphysics*, ed. Yirmiyahu Yovel, 133–60. Leiden: Brill.

Wirszubski, C. 1955. "Spinoza's Debt to Tacitus." *Scripta Hierosolymitana* 2: 176–86.

Wiszowaty, Andrew, Jr. 1980. "Rational Religion, or a Tract Concerning the Judgment of Reason to be used even in Theological and Religious Controversies." In *The Polish Brethren*. Harvard Theological Studies XXX, Document XXXIV, ed. George H. Williams, Cambridge, Mass.: Harvard University Press.

Wolf, A. 1935. *A History of Science, Technology, and Philosophy in the Sixteenth and Seventeenth Centuries*. With the cooperation of F. Danneman and A. Armitage London: George Allen & Unwin Ltd.

Wolf, Susan. 1979. "Asymmetrical Freedom." *Journal of Philosophy* 77: 151–66.

Wolfson, Harry Austryn. 1934. *The Philosophy of Spinoza*. 2 Vols. Cambridge, Mass.: Harvard University Press.

Woolhouse, R. S. 1990. "Spinoza and Descartes and the Existence of Extended Substance." In *Central Themes in Early Modern Philosophy*, eds. J. A. Cover and Mark Kulstad, 23–48. Indianapolis: Hackett.

1993. *Descartes, Spinoza, Leibniz: The Concept of Substance in Seventeenth-Century Metaphysics*. New York: Routledge.

Wurzer, W. S. 1975. *Nietzsche und Spinoza*. Meissenheim an Glan.

Yakira, Elkhanan. 1988. "Boyle et Spinoza." *Archives de Philosophie* 51: 107–24.

    1993. "Spinoza et les sionistes." In *Spinoza au XXe siècle*, ed. O. Bloch, Paris: PUF.

Yovel, Yirmiyahu. 1973. "Bible Interpretation as Philosophical Praxis: A Study of Spinoza and Kant." *Journal of the History of Philosophy* 11: 189–212.

    1989. *Spinoza and Other Heretics*. Vol. 1: *The Marrano of Reason*; Vol. 2: *The Adventures of Immanence*. Princeton: Princeton University Press.

    1994. *Spinoza on Knowledge and the Human Mind: Papers Presented at the Second Jerusalem Conference (Ethica II)*. Leiden: Brill.

Zac, Sylvain. 1965. *Spinoza et l'interprétation de l'écriture*. Paris: PUF.

Zweerman, T. H. 1983. *Spinoza's inleiding tot de filosofie. Een vertaling en structuuranalyse . . . benevens commentaar*. Leuven (thesis).

INDEX

.